NEWSWEEK CONDENSED BOOKS

JACK SMITH

_____

ARNOLD C. BRACKMAN

_____

JAMES P. O'DONNELL

_____

A. E. HOTCHNER

_____

PETER TOWNSEND

_____

SPEND ALL YOUR KISSES, MR. SMITH

THE LUCK OF NINEVEH

THE BUNKER

SOPHIA
LIVING AND LOVING
HER OWN STORY

TIME AND CHANCE
AN AUTOBIOGRAPHY

NEWSWEEK BOOKS, New York

NEWSWEEK CONDENSED BOOKS

Herbert A. Gilbert, Editor

Mary Ann Joulwan, Art Director

Elaine Andrews, Associate Editor

Danielle Woerner-Bobrick, Assistant Editor

Alvin Garfin, Publisher

The original editions of the books in this
volume are published and copyrighted as follows:

Spend All your Kisses, Mr. Smith
Published by McGraw-Hill Book Company
Copyright © 1978 by Jack Smith

The Luck of Nineveh
Published by McGraw-Hill Book Company
Copyright © 1978 by Arnold C. Brackman

The Bunker
Published by Houghton Mifflin Company
Copyright © 1978 by James P. O'Donnell

Sophia, Living and Loving
Published by William Morrow and Company, Inc.
Copyright © 1979 by Victoria Pictures, Ltd. and
A. E. Hotchner

Time and Chance
Published by Methuen
Copyright © 1978 by Peter Townsend

CONTENTS

Jack Smith, upstaged by his Airedale, Fleetwood Pugsley. Smith, a veteran journalist and a popular columnist for the Los Angeles Times, *resides in Los Angeles and Baja.*

SPEND ALL YOUR KISSES, MR. SMITH

A Condensation of the book by

JACK SMITH

CHAPTER 1

Nobody knows when middle age begins; not even the doctors and psychologists. It is said to be a state of mind as much as a physical condition, and its victim may be quite well into it before he realizes he is into it at all.

I know exactly the day on which I found out that I had already made this momentous passage, and in fact was well into it: Friday, May 23, 1969, rather late in the afternoon.

My discovery was heralded by the sound of our younger son Doug's motorcycle varooming up the hill. My wife and I heard him stop in front of the house and started out to greet him. He was living at that time in Westwood, where he shared a pad with two other UCLA students, and we were delighted by his occasional visits home.

We heard his familiar voice—young, playful, exuberant—and a second voice, the voice of a young, playful and exuberant girl, but a stranger. It was the first time he had brought a female home on his motorcycle. Usually it was books.

We hurried outside. What we saw unnerved us for a moment. They both wore glossy plastic helmets, his red, hers blue, with plastic visors distorting their faces. They looked like humanoid beetles. He kicked out the parking stand and settled the motorcycle and helped her off. She pulled off her helmet and shook out her hair. It was shoulder-length; a light reddish brown.

She rolled her eyes and made a little theatrical gesture of dismay. "I have ruin my permanent," she sighed.

She wore a shapeless blue windbreaker and blue jeans and chic brown boots; but despite this camouflage I made two hasty observations:

whoever she was, she was full-grown; and she spoke with a French accent. I had a feeling that events of which I had not even been aware had already gone past some point of no return.

We asked them to dinner and they stayed. The young woman's name was Jacqueline Joyeux, the Joyeux being French for "joyous." My sense of inevitability was deepened. Our son was half-French, his mother being the daughter of French immigrants, and it was not surprising that he would be attracted to a girl named Joyeux, perhaps fatally.

Her home was in Tours, and she had come to America, on her own, on a visitor's visa. To prolong her stay she had found work as a maid in a Beverly Hills home, which was of course illegal, and was rooming with a clutch of French girls similarly employed in domestic service. Our son, evidently, had serendipitously come upon this nest of nubile Gallic pigeons and soon cut Mademoiselle Joyeux from the flock. Where it would end one could only guess, and I already had.

While the women tidied up in the kitchen, getting acquainted in French, a language that excluded my son and me, we went down to the garage and began loading the motorcycle for their adventure. They were planning to drive up into the mountains to spend the weekend, cooking out and sleeping on the ground in sleeping bags. It was nothing for me to worry about. Doug was no novice. He had spent four summers in the Sierras as a packer, and he knew its moods and perils and its sanctuaries. Yet somehow I had a feeling that he wouldn't be perfectly safe this time.

I watched in wonder as the supplies vanished into the motorcycle's saddlebags. A dozen eggs, a slab of bacon, a loaf of bread, a sack of potatoes, and a large package of stew meat.

He found two sleeping bags in the garage and loaded them on the motorcycle, one on either side, for balance. Indeed, the motorcycle was beginning to look like one of the mules he used to pack for a trek in the high back country.

"Why a dozen eggs?" I asked.

"Well," he said, calculating, "four each for breakfast. That's eight."

"Of course," I said. "Four each."

They decided to stay the night and get an early start. Mademoiselle Joyeux was given the privacy of our spare bedroom and our son slept on the couch in my den.

"Well," I told Denny later, "it looks like she might be the one."

"Yes," she said, as if she had always known it.

We were all up early. Mademoiselle Joyeux was at home in the kitchen. She prepared breakfast with the skill to be expected of a French girl whose father, as she told us, was once a chef. I watched her make a four-egg omelet for Doug. "He always like four eggs for breakfast," she explained. It struck me as a strangely intimate piece of knowledge.

They were dressed and packed and ready to go and we were outside to wave them off when Doug decided to look in the garage for his old fishing pole. "I might try some fly-casting," he said.

"You have a license?" I asked, glad to be given some question of legality and prudence that I dared to offer advice on.

"Oh," he said, "I forgot that."

The problem really was, it turned out, that he didn't have enough money to pay for a license. He hadn't cashed his paycheck. I happened to have a twenty-dollar bill.

"I don't know how you can cash a twenty-dollar bill in the mountains," I said, "but you'd better take it anyway."

He took the bill and folded it into a pocket, and I realized that my status had changed: I was now an accomplice in the escapade.

They put on their helmets, lowered their visors, waved goodbye and trundled off down the hill. Denny and I were left standing in the empty street. The thrum of the motorcycle died out, and suddenly it was very quiet. I felt middle-aged, and slightly square.

It was a long weekend. I read two novels and the Sunday paper. It was growing dark on Sunday evening when we heard the sound of the motorcycle laboring up the hill.

Everything had gone well enough. They had taken the motorcycle as far as they could, then packed into the wilderness six miles on foot. Mademoiselle Joyeux was footsore but unrepentant.

He fished in a pocket and brought out the twenty-dollar bill. "Sorry it's wet," he said. "We had to ford the river."

Later I laid the twenty out to dry. It hadn't been much use. I realized I was dealing with a whole new set of values.

We saw Mademoiselle Joyeux rather often that summer and fall, mostly on weekends when Doug brought her by on his motorcycle. We were pleased to have her about. Our older son, Curt, was off with the Air Force in Southeast Asia, and we missed him. She helped to fill the house.

Denny had a woman to talk to, in French, and I was entertained by Mademoiselle Joyeux's buoyancy, her vivacity, and her Gallic impertinence. She happily regarded me as the embodiment of everything the French deplored in the American character. I was an easy target. When we fenced, which was often enough that I rather felt myself always en garde, she usually won the point. Her tactics were to pink me with a saucy thrust, unprovoked, as I saw it; and then, when I parried, to withdraw behind our language barrier, looking quite innocent, as if *she* were the injured party. Was it *her* fault if I didn't understand English? Meanwhile she kept me at my distance by calling me Mr. Smith, which came out something like *Mistair Smees*.

Part of her difficulty in understanding me, I thought, was that Europeans never quite grasped the American character. Their judgments were too hasty and too clouded by the European experience. That was demonstrated rather clearly one Sunday when Doug came by with Mademoiselle Joyeux and they found me watching football on TV, as they had more than once before.

"Mr. Smith," said Mademoiselle Joyeux that particular morning, "you do nozzing else?"

"What do you mean?"—I said—"I do nozzing else?" I did not mean to mock her, but her accent was contagious.

"Every time I come to your house," she said, "you watch football on TV. You do nozzing else?"

I explained that on weekdays I got in my car and drove over the freeway to work like any other good American. But since she had never quite understood what it was I did for a living, or why I was paid to do it, I knew she remained of the opinion that I really did nozzing else but watch football.

I got the impression in those weeks that she was not trying to understand me so much as trying to design me, to make me fit some stereotype for the middle-aged American male, especially one she might be appraising as a possible father-in-law.

She finally placed me in a category, but I wasn't to know what it was until late in October, after Doug had dropped out of college, quit his job and left town on his motorcycle with a vague announcement that he was going to see America before he was drafted. He meant to go all the way to New York.

It was warm in Lotus Land, but we knew the rest of the continent might grow cold in October. We worried about him, racing across the icy plains and through the bleak small towns of America. I thought I knew what compelled him. He was on an identity search. He had come to a crisis, and he needed to be alone in some vast space, to detach himself from his familiars, to discover the face and feel of his native land, to cross his horizons, to take his measure against a wider landscape. I had been caught up in the same kind of odyssey. I had gone all the way to the South Seas and Australia; but I had come back, and I knew he would come back too.

But we could see that Mademoiselle Joyeux was baffled and perhaps hurt by what must seem to her an act of desertion. It was her crisis too. We did not presume to probe or interfere, but we fetched her over to our house one evening for dinner, hoping the familiar setting and the wine and candlelight would make her feel at home and restore her confidence.

We dined outside in the patio. Denny had prepared a small French dinner, and Mademoiselle Joyeux had pitched in as usual to help with the table and make the salad. I started to open a bottle of champagne but thought better of it. Champagne might be too ostentatious, might make it seem that we needed too desperately to be cheered up. Instead I chose a Vouvray from the Loire Valley in which Mademoiselle Joyeux had been born and raised.

It was a lovely dinner. The evening was balmy, as October evenings are in Los Angeles. The sunset lingered, and when twilight came I turned on the light in my goldfish tank. The graceful little fish, so quick and vivid, added life and color to the scene, and we finished the wine by candlelight, talking softly.

Whatever anxiety any of us might have felt about our missing Galahad was muted in the conversation. Mademoiselle Joyeux was amiable and piquant. She personified that excellent phrase of her country, *joie de vivre*.

Then suddenly she grew pensive. She leaned toward me across the table, her eyes searching mine. "Mr. Smith," she said, still having trouble with it, pronouncing it *Smees,* "do you think your son will someday be like you?"

It was hardly a question I had anticipated. But I was touched. She was still a child, of course. It was only natural that she would be impressed by maturity. I thought about her question. Would our son someday be like me? Well, what young woman *wouldn't* want her mate to be kind and gentle, with a certain urban polish, a modest affluence, a mixture of dash and prudence, and beyond that, as the French would say, *je ne sais quoi.*

"What do you mean, *mon cher?*" I said gently, hoping the familiar French endearment would make her feel at home.

"You know, Mr. Smith," she said, "*bourgeois.*"

Bourgeois! I was shaken. *Me* bourgeois?

What did the word mean, anyway? I had never been quite sure.

Something to do with middle-class values and a banal life-style. And it probably meant something even less admirable in France.

"Bourgeois?" I said, hoping I sounded merely curious, rather than defensive.

Mademoiselle Joyeux looked uncomprehending. She turned to my wife. "What does your 'usban' say?"

"Bourgeois," my wife said. "I think he said bourgeois."

I tried to explain to Mademoiselle Joyeux. I was not bourgeois at all, as I understood the word. Perhaps she had judged me too hastily, on a superficial acquaintance. Or perhaps the word lost something in translation.

"I am sorry, Mr. Smith," she said, "if I say something wrong."

"You must not blame yourself, *mon cher*," I said gently, giving her my patient smile. "English is a very difficult language. More wine?"

We sat for a moment in silence, avoiding each other's eyes in the candlelight.

"Well," I said at last, "perhaps I'd better feed my goldfish."

"Oh, good!" cried Mademoiselle Joyeux, clapping her hands.

"You enjoy that?"

"Oh, *oui!* Mr. Smith. It is z'most exciting moment of z'day at your 'ouse—when you feed z'goldfish."

It really was rather exciting, I realized. Goldfish were such primitive little monsters. You couldn't domesticate a goldfish the way you could a dog. It was unnerving how the ferocious little nippers thrashed about, half-crazed with hunger. It seemed to me quite ridiculous to think that a man who kept goldfish could be bourgeois.

I opened the champagne after all.

It wasn't until we had driven Mademoiselle Joyeux back to her lodgings and were on the way home that my wife told me *mon cher* was the masculine form. I wondered how a man of urban polish could have reached middle age without knowing how to say "my dear" to a woman in French.

We knew Doug was all right when he phoned collect from New York City to ask if we could wire him some money—just a few dollars to make it home on. Once he was out of the city he could sleep off the road, so all he needed was enough for food and gasoline.

He had never been to New York before, and he was properly awed, like any other young American pilgrim. He had arrived without enough money for a room, but he had luckily met two girls in a Greenwich

Village coffee house and they had kindly put him up for the night.

"We needn't have worried about him," I told my wife. "He has a gift."

A week later he limped home on a sputtering motorcycle. He was dirty and bone-tired, but fulfilled, somehow; he seemed purged of whatever conflict had compelled him, and I sensed that he now was set on some new course.

So it was not surprising when he told us he and his friends were giving up their pad in Westwood. It had been a good arrangement: three young students living together in a yeasty sort of academic mulch. But such harmonies end. Now they were going their separate ways; not in anger, merely in acceptance of change. Doug came home with all his worldly effects in a rented truck.

"Can I put this stuff in the garage?" he asked. "Temporarily?"

"Why not?" I said, wondering what "temporarily" meant.

It was a formidable load. A great heavy green overstuffed sofa and chair, two desks, twin beds, bunk beds, bookcases, bureaus, odd chairs, and an enormous refrigerator.

"It seems like more than you started out with," I said.

"Yes. The other guys don't have any place to put things." ·

I was happy to provide a home, if only for a backwash of used furniture. But there was no room left for our Dodge. "We'll park it outside," I said. "Temporarily."

He had three large cartons stuffed with books. "Put them in the front bedroom," I suggested.

The front bedroom had been the boys' bedroom. My wife had turned it into a work and sewing room for herself. But it had soon become overstuffed. I opened the door cautiously. Sometimes things fell out on you. We squeezed in, edging around the ironing board and sewing table. There were piles of yardage and patterns on the bed. Books were stacked around the walls. They were mostly the fruits of book club memberships we had inherited from our older son when he went overseas. There was no room for them in the closets. The closets were jammed with eighteen years of precious memorabilia.

I picked through the books in the cartons from the truck. Elizabethan drama. The Greek plays. A history of Byzantium. Shaw, Galsworthy, Virginia Woolf. They were marked and dogeared.

I envied him: all those marvelous books, read or yet to be read. So they had really studied out there at Westwood, after all. I hefted a book on classic Greece. Maybe I could start all over, at the beginning. No. Too heavy. Too late.

We tumbled the books out of the cartons and got one of the bookcases from the garage and found room for it. It might no longer be possible to iron or sew in the room. But however long "temporarily" might be, we could never move from the house. We had a trust.

"If they ever get married," I pointed out to Denny, "all this stuff will come in handy. It's like a dowry."

"Yes," she said. "I might even throw in a sewing machine and an ironing board."

He also brought a rocking chair and a world globe that stood three feet high. I put the globe in my den, but there was no room anywhere for the rocking chair. I didn't know what we were going to do with it until I got up early the next morning, in the dark, and went into the kitchen for a drink of cranberry juice. As I groped toward the refrigerator, something struck the instep of my right foot. My first thought was that some intruder had been waiting in the dark and had struck me with a pickax. It was excruciating. I screamed. I grabbed the wounded foot in both hands and began dancing about on one leg in the dark. Lights went on. My wife burst in.

"What happened?" she cried.

What had happened was that I had hit my foot on the wedge-shaped point of a rocker. She had put the rocker in the kitchen.

"I thought it looked quaint," she said.

The garage, of course, was wiped out by Doug's impedimenta. It looked like the loading dock at the Salvation Army Thrift Shop. There wasn't even room for my garden cart, much less the Dodge.

Our life situation, it occurred to me, was a kaleidoscope. We kept shaking the little bits of colored glass about until they fell into a pattern that was pleasing to us—one we could live with. Then someone came along and gave it a bump, and the pattern was lost, never to be put back again in quite the same way.

We were bumped again that week. For a month past, bulky packages had been coming in the mail from our son Curt in Thailand. He was "short," as they said in the service, and was sending things home ahead of himself. He wasn't due for two more weeks, though, when the phone rang.

I have a collect call from Mr. Smith in San Francisco. Will you accept the charges?"

Less than two hours later I picked him up at Los Angeles International. He had thirty days' leave before reporting to a new base.

"I hope you can put me up," he said. "temporarily."

"Sure, if you don't mind sleeping in a warehouse."

It took him a day to unwrap the trove of packages he had sent home in the previous months. He had always had an eye for things of value. There would be no trash among his souvenirs. He had bought me a fine bronze Buddha, with one hand raised as a symbol of learning, and his mother a silver necklace the color of a twilight moon.

We adjusted. I even made peace with the rocking chair. In the mornings I sat in it in the kitchen and had my coffee and read the paper. The kaleidoscopic pattern kept changing, but the symmetry was always there, waiting to reveal itself, if you looked for it.

Then we were bumped once more. Doug told us that he and Mademoiselle Joyeux were going to France so she could be home for Christmas, and he could meet her parents.

CHAPTER 2

When Curt's leave was up I drove him out to Norton Air Force Base to catch a plane for his new post. He was going to England. It was a piece of luck. His original assignment had been to a base in Turkey, a bleak station out in the boondocks where men never saw anything but airplanes and goats. No one else wanted it, so he had volunteered. Then at the last moment a call had come from a base near London for a man of his rating, and his orders were changed.

We would miss him, but I was pleased that he was going. I thought of England as the country of my roots: I had grown up in England, through Dickens, Stevenson, and Conan Doyle, though I had never in reality been there. World War II had taken me the other way. For Curt it would be like a holiday. The war was behind him. He would see the sceptered isle at government expense, and perhaps have time to go across the Channel for a night in Paris, as every young man should.

But there was a thread of melancholy in my thoughts as I drove back to Los Angeles. For the first time, both our sons would be far away.

A letter awaited me in the box at home, and my spirits rose. It was from Doug, and it was postmarked London. He and Mademoiselle Joyeux were staying with her family in the village of Saint-Cyr, just across the Loire from Tours, but they had gone to Paris and taken the boat train to London for a holiday.

"Today we walked," he wrote. "Westminster Abbey is one of the most exciting things I have ever seen. We found it by accident, really. It is right across the street from Big Ben, all in the most ornate English Gothic style. . . ."

It wasn't a long letter, considering all he must have had to tell, and the real message was where I had learned to look for it in letters from distant sons—in the last paragraph.

"By the way, I hope you can both come to France for the wedding . . ."

They were going to be married in the *mairie*, or town hall, of Saint-Cyr. They would stay on in France for a few weeks after the wedding, then come back to America to live. Mademoiselle Joyeux's visa problems would be over.

We had three weeks to get ready. It was a fine excitement. Denny had never been to France, never seen Paris nor the mountain villages from which her parents had come, one in the Pyrenees, one in the Alps. She had to get a passport, and of course some luggage and some clothes, and all the time I was deciding that I couldn't go.

I finally told her. She would have to go alone. I was simply too busy to get away. For one thing, the house we were building down in Baja California, on the Bahía de Santa Tomás, was very nearly finished, and I would have to be nearby to see it through.

And of course, I pointed out, someone would have to stay home to take care of the automobiles and the motorcycle and the dogs. I had not only my own car, but also her car and our older son's car and our younger son's motorcycle. Also, who would feed the cats and goldfish?

She protested. She wouldn't go either. After all, it was going to be only a brief civil ceremony in the village mayor's office, not a big thing in the Tours cathedral. But I knew she had to go. Her roots were there, and now her grandchildren would have roots there too. Besides, she had bought new white boots and a white leather coat with a silver mink collar for the trip, and I knew that nothing, but nothing, should keep her from going.

I saw her off at the airport. As we said goodbye she told me, "Don't forget to put the trash out Tuesday morning."

It may seem a trivial thing to say at such an emotional moment, but getting the trash out was vital. If we missed on Tuesdays, we wallowed in trash for a week.

After the plane left I wondered how to remind myself to put the trash out Tuesday morning. It had always been her job. She had to get up earlier than I did in the morning, to get to work on time, so it was only natural. The trash truck came at seven o'clock, and it waited for no man.

It was not an easy task. We always had two or three barrels full, and sometimes four or five, especially if we'd had a big week for junk mail. Some Tuesday mornings it was touch and go. She would get up too late or forget it was Tuesday, and suddenly we would hear that galvanizing clank and grind and realize the truck was bearing down on us.

From the bedroom I could hear the entire drama—the cry of dismay, the opening and slamming of doors, the dash for robe and slippers, the clanging of the garage door, the groaning of the barrels as she dragged them out over the sidewalk, the anguished shout to the trash men:

"Wait! Wait for us!"

Once or twice I had put the barrels out myself, in emergencies, but it wasn't a good idea. If you have a system, you ought to stick to it. It's no good improvising so early in the morning.

Over the weekend, after she left, I could see that we were going to have a big trash. Three times the wastebaskets filled up and had to be carried down to the garage and emptied into the barrels. On the third trip I got my idea. I took one of the empty barrels and dragged it up to the house and through the front door and stood it in the middle of the living room.

It worked well. Whenever I walked through the room I dropped my trash in the barrel. When the mail came Monday morning I opened it over the barrel, setting the bills and personal letters aside and dropping the junk in.

Esthetically, a trash barrel in the living room may be controversial; but it is functional, and it might be considered an amusing pop comment on our civilization.

When the alarm went off Tuesday morning it reminded me of Denny. She would be in her small hotel in Paris. I wondered if she had awakened that morning in the City of Light and heard a truck rumbling over the Rue Saint-Simon and jumped out of bed, shouting, *"Mon dieu! It is the trash!"*

Suddenly I was aware of a clanging and scraping in our own street. I jumped out of bed.

It was too late.

My decision to stay home was hard enough to make, but I hadn't foreseen how much pressure would be brought to bear on me to change my mind—not just from members of my own family, but from colleagues at the paper where I worked and from strangers. They tried reason, sentiment, and shame. I was accused of everything from simple meanness of spirit to social alienation and psychic disassociation. One woman I didn't know sent me a two-word postcard saying "Go, Jack."

Oh, I wanted to go, all right. Except for the most urgent reasons I never miss a wedding to which I'm invited, though I will duck a funeral now and then. A wedding is a joyous rite. It is an honor to be invited and an act of cynicism as well as bad manners not to go. One might as well not care about the sunrise.

Some years back a young woman living in rural Indiana had written a letter to the *Post-Tribune* in nearby Gary, inviting me to her wedding. She had got the idea that I worked on that newspaper, which sometimes printed one of my pieces.

I thought it was quaint, a man living in Los Angeles being invited to a farm town in Indiana for the wedding of a girl he didn't know. The editor of my paper didn't think it was quaint at all.

"When a gentleman from the *Times* is invited to a lady's wedding," he said, "he goes."

I went. I flew to Chicago, took the electric train to Gary, and hired a car that got me to the church on time. There was a country breakfast afterward in the school gymnasium. I had never seen so much chicken. They must have decimated the chicken population of Indiana.

Yes, I thought, a wedding is a joyous occasion. And surely this one would be especially so. I pictured the wedding party climbing the steps of the little town hall. I could see my wife in her white boots and leather coat. How cold was it in France? Perhaps it would snow. I had never been to Tours, but I had read and heard that it was a beautiful and historic city. Mademoiselle Joyeux's parents would be there too, and her younger sister, Nanette. *Nanette.* I loved the name. Even our older son might be there, as best man. Surely he could get a pass for his brother's wedding and cross the Channel. The armed forces were civil about such things.

I wondered if everyone would cry. Yes, they would, I supposed. Except the two young men, of course. Young men didn't cry at weddings, did they? Only nice old bourgeois men were allowed to cry.

I supposed there would be a wedding breakfast afterwards, in some country inn, with much wine from the valley, and perhaps champagne. There would certainly be champagne if *I* was there. I really hated to miss the breakfast.

Within the week of Denny's departure a letter arrived on the stationery of the Hôtel Saint-Simon, 14 Rue Saint-Simon, Paris. I was surprised to find a slight tremor in my hands as I tore it open. I read rapidly down through the familiar handwriting.

". . . We walked around Notre-Dame last night and visited le Tour Eiffel, Rue Pigalle and Sacré-Coeur today. I'm finding the cold *cold,* but also bracing and exhilarating. Tomorrow we go first to the American Embassy, then the Champs-Élysées *et l'Arc du Triomphe et peut-être encore au* Tour Eiffel to go up on the elevator. Today there was a line waiting at least ten times as long as the one for *Midnight Cowboy.* . . .

". . . The hotel is charming and there's a darling little young concierge and what looked to me like a frightfully lumpy bed turned out to be the down comforter that has been keeping me cozy when I do hop in. *Mais il n'y avait pas du savon dans la chambre* (I told you so!).

"My God! It's two-thirty—and I want to get up at eight . . . Goodnight . . .

"P.S. Won't you change your mind? It isn't too late—if you *hurry! Spend all your kisses,* Mr. Smith."

I felt a strange surge of excitement as I read that final line. It was a phrase that had become something of a motto to us since that night, a year or two earlier, when I had come across it while reading by Coleman lantern in Mexico. I had never heard the phrase before, and it struck me as remarkably good advice. I read it aloud to her, wanting to share my discovery, but though she appeared to be listening, looking up from her own book, I had no idea that she would ever think of it again.

In the book I was reading the line was ascribed to some Roman poet, or Greek, perhaps. I must remember it, I told myself, and search out the poem at the library in Los Angeles. Sometimes, when I come across something I want to remember, I mark the page or make a note on a slip of paper, but more often I foolishly persuade myself that I can remember it without props. Then later I not only can't remember the book, but can't remember the thing to be remembered itself, having only a vague idea there was something I wanted to remember.

I remembered that quotation, and now and then I quoted it, or Denny did, when it seemed appropriate. But I soon forgot the name of the poet, and forgot what book I'd found it in. I looked in a dozen books, thinking it would turn up, but it never did. To this day I do not know the name of the poet, and I have never encountered anyone among my more erudite friends who knows it either.

And there it was before me again, a postscript to a letter. The phrase had many uses, we had discovered. It may have been purely a sensuous thought. Poets are not unknown to spend all their kisses. But surely it meant also that there is no point in taking any of one's riches into the next world. Why keep a kiss, a gesture, a word that might give a moment's pleasure or reassurance to someone else? Money you can't take with you. Kisses you can't leave behind.

I read the letter again and looked up a number in the phone book and dialed it, with a tremulous hand.

"Thank you for calling Air France," said a cool female voice. "Can I help you?"

"I want to fly to Paris," I said, "as soon as possible. Today. One person. First-class."

It might be difficult, she said. There was a steward's strike, and the airline was on a limited schedule. Perhaps I could wait a day or two?

"It's an emergency," I said. "A wedding. My son is marrying a Frenchwoman. There is no time to lose. I'm the father of the bride-groom."

Whatever their frailties, the French understand love and ceremony. She put me on a jet, nonstop for Paris.

CHAPTER 3

There was no one to meet me at Orly airport. No one knew I was coming. I had sent a letter to the Joyeux residence, where they were all to gather, but Denny had been somewhere in the Alps with Doug and Mademoiselle Joyeux, looking for her father's native village. The letter, I learned later, had been politely set aside, and waited unopened.

I had told them I would stay at Le Grand Hôtel, an elegant old palace near the Opéra. I took a taxi from the airport and spent a fitful night in my room. Global flights upset the human clockwork.

In the morning I bundled up and went out in the streets. My face turned numb. Paris was icy. I walked up the Boulevard des Capucines to a sidewalk café. It was glassed in for the winter.

I ordered coffee and croissants and took my time, like any Frenchman at his amenities, watching the shopgirls trotting off to their situations. They were armored against the cold in suedes and fake furs and shiny vinyl, like play soldiers in the opéra comique. Their cheeks were red and their legs flashed blue and pink through the slits in their flapping skirts.

I left the café and stepped into the quick parade. I felt an almost unbearable good humor. What a fine thing to be a member of this species, so chic and clever and vivid! The day was mine. Alone in Paris!

My eye caught a gaudy painted sign above a cinema that was showing *Bob & Carol & Ted & Alice*. It showed Bob & Carol & Ted & Alice, all in one bed . . . IMAGINEZ, it said, TOUTES LES POSSIBILITÉS!

Ah, Paris!

I walked till I came to the Arc de Triomphe and turned into the Avenue des Champs-Élysées and walked to the Place de la Concorde, vast and familiar under the towering pink obelisk from Luxor. Alas, the place was disfigured, like most of the urban world, by parked autos.

I walked on into the Tuileries Gardens. Its trees were sticks, its pools icy, its nudes cold. It was bleak and beautiful, quivering with the spring juices inside it, waiting to burst out.

I walked through the courtyards of the Louvre and took the Pont Neuf over the river to the Left Bank and walked in narrow streets to the Boulevard Saint-Germain. It began to rain. I ducked into a bar and ordered a café and drank it slowly, looking around at the other patrons.

Near the door a stocky man with a stiff gray beard and a face like pink granite was looking down through gold-rimmed spectacles at a paper on his table, working at it with a pencil in his rawboned hand. The likeness was startling. But the man was years dead!

As I left the café I gave him a closer look. It wasn't Hemingway at all, of course, nor even his ghost. It was only some lesser exile, working the crossword puzzle in the Paris *Herald-Tribune*.

I took a taxi back to the hotel. The evening was ahead. Alone in Paris. *"Imaginez toutes les possibilités!"*

"Ah, Monsieur Smith," said the man at the desk. "A message for you."

It was a telegram from Tours. ARRIVING YOUR HOTEL ABOUT 8 P.M. PLEASE WAIT IN YOUR ROOM.

It was nearly ten when they came in; my wife and both our sons. They had arrived in Tours and opened my letter that day. Curt had got a pass and come over on the boat train from London, arriving just in time to join them. Mademoiselle Joyeux had stayed in Tours to prepare for the wedding.

We walked to a café on the Boulevard des Italiens and had onion soup and mugs of Danish beer and were pleased with life.

In the morning my wife and our betrothed son set out to shop for a wedding ring and a pair of shoes. His old ones were down to the nails. I set out with Curt to see Paris. We were all to meet in the Louvre at noon.

Curt and I took the underground to Saint-Germain-des-Prés, on the Left Bank, and walked without plan in that exhilarating quarter, feasting on the scents of sausages and cheeses and the shop windows stuffed with the amenities of civilized life and the faces of people who seemed every one unique and valuable.

We paid three francs each to stand under the great dome of the Panthéon, not sure just which god we were to be in awe of, Yahweh or Bonaparte or Cybèle, and then walked a block to the Sorbonne, where students hurried down the sidewalks in their winter wraps, looking cold and hungry and exuberant, like extras in *La Bohème*.

We crossed the Seine to the Île de la Cité and entered Notre-Dame. It was cold. A mass was going on. Old men in red vestments sat in the choir stalls, singing the antique litany, their heads canted sideways on their necks, their faces old as stones.

We reached the Louvre on time. The others were late, and Curt suggested that we look into the hall of antiquity. We walked down an enormous corridor toward an atrium in which the Winged Victory of Samothrace soared headless against massive flights of stone stairs in a downpour of cloudy daylight. We climbed to another long hallway at the end of which the Venus de Milo waited for us in a vaulted chamber. We walked around her, seeing colors and scars and subtleties that a million copies had neglected.

Later, when the others came along, we lunched in the Louvre café on cold chicken and white wine. They had found a wedding ring in a shop on the Place de l'Opéra, but there had been some trouble about Doug's shoes. He had settled finally for a pair that were otherwise suitable, but squeaky.

"With every step," he said, "she's going to hate these shoes."

We started out in a little German Ford for Tours, escaping from the chaos of Paris traffic into the winter countryside. In midafternoon two spires appeared in the distance.

"Chartres," Doug said. "Isn't it fantastic!"

We drove into Chartres through medieval streets and parked below the cathedral and walked up to it and into the towering dim nave. We were alone, except for the ranks of stone angels and martyrs and one ancient woman lighting a candle before a patron saint.

It was tomb-cold. Only the candles and the light of the stained-glass windows gave any sense of warmth. It was utterly still. But I felt the presence of terrible and exalted spirits who had waited seven hundred years for this family of shivering Americans and an old woman lighting a candle.

It was dark when we reached Tours and crossed the river to Saint-Cyr-sur-Loire and drew up at the neat white plaster house on the Rue Foch where Mademoiselle Joyeux and her family awaited our arrival with a festive table.

"This is it," Doug said. He got out of the car and opened our door, and with every step his shoes squeaked.

My familiarity with Jacqueline's errant but engaging English had not prepared me for this first encounter with her parents. The Joyeuxs' lack of English was profound. Even Doug's prolonged visit had made no breach in that wall. Their English was no more abundant than my French, which is to say that between us there might have been a dozen words, in one language or the other, that were mutually understood, and these were soon battered beyond further service, like a shuttlecock in a doubles game between duffers.

My own ineptitude became apparent to me as soon as the door to the house was open and a small white feisty dog made for my ankles, yipping psychotically.

"Down," I muttered as he threw himself against my knees. He was not intimidated, however, and I realized with dismay that I didn't even know how to talk to a French *dog*.

"Clyde," scolded a girl who stood at the back of the crowd. She chastised the dog in his native tongue and he skulked away, biding his time.

Clyde? What a ridiculous name, I thought, for a dog.

But the warmth and hospitality of the Joyeux household soon transcended language. The house was two and a half stories high, but narrow, like a house in a medieval city. The lower floor was given over entirely to a dining room, which served also as the parlor, and a large kitchen. "My father," Jacqueline had told me, "he live to eat and drink."

Everything seemed almost clinically neat, but the table at the center of the stage was already set, dishes and flatware gleaming in the candle-light; and on a cabinet against the wall I saw a row of bottles, their contents ranging in color from palest yellow to deepest red. As my eyes fondled that lovely rainbow my tensions eased; here was the common language that Jacques Joyeux and I would share.

Maria Joyeux was as neat as her house, a well-kept woman, thin but well-shaped. Monsieur Joyeux was rounder than she, thanks, perhaps, to his love of food and wine, and bald as a monk. During the flurry of kissing and chattering that followed our entrance he said almost nothing, an activity in which I joined him, but our eyes met warmly. We knew we would find our meeting ground.

Monsieur Joyeux soon withdrew to the kitchen, our dinner being already on the stove. He was the village postman of Saint-Cyr, Jacqueline had told us, making his daily rounds on his bicycle; but he had once been a chef, and it was in the kitchen that he gave expression to the poet in the postman.

The girl who had rescued me from the dog soon sought me out. She was Jacqueline's younger sister, of course, Nanette.

"You speak French, yes?" she said in a burst of English which caused me to hope, for a moment, that we were about to engage in a long and enlightening conversation.

"No," I said. "But *you* speak English?"

"*Oui*," she said. "I am study her at school."

We made faltering progress, mostly over the steppingstones of her schoolbook English. I was soon enchanted. She was schoolgirl shy, but there was a boldness underneath, and wit, and she was vibrant with excitement over the visitors from America, the wedding, the sense of doors opening into a new world of unimaginable delights. She was a student at the Lycée Choiseul, which was in Tours beside the cathedral, but she was eighteen years old, or near it, and soon she would go to Paris to begin life.

Somehow the dog had got back in and was at me again. I gave him a knee in the muzzle, hoping Nanette wouldn't notice, and toppled him over, but he was up in an instant, more furious than before.

"You do not like Clyde?" said Nanette, laughing at me in her eyes.

"Clyde? Where did he get that name?"

"He is from your movie," she said. "I see *Bonnie and Clyde*, I say, Clyde is a good name for z'dog. Yes?"

Dinner began with onion soup. Monsieur Joyeux's pièce de résistance was a dish made of Belgian endive, ham, and Swiss cheese, and of course there was cheese and fruit and a pastry. But my memory is mostly of the wines.

He had seized upon my appearance as a God-given opportunity to demonstrate the wondrous variety and superior quality of the wines of the Loire, and he intended that I should not escape a single one. In this design, which both my wife and his regarded as insidious, I was wholeheartedly his accomplice.

My glass was never empty, except when my host emptied the dregs of one wine only to speed me to the next. Glass for glass we proceeded through his cellar, Monsieur Joyeux naturally asking nothing of me in the way of capacity that he was not quick to match himself. It became a ritual. The wine poured, the glass raised, the bouquet inhaled, the mouthful taken, the exclamation of approval; and all the while Monsieur Joyeux's eyes anxiously on mine, watching for their spontaneous tacit judgment.

For once in my life I was not unhappy to hear that there would be no champagne with dessert; but this turned out to be only because Monsieur Joyeux disdained champagne in favor of the sparkling white wine of his own valley. It was indeed a buoyant vintage, and it gave me the lift I needed, at last, to make it up the narrow wooden stairway to our bedroom on the top floor under the attic.

"Long live France," I sighed, and was soon as deep in slumber as all its kings.

I am an early riser, whatever my follies, and Jacques Joyeux evidently shared that virtue. When I went downstairs the next morning he was sitting at the table, drinking a milky-looking coffee from a cup the size of a cereal bowl. There was butter and jam on the table, and a great long loaf of bread. I guessed that he had already been out to the village bakery.

"*Bon jour,*" I said tentatively.

"*Bon jour,*" he said, not altering the tone.

We appeared to be the only members of the household who were up. He poured my coffee and we sat drinking and eating in silence, neither of us being noticeably well. Finally Madame Joyeux came down the stairs, then Nanette, then my wife, and one by one the others.

The wedding was not to be until the next day, and the drill for this morning, I was informed, was a visit to the nearby Château Langeais. Eager as I was to explore the medieval ornaments of the Loire, I had no stomach for a drive over icy roads that morning to tramp up and down stone stairways in an icy castle.

"I have a bit of jet lag," I explained.

But it was not thought proper for me to stay behind, and besides, we were first to take a taxicab into Tours, where I was to rent an automobile for the duration of our visit. The Joyeuxs had only their bicycles, and we would need a decent car for the wedding. As we left I envied Monsieur Joyeux, alone at his table with his third bowl of coffee.

We rented a fine new Renault sedan and drove over icy roads to the Château Langeais, a cheerless-looking stronghold built over the ruins of Fulk the Black of Anjou's keep, the oldest in France. It was tomb-cold, inside and out. A guide whose enthusiasm was no greater than mine led us from one cold chamber to another, wrapping us in shrouds of what he evidently thought was English.

Shivering and mildly vertiginous, I stood in the great chamber where Charles VIII had married Anne de Bretagne five hundred years before, and wondered that anyone could have fallen deep enough in love to get married in a castle without central heating.

It was extraordinary how quickly my spirits rose at lunch. Monsieur Joyeux had a repast waiting for us when we returned from the château, including, of course, the indispensable wine. Though I had misgivings about drinking any, I was reassured by the first taste; it warmed me to my toes. By the second glass I was euphoric.

Then midway through the meal something quite remarkable occurred. Monsieur Joyeux placed his knife and fork in his plate and sat still for a moment while his eyes seemed to cross slightly and his pinkish face went green. Up he got to his feet, without an *excusez-moi,* and hurried up the stairs.

"Your father is not well?" I asked my intended daughter-in-law.

"*Oui,* Mr. Smith," she said. "He is not well. Last night he 'ave *too* much wine."

"That is too bad," I said, trying not to sound triumphant.

CHAPTER 4

Our son and his betrothed were married on a snowy Saturday morning in the *mairie* (town hall) of Saint-Cyr, across the river from Tours.

They had considered marrying in the church, but the ecclesiastics of Tours were not propitiated by the bridegroom's credentials, or the lack thereof. I for one regarded this as a happy circumstance, suspecting that the town hall would be warmer than the church, and the civil ceremony briefer.

On the morning of the wedding the aunts, uncles, and cousins began gathering at the house on Rue Foch. There was an air of great excitement and much running up and down the stairs, and many bad jokes in two languages, and finally the bride descended in a full-length white satin fur-trimmed dress and white short jacket with fur-trimmed hood. Nanette, the bridesmaid, looked hardly less spectacular, and rather more worldly, in a chic black maxi coat and large-brimmed floppy hat. She carried a red purse and wore red mittens and a red band around her hat, and looked ready indeed to go to Paris and begin life.

We piled into four cars and drove through Saint-Cyr to the town square and parked directly in front of the *mairie,* the square looking as if it had been cleared of everything but a bicycle or two in expectation of our arrival. The *mairie* seemed larger than the Joyeux house. We climbed wooden stairs to the public meeting room where the ceremony was to be held. The room was spartan-plain, with rows of wooden chairs facing a long table.

A bust of La Belle France rested on a shelf above the table, and at the opposite end of the room, behind the chairs, a life-size bust of Anatole France stood on a pedestal with a plaque which noted that the illustrious writer had lived in Saint-Cyr, and at long last had wed his faithful housekeeper, Marie-Héloïse (called Emma), in this very room.

We settled into the chairs, and waited for the mayor to ascend the stairway for the ceremony. Two girls, the mayor's clerks, stood behind the table, turning the pages of a great register, and calling up the members of the wedding to sign in the proper places.

All was in order. We waited. Then we heard a measured step on the stairs. The mayor entered—a stately gray-haired woman in a beige and black dress with a silk sash—the tricolor of France—slanting down across her bosom.

Madame la maire walked with the dignity of Charles de Gaulle to her place at the center of the table and sat beneath the bust of La Belle France, symbol of la République. The resemblance was stunning. With her classic face, a face that might have been sculptured by Houdon, with the gray hair combed straight back from the noble forehead, *Madame la maire* was La Belle herself, though half a century older.

She beckoned the betrothed to come forward. The bridegroom took two curiously awkward steps, almost as if he were limping. Was something wrong? An instant later I remembered. The shoes. He was walking in a special way to keep his new French shoes from squeaking.

The *maire* began to read, rapidly, in French, the words coming out fluent and musical, like a jazz solo on the clarinet. She asked her questions and received, apparently, the right responses. *Oui.* Yes. *Oui.* I understood little, but once I caught my son's name. It was a question, followed by a momentary silence. *La maire* looked up expectantly.

"*Écrivain*," he said at last, as if having made an on-the-spot decision.

The *maire* finished. She beamed. She handed to the bridegroom a parchment stamped with the seal of Saint-Cyr. The ceremony was over. Chairs scraped on the wooden floor. There was much handshaking and hugging and kissing and laughing.

"Did you hear that?" my wife said aside to me as we moved toward the stairway. "*Écrivain?* He gave his occupation as a writer."

A writer. So that was what the word meant. Well, I thought, why not? It was better than being unemployed.

As we passed by Anatole France I gave him a wink. For a young *écrivain*, it seemed to me, the mischievous old skeptic would make as good a patron saint as any other.

We all gathered for a moment on the steps of the *mairie*, the bride like an enchanted white rabbit in her fur-trimmed hood. The icy air rang with joyous shouts and laughter.

Then snow began to fall; very light and beautiful and ephemeral. The flakes were tiny and bright and fell slowly, melting in the street.

We all hurried to our cars and drove out in the Loire Valley to Vouvray, where the wines are made, and sat down to a wedding feast in a warm inn called Le Val Joli.

On such a morning it was understandable why the French had invented the phrase *la joie de vivre.* It was a morning for weeping with joy, and of course some tears were shed; but there was more laughter as we gathered around a long table at Le Val Joli. It was a hunting lodge, or had been one, and the walls were hung with paintings of huntsmen in the woods with their dogs.

I had hoped to sit next to Nanette, so I might continue her English lesson, but the unattached girls in the party moved automatically to the side of my older son, the young American airman with the guardsman mustache. He sat between Nanette and one of her pretty cousins, and I observed that he seemed to have no trouble amusing both, though his French was no better than mine.

I found myself between an uncle and an aunt, I believe they must have been, who spoke no English. But fortune did not ignore me altogether, for my friend Jacques Joyeux was seated on the far side of the aunt I had drawn, and he, of course, was in charge of the wine. In the exercise of this responsibility, he performed with nothing less than the vigilance and generosity I expected of him.

That I would be grateful for a sip or two of wine became apparent as soon as the food began to arrive. First, for the appetite, we received plates heaped with seashells, some of them looking quite paleolithic, from which we were expected, I gathered, to extract the viscous flesh with an assortment of tools that lay beside each plate like instruments set out on a dental surgeon's tray. One of them, which appeared to be a nutcracker, was to be used, I saw by watching the others, for cracking the more stubborn of the creatures that had been wrested from the sea for this occasion. *Fruits de mer,* these delicacies were called. It is a term I am not likely to forget.

I eat shellfish reluctantly, since I am not fond of them to begin with, and there is some evidence that they give me hives. Thus, I made a perfunctory pass at a clam or two, then washed them down with a white wine from one of the two bottles which, thanks to Monsieur Joyeux, stood within easy reach of my plate.

The *fruits de mer* merely made me feel uncomfortable. I was afraid I would be thought quite rude, neither speaking the language nor eating the food. By polite exclamations of appreciation for the wine, however, accompanied by histrionic smiles and gestures, I hoped to express my good intentions. Indeed, all went well enough until the next course came.

I suddenly found myself looking into a plate on which lay two dead birds. They were hardly larger than sparrows, and for all I knew *were* sparrows. They had of course been plucked, but the remarkable thing about them, to my mind, was that they still had their heads and their feet. I was undone. I find it hard enough to eat fowl in any form, without thinking of the whole bird, soaring from tree to tree in glorious life. Never had I been asked to put knife and fork to a bird that looked as if he might put on his coat at any moment and fly away.

Not only was I unable to eat my birds, I was unable to watch my companions eat *their* birds; and when I heard my new daughter-in-law utter a tiny cry of delight as hers were placed before her, I wondered if after all our son hadn't made a mistake; if there were not cultural barriers one ought not cross.

It was only a momentary defection, of course, and my spirits returned as soon as I poured a glass from the bottle I had not previously tried. A most remarkable wine, I thought. It seemed to go straight to the head, and by the time I had drunk half a glass my fears and inhibitions were so thoroughly repressed that I might have tried one of the birds, if I hadn't already sent them away.

I had no idea how rapidly I was being anesthetized, however, until I essayed a scrap of conversation with the aunt on my left while pouring myself another glass, only to see her point, in great agitation, toward the bottle. Not quite in time, I saw that I was missing the glass and pouring that remarkable vintage, whatever it was, on the tablecloth of Le Val Joli.

Afterwards we piled into the Renault, and Doug drove us out to the Château Amboise, which is said to have been the first work of the French Renaissance in the valley of the Loire. In my judgment it was colder than the Château Langeais had been, if that was possible, and larger, and the English was no better. As I stood freezing on the balcony from which the Huguenots had been hanged, I groped for some profound observation on man's inhumanity to man, but all I could think of was the warmth of the Joyeux house, and the bed on the third floor under the attic. More than anything I wanted a nap.

At dinner that night I tried to find out from Jacques Joyeux, with Jacqueline interpreting, the name of the wine that had made such an impression on me. The question seemed to make him very merry.

"Mr. Smith," said Jacqueline, "my father say that z'bottle was not wine. It was *cognac*."

Everyone laughed, and Monsieur Joyeux raised his glass to me.

"He say," said my daughter-in-law, "you were *magnifique*."

On Sunday morning after the wedding, Denny and I took the train from Tours back to Paris to spend one last day. It was a Sunday, a day so cold and so beautiful that we ached from the cold and the beauty of it.

We had a room in a small hotel on the Left Bank, four flights up and no elevator, around a corner from the Place Saint-Germain-des-Prés, with its old cafés and old church, the oldest church in Paris.

Church bells woke us, the sound deep and measured; old bells, the same bells that had awakened Molière and Berlioz and Alice B. Toklas, and might at this very moment be waking a new Voltaire.

We walked down the Boulevard Saint-Germain to the Seine, and then across the bridge to Notre-Dame. A priest in red, the archbishop himself perhaps, was singing the mass in French.

We walked down the south aisle and stood in the light of the great rose window, beside the statue of St. Joan of Arc. The maid seemed supple and alive in the light of half a dozen votive candles.

The priest's voice was high and reedy against the deep distant voice of the great organ. Then he called the communicants to the altar and they streamed forward to receive the bread and wine.

The organ music soared. It grew wild and awful, like some cosmic river flooding. It filled the church. The very stones seemed made of sound. It burst into an exaltation that was almost unbearable, and then the power drained away and left only a plaintive aftersound, a few notes tumbling after each other in some playful fugue.

I was trembling, but not from the cold, as we walked out into the daylight.

"You seemed quite shaken back there," Denny said after a while, "for an unbeliever."

"Yes," I admitted. "But I'm not an unbeliever. I believe in Bach."

We had lunch in a glassed-in sidewalk café on the Avenue des Champs-Élysées, warming ourselves first with a *lait Gabrielle,* a nectar made of hot milk, honey, rum, and cinnamon.

The Sunday promenade was in full tide. Tens of thousands of Parisians were out on their splendid boulevard—the rich and the bohemian and the bourgeois; young lovers and old roués and married couples en famille, pushing red-cheeked infants in perambulators.

If this was all that civilization had brought us to, a *lait Gabrielle* in a sidewalk café on a cold Sunday in Paris, watching the people walk on the Champs-Élysées, it had all been worth it, all the centuries.

We descended into the underground and took the Métro back to the Place Saint-Germain-des-Prés, and when we came up to the street again it was snowing.

We had dinner in an old restaurant from La Belle Époque, looking at all the people and being looked at, sharing the communal sense of joy and excitement, and feeling quite lucky to be human.

The best part of any trip is the memory of it. Cold cannot be remembered, and minor disasters become diversions.

We flew home from Paris nonstop, and when I stepped out of the plane to the ramp I was kissed by a breath of warm air off the Pacific.

It was so pleasant, so reassuring, that I felt as if the world had never been any other temperature.

CHAPTER 5

It was a poignant April. First Curt came home from England and we went out to UCLA together for the annual Mardi Gras. He was due to leave the Air Force in the fall, and he wanted to go back to the university and get his degree. Like many of his generation, he had enlisted to resolve the uncertainty of the war and the draft. The beautiful Westwood campus, now tranquil after the turbulent '60s, stood for everything he hoped to come home to.

The Mardi Gras was held on the green field between the new dormitories and the old brick halls on the hills above the sunny splash of Janss Steps. We bought a string of tickets and tried a few rides and games of skill. It was early in the day and the other revelers were mostly children.

The booths were tended by UCLA girls; more cooks in every kitchen than were needed. They turned out to be the part of the Mardi Gras my son liked best. I was standing in line for a hot dog on a stick when I realized I had lost him. I walked back and found him looking at an ice cream booth.

SOPHOMORE SWEETHEART ICE CREAM, the sign said.

"You want some ice cream?" I asked.

"No. See that girl in the booth?"

She had Lady Godiva hair and a beach-girl figure and was wearing a demure white apron.

"Watch," he said.

She turned around and reached into the freezer to scoop up some ice cream. Under the apron she wore a little black mini. He sighed. So did I.

"All the time I was in England," he said, "it was winter."

We walked on.

"Step right up," a young man barked over a mike. "Win a Frisbee!"

For one ticket you got three chances to throw a Frisbee through a hole in a canvas wall. If one went through, you won a Frisbee. I got in line. Two small boys in front of me won Frisbees. My turn came.

"Sorry, sir," said the girl in the booth. "I'll have to charge you two tickets. You're—uh—not that young."

I thought she had handled it with tact. She might easily have said I was too old. I didn't win a Frisbee anyway.

We had pizza pie and teriyaki on a stick and then Curt said he was still hungry.

"You feel like an ice cream sundae?" he said.

We walked back to the Sophomore Sweetheart and ordered two chocolate sundaes.

"It's been four years," he said, watching the girl scoop up the ice cream. "I wasn't sure they still looked that good."

I could have told him he needn't have worried. They would always look that good.

Then Doug and Jacqueline came back from France. He found a job working nights, and for a few weeks, while they were house-hunting, they stayed with us.

It was a good chance for me to get better acquainted with Mademoiselle Joyeux, for I still thought of her as that. We weren't yet easy with each other. She still called me Mr. Smith, and though I called her Jacqueline, and grew more enchanted by her every day, there seemed to be a vague tension between us; a distance that neither knew how to cross. I imagined that she still saw in me the personification of everything difficult about America.

Like many Frenchwomen, she had developed a supple wit to protect her from male autocracy in a male chauvinist world, and often enough I felt its quick, light touch. She was elusive, though, and given to swift attacks followed at once by that disarming innocence. I was never sure whether to say "Touché" or "Sorry."

When she was home with us those evenings we tended to rely on television for entertainment. It eased the conversational strain, and at the same time gave our daughter-in-law a rather intensive course in American manners and morals.

One night we were watching a movie from the 1950s and I realized how far we had come since then in dealing with sex on the screen. I am not necessarily in favor of complete candor, but those old movies might have been easier to follow if the sexual encounters had been a little more explicit.

When movies were censored we never knew for sure whether anything had *happened* or not. There were clues—that look in Katharine Hepburn's eyes in *The African Queen;* lines like, "Please, Roger, don't spoil everything"; and music, always music, building up big and powerful and cascading over us in the fadeout.

I knew, and you knew, perhaps, that something had happened; that the plot had taken a critical turn, that it would never be quite the same with Clark and Ava again. But those scenes often went over the heads of innocents who didn't know life, or had just moved up from Hopalong Cassidy.

In one of the movies we saw on the television en famille, Richard Burton was a doctor who fell in love with Barbara Rush, the wife of Burton's best friend, Larry, who was dying of Hodgkin's disease.

Ordinarily I wouldn't have watched it. I'd had it with movies about doctors' dilemmas. But our daughter-in-law liked soap operas because everybody talked slow and said everything twice. "My God, Fred, I've suffered! How I've suffered! But I love you! I love you!" That made it easier for her to understand.

Everybody in the movie felt guilty. Burton felt guilty because as a boy he had seen his mother in bed with the gasman, Jimmy Dunn, and blabbed it to his father, who took it so hard he jumped to his death from a Cape Cod cliff. You didn't see all this, though. Burton told it in a choked-up monologue against a pounding surf of background music.

"Mr. Smith," said Jacqueline, "I do not understand. What does he say?"

"He said his father killed himself because his mother was unfaithful," I said.

"Really? For *zat* he kill himself?"

"This is Boston, Massachusetts," I pointed out, "not France."

Later it happened. Barbara Rush followed Burton down to his boat and he tried to comfort her over Larry being in such bad shape. They were standing on the deck in the daylight. He took her in his arms and the music rose and there was a fadeout to a Sleep-Eze commercial.

In the commercial a man couldn't sleep so his wife gave him a Sleep-Eze and he had a good night's sleep. "Tonight," the announcer said, "why don't you slip someone you love a Sleep-Eze? You'll both feel better in the morning."

Jacqueline left the room during the commercial and didn't get back until after a scene in which Barbara Rush told Burton she was going away to New Haven to have her baby.

"What 'appen?" she asked.

"Barbara Rush is going to have a baby," I told her.

"She is *enceinte*?"

"She is what?"

"*Enceinte*."

"Oh. *Enceinte*," I said, trying to copy her pronunciation. I hadn't come across that word but once or twice since high school days, when I was devouring the works of Guy de Maupassant. The French always had a better word for anything to do with women. *Enceinte* sounded so much more elegant than "pregnant."

"*Oui*," I said. "She is *enceinte*."

"Zen zay mus' have gone farzer zan I s'ought," she said. "I s'ought he only kees her."

"I could hardly keep from laughing," my wife told me later that night, "when Jacqueline wanted to know if what's-her-name was *enceinte*."

"Why is that?"

"Because *she* is, you know."

"She is what?"

"*Enceinte*."

"Who is?"

"Your daughter-in-law, of course."

I guess the grandfather is always the last to know.

Not long after that revelation, with its implications of my own changing status, I had yet another one to ponder.

We have always had a few heirlooms: a porcelain clock with gilded angels on it; a chamber pot now planted with some kind of succulents; a set of pewter—all kitsch but very precious. These things came down from some romantic past, beyond memory, where heirlooms are supposed to come from.

But it gives a man a start when he finds that something he bought in his youth is regarded already as a family heirloom. When one buys something new he does not expect it to become an heirloom in his own lifetime. The things we buy new *stay* new, don't they? Like the faces of friends we see every day, they never change.

True, my younger son has an easy chair that belonged to my father. My father left it to me, and I used it for years and then passed it on to Doug when he was married. So the chair is already in the third generation. It's as sturdy as ever and sound enough for a fourth generation, I'm sure. Then it will be an heirloom. I don't think you can call something an heirloom until it has seen four generations.

What worries me is the mirror.

I bought the mirror for my mother on her birthday, as I remember, a year or so after World War II. It was a large, oblong mirror to be hung on a wall. My mother hung it in her living room to give an illusion of space, a decorating trick that was then in vogue.

In time the mirror came down to Denny and me and we hung it in our living room to give an illusion of space. The mirror-space-illusion vogue had passed out in favor of Van Gogh prints, but we needed all the space and illusion we could get.

Later, when our sons grew tall enough to see over the top of a dresser, and vain enough to comb their hair, we put up a Van Gogh print where the mirror was and hung the mirror in their bedroom. There it had remained intact through all the many vicissitudes of recent years.

For a long time I hadn't given the mirror a thought. Now that my wife used the extra bedroom for sewing, she was the only one who frequently saw the mirror. I don't know whether she ever looked into it or not.

Then one day we were getting ready to visit Doug and Jacqueline in their new house. It was Jacqueline's birthday. There was a large, flat package against the wall. Denny was writing on a card.

"What are we giving her?" I asked.

"A mirror. You think that's all right?"

"Mirror?"

"Yes. All she has is a hand mirror. She needs a larger one."

She did indeed. She was expecting, and a young woman in that state ought to have a decent mirror, to watch the progress of her miracle.

"Do you mind putting it in the car?" Denny asked.

It seemed remarkably heavy.

"Where'd you get it?" I asked. "It weighs a ton."

"Where'd I get it? Why, out of the bedroom. It's ours. Didn't you know?"

Jacqueline was delighted. I saw at once how impossible it would have been for her without a mirror. She was before all else a daughter of France, and I could not imagine a Frenchwoman without one.

I sat in my father's easy chair watching her as she got acquainted with the mirror, regarding it first with apprehension, then with curiosity, then with a certain smile. Today, perhaps, the mirror was not at its best. Time would change that.

It struck me. Soon enough another person would look into that mirror, perhaps experiencing the same emotions, from fear to self-approval.

She would be—good Lord—my granddaughter! She would be the fourth generation to see herself in that mirror, that heirloom.

I got up out of my father's chair and looked at my mother's mirror. It had turned gray, I noticed, at the temples.

There are certain momentous events in a family's history at which the presence of the patriarch is not only unnecessary, but sometimes a nuisance.

I had been planning to go see the Rams play that weekend, but it was possible that in my absence I might become a grandfather.

"Why don't you just go ahead," Denny said. "It's no great problem. There wouldn't be anything you could do, anyway."

Of course she was right. I had been at sea, somewhere between Iwo Jima and Maui, when I became a father, and I did not get home to see our first son until he was nine months old. It was unlikely that I would be needed for the successful delivery of a grandchild.

"Nothing's going to happen this soon, anyway," she said.

"All the same," I said, "maybe it would be better if I just stood by."

She left for Jacqueline's house and I took off my shoes and sat in my rocking chair, looking out the window into a darkening sky. It was beautiful football weather.

I wondered how long I would have to wait. I got up and put on a Glenn Miller record and opened a beer. I turned the phonograph down low, so that the sound was more like an echo from the past, and found a dogeared Ross Macdonald mystery I had already read twice. There was no harm in nostalgia; not if you didn't try to live in it, but only used it to remind yourself that you had a past as well as a present, and a future.

But this time it didn't work. I couldn't get into the past. The present wouldn't let me go. I checked my watch. I gave the telephone ten minutes to ring.

I changed into slacks and an old tweed jacket and left a note: "Gone to the game after all. Don't worry. Love."

I found my field glasses and drove down to the freeway, wondering what it was I had meant her not to worry about.

I thought back to the war, when I was in the Pacific and Denny was expecting. She had taken advantage of my absence by vetoing my choice for a name, if our first child happened to be a boy. In the last letter I had written her before I was swallowed up in a landing, and we lost contact, I had suggested that we call him Lucky Jordan, after the hero of a recent motion picture starring Alan Ladd. Many weeks went by before our transport put my regiment back on Maui, and I found, among the dozens of letters in my mail-call packet, one that told me I had a son named Curtis Bresson Smith, the Bresson being his mother's maiden name. Actually, I liked it, though I realized it was two-thirds French. It seemed to me a good idea for all children, male and female, to preserve their mother's family name.

I knew my wishes would carry even less weight in the naming of my grandchild. Still, a grandfather has a right to make suggestions, and I had proposed Michele or Gabriele, for a girl, and Jacques for a boy, with Joyeux to be given as the middle name in either case. Jacques Joyeux Smith. It seemed to me to have a lot of class: and of course it would be an honor to both grandfathers.

It was a big game and I had to park more than a mile away from the Coliseum, but I didn't mind. Good football weather is good walking weather, and I was glad for the exercise, hurrying along the sidewalk with a stream of others, feeling an unspoken camaraderie.

I bought a ticket, a hot dog, and a program and found my seat. I was alone in a sea of empty yellow seats, but they soon began to fill. Even then I felt alone, isolated among noisy cliques and amorous couples.

It was all right, though, once the Rams took the field. A man can identify with his team. They were Arthurian knights; they wore my colors; they shouldered my cause. In my eyes they were chaste—a flight of 250-pound angels.

It was a good game; not a great game. I don't remember what the score was, or even who won, but I do remember that when I got home the house was empty. I phoned Doug's house but no one answered. I tried reading. I watched a movie on TV. The phone rang. It was Denny.

"I tried calling you earlier," she said. "Everything's fine. It happened sooner than anyone expected. You're a grandfather."

"It's a girl?"

"It's a boy."

"Jacques Joyeux?"

"No . . . Christophe Pierre."

"You mean Christopher?" I said hopefully.

"No. Christophe. It's French."

So there was no granddaughter yet to inherit the mirror. But maybe Christophe Pierre would like football in a few years, and I would finally have a relative who understood me.

It wasn't until a day or two later, when they got the birth certificate, that we found out it was really spelled Cristophe—with only the one *h*.

Jacqueline explained: "I am still dope up from my shot when this lady come to say, 'What is the baby's name?' and I forget how to spell Christophe. Now it is too late."

It didn't matter much to me. I planned to call him Pete.

CHAPTER 6

One art form I had long since grown beyond, I hoped, was the horror movie, but I found myself watching them again, though not by choice.

Horror movies were Jacqueline's favorite TV fare. Her English still wasn't quick enough to pick up all the thrusts and parries of fast dialogue, and in that regard horror movies are even better than the soap operas. They have very little dialogue at all, and it runs to freak and creature talk, which is quite slow; or to Fay Wray screams and hoarse cries of "My God, Dr. Peabody, it's come back!"

Our son was working until midnight, and Jacqueline often came to our place evenings with her infant to watch horror movies on TV until time to pick him up. She would not only watch the early ones, but also the late ones, which didn't begin until eleven o'clock. This was both a blessing and a curse.

By midnight, when she had to leave, the movie was only two-thirds over. Then she begged me to watch the last third, after she had gone, so she could phone the next morning and find out how it ended. Of course I hadn't seen the first two-thirds. I'd been shut up in my den, trying to read. When she left, and I took over, I never had the murkiest idea what was going on. In the last third the story always degenerated into an orgy of screaming and bloodletting and then it was The End.

The next morning she would phone.

"Ah, Mr. Smith! You see z'end?"

"Yes."

"What happen?"

"I don't know. It was horrible. There was this dreadful fight."

"Zey kill z'monster?"

"I'm not sure. Which one was z'monster?"

None of these conversations ever ended in a satisfactory way, for either of us.

On Monday nights, though, it was even more frustrating for us both, because of the conflict created by the regular Monday-night pro football game on the tube.

I couldn't always get home for the kickoff at six-thirty. So I would phone home and if Jacqueline was there I would ask her to turn the game on and watch it for me. I knew she wouldn't watch it. She understood football even less than my wife did. But she would turn it on for me. That kept her from turning on the early horror movie and being halfway through it when I got home. I wouldn't have had the heart to turn it off.

One Monday night I got home at half-time when the Browns were playing the Oilers.

"Who's ahead?" I asked. "What's the score?"

"I do not know who is the teams."

"The Browns are in white and the Oilers in blue."

"Zey all look purple."

She was right. she hadn't adjusted the color. It was hideous. The Oilers looked like eggplants.

Then she and my wife went shopping and left me alone with the baby. I had never been alone with him before.

"What'll I do," I asked, "if he starts to cry?"

"He will not cry."

As soon as the sound of the car died out, he started to cry. I couldn't even hear the quarterbacks calling signals. I put him in the bedroom. He cried louder. I picked him up and took him back to my chair and held him so he could see the screen, and rather to my surprise he stopped crying.

He was still watching the game when they came back. His mother beamed.

"Ah, you hold z'kid!" she exclaimed.

"Z'kid's going to be all right," I said. "He likes football."

She swept him up, away from such depravity.

There weren't any horror movies that night, but later I found them watching *Toys in the Attic,* that humid Deep South tale of murder and decadent love. Worse than horror. They were all watching it. My wife, my daughter-in-law, and my grandson.

I could see a battle shaping up for the kid's mind; or was it for my own?

In April our daughter-in-law's sister, Nanette, arrived from France to spend the summer. She had captivated me the night I met the Joyeux family in Tours, and I was delighted that I would be seeing her again. It was her first visit to America, and I was eager to introduce her to our culture in Los Angeles, so she could go back to France and tell them Paris wasn't the only city of light in the world.

On our first outing together I took her to the zoo. Given a language gap and a generation gap, it seemed to me that a zoo might be a good meeting ground. A zoo is a kind of United Nations. To the animals, French and English must seem quite the same. Animals remind us of the oneness of man. When you look into the eyes of an orangutan, you see neither Frenchman nor American, nor even the savage man of Borneo. You see us all.

"What would you like to see most?" I asked once we were inside.

"You have snakes?"

I saw that Mademoiselle Joyeux might turn out to be difficult, like her sister. "Yes," I said, without enthusiasm. "You like snakes?"

"Oh, no. I am afraid. But I like to *see* them. Yes?"

We walked entirely around the snake house, examining every exhibit. It seemed miles. My span of attention for snakes is very short. I know they are remarkable creatures, perfectly adapted to their function, which is to eat other animals alive. But I hope for more than that, even in reptiles.

Somewhere near the snake house, as we left it, I pointed out a weeping willow tree beside a lagoon full of swans and cranes.

"That's a weeping willow," I said. "Isn't it pretty? Weeping willow. It's called weeping because it looks sad. The branches are bent over and the leaves seem to be falling, like tears. You see?"

"Ah, yes. We have this tree in France. She is called *saule pleureur.*"

"What is it you say?"

She spelled it for me. "It is the tree who cries."

It was a good beginning. We had exchanged two of the lovliest phrases in one another's language. She had learned weeping willow, and I had learned the tree who cries.

I hoped to show my protégée the real Los Angeles beneath the pleasure-park artificiality of Disneyland, Knott's Berry Farm, Busch Gardens, Magic Mountain, and the zoo. So one morning I picked them all up—Mademoiselle Joyeux, Jacqueline, and the kid, and drove them down to Ports of Call. Nanette would be able to go back to Paris and say she had seen a New England whaling village in San Pedro, California.

With two naive Frenchwomen and an infant in my charge I felt a responsibility to be instructive. But I had learned already that somehow, in that particular company, I usually wound up feeling more ignorant than before.

We were no sooner parked and out on the wharf than we came to one of those stands where you pay a girl to dive for an oyster in a pool, and if there's a pearl inside, the pearl belongs to you. The two young women discussed it in French.

"Mr. Smith," my daughter-in-law said, "she doesn't want to try it."

"Why not?" I asked, wondering if she was always going to call me Mr. Smith.

"I think zey put z'pearl in z'oyster," said Nanette. "It is not really *belong to* z'oyster. No?"

"No," I said firmly. "I mean *yes*. It belongs to the oyster. Is that what they teach you in France? That Americans are dishonest?"

"No, zey do not say Americans are dishonest. But Americans do funny things. Yes?"

"Yes," I said, feeling lucky to get out of it that cheap, "we do funny things."

We climbed to the top of an old river steamer for a fish lunch from the snack bar and sat at a table by the rail, looking down at the harbor channel. A passenger freighter moved by us on her way out to sea, flying the flag of the American President Lines. PRESIDENT POLK was lettered on her bow.

"That's the *President Polk*," I told Nanette. "You know who he was?"

"No," she said, looking at me expectantly.

"I don't either," I said, "for sure."

Cristophe tossed a french fry overboard to a squadron of sea gulls. It was thirty feet to the water, and I was keeping an eye on him.

"Mr. Smith," his mother said, "what would you do if z'kid fall in? You would dove in to save him?"

"Dive in," I said automatically, wondering why she always called him the kid. It was just some Gallic perversity, I supposed. "No, I wouldn't dive in. It would break my neck. I'd jump in." And almost certainly drown, I realized gloomily. I hoped I wouldn't be tested. I had got through life so far without having to be a hero, and I didn't want to be one now.

We strolled through the village to the fishpond and walked up on the foot bridge. Large red koi carps were foraging in the murky water, smooth and quick as sharks. A man in rubber knee boots waded out and reached into the water to work on a pipe.

"It is not so profound," said Nanette.

"What is not so profound?" I asked, wondering if I had missed some thread of the conversation.

"Z'water," she said.

"Oh. Profound. In America," I explained, "we say the water is *deep*. We say profound for a deep idea, in the head." I pointed to my head.

"*Oui*," she said, pointing to her temple. "We say *profound* also for z'head."

It was one of our more profitable days. Mademoiselle Joyeux learned that we Americans do not put artificial pearls in our oysters, my daughter in-law learned that I would risk my life, if need be, to save her child, and all of us learned the meanings of profound.

CHAPTER 7

For years I have tried to phase out Father's Day. I consider it silly and commercial. If a man had the respect and affection of his wife and children, he would have it every day. If not, there was no use in setting aside one day of the year for perfunctory demonstrations.

But it isn't easy for a father to phase out Father's Day. The more he protests that he doesn't wish to be the object of any extraordinary attentions, the more he is suspected of inviting them. A man who is truly modest and self-effacing is rarely taken seriously.

So I thought of getting at Father's Day through Mother's Day, which fortunately comes first. I simply phased out Mother's Day. It seemed to me that if I gave up Mother's Day, the other members of the family would sooner or later get the idea and give up Father's Day. It's oblique, but I've discovered that in some families the oblique approach is best.

So I ignored Mother's Day completely, except to give my wife a jar of sweet pickles. Of course that was only a joke. I happen to love sweet pickles in liverwurst sandwiches, but she rarely remembers to keep them in good supply.

I also gave her the annual explanation of my attitude. It was just that I resented being obliged by some nationwide sales pitch to express, through merchandise, an essentially private sentiment engendered by years of proximity and interdependence.

"I know," she said.

I realized I had won her over when she decided to leave me on Father's Day and drive down to our house in Mexico alone. It was a symbolic act of liberation for us both. I could spend the day in solitude, reading and reflecting. Father's Day should be a day for introspection, for adding up one's wins and losses and striking one's balance.

I was carrying out this plan when the phone rang. It was Jacqueline.

"It is you, Mr. Smith? You are at home?"

"Yes, of course, I am at home."

"Good. We will see you later."

A few minutes later Curt phoned. "Are you going to be home?" he asked. "I thought I might drop by."

Curt was back in UCLA, determined to finish the education his time in the Air Force had interrupted, and was working on the side as well, so we hadn't been seeing as much of him as we would have liked. He arrived in an hour with a young woman I hadn't seen before. She had dark hair and eyes and a sunniness that made me think of Italy.

"This is Gail Paolucci," Curt said.

They were the Paoluccis of San Fernando Valley now, but they had come from southern Italy a generation or two ago, by way of Buffalo. She looked thoroughly American, this Miss Paolucci, but I had an idea she could put together a proper lasagna. She was taking physical therapy at UCLA, and they had met in chemistry. Evidently some chemistry was already at work. I was reminded of the day Doug had first come up the hill on his motorcycle with Mademoiselle Joyeux.

Curt and Miss Paolucci had brought me a large plastic bag full of water, with a rather fancy goldfish in it.

"For Father's Day," he said.

I had been phasing out my goldfish, much in the way Denny had been phasing out my pickles, by neglecting to replace them as one by one they disappeared. But this was a pretty fish; maybe just what I needed to restore my old enthusiasm.

Soon Doug arrived with Jacqueline, Cristophe, and Nanette. Nanette was carrying an enormous black puppy with a white spot on his chest.

"Not for me!" I said weakly, trying not to show my dismay.

"He is partly a Labrador retriever," said Jacqueline.

"A retriever?" I said, wanting to say that the last thing in the world I needed was a retriever.

"And part Dalmatian," said Nanette.

"Z'white spot," said Jacqueline, "zat is z'Dalmatian part."

"His name is Stephan," Doug said.

"Stephan?" It was all beginning to seem surreal, like a scene in a bad French movie.

"He's named after Stephan Bandera. You know, the Ukrainian rebel."

My familiarity with Russian history did not encompass Ukrainian rebels.

"He rebelled against the Soviet Union."

Much to my relief it turned out that Stephan Bandera was theirs. They had brought me something else. My daughter-in-law carried the gift into the house in a bulky sack. I viewed it with apprehension, but I knew it couldn't be worse than a dog.

"So you will not give them any more to your wife," she said.

It was three quart jars of pickles. I was touched.

So it turned out to be a rewarding Father's Day after all.

I soon grew fond of the goldfish. He would always remind me that he might have been a dog. And I had enough sweet pickles to last me to the next Father's Day, which I hoped to spend alone in quiet introspection.

Cristophe's first birthday party was held on a Saturday afternoon, and while it was to be mostly for his peers in the neighborhood, Denny and I were invited. I had never liked birthday parties when I was a boy, not even my own. They always produced too many tears and too much violence. But of course we had to go to this one.

Of all birthdays, the first is the most awkward. The honoree doesn't even know it's his birthday. It's impossible to buy a present for him. He isn't interested in anything he can't eat or break. In that respect a one-year-old boy is very much like a chimpanzee.

We decided to get him a swing. My wife went to Pasadena that morning to shop for one. I had to go out in the west San Fernando Valley on business. We agreed to meet at our daughter-in-law's house for the party.

"Maybe I'll stop at a store out there somewhere," I said, "and pick up something else, besides the swing, if I can find anything."

As it turned out I found myself in the neighborhood of Topanga Plaza and stopped to look in the toy shop. It was a busy day. No clerks were free to help me. I walked slowly up and down the aisles, looking for something that might engage the attention of a one-year-old and yet be sturdy enough to resist annihilation for a few days.

I picked up a football and gave it a spin in my hands. It felt good. A football is a beautiful object, and wonderful to touch, with its pneumatic tension and its pebbled surface. They don't smell as good as they used to, though, when they were made of leather instead of synthetics. I put it back on the shelf. Maybe in ten years.

Everything else suitable for infants seemed to be for girls. Women's liberation hadn't quite revolutionized the toy industry. They still made dolls and cuddly animals, objects designed to condition little girls for a woman's role in society as the stewardesses of love and warmth.

I saw a young woman looking at the hobby horses. She was pregnant and was pushing a stroller with a boy in it and had a small girl at her knee. It occurred to me that she might be a lot more help to me than a clerk. I could lean on her experience.

The hobby horses were made of hollow plastic. They were suspended on steel springs supported by a framework of metal tubing. They weren't as charming and sturdy-looking as the old wooden hobby horses used to be on their wooden rockers.

The woman put a hand on one of the horses and pushed it tentatively up and down, testing the bounce. She looked speculatively down at the infant in the stroller.

"I'm afraid he might fall out of that one," she said to the little girl.

"How old is the boy?" I asked.

"He's just a year," the woman said.

"What a coincidence," I said. "So's mine."

The little group pushed on. I thought of following to see what the woman bought, but I was afraid I might be mistaken for a nuisance.

I gave up and headed for one of the department stores to look in the boys' department. I could buy the lad some clothes. I happened to see a pair of white shoes in the window of a shoe store. They had an air of sporty elegance. I went in. As luck would have it, they had my size. I'm rather hard to fit.

"I'll wear them," I told the clerk. "I'm going to a birthday party."

I'd spent so much time looking for a present that I was late for the party. It didn't matter. I hadn't been missed. All was disorder. The moment I walked through the door I was attacked by Stephan Bandera, their phony Labrador retriever. He went for my shoes. I gave him a karate chop and saved the shoes, but he got an ankle.

It was a good party after all. There was a great deal of merriment. The kid was fine—never shed a tear; busted his beach ball and fell into the cake.

Nobody noticed my new white shoes, though, except the dog.

As intimidating as he was, Stephan Bandera was the kind of dog a man could admire, and he reminded me that I had always longed for a dog of my own. My wife's poodles hardly counted. What I had in mind was a large dog that would sit at my chair, walk with me, ride beside me in my car, be a companion in my mellow years. I wanted a dog that was stout of heart—one we could take to our house in Mexico as a guardian, one that could deal with rattlesnakes and shadows in the night.

Then one Sunday morning I found a promising notice in the classified:

AIREDALE PUPS. AKC.

I had always liked Airedales, but never owned one. Their virtues were well known. An Airedale was loyal, courageous, and tough. An Airedale had pride. He was no lickspittle lap dog. An Airedale was a terrier, with a taste for the hunt.

The ad led me to a shady street of ranch-style houses in the San Gabriel Valley. I knocked on a gate. Looking over the fence, I saw a grown Airedale in the yard. He gave me a sample bark. There was neither fear nor anger in it: simple authority. Other Airedales trotted out. It was a chorus.

A door slammed and a woman came into the yard from behind the house, quieting the dogs. "What is it?" she called out.

"Are you the lady with the Airedales?" I shouted, realizing at once how stupid the question must sound, with Airedales all about her.

She opened a gate and took me back to the kennels to see the pups. There were only two left, not quite four months old, a male and a female. The female seemed to like me better. She trotted over and nuzzled my hand and stood at my knee. The male paid me no attention until I called him, and then he checked me out briefly and trotted off.

"I'll take the male," I said a minute later, wondering why. Perhaps I felt I was already outnumbered by females in the family. It was a choice, though, that I sometimes had reason to regret, in the weeks to come.

"Does he have a name?" I asked.

"We call him Pugsley," the woman said. "You can give him a new name though. It's just a nickname. The children gave it to him."

"No," I said, "Pugsley it is." I thought it might be bad luck to change a dog's name, just as it was bad luck to change a boat's. Besides, I liked it: Pugsley. It sounded like a dog. They hadn't let me name my first son or my grandson; at least I could name my dog.

She took me into the house to fill out the papers and showed me Pugsley's family tree. His sire's name was Fleetwood Superson, and his dam's was Fleetwood Sun Maid.

"Fleetwood," she explained, "is the kennel name."

"You mean I have to call him Fleetwood?"

"Oh, no. But you can, if you like."

I put Fleetwood Pugsley in the passenger seat and drove him home. It wasn't an auspicious beginning. He seemed to prefer the driver's seat, and I had to keep fighting him off. As we neared home, the misgivings began to set in. No matter how mature and experienced a man becomes, he never foresees the pitfalls of an adventure he is drawn toward until it is too late to turn back.

At the moment I drove up in front of our house the first of many unforeseen but foreseeable complications became apparent. The sound of my car had brought our two cats running from their idle occupations, and as I walked around the car to open the other door the little beggars were whining at my ankles.

I opened the door. The Airedale fell out. One cat hissed and ran. The other bowed up like a horseshoe and lashed out with a paw, claws unsheathed. I rapped her on the head with a foot and she scatted.

Pugsley was unperturbed. I took it as a good sign, though there was a chance it only meant he was stupid. I took him through the house and into the back yard. The poodles were waiting at the door, leaping about and yipping idiotically. The male poodle ran into his house. The female bared her teeth, frightened herself with a bark, and followed her craven mate into their disenchanted cottage.

That evening I made drinks for Denny and me, to ease our tensions. Everyone's nerves were taut. The cats remained hostile and furtive. The poodles cowered in their house, prostrated by fear and jealousy. Only the Airedale remained unperturbed.

"Don't forget," Denny said, "he's yours."

In the next few weeks the amount of mischief he thought up was beyond belief. He visited one calamity after another on us, dismantling furniture, shredding garments, peeling the covers off magazines, polkadotting carpets, excavating some articles and burying others, and keeping the cats and poodles—not to mention me—in a state of unrelieved anxiety.

His excesses seemed to me to go so far beyond the normal patterns of canine adolescence that finally I took him down the hill to Dr. Morehouse, who had doctored all our other dogs and was no stranger to psychotic behavior.

"I expected him to be frisky," I told him, "being a terrier, but I'm beginning to think it's a disorder—maybe something glandular."

Dr. Morehouse sat him on a steel table and thumped him here and there and looked into his eyes and mouth.

"Good dog," he said. "Good temperament. Intelligent, too, I'll bet."

"Intelligent?"

"That's one reason he's so aggressive. You should consider yourself lucky to have finally got yourself an intelligent dog—this late in life."

"I suppose he'll calm down then—when he's older?"

"Oh, yes. That is, until the sex drive sets in. Then he may get worse."

CHAPTER 8

After the Airedale chewed up the poodles' doghouse I knew I would have to do something about the acute housing problem.

It was obvious there would be no point in buying another wooden doghouse, since it was likely to meet the same fate. I looked at various types of houses in a catalog at the pet shop, but they were all too expensive or too vulnerable. One had a tin roof, but the Airedale would have chewed out the sides and let the roof fall in.

I was putting it off, hoping to get a house built before the next storm came. What I had in mind was a duplex made of cement blocks with a galvanized iron roof. The Airedale could live in one side and the poodles in the other.

Two events occurred, however, to intervene in the execution of that program. First, the construction men digging up under the foundation to repair some old earthquake damage stopped work for the holidays, leaving a mountain of dirt in the middle of the dog yard. Construction on the doghouse had to be postponed.

Then the rains came. We got home in the middle of the storm and opened the door to let the dogs in as usual. The result was disaster. The rain had turned the mountain of dirt into mud. The three of them raced past us like horses pounding home in the mud at Santa Anita. We shouted and screamed but the damage was done.

Then the rain grew worse. The dog yard turned into a quagmire. When I looked out the window I couldn't even see the dogs. I fed them by setting their bowls out on the step and getting back inside and slamming the door before they could reach me.

It wasn't till Christmas Day that we began to sense that something mysterious was afoot. Now and then we could hear the Airedale barking but it sounded strange, like a dog barking over the telephone.

"He's in the attic," Denny said.

"Don't be silly," I told her.

Then we began to hear thumps, like someone dropping heavy boots on a floor. Then we heard metallic clunks like the sound of balky plumbing. I started to get the stepladder to look in the attic, but I realized the sound was coming from the bedroom wall.

"Where are they, anyway?" Denny asked later, looking out the kitchen window into the dog yard. The dogs were not in sight. Either they were so muddy as to be indistinguishable from the mud, or they had escaped. Suddenly all three appeared out of nowhere. They looked quite dry.

"I've got to get at the bottom of this," I said. I put on my boots and rain gear and went out. They were gone again. Then the three of them suddenly appeared, dry as turnips.

I slogged around in the mud till I found the answer. It was really quite simple. The workmen had neglected to replace the screen over the crawl hole and the dogs had found the opening. They were living under the house.

Meanwhile our color TV had freaked out during the rainstorm. The picture turned snowy, distorted and unstable. It was a cruel irony that this breakdown should occur just ahead of Super Sunday. It was also ironic that the picture had been better than ever since we had hooked up with Theta Cable, thus bypassing our flighty rooftop aerial. At any other time of year I might have been in no hurry to get it fixed, but I didn't want to spend Super Sunday watching the Super Bowl game in a bar.

I phoned Theta Cable. They said they'd have a man out Friday. Just before he arrived, though, we stumbled onto the trouble.

Curt had come over to work on the doghouses. He was building one for the poodles and one for the Airedale, so we wouldn't have to let them stay underneath the house again the next time it rained. I was afraid the Airedale might chew some of our water pipes. They're nothing but iron and copper—no problem for an Airedale.

"Would you mind crawling under the house," I asked Curt, "to see if everything's all right?"

He crawled under the house while I waited nervously outside, holding back the Airedale. I heard a whistle. He crawled out, dragging a heavily insulated line. Its end was frayed and gnawed, its copper core exposed.

"Here's what's wrong with your TV," he said. "The cable's been chewed through."

"Good Lord," I said. "What about the pipes?"

"They seem to be all right. He was working on the telephone lines, though. It's a good thing it stopped raining."

"What will I tell the man from Theta?" I wondered.

The question no sooner occurred to me than a van pulled up in front of the house and the Theta man stepped out in his spotless blue coveralls. He was carrying what looked like some kind of electronic testing device.

"You won't need that," I told him. "We've found the trouble."

He stopped short, looking mildly irked. He'd probably had enough of people calling up with emergencies, only to find out they had forgotten to plug their set in.

"Your cable's been chewed in half," I said, realizing I had made it sound like his fault.

"That happens," he said amiably. "Little animals get under the house."

"Yes," I agreed. "There's a lot of wildlife on this hill. We have raccoons, you know."

He nodded.

"And possums. They're something like a rodent."

"No problem. We'll put you in a new cable."

I heard a commotion. Curt was shouting. "He's out!" The gate was open. The Airedale bounded up. He made for the cable man and embraced him, leaving two muddy prints on his laundered coveralls.

"Of course," I said, wrestling the dog down, "it could have been my wife's poodles. We've been doing some work and the men left the crawl hole open."

"No problem," he said, wiping at his blouse with an open hand. He crawled under the house with a roll of cable and came out fifteen minutes later.

"Now try your picture," he said.

We went inside and I turned the tube on. In a minute the picture came in—wonderfully gaudy, good as ever. I wouldn't have to spend Super Sunday in a bar after all.

Some animals, I've read, can be fooled by experiments in which their environment is altered. Thus, if you put a bear in a cold dark room he thinks it's winter and begins to hibernate. Our springlike weather held; and on Super Sunday, as the temperature rose to the high eighties, my system evidently was fooled, like the bear's. I thought it was spring. For a while on Sunday morning I was actually irrational. I had an irresistible urge to go down to the garage and clean it out again.

"What about the Super Bowl?" my wife asked.

"I really don't care that much," I said. "What kind of man could sit in front of the tube on a day like this? It's a betrayal of the senses."

It was ten o'clock when I went down to the garage. It gave me a strange, heady feeling. I had triumphed over indolence and addiction. I wasn't going to spend a rare day like this in my chair, watching the little toy men play football in a darkened house.

I stood a minute on the front porch, absorbing the day. It was like a gift. The sky was the color of Montana's in June. The air was pure and balmy. The mountains were white over the rooftops.

I walked down to the garage and opened the door. The disorder was stunning, like a physical blow. It looked like a museum set up to illustrate the materialistic glut in which mid-century Americans had lived.

How many times over the years had I faced this Herculean task? Each time thinking it would be the last. But always afterwards there was some calamity that struck like the Johnstown flood, wiping me out.

Had we needed all this junk? There was my electric lawnmower, the orange paint still new-looking under the dust. The power saw, still red and silver, like a Christmas toy cast aside. The files and boxes and trunks. The piles of dusty books.

The job had never seemed more awesome. It wasn't only that the physical effort would be prodigious. What really cowed me was all the decisions I'd have to make. What could be thrown away? What must be saved? Cleaning out a garage is finally an ordeal of agonizing judgments.

"It looks hopeless," Denny said. She had come down from the house, ostensibly to help, but actually, I knew, to guard her treasures.

She began picking up old clothes. She held a yellow skirt to her waist. "I think I might be able to do something with this," she said.

It was the same old story. Every time we had gone down to the garage to get rid of the impedimenta of the years, she had weakened, and behind my back the castoffs were retrieved.

We wrestled the barbecue and a garden table out of the way and I saw two cartons of big books, long forgotten. I slipped one out. It was Volume XVI of my complete set of the 1892 edition of *Encyclopaedia Britannica*.

"My God," I said, blowing the dust off the leaves and rifling through the closely printed pages with their wonderful engravings. "Do you realize that when these books were printed Victoria was still Queen?"

"Why keep them?" she asked. "Aren't they terribly out of date?"

"Are you serious?" I said. "They're not out of date for anything that happened before 1892."

In the old plywood wardrobe closet the boys had used in their bedrooms I found a row of Curt's uniforms from the recent war and my forest-green Marine Corps blouse from World War II.

"I didn't know I'd saved that," I said.

"Don't you remember? The last time you cleared out the garage you said everything had to go, but we compromised. You kept your blouse and I kept my wedding gown."

I saw a stack of old school papers in a ruptured cardboard carton. I reached down and picked up a handful. They were book reviews, handwritten by one of the boys. *Cannery Row, Bridge of San Luis Rey, The Red Badge of Courage*. I felt a stab of envy for a lad reading those books for the first time.

Then I came to a theme, carefully typewritten, a dozen pages long. It was evidently a term report; a matter of the greatest weight. The title was carefully typed across the first page in capital letters: HENRY

THOREAU'S CRITICISM OF A MATERIALISTIC SOCIETY.

I sat down on a sack of cement and read it through. He stated his thesis in the final paragraph.

"Thoreau accuses us of trying to solve the problems of life by making them more complicated than they are. It is true. Our lives are cluttered with things that we accumulate trying to find happiness and comfort. I think, as Thoreau did, that we would be happier and our lives would be better if we pursued only the real necessities of life, which in his words are 'food, shelter, clothing and fuel.'"

"No use trying to do it all today," I said. "It isn't that important."

We went back to our shelter and I turned on the Super Bowl game.

"Would you mind getting me some cheese and crackers and a beer?" I said. "The game's already started."

"Is that all you want?"

"Yes. My needs are simple."

I was content. I had food, shelter, clothing, and the Super Bowl.

CHAPTER 9

From the beginning Denny and I sensed that Curt and Gail had serious intentions, and they did not keep us waiting long.

Any doubt about the outcome of the acquaintance was put to rest when she invited us to the home of her parents, far out in the San Fernando Valley, for Thanksgiving dinner. In American culture, a young couple who failed to marry after bringing their parents together at the Thanksgiving table would be seriously compromised.

So it was with that feeling of meeting a new set of relatives-to-be that we drove out to the Paolucci house. Like the Joyeux, Bernie and Mary Ann Paolucci had two daughters, Gail's sister, Bernadette, being also the younger. Thus, when we entered the Paolucci household, the situation was reminiscent of that first evening in Tours.

But this time I was on my good behavior. There would be wine, of course, or Paolucci's name wasn't Paolucci. But there would be no language barrier, so it was not expected that he would ask me to sample every wine of the Italian campagna as a substitute for conversation.

It was evident that Gail was very close to her family, and would remain so, which meant that they would inevitably become a part of our family too. If it was not wine, I wondered what common ground I would have with Bernie Paolucci, or would there, perhaps, be none at all? We were no sooner through their front door than my concern evaporated.

Paolucci and I shook hands, but he seemed to be straining to hear a sound emanating from the door of what appeared to be a man's den, just off the entry hall. I recognized the sound: a crowd roar and the frantic voiceover of the announcer. He had the Ram game on TV.

"What's the score?" I asked.

"Dallas was ahead one touchdown," he said. "But it sounds like something just happened."

We moved into the living room for the perfunctory introductions and exchanges.

"Well, Jack," Bernie said, when the conversation lulled, "we might as well watch the game. They don't need us in the kitchen."

As we headed for Bernie's den, I thought of that great last line in *Casablanca,* when Claude Rains and Humphrey Bogart are walking arm in arm into the night, and Bogart says: "Louis, I think this is the beginning of a beautiful friendship."

Curt and Gail were married on a Saturday afternoon in the Presbyterian Church of Pasadena. They were not members of the congregation, but the church is English Gothic, in gray stone, and they chose it for its beauty.

I was almost late, which would have been embarrassing, since being on time is the last of my virtues I can boast of as intact. Denny was waiting for me on the steps, looking like a woman who has just begun to worry. She had gone ahead of me, in her own car, to take Doug a white shirt. He was to be the best man, of course, and at the last minute discovered that a white shirt was not in his wardrobe.

"I was beginning to wonder," she said. "Everyone's already seated."

We entered the church and an usher, one of Curt's college friends, took her arm and led her into the wedding chapel and down to a pew at the front. I followed, feeling unnecessary. A man is always upstaged at a wedding—even the bridegroom.

It was a simple vaulted Gothic chapel with oaken beams and panels. Sunlight filled it softly through stained-glass windows. All was ready. Suddenly there was a burst of organ music, something antique and exuberant, pierced with joyous trumpeting. It was heraldic music, the music of beginnings.

The minister walked out to the altar, looking like a proper Edwardian baronet in his gray suit and his trim brown beard. Like the music and the church, he had been their choice, the Reverend John Wareham, a

Unitarian of free spirit. He had been the minister at another wedding we had attended one windy day on Point Dume. The ceremony had been held in the open, in a garden by the sea, and he had worn an open shirt and read from e. e. cummings.

The bridegroom and the best man took their places, and I noticed that Douglas was wearing a blue shirt after all. Perhaps the white one hadn't fit. At least his shoes didn't squeak.

The bridegroom's shirt was red, one more touch of the unorthodox that seemed to characterize this ceremony, although the setting was richly traditional. How handsome he was, I realized, with steadfast eyes and a mustache of a baroque fullness and panache that my own lip, in my youth, had never been able to produce. He turned and looked up the aisle.

The bride was approaching on her father's arm, walking behind her sister. Gail's gown was white and traditional, but the veil was off her face. Her eyes were dark but full of light. She smiled without self-consciousness, as if from sheer delight. It was a Neapolitan look, I thought. She was a true Paolucci, soon to be a Smith.

Music filled the chapel like a sunburst. It was Bach, I supposed, if Curt had chosen it. Or perhaps it was something older—something from the Renaissance. It was stately, yet light as a flight of bees.

Her father surrendered the bride to the waiting young man and Mr. Wareham read some lines from a love song by Elton John.

Then, as Gail had wanted, he read from *The Prophet,* his voice supple and resonant, riding easily over the seas of Kahlil Gibran's poetry. It was a passage urging that love should be followed, that they should love one another but not let love become bondage; that they should keep their separateness in their togetherness.

"In these days of zero population growth," said Mr. Wareham, "not everyone is speaking of children as the natural outcome of marriage. But Gail and Curtis want children and hope that in due time they will be so blessed."

A few more lines, then, from Gibran, admonishing that they were to love their children but not try to make their children in their image; that they were the bows from which their children would be sent forth as arrows.

Then all of us in the chapel were asked to come forward and stand close about the bride and bridegroom for the ceremony of the ring and the vows.

"The ring?"

Mr. Wareham was looking expectantly at the best man. A silence fell. A hand went deep into a coat pocket, groping. My breathing stopped. And then—an eon later—the ring came up in the best man's hand, a sapphire flashing.

It is always the critical moment in a wedding, when the ring appears, like that instant when a jet of water in a fountain attains its peak, shatters, and comes glittering down in the sunlight. It is too late for temporizing, and those who might have spoken out against this union have been admonished forever to be silent.

The vows were made and the minister pronounced them man and wife, invoking the laws of God and California. It is an ending that always takes me by surprise at weddings, in its suddenness, the fullness of its meaning, and its finality.

We all drove over the freeways to an Italian restaurant in the valley for a champagne reception and an Italian wedding dinner. The wine was chianti, which doesn't look at all like cognac, but I was very careful not to pour it on the tablecloth.

Bernie Paolucci and I were happy men. It was a matter of record, vouchsafed in the ceremony itself, that time would bring him a grandchild. And I had reason to be pleased with both my sons. Even as they left us, they had enriched our lives: one of them had brought French cooking into the family, and now the other had brought Italian.

CHAPTER 10

When Cristophe started to talk his Grandmère Joyeux, who had never ventured farther from home than Paris, flew to Los Angeles to see her grandson and her daughter, who was *enceinte* again. Madame Joyeux had recently lost her husband. Jacques had suffered a heart attack on his postman's rounds one morning, and fallen from his bicycle, fatally stricken. His absence, following upon the departure of her daughters, one to America, the other to Paris, had kindled in Madame Joyeux an understandable desire to get acquainted with her only grandchild.

In thinking that I had been prepared for her visit by my exposure to Jacqueline and Nanette, however, I seriously overestimated the fruits of that experience. I was soon to realize that since our first meeting at the Joyeux home I had learned almost no French, and Madame Joyeux had learned no English whatever. Our language barrier was all but impenetrable.

This was demonstrated one morning when I drove to Jacqueline's house to deliver a French poster I had bought for her bedroom, or *chambre,* as she called it. The poster had been an advertisement for a show called "Tournèe du Chat Noir," a coming attraction at some nightclub in Mont-martre. It was red, white, and black, and featured a magnificent black cat.

In decorating her chambre, Jacqueline had chosen stark black and white, with touches of vivid red. I felt sure Le Chat Noir was just what it needed. I had bought the poster and taken it by for inspection. She was delighted. I had promised to have it framed. She had hoped it would be ready before her mother arrived. Unfortunately, though, it wasn't until several days after the arrival of Madame Joyeux that I could pick it up.

With that fine feeling a man has when he bears gifts, I drove over to my daughter-in-law's house with the poster. It looked splendid under glass in its thin black metal frame. I rang the doorbell. There was no response. I heard Stephan Bandera bark. I was about to leave. Then I heard a child shout. My grandson. In a moment a shape appeared through the amber Flemish window in the door. But the handle did not turn.

Suddenly I knew what was wrong. Jacqueline had gone out, leaving the dog to watch over her child and her mother. She had no doubt given Madame Joyeux strict instructions not to answer the door. One never knew who might knock at one's door in that neighborhood, and, confronted by a stranger, across that language barrier, Madame Joyeux would be confused, at least, and perhaps frightened.

What to do? I would have to let her know it was me.

"*C'est moi!*" I shouted at last, expending possibly one-third of my French vocabulary.

A minute went by.

"*C'est moi!*" I repeated, somewhat louder. "Mr. Smith!"

I heard a commotion inside the door. The handle turned. The door opened three inches. It was Madame Joyeux, peering through the crack. We both smiled like silent screen comedians. The door swung wide.

"*Bon jour,*" I said, expending another third.

"*Bon jour! Bon jour!*" exclaimed Madame Joyeux.

I patted my grandson on the head. The dog bounded toward us from somewhere back in the house and leaped up against my chest, driving me back to the door frame.

"He's got his growth," I said, wrestling him down to the floor.

"*Comment?*" said Madame Joyeux.

"The dog!" I said. "He is a monster!"

"*Oui,*" she said, beaming down at the dog as if I had paid him a compliment.

"Goggie!" shouted Cristophe. I had hoped he would be talking better than that at his age, but I was gratified to hear a word of English, at that moment, infantile as it might be.

I showed the poster to Madame Joyeux. She nodded enthusiastically and expatiated upon it in French.

"It's for your daughter's bedroom," I said. "*Pour* Jacqueline."

She regarded me intensely, trying to get my meaning.

"*Pour la chambre,*" I explained.

Her eyes failed to light up. It must be my accent, I thought. Perhaps it was too Parisian for her. After all, Madame Joyeux was a provincial.

It occurred to me that a glass of wine might put us both at ease and improve communication.

"Wine?" I said. "Is there any wine?"

Madame Joyeux looked blank.

"*Vin,*" I said, though I knew it was not as easy a word to pronounce as it looked. "*Avez-vous vin?*"

I saw no comprehension in her eyes. I certainly would have thought a woman from the Loire Valley would know the French word for *wine.* I made the motions of opening a bottle and pouring and drinking. She had seen me drinking enough of it in her house, after all.

"Ah, *vin!*" she exclaimed.

I was pouring a glass of California rosè when the phone rang. I picked it up and said, "*Bon jour.*"

There was a silence; then finally my daughter-in-law's voice, alarmed: "Who is it?"

"It's me. Your father-in-law."

A long silence. "Mr. Smith! I cannot believe it! My mother lets you in?"

"Yes. I spoke French to her."

"You speak French? What did you say?"

"I said, '*C'est moi.*' "

"Mr. Smith! I cannot *believe* it! That is *excellent!* Wonderful! How are you getting along now?"

At that moment the dog had another run at me, giving me what the quarterbacks call a blind-side sack.

"Goggie!" my grandson shouted.

"Oui—goggie!" shouted Madame Joyeux.

"Don't worry," I told my daughter-in-law. "Your mother and I are drinking, and your son is teaching your mother how to say dog in English."

Later, as I was leaving, I turned to Madame Joyeux at the door and said, "*Au revoir*." There was no point in leaving without having used all the French I knew.

Madame Joyeux frowned and wagged a finger in reproach. "*Ce n'est pas au revoir*," she said. "Gootbye!"

"Ah, *Oui*," I said. "Gootbye."

That interlude strengthened my idea that one reason most men are baffled by the housewife's yearning for freedom is that they're unable to think of the house as a trap. They see staying at home as an adventure, and can't understand why their wives want to escape into the monotony of factory or office.

Late one afternoon in October I was reminded of what improbable and charming things can come to a man's front door. I was in my den in the declining throes of a fever, sliding gradually back to normal, when the doorbell rang.

I couldn't remember hearing any sounds of approach. I was hoping my wife would answer it. Then I realized the house was rumbling and gurgling and I remembered that she had gone outside to run the hose up the pipes again. It was up to me.

I got up and lurched to the door and yanked it open. It had been out of plumb since the last earthquake and responded only to violence. I always yank it open anyway, to gain a psychological advantage over whoever is at the door.

It appeared to be a small boy of eight or nine. He was holding a live snake, one small fist clenched around its neck. Its head bulged out at the top of his fist and the rest of it hung out, wriggling like a loose spring. It took the starch out of me.

"Can I use your telephone?"

"What for?"

"I have this snake."

"So I see."

"I want to phone my mother to come after me. I'm afraid if I walk home he'll get away. He's really strong."

"Come on in," I said. He followed me in to the phone. He looked at the phone and moved the snake with elaborate care from one hand to the other. They both looked up at me. It was obvious he could not dial his mother and hold the snake. One of us would have to hold the snake while the other dialed.

"What's the number?" I said. "I'll dial."

I dialed and put the phone in his free hand. Evidently his mother answered because he told her where he was and asked her to come and get him. "I have this snake," he said. "What? . . . Yes . . . A snake . . . What? . . . Yes. He's alive . . . Okay." He put the phone down. "She's coming," he said.

We waited on the porch. In a few minutes his mother drove up the hill in a station wagon. He said thanks and got in beside his mother.

"We'll keep it forty-five minutes," she shouted at me, and drove back down the hill.

How could a housewife find drudgery in a day like that?

A day or two later, when I was home alone, the doorbell rang again. It was afternoon, and the schoolchildren were on their way home from the school at the top of the hill. I heard at least two sets of shoes on the steps and porch, and then the ring. It was extra loud.

I guessed it was a couple of girls. Girls ring a doorbell louder than boys. I don't know why that is. Electronically, it doesn't make sense. A doorbell either rings or it doesn't. You can't make it ring louder by pushing the button harder. They do it, though.

It's much the same principle by which a woman who thinks the house is too cold will turn the thermostat up to 90 degrees, thinking it will heat up to 70 degrees faster than if she merely turned it up to 70. You cannot convince a woman that this will not work.

I went to the door. It was two girls, just as I suspected. I recognized them both. They had nicked me several times for Girl Scout cookies, and I supposed that's what it was this time.

"What's up?" I said.

It was the smaller one who spoke. The other girl happened to be about the best cookie salesman in the neighborhood—maybe the best; and it was evident she was being held in reserve, in case I proved difficult. They had me set up for the old one-two.

"Could we pick a pomegranate from your tree?"

All I could do was laugh. I was surprised by the question. For one thing, I was so sure it was cookies, and also I was surprised that they would come to the door and ask permission to pick a pomegranate.

"I was laughing," I explained, "because nobody ever asked before, if they could have a pomegranate. They just take them, and that's that."

I sometimes forget we have a pomegranate tree, until it is heavy with fruit. It was a volunteer, like our palm trees and our Chinese elms. It had simply grown up through the ivy on the north bank and I hadn't the slightest idea what it was until it revealed itself by bearing its first fruit.

It is up near the sidewalk the children use on their way to and from school. Even though the tree has grown taller and filled out, they still have to take a step or two into the yard before they can reach the fruit. They can't quite reach it from the sidewalk. So technically it's trespassing.

But I don't care. It is my belief that the pomegranate was created to be stolen. It is red and tempting. It is sealed, and must be broken open. Its contents are like jewels in a treasure box, to be spilled out or plucked out one by one. It is the antidote for Eve's sin. Its theft from a tree by a sidewalk on the way home from school is an act of innocence.

I thought of telling the little girls about my theory, but I realized, just in time, that it might sound odd if they went home and told their mothers that Mr. Smith, on the corner, was talking to them about sin and innocence and stolen fruit.

"Help yourselves," I told them. "It's God's will."

I am not what might be called gadget-happy, but finally, for what seemed to me a number of good reasons, I bought one of those machines that answer the telephone for you.

Too many times I have come pounding up from the garage to answer a persistent ring, rasping out my hello with the last remnant of my breath, only to hear the click of a wrong number hanging up or a stranger's voice asking if I am the man of the house.

I hoped to escape the sales pitches; the people who wanted to sell me six more magazine subscriptions or a new roof, or wanted me to put aluminum siding on my house or have my termites inspected.

The main advantage, I thought, would be the harvesting when I got home at the end of a day out, or an evening, of all the calls that had come in during my absence.

The machine I purchased is simply a recorder that plugs into the telephone. You first put your own message on it, and when someone calls, the machine takes over after a ring or two, answers the phone, and delivers your message.

But taping the message wasn't easy. I didn't want to sound too formal or too casual. I wanted to be cheerful, but businesslike. If it was a sales pitch, I didn't want to sound like an easy mark. If it was a friend, I didn't want to sound rude.

I plugged the microphone into the machine and spoke my message: "Hello. This is a recording. This is Jack Smith. He is unable to answer the telephone at the moment. If you like, wait until you hear the tone, then leave your message."

I played it back. It sounded fairly good. A little halt, perhaps, with a stutter here and there, but it got the message over.

I dialed our neighbor Dalton. Mrs. Dalton answered.

"Is Dalt there?" I asked her. "It's me, Jack."

"Just a minute," she said. "I'll get him."

"No," I said. "Never mind. Just ask him to give me a ring when he isn't busy."

"He isn't busy now."

"Never mind. Just tell him to call me."

I hung up. In a minute the ring came. I picked up the receiver to eavesdrop. There was a click and the machine started playing my message. Then silence; and then the go-ahead tone. I wondered what Dalton would say. Suddenly there was a familiar buzzing. It was the dial tone. Either the machine wasn't working properly or Dalton hadn't left a message.

I phoned the Daltons again. Mrs. Dalton answered.

"Did Dalton call me?" I asked.

"Yes."

"What happened?"

"He hung up. He said he got a machine and he doesn't want to talk to a machine. Are you all right?"

I was wondering who else I could try when the phone rang again. Once again I eavesdropped. The machine answered and played my message. After the tone I heard a familiar voice. It was Curt.

"Who's that?" he said.

I turned off the machine. "That was me," I said. "I've got one of those answering machines. How did it sound?"

"Terrible," he said. "You sounded like you were reading something off the back of a box of corn flakes."

Maybe, I thought, I should have Denny tape the message. She had a resonant voice and enunciated clearly. I wrote a new message: "Hello. Thank you for calling the Smiths. We are unable to answer the telephone at the moment. You may wait for the tone, and then leave your message."

I thought it had class. I especially liked the "Thank you for calling the Smiths." It was the way the airlines answered the phone when you called for a reservation.

Denny put the message on the tape, and I had to admit it was better than mine had been, although Dalton still refused to leave a message. I suspected it was merely envy on his part.

For a time I wondered if the thing was really going to be of any use. Then one afternoon I came home and turned it on and got the message I'd been expecting any day. It was Doug. He sounded tired and harassed but happy.

"It's a girl," he said. "Everything is fine."

A girl! It was about time. We hadn't had a female Smith born into the family since 1907. I had been delighted with my sons, but I had always rather regretted not having had a daughter, too. There was so much I knew about life to tell a girl. I would hardly be able to wait for her to get through her Terrible Twos. They never understood me until after they were three.

"That's wonderful!" I said. "What's her name?"

There was a click and a dial tone. I had forgotten I was talking to a machine.

Her name turned out to be Adriana Estelle. So they had rejected my suggestion of Gabriele or Michele, if it was a girl. I had thought it would be fun to call her Mike or Gabby.

But Adriana was fine. I could call her Andy.

CHAPTER 11

It is said that most injuries occur in the home, so I suppose I shouldn't have been so surprised that I hurt my arm watching television one night at Jacqueline's. Being in the neighborhood, we had dropped in to say hello and were seduced into staying for dinner by the aromas from her kitchen.

Doug was away at night school and Denny joined Jacqueline in the kitchen, so to entertain myself I sank into the living room couch and started staring at the tube. It was on, but nobody was watching.

Suddenly my heart thumped. The scene was familiar. I had blundered onto one of my favorite movies. It was Clark Gable on the screen, in his white hunter outfit, and Ava Gardner. Ava was in pants and a safari jacket, but nothing could conceal the grace of that long graceful body.

The sound was too low to hear, but it was easy to see that the conversation was nearing a climax; then suddenly Ava was in Clark's arms; an impulsive thing. He shoved her away. No time for women here in the veldt. Then Ava gave him that slow, sly, devastating smile, and you knew she had scented the prey. I lurched toward the set and turned up the sound.

"You're watching television?" my wife said, looking in from the kitchen.

"Yes. It's *Mogambo*."

"*Mogambo!* Haven't you seen that—two or three times?"

"More like four or five."

"How can you take it?"

She doesn't understand. It's the genre. I have always loved high-humidity movies. The steamy jungle. The wild cries in the night. The long iced drinks on the verandah. The troubled sleep behind the mosquito netting. Alan Ladd in a limp white suit. Sidney Greenstreet delicately mopping his face under a revolving fan at the back of a nightclub in Macao.

"The trick is," I explained, "to forget how it turns out."

Gable actually orders Miss Gardner to leave his house, and she packs up in a huff and boards the riverboat. "Maybe sometime," he says, "I'll get to Paris. Look you up."

Suddenly I was struck in the left ear by a soft round pink sponge-rubber ball. It was the kid. He wanted to play catch. "Not now," I said, "I'm watching *Mogambo*. Don't you want to see the animals?"

He got the ball and hit my ear again. He didn't want to see the animals. He wanted to play catch. I felt guilty, watching a movie I'd already seen four times when my only grandson wanted to play catch.

"Okay," I said, picking the ball up off the floor. "Catch."

He was standing off to my left, but I found that I could keep my eye on the TV screen and toss the ball to him with my left arm, though it was rather an awkward movement, something like trying to roll up the left rear window of a car from the driver's seat. I once crippled my arm for a week that way.

Still, it went quite well. I'm not left-handed, but every basketball player develops left-handed skills, and I was getting it to him, my peripheral vision being almost as good as ever. His returns were more erratic. Some were true, and I one-handed them, as the baseball announcers say. Some fell in my lap. But most either hit me in the ear or went wild.

I was soon engaged in a more or less rhythmic exercise of getting up, bending over to fetch the ball, sitting down, cocking my arm, and throwing sideways at a ninety-degree angle to my left, all the while trying to watch *Mogambo*.

Finally Grace Kelly showed up. Grace Kelly was the queen of humidity movies. No matter how narrow her escapes, how strenuous her exertions, how cruel the equatorial sun, Miss Kelly never lost her lovely porcelain facade. No bead of perspiration trembled on her upper lip. And yet, when she looked up at Gable after he'd shot the lion to save her life, there was the promise of something animal and reckless in those pale cool eyes.

The picture wasn't over yet when dinner was served. When we sat down at the table it occurred to me that my left arm felt hot and tingly. By the time I finished the wine it was numb.

"I think you'd better drive home," I told my wife.

What I had, I learned the next day, was tennis elbow. It may sound trivial, but tennis elbow is what forced Sandy Koufax to quit baseball, at the top of his career. In the same arm, too.

What really annoyed me, though, was that I still didn't know how *Mogambo* turned out.

My elbow was on the mend when Jacqueline invited us over to dinner for Cristophe's fourth birthday (I no longer called him Pete). I suggested that Denny buy the presents for him and I would pick up something for Jacqueline. It has been my observation that at small boys' birthday parties their mothers are at least deserving of a consolation prize.

The only gift I could think of was flowers. They're always in good taste, and even though a person may like daffodils better than marigolds, for example, it is hard to imagine a person actually disliking any kind of flower.

I explained the situation to our florist down in Highland Park. "What about some of these?" he said, showing me a bunch of pink, red, and white carnations.

I felt a surge of melancholy. Carnations always affect me that way. I suspect it's because when I was a small boy my mother used to take me to church on Mother's Day and if your mother was still alive you wore a red carnation and if she was dead you wore a white one. So every time I see carnations I think of somebody's mother, dead or alive.

"What about those?" I asked, pointing to a clump of big yellow chrysanthemums in a pot.

I have always loved chrysanthemums, especially the big yellow ones, so exuberant and bouffant. They are, after all, the flower of our most exciting festival in America—football. I never see big yellow chrysanthemums without thinking of football seasons of long ago, with the pink-cheeked cheer girls in their woolly sweaters and pleated skirts, shaking pompons and turning cartwheels.

"Those will last in the house for weeks, you know," the florist said, "And then she can plant them outside."

When Denny came home the pot of chrysanthemums was on the bar. I wanted to see her reaction.

"Oh, dear," she said. "You got those for Jacqueline?"

"Yes. Aren't they great?"

"They're very nice."

"What d'you mean they're very nice? Is something wrong with them?"

"Well," she said, "in France, you know, you only see chrysanthemums at funerals."

"Well, this isn't France."

"I know. But she can't get over the way she feels. She's told me. Chrysanthemums make her sad."

"That ridiculous. It's time she got over those French prejudices. This is America."

That evening I was holding the pot of chrysanthemums when Jacqueline opened her front door. Her face fell.

"Oh, Mr. Smith," she said. There was no joy in it.

"You don't like chrysanthemums?"

"Someone has died?"

"No one has died, for God's sake. Where'd you get that idea?"

"I am sorry, Mr. Smith. In France chrysanthemums mean there is a funeral."

I carried the pot in and set it on a table. "You've got to get over that idea," I told her. "In American chrysanthemums are a symbol of life at its most exuberant. They're the flowers of our most joyous festival."

"Z'Fourth of July?"

"Football."

"I am very happy no one is dead," she said.

After dinner our son took movies of the kid opening his presents and of all of us sitting around the living room with the pot of chrysanthemums in the middle of the table.

As we were leaving I offered to take the flowers home. "We can plant them," I said, "and I'll bring you something else."

"No, Mr. Smith," she said. "You are right. I must get over my feelings. Don't worry. I will write my mother."

"What do you mean—write your mother?"

"We must send her the movies, of course," she said, "and when she sees the chrysanthemums in the movies she will think there has been a funeral. I will write her a letter and tell her nobody is dead."

The next time, I thought, I'd take carnations. If anyone had to feel melancholy, it might as well be me.

As a man who tries to turn all adversity to profit, if only the improvement of his own character, I emerged from a prolonged attack of laryngitis with a deepened respect for the power of the human voice.

Being temporarily speechless, I must admit, did turn out to have its compensations. It is amazing how many trivial questions can be answered with a shrug, a rasp, or a gesture in which the index finger is pointed at the open throat.

Also, without fear of inspiring hard feelings, the victim may decline a summons to the telephone. He may lie safely in his bed, eavesdropping as his wife tells whoever it is on the line, "I'm sorry, he can't talk. Yes. It's laryngitis." He is gratified at these moments by righteous self-pity and a sense of freedom.

Those small compensations aside, however, I did begin to gain a new appreciation of the voice as an instrument of command. Household discipline virtually broke down while I was incapacitated. I hadn't realized how much the harmony of our simple life depended on my spoken orders, even when they were disguised, humanely, as amiable observations.

This came to me one evening when my wife served a ragout of leftover beef. Finding it rather in need of seasoning, I whispered, "Are we out of salt?" Ordinarily that would have sent her off to the kitchen. Instead, she merely looked up and said, "What?"

"I asked if there was any salt."

She leaned toward me. "What?"

I made a gesture of shaking salt in my plate.

"You want the pepper?"

By then I was on to her game. I could have brought her off it with a few words, but I knew they would have to be delivered with a tone of restrained but intimidating reproach. My voice wasn't up to it. I went into the kitchen and got the salt myself.

Oddly, it was the dog, with whom I was accustomed to communicating only on the most elementary level, that made me see how much authority I had lost. I was teaching him not to bark at trifles, and we had made good progress. Whenever I heard him start what sounded like a bout of senseless barking I needed only to switch on the outside floodlight, yank the door open, and shout "Quiet!" at the top of my voice. At this command, with its ring of mastery, he would lower his head and go into his house.

Something set him off that night, and, without thinking of my handicap, I switched on the light, yanked the door open as usual, and shouted "Quiet!" What came out was not quite as loud as a stage whisper.

The dog stopped barking but he didn't go into his house. Instead he bounded toward the door and leaped past me into the kitchen.

"Out!" I whispered. "Out!"

My wife staggered into the kitchen, sinking half to her knees in a paroxysm of callous laughter. "His master's voice," she whimpered, evidently overcome by some sadistic joy at my helplessness.

It taught me something. There was a touch of Delilah in the best of them.

Finally one morning, when I had reached the point where I thought I could feel my vocal cords vibrating again and could hear a slight, hoarse sound, I decided to answer the phone and try my wings.

"Hello," I said, sounding like a breather in one of those suspense movies.

There was a pause. "Allo? . . . Mr. Smith?" It was Jacqueline.

"Yes. It's me."

"You are all right?"

"I have laryngitis."

"What do you say?"

"Laryngitis. I can't talk."

"Mr. Smith, you don't sound like yourself. Are you all right?"

"What do you want, Jacqueline?"

"Mr. Smith, do you have some snails?"

"What?"

"I would like to borrow some of your snails."

It turned out she had suddenly been overcome by a hunger for escargots, but they were of course too expensive. So she had gathered some wild snails from her back yard. But there weren't enough. She wanted to come over to our house and gather some of *our* snails.

"Mr. Smith," she said, "you have hundreds of snails. I have seen them many times."

"My God," I said.

"What?"

"I can't talk. I'll call you back."

A day or two later Jacqueline came by with her children and a small kitchen pail.

"We have come for the snails," she said. "You are all right, Mr. Smith?"

I had forgotten her telephone call about the snails, or I tried to. It had only been a joke, or perhaps a hallucination, from my laryngitis. It was no joke. She was there, with her pail and her helpers, ready to plunder my backyard.

I shouldn't have been surprised. She was French. She was a good cook, the daughter of a chef. She was frugal. And like everyone else, she was squeezed by inflation. She had seen the snails crawling about her backyard in North Hollywood, fattening on her flowers, and said, "Why not?"

Her husband wisely had questioned whether it was safe to eat backyard snails, even if one had the stomach for such a dubious adventure. He had insisted that she telephone the Public Health Department. She had done that, though it was something she dreaded, trying to cope with bureaucratic English over the telephone.

"Zey say it is all right to eat zem," she told me, "as long as zey have not been poison."

"How do you know they haven't been poisoned?" I asked.

"Mr. Smith!" she said. "You would not poison a poor little snail?"

I let them go out into the backyard and they gathered two or three dozen of them, much to my surprise; I'd had no idea we were so well stocked.

By an unnerving coincidence, the next day happened to be Adriana's birthday, and Jacqueline invited us that evening for dinner.

"You must promise me," I told her, "that you will not serve snails."

"Mr. Smith," she said, "I cross my heart. I will fix something else, special for you."

"I'm not joking," I told her as severely as I could.

Despite her promise, I had serious misgivings as we sat down. However, I studied everything carefully before eating it, and except for a moment of uncertainty about the chopped mushrooms, I felt secure.

Over champagne and birthday cake I was relaxed enough to pretend a sophisticated interest in her snails. After all, I might not be French, but I was not a barbarian, either.

"Just as an academic culinary question," I said, "how do you prepare them?"

Somehow she made it sound like a Grimm's fairy tale: "First," she said, "you go in the garden and you look for snails. And if you find some little snails you wait till they grow up and you put them in a box and you feed them for two or three days."

"You feed them? What?"

"Spinach. *Salade.* Apple peels. Then you starve them for two days."

"You starve them?"

"*Oui.* So all the stuff gets out of their body. Yes, they must not eat for two days. Then at the end of two days of starvation you put them into a big container of water that is soaked with salt. So all the saliva and stuff gets out of their bodies. You have to rinse them at least ten times in clear, cold water. Because if you don't, they are still slidy."

"Slidy?"

"*Oui.* Slidy. And then you cook them for about forty-five minutes in hot water, and when they are cooked you put them in cold water right away and put them in your refrigerator, so when the water is cold, you take them out of the refrigerator and then take them out of the shells."

I had a feeling that she had neglected the more repulsive instructions, and pushed her for utter honesty.

"Oh. You do not eat the heads. You have to cut the head off, and the intestines. The only part you eat is the part that crawls on the ground. In the restaurants they do it with just garlic, parsley, and butter. But me, I do it with a little touch of my father, which I think is much better; I put some bread crumbs in it, and I do something that nobody else does—I put in some Pernod."

So that was her secret. A touch of her father, and a touch of Pernod. The thought of Jacques Joyeux and Pernod brought on a twinge of nostalgia in me for that glorious night in Tours, when the two of us sampled the wines of the Loire. But it was not an emotion quite urgent enough to make me try snails.

Not long after the snail incident, I bought a tree house for my grandson. He wasn't old enough to build his own, and I couldn't wait. I had always wanted a tree house when I was a boy, but there was never the right kind of a tree, or if there was, we always moved away. I didn't want that to happen to the kid.

Every child needs a retreat, a place where he can escape adult logic; where he can be alone to fantasize, to create his own universe, with himself at the center. A good tree house, I always thought, ought to be equipped with a spyglass, so its occupant could look out upon his realm and familiarize himself with its every detail.

Two men delivered the house one morning by truck. Like most things these days, it came unassembled, but it was said to be easy to assemble with instructions. I will say there seemed to be more pieces to it than I had imagined when I saw the model on the sales lot out in El Monte. Before I gave it up I counted seventy separate pieces of wood, and there were three cartons of nuts, bolts, and washers.

"You think we can put it up in a day?" I asked the driver.

"Well," he said, not sounding too sure, "you ought to. It's about a six-beer job."

They left it in the backyard under the deodars. It looked like something blown down by a cyclone. I wondered where to begin. The sensible thing, I decided, would be to start with the first beer.

I had asked our two sons to come over in the afternoon to help, so I did nothing until they showed up. Then we moved all the parts down to the second level above the canyon. I wanted the tree house to have a good view.

I must explain that the house is not assembled in a tree, but sits up on wooden legs, so that its floor is six or seven feet above ground. It is a tree house without a tree, but it does have a slide, so you can come out of the door and slide to the ground, and also a fireman's pole; and, suspended below the house, a glider and a swing.

Our sons are good with their hands, and the thing seemed to move right along. But we made a mistake or two and had to back-track, and when dark fell we had nothing but the supporting structure in place, with the slide and the swing. The house itself was still in sections, leaning against the sundial. The truck driver had been right. We were only half finished, but among us we had only drunk three beers.

The next day was Sunday and we might have finished the job, but both of my sons had other obligations. In the morning I went down to the site and looked it over. I knew I could never finish it by myself. I sat in the swing to think, and the next thing I knew I was swinging. Gradually, without realizing it, I gained momentum. Higher and higher I went, feet flying up against the sky. At last I slowed to a stop. I heard a woman's laugh and turned around. The Millers had walked up the hill to their mailbox and were looking down at me from the road.

"It's for the grandchildren," I said.

"Of course," said Mrs. Miller.

One weekend after the tree house was built we had the grandchildren over, and I became more inclined than ever to believe that boys and girls are not the same.

Neither the feminists nor the psychologists in their camp have persuaded me that boys and girls are the same kind of people inside their heads, and that little girls would behave exactly like their brothers, unless we taught them not to.

What got me thinking about it again was an incident that occurred about six o'clock on Sunday morning, not long after the sun was up and I had become vaguely aware that a new day was on us.

"Grampa," said my granddaughter in my ear.

I don't much like being called Grampa. If I have to be given a new familiar name, simply because one of our sons has seen fit to have children of his own, I would prefer to be called Grandfather, or Jack. I don't see why having grandchildren should deprive a man of his dignity.

"What do you want?" I asked, sure that whatever she wanted, it most probably should be referred to my wife, who was still asleep.

"Will you put this flower in my hair?"

She held out a plastic daisy, white and blue, and some kind of hairpin. As I had foreseen, it was a task for my wife; but my granddaughter's eyes were in their appealing phase, soft and helpless, and I thought, "Oh, what the hell."

I sat on the edge of the bed in my pajamas and pinned the flower in her hair. It wasn't a very good job. The daisy seemed to dangle, rather than float upright, but I doubted I could do any better.

"There you are," I said, and she trotted off, looking innocent as the morning; but it has been my experience that a girl who sets out with a flower in her hair, like a badge of good intentions, can do a lot of mischief.

My granddaughter returned. She was holding a clutch of articles between her hands, the way you hold a wet kitten, and pushed it toward me. It turned out to be her shoes and socks. She wanted me to put them on. I looked at my wife, hoping she was awake. If she was, she wasn't letting on. Her head was under the pillow.

"Oh, all right," I said, and took the shoes and socks. I couldn't remember that I had ever put a small girl's shoes and socks on, not having had any daughters, but I assumed it wouldn't be a lot harder than putting on a boy's. That didn't turn out to be true.

I tried to put a sock on, but it seemed to be the wrong size. Then I saw why. She was squiggling her foot ever so little, not enough to appear openly uncooperative, but enough to frustrate operations.

"Keep your foot still," I said sternly. Her face clouded, but her foot went limp. In less than five minutes I had her shod. The feminists can say what they like, but it is harder to put a little girl's shoes and socks on than a little boy's, and I think it's congenital.

She skipped off and my grandson appeared in the doorway. He had dressed himself, being six, and I noticed that he had a rather wicked-looking pirate knife stuck under his belt. I hoped it was made of rubber.

"Can I play in the tree house," he asked, "Grampa?"

"Yes, of course," I said, thinking that if I worked with him on it I could get him to say Grandfather or Jack. "That's what it's for."

My wife's eyes were open. I think she knew the first wave had broken, and that there would be a lull. I told her about having to pin the daisy in her granddaughter's hair while her grandson armed himself with a knife and went out to play. "Why do you think she wanted to start the day with a flower in her hair?" I asked.

"I imagine it's something she got from her mother," she said.

"You mean heredity?"

"No. It's something her mother taught her."

"I don't believe it," I said. "It's in her genes, or hormones, or whatever it is."

I was thinking of getting dressed when a startling sound came from the living room. It was a rapid series of clicking sounds, like beans being spilled on the kitchen floor. I hurried out, baffled and alarmed. She was standing on our newly restored floor in a pool of spilled pearls.

"My pearls broke."

"I see."

"Why do you only have one sock on?"

"Because," I said, knowing I was being diverted from the pearls, "you've kept me so busy I haven't had time to put the other one on."

"I'm going out to play in the tree house," she said.

She went, without her pearls but with her flower, to see what she could do, I expect, to exasperate her brother.

I tell you, they're different.

CHAPTER 12

It was Jacqueline's love of French cheese that led to her employment as a cheese importer's representative in gourmet grocery stores, and indirectly to her first contact with the French-speaking community of Los Angeles.

This in turn led to a situation in which I was able to give her some advice and support, and which, I believe, ultimately gave the two of us a heightened respect and affection for each other.

She had been asked by a group of French-speaking teachers to give a talk on cheeses at one of their meetings, speaking in French, of course, and she had accepted, only to regret it at once.

As the day grew near she became sick with anxiety. She had never before talked to a group larger than her family, afraid she would be too nervous to utter a sound. She simply could not go through with it.

"But it ought to be a piece of cake," I told her. "You'll be speaking in French, after all."

"Zat is z'problem," she said. "Zey are all teachers of French and I am just a poor uneducated little girl from Tours."

I am no judge of the quality of her French, of course, but I had heard that Touraine French was the purest French of all, and even if she hadn't been at the top of her class at the Lycée Choiseul, she ought to be able to give a little talk on cheeses without embarrassing herself.

"Mr. Smith," she said, "I cannot do it. I will say I am sick."

"No," I said. "You can't do that. You have committed yourself, and you must do it."

"You are right," she agreed wretchedly.

"Would it help," I asked, "if I went with you? You can pretend you're talking to me."

"You would do zat?"

Her apprehension, I noticed, had brought back her z's.

"If you like," I said.

Actually, I was well qualified to help her. I too had once been pathologically afraid of talking before groups. but I had had to do it, and in time had overcome my fear.

"You simply tell them a funny story to begin with," I advised, "and make them laugh, and they will be your friends from then on."

"What if zey do not laugh?"

"They will laugh," I said, though I knew they were unpredictable, and might not.

I tried to make her see that she was a very charming and amusing woman, with a gift for telling funny stories. I remembered how funny it had seemed to me when she told the story of her trip to Baja with her three friends.

"You can tell a funny story about *me*, if you like," I said. "You must know one or two."

"You would not mind?"

"Of course not. Not if it will put you at ease."

It was an all-day meeting at a school in the elegant old Hancock Park neighborhood, and my daughter-in-law could hardly have been more intimidated than I was. There were perhaps 150 others present, a rather chic and sophisticated-looking crowd, I thought, and even the casual conversation in the hallways was limited to French. The morning seminar was on various topics of interest to the French community, and Jacqueline was on the program to follow a writer who discussed her most recent cookbook. I could not understand a word the cookbook author said, but I could sense her skill, and her audience was obviously entranced.

All this time my daughter-in-law sat beside me, twisting a handkerchief in her hands and expelling a series of taut little sighs.

The applause for her predecessor died out. Her time had come. She rose and walked to the podium. Joan of Arc, walking to the stake. I am familiar with the silence that falls between one's introduction and one's opening words. It is awesome. The introduction was over. She stood alone before her silent audience.

She began. I was surprised at the measure of my own anxiety. I was almost glad it was Jacqueline up there, not me. My chivalry was gone. She had managed to get started, and the telltale signs of nervousness were there. But she flew on, stalling for a terrifying moment, like an old biplane at a flying circus, then spinning out and leveling off, only to stall again.

But something was happening. A scattering of laughter, tentative. Then another. Then it was louder and intermittent. Finally, as my daughter-in-law waxed on, warming to her story, whatever it was, the laughter erupted. The hilarity was genuine.

I was sitting at the back, and faces turned toward me, laughing, their eyes searching me out as my daughter-in-law sailed on. They wanted to share their delight with the lucky father-in-law of such a treasure. It was contagious. I was laughing too, though I hadn't the slightest idea what she was saying.

The story ended. The laughter subsided. But she had weathered her fright. Now she was coasting; I could tell. She finished quite gracefully, and left the podium to what sounded like sincere applause.

"You were great!" I told her afterward. "Just great! What were you telling them, anyway, that was so funny?"

"Oh, Mr. Smith," she said, "I hope you will forgive me."

"Forgive you? For what? I'm *proud* of you."

"Mr. Smith, I tell zem the story about how you cannot eat the little birds with their little heads and their little feet and you think the cognac is wine and you get *smash* and pour cognac on the table at my wedding breakfast."

So I had helped her after all.

"I'll tell you what," I said as I drove her home. "I'll forget you ever told that story if you forget it ever happened."

"Mr. Smith," she said, "it's a deal."

"By the way," I said, "now that we're such good friends, you don't have to call me Mr. Smith any more."

"Mr. Smith," she said, "I cannot help it. It is the way I am brought up. The fazher-in-law must be treated with respect. To me you will always be Mr. Smith."

Looking at it that way, I rather liked the idea.

Curt has a sense of theater, and sometimes he enjoys breaking the most exciting news in an oblique or offhand manner, so that one does not get it directly, and the effect, when it does come through, is all the greater.

Late one afternoon he phoned to ask me about a business matter, and when we had finished with that he said, "Oh, there's something else."

"Yes?"

"Gail's in labor."

My response was a prolonged silence. My clock was not set for that revelation. It was premature. The baby had not been expected for another ten days, and babies in my family had always been on time, or late.

The way he had broken the news reminded me of a day in April thirty-two years earlier, when a corporal named Jones sauntered into a Dallas hut on Maui, where our division was recuperating after Iwo Jima, and said casually, "You guys hear the news? Truman's President."

First, one had to think who Truman was. Then one had to wonder how Truman could suddenly be President. Only then did the shocking truth sink in. Roosevelt, somehow, was dead.

I remembered also that only the previous September Curt had invited all of us out to dinner, including the Paoluccis and Bernadette, and

Douglas and Jacqueline and the two children. The scene he had chosen was rather an expensive restaurant at the Marina, and my feeling that he was being frightfully extravagant was heightened when he ordered Mumm's champagne. I had raised him to believe that a good California champagne was suitable for any occasion.

By no amount of wheedling could he be induced to disclose the reason for this festive gathering before he was ready. Only when he stood up, at last, champagne glass in hand, did the explanation come, and even then it was indirect.

I had guessed, by then, that he had been given a substantial raise, if not actually elevated to chairman of the board. At UCLA he had changed his major to environmental geography after the war, and then had done a graduate year in that field and was now employed as an environmentalist with a large utility company.

Gail had been steadily employed in physical therapy after graduating, and their combined incomes had given them a level of affluence that my wife and I could only have dreamed of when we were their age. Perhaps, I guessed, he was going to announce that they had bought a house in Bel-Air, or at least a yacht.

We all fell silent at the table. Even the children sensed that something exciting was about to be said, and turned their faces expectantly toward their uncle.

"Cristophe and Adriana," he said momentously, smiling down at the two children, now enchanted by the sound of their own names, "are going to have a cousin."

Mary Ann Paolucci was seated at my right. She looked at me, and I watched her face turn from uncertainty to comprehension to joy. She and Bernie Paolucci had long made it clear that they were ready for such an event.

I remembered the lines from Kahlil Gibran, which of course had been read into their wedding ceremony at their request, that they were the bows from which their children, like arrows, would be sent forth.

"It's probably a false alarm," I told Curt over the phone. Ten days early wasn't like the Smiths. But somewhat after five o'clock he called back to say that he and Gail were leaving for the hospital. I was about to advise against this, pointing out that it was a bad hour for traffic; but I realized they were dealing with an urgency that was oblivious to such inauspicious factors.

Denny and I decided not to go to the hospital. We knew the Paoluccis would be there, and one set of grandparents ought to be enough. But we spent a restive night.

Curt phoned at five o'clock in the morning. The delivery had been made. It was a girl, and her name was Alison Paolucci Smith.

For a moment I indulged myself in the notion that I had been influential in the choice of that name, remembering my suggestion that they preserve Gail's maiden name as a middle name for the child, whatever its sex. But it was probably only a coincidence. I couldn't remember that either of my daughters-in-law had ever taken any advice of mine, and certainly not in a matter as serious as naming a baby.

"And now," I thought, counting on my fingers, "there are nine of us."

I soon found out what my function was to be in greeting this new member of the family. All of us gathered that evening at the hospital in Santa Monica to see the principals, and since small children are not allowed in maternity wards, it was decided that I should wait in the downstairs lobby with the cousins.

I might have managed it with poise, I believe, except that someone else had left two small children down below, without a guardian. I found myself suddenly trying to manage four children, instead of two, and quickly discovered that the amount of energy and mischief released by four children is a quantum jump over the amount released by two.

The critical point came when Adriana, who had proposed a game of hide-and-seek, not only found a place to hide from the two strange children, but also from me. My annoyance soon turned to alarm. I could find her nowhere.

"Where is she?" I demanded of her brother.

"She's in the praying room," he said.

"She's in the what?"

He showed me. She had hidden in the dimly lighted chapel off the lobby, from which I furtively retrieved her. I was about to ask my grandson where he had picked up that extraordinary phrase "praying room" when the hospital security officer appeared, looking every inch an authority figure in his blue uniform and leather harness.

"Here now!" he barked. "Stop that noise!" There was no chuckle in his voice and no friendly twinkle in the reproachful glance he sent my way.

"I'm only responsible for two of them," I pointed out.

"They'll have to be quiet," he said, making it plain that he considered me responsible for the whole lot. I was glad he hadn't come along while my granddaughter was hiding in the praying room.

Finally Doug came down in the elevator and took over and I went up to see my new granddaughter through a window. Alison Paolucci Smith. She looked as if she'd been in a fight and lost the first round. She also looked like a winner. I decided to call her Lucci.

The others moved down the corridor to talk to a nurse, and for a moment I was alone with my granddaughter. I blew her a kiss through the window.

It seemed like a good time to spend one.

A stone bas-relief
depicting Assyrian
cavalrymen in the
mountains, from the
palace of the great king,
Sennacherib, at Nineveh.
Nearly two miles of such
reliefs were found on the
walls of the immense
palace.

THE LUCK OF NINEVEH

A Condensation of the book by

ARNOLD C. BRACKMAN

FOREWORD

In 1817, when Austen Henry Layard was born, there was no tangible proof that Nineveh, the seat of the Assyrian empire, which reputedly had endured longer than any empire before or since, ever existed.

The Bible, of course, contained numerous references to Nineveh as "that great city," and fragments of its history, preserved by classical Greek and Roman geographers and historians, attested to its former glory, grandeur, and notoriety. Thus, although Nineveh and Assyria had been "familiar to us from childhood," as Layard expressed it thirty-four years later, "it is only when we ask ourselves what we really know concerning the Assyrians that we discover our ignorance of all that relates to their history, and even to their geographic position."

Indeed, Layard considered it one of the most remarkable facts of his day that the records of an empire, so renowned for its power and civilization, were entirely lost.

It was in the course of working on a biography of Heinrich Schliemann, the discoverer of Troy, that I stumbled onto the personal relationship between Schliemann and Layard, the discoverer of Nineveh. The link between them had been lost in history just as had the capitals of the Trojans and Assyrians.

Schliemann's story is the rags-to-riches epic in archaeology; Layard's story, the tale of the greatest adventurer in archaeology.

Schliemann, in his dreams and in the field, spent a lifetime in search of noble Troy—and found it late in life. By contrast Layard, as he openly conceded, "accidentally discovered" Nineveh in his youth. In contemporary argot, he lucked into it. In the process, like Schliemann, Layard brought to light a new world.

Just as Nineveh and Troy are insolubly linked in the legends and history of Western man, so are Layard and Schliemann. I have told Schliemann's story elsewhere.

This is Layard's story.

May the gods lead him.
—ASHURNASIRPAL

CHAPTER 1

In 1825, Austen Henry Layard embarked on his first solo journey. He took a coach from London to Dover, crossed the English Channel by packet, and traveled from Calais to Paris. He put up one night in the French capital and ordered the concierge to bring him a bottle of champagne. By diligence the following morning, he proceeded to Moulins, arriving in the middle of the night. "In the crowd," he recalled later, "I recognized my father, who was waiting for me."

Layard was eight years old.

The journey gave him a large measure of self-confidence, and a taste for travel and adventure. The champagne incident also illuminated his precocious appreciation of life's pleasures. "I well recollect asking for that bottle, which my father, to his amazement," Layard said laughingly sixty years later, "found charged in the bill."

In many ways, the journey was a microcosmic forerunner of his future life style.

As Layard's surname suggests, his family was of French origin; indeed, the family claimed to be of ancient stock, descended "in a somewhat mythical way," his relatives used to say, from Raymond of Toulouse. Whatever the case, when Louis XIV revoked the Edict of Nantes in 1685, and thereby removed the shield that protected the Protestant minority from religious persecution, the French king set in motion a mass flight of Huguenots, as they were called, from France. Among the refugees was Peter Raymond de Layarde, who slipped across the Dutch border with the assistance of a French Catholic friend, and fled to England.

De Layarde Anglicized his name and entered the British army, rose to the rank of major, married the daughter of a French refugee like himself, and settled in Canterbury, where a French community took root after the Huguenots were granted permission to use a crypt of the cathedral for their service—a service they conduct there to this day.

The Layard family flourished on English soil. By the turn of the eighteenth century, two Layards had risen to the rank of general in the army and a third, Charles, entered the church, became Prebendary of Worcester, Chaplain-in-Ordinary to King George III, and Dean of Bristol. Like many of the orthodox clerical dignitaries of his day, he lived comfortably, frequented good society, enjoyed good food, and, as his grandson Austen Henry Layard was wont to say, "drank freely of old port."

In truth, the dean was a pompous and overbearing figure who was in constant conflict with Christian values. He was not especially fond of children, particularly his own. He solved their interference in his own life by bundling them off at an early age to respectable country families. His second son, Henry Peter John Layard, was dispatched to Ramsgate. The dean never corresponded with him and rarely visited him. Incredibly, he never invited his children home for the holidays, not even Christmas. If his wife had any say in the matter, there is no record of it.

Young Henry Peter John was fortunate, however. His proxy family was well read and fostered in the boy a taste for English literature and the fine arts. The child also developed a deepening affection for a playmate with merry blue eyes, Marianne Austen, the daughter of a neighbor and local banker.

While he was growing up at Ramsgate, France invaded the Netherlands and in 1795 reduced Holland to the status of vassal. Automatically, the Dutch overseas empire, which was spread from Surinam on the northern bulge of South America to the Malay archipelago in Southeast Asia, became fair game for the British, who warred incessantly with the French on a global scale. One of the jewels of the Dutch empire was Ceylon, "Pearl of the Orient," rich in spices, tea, rubber, pearls, and other exotic treasures. The British East India Company lost little time in driving its Dutch counterpart from the island.

To the British, Ceylon was a kind of paradise, and their acquisition of the territory set off a wild scramble for postings to the island, particularly for appointments to the newly founded Ceylon Civil Service, which administered the treasure trove. The civil service was considered a shortcut to riches, and the dean shrewdly applied the right pressure in the right places in obtaining appointments for two of his sons, Henry Peter John and Charles Edward, both of them now teenagers.

In short order, the Layard name became a force in the crown colony. Through the years, Layards held key posts in the civil service, served as senior officers in the Ceylon Rifles, played prominent roles in the island's judiciary system, from district judges to chief justice, and prospered as tea-and-coffee planters and traders.

But this was not to be the case with Henry Peter John. His brother Charles and Charles's descendants reaped the good fortune, while Henry was compelled by poor health—notably an unfortunate mix of asthma and malaria—to leave the tropical paradise. He returned to England with a modest pension, and little else.

In Ceylon, however, the youthful Layard's thoughts had turned on more than making a fortune. No sooner had he disembarked from a square-rigger in the Thames' roadstead than he took the first available stage to Ramsgate and proposed to Marianne. She promptly accepted the offer. Attractive, diminutive, she possessed an uncomplicated and unassuming nature, and despite a parochial upbringing, she was quite cosmopolitan in outlook. Marianne was a voracious reader—and rarely forgot anything she read. Her weakness was a susceptibility to family pressures, real or perceived. The Austens were a large, well-to-do, close-knit clan. Fortunately for Marianne they approved of "the young man from Ceylon," whom they had known and liked as a child and whose father had impeccable Church of England credentials.

Soon after their betrothal, with Napoleon's defeat and the restoration of peace on the Continent, the asthmatic Henry and his bride sailed for France with a view to stretching out his small pension and escaping England's miserable climate. In Paris, on a blustery Wednesday, March 5, 1817, on Rue Neuve des Petits Champs, Marianne gave birth to the couple's first child, a boy, dutifully christened Henry Austen.

The senior Layard's health, however, fared no better in France than in Ceylon or Britain. In quest of a milder climate, Layard and his family gravitated south, and in 1821, when Henry Austen was four years old, they settled at Florence, where, for the first time since he quit Ceylon, the father was overjoyed to find himself free of chronic asthmatic attacks.

Unlike his own father, the senior Henry Layard was a doting father, who cultivated in his children a lively interest in the fine arts and the world. With young Henry Austen in tow, the father employed Florence's renowned museums and picture galleries as classrooms.

These happy days in Italy, however, were short-lived. Marianne's family was horrified at the thought of her children being raised in a foreign country; worse, among foreigners. Her brother Benjamin and his wife, Sara, a childless couple, were particularly upset. As young Henry's godparents, they felt a special responsibility toward the boy.

Benjamin Austen was a prominent London solicitor, and he entertained big plans for the lad. When the boy was of age, he proposed to take him on as an articled law clerk. In the back of Austen's mind was the hope that the young man might become a partner in his firm and eventually take over the law business. Like her husband, Sara Austen, a socialite who collected young writers and artists around her dining room table, insisted that the boy's place was in a proper English school where he would obtain a proper education before taking up the law. "Proper" was one of Sara's favorite words.

The affluent Austens brought pressure to bear on Marianne, and the Layards returned to wet and dreary England. But the father suffered so from a fresh series of asthma attacks that on medical advice he and his family fled back to the Continent for relief and settled in Moulins.

During the family's residence at Moulins, young Henry entered a French school. Sheltered through infancy and childhood, Henry Austen Layard came into contact with a new world. Suddenly, he found himself a member of a detestable and detested minority. The Napoleonic wars were over, but the French and English continued to view each other suspiciously, even with contempt and hatred. At school, Layard was denounced as a Protestant and heretic.

He was often beaten up by school bullies, and whenever a scuffle erupted, the headmaster meted out to him a double punishment.

Informed that they possessed a "rebellious and unmanageable" son, the surprised Layards eventually got to the bottom of the trouble and withdrew him from school. But the experience gave young Layard a new perspective on life. He developed a persecution complex and, as a defense mechanism, a hot temper and aggressive attitude. Thereafter, in dealing with the world, he was outwardly on the offensive, although inwardly on the defensive.

If the Moulins school episode was disastrous for the son, so was the French climate for the father. The family packed their belongings and, after a brief residence in Switzerland, returned to their beloved Italy and their old haunt, Florence.

This second sojourn in Florence was the happiest period of Henry Austen Layard's youth. He was immersed in a world of painters and soon became as fluent in Italian as in French and English. In a house filled with books, he was drawn irresistibly to volumes about travel and high adventure—the sort of books his mother feasted upon until her death in 1879 at the age of eighty-nine.

One of Layard's favorite authors was Johann Burckhardt, the Swiss explorer who wrote a string of travel books on Asia Minor and had recently discovered the lost city of Petra, built by the Nabataeans, in what is now the Jordanian desert. Petra, he wrote, was a mass of glorious ruins of undetermined vintage and lay in an utterly desolate region.

Burckhardt's account stirred within young Layard a desire to see Petra for himself and perhaps find a "lost" city of his own. But his favorite book was *The Thousand and One Nights,* that composite of Persian and Indian tales, transmuted into Arabian fables, which to this day, in expurgated form, serves as a Western child's introduction to the Arab world. As a result of his passion for the *Arabian Nights,* he thereafter devoured every available book on Near Eastern travel.

Immediately after having resettled in Florence, the father and son had fallen back into a familiar routine, touring galleries and museums. By the age of nine, young Layard knew the identity of every painter of the Florentine school, and was at home with all the pictures in the great Uffizi and Pitti collections. By the age of twelve, he was an accomplished art connoisseur and critic. He could distinguish the subtle difference between the paintings of such minor artists as Carlo Dolci and his daughter Agnes. Indeed, for a time, the boy considered becoming a painter. But his father, who envisioned his son as an established London solicitor, with wood-paneled office, discouraged the idea. Beauty in art, yes; money, no.

Nonetheless, the father let the son down gently and arranged for the youth to take drawing lessons with a local, indifferent painter who lived in a cell at the Convent of St. Croce. The artist taught the child to copy lithographs of human figures and animals, an accomplishment that proved invaluable to him in later life. Young Layard also visited the studio of Seymour Kirkup, an English painter and student of Dante who is best remembered for his illustrations of the Vernon edition of the *Divine Comedy.* A local celebrity, Kirkup enthralled the boy with the story of how he discovered a lost fresco by Giotto. It was hidden by centuries of whitewash on a wall in the chapel of Borgello. Little did Layard realize that he was destined to repeat Kirkup's actions far afield, and on a stupendous scale, recovering not simply a lost work of art but enough lost art to fill several museums.

In Italy, Layard's father retained his Ceylonese habits and, despite his limited income, crowded his lunch table regularly with local and visiting personalities. They were largely big fish from small ponds, among them, Morgan, a landscape painter; Niccolini, a dramatist; Trelawny, a friend of Byron; and Migliarini, who was in charge of the "department of antiquities" at the Uffizi, the word "archaeology" yet to come into popular usage.

Table talk centered on the fine arts, and travel. These luncheons excited the boy's imagination, instilled within him an intense desire for travel, and turned him, prematurely, into a cosmopolitan lad.

Through their friendship with Migliarini, father and son visited the Etruscan excavations in progress in the region and inspected the ancient walls of Florence, Layard's first contact with "the dig," as modern archaeologists term it.

Archaeology, of course, was in its infancy, stimulated largely by the casual discovery of the ruins of Pompeii at the end of the eighteenth century, an event which stirred the imagination of Europe. But these ruins, covered with volcanic ash, were essentially aboveground. The idea that lost cities and lost civilizations could be brought to light by digging into the core of the earth was novel.

Thus, in the formative phase of Layard's life, fate appears to have pushed him in the direction of archaeology, and its outriders, travel and adventure.

As the years slipped by, his godparents back in England were aghast at their godson's freewheeling education. The Austens applied new pressure on Marianne and her husband to reconsider the boy's future. The choice was theirs—either ship him to England for a proper education or raise him among dirty foreigners. True to her character, Marianne retreated and, true to his, her husband retreated with her.

In 1829, at the age of twelve, young Layard's Italian idyll collapsed for the second time. He was packed off to England.

Like a caged bird—shut up.
—SENNACHERIB

CHAPTER 2

In England, the Austens placed their heir in a school maintained by the Reverend James Bewsher, like themselves, a proper Tory and member of the Church of England. "I found myself," Layard said with understatement, "among boys who had been brought up differently from myself."

Not only did he have nothing in common with them, but the students regarded him darkly. His fluency in French and Italian made him suspect, the butt of unending harassment, and Layard was introduced to reverse discrimination.

Since he was never destined to wear a school tie—the Layards could not afford to send him to college, and the Austens saw no need for it—his tutors at Bewsher's school took little interest in his classical education. "I have regretted it through my life," he often said.

Layard usually spent Christmas and other holidays at the Austen town house or country estate, where Layard discovered he possessed a natural gift for horsemanship. He also regularly visited the British Museum, then located at Montague House, within a few minutes' walk of the Austens' London residence. There he gazed, for the first time, on all that remained of the "great cities" of Nineveh and Babylon, which was scant indeed. The collection had been purchased—the year he was born—by the Museum from the widow of Claudius James Rich. To Layard, the name Rich meant nothing.

The collection filled a solitary display case and consisted of four baked clay cylinders, thirty-two clay tablets, thirteen bricks, one boundary marker and several smaller bits and pieces. The relics were covered with arrow-headed characters thought to be of Assyrian origin.

In the Book of Genesis, Assyria is identified as the first great empire to come into existence after the Flood, and the founder is singled out as Nimrod, a great-grandson of Noah. Nimrod established his kingdom in the "land of Shinar," the Mesopotamian delta, but, as a Greek writer later observed, he was seized "with a powerful desire to subdue all of Asia that lies between the Don and the Nile." According to Genesis, whatever his true motivation, "out of that land he went forth into Assyria and builded Nineveh." Situated along the east bank of the Tigris, some 220 miles north of the delta, Nineveh became the seat of empire and the greatest city of its day.

Dotted with majestic palaces, temples, canals, and gardens, its walls rose 220 feet above the West Asian plain. Fortified by 1,500 watchtowers, the walls were so thick, it was said, that three chariots easily drove abreast upon them. Nineveh was defended by five walls and three moats. Each of the city's fifteen gates was guarded by ramparts. And within its perimeter were more than thirty temples "shining with silver and gold."

For more than 1,300 years Assyrian monarchs ruled from Nineveh and other royal cities within the immediate vicinity. Then, as swiftly as the empire rose, it fell—and disappeared.

Although Layard did not know it at the time, the British Museum's lonely case of Assyrian relics gave Rich immortality. It marked the first stirrings of Assyrian archaeology.

Layard spent four years at Bewsher's in a desultory fashion. Then in 1834, Layard's parents and brothers returned to England at the insistence of the Austen clan. Layard met his parents at Dover, and a warm reunion ensued. The parents were proud. Their oldest son, approaching his seventeenth birthday, had developed into a handsome youth, who wore his golden locks à la Byron and sported a mustache in the dashing style popularized during the early Victorian era.

Benjamin and Sara Austen had virtually adopted young Henry in his parents' absence. At Benjamin's request, he had even reversed the order of his Christian names and signed himself Austen Henry, although family and friends continued to call him "Henry." He was ready to embark upon his apprenticeship in law, and clearly he was being groomed to take over his uncle's firm. At least, that was the family game plan. "My own tastes and inclinations . . . were not considered or consulted," Austen Henry observed with misgiving. "Nor was my character and disposition taken into account."

On January 24, 1834, he was "articled" to his uncle for a period of five years, during which Layard diligently and desperately applied himself to the law. The effort was a disaster.

His father bestowed on him an allowance of £2 ($10) a week. From this amount, he was expected to pay for his lodging, food, clothing, carfare, entertainment, books, and incidentals.

Each morning, promptly at nine, like a young Bob Cratchit, Austen Henry was at his stool in his uncle's chambers, quill in hand, ready to partake in the routine of an attorney's office. His principal activity was to copy legal documents and to accompany the firm's clerks to public offices to transact business. When not entwined in seemingly endless piles of paper, he was expected to read and master the law.

At quitting time, late in the day, his uncle and staff departed for their homes and the warmth of their winter hearths while Layard went to dinner alone at a dingy eating house just down the street. Dinner was always the same, a single chop and a glass of tepid water, at six pence (12 cents), the cheapest fare he could find. After dinner, he was expected to return to his uncle's offices at Gray's Inn and spend the evening studying

Blackstone, before retiring to his cheap boardinghouse on New Ormond Street. His only escape from the drudgery of the law was Sunday, when the Austens held open house.

These Sunday dinners were glittering affairs, the more surprising since the puritanical outlook of the Victorian age was beginning to take hold and Parliament had just narrowly defeated the 1837 Sunday Observance Bill which would have barred entertainments, public or private, on the Sabbath.

But like Layard's parents, his aunt and uncle were gracious hosts and crowded their table with a wide circle of writers, painters, and politicians, the latter invariably staunch Tories. He dined with such celebrities as Turner, the painter; Robert Plumer Ward, auther of *De Vere;* Charles Fellows, who had found Greek ruins in Turkey; Isaac Disraeli, the literary critic, and his foppish son Benjamin, who wrote *Vivian Grey,* with the editorial assistance of Aunt Sara, a book that catapulted him into the limelight and, ultimately, into 10 Downing Street. On one occasion, in the course of a spirited debate, young Disraeli brought down the Austens and their guests with the outrageous declaration that when he became prime minister, he would do thus-and-so. As the laughter reverberated around the table, an angered Dizzy, as he was called, shouted, "Laugh as you may, I shall be prime minister!"

Among the Austens' inner circle, the two personalities whom Layard envied the most were Disraeli and Fellows.

Layard, then seventeen years old—Dizzy was thirty—was secretly jealous of the brash, confident young Tory who knew what he wanted and was determined to get it. Like himself, Disraeli had been an articled clerk. One day, however, Dizzy was caught reading Chaucer instead of Blackstone, upbraided for breech of discipline, and told he was unfit for the law. Dizzy required no encouragement to abandon the profession. He fled Gray's Inn and took refuge in the worlds of literature and politics. If only someone would tell Layard that he, too, was unfit for the bar.

As for Fellows, then 35, he regaled the Austens and their guests with fascinating accounts of exploration in Turkish Asia and the discovery of such Greek ruins as Xanthus, the ancient capital of Lycia. Layard was fascinated by Fellows. Secretly, he nurtured the hope of emulating him.

After these stimulating Sunday dinners, young Layard returned to his boardinghouse more depressed than ever.

Layard's father, within a year of his reluctant return to England's inhospitable climate, sustained a fresh series of asthmatic attacks. These bouts left him weak, and he contracted tuberculosis, the curse of a rapidly industrializing England.

Young Disraeli, in the hustings during the 1835 election campaign, visited the elder Layard at his Aylesbury home, on the outskirts of London, and was aghast. "Layard in bed," he penned the Austens in his familiar staccato style, "& really dangerously ill."

Austen Henry rushed to his father's side. Shortly thereafter, at the age of fifty-one, he was dead. His death stunned the boy. The shock, coupled with a rapidly declining interest in the law, induced a severe depression. Alarmed, the Austens summoned their physician and the doctor prescribed "a change of air."

In the company of a friend of the Austens, William Brockeden, an author and illustrator, Layard spent part of the summer that year on the Continent, chiefly in the Italian Alps. Through "Brock," as his friends called him, he met Camille de Cavour, learned of the Italian struggle for independence, and was quickly enlisted to Cavour's side.

It was during this journey that Layard's serious interest in the world of the distant past surfaced. Brock was gathering material for a new book. In particular, he wished to verify the theory that Hannibal had crossed the Alps during the Second Punic War through a pass now known as the Little St. Bernard.

During their Alpine sojourn, Brock introduced Layard to Henry Crabb Robinson, a former foreign correspondent of the London *Times*. Robinson took an immediate liking to the young man and extended him an invitation to breakfast with him in London. Despite his "retirement," Robinson contributed regularly to journals and frequently employed Layard as a research assistant. "Soon," Layard recalled, "each moment that I could spare from my work at Gray's Inn was devoted to general reading."

German was hardly a popular language in that era. But as a result of his association with Robinson, who talked endlessly about Goethe and other German writers, Layard sought to acquire a knowledge of it. For the price of a cup of tea and a slice of bread and butter, he recruited a destitute Polish refugee to give him evening lessons in German. Through the Pole, Layard learned of Russia's network of Siberian prison camps and of the Polish struggle for independence. Thus, he received lessons not only in German but also in foreign affairs.

The change of air that summer had done him wonders, and thereafter he spent his summers on the Continent, missing an occasional chop at dinner or squirreling away a few pence to finance these journeys. In

1836 he spent July and August in France, and the year after that he revisited Italy, his true home.

During this Italian airing, Layard met Silvio Pellico, whose *Francesca da Rimini* was an Italian literary sensation. "The conversation," Layard recalled, "turned upon Botta, the historian." Carlo Botta had recently died at Paris at the age of sixty. It was the first time Layard had heard the name, but five years later, his meeting with Botta's son, Paolo Emilio, was destined to mark a turning point in his life.

The following summer, in 1838, with the advance of a few extra pounds from his widowed mother, Layard booked a second-class passage on a British steamer for an excursion to Scandinavia and Russia for the purpose of "seeing something of northern Europe."

Other than short summer excursions, Layard quenched his thrist for travel by haunting London's secondhand bookshops. His focus centered on books about travel and adventure in Asia Minor. At a book stall near the British Museum he found worn copies of Sir Robert Ker Porter's two-volume work on Persia and ancient Babylonia. The set had been published in 1821, when Layard was four years old.

Not only Sir Robert's book but his adventurous life style appealed to Layard. Porter had married a Russian princess, and he himself was a character as fanciful as any in Scheherazade's tales. An incurable romantic and adventurer, Sir Robert also described himself as "an ardent lover and sedulous practitioner of the arts and the study of antiquity."

During his Near Eastern travels, Porter traced the route of Xenophon and the Ten Thousand Greeks, a land march that took him to the nondescript Turkish town of Mosul, on the west bank of the Tigris. There, to Porter's astonishment, he discovered that according to local legend the large mound on the opposite bank was the site of lost Nineveh. Out of curiosity, Sir Robert crossed the Tigris and found scattered on the mound a number of odd bricks inscribed with chiseled characters "known by the several names of cuneiform, nail-headed, arrow-headed." With astonishing perspicacity, he surmised that the characters might be of Assyrian origin and speculated: "We might not be extravagant in believing these characters to have been used before the Flood."

He also reported the discovery of "curious relics," the fragments of cylinders covered in cuneiform characters and depicting such fantastic figures in combat as a bull, half-man, half-beast.

Porter's book captivated Layard. He was also moved by the last paragraph of this 1,589-page tome, in which, in the form of an afterthought, Sir Robert grieved over the death of Claudius James Rich, the East India Company representative who had often been Porter's host at Baghdad and who had succumbed to cholera at the age of thirty-four. Rich had left behind some "literary papers," and Sir Robert ended the postscript with an appeal that the papers be published.

Rich? The name plucked at Layard's memory. Suddenly, he remembered: Rich's name adorned the odd collection of cuneiform tablets in the lonely vitrine in the British Museum.

Layard scurried about in search of Rich's literary papers and learned that they had just been published by his wife, fifteen years after Rich's death. When Layard got his hands on Rich's memoirs, the title alone whetted his appetite: *Narrative of a Residence in Koordistan, and on the site of Ancient Nineveh; with a Journal of a Voyage Down the Tigris to Baghdad and an account of a visit to Shirauz and Persepolis.*

Layard sat up through the night reading Rich and the following day fell asleep on his stool at Gray's Inn.

Like himself, Rich had been born in France—near Dijon, in Burgundy. An extraordinary linguist, Rich was fluent in Arabic by the age of nine. By fifteen he had mastered the Babel of Asia Minor—Persian, Hebrew, Turkish, etc. Two years later he joined the East India Company, rose quickly through its ranks, married the comely Mary MacIntosh, daughter of a company official, and at twenty-five was appointed the Company's resident at Baghdad.

In his journal, Rich referred to the collection of relics he had donated to the British Museum as "the curiosities of Nineveh." But, he confided, "Whether they belonged to Nineveh or some other city is the question."

Layard's adrenalin flowed as he read these passages. The journals, edited by Mary as an imperishable monument to her husband, stirred not only Layard but England.

Layard was now permanently hooked on Asia Minor. "I greedily read," he said, "every volume of Eastern travel that fell my way." And the more he read, the more he railed against his fate as a law clerk.

In 1838, after four years of legal training, he reached the breaking point. "I could not conceal my feelings on the subject from my uncle and my friends," he said. Even Uncle Benjamin realized that the boy no longer even attempted to apply himself seriously to the law. Forthrightly, the uncle told his godson, as a young Disraeli had been told a decade earlier, that he was unsuited to be a solicitor and, for that matter, probably unsuited for any other kind of work.

For Layard, the present was bleak, and the future bleaker. "I was almost in a state of despair," Layard said. "My position in England seemed to me hopeless and caused me so much misery that I thought only of getting away." He was twenty-one and he felt his life was behind him.

As his personal crisis deepened, a paternal uncle, Charles Layard, who had journeyed to Ceylon with his father forty-two years earlier and amassed a fortune, reappeared in London on holiday. The Austens confided in him their concern about their mutual nephew, and Uncle Charles took young Layard to lunch to sound him out. Downing a tankard of bitters, Uncle Charles advised his nephew to consider Ceylon, as his father before him. "The island is flourishing," the uncle reported. Moreover, there was no need for young Layard to pass the bar examination to practice law in Ceylon. He needed only a certificate, and surely, after nearly five years of drudgery, he could obtain that modest recognition of his apprenticeship.

Surprisingly, despite his passion for travel and adventure, Layard had never considered Ceylon the solution to his problems. Now the solution was manifest, or so it seemed.

But as the fates were to have it, he never got there. He set sail, but instead of a journey to Ceylon, Austen Henry Layard embarked on a journey into history.

> *A district on the other side of the sea,*
> *a distant place.*
> —ASHURBANIPAL

CHAPTER 3

In the great age of sail, before the opening of the Suez Canal in 1869, the quickest way to reach Ceylon from England was also the most inconvenient. The traveler embarked in England and sailed to Alexandria, since pharaonic times Egypt's principal port of entry. Then he proceeded overland across the Isthmus of Suez, and caught a ship bound for India via the Red Sea.

But chance intervened, and Layard found himself contemplating an altogether different route.

As a formidable Ceylonese figure, Uncle Charles was in great demand in London for counseling about opportunities on the island. Among those who introduced themselves was an adventurous Englishman of twenty-eight named Edward Ledwich Obaldeston Mitford, staunchly Tory and Church of England, who had spent five years on the Barbary coast of North Africa, largely in Morocco, and was currently unemployed. Uncle Charles was impressed with his experience and thought he would make an ideal traveling companion for his nephew.

They quickly discovered strong bonds. They were, in Layard's words, "equally careless of comfort and unmindful of danger, curious, enthusiastic, and anxious to leave England as soon as possible." But Mitford dreaded the sea. He proposed reaching Ceylon by a land march through Europe, Asia Minor, Central Asia, down the Indian subcontinent, and then across Adam's Bridge, the chair of treacherous sandbanks separating India from Ceylon.

The plan appealed to Layard. It was vast, romantic, and extravagant. It contained elements of high adventure—danger—since some of the areas they would traverse were unmapped and Europeans in those regions were regarded as no less strange than visitors from a distant planet.

Layard and Mitford, their spirits soaring, plunged energetically into preparations for the journey, heedless of the dangers. They would be without even elementary forms of communications. No telegraph lines had yet been strung across the region. There were not even any post offices along the route—and there were no road maps available.

But, they obtained introductions to a number of old Asia hands and picked their brains. Among them were the aging James Baillie Fraser, whose works Layard had devoured as a child, and Sir Charles Fellows, whom Layard had met at his godparents' Sunday dinners. Probably at Fellows' suggestion, Layard contacted the Royal Geographic Society and outlined the route of their proposed journey. Layard's interest in exploration excited the Society's secretary, who informed him that "the ruins of ancient cities and of remarkable monuments" were certain to exist along the route, especially in western Persia, where "all attempts to reach them have hitherto failed."

The secretary supplemented his meager knowledge of the area with the field reports of Major Henry Rawlinson, a former military adviser to the Shah's court in Persia, a soldier-scholar who would emerge as one of the great Orientalists of the Victorian period. In the course of his activities in western Persia, Rawlinson had discovered many ancient ruins. But he was unable to visit the highlands that were inhabited by the Baktiyari, a tribe that was in an almost perpetual state of rebellion against the Shah. Nonetheless, Rawlinson had received secret descriptions from Baktiyari chiefs of ruins and rock-cut inscriptions in the area around Shushan. These reports excited the Royal Geographic Society, and the clergy, too, for it was at Shushan that Daniel saw the vision of the ram and the goat. The Society urged Layard to try to penetrate the region, and he promised to do so if possible.

Layard did his homework. He read everything available on Asia Minor. He also took lessons in Arabic and Persian; however rudimentary, the lessons gave him an ear for those exotic languages.

There were other things to consider before setting out. For one thing, there was the question of money. Layard, who had no funds of his own, was determined to make the journey pay for itself. Accordingly, he took lessons in taxidermy with the hope of shipping stuffed birds and small mammals to the British Museum. He also accepted a mapmaking commission from the Royal Geographic Society. A sea captain gave him lessons in the use of the sextant, and Layard invested in an artificial horizon, a compass, an aneroid barometer, a Fahrenheit thermometer, a telescope, and a pocket sextant. Since a sextant is useless without a chronometer, he put his last savings into a reliable watch.

Again with an eye to financing the venture, Layard and his companion solicited an advance of £200 ($1,000), a goodly sum in that day, from the publishing house of Smith-Elder. Under the terms of the contract, the pair agreed to "forward to the said Messieurs Smith-Elder Company, within six months after their arrival in the island of Ceylon, a manuscript of their journal in an intelligible and prepared condition for the press." If they failed to produce the manuscript, they agreed to repay Smith-Elder the advance, with interest.

Part of the advance was invested in a couple of double-barreled shotguns, both for protection and with a view to procuring fresh meat. Layard contributed two double-barreled pistols of his own to the arsenal, and to supplement their diet with fresh fish, he also packed away a light rod and flies.

Layard visited the Austens' physician and asked for lessons in medicine. The doctor took the young man with him on his rounds of the University of London Hospital, pointed out various illnesses, demonstrated how to mend broken bones, and provided him with a do-it-yourself kit for treating the three curses of Eastern travel: dysentery, eye inflammation, and fever (the discovery of malaria and its transmission by the female mosquito was still a half-century away).

Both Layard and Mitford agreed to travel lightly, carrying only as much as they could cram into saddlebags. Layard's wardrobe consisted of a change of clothes, some linen, a change of stockings and boots, powder and shot, a cloak or poncho for protection against the rain, and a contraption, popularized by the East India Company, called a Levinge bed. This consisted of a pair of sheets sewn together and attached to a mosquito curtain that was hung from a tree or a nail on a wall—in effect, a primitive sleeping bag.

On June 1, 1839, all was at the ready except for one odious detail. Layard had still to obtain his accreditation as an attorney. For five days he crammed, took the examination, and, as much to his surprise as relief, passed with flying colors. Nine days later Layard was formally "sworn, admitted and enrolled as attorney of Her Majesty's Court of Queen's Bench at Westminster." That was the last the law ever saw of him. He never practiced for a day.

If Layard entertained any misgivings about the journey, it was the separation from his mother. Marianne Layard recognized her son's spirited nature and made no attempt to dissuade him from the adventure. On July 9 she arrived in London to bid her son farewell. She gave him her blessings and, much to his surprise, a going-away gift of £300 ($1,500). This, coupled with his share of the Smith-Elder advance, and a credit of £300 which Uncle Charles had drawn on Coutts & Co., bankers, was his total capital.

The following day, Layard and Mitford embarked—but in different directions. Mitford, whose aversion to the ocean was total, took the shortest sea route to the Continent and landed at Calais. Layard took a steamer for Ostend. They agreed to rendezvous at Brussels.

Three days later, July 13, Layard landed at the Flemish fishing port of Ostend and joined Mitford at Brussels. The rigors of early Victorian travel notwithstanding, they moved effortlessly through central Europe and on August 10 reached the southern limits of the Austro-Hungarian empire. It would take them eight months more to reach Mosul, the halfway point to Ceylon.

When they crossed into the world of Islam, the Fertile Crescent, stretching from the northern rim of Africa to the Malay archipelago, Layard wrote, "The change since passing the borders of Christian Europe is now complete, and I feel myself, as it were, in a new world—in a world of which I had dreamt from my earliest childhood."

The bazaars through which they passed were crowded with Turks,

Albanians, Greeks, and others. The women wore veils across their faces, merchants sat cross-legged in front of their wares smoking the narghile, or water pipe, Albanians carried yataghans (short sabers without cross-pieces) tucked into their belts, and savory, enticing aromas exuded from food stalls.

At the *serai*, the official residence of the pasha, the chief administrative officer in the area, they were served heavy black Turkish coffee and amber-mouthed water pipes. The pasha questioned them briefly about the nature of their journey, and issued a *bouyourouldi*, or official pass, for post horses. One of the strengths of the Ottoman empire was its superb communications system. A pony express served the empire. At intervals of eighteen miles were caravansaries, rest and relay stations for the quick change of horses or for spending the night. But travelers could use the system only with official approval.

On August 30, the pair set off for Constantinople, the seat of the Sublime Porte. A fortnight later, they rode within sight of the minarets and domes of St. Sophia and entered the Ottoman capital through the Gate of Seven Towers.

Layard and Mitford found lodging at Roboli's, a small hotel run by an Italian. There Layard came down with his first bout of what would develop into chronic fever. He suspected that he had contracted the malady at a caravansary adjacent to a marshy plain. The ague—malaria, really—was accompanied by dysentery.

Layard was attended by an Armenian physician who proudly displayed a diploma from Edinburgh University. The method of treating most illnesses at that time was bleeding. Like a mystic, the doctor made a large circle with pen and ink on Layard's stomach and ordered the circle filled with leeches. Layard was bled twice. His loss of strength was so great that he was unable to continue the journey. For several days he was delirious and was once considered in grave danger.

By early October Layard had regained his strength. He and Mitford agreed to abandon the pony express and purchase their own horses, making themselves independent of the caravansaries and enabling them to follow any route that suited their fancy. For £20 they purchased three sturdy animals. They also hired a garrulous Greek, Giorgio, as combination dragoman, servant, and cook. Mitford departed with Giorgio and the horses overland while Layard gained extra rest by following the Turkish coast in a caïque. They were reunited at the dingy port of Mudiania.

The pair were ignorant of the language and customs of the people, the maps of the interior of Turkey and Asia Minor were almost blank, and they could not have selected a worse time to travel through Turkish Asia. The empire's Egyptian provinces had rebelled, and the insurrection had spread across the Middle East. The region beyond Turkey proper was on the edge of anarchy.

Traveling by horses at the speed of Nelson's ships at Trafalgar, a modest three knots, Layard and Mitford set off across Asia Minor. Their only concession to the warnings of the British embassy was to adopt the prominent red fez of the Turk, with its tassel of blue thread, not only because it was more comfortable than their European riding caps but primarily in the hope that they would be less conspicuous as they passed through the countryside.

As the party pressed ahead, Layard maintained a journal of the route for the Royal Geographic Society, mapping streams and rivers, taking bearings on mountains and other conspicuous objects. He jotted the information down in a notebook which was ruled into equal spaces, each representing half an hour's progress, or about one and a half miles.

On the outskirts of Adana, they came upon classical ruins, a Greek temple of the Ionic order. "I was greatly excited," Layard recalled. "This was the first Greek ruin that I had seen."

In Layard's accounts of the journey there are animated passages about the various ruins they stumbled upon along their route. In Mitford's writing, the most exciting pages deal with the flora and fauna. Mitford was a naturalist, and an ornithologist of some authority. Thus, while Layard wrote glowingly of Adana's ruins, Mitford observed that one of the eighteen Ionic columns, standing 24 feet high, "is crowned with a stork's nest."

And while Layard studied the ruins at Adana, Mitford was busy freeing a golden eagle, measuring 7 feet across the wings, from a trap. "He lay quite still, not attempting to strike, while I opened the trap, seeming to understand my good intentions," Mitford noted, "and as soon as he felt himself free, he soared slowly into the sky."

As they moved across Turkey, Layard was shocked and angered by the injury caused to many classical ruins in Asia Minor by treasure seekers and others. There was hardly a temple in the region that had not been smashed in the search for hidden treasure. In Adana itself, to Layard's consternation, he discovered that almost every cottage was built of fragments of marble from local temple ruins, some of the slabs exquisitely carved, others bearing Greek inscriptions.

In southwestern Turkey they encountered their most extensive ruins, and Layard spent a whole day copying inscriptions near a colossal headless statue of Hercules.

As the pair approached Tarsus, they entered a region contested by the rebellious Egyptians, an area which today encompasses Syria, Lebanon, Israel, Jordan, and, of course, Egypt itself. At Tarsus the character of the people dramatically changed from predominantly Turkish to Arabic. Layard now inspected a great mass of rubble which some local villagers believed to be the remains of an Assyrian monument. But there were no cuneiform inscriptions to prove their suspicions, and even if there had been, nobody would have been able to read them. According to the credulous inhabitants of Tarsus, this was the funeral pyre upon which the Assyrian king Sardanapalus, the founder of Tarsus, had consumed himself, his wives, and his wealth.

This was Layard's first brush with Assyria in the rough, and he wrote, "I viewed the ruins with particular interest." Yet he realized that despite all his reading, he was inadequately prepared for exploring a region so rich in Biblical and classical traditions. "I had turned my attention but little to archaeology," he reflected, "and I had but a mere smattering of scientific knowledge of any kind. I never regretted more the incompleteness and neglect of my early education."

But this burgeoning interest in lost worlds was taking a toll. When he and Mitford reached Aleppo, Layard came down with a second—more violent—attack of ague. Once again he was bled. This time fifteen leeches were applied to his stomach, twelve to fourteen ounces of blood drawn from his body, a strict diet imposed, and heavy doses of quinine prescribed. "It is wonderful," he wrote to family and friends in England, "that I survived this treatment!"

In a figurative sense, Aleppo was their first crossroad. Before them lay two roads, and two worlds. One road, running due east, led across Mesopotamia to Mosul, Baghdad, and the Indian subcontinent. The other led south to the Holy Land. By mutual agreement, they turned south. This was an opportunity neither felt he could afford to miss. Mitford was moved by a natural Christian desire to make a pilgrimage to Bethlehem, Golgotha, and in between. Layard was seized by a passion to visit the ruins along the Jordan that he had read about as a child.

They crossed into the Holy Land in a spirit of high enthusiasm, taking the same trail as Roman legions and Crusaders before them. But their visit was disillusioning.

Layard found the place distasteful, the countryside an impoverished wasteland, and the towns dilapidated and in serious disrepair. Jerusalem itself was filled with religious fanatics and imposters. Quarrels and scandalous broils among various denominations for control of shrines offended Layard's Christian sensibilities. Only the previous Easter, he learned to his disgust, the Egyptians had been forced to dispatch armed troops to the Church of the Holy Sepulchre to keep peace among warring religious factions. The principal struggle was waged between the Roman and Greek Catholic churches. Behind them lurked France and Russia, preparing the groundwork for what later became the Crimean War.

They were both eager to move on, but they narrowly missed ever leaving. One morning their innkeeper summoned them to breakfast and, Mitford recounted, "We could not lift our heads from the pillow, from giddiness and racking headache, accompanied by retching, faintness and spasmodic pains in the chest." On account of extreme cold that night and in the absence of fireplaces, they had adopted the local habit of burning a large pan of charcoal in their room. They were almost asphyxiated.

While they recovered, they argued over their next objective. Mitford favored resuming the overland march directly to Ceylon, and by the most expeditious route. Layard, however, was determined to visit Petra, the lost city which Burckhardt had rediscovered less than a generation earlier in the area of the Dead Sea and which he had read about as a child in Florence.

On all sides Layard received dire warnings against his plan. The British consul denounced it as "foolhardy," as did the Egyptian governor of Jerusalem. The Dead Sea was a no man's land, the pasha warned, controlled by neither Constantinople nor Cairo. It was the hunting ground of fanatical Bedouin marauders who were hostile to the "unbelieving" Franks. The Bedouins, who claimed to be descendants of Ishmael, wandered across the deserts with their flocks and herds, dwelt in tents, and subsisted largely on plunder.

In the face of this counsel, Mitford considered it rash and stupid to visit the region. And for what? To look at ruins?

On January 15, 1840, while Mitford took the road back to Aleppo before turning due east, Layard left for Petra. His first stopover was Hebron, where he hired two camels for the journey to Petra and to the Dead Sea. This was Layard's first camel ride, and he learned one of the reasons these animals are referred to as "ships of the desert." He experienced *mal de mer*.

Along the route he reached a wadi or depression in the desert, and found it dotted with the black tents of nomadic Arabs. In storybook fashion, the sheik invited the stranger to his tent and served him bowls of rice and boiled mutton. Layard felt he had crossed the threshold of reality and had entered the fabled world of a thousand and one nights.

The sheik, as it turned out, was also concerned about the young Englishman's ambitious plan; as Layard discovered, many of the Arab tribes in the region were as wary of roaming Bedouin war parties as Turks and Franks. He took a liking to the youngster and provided Layard with two armed guards to guide him to the next friendly Arab encampment.

As the small party approached the Dead Sea area, Layard found himself engaged in one cliff-hanger after another.

He was attacked by a war party of marauding Bedouins who stole many of his belongings. He saved his life—and those of his two companions—by seizing the leader of the Bedouin band in the melee and pointing his rifle at the chieftain's head. Layard threatened to blow the man's head off unless his followers withdrew—which they promptly did. While being constantly tracked from just over the horizon, Layard marched his hostage at gunpoint across the searing desert to the safety of the next friendly Arab encampment.

By this time, the hostile Bedouin was famished. Applying the textbook psychology he read about as a child in Burckhardt and other writers on Araby, Layard invited his prisoner the following morning to join him at breakfast. Out of hunger, the Bedouin leader accepted.

The youthful Layard had outfoxed the older, wiser warrior; for it is the sacred duty of the Arab, including the Bedouin, to protect at all costs a person with whom he has broken bread.

Layard now demanded that his hostage arrange for the return of all his personal belongings. At first the Bedouin resisted, but the Arabs in the camp shouted, "You have eaten bread with this man—he walks with God while you walk with the devil!" Sheepishly, the Bedouin leader arranged for the restoration of Layard's stolen articles.

As a result of this, and similar, incidents, Layard acquired a deep insight into Arab character. The same man, Layard found, "who at one moment would be grasping, deceitful, treacherous and cruel, would show himself at another generous, faithful, trustworthy and humane."

Ultimately, by keeping his wits about him, Layard reached his objective—Petra. The silence and solitude of Petra, with its fallen cornices and broken columns, excited his imagination. In a statement he was destined to amend later, but which mirrored his unlimited enthusiasm for art and antiquities, he wrote in his journal, "The ruins of Petra are unlike those of any other ancient city in the world."

Layard continued on to Tiberias and thence to Damascus, where he presented himself to the British consul. The consul reported that Mitford, after waiting several days, had pressed on to Aleppo, where Layard was to meet him.

At Aleppo Layard finally found Mitford, who was completing preparations for crossing the Euphrates and marching on to the banks of the Tigris.

This time there was no argument between the two about the next stage of their journey. They would plunge into Mesopotamia and head straight for the trading post of Mosul on the west bank of the Tigris.

In the course of their long trek to Mosul, they stopped to explore the ruins at Nisbin. The town was once the eastern strongpoint of the Roman empire, the residence of the Emperor Trajan during the Parthian War. All that remained were a few splintered shafts of columns, friezes, and fragments of architectural ornaments.

Finally, on April 10, twenty-three days out of Aleppo, the pair came in sight of Mosul. It was built against a backdrop of vast mounds. Layard had read about them in the works of Rabbi Benjamin of Tudela and Claudius Rich, but this was the first time he had seen them. "I was deeply moved and impressed," he said, "by their desolate and solitary grandeur."

He would have been astounded to learn that in this desolate and solitary setting, he would find his place in the sun.

> *This mound was visible for a distance of many*
> *stadia, and this mound,*
> *they say, stands even to this day.*
>
> —STRABO

CHAPTER 4

From a great distance, as Layard and Mitford approached Mosul, its walls, minarets, and gardens glittered alluringly along the right bank of the river. "It was only when we entered it," Layard said, "that we realized the condition of ruin and decay to which it had been reduced by long misgovernment and neglect." Mosul was a backwater.

The interior of the town was no more appetizing than the riverfront. Most of the people dwelt in hovels. There was not a hotel in town worthy of the title. The caravansaries crawled with vermin. Mosul did not even possess a mosque of distinction, although one, curiously, was shaped like an octagonal pyramid. The two banks of the Tigris were linked by a makeshift pontoon bridge of boats, moored head and stern abreast. In a seemingly endless procession, people, donkeys, horses, and camels crisscrossed back and forth.

But although Mosul was impoverished, it had a cosmopolitan air. Among the fifty thousand citizens were Moslems, Jews, and members of various Christian sects. The Christians were largely Jacobites, Papal Syrians, and Chaldeans, as Nestorian converts to Roman Catholicism were then called.

Despite its shortcomings, for a weary traveler Mosul had its compensations. Almost on the eve of Layard's arrival, the British had opened a consulate, the city's first foreign diplomatic mission. High over the city, as if capable of swathing it in its folds, floated the British flag.

The new consul, Christian Rassam, was an extraordinary figure, one of eight children and the son of Anton Rassam, archdeacon of the Chaldean Christian community. Christian Rassam was well selected by the British to represent their interests. He spoke a half-dozen languages fluently, and had served as interpreter and guide to the Royal Navy's first charting expedition on the Tigris. Rassam insisted that Layard and Mitford put up at the consulate. There was one other European visitor in town, also a guest of the Rassams, Roger Ainsworth, who had arrived only recently with a commission from the Royal Geographic Society to explore the ruins of Hatra, a Parthian desert fortress which had resisted the Romans until A.D. 195.

Rassam's consulate, clean and spacious, boasted several splendid terraces and a huge courtyard. In a slum like Mosul, it was a veritable palace and impressed upon the local inhabitants the power, authority, and majesty of Queen Victoria.

That first evening in Mosul, over cups of thick black Turkish coffee, Rassam entertained his guests with the checkered history of the town. Gibbon, for example, assumed Mosul to have been a suburb of Ninus, the city that presumably gave rise to Nineveh, and Rassam recalled that he had once read an old Syriac manuscript that claimed that Mosul rose on the very ruins of Nineveh.

As he listened to these tales, Layard's mind raced back to the mysterious cuneiform tablets in the British Museum and to Rich's speculation about Nineveh's former existence on the bank opposite Mosul. His first impulse the following morning was to rush across the pontoon bridge and inspect the two huge mounds that dominated the left bank, Nebbi Yunnus [Prophet Jonah] and Kouyunjik [a bastardized Turkish word for sheepfold].

Nebbi Yunnus covered an area of about 40 acres and was the loftiest of the two mounds. According to local tradition, this was the burial place of Jonah, who preached Nineveh's destruction if it did not mend its ungodly ways. The eastern half of the mound was a Moslem cemetery, and the prophet's tomb occupied the northwest corner, surrounded by several dilapidated houses. Their inhabitants were Kurds and Turcomans, and they owned the sheep pastures on both mounds.

Kouyunjik lay just to the northwest of its sister mound, 95 feet above sea level, and embraced about 100 acres.

The two mounds fascinated Layard beyond description. He had never before seen anything comparable, and he spent a week searching for fragments of marble and bricks with those curious arrow-headed characters he had seen at the British Museum eons ago whenever he escaped from Uncle Benjamin's dungeon. But he found nothing, not even a clue to indicate that the mounds were anything more than monstrous heaps of rubbish.

If Kouyunjik was truly the ancient site of Nineveh, Layard concluded, "the city had perished with her people and left no wreckage behind."

But as he wandered back and forth across the vast mounds, intuitively he changed his mind and became increasingly convinced that they must cover some vestiges of the past, that they had some story to tell the present. "I felt an intense longing to dig into them," he wrote in his journal. But the idea was out of the question.

In his physical condition, it is remarkable that he spent so much time among the mounds. No sooner had he and Mitford arrived at Rassam's house than Layard came down with another bout of ague. Each night he was racked by fever and chills, and all the blankets of Rassam's household failed to melt the ice in his bones.

That week Ainsworth and Rassam completed their plans to ride into the desert and explore Hatra. Mitford agreed to go along with them, and despite his fever, Layard insisted on joining the party also. On the day they left for Hatra, Layard suffered another sharp attack of malaria and was delirious for several hours. "I was consequently very weak," he admitted, "but in the fine air of the desert I soon regained my strength."

Hatra's remains had been originally discovered a few years earlier by Dr. John Ross, the resident physician attached to the East India Company's Baghdad station. He published an account of his discovery in *The Journal of the Royal Geographic Society*. But he was unable to linger at the site, because it was infested by marauding Bedouin tribes. Since then, as a result of an outbreak of plague at Hatra, the ruins were reportedly deserted, affording the Society the opportunity of a comprehensive study of the place.

On their first night out of Mosul, the party slept at a hot sulfur spring, and from that campsite, on the horizon, Layard saw his third mound. Tradition, Rassam told him, attributed the mound to Nimrod. Nimrod! The legendary founder of the mighty Nineveh.

"As the sun went down, I saw for the first time the great conical mound of Nimroud rising against the clear evening sky," he said. "The impression it made upon me was one never to be forgotten."

The following day, the party struck deeper into the desert. Their *cawass*, provided by the local Turkish governor as an armed escort, panicked and deserted them, fleeing back toward Mosul. He never got there. He was captured and murdered by Bedouins.

In search of Hatra, the party pressed ahead, deeper into the Mesopotamian wasteland.

At daybreak one morning, they awoke to find themselves enveloped in a thick white mist. Like vessels at sea, they were immersed in fog. Suddenly, as also occurs at sea, a light wind sprang up and lifted the mist before them like the lifting of a windowshade. "Not far from us rose a vast and magnificent pile of buildings, and a long line of walls," Layard recorded, ". . . the walls had equidistant towers." They had found the Hatra of the Parthians.

Along the outer edge of the ruins were flocks of sheep, herds of camels, and a series of Bedouin tents with spears, tufted with ostrich feathers, implanted in the ground before them. "It was so fairy-like and unexpected that I could scarcely believe my senses," Layard said, "and [I] fancied myself in a dream."

If Layard and his group were surprised by the presence of Bedouins, so were the Bedouins surprised by the presence of Franks. What brought the Franks to Hatra?

Rassam, who acted as diplomat and interpreter, explained that the travelers had come to study the ruins and to gratify their curiosity. Nonsense, the sheik said. Obviously, the Europeans were in search of buried treasure. As the Franks toured the ruins, the Bedouins tagged along and waited impatiently for the Europeans to reveal the location of the gold. When Layard and Ainsworth began to make sketches of the ruins, and take measurements with a tape, the credulous Bedouins suspected that they were employing black magic. By midday, the sheik and his followers had convinced themselves that the strangers were probably the reconnaisance party of a Frank army or how could their audacity be explained? The Bedouins hurriedly folded their tents and stealthily slipped away. Ainsworth and his party were relieved to see them withdraw.

After several days at the site, the party returned to Mosul. While Layard was content to tarry among the mounds there, Mitford was impatient to push on toward Ceylon via Baghdad, which lay 250 miles south of Mosul. The desert route was too dangerous, too costly, and too time-consuming, so they decided to make the journey down the Tigris in quaint but traditional fashion, on a raft.

Two millenniums earlier, Herodotus wrote about this style of travel: "The boats which come down the river to Babylon are circular, and made of skins," he reported. "The frames, which are of willow, are cut in the country of the Armenians above Assyria, and on these, which serve for hulls, a covering of skins is stretched outside, and thus the boats are made, without either stem or stern, quite round like a shield. They are then entirely filled with straw, and their cargo is put on board, after which they are suffered to float down the stream. When they reach Babylon, the cargo is landed and offered for sale; after which the men break up their boats and sell the straw and the frames. The current is too strong to allow a boat to return upstream, for which reason they make their boats of skins rather than wood."

In Layard's day the circular raft called a kelek was as popular as ever. For 400 piasters, about $20, Layard and Mitford ordered a small raft of sixty skins. It was 12 feet long, had an 8-foot beam, and required only one boatman. For the next four days, as they floated downstream, this was to be their home.

Insouciantly, the pilot pushed off and they shot down the river as though they were riding a canoe through the Grand Canyon rapids. The water boiled furiously as they were swept over an ancient barrage and the ruined foundations of a bridge built by the Assyrians.

Then, within a short distance of Mosul, a great conical mound appeared abeam of the raft. Layard immediately recognized it. "The ruins of Nimroud," he said. Once again he felt a longing to dig into the mound and find what, if anything, was hidden within its core. He was overcome, as he said, by "a kind of presentiment that I should one day seek to clear up the mystery." Now he knew the where of his fate. He still did not know the when and how. And, like everyone else, he would never truly understand the why.

During the first day's journey, they passed, to Layard's surprise, other mounds. He obtained a fix on them, using his compass and chronometer, and made pencil sketches of them in his journal. The Arab boatman at the tiller recognized Layard's unusual interest in the mounds and, as they swept along, pointed out traditional sites.

The banks of the Tigris were covered for long stretches with tamarisk jungle, and occasionally the party tied up to shoot game and cook dinner. On the first night out they reached an Arab riverine village and Layard saw his first palm grove. Beneath the shady fronds were clusters of orange, lemon, and pomegranate trees. They were filled with spring blossoms.

The Arab villagers, Layard wrote, were "kind and obliging." The girls wore no veils and were usually not afraid to show themselves to strangers. Layard found them "singularly graceful and well-made," and he noted that their faces as well as their bodies were tattooed with designs. He learned about their tattooed bodies because occasionally an Arab girl raised her solitary blue shirt and brought it over her head to hide her face from the inquisitive Frank. She wore nothing underneath. (He also may have learned about their tattoos in a more intimate fashion. "All my *Arabian Nights* dreams were almost more than realized that first night ashore," he said.)

On the fourth day of their journey, the fabled Baghdad of Haroun Al Rashid rose majestically from the banks of the Tigris, her domes and minarets sparkling and glittering in the sun.

In the river's roadstead, as they drifted along on the current, was a gunboat flying a British Jack at her bow staff. She bore the name *Nimroud*—again that tantalizing name—and she was one of two British ironclad paddle-wheelers controlling the sea route between Baghdad and the Indian Ocean.

Layard and his companion landed on the left bank of the river, beneath an enormous white building that flew a British flag, the residence of the East India Company's political resident in Turkish Asia, Colonel Geoffrey Taylor. Taylor warmly welcomed Layard and Mitford and gave them free run of his impressive residence.

The pair lingered at Baghdad for almost two months. Layard spent much of the time fighting recurring malarial attacks, studying in

Taylor's library, and, whenever he felt fit, inspecting mounds in the vicinity and engaging in what he himself described as "riotous living." The officers and crews of the English gunboats knew all the proper dens of iniquity operated by Hindustani, Arabian, and Persian madams.

A French mission was the only other European diplomatic representation in the city, and through its members Layard learned that the French planned to open a consulate upriver, probably at Mosul.

Taylor arranged for Layard and Mitford to call on the local pasha, or governor. On the day of the audience, the temperature in Baghdad's streets was 104 degrees Fahrenheit and the pasha greeted them from a divan, his hairy chest naked from the waist up. Layard found him repulsive. "Masses of fat hung about him," he wrote, and, aside from food, he "thought of little but the delights of the harem." For the first time, Layard understood the rot that was eating at the Ottoman empire.

The situation in Baghdad was a classic example of that rot. Although Baghdad was one of the richest pashaliks of the empire, it was being reduced to ruin by corruption and maladministration. Roads were insecure, the people restless, the regime repressive, commerce almost at a standstill. Only the presence of British gunboats maintained a veneer of order. To the politically astute Layard, Baghdad, like Singapore and Gibraltar, could serve as a linchpin of the expanding British empire. It linked the Mediterranean and the Indian Ocean. Layard was convinced that in time the city would revive as a commercial center.

During their sojourn at Baghdad, Layard was intrigued by Taylor's reports of the existence of mounds in the vicinity, especially at Hillah, the site of ancient Babylon, and Ctesiphon, where the Sassanian rulers of Persia built their palaces.

Layard succeeded in talking Mitford into joining him on an excursion to Hillah. It was May 16, 1840. Layard was stunned by what he saw. The desolation, the solitude, the shapeless heaps—this was all that remained of one of the greatest and most renowned cities of antiquity. Regularly, he learned, the few inhabitants of Hillah dug into the mounds for bricks, either for their houses or to sell at construction sites in Baghdad. Many of the bricks bore "nail-headed designs," he was told.

"The characters had not been deciphered, and the meaning of the legend was unknown," Layard observed. They were the first examples of cuneiform that he had ever collected, and he would have been astounded to know that most of them bore the name of Nebuchadnezzar, the Babylonian king who leveled Solomon's temple.

Itinerant Arabs also occasionally discovered cylinders covered with strange figures, and other odd objects baked in clay or fashioned from bronze. Many of these relics turned up in Baghdad's bazaars and were eagerly bought up by Europeans as souvenirs and conversation pieces. Colonel Taylor, for example, possessed a large collection of them; so did the mission's surgeon, Dr. Ross, the same Ross who was the first Westerner to discover and explore Hatra.

As Layard and Mitford rode back to Baghdad, Layard was again struck by the long lines of mounds which traversed the plains around Hillah in almost every direction. Suddenly, he realized that these were the remains of great canals and his thoughts turned to the Hanging Gardens of Babylon.

Upon returning to Baghdad, Layard immediately arranged to visit the ruins of Ctesiphon. But Mitford's interest in ruins was waning, and Layard decided to make the short journey alone.

Since Ctesiphon was situated along the Tigris and the *Nimroud* was scheduled to pass the spot en route to Baghdad late in the day, Colonel Taylor arranged with Captain Felix Jones to pick him up on his return, so that Layard would be spared the fatiguing ride back to Baghdad by donkey. Accordingly, at dawn that day Layard set out for Ctesiphon with an Arab guide. At the site of the ruins he dismissed the guide, who returned to Baghdad with Layard's mule.

Despite the intense heat, Layard spent the greater part of the day scrambling over the ruins of the ancient Sassanian palaces, some of which rose 106 feet above sea level. The palace foundations were a solid mass of compacted brickwork, almost indestructible.

In late afternoon, atop the ruins, Layard detected a wisp of smoke on the horizon—the *Nimroud* was churning upriver on her way to Baghdad. Layard quickly descended from the top of the ruins and, to his surprise and dismay, discovered that a broad and deep marsh, formed by the incoming tide, separated him from the main bank of the Tigris. He had no choice other than to wade across the marsh. He stripped off his clothing and plunged into the morass with its leeches and occasional water snakes. Waist high and sometimes up to his armpits, he struggled through the water, his footing in the deep mud insecure and the sun beating overhead. He was genuinely frightened, and almost panicked. The paddle-steamer was rushing along, and Layard was afraid the vessel's lookout would take him in the distance for an Arab buffalo keeper and pass him by. In desperation, he waved a handkerchief to attract attention. The vessel stopped, and Captain Jones dispatched a boat to rescue the drowning figure. Jones never quite got over the incident and for the rest of his life told the story of how, "seeing something white waving in the marsh, I looked through my telescope and perceived the head of a European just above the level of the water. I had landed and had fished an English-traveler out of the morass, drenched to the skin and shivering with ague."

According to the law of the Medes and Persians.
—ESTHER

CHAPTER 5

L ayard and Mitford now entered upon what was, in Layard's words, "the most difficult and dangerous part of our journey"—the trip through Persia, the last barrier before crossing into British India. Once in India, Ceylon was just a step down the pike. The Persians, however, were a law unto themselves. They were hostile to Christians in general and Europeans in particular. To make matters worse, as a result of Russian machinations, Persia and Britain teetered on the edge of war.

Since Layard felt he would attract less attention in local dress, he discarded the Egyptian uniform he had assumed earlier in his travels, and donned the garb of the Persians—long flowing robes, shalwar, or loose trousers, and a black lambskin cap, Persian-style. He shaved the crown of his head and dyed his blond hair and beard deep black. With a boyish enthusiasm that persisted through his maturity, Layard relished the guises in which he traveled across Asia Minor.

He and Mitford joined an armed caravan of seventy men, women, and children, and fifty-five animals, on June 22, 1840, bound from Baghdad to the Persian frontier town of Kermansha. In the party were two litters slung across mules, each containing a young woman, the wives of an old Turkish merchant. In a letter to his mother, a frustrated Layard complained, "I haven't been able to find out whether any beauties may be concealed by the obstinate veil which is down day and night."

At Kermansha their journey came to an abrupt end. Britain and Persia had suspended diplomatic relations. Layard and Mitford were ordered to proceed no farther into Persia without the approval of the shah-en-shah or Persian king-of-kings. Under armed guard, they were bundled off to the Shah's camp, a three-day march from Kermansha.

For more than a month, Layard and Mitford, suspected of being British agents, were detained as the Shah's "guests."

During their forced detention in the Shah's camp, they were given permission to journey, under armed escort, to nearby Behistun, where Major Rawlinson had reported trilingual cuneiform inscriptions on a lofty, smooth-surfaced cliff. "The . . . bas-reliefs and cuneiform inscriptions . . . were at so great a height from the ground, and so completely inaccessible, that it was impossible to make copies of them," a disappointed Layard reported. The rock was destined to become a Rosetta Stone of Assyriology. It contained inscriptions in Median, Babylonian, and Persian. Scholars—among them Rawlinson, who was the first to succeed in making a copy of the legend—would later determine that it was signed by Darius the Great.

Other than the excursion to Behistun, Layard and Mitford were confined to the Shah's camp. The pair had left England almost a year before and were now hopelessly stalled halfway to Ceylon.

On July 10, the first anniversary of their departure from London, the Shah broke camp and marched to Hamadan. Layard felt in luck. He had longed to visit Hamadan, which, as Ectabana, the capital of the Medes, was as famous in antiquity as Nineveh and Babylon. According to the Old Testament, Hamadan was the burial place of Esther and Mordecai. Both Jews and Moslems had built a shrine at the spot and squabbled incessantly over its possession.

After the Shah's entourage reached Hamadan, Layard went off to visit the celebrated tombs and came away disappointed. "I found nothing in the building except a vault filled with rubbish," he recorded in his journal.

Fortunately for Layard and Mitford, Baron de Bode, the first secretary of the Russian embassy in Persia, arrived at Hamadan on a special mission to the Shah. He was surprised to find the two Englishmen in camp and interceded with the Persians on their behalf to obtain a firman.

A firman was an imperial decree—in this instance, a travel document. Without it, Mitford mused, "we might have been detained an indefinite period."

The firman had a catch. The pair could travel through Persia to India but only along the well-worn caravan routes of northern Persia which stretched into Afghanistan. They were barred from pursuing their original plan of cutting directly through the heart of Persia via Yezd and Seistan, a route rarely glimpsed by Europeans. Before their departure from London, the Royal Geographic Society had expressed to Layard a special interest in having him map the Seistan route.

Mitford eagerly accepted the firman's condition. He was anxious to get on to Ceylon. But Layard, as brash as ever, was unwilling to renounce the attempt to cross the Seistan. Instead of accepting the firman to cross northern Persia, he boldly asked for—and received—a firman to travel south to Bushire, a Persian Gulf port on the road back to Baghdad. Layard had concocted a wild plan of returning to Baghdad with a detour through the forbidden Seistan. He sought to cajole Mitford into the journey, but Mitford had had enough of Layard's detours, and the companions parted company.

"We had been together for above a year," Layard wrote later, "and I much regretted that we had to part."

Mitford also expressed regret, but in fact a strain developed between the two men. While they remained in touch with each other for the rest of their lives, the warmth was gone from the relationship.

Nine months later, May 2, 1842, Mitford reached Ceylon, his coveted destination. "[I was] kindly welcomed by the Governor, Sir Colin Campbell, who informed me that he had received a notification of my appointment to the Civil Service of the Colony."

As for Layard, for the next year or so, he wandered through the remote mountain districts of western Persia, crossing terrain that no European had trod since the days of Alexander. He searched for ancient ruins, and found them, and he discovered, to his astonishment, new mounds.

He left Hamadan August 8, with only a horse and a pair of small saddlebags, and soon came down with yet another attack of intermittent fever and dysentery. He pressed ahead toward the Persian Gulf, but, once beyond Hamadan, he made a detour east and headed for Isfahan, taking notes for the Royal Geographic Society. It was a dangerous sojourn, for although his travel documents gave him permission to travel south, he might easily have been taken for a British spy and been tortured and shot. He did, in fact, have some close calls.

At Isfahan, for example, he paid a courtesy call on the *matamet* or governor of the province, a eunuch of Georgian birth, born of Christian parents, who had been purchased as a slave and raised as a Moslem. The *matamet* displayed remarkable administrative abilities, enjoyed the Shah's confidence, and had risen rapidly in the Persian hierarchy.

But the governor was feared and hated. Insensible to human suffering, he spent idle hours inventing new forms of torture, as though he sought vengeance against normal members of his sex. His most recent triumph was a tower which he had constructed of three hundred living prisoners. The prisoners—mountain rebels—were laid on stones in layers of ten, mortar being spread between each layer, their heads left free.

The wily *matamet* entertained suspicions about the young Englishman and detained him, although he was allowed to roam through the city.

Layard took advantage of the situation, devoting the days to studying Persian and the evenings to a cram course in the lifestyle of the Persian elite. Members of the Persian nobility often invited him to dinner, which was served in the *enderum,* or harem. While dancing girls performed, bottles of arak (a strong, bitter liquor) and platters of sweetmeats were served.

"Many of these girls were strikingly handsome," Layard observed. Their costumes consisted of loose silk jackets, entirely open in front so as to show their bare breasts. Their eyebrows were colored black. Their eyes were large and dark and rendered more brilliant and expressive with the use of kohl. "The dancing," Layard recorded, "soon degenerated into outrageous indecency, for these dancing girls did not refuse the wine and arak that were liberally offered to them."

The *matamet* appeared to be playing a cat-and-mouse game with his compulsory visitor. The governor granted him several audiences and at each audience, Layard's dislike of him deepened.

Unable to receive permission to proceed through the Seistan, which lay to the east, Layard tacked. As the Shah's military adviser, Major Rawlinson had heard of the existence of ancient ruins in the wild Baktiyari mountain district of Persia and had sought to explore them but was unable to do so because of the anarchy that prevailed in the mountains. For young Layard to accomplish the feat would be a rather large feather in his cap. It would also get him out of Isfahan. Accordingly, after a month's detention by the *matamet,* Layard asked whether he might have permission to visit the Baktiyari mountains. To his surprise, the governor acceded to his wish. Unknown to Layard, the *matamet* was plotting a punitive war against the Baktiyaris. Certain that the Englishman would meet with death among them, he planned to use Layard's murder as a pretext for a pacification expedition.

The *matamet*'s permission coincided with the departure of a caravan to Kala Tul, the headquarters of the Baktiyari's paramount chief, Mehemet Taki Khan. Layard joined the trek and for the next several months dwelt among the mountain tribes, the first Christian and Frank to do so.

Much to the *matamet*'s discomfort, Layard was not only unmolested but, on the contrary, was treated as an honored guest. He exhibited in the mountains the same uncanny ability he displayed among the Turks, Arabs, and others to make fast friends among non-Westerners.

The Baktiyari, he found, were "a splendid race," the men chivalrous, tall, finely featured, and the women fair-skinned and graceful.

A genuinely intimate friendship developed between Layard and the paramount chief. Indeed, their relationship grew so strong that Mehemet Taki Khan sought to convert Layard to Islam and, as a tantalizing bribe, offered him in marriage the most stunningly beautiful young woman among the Baktiyari, the famed Khanumi. She possessed exquisite features, her eyes large, black, and almond-shaped. She was as intelligent and lively as she was sexually desirable.

"The inducement was great," Layard conceded, "but the temptation was resisted."

Layard's interlude in the mountain districts of western Persia were among the happiest days he had spent since his childhood in Italy. Much of the time was spent exploring ruins, sites never before seen by a European. For example, he visited Manjanik, where—according to tradition—Abraham was cast into the fiery furnace by Nimrod. He also visited what was purportedly Daniel's tomb and nearby, in a gorge near Kala Tul, he discovered a carved figure, larger than life, and thirty-six lines of unintelligible arrow-headed characters. At another place, he came across a set of rock sculptures which he attributed to "the most remote antiquity."

As he went from site to site with his pencil, sketching the cuneiform characters and rock-cut sculptures, his name spread rapidly through the mountains. Many of the tribal peoples considered him a magician to whom the jinns had given extraordinary powers: he wrote with a dry stick from which ink flowed freely.

Mehemet Taki Khan, the Baktiyari chief, was also a pragmatic man. He knew there was friction between Britain and Persia, and he regarded Layard as a hedge against a Persian invasion of his mountain retreat. When reports reached Kala Tul that a British sloop-of-war, on a charting expedition, had temporarily dropped the hook at Karak, a Persian gulf port about 175 miles to the southwest, Mehemet Taki Khan revealed to Layard his plans to throw off the Persian yoke and proclaim the independence of the Baktiyari. He persuaded Layard to visit Karak and offer the British special commercial relations in return for English support of Baktiyari independence.

Layard, who always empathized with the underdog, required little encouragement to rally to the Baktiyari cause.

Accompanied by a small detachment of Baktiyari escorts, in December Layard made the perilous journey to Karak. In the roadstead, indeed, was a British sloop-of-war. For Layard, it was a heartening sight. "My first thought was a bath," he said. And on Christmas Day, 1841, he dined with the expedition's officers aboard H.M.S. *Coote,* the flagship of the East Indian Company's Persian Gulf flotilla.

Layard's mission, however, was a failure. The *Coote*'s commander advised him to tell the Baktiyari that British policy was to avoid a conflict with Persia and that the Baktiyari could not expect British support for their war of independence.

A disappointed Layard returned to Kala Tul only to learn that the *matamet,* at the head of a large Persian army which included horse-drawn artillery, had invaded the Baktiyari lands. Mehemet Taki Khan was taken prisoner and placed in chains. As for his people, many were taken prisoner; others were slaughtered like livestock.

To free their chieftain, a band of Baktiyari attacked the *matamet*'s camp. Impetuously, Layard joined in. The raid was a failure.

Arise, go to Nineveh, that great city.
—JONAH

CHAPTER 6

Like a Daniel in the lion's den, the audacious Layard rode to Shuster, where the victorious *matamet* now made his headquarters. The governor's camp was given over to feasting, drinking bouts, sexual orgies, and the torture of prisoners. Layard coolly informed the *matamet* that since the mountain districts were in disorder, he had abandoned the idea of examining ancient sites and planned to "push on."

The *matamet,* if nothing else, had a superb intelligence system and was aware of Layard's political activities on behalf of the Baktiyari. "You Englishmen," the *matamet* admonished Layard, "are always meddling in matters which do not concern you." In fact, Layard might well have found himself roasting on an open spit, but fortunately the Shah was set on trying to avoid an Anglo-Persian war.

Instead Layard was once again detained by the governor and spent one of the most terrifying months of his life at his camp. The torture of prisoners was an almost daily occurrence, their shrieks of pain heard at all hours of day and night. The bastinado was commonplace; often, after this form of pillory, the prisoner was revived with buckets of water and hot irons were applied to his penis and testicles. For good measure, needles were driven under his fingernails and toenails.

"The cries of these wretched victims of Persian cruelty," Layard said, "were ringing in my ears when I escaped from Shuster." After a month's "education"—most probably as a warning to keep his nose out of Persia's internal affairs—the *matamet* provided Layard with travel documents for Basra, the Persian Gulf port situated just below the confluence of the Tigris and Euphrates. Layard retreated across western Persia to the friendly confines of Turkish Asia.

His spirits soared as he reentered the domains of the Ottoman empire. "To my great joy," he recorded as he reached Basra in the spring of 1841, "a merchant ship flying an English flag was anchored in the middle of the stream." He hired a small boat and rowed to the ship. Aboard the *Lord Elphinstone* that night, for the first time in months he enjoyed the pleasant sensation of sleeping between clean sheets. Except for his brief visit to Karak, he had been out of touch with the Western world for what seemed a millennium.

An Arab courier was leaving Basra the next day for Baghdad, a two-day ride, and Layard opted to join him rather than wait for the vessel to weigh anchor.

Layard was now in a quandary. Ceylon was out of the question. His funds were running low. Physically, he was exhausted. He had no job. His life was still a succession of failures. And he had a touch of homesickness.

"You will be surprised to find me again writing to you from Baghdad," he wrote his mother September 9, 1841. "I have seriously and after much reflection determined to return to England if my uncle and yourself should approve of my doing so." On the same day he posted a letter to "Uncle Ben" in which he observed, "You must have seen from my last letter that I was proceeding but slowly towards India." Consuming spoonfuls of crow, he requested his godfather's "sanction to my returning."

While he awaited word from his mother and Uncle Ben, he engaged a munshi to teach him Persian and Arabic. He talked incessantly about the artificial mounds that dotted the region and sought to organize a consortium to finance their exploration. One English trader at Baghdad, Alexander Hector, was so impressed that he wrote to Sheffield, England, to raise interest and money for the project. "[I] believe that the objects of antiquity to be discovered would easily repay the expense," Layard told Hector with confidence.

Once in England, Layard hoped to land a job and raise funds for the scheme himself.

It was now 1842, and Layard made preparations to return to England by the shortest and cheapest route possible, via Beirut. These plans, however, coincided with news from Constantinople of a border clash between the Turks and Persians and rumors that the Sublime Porte and the Shah toyed with declarations of war against each other.

Colonel Taylor, the British resident at Baghdad, was anxious that the British ambassador in the Turkish capital, Sir Stratford Canning, be fully apprised of the latest situation in Mesopotamia. The colonel asked Layard whether, instead of proceeding to England via Beirut, he would consider taking the longer route via Constantinople. Taylor said he had a number of secret dispatches that must be placed in the ambassador's hands and that once Layard reached the Ottoman capital he might furnish Sir Stratford "at the same time, personally, with any information that he might require should he think fit."

"I at once consented to do so," Layard said.

The Turkish pasha at Baghdad also planned to dispatch a *tatar*, or pony express rider, to the Sublime Porte with reports on the situation and, at Taylor's request, the governor permitted Layard to accompany the Ottoman courier.

On the eve of his departure, Layard checked with Alexander Hector to see if there was any reply to his proposal to dig up the mounds. There was none.

With the *tatar* setting a breathless pace, they rode day and night and in fifty hours arrived at their first caravansary, Mosul. Fate had thrown Layard back among his "mysterious mounds."

Mosul was as depressing and evil-smelling as ever. But there was a change. No longer was the British consul, Christian Rassam, the only foreign representative on the Tigris's west bank. A French official, Paolo Emilio Botta, had raised the tricolor, and, to Layard's utter astonishment, Botta was excavating the great mound of Kouyunjik on the opposite bank!

Layard immediately called on the new French consul and discovered in Botta "a delightful companion." The two struck it off magnificently and became enduring friends. Botta was flexible in his views, large-minded and willing to impart what he knew.

Botta's name struck a chord in Layard's memory. This was Paolo Emilio Botta, the Turin-born son of the Italian historian whom he first came across a dozen years earlier during his youthful escapades in Italy. The son, now thirty-seven years old, twelve years Layard's senior, was an unusual figure. An accomplished botanist, who opted for French citizenship during the Napoleonic wars, he entered the French foreign service and held various consular posts in Egypt, Yemen, Syria, and China before his posting to Mosul. China was his undoing. There he became addicted to the poppy, "a fatal habit," Layard called it, "which ruined his health and rendered him liable to occasional fits of melancholy and despondency of the most painful nature."

Layard and Botta spent three days engaged in a running conversation about the mounds. Botta was the first person Layard ever met who was willing, indeed eager, to engage in speculation about what might lie within them, and Layard was puzzled about Botta's interest. Julius Mohl, Botta explained, was the catalyst.

Mohl, a German-born Orientalist, had settled in France and, like Botta, adopted French citizenship. During a trip to London, Mohl spied the single vitrine at the British Museum containing all that was known about Nineveh and the Assyrian empire. It was, of course, the collection of the late Claudius Rich. Mohl read every line of Rich's memoirs and concluded that Rich had discovered lost Nineveh and that archaeological treasure lay buried beneath the mounds, even though many people considered Nineveh a fable.

Mohl, however, persisted in his belief and in 1840 was named secretary of the French Asiatic Society. Two years later the French decided to establish a consular office at Mosul, and Botta, in disfavor with the Quai d'Orsay because of his drug problem, was assigned to that backwater of the Ottoman empire as a form of punishment.

Julius Mohl saw his opportunity and seized on the appointment to impress upon Botta that a great opportunity lay before him and *la belle France*. Botta must not merely explore, observe, describe, and measure the size of the mounds opposite Mosul. He must *dig* into them. Botta, who was amenable to almost any suggestion, promised to do so.

Botta told him how he had searched the mounds of Kouyunjik and Nebbi Yunnus and found nothing but potsherds and kiln-dried bricks and a few fragments of alabaster inscribed with cuneiform characters. These items could hardly be taken seriously. For Mohl's benefit, however, he meticulously numbered the cuneiform fragments. The potsherds he threw aside as valueless. [It was not until the late nineteenth century that Heinrich Schliemann at Troy and other embryo archaeologists recognized potsherds as time-prints of past civilizations.]

The following day he and Botta crossed the Tigris to inspect the Frenchman's trenches. Botta was right; there was nothing to see.

Layard was somewhat dismayed. Yet, intuitively, he clung to certainty that *something* must be hidden in those artificial mounds.

He sought to buoy Botta's spirits, and his own. "I am convinced," he told Botta, "that remains of great interest and importance are concealed within these shapeless accumulations of earth and rubbish."

But despite Layard's encouragement, Botta, especially in fits of drug-induced despondency, was overwhelmed by quiet desperation. He told Layard he felt he was looking for the proverbial needle in a haystack. The mounds were so large that they discouraged aimless digging. But without clues he had to dig aimlessly. The more he trudged around Kouyunjik, putting his spade here and there, the greater his frustration at not finding anything. And the more despondent he became, the more he turned to his Chinese pipe for solace—and escape.

The Layard-Botta dialogue was interrupted by the *tatar*'s announcement that he was ready to resume the dash to Constantinople. Before galloping off, Layard implored his newfound friend to dig, dig, and dig again. He also extracted a promise from Botta to write him at Constantinople if anything turned up.

His enthusiasm rekindled by Layard's infectious optimism, Botta resumed his single-handed exploration of Kouyunjik.

Thou third great Canning, . . .
who wert the voice of England in the East.
—TENNYSON

CHAPTER 7

Layard arrived back at Constantinople on July 10, 1842, bronzed and unkempt after the long trek across the deserts and plains of Asia Minor. No sooner had he dismounted than he presented himself at the British embassy with Taylor's dispatches.

An embassy clerk peered down his nose. "Wait a moment," he sneered. Layard waited, and waited. At length a fashionably dressed young prig appeared, cavalierly accepted the dispatches, and remarked that the ambassador, Sir Stratford Canning, was "too much occupied to see anyone." He turned abruptly and left the room.

Layard was stupefied. He left the embassy for Roboli's hotel, where he and Mitford had stayed during their first visit to the Ottoman capital. Upset by this rude and discourteous treatment after so long and arduous a journey, Layard wrote the ambassador a bristling letter.

"After suffering considerable hardships for three years my face may be somewhat bronzed and my dress after a long absence from Europe might not be within the rules of fashionable elegance," Layard sputtered, "but I cannot admit that my outward appearance could warrant the insolent contempt with which I had the honor to be treated."

Three years of dealing on his own, from the top to the bottom, from camel drivers to pashas, taught Layard to treat the apex and base of the social pyramid with equal trenchancy when the situation demanded it.

Sir Stratford, then fifty-nine, was the terror of the Ottoman empire. In Turkey, each ambassador is designated *buyuk elchi,* great envoy. During three tours of duty at Constantinople, the phrase Great Elchi referred to only one ambassador, Sir Stratford Canning.

Not unlike Layard, Canning was impatient and quick-tempered. He was also a cultivated scholar, a workaholic, and angered by trifles. Small talk annoyed him, and he chafed at red tape. Committee meetings bored him completely. Surprisingly for a skilled diplomatist, he was often brusque to the point of rudeness.

As necessary, however, he displayed the charm, courtesy, and tone of a *preux chevalier.* Canning, unlike his petty aides, suffered no inferiority complex. On receipt of Layard's letter, he dispatched an embassy *cawass* to Roboli's with a note inviting Layard to tea.

"Sir Stratford received me immediately," Layard wrote some fifty years later. "I was greatly struck by his appearance, and thought him one of the handsomest men I had ever seen." Sir Stratford's hair was silver, his frame tall and spare, his eyes gray and penetrating, his brows massive and overhanging, and his air calculatingly reserved and intended to impress callers with awesome respect for his queen, Victoria.

Sir Stratford apologized for the embassy's bad manners and immediately began to pick Layard's brains about the Turco-Persian frontier. Canning was impressed with his intimate grasp of "the great game," as Kipling later called geopolitics.

When Layard was about to leave, the ambassador suggested he remain in Constantinople for a few days, since Britain planned to mediate the dispute between the Shah and the Sultan and Layard could, perhaps, play a useful role in the negotiations.

Layard tarried at Roboli's for a week, his funds running low. A steamer was making ready for England, and Layard sent Canning a polite note informing him that unless the ambassador desired to see him again he was sailing within a couple of days. Receiving no reply, Layard packed his meager belongings, paid his hotel bill, and headed down the steep street leading to Tophane wharf.

As Layard placed his foot on the gangplank, an embassy *cawass*, slightly out of breath, caught up with him and handed him a note from the Great Elchi. "Come and dine here tomorrow," the invitation read.

"After a moment's reflection," Layard said, "I determined to return to the hotel and to accept Sir Stratford's invitation."

At lunch, Sir Stratford disclosed that Britain and Russia agreed to mediate jointly the Turco-Persian row; but, he observed, some time would elapse before the negotiations gathered headway. Canning made a startling proposal. While marking time, would Layard be interested in carrying out a confidential mission for him, visiting the Balkans and gathering political intelligence on the growing restiveness of Turkish rule? Sir Stratford stressed that the mission would be unofficial. If something went awry, Layard could not appeal to the embassy for assistance.

"My taste for travel and adventure had not been satiated," Layard said, and he readily accepted the proposal. The idea of embarking on a "secret mission" appealed to him and suddenly he saw his future as a member of the foreign service.

His travels took him through Albania, Bulgaria, Bosnia, and Serbia. The area was in turmoil as Turk and Russian contested for power.

Layard reconnoitered the political situation at Belgrade and found the local British consul unimaginative and insensitive. The Belgrade situation was critical and demanded Canning's immediate attention. In the grand tradition of Verne's Michael Strogoff, Layard rode *tatar*-style day and night to Constantinople bearing the news to Canning.

The gist of Layard's reports was that England should stand up to Russian encroachment in the region and support the Serbian independence movement, a conclusion Sir Stratford arrived at independently. But Lord Aberdeen, the foreign secretary, was bent on a policy of appeasing Russia's expansionist appetite, and he rejected the policy.

Nonetheless, Canning was so impressed with Layard's raw ability that he proposed to the foreign secretary the young man's appointment to the embassy as an attaché.

Layard was now introduced to the dirty politics of the large bureaucracy. The consul he had criticized complained directly to Aberdeen that Layard carried on at Belgrade as an official of the British embassy and that he actively worked to undermine British policy. Layard had no difficulty in disproving the charges. "But," as Layard put it, they had "produced an unfavorable impression" on Aberdeen.

The Scot probably would have overlooked the incident had it not coincided with another episode which almost wrecked Layard's diplomatic career before it started.

When Layard left England in 1839, he had deposited with Coutts & Co., bankers, half the £300 his mother advanced him. The bank extended a letter of credit, and when Layard was in need of funds during his Persian adventures, he drew against the letter. But the documents were improperly endorsed and Coutts refused to honor them. Layard was ignorant of the affair when Sir Stratford received a letter from Coutts denouncing Layard as a swindler.

Layard begged Sir Stratford to withhold his judgment until he could exchange letters with Coutts & Co. For months, he was, in his own words, "under a cloud." Finally, the matter was cleared up. The London bankers expressed regret at what happened and tendered him a formal apology, but the damage was done. In Aberdeen's view, and that of the foreign office, Layard was a "controversial" figure, clearly unfit to serve in Her Majesty's service.

Everything appeared to be working against him. But Sir Stratford's confidence in Layard was unshaken, and he advised him to remain at Constantiniple as his attaché "with every prospect," Canning assured him, that Aberdeen would eventually come round to his appointment to the embassy.

A disheartened Layard agreed to mark time in the unpaid, unofficial post. This was, at least, an opportunity to remain in the East. It mattered little to him what he did as long as he remained in Asia Minor, where he felt free and independent.

On his first visit to Constantinople, Layard had met J. A. Longworth, the Near East correspondent of the London *Morning Post*. Layard looked him up. Longworth welcomed Layard and suggested he share his digs. Longworth lodged with an Armenian widow who had a vacant room and three daughters; the youngest, a girl of sixteen, quickly caught Layard's mobile eye. "She was," he said, "of exceptional beauty."

The other member of Longworth's mess was Charles White, the correspondent of the *Morning Chronicle,* who was a student at Eton with Sir Stratford Canning. Like Layard, Longworth and White were free spirits, and theirs was an uproarious relationship.

Layard, meanwhile, had abandoned plans to return to England. "I find," he wrote Uncle Benjamin, "that my mind is too active to admit of my returning cheerfully to any sedentary employment unaccompanied with an extraordinary degree of excitement, and I fear that I should be unable to settle down to the law."

Uncle Ben, who shared the same fears and considered his godson flighty, was hardly surprised by the change in plans. Nonetheless, he encouraged Layard to follow up his relationship with Canning.

For Layard, the next three years, 1842-45, were crowded like the masts of a full-rigged ship with sail. Unofficially, he worked as Canning's private secretary; Canning met his food and lodging bills and paid him a retainer of £200 annually. He also worked on a book about his adventures in Persia.

Nor did he forget the mounds. He continued to search for a financial backer, and he infected Canning with his enthusiasm for the project. With an eye to future exploration in Mesopotamia, he took lessons in Turkish, Hebrew, and Syriac, convinced that the latter two Semitic tongues were linked to the arrow-shaped characters of the Assyrians.

In the midst of these activities, Layard also worked as a part-time journalist. When White was recalled to London, he inherited the position of *Morning Chronicle* correspondent. When Longworth was reassigned, his job also fell to Layard. Thereafter, Layard's reputation as a free-lance journalist spread rapidly, and he was appointed Constantinople correspondent of the *Malta Times,* the most influential and widely read English-language newspaper in the Near East.

Through his contacts as a foreign correspondent, Layard made many friends among leaders of the Turkish, Armenian, and Greek communities in the Ottoman capital, including Ahmed Vefyk, eight years Layard's junior, who worked at the Turkish foreign ministry. In a manner reminiscent of young Disraeli's outburst at Uncle Benjamin's, Vefyk proclaimed, "One day I will become grand vizier!"—a role in a sultanate equivalent to that of the prime minister in a parliamentary government.

Vefyk's family belonged to the Turkish reform movement. Unlike most families of their rank and station, for example, the Vefyk household included neither eunuchs nor slaves. Through his young friend, Layard came into subrosa contact with the leaders of the Turkish reform movement. In short order, Layard became a secret conduit between the reformists and the British ambassador.

Through Layard, Canning sought to throw England's support behind the reformists. Canning was convinced that unless the indolent, corrupt bureaucracy was streamlined its fall would not be far distant. Layard was of the same opinion.

Layard still had no regular job, no regular income, no future. But he had grounds for hope. Major Rawlinson, the renowned soldier-scholar, had replaced Colonel Taylor at Baghdad as British resident in Mesopotamia, and he took the initiative to contact Layard. Rawlinson had been impressed with the copies of cuneiform inscriptions Layard had collected on his travels and deposited in Taylor's library.

But Canning, try as he did to obtain Layard an attachéship, was still unable to overcome Lord Aberdeen's prejudices. When a Turco-Persian border commission was established to delimit the frontier between the two quarrelsome neighbors, Canning proposed Layard as a member of the commission because of his firsthand knowledge of the troubled theater. But the foreign secretary passed over him. Lady Canning and her three school-age daughters had left for England, and Sir Stratford was making plans to follow suit on home leave. Canning, who never lacked confidence in his diplomatic skill, was convinced that once he talked to Aberdeen, he would remove the difficulties which had stood in the way of Layard's appointment as an attaché. But, Canning conceded, this might take two or three months.

Sir Henry Wellesley was already en route from London to take charge of the Turkish mission during Sir Stratford's absence. "I was not desirous of remaining at Constantinople after Sir Stratford Canning's departure," Layard said, "and I was anxious to find some means of spending my time profitably until he had been able, after his return to England, to obtain for me from Lord Aberdeen the permanent appointment in the Constantinople embassy, of which I had the promise."

But how was he to mark time "profitably"? Suddenly, it struck him. Layard proposed to Canning that during his absence he proceed to Mosul and dig up the mysterious mounds.

His proposal to excavate the mounds was hardly surprising. Rarely, during his three years of aimless drifting in Constantinople, was Nineveh far from his thoughts.

Botta had kept his word and had maintained regular contact. The tone of the Botta-Layard letters was almost invariably the same. Botta complained that his excavations turned up nothing. Layard entreated him to continue to dig. Layard even suggested that Botta shift his operations from Kouyunjik to the strangely shaped mound at Nimrod, the artificial heap that fascinated him above all others and that he considered—however irrationally—*his* mound. But Botta, his energy drained by opium as much as by Mesopotamia's climate, argued against it because, he said, it was "too far away." The distance between Mosul and Nimrod was 14 miles.

Then, in the spring of 1843, Layard received the dismaying news that Botta had abandoned Kouyunjik. Layard railed against his decision. So did Mohl. If Botta thought of Layard and Mohl wining and dining in Constantinople and Paris, while he dwelt in sweltering, foul-smelling Mosul, he kept his opinion to himself.

For months, Botta's activities at Mosul had kept the town's coffeeshops filled with gossip. What did the crazy European want with nail-headed inscriptions? The previous December, in the midst of his explorations of Kouyunjik, an inhabitant of Khorsabad had turned up at Botta's house with two kiln-baked bricks inscribed with cuneiform characters. He claimed that he had found them near his village and offered to procure for Botta, at a modest price, as many as the crazy foreigner desired. Khorsabad was filled with them, he alleged. Botta was accustomed to the soaring imagination of Arabs and stifled a yawn.

But when he abandoned Kouyunjik, he recalled the incident, and he sent several of his workers to Khorsabad, a place about as far from Mosul as the Nimrod mound.

Three days later, his workers returned in a state of frenzy. They had dug up a statue inlaid with nail-headed inscriptions. Botta dispatched his foreman, Naaman ibn Naouch, to make an investigation.

Botta had complete faith in Naaman. "He has two qualities which are very rare in this country," Botta said, "namely, intelligence and probity."

Naaman returned from Khorsabad highly agitated. Botta hestitated no longer. He journeyed to the mound. There he saw what his workmen had uncovered: an incredibly magnificent alabaster bas-relief. As he gazed on the sculpture with disbelief, he realized that he was looking at a lost world.

The bas-relief depicted scenes of a monarch, accompanied by soldiers attired in strange garb, leading a column of prisoners into captivity. Botta realized that it was a mere fragment of what must be a large building buried in the mound. He tested his theory by sinking shafts at random. "I caused a trench to be dug," he said, "[and] . . . my workmen immediately found a wall displaying two very remarkable colossal figures, eight-and-a-half metres [27.5 feet] high."

On April 5 Botta announced his discovery in a letter to Mohl. He sent it by *tatar* to M. de Cadalvene, the director of French overland posts at Constantinople, who arranged to forward it by ship to Paris.

Botta had unearthed objects that had not been seen for thousands of years, among them, two figures, nearly 9 feet high, one of a winged personage with the head of a bird and the other a bearded king who held a trident terminated by three balls.

In Paris, Mohl was elated. His belief in the mounds was vindicated.

Mohl rushed to the Academy of Inscriptions and Belles-Lettres with Botta's letter and characterized Botta's work as "a discovery destined to throw a great light on one of the most obscure and interesting portions of ancient history."

Botta's discovery electrified Paris. On May 24, 1843, barely six weeks after Botta broke the news, the French cabinet authorized a 3,000-franc grant to Botta to continue the excavations. This was soon followed by other grants totaling 140,000 francs. Eugene Flandin, a volatile, young, Italian-born artist, was ordered to proceed to Mesopotamia to make drawings of Botta's finds.

But Flandin's journey to Khorsabad was to be postponed. In July, as the Mesopotamian summer lengthened, with temperatures above 155 degrees Fahrenheit, Botta wrote, "[I] am now desperately ill." He was down with "a sort of cholera" and, in delirious condition, was carried by litter to Mosul. He no sooner recovered than he was mired in political problems.

Botta's difficulties started when rumors spread that he had either found buried treasure or that the inscriptions he busily copied were ciphers which revealed the location of the treasure. Wilder stories circulated among the more credulous. The most fantastic claim was that the inscribed bricks were ancient land deeds and that by acquiring them, the Franks would lay claim to the whole of Mesopotamia. Still another tale was that Botta built secret fortifications at Khorsabad.

In October 1843 the governor of Mosul, backed by Constantinople, prohibited Botta from continuing his excavations. In the Turkish capital the French ambassador labored for months before he could dispel these wild stories and obtain a firman permitting Botta to resume the dig and Flandin to join him. As a result of these political idiocies, Flandin did not reach Mosul until May 4, 1844, almost a year to the day he was commissioned to rush to Botta's assistance. During that interval much of what Botta had unearthed had dissolved as a result of desert winds, searing heat, and a harsh winter.

For the next six months Botta and Flandin engaged in a remarkable collaboration. Flandin made copies of the sculptures; Botta, the cuneiform inscriptions. On October 31 they completed their work and abandoned Khorsabad to the weather. Nine days later Flandin left for Paris, via Constantinople, with their precious collection of drawings.

Before his departure from Khorsabad, Botta had selected several pieces of sculpture to be shipped to the Louvre. Working alone after Flandin's homeward passage, Botta prepared the objects for the journey to Paris. Several sculptures weighed as much as three tons, and he sawed them into manageable blocks. Yet transportation was so primitive that Botta spent six weeks forging axle trees strong enough to support the loads. Even so, he was compelled to abandon many pieces of sculpture along the way. He also had to build special keleks to carry the objects downstream to Baghdad. During the loading of one raft, a worker was crushed to death and several others injured. It was not until June 1845, eight months after he abandoned Khorsabad, that the sculptures arrived at Baghdad, where they sat on the riverbank until a French man-of-war picked them up for the voyage to France.

Botta's discoveries excited Canning almost as much as they did Layard. Major Rawlinson, assigned to Baghdad as Taylor's successor, was also agitated by Botta's finds. He wrote Layard to urge Sir Stratford "to take an interest in the antiquities of this country. It pains me grievously to see the French monopolize the field, for the fruits of Botta's labor, already achieved and still in progress, are not things to pass away in a day but will constitute a nation's glory in future ages."

While Layard and Rawlinson vied for Canning's support, Flandin appeared on the Constantinople scene and triumphantly showed Layard his drawings. Layard promptly reported the matter to Canning. The French had pulled the archaeological coup of the year.

If Layard was bitter, it was not toward Botta and Flandin, but toward his compatriots. British capital, private and public, was available for industrial expansion, new trade routes, and colonial acquisitions. Digging up worlds of the past? This hardly merited discussion.

But the more Layard thought about Botta's discoveries, the more he was convinced, as Botta suspected, that he had not discovered Nineveh. The site was too far from the Tigris and did not conform with historical accounts of its location. The extent of the ruins was also limited, yet Nineveh was a "great city." Nineveh still awaited the pick and shovel.

It is against this background, in the summer of 1845, as Canning packed his bags and made ready to join his wife and children on home leave in England, that Layard proposed to the ambassador that, with a couple of months to kill until Sir Stratford won over Aberdeen to Layard's appointment as an attaché, he proceed to Mesopotamia and continue the explorations Botta had abandoned.

Layard estimated that the job of excavating Nimrod—he thought the traditional name of the mound itself a significant clue—would cost about £150 ($750), a figure based on Botta's pay scale of 4½ piasters (20¢) a day per worker. "Sir Stratford not only approved my proposal," Layard said jubilantly, "but offered to share in the expenses which would be incurred in making tentative excavations."

Initially, Canning contributed £60 to the project; later, he doubled it. Layard put up the difference (£30).

Canning and Layard also drew up a compact, dated October 15, 1845. Under its terms, Layard was "to inform Sir Stratford Canning of his operations and to give him a full account of any objects worthy of curiosity which he might see or discover."

Both Layard and Canning thought the excavations would be completed in two months. "Should he [Layard] have reasons for adding another ten days or fortnight," Canning's *aide-mémoire* said, "he is at liberty to follow his own discretion."

As it developed, Layard was to spend the next seven years among the mounds of Assyria.

> On the solitary pastures where our sheep [are] half
> asleep . . .
> was the site of a city great and gay (or so they say).
> —BROWNING

CHAPTER 8

Canning, concerned lest Layard's sudden return arouse the French to resume their excavations, deemed it "most prudent" that Layard leave for Mosul furtively.

Prior to his departure, Layard took a crash course in map-making from an English officer in the Turkish service. His plan was to make surveys "of any ruins I may discover and of the many ruins on the banks of the Tigris which are believed to represent the site of Nineveh."

Once again, as was his style, Layard traveled alone. He also traveled lightly. He crammed his effects into two leather saddlebags—some linen, a change of clothes, a few books, maps, surveyor's instruments, and a coverlet for sleeping. He arrived at Mosul October 27, covering 900 miles in twelve days. The weather was miserable along the way, raining almost constantly, and he rode "usually wet to the skin."

Christian Rassam was surprised to see him back in Mosul and greeted him warmly. It was good to see a friendly face.

On November 8, with Rassam's help, Layard secretly procured several picks and shovels, engaged a mason, a *cawass*, and a servant, and floated down the Tigris to Nimrod on a small kelek. Henry Ross, a Baghdad merchant who arrived in Mosul the day after Layard set out, joined the expedition. It took six hours to float downriver to Nimrod.

The group arrived at dusk and took shelter in the miserable nearby village of Naifa, putting up at the hovel of the local sheik, Awad abd-Allah. Awad spoke a little Turkish and was "intelligent and active." Layard hired him on the spot as "superintendent of the workmen." That night Awad regaled the party with the traditions connected with the ruins of the Nimrod mound. Truly, he said, the mound was the site of a palace built by Ashur, the lieutenant of Nimrod, "the mighty hunter." This was the place where Abraham—peace be with him!—cast down and broke into pieces the idols worshiped by unbelievers.

Layard slept little that first night as he dreamed of underground palaces. When Awad summoned him to breakfast, the sun was just breaking. "The lofty cone and broad mound of Nimroud broke like a distant mountain on the morning sky," Layard recorded. The great mound, shaped like a parallelogram, stretched 1,800 feet in length, 900 in breadth, and about 65 feet in height.

Awad had augmented Layard's group with a work party of six Arabs. In stupefaction, they watched as Layard crawled around the mound collecting fragments of bricks and other rubbish. With a shrug, they joined in the search and were amazed as Layard jumped joyously when one of the workers brought him the fragment of a bas-relief. Awad pointed to a piece of alabaster which appeared sticking above the soil. Layard ordered the men to dig it up. They put their spades to the earth. It proved to be a huge slab covered with cuneiform inscriptions. At

Layard's command, they dug deeper and faster, uncovering one slab after another. "[Then] we came almost immediately to a wall, bearing inscriptions," Layard said. Parts of the wall were seared, evidently scorched in antiquity. As night fell, Layard was convinced that something immense was buried within the mound, but precisely what it was or what he was looking for he did not know.

The following morning, November 10, Layard's work force was increased by five new workers. Before the day was out, Layard found himself in a room built of slabs. In the bottom of the chamber, amid the rubbish, he said, "I found several ivory ornaments" (they are now part of the collection of famed Nimrod Ivories, among the world's greatest archaeological treasures).

That night, in the glow of a campfire, in a mood of triumph, Layard wrote his skeptical godparents, Aunt Sara and Uncle Ben, "As yet no figures, but, from fragments discovered in the rubbish, I have no doubt they will come. [The mound] appears to be one great palace, principally of marble, which has been plundered, destroyed as far as possible by fire and has remained ever since under the accumulated dust of ages."

He continued to excavate the mound, and he continued to find walls and chambers. On the fourth day, at Ross's insistence, Layard was compelled to call a halt and return to Mosul. His body was racked by fever and chills. Ross considered his physical condition dangerous. He had seen too many Europeans fall by the wayside, victims of ague.

In Mosul, while recovering from this latest attack of malaria, Layard wrote Canning his first report on their joint "speculation." The report filled twelve pages. "As yet I have not found sculptures, but from several fragments, which I discovered in the rubbish of the mound, I have every reason to think that figures exist," he said. "Indeed, I have found an old man here who pretends to have buried, fifty years ago, slabs similar to those of Khorsabad which he discovered when digging for building-bricks. He has promised to show me the spot."

He wrote that "the ruins of Nimroud are very extensive," and that it would take "at least a month" to explore them. "Should I be fortunate enough to discover sculptures worth transporting," he continued, "Nimroud would be particularly adapted for the work as it is within three-quarters of a mile of the river."

Canning replied with a letter of encouragement. "What I would not give to be with you . . . ," the ambassador said. "My curiosity is not only on tiptoe, but on stilts."

More bouyant than ever, Layard returned to Nimrod on November

19 and moved his headquarters to a new village, Selamiye, which was encircled with a mud brick wall and afforded protection should Bedouins hear of treasure and stage a night raid on his camp. He moved into the largest hovel in the village. It was little more than a barn. He occupied one half and the other half was inhabited by cows, bullocks, and mules. A second hovel was occupied by the wives, children, and poultry of his laborers. A third served as mess hall and workers' quarters. The fourth building was turned into a stall for Layard's horses. The roofs of these buildings leaked badly when it rained, and Layard frequently passed a wet night under a rude table which he had himself constructed.

The work at Nimrod proceeded apace. His Christian workers, Chaldeans he called them, were strong and hardy and manned the picks. The Arabs carried off the debris in baskets and threw it over the side of the mound, including, unknown to Layard, potsherds of inestimable archaeological value.

On November 28, Layard hit his first jackpot. The first stroke of the pick that morning revealed the top of a bas-relief. The workers were caught up by Layard's infectious enthusiasm. Despite a violent rainstorm, they worked until dark to bring the sculpture to light. One slab depicted the siege of a walled city; the second slab, a battle scene.

On December 1 he wrote Canning, "I am happy to inform your excellency that on Friday last I was sufficiently fortunate to find sculptures at Nimroud." And he added more good news: "The marbles sent by M. Botta are stuck at Baghdad waiting for a ship." Clearly, like Canning, Layard also had visions of the British beating the French to Europe with the first "Assyrian marbles."

In the midst of this elation, the governor at Mosul accused him of digging up a Moslem burying ground and ordered him to cease all excavations. Layard encountered little difficulty in circumventing the order, which was brought to him by the governor's aide, Daoud Agha. He simply bribed the aide and resumed digging.

Astride the elongated mound, Layard arbitrarily selected a new spot to dig. His workers put their picks to the soil, and to their amazement, as well as Layard's, they immediately struck a piece of sculpted granite. They had stumbled on a pair of fantastic winged bulls and winged lions, 14 feet in height, forming the entrance to a huge chamber. The walls of the chamber were covered with carved human figures, each 9 feet tall.

When Layard returned to Mosul shortly before Christmas, a letter from Rawlinson awaited him. "I can come to no other conclusion than that Nimroud is the original Nineveh," he wrote, and he invited Layard down to Baghdad to deliver a firsthand account of the discoveries. Layard readily accepted. He was anxious to make arrangements with the East India Company's representative for transporting the winged bulls to England. He also felt he deserved a night on the town, and what could be a better place than Baghdad?

Layard spent Christmas week at Rawlinson's imposing residence. Although they had corresponded frequently, this was the first meeting between Layard, the founder of Assyrian archaeology, and Rawlinson, the Assyriologist, among the first to decipher Assyrian inscriptions. "It was a happy chance which brought together two such men," Rawlinson's older brother George, Canon of Canterbury and professor of ancient history at Oxford, later remarked. "Each [was] strongest where the other was weakest."

Layard was the excavator, robust, determined, energetic, inured to hardship by travel in remote areas. Rawlinson, who had joined the East India Company at the age of seventeen, who, like Layard, had never attended college, was scholarly by nature, a self-taught classicist and linguist who was fluent in modern and ancient Persian, Hindi, Hebrew, and lesser-known tongues, a man of wide reading and deep insight.

Rawlinson's fixation was cuneiform. He was as determined to decode the nail-headed characters as Layard was to probe the core of the mound at Nimrod. Rawlinson thought of archaeology in terms of unearthing lost literature. He considered recovery of art a happy by-product, nothing more.

This blind spot infuriated Layard and others who argued that one picture is worth a thousand words. The conflict came to a boil some years later when both sides tried to establish a chronology for Assyria.

Layard's ability to keep up with Rawlinson in the matter of cuneiform, however, impressed Rawlinson and was a tribute to Layard's scholarship. That week Rawlinson and Layard identified together the arrow-headed characters for god, king, and city. In a letter to his mother, Layard boldly expressed confidence that "with the assistance of the materials furnished by the joint stock of Rawlinson and myself, I hope very shortly to have the alphabet." Rawlinson was less sanguine. In his diary, he wrote that he expected to crack cuneiform in "another two or three years." Was cuneiform Chaldean? Some dialect, long forgotten, of an existing language? Some unknown language? Endlessly, or so it seemed, both men discussed these questions. At the time neither realized that the Assyrian language possessed no alphabet.

Early in January, before returning to Mosul, Layard and Rawlinson entered into a pact. Layard promised to tranship his finds through Baghdad so Rawlinson could personally inspect each new cuneiform inscription. In return, Rawlinson promised to send a steam-driven vessel upriver to collect the art treasures and transfer them at Baghdad aboard a homeward-bound East Indiaman. Botta's collection was still sitting on a Baghdad wharf waiting for a French ship. Rawlinson—like Canning and Layard—relished the idea of the British Museum's beating the Louvre to it with the world's first exhibition of Assyrian relics.

His batteries recharged, on January 17, 1846, Layard returned to Nimrod. During his absence, Hormuzd Rassam, the seventeen-year-old younger brother of the British vice-consul, had taken charge at Nimrod and had established a new base of operations atop the mound itself. Layard was given the most luxurious of the new dwelling places. "A few rude chairs, a table, and a wooden bedstead, formed the whole of my furniture," he said. Layard admired the young Hormuzd's eagerness and industriousness and appointed Hormuzd his agent at Nimrod, inviting him to share his primitive quarters.

The Nimrod mound covered 60 acres. Lest the vein he worked run out—Botta's experience at Khorsabad—Layard thought it prudent to make some fresh experiments elsewhere on the mound.

Once again, luck, that fickle goddess, was his outrider. Arbitrarily, he pointed to a new spot and ordered another trench dug. With the first shovel of debris, his men struck a wall covered with bas-reliefs. But Layard was puzzled. Just as he could distinguish at the age of twelve the different styles of the Venetian school of painters, he promptly recognized that the artistic style of the new reliefs belonged to a period other than his earlier discoveries.

The new figures were 3 feet 8 inches high and were superbly executed. They appeared to have stepped from a nightmare—winged creatures with human bodies and the heads of either vultures or eagles. The curved beak of one was half open and displayed a pointed tongue covered with red paint. Clearly, he had discovered another Assyrian period.

Early the following morning, Layard rode off to parley with a local sheik, a feature of his continual shuttle diplomacy aimed at maintaining friendly relations with the various tribes in Nimrod's vicinity. As a matter of policy, he regularly presented gifts to local chieftains—a piece of silk or embroidered material, a pair of boots. The Arabs were delighted.

Returning to Nimrod from the parley late that morning, Layard spied two Arab horsemen flying from the mound at full speed. Abruptly, they pulled up as they approached. "Hasten, O Bey!" exclaimed one panting rider. "Hasten to the diggers, for they have found Nimrod himself!"

At the mound, Awad, his foreman, stepped forward and proudly announced that they had unearthed the mighty hunter himself, the father of Ashur. Layard hastened to the spot. Protruding from the bottom of the pit was an alabaster head, 8 feet in height, which he promptly recognized as belonging to a gigantic, human-headed winged lion. "The expression was calm, yet majestic, and the outline of the features showed a freedom and knowledge of art, scarcely to be looked for in the works of so remote a period," Layard wrote.

Layard's credulous Arab workers were terrified by the apparition. "It required no stretch of imagination [for them] to conjure up the most strange fancies," Layard wrote. In the tradition of the countryside, the head conjured up a visitation from the lower depths, from hell itself.

As Layard studied the head, the sheik with whom he had conferred earlier in the morning rode up with his warriors to view the wonder. "This is not the work of men's hands but of those infidel giants of whom the Prophet, peace be with him! has said, that they were higher than the tallest date tree!" he exclaimed. "This is one of the idols which Noah, peace be with him! cursed before the Flood."

Mosul was thrown into bedlam by the news. The Cadi, or titular orthodox religious leader of the pashalik, protested to the governor that Layard's activities ran counter to the teachings of the Koran, although the Cadi was hard put to explain precisely in what way. Nonetheless, with Mosul in agitation, the governor summoned Layard and advised him to quietly suspend his activities until the sensation subsided.

On April 21, 1846, Layard wrote his mother a lengthy letter and singled out his winged, human-headed lions as "the most magnificent specimens of Assyrian sculpture that could be found above or under the ground." The sculpture of Nimrod, he wrote triumphantly, far exceeded that of Khorsabad. "The lions . . . for instance, are admirably drawn and the muscles, bones and veins quite true to nature and portrayed with great spirit," he said. "There is also great *mouvement*—as the French well term it—in the attitude of the animal."

Mosul, meanwhile, refused to calm down, and Layard became increasingly restless. He appealed to Canning for a firman permitting him to resume the excavations and remove the finds. He also took the opportunity to touch on that hardy perennial, money. In a letter to Canning dated April 21, 1846, Layard wrote that he was running low on funds, and drawing on his own meager resources in the hope that, "should the government carry on the excavations, I shall be refunded."

Canning appreciated Layard's difficulties and replied: "I shall do my best to come to your aid."

But even the Great Elchi could not wave a magic wand and produce a firman and funds. Canning, quite rightly, felt it would be gross to press so quickly for another firman. The Sultan, at the top of a tottering empire that stretched from Egypt to the Persian frontier, had other matters on his mind.

But Layard was particularly anxious about acquiring a firman, since the French had dispatched a new vice-consul to fill the vacancy left the year before by Botta's departure. The new consul, M. Guillois, shocked Layard by disclosing his intention to reopen Botta's dig at Kouyunjik, and announcing that the French were already in the midst of negotiations at Constantinople for a firman. Layard considered these moves a threat to British interests and decided to take matters into his own hands. The situation demanded a dramatic diplomatic gesture. Accordingly, he decided to throw a monster bash. He issued a general invitation to all and sundry to attend the gala: the governor and his Turkish staff, Arab sheiks, Kurdish chieftains, leaders of the Christian minority, members of Mosul's old-line Jewish families, and the diplomatic community. Fourteen sheep were roasted and boiled. Musicians and dancers were hired. The party lasted three days.

Layard's reputation, already high, acquired new stature throughout the pashalik. He was the talk of the bazaars and coffee shops. Impressed by Layard's popularity, the pasha concluded that "the dust had settled" and that Layard could resume his digging at Nimrod.

The governor no sooner flashed the green light than an official authorization, in Layard's name, arrived from Constantinople. Canning was finally ready to embark on home leave. He realized that there was insufficient time to obtain a firman and, in desperation, had approached the grand vizier, his intimate friend, for the next best thing, a vizierial letter. It was immediately forthcoming.

"In the vicinity of Mosul there are quantities of stones and ancient remains," the vizierial letter addressed to the governor of Mosul began. "There is also an English gentleman who has come to the area to look for stones of this kind . . . The British ambassador has prayed that there be no obstacles placed in the way of the above-mentioned gentleman's taking some stones which can be of use to him, such as those which he may be able to discover in the midst of the excavations he will make in places believed to enclose stones of this type, and to his putting them on shipboard in order to transport them to England."

Neither Canning's nor Layard's name actually appears in the document. No need. In 1846 there was only one British ambassador in Constantinople and only one Englishman in Mosul collecting "stones." Nevertheless, much later the letter became a bone over which lawyers and academicians endlessly scrapped. Did the "stones" belong to Canning, who financed the expedition and extracted the vizierial authorization from Constantinople? Or to Layard, who labored in Mesopotamia and dug them up?

In a note accompanying the authorization, Canning urged Layard to exploit the letter to the fullest, to dig, shotgun style, into every mound that might contain Assyrian antiquities so that Britain could secure a prior claim to excavation. Even in this formative period of archaeology, a rule was generally accepted that whoever dug at a site first exercised a prior claim to it unless he relinquished it to another. But Canning also urged him to act circumspectly, not to be "too greedy" and to respect the claims and jealousies of others. "I need not tell you," he said, "that our Gallic neighbors are particularly in my thoughts."

They were also in Layard's. Guillois was surprised by the vizierial directive. The damn Anglo-Saxons had beaten the French to it again. Nonetheless, he warned Layard, France held a prior right to Kouyunjik in the light of Botta's earlier excavations, even though he had found nothing at the site.

Layard considered the French claim without merit. Botta, he argued, abandoned Kouyunjik. Guided by Canning's instructions, Layard invited Guillois to join in a joint Anglo-French excavation of the mound, but the Frenchman rejected the olive branch.

Like petulant children, the two Europeans rushed to the mound and began to dig in opposite directions. Layard had distinct advantages over his rival. He was a keen observer, connoisseur of art, and, by now, a relatively experienced digger. He was learning to read a mound the way a fisherman reads the ocean. For example, he had noticed that each mound appeared to have a pyramidal-shaped high point, and although he did not know what it meant, he suspected that by clearing the debris from around that spot he was likely to increase his chances of making a significant discovery. Today the high point is known as the ziggurat, or temple tower; in a sense, the Assyrian and Babylonian stairway to heaven. Accordingly, in the race to dig up Kouyunjik, Layard staked out a claim to the high ground.

The race, however, ended in a dead heat. "We both continued our research for about a month without success," Layard reported. He was baffled. Of all the Mesopotamian mounds, Kouyunjik, known to travelers from Xenophon to Rabbi Benjamin to Claudius Rich as a possible site of Nineveh, should have contained the richest lode. Yet, like Botta before them, they found only a few potsherds, kiln-baked bricks, and chips of sculptures.

It was now summer, and a lesser individual would have put off work until autumn, given the almost intolerable heat in Mesopotamia in the middle of the year. Not Layard. He had his authorization and he was determined to continue his explorations. Judiciously, however, he shifted his operations from Kouyunjik to his beloved and productive Nimrod, where he could work in complete freedom.

But back at Nimrod, even Layard had to make concessions to the sun. The rickety dwellings Rassam had erected atop Nimrod were stifling, and life in an Arab tent was no improvement. Layard ordered caves cut into the Tigris's bank, and he converted one of these recesses into summer headquarters. "I was much troubled, however, with scorpions and other reptiles which issued from the earth forming the walls of my apartment," he said, "and later in the summer by the gnats and sandflies which hovered on a calm night over the river." But the apartment had a consolation: it was between 30 and 40 degrees cooler than outside.

As the summer lengthened, the heat took its unmerciful toll. Searing desert winds blackened the sky, accompanied by flights of locusts. Whenever a whirlwind approached, activities at Nimrod came to a complete halt. Layard watched in fascination as the column of sand swirled toward him. If the tornado struck while he was working on the mound, his favorite refuge was beneath a fallen lion. His workers huddled in trenches, blinded by the sand and almost on the verge of suffocation.

In these terrifying conditions, Layard pressed ahead. His hardships were compensated. His finds were spectacular. The mound was honeycombed with chambers and blackened walls. There were accumulations of ashes in places where wooden beams had been inserted to support a roof or wall. The city or palace, or whatever it was, had been put to the torch in antiquity.

Each day brought forth new wonders, deeper mysteries.

Gods, kings, warriors, and captives emerged from the depths of the mound, a fantasia of elaborately sculpted and richly ornamented figures, some 8 feet in height. Under a broken slab, for example, he discovered a magnificent yellow limestone human-headed ox or bull with wings. "I lifted the body with difficulty," he recorded, "and to my surprise I discovered under it sixteen copper lions, admirably designed, and forming a regular series, diminishing in size from the largest, which was above one foot, to the smallest, which scarcely exceeded an inch."

The origin of the mound continued to baffle him, and he referred to the objects he unearthed as "Assyrian or Chaldean." Despite Rawlinson's heady conclusion earlier that Layard had rediscovered Nineveh, Layard—like Botta before him at Khorsabad—was reluctant to claim that he had found "that great city" of Genesis.

While Nimrod's original name was uncertain, there was no doubt that Layard had found himself. "I live among the ruins," he wrote Aunt Sara, "and dream of little else. For the time being, my hopes and fears and joys center in them."

Although he did not know it, he was finding not only himself but also a place in history.

> *I crossed rivers . . . I climbed mountains.*
> —SHALMANESER III

CHAPTER 9

While Layard was rummaging through Nimrod, Rawlinson made arrangements for the *Nitocris*, a steam-driven coaster of the East India Company named for a mythical queen of Babylon, to sail upriver "to assist in the conveyance of Mr. Layard's sculpture and other antiquities from that site to Baghdad." Layard's good friend Lieutenant Jones, who had fished him from the Tigris two years earlier, commanded the vessel.

But the *Nitocris*'s voyage was a complete failure. The river's ebbing current that year was exceptionally strong, and the vessel did well to maintain headway. Worse, engine breakdowns were frequent. Employing auxiliary sail was useless. When *Nitocris* got halfway to Nimrod, she was compelled to put about and return with empty holds to Baghdad. Layard was now confronted with the awesome problem of how to remove the immense winged lions and bas-reliefs, each weighing several tons, in the absence of transportation. Some of the blocks of sculpture were 9 feet square and 1 foot thick. The few ropes Layard procured were of such poor quality that they snapped like threads. And the carts used by the Arabs could "scarcely be used for carrying a load of hay."

He solved the problem as Botta had. Importing several Mosul stonecutters, he ordered them to saw the sculpture into manageable portions. Damage was unavoidable. "The inscriptions being mere [sic] repetitions," Layard said, "I did not consider it necessary to preserve them as they added to the weight." Two stonemasons broke them off and tossed them aside.

The blocks were packed in felt and straw and transported in twelve cases to the river's edge on rude buffalo carts. Special keleks, rafts of skins similar to the raft he and Mitford had floated down the Tigris on, were built. The crates of art, awash, were made fast. Down the Tigris the cargo went—at the mercy of currents and rapids. As much to Layard's surprise as Rawlinson's, the convoy landed safely at Baghdad.

The British resident immediately took charge of the shipment and, after inspecting them (and no doubt lamenting the loss of the inscriptions), Rawlinson arranged for their transfer to a ship bound for England.

By now summer had lengthened and the heat at Nimrod had become so unbearable that even Layard complained. Finally, he hit on a novel plan to defeat the sun. He decided to dig by lamplight from dusk to dawn.

The first weeks of nighttime digging at Kouyunjik were as unproductive as his earlier excavations and those of Botta and Guillois. Yet Layard was convinced that within this mound of mounds, the traditional site of Nineveh, there must be some clue to antiquity.

Once again, luck was with him. An aged Mosul stonecutter, whom Layard had employed at Nimrod, recounted how he was present when Rich found a bas-relief and that afterward, as a true believer, he had joined others in smashing the idol to pieces. "He offered to show me the spot," Layard reported, "and I opened a trench at once into a high mound which he pointed out in the northern line of ruins."

Layard's workers touched their shovels to the spot and promptly struck fragments of sculptured alabaster. For the next seventy-two hours, oblivious to the sun and moon, Layard worked around the clock to excavate the area.

The first major discovery was the entrance to a chamber guarded by two winged creatures, half-human, half-beast. They had been battered to pieces with hammers. The size of the sculpture—20 feet in height—

astonished Layard, who thought he had grown accustomed to surprises. "The proportions were gigantic, and the relief higher than that of any sculpture hitherto discovered in Assyria," he recorded. The chamber was filled with broken pieces of sculpture, many bearing cuneiform inscriptions. A pavement of limestone led from the chamber into the interior of the mound. In high expectation, Layard followed it, but it petered out. Not another piece of sculpture was found.

A modern archaeologist would be ecstatic over such a discovery, but Layard was dismayed. In this early period of archaeology, the success of a dig was measured by the amount of freestanding sculpture recovered. Potsherds meant nothing; inscriptions or designs were unintelligible curiosities except to a handful of people like Rawlinson; stratigraphy was unheard of; no detailed records of the dig were kept. This was one of the reasons Layard and his contemporaries were unable to put the Assyrian jigsaw puzzle together. They saved and studied only the big pieces and ignored or discarded the smaller ones. As a child knows, every piece of the puzzle, big or small, serves as a clue to completing the picture.

Layard's insistence that he work at the mounds in the middle of summer had taken a personal toll. He had lost considerable weight and was ravaged by recurring bouts of malaria. Christian Rassam and his wife Matilda were alarmed by the deterioration in his health and strongly advised him to emulate the Assyrian kings of antiquity and take to the hills, especially since a cholera epidemic had broken out at Baghdad and would probably spread to Mosul. He was in no condition to resist that dread disease. Disappointed over the meager results of his second assault on Kouyunjik, Layard bowed to their advice.

In September, accompanied by Rassam's younger brother Hormuzd, Layard left for the Tiyari Mountains, a district inhabited by the Nestorians, or Chaldean Christians, who claimed to be the nearest descendants of the ancient Assyrians.

While Layard was traveling in the mountains, Canning was in London bringing influence to bear to get the crown to underwrite a massive excavation of the mounds. He pressed the Prime Minister, pestered the Treasury and Foreign Office, put pressure on scholarly friends at his alma mater, Oxford, and visited the trustees of the British Museum.

The obstacles were considerable. However unfairly, Layard's reputation in London was suspect. Although Lord Palmerston had replaced Lord Aberdeen as foreign secretary, the Foreign Office remembered the incident involving the jealous British consul at Belgrade who falsely

Austen Henry Layard, standing at top right, supervises the moving of one of the gargantuan stone figures which he found flanking many Assyrian palace gateways. The task of transporting this 14-foot tall, 10-ton winged bull, and a similar lion, from the Nimrod excavation site to the British Museum in London, was a formidable undertaking. Layard's methods mirrored those of the ancient Assyrians. He was later to discover, on panels at the palace at Nineveh,

engravings which showed that they, too, had employed a combination
of rollers, levers, blocks and tackles to move the statues into place. For
advice on how to transport the colossi to the sea (where modern steamers awaited them
for the ocean voyage) he followed Queen Semiramis, who centuries before had floated
such stones downriver on huge rafts. Despite occasional mishaps, Layard's oversized
treasures reached their new home safely.

These stone bas-reliefs from Assyrian palaces
depict common motifs—though perhaps less
common than the scenes of conquest that graced
many of their walls. At left, a slab from the
threshold pavement of King Sennacherib's palace
at Nineveh shows an eagle-headed winged being
with a man's body, pollinating the Sacred Tree.
Another winged being, center, from the Palace of
Ashurnasirpal II at Nimrod, pollinates the
Sacred Tree next to an attendant carrying the
King's arms. The cuneiform writing on the slab
is the standard inscription of Ashurnasirpal II
(884–859 B.C.) At upper right, another stone
relief from Ashurnasirpal's palace shows the
King, at left, and an attendant. See detail, right.

A winged human-headed lion, above left, and bull, above right, from the Palace of Ashurnasirpal II. This pair of stone creatures, each standing about 10 feet high, is in New York's Metropolitan Museum of Art. The limestone sculpture below is a drinking cup (7th century B.C.) in the shape of an antelope head.

A Median leading a pair of horses, above, as tribute to
Sargon II, another Assyrian king (722–705 B.C.)
This stone bas-relief is from his palace at
Dur-Sharrukin (modern-day Khorsabad). The
relief below, showing a cavalryman fording a
stream, is from the Palace of Sennacherib
(704–681 B.C.) at Nineveh.

A detail of the standard inscription, in cuneiform, of Ashurnasirpal II, the king who proclaimed, "I am merciless . . . first in war, king of the world . . . who has trampled down all who were not submissive to him . . ."

The stone relief above, in a floral motif, is from the threshold of the Palace of Sennacherib at Nineveh. This city was built on a grander scale than others discovered by Layard, and Sennacherib himself was described by contemporaries as "a mighty hero clothed in terror." The profiled head below is that of a royal attendant in the court of Sargon II, at Dur-Sharrukin.

accused Layard of impersonating a British embassy official. The Treasury recalled the Coutts affair, although the bank had exonerated Layard and conceded it was their error. The Museum's trustees viewed Layard uneasily as a hotspur who would embroil them in all sorts of difficulties.

When the Museum waffled, Canning circulated Layard's private reports about the preliminary discoveries in the mound. The trustees were impressed and came down on Layard's side, but the niggardliness of their offer was profoundly disappointing. The Museum authorized an expenditure of £2,000 ($10,000) to meet the costs of excavating the mound and set a deadline of ten months, June 30, 1847, for its completion. The money was to be cut four ways—£400 for Canning, to repay him for his out-of-pocket outlay; £500 for Layard as compensation plus £100 in travel expenses for his return to England at the completion of the project; and £1,000 for the excavation itself.

The authorization was a joke. In effect, Layard was provided with £100 monthly to cover all his expenses at Nimrod. Out of this amount he was expected to hire and pay more than a hundred workers; superintend the dig; make drawings of bas-reliefs in duplicate (the Museum refused to send an artist, as the French had sent Flandin to Botta); copy all cuneiform inscriptions; make duplicate casts of sculptures and bas-reliefs which could not be removed; pack and move the sculptures; and arrange for the embarkation for London of "the spoils," as Canning referred to the treasures. By contrast, the French government had presented Botta and Flandin with £5,000 simply as a token of the nation's appreciation of their effort at Khorsabad, in addition to the thousands of pounds freely spent to produce the incomparable *Monuments of Nineveh*.

Canning was appalled by the British Museum's insensitivity to the problem. But as a skilled diplomat he sought to convince Layard of the wisdom of accepting the arrangement. "The British Museum undertakes Nimroud in my stead," Canning wrote Layard. "You are the agent. I shall be disappointed if you are not satisfied."

When Layard returned from the mountains, Canning's letter and a contract from the British Museum, dated September 21, 1846, awaited him. As he held the envelopes in his hand he was ecstatic. The great moment had arrived. When he read the contents, he was plunged into a state of deep depression. His first reaction was to reject the Museum's contract out of hand. But then what? Clearly, he would forfeit his great dream of exploring the mounds. Gorging on his disappointment, he finally accepted the Museum's proposal. Nonetheless, his pride and desire for independence impelled him to strike back at the Museum. He told the trustees to keep his £600 salary and travel expenses. Better still, Layard wrote, he would add that sum to the amount they allocated for the excavation of the mound. He would spend it on equipment and manpower.

On November 1, 1846, Layard reopened excavations at Nimrod on a massive scale.

The first order of business was to establish a permanent base camp and recruit workers. For his headquarters, Layard erected an elaborate house of mud bricks on the outskirts of Nimrod. Ross, the Baghdad merchant who had joined Layard on his first inspection of Nimrod, described it in a memoir: "It was run up in a hurry, the bricks were not properly dried and it rained before the roof was done, so when it was inhabited inside walls were quickly clothed with sprouting barley which, for want of light, grew longer and whiter every day and hung down the walls in fantastic festoons."

Adjoining the Layard residence was a series of huts built for his *cawass* and servants. A stable and a "guest house" for important Arab visitors completed the complex.

In the course of construction, the builders made equidistant holes in the walls of the buildings, in a style popularized on the other side of the world in the same period by the Alamo in Texas. The warlike appearance of the houses was designed to frighten off Bedouin raiders. Although the bricklayers had the best of intentions, Layard was horrified. He feared rumors would get back to Constantinople that he was erecting fortifications at Nimrod—the problem Botta had had at Khorsabad. "I immediately ordered the holes filled up," Layard said. But he did not neglect the need for defense in case of Bedouin attack.

Forty workers and their families were ordered to pitch their tents around Layard's camp. Forty more Arab families were instructed to erect their tents atop the mound itself, and the remainder of the Arab work force were directed to peg their tents along the banks of the Tigris, where they busied themselves building keleks for moving the Assyrian relics downstream to Baghdad. The Arab men were all armed.

In addition, with Turkish permission, Layard recruited the *bairakdar*, or standard-bearer, of the Turkish irregular garrison at Mosul. The *bairakdar* was authorized to keep the camp in a state of readiness against Bedouin marauders and to guard whatever art treasures were recovered from the depths of the mound.

On the mound itself, immediately above the colossal winged lions he had discovered earlier, Layard ordered a barracks built for his fifty Nestorian diggers and their families. He also directed the construction of a godown atop the mound for storing relics.

The workers were paid abysmal wages. The wage scale ranged from three to five piasters daily—roughly 13 to 22 cents. But, as Ross put it, "The people about were very poor and only too glad to gain a few piastres by working for Layard." Within a matter of days, Layard recruited 130 workers and an extra couple of dozen guards and servants.

Hormuzd Rassam, now eighteen, Layard's chief of staff, lived in Layard's house and assisted in keeping the books. As an agent of the British Museum, and therefore the crown, Layard was responsible for the disbursement of public funds, and he maintained meticulous ledgers. The cost of establishing the camp was 2,407.20 piasters ($108.31), including 590 piasters for his hovel and those of his workmen; 1,369 piasters for wages, tools, and supplies—wicker baskets, felt, wood, iron screws, mats, and so on.

Layard freely engaged in payola. His workers expected it, it was sound diplomatic policy, and he enjoyed the role of a Santa Claus. Thus, the first monthly financial statement he submitted to the trustees recorded disbursements such as these: "37.20 piastres for a present to Arab sheikh; 100 piastres for gift for sheikh's daughter; 103.20 piastres for a present to servants for cooking for staff." After having been put down by Layard, the trustees accepted these expenses without protest.

Layard divided his workers into gangs. Each party contained two to four Chaldean diggers—the strongest and most active men in camp—and between eight and ten Arabs who carted off the earth in baskets. The debris was either piled in fresh heaps atop the mound or flung over the side of the artificial mountain to the desert floor below.

Layard attacked Nimrod on all sectors. He darted around the mound, issuing orders, boring holes here, digging trenches there. This, of course, was the era of the shovel and kerosene lamp, and he played the dig by ear. There were no infrared photographs, radioactive isotopes, carbon dating, bulldozers, or forklifts.

The Layard strategy was simple and direct: dig pits until walls were struck and then follow the walls with trenches. With his modest financial resources, Layard could never truly explore each uncovered area. His plan was to dig around the walls in search of bas-reliefs and sculptures without removing the earth from the center of a chamber or building, a rather primitive manner of excavation. Moreover, he no sooner uncovered a chamber than he quickly explored it and hurriedly filled it in, moving on to a new pit.

His method of digging left much to be desired. His techniques were not only primitive but crude. They never approached scientific methodology. In some respects Layard's work was disastrous; many inscriptions and art objects were either buried under new avalanches of debris, bypassed completely, or unnecessarily broken into unrecognizable pieces.

After a week into the dig, with rising spirits, November 7, 1846, Layard announced in a letter home: "I am now exploring Assyrian ruins in the neighborhood of Mosul on the Tigris."

Nimrod was about to yield its secrets.

She saw men portrayed upon the wall,
the images of the Chaldeans portrayed with vermilion.

—EZEKIEL

CHAPTER 10

In the last century Sir William Matthew Flinders Petrie, a founder of Egyptology, complained that too many people exhibit quaint notions about archaeology. As a case in point, he cited a London matron who once asked him how she should excavate a ruined town—should she begin to dig at the top or the side? A cake or pie was apparently in her mind, and the only question was where to best reach inside it.

The young matron probably gained her impression about archaeology from Layard's exploits. Layard simply put his thumb into Nimrod and pulled out a plum.

His first six weeks of digging on a large scale produced a cornucopia of art. Within that breathless period he discovered three palaces, twenty-eight immense chambers and halls, thirteen pairs of colossal man-headed winged bulls and lions, walls covered with bas-reliefs, the renowned Black Obelisk, and enough vases, weapons, cuneiform tablets, and Assyrian artifacts to fill a museum—which he did. The results of his excavations stirred Europe and set in motion an irreversible curiosity about the worlds of the past.

At one point his workers uncovered a bas-relief and "saw men portrayed upon the wall." A portion of the bas-relief retained its original color, flecks of vermilion. In the pictures, the Assyrians battled against some strange people. Layard's description has a scriptural ring. "The king stands gorgeously attired, in a chariot, drawn . . . by three horses richly caparisoned," Layard said. In the Book of Ezekiel, the sinful Samaria talks of "the Assyrians her neighbors, captains and rulers, clothed most gorgeously, horsemen riding upon horses, all of them desirable young men."

The battle scenes on the bas-reliefs depicted castles and battlements; warriors riding upon horses; the enemy on foot, some wounded, some dead, some in fetters; engineers undermining the walls of an adversary's fortress; engines of war spitting fire; and vultures hovering in the sky above the killing ground. "They are designed with great spirit," Layard marveled, "carefully executed."

Not all the bas-reliefs were of battle. There was a scene of a victory banquet, showing butchers butchering a lamb and bakers baking bread. Assyrian boats were shown in rich detail, down to the construction of the vessel's rudder. Layard was amazed: "It is singular that this is precisely the mode adopted by the inhabitants of Mosul in this day when they cross the Tigris in barques, perhaps even more rude than those on the same river three thousand years ago."

As the workers strained to lift one slab from the bottom of a trench, Layard immediately recognized scales of armor. Each scale was separate and was of iron, from 2 to 3 inches in length, rounded at one end and squared at the other with an embossed line in the center, not unlike the mail employed by Crusaders in the Middle Ages.

"The iron was covered with rust," he reported, "and in so decomposed a state, that I had much difficulty in cleansing it from the soil." He collected three baskets of these relics.

Other portions of armor were also found in the pit, some of copper, some of iron, and others of an alloy of copper and iron. Unexpectedly, he came upon an Assyrian helmet in a perfect state of preservation. It was shaped precisely like the pointed helmet represented in the bas-reliefs. Layard touched it and the helmet crumbled before his eyes. Carefully, he collected the fragments. Soon other helmets were found, but they also fell apart on exposure to fresh air. Helpless to prevent the decay, Layard was heartsickened by these losses. History was being lost as quickly as it was recovered.

Layard also stumbled across thousands of potsherds. Without realizing their value as time-prints of civilization, he and his workers cast them aside—"curious relics" is how Layard described them. On one occasion, however, he felt compelled to collect the fragments, not because he was interested in potsherds but because they bore cuneiform characters. He spent hours trying to match the pieces but found the task "impossible." He put them aside only to return to them again and again. Finally, one evening, under a hot and smoky kerosene lamp he completed the puzzle and, to his surprise, found that the characters were similar to those on some of the pottery Botta had found at Khorsabad. Like a ten-year-old child who remembers each and every stamp in his philatelic collection, Layard filed away in his memory vault every arrow-headed character he came across.

He speculated that the name inscribed on his and Botta's pottery was the name of some king. And, it was later developed, it was—Sargon the Great.

Whichever way Layard turned on the mound, he entered a new art gallery. Indeed, he grew so accustomed to finding bas-reliefs, sculptures, and cuneiform tablets that sometimes he was blasé. "The shape of this chamber was singular," he reported, adding, "it has two entrances . . . nothing of *any* importance was discovered. The slabs were unsculptured; upon each of them was the *usual* inscription" (italics added).

While a party of workers cleared the debris from around the slabs, Layard rushed off to the center of the mound to superintend the excavation of the spot where, earlier, he had discovered his first pair of man-headed winged bulls, the logo of the Assyrian empire. As he helped clear the rubbish from around the monsters, he discovered that the backs of the bulls were adorned with inscriptions in large and well-formed nail-headed characters. He suspected that the bulls were sentinels who guarded the entrance to a palace or chamber. Accordingly, he ordered a trench dug at right angles to the bulls in the hope of discovering what they protected. The work was hardly under way when his diggers struck a winged figure of a bird's head which towered 14 feet above them. Then they bumped into the beard and one of the five legs of another winged bull, this one carved from an immense block of yellow limestone. Layard was elated. "These remains, imperfect as they are, promise better things," he recorded.

But the next several days produced nothing, the only dry spell he encountered during those first forty days of digging. By now the trench extended for 50 feet at a depth of 10 feet. Before abandoning it, Layard decided to continue in another direction. Only minutes after he made his decision, the workers uncovered the corner of a piece of polished black marble. Tearing away the earth and rubble with shovels and hands, they uncovered a magnificent monolith, 6½ feet in height, lying on its side.

With the aid of ropes, and extra teams of workers, the obelisk was carefully raised from the bottom of the trench. It was sculptured on four sides. There were twenty small bas-reliefs and 210 lines of inscription, which Layard meticulously copied. The obelisk was in a superb state of preservation. "Scarcely a character of the inscription was wanting," Layard said, "and the figures were as sharp and well defined as if they had been carved but a few days before."

The monolith depicted a king, a prisoner at his feet, reviewing a procession of exotic animals—the elephant, the rhinoceros, the two-humped camel, the wild bull and lion, the stag, and various species of anthropoid apes. Layard concluded it had been erected to commenorate the "conquest of India or some country far to the east of Assyria."

The monolith's discovery encouraged Layard to dig deeper and to extend his trenches across the mound. Again his energy and enthusiasm were rewarded. The southeast corner of the mound was a horn of wonders, including a pair of winged lions about 5 feet high and 5 feet long. These lions, moreover, had the usual four legs, not the five legs he found on all the other Nimrod lions and bulls. They were carved from coarse limestone.

Behind the lions was a stone monster, with the head of a vulture, the body and arms of a man, and the tail of a fish. Between the two lions was a pair of crumbling sphinxes. "They differed from all Assyrian sculpture hitherto discovered," Layard said. "Nor could I form any conjecture as to their original use." They were not in relief, but freestanding. The human heads were beardless, but Layard could not determine whether they represented man or woman. The body of each sphinx, like the great Egyptian sphinx at Giza, on the outskirts of Cairo, was that of a lion. But unlike the Egyptian sphinx, the Assyrian version boasted a pair of graceful wings, forming a platform which Layard suspected was a sacrificial altar. The area around the altar was buried in charcoal, and the fire which obviously had destroyed the temple (he found traces of fire everywhere in the mound) "appears to have raged with extraordinary fury," he observed.

Of the two sphinxes, one was completely damaged and the other worthy of rescue. But both sphinxes proved evanescent.

"I endeavored to secure [the intact one] with rods of iron, and wooden planks; but the alabaster was too much decomposed to resist exposure to the atmosphere," Layard said. "I had scarcely time to make a careful drawing, before the whole fell to pieces; the fragments were too small to admit of their being collected, with a view to future restoration." In the charcoal debris, however, he recovered a small head of alabaster, and to his delight, the body of another winged sphinx—a miniature or model of the large ones that had decomposed.

A few days later workers reported a new find, this time in the northwest corner of the mound—bricks bearing the same cuneiform characters as those Layard had found earlier among the ruins of Kouyunjik opposite Mosul. This discovery linked the traditional site of Nineveh—Kouyunjik—with Nimrod, the suspected site of the real Nineveh. But the discovery left Layard confused.

He had little time to analyze his confusion. As he studied the problem, a cry went up from another part of the mound. Layard hurried off to find a huge slab with an inscription on it, probably the name of a monarch. "I ordered it to be raised with the intention of copying it," he said. Crowbars were employed, and amid the usual grunts, groans, and curses the stele shifted. Layard and his workers were dumbfounded, and almost dropped it. Beneath the slab was a narrow earthen sarcophagus and in it a well-preserved skeleton. As they stared at the skeleton, it fell to pieces on exposure to the air. The trench was lengthened and another earthen sarcophagus was discovered, lined with vessels baked in clay. It contained two skeletons. "Although the skulls were entire when first exposed to view," Layard said with disappointment, "they crumbled into dust as soon as touched, and I was unable to preserve either of them."

These finds baffled Layard completely. The burned walls, the skeletons, the Black Obelisk, the sphinxes—they told a story, but he could not fathom it.

Intuitively, however, he sensed, especially in the Black Obelisk, that he had uncovered one of the great prizes of archaeology. Only later, when the cuneiform code was cracked, would he learn that the monolith was erected in 841 B.C. by Shalmaneser III and showed him receiving tribute, including gifts from Jehu, the son of Omri, king of Judah.

When Rawlinson, with the help of others, made the initial breakthrough in deciphering cuneiform, the whole of Europe would be thrown into uproar and confusion. The inscriptions incontrovertibly revealed that Nimrod was Calah, the Calah of Genesis 10:11, and the first of the four cities built after the Flood. But if Nimrod was Calah, and it was, then where was Nineveh?

Layard's work pattern at Nimrod would have exhausted the most indefatigable of explorers. Daily he rose with the sun, and after a hasty breakfast spent the remainder of the day in the searing heat superintending the dig, making copies of inscriptions, preparing rubbings of bas-reliefs, arranging for the removal, packing, and shipment of finds. He jumped into freshly dug pits, struggled out of 15-foot trenches, handled the pick and shovel himself as the occasion demanded. Nightly he sat by a hot kerosene lamp comparing the inscriptions in his notes with the paper impression he had made earlier in the day, finishing rough sketches, going over the camp's accounts with Hormuzd Rassam, ordering supplies from Mosul and Baghdad, handling correspondence with the trustees, Canning and Rawlinson, and planning the next day's digging strategy. These tasks were rarely completed before midnight. Exhausted, he fell asleep in his rough-hewn bunk and slept soundly for five solid hours. As the sun's first rays touched down on the barren mound, Layard leaped from bed and embarked on another nineteen-hour work day.

Since Layard alone at Nimrod possessed even a superficial knowledge of "modern" medicine, he quickly acquired the role of country doctor. He himself was frequently downed by fever and chills; yet, the workers and their families had complete confidence in him. He treated them as best he could for trachoma, dysentery, and other chronic West Asian diseases.

He also found himself pressed into the role of justice of the peace whenever fights broke out. Domestic fights accounted for most of the disputes. As soon as a worker saved a few piasters, his thoughts turned to the purchase of either a new wife, new spear, or new cloak, usually in that order. "The old wife naturally enough raised objections," Layard said, "and picked a quarrel with the intended bride, which generally ended in an appeal to physical force."

Fathers and brothers of the bride-to-be were drawn into the affair to protect the family's honor. Their clan would soon join the fray to protect the tribe's honor. "I had almost nightly to settle such questions as these," Layard said. "Only on one occasion did either of the parties refuse to abide by my decision."

Free spirit himself, Layard also recognized that all work and no play would make his workers restless, if not dull. "I frequently feasted the workmen," he said, "and sometimes their wives and daughters were invited to separate entertainments, as they would not eat in public with the men." And the workers sometimes organized a party of their own.

After the day's work, Kurdish musicians frequently strolled through the camp and spontaneous dances were the order of the night. The dances lasted through a greater part of the evening, and Layard often felt compelled to exhort his men to get rest and save energy for the next day's work. Occasionally, the sheik of a neighboring desert tribe visited Nimrod. Around campfires, the sheik and his lieutenants would pass the latest gossip, news of vendettas, plundering expeditions, and assorted tidbits. By nature the Arabs are great storytellers, and Layard listened with enthusiasm.

When the nomads moved on, they in turn spread tales about the great wonders disgorged daily from Nimrod and about the all-powerful Frank who had been befriended by a jinn and had learned the secrets of the mound. Like a windstorm these stories swept across the desert, and Layard's "guest house" was almost perpetually occupied by visiting sheiks and others.

Often Layard's impoverished Arab workers entertained him at a "feast," a term pathetically misused in this instance. If a worker saved enough piasters to buy a handful of raisins or a piece of camel meat, or if he had a cow which occasionally yielded butter or sour milk, he would immediately summon his co-workers and Layard to share in his good fortune. "The whole dinner, perhaps, consisted of a half a dozen dates or raisins spread out wide, to make the best show, upon a cornsack; a pat of butter upon a corner of a flat loaf; and a few cakes of dough baked in the ashes," Layard said, describing such an occasion. "And yet the repast was ushered in with every solemnity—the host turned his dirty keffiah, or head-kerchief, and his cloak, in order to look clean and smart; and appeared both proud of the honor conferred upon him, and of his means to meet it in a proper fashion."

Layard knew and appreciated the meaning of poverty. His ability to empathize with downtrodden people largely accounted for his extraordinary acceptance in western Asia's melting pots. Although a Christian and a Frank, his workers spoke of him as "one of us."

By early December Nimrod's godown was bursting with so many sculptures, bas-reliefs, and other relics that Layard considered the moment propitious to send a convoy of treasures downstream. He rode to Mosul for supplies—mats, felts, and ropes. These were sent by raft to Nimrod while Layard returned to base by a fresh horse to superintend the movement of the treasures to the bank of the river.

The supply convoy, however, never arrived. En route from Mosul, the rafts were attacked and plundered by Bedouin marauders. Layard appealed to Mosul's governor to track down the culprits and recover his property. The appeal was in vain. "The Arabs of the desert," the Turkish governor said, "are beyond our reach." Although the loss amounted to only a few pounds, Layard considered the situation precarious. "If this robbery passed unnoticed," he said later, "the remainder of my property, and even my person, might run some risk." He foresaw a Bedouin attack on Nimrod itself, and an end to the excavations.

Several days later, Layard learned the name and location of the band that had pillaged the convoy. Accompanied by the *bairakdar* and another irregular—both heavily armed—Layard rode straight for the Bedouin encampment. The ensuing swashbuckling action belongs to Rafael Sabatini.

"We reached the encampment after a long ride," Layard said, "and found the number of the Arabs to be greater than I expected."

Layard's audacity stunned the Bedouins. No stranger, certainly no Frank, dare enter their turf.

"Peace be with you!" Layard signaled as he dismounted in front of the sheik's tent. "I know the laws of friendship; that which is my property is your property, and the contrary." Politely, he asked for the return of his stolen supplies. The sheik feigned ignorance. "O Bey," he replied, "no such things as mats, felts, or ropes have ever been in my tents." As he spoke, Layard noticed a new rope supporting the principal pole in the sheik's tent.

At a prearranged signal, Layard, the *bairakdar,* and the irregular drew cocked pistols, handcuffed the sheik, pointed a gun at his temple, rushed out of the tent, mounted their mares, and dragged the sheik after them at "an uncomfortable pace," with guns trained on him.

Layard's impudence paralyzed the sheik's followers. The sheik was taken to Nimrod, where he was given the option of freely returning the supplies or being handed over to the Turkish authorities at Mosul. With visions of the bastinado, the sheik quickly acquiesced to Layard's demand. The following day all supplies were returned together with a lamb and a kid as a good-will gesture. "I dismissed the Sheik with a lecture," Layard said, "and had afterwards no reason to complain of his tribe—nor indeed of any tribes in the neighborhood."

A week later, Christmas Day, he recorded the "satisfaction" of seeing the twenty-three cases, including the obelisk, floating downriver. As the keleks vanished from sight, Layard mounted his mare and galloped off to Mosul to celebrate the Feast of the Nativity with the few Europeans "whom duty or business had collected in this remote corner of the globe." His hosts, Christian Rassam, the consul, and his wife Matilda, prepared a banquet for the occasion.

But Layard worked even through Christmas week. He completed notes, wrote up his account ledgers, redrew his map of Nimrod, and dispatched a lengthy report to London on his work.

The trustees were delighted with his work and directed their secretary, the Reverend Forshall, "to express to Mr. Layard the satisfaction of the Trustees with the progress he is making and to enquire as to the intentions of Mr. Layard respecting the manner and time of conveying these cases to England in order that the antiquities may be insured against sea risque."

How long shall Ashur take you away?

—NUMBERS

CHAPTER 11

When Layard's convoy of rafts, bearing the first shipment of sculptures and inscriptions, reached Baghdad safely, Rawlinson was overwhelmed. Since the "marbles" belonged to the British Museum, he hastily wrote Forshall on January 27, 1847, for permission to write up the discoveries for scholarly journals. "Naturally I am anxious to communicate this information to the world," he said.

The trustees were delighted. They directed Forshall to "acquaint Major Rawlinson that he is at liberty to make any use as he thinks proper of the information he derived from the Antiquities which passed through his hands and that it is gratifying to the Trustees to hope that by means of Major Rawlinson's search, these antiquities may be soon made to contribute to the increase of historical knowledge."

Perhaps no stronger evidence of Layard's incredible successes may be found than in a letter to him from the Reverend Forshall. "[We] desire to compensate you upon your happy success," Forshall wrote, and announced that over Layard's objections about receiving payment for his work, the Museum had deposited £500 to his personal bank account as compensation for a job "well done."

When Canning learned how hard Layard was driving himself, he expressed alarm. "There is nothing," he wrote Layard from London February 9, "like taking things in time." But Botta, in a *"mon cher Layard"* note, congratulated his English friend and encouraged him to press ahead.

And onward Layard pressed.

During this second phase of the Nimrod dig, Layard made a remarkable discovery—a number of strange, white-yellow ornaments of "considerable beauty and interest." The objects, when uncovered, adhered firmly to the soil and were in so advanced a state of decomposition that Layard encountered great difficulty in extracting them, even in fragments. "I spent hours lying on the ground, separating them with a penknife, from the rubbish by which they were surrounded. . . . With all the care that I could devote to the collection of the fragments, many were lost, or remained unperceived, in the immense heap of rubbish under which they were buried."

After spending most of the day on his hands and knees in a trench some 20 feet below the earth, gathering up these curiosities, Layard retired to his shack and spent the night trying to piece them together and to determine their composition. Ross made one of his irregular visits to Nimrod at this time and joined in the game. "We often sat up at night trying to piece bits of inscriptions together," Ross said in a memoir published posthumously by his wife Janet in 1902. "But the greatest puzzle we ever had were strange bits of what seemed to be brittle whitish stone or porcelain.

"In vain they were turned and twisted," Ross wrote, "until one night the light fell at an angle on a splinter I had in my hand, and I recognized the waving texture of ivory." These were the fabulous Nimrod Ivories. They rank today among the world's greatest archaeological treasures.

When the objects reached England, chemists at once saw that age had completely broken down the animal gluten, leaving nothing but the calcerous substance of the ivory. Museum officials boiled the fragments in a glutinous compound—a form of Jello—and restored what centuries of burial had exhausted. The restoration was so admirable that when Layard ultimately returned to England, he hardly believed his eyes.

Layard also discovered in those first weeks of 1847 numerous clay-baked vessels containing human remains. The sarcophagi were generally bowl-shaped. "In nearly all were earthen vases, copper and silver ornaments, lachrymatories and small alabaster bottles," he said. He was able to preserve two skulls, although most of the remains crumbled on exposure to the air.

Among the coffins he found a well-constructed tomb, built of bricks and covered with a slab of alabaster, apparently the grave of a person of high rank. He sifted the human dust through his hands and found beads and small ornaments belonging to a necklace. The beads consisted of agate, carnelian, amethyst, and opaque colored glass. The prize was a magnificent lapis lazuli pendant shaped as a couchant lion. He also found copper ornaments.

Some of Layard's discoveries were breathtaking, among them the large ceremonial hall to a palace whose entrance was formed by gigantic winged bulls and lions. Between them stood a pair of *double* sphinxes, something he had not found before (nor has anyone since). The sphinxes were carved out of coarse, gray limestone.

Every wall of the huge hall had been scorched by flames. Clearly, the whole of Nimrod had been put to the torch in antiquity. The smoke and cinders of the city's destruction spread over Mesopotamia like an ominous mushroom-shaped cloud.

One evening, after a particularly exhausting day, an old desert nomad arrived at the dig and spent the night with Layard's workers. Nimrod's idols and jinns did not impress him. The Arab said he had seen the same thing at Khalah Sharghat years before. Layard, who had visited that mound two years earlier and returned to Mosul empty-handed, attributed his tale to "the fertile imagination of the Arabs." But the man persisted and wagered that he could show Layard the exact spot of one great piece of sculpture, carved in black stone.

Layard accepted the bet. Khalah Sharghat, he recalled from his first visit there, was infested by Bedouin marauders, notoriously dangerous. Nonetheless, he felt the marbles worth the game, especially since the latest reports indicated that a friendly and powerful sheik had pitched his tents near the mound. Accordingly, Layard sent ahead a small reconnaisance party while he led a well-armed column, including Rassam and his *bairakdar,* to the spot, several miles south of Nimrod.

Layard's party found the friendly Arab encampment about 10 miles from Khalah Sharghat. The sheik warmly greeted the Frank and his party and showed the Englishman off to his harem and even to his sister.

In the afternoon of their arrival they rode to the mound. The old Arab storyteller won his bet. He directed Layard's workers to a particular spot, and after an hour's digging they uncovered a sitting figure in black basalt, the head and hands missing. It was a beautiful piece of sculpture. The square block of stone upon which the figure sat was covered on three sides with cuneiform. Layard did not know it at the

time, but the figure was that of the Biblical king of Assyria, Shalmaneser
II. It was novel in one respect. It was the first life-sized figure of an
Assyrian Layard had ever seen. All the other figures were either
miniatures or colossi.

Impressed by the discovery, Layard ordered trenches dug at right
angles to the statue. His workers soon came upon walls, bits of basalt
with small figures in relief, portions of cuneiform-covered slabs, and
a series of now familiar tombs, shaped like dish covers.

In one coffin he found a superb copper cup, identical to one he saw
held by a king in a bas-relief at Nimrod. The cup linked Nimrod and
Khalah Sharghat.

Studying the mound with the eye of a seasoned excavator, Layard
suddenly understood the general plan of these Assyrian complexes.
"The principal ruin at Khalah Sharghat, as at Nimrod, Khorsabad, and
on other ancient Assyrian sites, is a large square mound, surmounted by
a cone or pyramid," he said.

Actually this was the terraced ziggurat, or temple tower, a distinctive
feature of Assyrian and Babylonian temples, that Layard was to learn a
great deal more about during the course of his excavations.

Layard was convinced that if he dug deeply he would make a
spectacular discovery. But he lacked the manpower to do the job. He
didn't even have the means of transporting the black basalt figure to
Nimrod and had to leave it where he found it.

As he departed, he speculated about the mound's identity in antiquity.
Judging by the fragments he found, as compared to those at Nimrod, he
concluded—rightly—that the mound was "one of the most ancient cities
of Assyria." It would have boggled his mind to know that Khalah
Sharghat was Ashur, the first capital of the Assyrian empire.

The spring of 1847 advanced rapidly across the land between the two
rivers, accompanied by severe drought. The water level of the Tigris
sank, and Bedouin raiders, driven from their waterholes deep in the
desert, encroached upon more permanent settlements, including the
villages near Nimrod. Not only were the Bedouins moving too close for
comfort, but in the light of crop failures, the peaceful Arab tribes, from
among whom Layard recruited most of his manual labor, planned to
move north to Mosul and beyond in search of water.

Once these tribes departed, Layard surmised, "the country would not
be only very unsafe but almost uninhabitable and I should be compelled
to leave Nimrod."

In this situation, Layard decided to terminate his excavations and focus on shipping the rest of his treasures to England.

To their credit, Forshall and the trustees of the Museum did not expect Layard to remove the winged bulls and lions from the mound. Botta had tried to do so at Khorsabad, they were aware, and the results were disastrous. Botta left one winged bull abandoned on the road between the mound and the Tigris. The other, which he had sawed into pieces, was still sitting in the sun at Baghdad awaiting a French vessel. In any case, the idea of sawing the winged colossi offended the British Museum's artistic sensibilities, and Layard was instructed to leave the fabulous creatures *in situ* and cover them with earth.

"I was loath, however, to leave all these fine specimens of Assyrian sculpture behind me," Layard said. His credibility was at stake. If he returned to London without these grand prizes, he was afraid that people would be "half-inclined to believe that I have dreamed a dream, or have listened to some tale of Eastern romance."

But how could he get the gargantuan statuary to London? The answer, he felt, was in the classics. Specifically, in the writings of Diodorous. "Semiramis, the Assyrian queen," Diodorous wrote in 50 B.C., "quarried out a stone from the mountains of Armenia which was 135 feet long and 25 feet wide and thick; and this she hauled by means of many multitudes of yokes of mules and oxen to the river and there loaded it on a raft, on which she brought it down the stream to Babylonia."

If Semiramis could move the stones in antiquity, why couldn't Layard do the same some three thousand years later? "I resolved," he said, "upon attempting the removal and embarkation of two of [them]."

From among the thirteen pairs of human-headed winged bulls and lions, Layard selected one bull and one lion, the smallest and best preserved, each about 14 feet in height and weighing about ten tons.

A working party was sent into the mountains north of Mosul to fell mulberry trees, the same trees employed by the Assyrians in the construction of roof beams for their palaces and fortifications. Layard also acquired the rusty iron axles Botta had used in transporting his sawn blocks to the Tigris. Each wheel was constructed from three solid pieces of wood, nearly a foot thick, and bound together, like a beer barrel, with iron hoops. Beams were laid across the axles and, in turn, crossbeams above them.

"Simple as this cart was," Layard said, "it became an object of wonder in the town." Like Lilliputians, crowds of Mosul residents gathered daily to inspect the gargantuan cart. When the cart, drawn by a team of bulls, was ready to leave the city, a local holiday was proclaimed. The governor's indolent aides lifted themselves from their divans; guards abandoned posts; bazaars were emptied; and half the population of the town assembled at the gates of Mosul to witness the spectacle.

Layard ordered the digging of a trench some 200 feet long and 15 to 20 feet wide from the base of the colossi to the plain below. He also directed the construction of a miniature railroad bed of greased roller ties over which to move the sculptures through the massive trench to the waiting cart. Incredibly, the Nimrod mound was so rich in archaeological treasure that in the midst of this new flurry of digging, Layard discovered another chamber and new slabs of magnificent bas-reliefs.

From Baghdad, with the compliments of Lieutenant Jones and the Royal Indian Navy, Rawlinson shipped Layard naval spares, including hawsers, jackscrews, blocks, and tackle. While waiting for the shipment to arrive overland, Layard superintended the packaging of the colossi. They were mummy-wrapped in felt and mats to protect them as far as possible from injury during transport.

By mid-March all was in readiness. The bull was the first to be moved. The earth and debris around the foundation were scooped away; thick beams were placed against the bull to support it; and a myriad of ropes were made fast around it's waist. Layard's three-hundred-man work force was now augmented by large numbers of Arab horsemen who descended, out of curiosity, to lend a hand.

Layard took a position on a high pile of earth overlooking the pit containing the bull, from where he planned to orchestrate the operation. "It was a moment of great anxiety," Layard said. And also of great din. There was so much noise that Layard could not be heard above the tumult and, in desperation, threw bricks and clods of earth at the working parties to draw their attention. "But," he conceded, "it was to no avail."

As the operation got under way, the drums and shrill pipes of the Kurds sounded like the advance of Scottish infantry; Arab workers, stripped to the waist in the broiling sun and half frantic with excitement, raised chilling war cries; women and children congregated on the sidelines shouting encouragement to the men.

The wedges were knocked away from the bull and the Arab workers strained to hold the ropes as it began to tilt over. Frantically, the Chaldeans threw water on the ropes to ease the strain, but the hawsers snapped like kite string and the workers holding the ends were catapulted backwards, like acrobats. The bull toppled from its foundation, and a cloud of dust swirled up from the bottom of the trench. "I rushed into the trenches," Layard said, "prepared to find the bull in many pieces."

The gods of Assyria, however, hovered over the dig: the bull was not damaged. "I saw it lying precisely where I had wished to place it," Layard said, "and uninjured!"

The Kurdish pipes and drums started up again, the women shouted and clapped hands, and the workers danced with joy. The sun was going down and the occasion demanded a party. Several lambs and cows were slaughtered, boiled, and roasted. Despite Layard's exhortations, the workers danced until dawn as if to demonstrate their ability to resist fatigue.

The following morning the bull was skillfully moved over the greased rollers, and as the stone monster reached the bottom of the mound, lowered safely onto the waiting cart. The oxen harnessed to the yoke, however, felt the enormous weight behind them and refused to budge. They were replaced by several hundred men, who proceeded to haul the great cart across the scrub desert.

With the *bairakdar* at his side, Layard rode at the head of the colorful procession. Then came the Kurdish pipers and drummers, followed by the cart itself. Tracking behind the vehicle were the women and children, shouting encouragement. The procession was closed by a troop of Arab horsemen who executed daring field maneuvers, raising swirls of sand as they raced up and down the column, their tufted spears held high, simulating cavalry charges.

Abruptly, the procession came to a dead halt. Two cart wheels sank in a rut, and every effort to dislodge them failed. Ropes snapped, men cursed. The sun set. Layard called it a day and left behind his *bairakdar* and a company of armed Arabs as custodians lest some Bedouin raiders make an effort in the middle of the night to steal the ropes, mats, and felts.

"My suspicions did not prove unfounded," Layard later reminisced. Scarcely had he returned to the base camp when rifle fire crackled across the desert wasteland. Hastening back to the mired bull, Layard discovered that a band of Bedouins had been driven off after a sharp exchange of musketry. One ball passed through the matting and felt and left its mark on the side of the bull.

The following morning after hours of backing and filling, the cart finally resumed its journey to the Tigris—and made it. It was a prodigious accomplishment.

In a letter to his mother, Layard expressed satisfaction with his work. "I have just moved one of my great winged bulls to the river and he is now ready to be embarked. I have succeeded in my attempt," he gloated, "while the French bull is still sticking half-way between the river and Khorsabad."

Next he set to work on the lion. To avoid a second spill, he doubled the number of ropes. Again, while clearing the rubble from around the base of the lion, he made a new discovery, inscribed slabs. Two days later the lion was sitting on the bank of the Tigris as complacently as the lions of Trafalgar Square.

While these activities were in progress, Layard directed another party of workers to build two enormous rafts, each consisting of six hundred inflated goat and sheep skins, for the more than 500-mile journey downstream from Nimrod to Basra, at the mouth of the Tigris. Layard estimated it would take about ten days for the rafts to negotiate the rapids and currents to Baghdad and another two weeks or more to complete the second leg of the journey from Baghdad to Basra, largely because the last 60 miles was a tidal current, ebbing and flowing alternately every six hours.

On April 20 there was a slight rise in the level of the river, and Layard rushed to exploit it. Very much in the style of launching a boat on a well-greased slipway, the bull and lion were slid onto the rafts as hundreds of workers held back their rapid descent with ropes. Two days later the keleks were pushed offshore and sent on their way—at the mercy of the gods.

For all practical purposes, the work at Nimrod was completed. Not too soon, either. In May, Layard brought the Nimrod excavations to an end when, in accordance with the instructions of the Museum's trustees, he began to fill in the trenches and pits and cover up the winged figures and bas-reliefs he was compelled to leave behind. The precaution was necessary to preserve the sculptures not only from the weather but also from the clubs of the Bedouin marauders and other Moslem zealots who were always quick to smash the idols of unbelievers. He also leveled his huts and fortifications. When the trenches were filled, the mound reverted to its former appearance, a barren, windswept escarpment. [A century later the British School of Archaeology in Iraq, headed by M.E.L. Mallowan, resumed the work left behind by Layard, and dug up anew the objects he had buried.]

Closing down the camp gave Layard and those around him a time for reflection. The sheik whom he had visited at Khalah Sharghat confessed that he was mystified. "In the name of the Most High, tell me, O Bey," he asked Layard, "what are you going to do with those stones?"

But something far deeper disturbed the sheik.

"Here are stones which have been buried ever since the time of the holy Noah—peace be with him!" the sheik said. "Perhaps they were underground before the Deluge. I have lived on these lands for years. My father, and the father of my father, pitched their tents here before me; but they never heard of these figures. . . . Lo! here comes a Frank from many days' journey off, and he walks up to the very place, and he takes a stick and makes a line here, and makes a line there. Here, says he, is the palace; there, says he, is the gate; and he shows us what has been all our lives beneath our feet, without our having known anything about it. Wonderful! Wonderful! Is it by books, is it by magic, is it by your prophets, that you have learnt these things? Speak, O Bey; tell me the secret of wisdom!"

Halfway to Mosul the road crossed a low hill, and from its crest both the town and the ruins were clearly visible. The long, dark and brooding line of mounds moved Layard deeply. He reined up his horse and looked upon them for the last time.

Back in Mosul, however, the mounds on the left bank continued to fascinate Layard. So thrifty had he been at Nimrod that he still had a little money left from the Museum's meager funds. "I proposed, therefore, to devote my last piasters to an examination of the ruins opposite Mosul," he said, "particularly the great mound at Kouyunjik."

After more than a year of digging, Layard still had not discovered the true site of Nineveh. Now, though he would not know it for some time to come, he was about to realize a lifelong dream. Kouyunjik had proved elusive to everyone who had dug there. When Guillois, the French consul, had heard of Layard's incredible successes at Nimrod, he had resumed digging at Kouyunjik, but, like Botta and Layard before him, he turned up nothing. He would dig a few feet at one spot, find nothing, and then go off in another direction and dig another hole. By the time Layard reappeared in Mosul, Kouyunjik resembled a Swiss cheese.

But the discovery of the "pyramid" or ziggurat at Nimrod and Khalah Sharghat had provided Layard with the ultimate clue. When he retackled Kouyunjik in June, he was convinced more than ever that great treasures were locked within the mound, palaces and sculptures that had eluded the spade because no one understood how the Assyrians built their acropoli.

Poking around the "pyramid" at Nimrod, Layard had learned the secret of digging up a Mesopotamian mound, a secret exploited to this day by contemporary archaeologists. Whenever the Assyrians erected a palace or temple complex they first constructed a platform of sun-dried bricks 30 to 40 feet above sea level. When the Assyrian acropoli were overrun and destroyed, the ruins remained on top of the platform and in time were covered by wind-blown sand and dust, forming great artificial mounds. "Consequently," Layard reasoned, "in digging for remains, the first step is to search for the platform of sun-dried bricks. When this is discovered, the trenches must be opened to the level of it, and no deeper."

At Kouyunjik, Layard put his men to work in search of the platform rather than sculptures and inscriptions. He was becoming a sophisticated excavator. After several days of digging he struck pay dirt, a platform of unbaked bricks some 20 feet below the crest of the mound.

Soon his workers reached the entrance to a chamber and uncovered a sculptured slab which had been almost completely destroyed by fire. Layard directed his men to follow the burnt wall. Next they stumbled across a foyer formed by enormous winged bulls, the largest Layard had ever seen, almost 17 feet in height. By mid-June, Layard had opened nine chambers, each fire-damaged. Many of the sculptures and reliefs had been defaced, apparently hacked by an enraged mob or a revengeful adversary. The architecture and sculptures closely resembled those found in the palaces of Khorsabad and Nimrod. But there was a notable difference. Everything at Kouyunjik was on a grander scale. The figures in the bas-reliefs, for example, stood fully 10 feet high.

Whichever direction he dug, new sculptures emerged, among them four pairs of fantastic man-headed winged bulls. The chambers were strewn with earthen vases and fragments of pottery, bottles and pieces of broken glass, and curious oblong tablets of dark unbaked clay covered with nail-shaped characters. The tablets looked like leaves of a book. As it turned out, they were.

The scenes depicted in the bas-reliefs were gruesome—foreign cities put to the torch by victorious Assyrian armies, lines of prisoners with their hands bound, people and cattle driven before their conquerors with rawhide whips, long lines of captive women cradling their children in their arms, the severed heads of the vanquished tabulated by Assyrian scribes. The scenes recalled the Old Testament's admonition about the Assyrians: "All who see ye shall flee." As at Nimrod and Khalah Sharghat, Layard was confused as to the true origin of Kouyunjik.

Unknown to him, he had found the exact site of Nineveh! The ruins were those of Sennacherib's palace, the Sennacherib of the Books of Kings, Chronicles, and Isaiah.

Earlier, influenced by Rawlinson, Layard had considered Nimrod to be Nineveh. Then he revised his scheme of things to make Nineveh an immense city, in conformity with Jonah's description of it as an "exceedingly great city of three days' journey." Now he wrote, "The position of the ruins [of Kouyunjik] proves that at one time this was one of the most important parts of Nineveh; and the magnificence of the remains shows that the edifice must have been founded by one of the greatest of the Assyrian monarchs."

Layard now considered Kouyunjik a "part of Nineveh," and he viewed the latter as encompassing an area stretching from Nimrod to Kouyunjik.

Of one thing he was certain: his funds were being rapidly depleted, his staff was inadequate for the task that lay ahead, and he had barely scratched the mound. Yet he was more than satisfied by his new discoveries. "The discovery of this building and the extent to which the excavations have been carried out," he wrote the British Museum in June, "I conclude establishes our claim to the future examination of the mound should the trustees be desirous to continue research in this country."

It only remained for him to wind up his affairs at Mosul. The winged colossi had safely reached Basra on the first leg of their journey to England.

England. He had not seen the white cliffs of Dover in almost eight years. If he was ever able to capitalize on his discoveries and land a diplomatic post, this was the moment to be in London. He even had money for the trip home. As another reward for his labor, the trustees of the British Museum, much to his surprise, had deposited an additional £500 to his personal account. It was a reward for moving the bull and the lion. Yes, the moment was ripe to return to England.

On June 24, 1847, Layard abandoned Mosul, accompanied by the bright-eyed, eighteen-year-old Hormuzd Rassam. Layard had proposed to Christian, the vice-consul, that he take the boy with him to Britain for a "proper education," the very same phrase the Austens used in discussing his own childhood. Christian Rassam readily accepted the generous offer.

Almost the whole town rode out with him to some distance from Mosul as a farewell gesture. His workers followed on foot, and as he passed through the gates of Mosul their wives and daughters, in an emotional outburst, clung to his horse, kissed his hand, and wailed their grief at his departure.

Layard reflected on his labors in Assyria. Scarcely a year before, with the exception of the ruins discovered by Botta, not one Assyrian monument was known.

Layard was neither deeply religious nor unusually superstitious. Yet his luck at Nineveh troubled him. For thousands of years the Assyrian cities had lain hidden under the Mesopotamian plains, awaiting a deliverer. Why him? "It had often occurred to me during my labors," he later confessed, "that the time of the discovery of these remains was so opportune that a person inclined to be superstitious might look upon it as something more than accidental."

In any event, Layard had produced convincing evidence in an age of increasing skepticism that the magnificence and puissance of the Assyrian empire, which had made Nineveh the envy of the ancient world and her fall the theme of prophets and poets, was not a myth.

> *Weary and worn,*
> *all his toil he engraved on a stone.*
> —GILGAMESH

CHAPTER 12

Fittingly, Layard reached London during the most joyous season of the year. He took a brougham directly to the stately Austen house at Montague Place, in Bloomsbury, a pebble's throw from the British Museum.

At Christmas dinner, over roast beef and Yorkshire pudding, Layard regaled his family with tales of adventure and discovery among the lost cities of Assyria. The Austens beamed. He was no longer their idle, drifter nephew. He was their godson again, and they took pride that he bore their name.

Layard not only talked of Assyria that day but also of another love, foreign affairs. He warned his listeners about Russian designs in the Near East and the need for speedy reform if the Ottomans were to save their empire, and he forecast impending revolution in France. (Layard stopped off in Paris on his way home—where he received a hero's welcome from French scholars who witnessed his presentation of his discoveries—and so his impressions of the political situation were fresh and first-hand.) His views on France shocked the Austens, who thought the royalists were in firm control.

Layard's fame extended beyond Montague Street. Oxford University, where he had placed Hormuzd Rassam for schooling, bestowed a Doctor of Canon Laws upon him, an honor he especially relished when he recalled his days at the Reverend Bewsher's school. He was also elected a member of the Athenaeum, a society founded some twenty-odd years earlier by Sir Walter Scott and Thomas Moore. Layard's name had also crossed the Atlantic. Miner Kellogg, an American painter friend, wrote from New York: "The Ethnological Society here have a *deep* interest in your discoveries and your letters to me have been read before it."

Sir Stratford Canning, returning to his post, wrote a note of encouragement from Switzerland dated January 2. "You must make the most of the Assyrian antiquities," Canning counseled. "Do them justice and yourself credit, and make the public understand that they got a prize."

His enthusiastic receptions in Paris and London, coupled with Canning's letter, suddenly made him acutely aware of the possibilities of using Assyria for a leverage in ascending the diplomatic ladder.

New Year's Eve he wrote Viscount Palmerston, the new foreign secretary, and requested a personal interview. Before Layard left for England on a stopover at Constantinople, he was informed that Canning had finally secured an appointment for him through Palmerston, and he wished to thank his benefactor. Admittedly, the letter was obsequious. "Although I have not had the honor of receiving your lordship's dispatch appointing me an attaché to Her Majesty's Embassy at Constantinople," Layard wrote, "an account which I have received at the Foreign Service will, I trust, be sufficient to authorize me to express my sincere thanks to your lordship not only for the appointment but for my nomination."

He also dropped by the British Museum and introduced himself to the secretary, the Reverend Forshall, who greeted him warmly and arranged immediately for a formal meeting between Layard and the trustees January 8. The meeting was chaired by no less a figure than the Duke of Cambridge, Victoria's first cousin and one of the Queen's favorites, who, behind his back, was called "Royal George." Others present were the Marquess of Northampton, the Viscount Mahon, Sir Inglis Bar, and the Dean of Westminster. Layard was moving in high circles. A record of the meeting reports that Royal George conveyed to Layard the "best thanks of the Trustees for his zealous, successful and in every respect satisfactory services. . . ." Thereupon Layard unrolled his collection of Assyrian drawings and launched into a description of his discoveries. The trustees were fascinated.

At that moment, however, the "Nimroud marbles" were encountering the same obstacles that earlier had confronted Botta. Layard's winged bull and lion were stuck at Basra with no ship on the horizon. So were the Black Obelisk, the Nimrod Ivories, and the lion-hunting scenes. Layard estimated there were "from 70 to 80 marbles and from 30 to 40 smaller objects." He appealed to the trustees to put pressure on the Admiralty to give the transport of the relics to England a naval priority.

A cloud partially darkened his otherwise bright homecoming: repeated malarial attacks. The disease now affected his liver and forced him to give up social drinking. It also forced him to postpone plans to return to Constantinople.

Although the state of his health improved over the next few months, Harley Street physicians insisted that he was still not strong enough to take up his post. Finally, in May, on the advice of his doctors, the foreign office extended his home leave six months. The extension dovetailed beautifully with his plans to write a book on his adventures and cash in on the excitement created by his discoveries.

During the writing of the book, he spent most of his time at Canford Manor, Dorsetshire, near Bournemouth, the home of a cousin, Lady Charlotte Guest, and her husband, Sir John, both of whom he had recently met in London. Layard regaled Charlotte's children with tales from the Arabian Nights. He recounted his own adventures in the East, and enthralled them with stories about the stone monsters he found buried in the earth—lions with wings, bulls with human heads.

Among the children, one in particular took a special fancy to "Uncle Henry," five-year-old Mary Enid Evelyn, whom he bounced on his knee and who bore a striking resemblance to her mother. Enid, as she was called, fell madly in love with her mother's Ninevite.

Though Layard's move to Canford Manor raised some Victorian eyebrows, there is no reason to believe that his relationship with Charlotte went further than an endearing friendship. Through Charlotte, he renewed his acquaintance with Disraeli, and he found his stay there pleasant and comfortable. As he wrote to Ross, back in Mosul: "The pleasure of English country life spoils one for the adventures and privations of the East."

In truth, however, Assyria was rarely out of Layard's thoughts. At Canford he worked steadily and happily, almost effortlessly, on his two-volume epic, *Nineveh and Its Remains*. He also produced a companion piece, *The Monuments of Nineveh: From Drawings Made on the Spot*, which contained one hundred plates and which was probably partly financed by the Guests.

While working on *Nineveh* and *Monuments*, Layard worked simultaneously on a third book, *Inscriptions in the Cuneiform Character*, a collection of the texts he had copied at Nimrod, Kouyunjik, and elsewhere. Any one of these three projects would have been more than enough for a professional writer to handle—and Layard was working on all three projects while recovering his health.

In a note to Forshall, he described the Nineveh manuscript as "a popular description of the objects discovered in the operations in Assyria." As usual, Layard's modesty failed to do him justice. His account of Nineveh was more than another travel book. Layard was creating a new genre in literature, the book on archaeology, in narrative form, which interwove scholarship, travel, romance, and high adventure. His impact on the literature of archaeology is as deep today as that of Edgar Allan Poe on the development of the detective story.

While Layard maintained an incredibly tight writing schedule at Canford Manor, he still found time to orchestrate further excavations in Assyria by remote control. Through Ross, Layard arranged for the reopening of the Kouyunjik excavations and the removal of the headless statue of Shalmaneser II from Khalah Sharghat (Ashur).

The extent of Layard's involvement with the mounds during this period is reflected in the exchange of letters and reports between Layard at Canford and Ross in Mosul.

On January 24, after inquiring about Layard's health, Ross wrote: "The excavations are much more promising than they have been for a long time past. I am digging in the S.W. corner, and half tablets of chariots and horsemen are coming out in regular series, and apparently leading to something good. But the depth of the trench is tremendous; and with the few men I have the work proceeds slowly."

The report ended on a familiar note. "I am at the last gasp for funds."

In March, Ross dispatched a work gang with mats and ropes to Khalah Sharghat to retrieve the headless statue. Layard had hoped to complete the job for under 2,000 piasters ($92). But Ross complained that "the Khalah Sharghat [sic] stone will cost a good deal more than you thought." He did not give the cost figure, but it probably cost another

179

$15 or $25 to excavate and transport to Mosul.

Meanwhile, Ross, in high excitement, reported that he had struck another mother lode at Kouyunjik. "The ground is so deep that we are digging in tunnels, breaking a hole here and there to give light," he said. "The roof is six or seven feet thick." Ominously, he reported that the frustrated French vice-consul had resumed digging at Botta's old stamping ground, Khorsabad, and that "Guillois has found a bull with an eagle-headed figure in one of the little mounds near Khorsabad."

By May 20 Ross was working so deeply underground that he could have used a Newcastle miner's lamp. "The excavations are regular catacombs," he said, "and in spite of the perforated skylights, I have to examine some of the slabs by candle light." The bas-reliefs were covered with scenes of sieges, with the Assyrians scaling ladders, and "headless corpses falling to the ground. The scenes," Ross wrote, "[are] in fact, just like the Nimrod ones, but completely charred."

On a lighter note, Layard inquired about his girlfriends. Bachelor Ross reported back that he was having so much trouble with the free and easy ladies of Mosul that he had barred his room to them and pledged "not another woman shall put her foot within my door."

Summer descended rapidly on the Mesopotamian plain, and the temperature soared. In June, Ross was forced to quit the dig—not because of the heat—but his father needed him at the Malta branch of their trading company. Ross left for Malta overland, via Constantinople, and in his first letter from the Mediterranean island, he wrote Layard, "Fancy at Kouyunjik, on the last day I was there, fragments of what must have been a barrel-formed terra-cotta cylinder with very small and beautiful inscriptions turned up." This was one of the Assyrian cylinders, among the most fabulous treasures in archaeology.

At Canford Manor, in the comfortable surroundings of Lady Charlotte and her children, summer slipped gently into autumn. Layard's health was restored and his maunscripts completed. The malarial bouts ceased, and he put on weight. Although he would have preferred to remain at Canford through Christmas, he could no longer delay his return to Constantinople. Canning was impatient.

As Layard prepared for his departure, the brig H.M.S. *Jumna* docked in October in Chatham, on the right bank of the Medway, 10 miles above its confluence with the Thames and about 30 miles from London, a principal Royal Navy station since the reign of Henry VIII. Her holds were packed with fifty-five cases of Nimrod treasures. Aboard was the most precious Biblical treasure unearthed at Nimrod, the Black Obelisk.

Layard rushed to Chatham to arrange personally for the transfer of the cargo to the British Museum.

At the Museum, on a fog-shrouded October 12, Forshall, the trustees, and other officials gathered around Layard as he pried open the cases. But when Layard looked inside, his temper flared. The treasures had been carelessly packed, the order in which he had crated them scrambled, and several pieces were missing! Suddenly he recalled a letter Ross had written from Mosul which had puzzled him at the time and which he had laughed off as bad reporting. According to the *Bombay Monthly Times*, Ross said, the local branch of the Royal Asiatic Society had conducted a seminar on "the remains found by Major Rawlinson [sic] at Nimrod" and that a rubbing of the Black Obelisk showed the inscriptions were probably Egyptian hieroglyphics. "So much for learned societies," Ross, the businessman, said.

As Layard stood in the basement of the British Museum in the midst of the opened crates, he realized that they had been opened and pilfered in Bombay on their way from Basra to London.

Pilferage aside, the trustees were delighted by the contents of the shipment (the winged bull and lion were still to come). In a letter to Foreign Secretary Palmerston, the Museum described Layard's collection as "one of the most important contributions to . . . archaeological science . . . in recent times." And it was.

The name of Nineveh will last to the latest ages;
and now the name of him who laid bare,
who brought to light its treasures,
will be handed down with it.

—WALPOLE

CHAPTER 13

In November Layard sailed for Turkey and on Christmas Day dined with the Cannings at the embassy. As Canning's indefatigable aide, Layard quickly returned to familiar routine. At 6:00 A.M., sometimes an hour earlier, he and Canning shared a pot of tea and went over a daily mound of dispatches. On occasion they postponed lunch until it was almost time for dinner. Nightly, Lady Canning retired at 10:00 P.M., but

Sir Stratford often worked through the night. "It was no uncommon thing for an attaché to enter his excellency's room in the early morning," a friend of the ambassador recalled, "and find him still in his evening dress. . . . Few men could toil as he did."

Few, except Layard.

Incredible stamina and unrelenting drive were among the bonds between Canning and his protégé. Canning also respected Layard's political judgment and increasingly relied on him to check his own impulsiveness. At the close of his lengthy career, Canning remarked that Macaulay and Layard were "the two most brilliant men I ever met."

Canning went out of his way to develop Layard's diplomatic contacts. For example, he arranged for Layard to be presented to the Sublime Porte, Sultan Abdul Mejid, in the ornate setting of the fabulous Seraglio. The audience had an amusing twist. Canning delivered an eloquent discourse on the illustrations of history furnished by Layard's discoveries and the moral to be derived from the fall of great cities. The official interpreter pithily summed up the oration. "This is the man who dug up the old stones." The Sultan nodded sleepily.

But it seemed questionable how long the strange relationship between the headstrong ambassador and the unpaid attaché would continue. Layard gave the impression of the independent dollar-a-year man, but he lived uncomfortably on handouts from Canning. Layard, now "middle-aged"—he was thirty-two—descended into increasingly frequent periods of melancholy over his inability to get a regular paying job, the nightmare that had haunted him since his days as an apprentice law clerk.

Suddenly and unexpectedly, the years of struggle and sacrifice paid dividends. In early 1849 his publisher, John Murray, brought out Layard's *Nineveh and Its Remains*. The book was such a brilliant success that even Murray was surprised. Nearly 8,000 copies were sold the first year, making it a runaway best seller.

"It is rarely once or twice—it may be in a century—that a book of this high character is brought before us," *Bentley's Magazine* said. The London *Times* was ecstatic. "The most extraordinary work of the present age," the reviewer said. "We question whether a more enlightened and enterprising traveller than Mr. Layard is to be met with in the annals of modern history." And the *Tribune* added, "The book has a rare amount of graphic, vivid and interesting narrative."

"No one speaks of any other book," Aunt Sara wrote from Montague Place. ". . . your course, my dear Henry, is now clear. *Nothing can stop you.*" The Royal Geographic Society honored Layard with the Gold Medal, and Uncle Ben accepted the award on behalf of the absent Layard. Benjamin Austen, who had spoken despairingly of his godson as a shiftless romantic, now saw him differently. "When he left England, he had no letters of introduction, and no patronage or assistance of any sort," Uncle Ben proudly told the Society's dinner. "But . . . he combined an indomitable and enterprising spirit . . . with courage."

The foreign office was also impressed. "Nobody asks: 'Have you read it?' " a colleague in the department wrote Layard. "That is taken for granted."

Coincidentally, with the publication of *Nineveh,* the schooner *Apprentice* docked at Chatham with seventeen more cases of Assyrian sculptures aboard, including the headless figure of Shalmaneser from Khalah Sharghat, the Ashur of Genesis. The relics were immediately placed on display at the British Museum. Book sales spurted.

By mid-year, *Nineveh* had run through four printings and Murray tore up his contract with Layard. He had agreed to publish the book on the usual terms of half profits. After the sale of the first edition, he wrote Layard that the sale had so far exceeded his expectations that he considered it right to give Layard two-thirds instead of half the profits.

Murray also sold the American rights to George Putnam, who dropped everything at New York and rushed into print with it.

As the adulation filtered down to Constantinople, Layard was embarrassed. "I am inclined to feel ashamed of myself," he wrote home, "as if I were humbugging the public, when I read the flattering notices in the press."

The adulation also embarrassed the government and the British Museum, both of which had treated Layard shabbily. Lord Palmerston, the foreign secretary, now described Layard glowingly as "extraordinary . . . enterprising . . . accomplished" and announced that he had been promoted, effective April 1, to the rank of *paid* attaché—still only £250 better than an unpaid attaché. Lord John Russell, the prime minister, was so overwhelmed by the Museum's exhibit that he ordered the first lord of the admiralty to dispatch a naval vessel to Basra immediately to pick up the winged lion and bull. And the Museum, with the government's endorsement, proposed that Layard lead a second expedition into Assyria, complete with staff artist, assistants, and medical officer.

Layard and Canning were elated by the news, especially the government's decision to underwrite a second expedition. Details were still forthcoming, but letters from Layard's relatives and Canning's foreign office sources indicated that the Russell ministry was pulling out the stops. There was talk that £20,000, and more, would be made available for a two- or three-year Assyrian campaign.

Hormuzd Rassam was instructed to return to Constantinople and assist Layard in organizing the expedition. On the voyage to Constantinople, Rassam was accompanied by Frederick Charles Cooper, twenty-eight and newly married, who had been hired by the Museum as the expedition's artist at £200 per season.

These developments elated Layard and Canning and restored their faith and confidence in Britain's national concern about art and archaeology. By God, who said the English were no match for the French when it came to spending money on culture? Here was the proof. The British lion held high its head not only as a military and economic power but also as a cultural force in world affairs.

Then the sky came tumbling down.

On April 1 the Museum sent Layard a copy of the expedition's proposed budget for two years. For the first season's dig, September 1849 to April 1850—the "cool" months—the government authorized and appropriated an expenditure of £1,500. The sum was to cover outfitting the expedition with new guns, spades, pickaxes, saddles, notebooks, transport animals, food, medical and other supplies; the salaries of Cooper, Rassam, and physician, still to be selected; the wages of 150 workers; and the costs of packing, crating, and shipping the finds downriver to Basra.

Canning lost his diplomatic aplomb. "Incredible," he roared.

Layard wrote the Museum: "Utterly impossible."

In Baghdad, Rawlinson heard the news, and could not believe it.

Layard and Canning sat up through the night working on the figures. After paying for general expenses, they estimated that the expedition would have left between £300 and £400 for workers' wages, and about half that amount would go to the cost of building rafts. The budget was utterly ridiculous.

The Museum sought to ease the tension. Sir Henry Ellis, the principal librarian, noted that the £1,500 would only be the first payment and that a similar amount would be appropriated for the second season, 1850–51. Layard thought Sir Henry was putting him on. But, in a private letter, Hawkins, the Museum's new secretary, cautioned Layard that the Museum was besieged by so many requests for funds that failure to accept the offer meant the money would be quickly diverted elsewhere.

Layard wavered for weeks. While he vacillated, *Nineveh* went into several new editions, and Layard suddenly had an unexpected source of income. (Layard was to earn £1,500 a year in royalties for many years—ironically, the very same amount the Museum proposed for the expedition's operations.)

On August 20, as the summer's heat waned on the Assyrian plain, Layard made up his mind. He would use the royalties to underwrite the expedition. Just as he made the trustees look small once before when he told them they could keep his salary, he again held a mirror up to their faces. "My private resources are far from considerable," Layard wrote, "but such as they are they shall be devoted to the undertaking." The trustees and the government climbed back in their hole.

A week later, Layard and his party bade farewell to Canning and prepared to embark on the journey to Mosul.

In addition to Cooper and Rassam, Layard had acquired the services of Dr. Humphrey Sandwith as the expedition's medical officer. Sandwith, it developed, was a bumbling, good-natured Dr. Watson, more interested in shooting parties than medicine. Four others completed the party: Layard's faithful *bairakdar,* who rode shotgun; his old *cawass;* and two new faces, a Catholic Syrian and an Armenian, as servants. Layard felt that after the hardships of the past decade, he was entitled to travel in a bit of style.

The British Museum's instructions to Layard were direct and simple. He was to "return to the site of Nineveh" and ship "selected specimens" of Assyrian sculptures and inscriptions to the Museum on Great Russell Street. Everything the party discovered and all the drawings made by members of the expedition were the property of the Museum.

On the morning after the party's arrival in Mosul, Layard rode to Kouyunjik and reopened the dig. "Little change had taken place in the great mound since I had last seen it," he wrote in his journal. "It was yellow and bare, as it always is at this time of year."

After Ross's departure, the digging had progressed under the direction of Hormuzd Rassam's brother Christian, largely to retain the British right to excavation, pending Layard's return. The elder Rassam, however, had hit upon a novel scheme for extending the operation and skirting the problem of removing thousands of tons of earth and debris. He tunnelled along the walls, sinking shafts at intervals to admit light and air. The tough soil, mixed with potsherds, bricks, and the remains of buildings erected atop the Assyrian ruins, rendered the technique simple and safe. When Layard visited the site, he marveled at Rassam's ingenuity. He felt he was in a Welsh coal mine. "The subterranean passages were narrow, and were propped up when necessary either by leaving columns of earth, as in mines, or by wooden beams," he observed.

The galleries were dimly lighted and lined with Assyrian art. Broken urns projected from the walls. Potsherds were strewn along the palace corridors. Strange statues occupied recesses and corners. Layard strolled through a unique underground museum. His heart throbbed with excitement.

"I lost no time in making arrangements for continuing the excavations," he said. He considered Rassam's method so effective that he imitated it.

Unannounced, his former work crews reassembled on the mound that morning and Layard soon put his old gangs to work in the bowels of the stifling mound, one hundred men divided into a dozen work parties.

Layard's luck at Kouyunjik continued to hold. Work no sooner resumed than he ran into a fantastic series of bas-reliefs in which "the history of an Assyrian conquest was more fully portrayed than in any other yet discovered." The king, accompanied by chariots, cavalry, and infantry, marched through forests and across mountains, storming enemy castles, occupying towns, carrying the war into the heart of the enemy countryside. The heads of the slain were piled up in pyramid fashion. The wounded fell under the feet of advancing cavalry. The bas-reliefs showed columns of prisoners: men chained together or bound singly in fetters, and women, some on foot, carrying into captivity children on their shoulders. The dominant Assyrian theme was war, and the horrors of war.

In a nearby chamber, which turned into a great hall, Layard found a new collection of gigantic human-headed bulls and eagle-headed and lion-headed monsters. One creature had a human head and the legs and paws of a lion. In the half-light, underground, Layard was reminded of the gargoyles adorning Notre Dame. The strange creatures provided an eerie backdrop to the proceedings as Layard and his workers shoveled away debris, propped up wooden beams in the shafts, and went about their work like groundhogs.

An engrossing eyewitness account of Layard at work in this period turned up in 1851 in the journal of Lieutenant F. Walpole, Royal Navy, who used his home leave to travel in the region.

Walpole inspected the subterranean passages firsthand. "Descending a few rudely cut steps, a narrow passage leads to one of the regular excavations; these were long galleries, some ten or more—perhaps fifteen feet high, and four or five broad, with the earth cut in an arch overhead, so as to render it less likely to fall in," he recorded. "Every fifteen or twenty feet a hole was cut in the top, open to the surface. . . . It was impossible to enter these [tunnels] without a feeling of awe." He described the bas-reliefs *in situ* as "beautifully cut" and added, "The inscriptions are as fresh as on the day they were executed." They recalled to him passages from the Books of Nahum and Ezekiel. "These [passages], as I sat," Walpole said, "I saw portrayed on the walls."

On October 18, with Hormuzd Rassam at his side, Layard rode off for Nimrod, the mound closest to his heart. The people of the area slew a sheep to celebrate his return.

Like Kouyunjik, nothing there had changed either. Assyrian sentinels astride the mound greeted him. "A few colossal heads of winged figures rose calmly above the level of the soil," he wrote. They were the two pairs of winged bulls, which had not been reburied on account of their mutilated condition.

Layard and Rassam hastily recruited their old work gangs and reopened the excavation. The pay scale was still pitiful, but so was the local economy. First-class diggers, exposed to hard labor and danger, received the equivalent in piasters of 13½ cents per day; second-class diggers, 9 cents. Those who filled baskets with debris also received 9 cents; general workers, 7 cents; and young boys, who sifted rubbish for treasure, 4½ cents daily.

For the first several days, Layard stayed at the nearby village of Nimrod—until the vermin drove him to living in a tent atop the mound.

On the second morning of his return, as he ascended the mound at dawn, he spied a group of travelers on the summit, their horses picketed in the stubble. He approached warily but was relieved to recognize his *bairakdar,* who pointed excitedly to an excavated chamber in the mound. Layard peered in and saw a man wrapped in a great cloak, deep in slumber. It was Rawlinson, wearied by a long and harassing night-long ride, exhausted after a bout with chills and fever.

"For the first time," Layard said, "we met in the Assyrian ruins."

The East India Company's resident was en route from his post in Baghdad to London, via Constantinople. Layard and Rawlinson spent three days together, but for the first couple of days Rawlinson was too ill to walk among the ruins. On the third day, his health improved slightly, and he and Layard made a hasty survey of the excavations. Rawlinson then continued his journey, wishing him well and lamenting that Layard had not been assigned to replace him at Baghdad.

At Nimrod Layard was also visited by Walpole, whose journal again supplied some interesting details. "I ought to mention," he wrote, "that the Arabs on the mound are all well armed, all have good serviceable muskets; these are long barrelled, and the stock short and light. It is a cumburous weapon to use without a rest." The young naval officer found the barrels "excellent" but observed that the springs in the locks were often faulty. "The shots, however, they make with ball are wonderful, and our table was supplied with hare or gazelle daily." The game, he added, was washed down with strong coffee "cooked on splinters of cedar wood, dug from the [ancient] buildings."

The camp itself was lively. The Arab workers shouted as they carried their loads. "They cursed the people who had made the place so strong, and the work so hard," Walpole wrote. Layard, if he was not directing the digging of a new tunnel or studying a new find, "was hard at work copying off inscriptions."

With the excavations at Kouyunjik and Nimrod reopened, Layard set in motion a whole new series of digs. He inspected the Assyrian ruins near Baasheikah, where a mound about the size of Nimrod stood, irregular in shape, furrowed by deep ravines worn by winter rains. He surveyed the Makloub Mountains, where he suspected the Assyrians quarried their stone. He scurried over the countryside, sextant in hand, taking bearings on the location of mounds (called *tels* in Arabic), among them Tel-Ermah, Tel-Shibbit, Tel-Duroge, Tel-Addiyah, Tel-Abou-Kubbah, and Tel-Kharala. He also revisited Khorsabad, the scene of Botta's triumph, and picked his way through his old friend's debris. "The sculptures in the palace itself had rapidly fallen to decay," Layard wrote, "and of those which had been left exposed to the air after M. Botta's departure, scarcely any traces remain."

Fortunately, however, in some places, Botta's trenches had collapsed, recovering and preserving the bas-reliefs. "Here and there a pair of colossal bulls, still guarding the portals of the ruined halls, raised their majestic but weather-beaten man-heads above the soil," Layard said.

Once again Layard waved his magic wand. He assigned several workmen to an unexplored part of the Khorsabad mound and—presto!—they no sooner touched their shovels to the ground than they found inscribed tripods and a collection of magnificently ornamented bricks with Assyrian figures and designs.

Layard spent Christmas Day, 1849, at Nimrod, with Stewart Erskin Rolland, late of the 69th Regiment, and his attractive wife Charlotte—a pair of English travelers who had attached themselves to the expedition—Rassam, Cooper, and Sandwith.

By February, within six months of reopening the excavations, Layard had collected enough new archaeological treasures to fill another wing of the British Museum.

At Kouyunjik, he discovered panels which showed in detail how the Assyrians moved the winged bulls and lions into their palaces—man-hauled on rollers with an assist from levers, blocks, and tackle. "I used almost the same means!" he exclaimed.

He also unearthed a facade of the Nineveh palace which consisted of ten colossal bulls and six human figures, some of them more than 20 feet high, grouped together and extending a length of 180 feet. One figure in particular took his fancy, that of a bearded giant holding a struggling lion in one arm and a sickle-shaped saber in the other. Layard dubbed him "the Assyrian Hercules." Actually, the giant was Gilgamesh, the hero of the epic poem of the same name, of Sumerian and Babylonian origin, which dealt with the Creation and the Flood.

Among the important finds was a continuous cuneiform inscription of 152 lines which neither he nor anyone else could yet read but which soon would be deciphered and would turn out to be the annals of the Assyrian king Sennacherib.

Many of the colossal figures in the chamber had been knocked over, and Layard felt the havoc had been wrought by a terrestrial catastrophe. "The same convulsion of nature—for I can scarcely attribute to any human violence the overthrow of these great masses—had shattered some of them into pieces, and scattered the fragments amongst the ruins," he said.

Layard also discovered a complete series of thirteen bas-reliefs, "sculpted with a spirit and truthfulness worthy of a Greek artist," depicting the Assyrian assault on Lachish, which, according to the Book of Joshua, was among "the uttermost cities of the tribe of Judah." Other finds included several glyptic or cylinder seals, which looked like a roll of postage stamps. Four bore Egyptian hieroglyphics, and one contained the seal of an Assyrian monarch and the cartouche of an Egyptian pharaoh. The double seal had apparently been affixed to a long-forgotten treaty.

At Nimrod, Layard unearthed another spectacular find—a chamber which appeared to serve as a repository for royal arms and sacrificial vessels. The room was a treasure chest of Assyrian history and art. Among the numerous items in it were a throne chair of wood overlaid with bronze; copper jars; bronze plates, cups, goblets, tripods, and cauldrons. The cauldrons looked as if they belonged in Homer's *Iliad*. Many of the bowls were covered with figures; on one, Layard counted six hundred. Some vessels were ornamented with bosses of silver and gold.

The chamber also disgorged objects of ivory and glass. One glass bowl, he would soon learn, bore the name of Sargon the Great, the scourge of the East, who lived almost a millennium before Christ.

As he studied these works of art, especially the repoussé work, Layard marveled at the detail. How did the artists of Assyria work in such microscopic detail? He found part of the answer in that same chamber: a rock-crystal lens. The convex side had been fashioned on a lapidary's wheel and was tolerably well polished. It had been employed as a magnifier.

Another prize in the chamber was a stockpile of arms, including swords, daggers, shields, and the heads of spears and arrows, "which being chiefly of iron fell to pieces almost as soon as exposed to the air," he recorded. The shields stood upright, one against the other, just as they had been stacked thousands of years earlier. They were bronze and circular, the iron handles fastened by six nails, the heads of which formed an ornament on the outer face of the shield. The diameter of the largest and best-preserved shield was 2 feet 6 inches. But the shields were in such an advanced state of decay that with "great difficulty" Layard was able to preserve only two of them and ship them to England.

In his own mind, however, his most important discovery was learning more about the secret of the strange "pyramid" which rose in the northwest corner of the Nimrod mound. Thirty men tunneled into it, and after penetrating 84 feet into the base, ran into a wall of solid stone masonry. They burrowed another 34 feet into the masonry and, in the process, discovered a flooring of sun-dried bricks. Among the bricks was a yellow earthen jar, rudely colored with simple black designs. "And in it [I] found bones, apparently human," Layard wrote.

Then it dawned on him. The cone was "a square tower, and not a pyramid." The ruin, because of its structure, had simply taken a pyramidal form. He pressed ahead. Finally, within the core of the tower at the base, he uncovered a vaulted chamber, 10 feet long, 12 feet high, and 6 feet broad. "No remains whatever were found in it," he said, "neither fragments of sculpture or inscription, nor any smaller relic."

But he uncovered evidence that the chamber had once been broken into and he surmised that, like the pyramids of ancient Egypt, which housed the pharaohs, tomb robbers had rifled the chamber of its embalmed king and treasure.

In the midst of these activities Layard still found time to arrange for the removal of the two great human-headed lions he had discovered earlier at Nimrod and for the transportation of these great objects by raft to Basra.

To protect them from the weather, prior to his departure in 1848 he had covered them with earth. The British Museum had directed Layard "to remove them entire," and in December his laborers had started building a road through the ruins to the edge of the mound. By the end of February the road was completed and the lions man-hauled down it with enormous levers and tilted over the mound onto two carts, their fall restrained by blocks, tackle, and curses. The carts were then dragged to the bank of the Tigris. The Arabs insisted that Mrs. Rolland, an object of uninterrupted attention and curiosity, ride the lions for good luck. She did so, and in this manner the carts finally reached the bank. But it was not until April, when the torrents of spring flooded the Tigris, that the lions were sent on their way aboard two keleks. One raft went aground in the delta and was given up for lost. But Felix Jones, Layard's old friend who had been promoted from lieutenant to captain while Layard was in England, skillfully sailed his steamer abeam of the shoal and rescued the precious cargo.

While removing the lions from Nimrod Layard again confronted the question which has haunted archaeology from its inception: the morality, or immorality, of disturbing the dead, the past.

In *Nineveh and Babylon,* Layard expressed his feelings about the lions solemnly, eloquently, and romantically: "We rode one calm cloudless night to the mound, to look on them for the last time before they were taken from their old resting-places. The moon was at her full, and as we drew nigh to the edge of the deep wall of earth rising around them, her soft light was creeping over the stern features of the human heads, and driving before it the dark shadows which still clothed the lion forms. One by one the limbs of the gigantic sphinxes emerged from the gloom, until the monsters were unveiled before us.

"I shall never forget that night, or the emotions which those venerable figures caused within me. A few hours more and they were to stand no longer where they stood unscathed amidst the wreck of man and his works for ages. It seemed almost a sacrilege to tear them from their old haunts to make them a mere wonder-stock to the busy crowd of a new world. They were better suited to the desolation around them; for they had guarded the palace in its glory, and it was for them to watch over it in its ruin."

While clearing out the repository for royal arms and sacrificial vessels at Nimrod, Layard's workers accidentally discovered two doorways leading from the chamber into separate apartments. Layard, the first to cross the threshold of the first doorway, found himself in a hall which led to two small chambers, each opening into the other. The chambers were paneled with bas-reliefs, but the greater part of them had been destroyed. Layard beheld a strange sight: the two chambers were entirely filled with cuneiform tablets. Layard had entered the royal library of Assyrian kings!

The electrifying discovery recalled to his mind Darius' order in the Book of Ezra to search "the house of rolls," and Layard christened the twin rooms "the chambers of records."

"We cannot overrate their value," he said jubilantly. "They will furnish us with materials for the complete decipherment of the cuneiform character, for restoring the language and history of Assyria, and for inquiring into the customs, science, and we may perhaps even add, literature, of its people."

The bricks, or tablets, were in different sizes. The largest measured 9 inches by 6½ inches; the smallest, not more than an inch in length and containing one or two lines of writing. The nail-shaped characters were in pristine condition, singularly sharp and well defined. In some instances, the cuneiform was so minute it could be read only with a magnifying glass. He collected more than 25,000 tablets from the library.

News of the discovery spread to the Continent rapidly. When Rawlinson heard of the find he was overjoyed. "A perfect cyclopaedia of Assyrian science," he forecast.

And he was right. When the cuneiform code was shortly cracked by Rawlinson and a tiny band of scholars, including, notably, Hincks and Fox-Talbot, it turned out that Layard's library contained dictionaries and grammars, treatises on botany, astronomy, astrology, metallurgy, geology, geography, chronology, tracts on religion and history, and a collection of royal edicts, proclamations, laws, and decrees.

Layard's discovery confirmed the tradition of Seth, the third son of Adam and Eve, who wrote the history and wisdom of the ages before the Flood on burnt and unburnt bricks so that the record should never perish. If water destroyed the unburnt bricks, the burnt would remain. If fire destroyed the baked tablets, the unburnt ones would harden.

At Kouyunjik, the site of Nineveh, Biblical archaeology was born.

Love among the ruins.
—BROWNING

CHAPTER 14

With the excavations at Kouyunjik and Nimrod running smoothly, the impatient Layard undertook a series of short forays into the countryside in 1850 in search of more mounds, more ruins—and more adventure. He found them all.

But these sojourns were hit-and-miss forays. In the back of his mind was a more ambitious project. He longed to mount a major expedition into untrod country, in particular the terrain along the uncharted Khabour River, which rose in northern Mesopotamia and ran west of the Tigris. But he needed an excuse to satisfy the trustees of the British Museum.

In March 1850, Layard received his excuse. A band of Bedouins from the friendly Shammer Arab clan descended on Mosul bearing a letter from their sheik. The sheik announced that "two colossal idols, similar to those of Nimroud," had suddenly appeared in a mound along the Khabour's banks, and he invited Layard to come to see for himself.

"I lost no time in making preparations for the journey," Layard said. He selected fifty of his best Arab excavators and a dozen Tiyari and Chaldean workers to accompany him. The party also included several Bedouin guides, as well as the indispensable Hormuzd Rassam, the Rollands, Cooper, and Dr. Sandwith.

The desert air exhilarated Layard like nothing else. The feeling of independence which he had first experienced when he and Mitford embarked on their journey to Ceylon a decade earlier again coursed through him. Like the nomadic Arab, Layard was a son of the desert. The desertscape was uncluttered, unlittered. Only in the desert did he feel as free as the air he breathed.

On April 3, the caravan reached its ultimate destination, Arban, on the banks of the Khabour, the encampment of Sheik Mohammed Emin, Layard's host and a leader of the Shammar Arabs. Layard immediately went to the spot where the colossal stone monsters were said to have suddenly risen from the earth. He was not disappointed. The river had gradually worn away the mound astride its bank and, during a recent flood, left uncovered a pair of winged, human-headed bulls, some 6 feet above the water's edge and fully 50 feet beneath the level of the ruin.

They were pygmy-sized bulls, sculpted from coarse limestone and about 5½ feet in height and 4½ feet in length. Their style of art also differed considerably from previous bulls he had found. The wings on the Arban specimen were small in proportion to the body and did not have the majestic spread of the Ninevite bulls. Also, the sockets of their eyes were deeply sunk.

Layard's first impulse was to start excavations. But, ever sensitive to the culture of the people around him, his first order of business was a reception for the sheik and his camp. Accordingly, he pitched a tent large enough to hold two hundred people. The party lasted two days. Charlotte Rolland, in her European costume, drew much attention from the Bedouins. So did the European men. It was the first time the sheik's camp had ever gazed on the notorious Franks. "They soon, however, became used to us," Layard said, "and things went on as usual."

At Arban Layard hired fifty of the Bedouin warriors to supplement his work force and launched a massive attack on the mound with spades and picks. Tunnels were opened behind the bulls. Trenches were dug into the surface of the mound. Immediately, a number of objects were recovered, including fragments of bricks with arrow-headed characters, jars, vases, funeral urns, and highly glazed pottery. On the fifth day a second pair of pygmy-sized winged bulls was discovered and a few days after that a magnificent lion in bold style with five legs. The lion was about 5 feet in height.

Among the most startling discoveries was a collection of Egyptian scarabs, some bearing the cartouche of the pharaoh Thotmes III, the Egyptian Napoleon, and another that of Amenophis III, who was succeeded to the throne by the heretic Akhenaten, the first monotheist in history, a precursor of Moses and father-in-law of Tutankhamen, whose gold-filled tomb was not discovered until a half-century ago.

Several tombs were also found in the ruins. "They contained human remains turned to dust," Layard reported, "with the exception of the skull and a few of the larger bones."

As April drew to a close, hot weather approached uncomfortably near, and Layard and his party broke camp for the return journey to Mosul.

The expedition ended, however, on a troubled note.

Layard was disgusted with Cooper and Sandwith. During the trip neither of them contributed much to the proceedings. Sandwith spent almost all his time on shooting parties, and Cooper kept mooning over his bride. Worse, on the return journey, Cooper and Sandwith came down with fever. So did Rassam, who became "dangerously ill." The caravan halted for five days while Layard and Charlotte nursed Rassam back to health.

These troubles were compounded by deepening tension between Stewart Rolland and Layard over Rolland's wife. During the two-month-plus journey, Rolland's admiration for Layard had developed into open hatred and jealousy as Layard's attentions to his wife became more and more obvious.

On one occasion in mid-April, as Rassam and the others recuperated from a bout of malaria, Layard, with Charlotte mounted behind him and clinging onto him for support, took off across the desert on a swift camel to visit a neighboring sheik's encampment.

Rolland apparently thought he had been made a cuckold, and several days later Layard reported a "painful scene" between the Rollands. Rolland beat her "most cruelly," Layard said in a private letter to a friend, adding, "I was alarmed by her screams and, seeing her struggle with him in an open tent, had him immediately seized."

When Rolland recovered from what Layard described as "his mad fit," he apologized, but Layard refused to accept the apology unless he packed his bags and left for England immediately. This is the chord on which the expedition arrived back in Mosul on May 11. The Rollands left the following day.

Several weeks later, in a letter to Henry Ross, who was then in Constantinople, Layard confessed, "I shall feel her loss as she is the only [English] person who has given me the slightest assistance—copying inscriptions, notes, M.S., and taking bearings."

Layard enclosed a sealed letter for Ross to give to her and added, "She will probably write a few private lines to let me know how they have got on, which she will entrust to you." Layard underlined the word "private." If Charlotte wrote, there is no record of it. In any event, she dropped out of his life.

After the Rollands departed for England, things at the camp grew progressively worse. Cooper and Sandwith came down with new attacks of malaria. During the frightful heat of the summer of 1850 they retreated into the hills around Lake Van, where Layard mounted another excursion in search of far-flung Assyrian sites while they tried to recover their health. But the mountain air did them little good, and they informed Layard of their intention to "throw in the sponge" and return home. Layard was disgusted. He and Rassam were as ill as they were, but clearly Sandwith and Cooper lacked the desire and drive to see the expedition through to the end.

Sandwith was not replaced. But in November the British Museum dispatched T. S. Bell, a former student at the government's School of Design, as Cooper's replacement. Bell turned out to be a young, brash, insensitive colonial type who lorded it over the misbegotten "natives." He reached Mosul at the end of February and barely lasted three months. Against the advice of the "natives," he took a swim in the Gomel River, a tributary of the Tigris, was swept under by the swift current, and drowned. His drawings were lost en route to London.

Except for the dedicated and devoted Hormuzd Rassam, Layard was now alone.

Both men were ill with malaria. "Fortunately our ague attacks did not coincide," Layard said later. "We were prostrate on alternate days, and were therefore able to take charge alternately of the work."

By the end of summer, however, half delirious from malarial attacks, the depressed Layard himself retreated from Mosul and took refuge in the mountains. "Few European travellers can brave the perpendicular rays of an Assyrian sun," he apologized.

And yet, in England and the Continent, as Rawlinson soon discovered on his return to London, Layard was a hero of the day. He was popularly referred to as either "the lion" or as "Mr. Bull," a nickname which stuck. His first winged bull and human-headed lion had just arrived at Chatham aboard H.M.S. *Apprentice.* They were quickly put on display to the delight and astonishment of the general public. Layard's "duplicates" also arrived, crates of Assyrian relics as gifts to Oxford University in repayment for their honorary degree and to the Guests at Canford. Indeed, Charlotte Guest added a new wing to Canford Manor and filled it with Assyrian antiquities—a lion, bull, bas-reliefs, and cuneiform tablets. She called it their "Nineveh Porch." Enid, her third child, seven years old, played hide and seek among her uncle's strange gifts.

That summer, too, a new edition of *Nineveh and Its Remains* rolled off Murray's presses and was soon followed by Layard's first foray into the scholarly world, *Inscriptions in the Cuneiform Character from Assyrian Monuments,* a handsome, coffee-table tome bearing the imprint of the British Museum and edited by Edward Hawkins, the Museum's new secretary.

To his surprise, the British Museum appropriated another £500 to his fieldwork and implied that there was more to come. With the infusion of new funds, Layard turned his eyes southward. "The winter was now drawing near," he wrote in his journal, "and the season was favorable for examining the remains of the ancient cities in Babylon."

On December 5 he formed a caravan to travel to Hillah, 60 miles south of Baghdad, just north of the ruins of ancient Babylon. There he established "winter quarters" and celebrated Christmas, 1850.

Layard's initial focus of interest was a great ruin about 5 miles from Hillah which dominated the horizon and was the first great mound he had seen on approaching Babylon from the north. The Arabs told him it was the Mujelibe, "the overturned," the site of the Tower of Babel.

Layard went to the spot and assaulted it with pick and spade. He employed Rich's memoirs as a guide and in particular searched for the underground chamber where Rich had found a wooden coffin and skeleton. Success was almost immediate. Within a few days Layard had not only located the lost chamber but had also amassed a splendid collection of burnt bricks inscribed with two lines of cuneiform. In another year or two, with the deciphering of cuneiform, the lines turned out to be the name and titles of Nebuchadnezzar.

Beneath the chamber Layard unearthed several coffins. "They still held skeletons, more or less entire, which fell to pieces as soon as exposed to the air," he said. "No relic or ornament had been buried with the bodies. The wood of the coffins was in the last stage of decay, and could only be taken out piecemeal. A foul and unbearable stench issued from these loathsome remains."

Clearly the coffins were of a comparatively recent period. But Layard's disappointment was assuaged by the discovery of small glass bottles, bronze and iron arrowheads, earthenware in different forms and shapes, and some vessels glazed with an especially rich blue color, like a Tintoretto painting.

Then he realized that if original ruins existed in the mound they must be at ground level. He abandoned his ghoulish work in the trench atop the mound, and opened tunnels at the base.

"A few days' labor enabled me to ascertain that we had at last found [an] ancient building," he said. In great excitement, he and his workers tore at the mound and were rewarded by the discovery of a series of walls. Layard had reason to believe that he was hot on the trail of a major discovery. "But I failed to trace any plan," he said in disappointment, "or to discover any remains whatever of sculptured stone or painted plaster."

Layard now turned his attention to the site of Babylon itself. The area was a shambles of debris. "On all sides," he recorded, "fragments of glass, marble, pottery and inscribed brick are mingled with that peculiar nitrous and blanched soil which, bred from the remains of ancient habitations, checks or destroys vegetation and renders the site of Babylon a naked and hideous waste."

Once again, however, an area of promise turned into a quagmire of futility. His prize discoveries there were fragments of glass inscribed on the inner surface with letters "in form not unlike Hebrew." He shipped the fragments to England, where Thomas Ellis, a celebrated mid-Victorian Hebrew scholar in the British Museum's manuscript division, identified the writings as belonging "to the descendants of those Jews who were carried captive by Nebuchadnezzar to Babylon and the surrounding cities."

But beyond these bits and pieces, Babylon was a bust.

Layard was now thirty-four years old, lean and bearded. He missed the creature comforts of mid-Victorian England, of the cricket on the hearth, and, above all, Canford Manor. He recognized that for a true archaeologist and Assyriologist there was no journey's end. Yet he had reached the end. The terrible heat, the vermin, the repeated bouts of ague, the coarse way of Mesopotamian life, the parsimony of his financial backers, his uncertain future—all combined to bring him to a dead end in his search for a lost world.

The moment had come to return to England.

By the middle of March, Layard was back in Mosul. He stayed long enough to put his affairs in order, and a month later, he left for England via Constantinople, just before the heat of summer descended on the Assyrian plain.

He knew he would never return. But Assyria was not done with him—nor he with her.

I can forgive Layard for finding Nineveh;
I cannot forgive Nineveh for finding Layard.
                                        —EMILY EDEN

CHAPTER 15

The thirty-five-year-old Layard could not have timed his return home more dramatically. In 1851 a new mood of national pride and unity swept England. He arrived in London in July, two months after the opening of the Great Exhibition, the first modern world's fair. The fair's central attraction was the Crystal Palace, a towering mass of iron and glass which rose 282 feet above Hyde Park.

Much to Layard's astonishment, Nineveh was the topic of the moment. Public schools offered prizes for essays based on Ninevite themes— composed, of course, in Latin. Walter Savage Landor, the author-hero of an impressionable young Layard when he struggled with Uncle Ben's law books, published a poem in Layard's honor. "Layard!" he sang, "who raisest cities from the dust." Layard was made a Citizen of London and given the keys to the city.

But Layard's first thought on reaching London was neither the Great Exhibition nor Nineveh. It was on Canford Manor and Lady Charlotte Guest.

Ignoring his mother, brothers, and the Austens, Layard beat a track straight to Dorsetshire. Charlotte, now thirty-seven, as lovely as ever, warmly greeted her "Ninevite," as she called him, and, despite his state of weariness, arranged a swirl of soirees for him. He was put on display like an Assyrian trophy. After a fortnight of this, Layard threw up his hands. "I am heartily sick of London," he wrote, "and its great people."

Thereafter, life at Canford Manor quieted down. Layard contented himself playing games with the children, eight-year-old Enid, her brothers and sisters, and their friends.

John Guest was bedridden at the time, and Layard spent Christmas week that year at Canford. Lord Bessborough, a relative of Charlotte's and the editor of her diaries, said, "He made himself responsible for entertaining the ten children, so leaving Lady Charlotte to look after her husband."

When Sir John died the following year at the age of sixty-seven, Charlotte went into mourning for six months, and on her first venture in public, she joined Layard at Covent Garden to hear *Fidelio*. "I felt some scruples on the matter of this first going out again," she wrote in her diary, "but I muffled up going and coming, and sat at the back of the box, and so escaped notice." The gossips were having a field day, however, and Layard's name became linked romantically with his cousin's.

In London, Layard made the rounds—his mother's place, the Austens, the British Museum, the Foreign Office, and John Murray, who urged Layard to cash in on the Nineveh craze by coming up with an edited, popular account of *Nineveh and Its Remains*. While recovering his health, Layard worked on the project and completed the editing in September. Murray rushed it into print. Fourteen thousand copies were sold within a year. The book was so popular it was reissued in 1867. In New York, Harper's brought out an American edition; at Leipzig, a German edition appeared.

Simultaneously, in a tour de force, Layard also worked on two other books, his mammoth *Discoveries in the Ruins of Nineveh and Babylon* and a new coffee-table volume, *Second Series of the Monuments of Nineveh.*

Archaeology's growing popularity prompted the British Museum to put Layard in charge of a third expedition into Assyria. To the trustees' consternation, however, Layard balked. He had at last had his fill of the Arab world.

"I shall certainly not leave England again if I can help it," Layard confided to Ross. He also made known his views to Rawlinson, who was about to return to Baghdad for another tour as British proconsul in Mesopotamia, and Hormuzd Rassam, who had recently returned to England, with Layard's connivance, and hoped to take up permanent residence there.

Matters quickly came to a head.

A subcommittee of the trustees met with Layard and Rawlinson at the British Museum, Saturday, August 2, 1851, "to confer with Mr. Layard and Colonel Rawlinson as to the continuance of researches in Assyria." The Museum passed the ball to Rawlinson and agreed to finance a new, two-year expedition under his charge at a rate "not to exceed £1,500 per annum."

Layard's decision not to return to the East left him in an awkward and familiar predicament. Other than royalties from his books, he had no source of income. But what kind of employment should he seek? "I should like," he confessed to Ross, "to get into Parliament in England and think that, if once there, I could push my way."

With the new year Layard's fortunes altered, abruptly and favorably. On January 2, 1852, the prime minister, a liberal, invited him to No. 10 Downing Street for an interview. Lord Russell had heard much about the young man from Canning, and Canning's replacement, Lord Cowley, who was now taking up a new post as Her Britannic Majesty's envoy to France, the foreign office's most attractive and sensitive mission.

Cowley promptly offered Layard a plum, the position of embassy secretary at Paris at £500 pounds a year. Before Layard could leap at the opportunity, however, Russell's foreign minister, Lord Granville, astonished Layard—and London—by naming Layard undersecretary of the foreign office.

The reason for surprise was Layard's lineage. His family did not belong to that small cluster of names that ruled the empire, a coterie of power brokers who played musical chairs as Liberal and Tory governments rose and fell during Victoria's reign. Indeed, nepotism was one of the critical weaknesses of Victorian England, not only at the top but right down the line. The spoils system, based on family connections, was encouraged; advancement on merit, discouraged. On occasion new blood was pumped into the system. Layard was one example; Disraeli another.

Layard's appointment was enthusiastically received by public and press, Canning wrote a note of congratulations; so did Disraeli, who was pushing his way in Parliament in a manner that Layard envied. The Austens were delighted. Sara told everyone that the Austen influence during his adolescence probably had much to do with sweeping him into the corridors of power. Uncle Ben termed the appointment "an accomplishment of all my hopes."

The euphoria lasted nine days. On February 20 Russell's ministry fell. But when the House of Commons was dissolved, Layard saw the opportunity to enter politics, and grabbed it.

Layard contested in Aylesbury township, where his parents had lived and his father had died eighteen years earlier. Although Aylesbury was considered a safe Tory seat, Layard was confident of victory. He swept the polls. "It was a complete triumph," Layard said July 9, "and most gratifying."

In Parliament, he lived up to his nickname Mr. Bull. He was a bull in a china shop—and was thus depicted in a cartoon in *Punch.* He was a maverick, a liberal conservative and a conservative liberal. No label, no slot, no pigeonhole, no political party fitted him. Ardent liberals and conservatives misunderstood him. "My position is . . . a delicate one," he told Ross. "Taking an independent line, I cannot, of course, expect much from the government that is now in power, and, on the other hand, I have completely broken off with the other party."

He was denounced on both sides of the House. In a classic remark, one of his critics, the author Emily Eden, declared that she could forgive Layard for discovering Nineveh but she could not forgive Nineveh for discovering Layard.

In parliamentary debates, Layard bristled. He descended into personalities, and on one occasion his remarks in the house had to be bowdlerized for the permanent record.

Lord Aberdeen, who had blocked his appointment to the diplomatic service more than a decade earlier, was his *bête noire*. He assailed Aberdeen's appeasement of Russia. "Where are you to stop Russia?" Layard asked. "How many centuries did they not throw back the civilization of mankind!" During the Crimean War he visited the front and was appalled. He accused the government of sacrificing thousands of British lives "on the shrine of inconsistency and neglect." He toured India, the jewel of empire, shortly after the Indian mutiny of 1857, and was shocked. "The people we govern are treated like a distinct race, inferior to us—more, indeed, as if they were a lower order of creatures," he declared.

Layard defended Cavour and the emergence of liberal institutions in Italy, and he rallied to the cause of the Turk while a horrified, evangelical Gladstone denounced the Sublime Porte as a "barbarian." Layard raised almost everyone's hackles, including Victoria's, on about every issue that came before Parliament.

Yet in private, he had admirers. Disraeli, who soon emerged as the most colorful and powerful prime minister of the century, described Layard as "a genius" and often joshed him for not joining the Tories.

In 1857, when Layard opposed reprisals against India for the "mutiny," he was defeated for reelection.

In 1860, after an absence of three years, he was returned to Parliament. The advancing years had softened him, although he was always at the ready to mount a barricade if he felt the issue before the house warranted it. Primarily he spoke out on the need for administrative reform (the domestic issue of the day) and foreign affairs. His expertise in the latter field attracted the notice of both sides of the house. "The ability, and what is more, the personal knowledge and experience, which he brought to bear on [various] subjects, drew general attention to him," Lord Aberdare, a close associate, later wrote in a memoir. Disraeli, moving to the pinnacle of imperial power, watched him carefully.

Layard's vision of foreign affairs was a mix of imperialism and reform. Observers of the post-mid-Victorian period took to calling him "the first Liberal Imperialist."

In 1861 Palmerston formed a new Liberal government and Layard's old admirer Lord Russell was named foreign secretary. The new government offered back Layard his old post as undersecretary of state for foreign affairs. Layard jumped at it. Public, Parliament, and press applauded the appointment. But behind the scenes Palmerston had engaged in a push-and-shove match with the Queen. Victoria thought of Layard as a brash, incandescent critic of her regime. She did not understand that his endless calls for reform were designed to preserve the empire. In an exchange with Palmerston, she tartly reminded the prime minister that the post should be held by "a thorough gentleman," and in her view, Layard was no gentleman.

But Palmerston had his way. The age of the divine right of queens was long past. Layard's polished performances in the foreign office, however, soon won over Victoria, and the Queen became one of his ardent admirers, although she never forgave him for his past indiscretions, especially his attacks on the bloated aristocracy and its blundering in the Crimean War.

Aunt Sara, now seventy, beamed over her godson's appointment and predicted that Layard was on the high road to No. 10 Downing Street. A month later, however, the joy was taken out of her life. After a long illness, Benjamin Austen passed away. In his last will and testament he left Layard, his apprentice law clerk and godson who bore his cognomen, a token bequest of £500. Sara died seventeen years later.

Layard plunged into foreign affairs, his forte, with zest. He profited from his early travels and adventures. With aplomb, he dealt with the election of the Greek king in 1863, the Serbian Question (which ultimately led to World War I), the American Civil War, Bismarck and Schleswig-Holstein, King Theodore of Abyssinia, and so forth. But Layard still had some rough edges.

"Endowed with an independence of character, which was often rather rough in its manifestations . . . ," Lord Aberdare, who edited some of Layard's papers, wrote later, "he was also hampered in his political career by the fact that he represented a combination of views and opinions which was in his time quite strange and exceptional."

In 1868, when Gladstone assumed the prime ministership for the first time, the new head of government promptly removed Layard from politics and shunted him into the post of chief commissioner of works and buildings, a position which admitted Layard to the Privy Council and empowered him to rule over urban renewal and the construction of new buildings in the seat of empire.

Layard took the new appointment in stride. He had always considered the British Museum "a monstrous building" and London an architectural mess. He immediately drew up imaginative—and costly—plans to beautify the Museum and the capital. Based on his excavations in Assyria, he entertained definite ideas on the subject. But the cost of the projects horrified the treasury. When the exchequer informed Gladstone, the prime minister blanched.

Layard lasted on the job ten months.

He was accused of throwing away public funds on architects, sculptors, painters, and "market-gardeners," i.e., landscapers. When he ordered mosaics to be imported from Italy and installed in the Houses of Parliament, there was an uproar over waste. "The only condition is to be," Mr. Bull bellowed, "not how well but how cheaply can a thing be done and that will not do for the arts!" His political enemies unjustly accused him of profiting from the mosaic project because of his financial interest in Murano, the Italian company which received the contract.

Layard was outraged. He was fed up with domestic politics.

He was also an embarassment to Gladstone, and in 1869, a year after taking office, the prime minister eased him out by offering him an appointment abroad, as minister in Spain.

I caused my lady to dwell . . .
in joy and happiness.
—TUKULTIURTA

CHAPTER 16

For Layard, the year 1869 was a watershed. Not only did he give up his desire to "push his way" through politics, but he also abandoned his bachelorhood.

For years, there had been gossip about Layard's incessant visits to Canford Manor. Lady Charlotte, of course, was the focus of the petty talk. But within two years of Sir John Guest's death, she silenced that gossip and provided rumormongers with another field day—by marrying her son's tutor!

At the time of her husband's death, Charlotte had engaged one Charles Schreiber, at a salary of £400 a year, to coach her sixteen-year-old son Merthyr. Schreiber was eleven years Merthyr's senior and fourteen years Charlotte's junior. On April 10, 1855, she married him. Schreiber's mother was ambivalent about the wedding. "This is nothing to be ashamed of, though there may be much to be said for and against, on both sides . . .," she had written the couple when they revealed their plans to her the previous November.

Layard had no such ambivalence. He strongly disapproved of her action, and relations between Layard and Charlotte cooled appreciably. Charlotte felt hurt. There were stories, unsubstantiated, that he had hoped to marry her.

Apparently Charlotte's ten children also took a dim view of their mother's remarriage, and life at Canford Manor lost much of its festive air and attractiveness for the Guest children, just as it had for Layard.

In 1857, in an August 1 diary entry, Charlotte again expressed dismay over Layard's behavior. "He cannot forgive my marriage," she wrote.

But not longer after, Layard appeared to have undergone a change of heart. Within two years he was visiting Canford Manor frequently as in the past. Victorian tongues wagged the more—but inconclusively. Now what was the object of Layard's incessant trips to Canford?

During this period the ranks of Layard's bachelor friends from his adventurous days in Constantinople, Baghdad, and the other fleshpots of the East thinned noticeably. Henry Ross, at the age of forty, had wed eighteen-year-old Janet Duff Gordon; Rassam, at forty-three, married a girl half his age, Anne Elizabeth Price, the daughter of a captain formerly in the 77th Highlanders; Rawlinson, at the age of fifty-two, wed a twenty-three-year-old beauty, Louisa Seymour.

Then, in early Janaury 1869, Layard titillated London Society. He proposed—to Enid, Lady Charlotte's daughter, the tyke he had bounced upon his knee when he first returned from Assyria. Tiny Enid had ripened into a tall, slender, and lovely young woman of twenty-five. She possessed classic features, an aquiline nose, blue eyes, and honey-colored tresses that fell to her shoulders. Mr. Bull had always been the love in her life, first paternally (her father died when she was eight), and, after adolescence, in a surprisingly and completely different way. Whether or not she was waiting for him and whether or not he was waiting for her is not known and will never be known. Layard and Enid were private about their most intimate relationship.

Whatever the case, Enid did not hesitate a moment. She readily accepted Layard's proposal. As an engagement present, he snapped around her thin left wrist—it was slender enough for him to encircle it with his thumb and index finger—an exquisite bracelet fashioned from Esarhaddon's seal.

The reaction of the prospective in-laws was mixed. Now it was Lady Charlotte's turn to be discomfited. Her daughter's decision took her by surprise, and it took a couple of months to turn her around. Layard's mother, who had never remarried and was now sixty-six (she died in 1879 at the age of eighty-nine), also harbored reservations. "I hope that she [Enid] will never regret the change," Marianne Layard wrote Charlotte.

Many of the couple's friends entertained similar misgivings. Not only was Enid twenty-seven years younger than Layard, but she had led a relatively sheltered, almost cloistered existence at Canford. By contrast, Layard was worldly, roisterous, restless, and explosively aggressive.

Marriage bonds were posted March 3 and the wedding took place swiftly, six days later. As a wedding gift, Layard presented his "darling Enid," as he fondly called her, a unique piece of jewelry, a necklace fashioned from several cuneiform cylinders.

The couple honeymooned at Dorking, in Surrey, then the lush valley of the Mole River, between the escarpment of North Downs and the sandy heights of Leith Hill. Layard found time to drop Lady Charlotte a note; he apparently always had time to write letters. "I am," he wrote unabashedly, "more in love with her than ever."

The marriage was a brilliant success and outlived many of the gossipers of the day. It was an idyllic union. Layard never left her side and never looked at another woman. Early in their marriage, Enid confessed "with astonishment" that her happiness with Layard was complete, although they were destined to be childless.

In physical appearance they were in striking contrast. She stood a head taller than he, and she retained a slim figure while Layard's silhouette grew increasingly rotound. She frequently dressed in sparkling white, a color that matched Layard's egret-white hair and beard. In company, Layard was his usual witty and explosive self; she, low-keyed, demure, and radiant.

When Gladstone offered Layard the Spanish embassy with the rank of minister extraordinary, Layard talked it over with Enid at breakfast, their most intimate meal. This was their first big decision together. He deferred to her. She approved and he promptly notified the prime minister that he accepted the appointment.

Layard's career in domestic politics was at an end. So was his life in England. Thereafter, like Canning before him, he lived largely abroad. Inevitably, power politics led him back to Constantinople and, from there, by remote control, back to Assyrian archaeology.

During Layard's early years in Spain, Assyrian archaeology continued to languish in the doldrums which enveloped it during the Crimean War—despite the breakthrough in the decipherment of cuneiform. Logically, that wonderful discovery should have dictated burgeoning interest in Assyriology. But logic is not mankind's strong suit.

Layard recognized this human condition. Interest in Assyria, he forecast, will revive only when there is "some discovery so important as to excite attention and curiosity."

In 1873, three years after Layard and his bride settled at Madrid, the "exciting curiosity" exploded on the front pages. The trigger was pulled by George Smith, who flashed across the archaeological firmament like a meteor.

Smith was born into an impoverished Chelsea family in 1840 and was apprenticed to Bradbury & Evans to learn banknote engraving. This was the firm that in 1854 published Layard's guide to the Nineveh Court at the Crystal Palace. The booklet fascinated Smith. Just as Layard's imagination had been fired from an early age by the *Arabian Nights*, Smith's was set aflame by Layard's discovery of Nineveh and his adventures in Assyria.

Smith spent the greater part of his lunch hour each day at the British Museum, studying Layard's finds. He spent the greater part of his modest earnings on books by Layard, Rawlinson, Ferguson, Vaux, Loftus, and others. Over a period of time, Rawlinson, who maintained a workroom at the Museum, took notice of the youth's almost daily visits to the Assyrian section. Impressed by Smith's enthusiasm, Rawlinson gave him permission to study paper casts of cuneiform tablets in his workroom. There Smith displayed a rare gift for deciphering cuneiform, and after a short while Rawlinson (who, it will be recalled, was one of the original decipherers of cuneiform) landed him a position as an assistant in the Museum's department of antiquities.

"Everyone has some bent or inclination which, if fostered by favorable circumstances, will color the rest of life," Smith wrote later. "My own taste has always been for Oriental studies, and from my youth I have taken a great interest in Eastern explorations and discoveries, particularly in the great work in which Layard and Rawlinson were engaged."

In 1872, while rummaging through the thousands of cuneiform tablets Layard and Rassam had recovered from the royal libraries of Nineveh, Smith made an earth-shattering find. Among the items collected by Rassam was "a curious tablet" which recounted a story with a familiar theme: a great flood, a ship aground, a dove sent out when the waters subsided . . .

Smith had found the Assyrian version of Noah's Ark!

That December, at a meeting of the Society of Biblical Archaeology, Smith announced his discovery.

It created a sensation. Smith casually remarked, however, that about fifteen lines of the story of the Flood were missing.

This was an era of robust circulation wars. Newspaper publishers underwrote expeditions to the North Pole and engaged in other stunts. In New York, for example, James Gordon Bennett's *Herald* assigned Henry M. Stanley, a reporter, to join the British 1868 expedition against King Theodore of Abyssinia, who had taken several British subjects hostage, among them none other than Hormuzd Rassam. This was the Stanley that the *Herald* later sent in search of Dr. Livingstone.

In this atmosphere, the London *Daily Telegraph* proffered Smith £1,000 if he would take charge of an expedition to Assyria in search of the missing fragment.

On May 7, 1853, Smith, who had never before been outside of England except on a short visit to Wales, arrived at Mosul and two days later descended into one of the old Layard-Rassam trenches at Kouyunjik. In a denouement that Hollywood producers would reject out of hand as belonging to the theater of the absurd, five days later, while poking around in the trench, Smith recovered the missing piece.

"I sat down to examine the store of fragments of cuneiform inscriptions from the day's digging, taking out and brushing off the earth from the fragments to read their contents," he said. "On clearing one of them I found to my surprise . . . that it contained the great portion of seventeen [sic] lines of inscription belonging to the first column of the Chaldean account of the Deluge, and fitting into the only place where there was a serious blank in the story."

Naïvely, Smith expected his newspaper to continue to lavish money on further exploration in Assyria. But Edwin Arnold, the *Telegraph*'s editor, had his circulation-builder, and was already in search of a new sensation. Arnold ordered Smith home.

On his return to London Smith, in the tradition of Layard, rushed into print with a two-volume *Chaldean Account of Genesis*. John Murray, of course, was the publisher, and the book was an immediate success.

Victorian England was then riding the crest of the Evangelical wave. The public clamored for the government to return Smith to the field. The British Museum bowed to public pressure and underwrote two more Smith expeditions to Mosul. On the second of these, in 1876, Smith fell ill and died at the age of thirty-six.

Smith's death did not stifle interest in Assyria; on the contrary, the perils of archaeology excited the public. The Museum was in a quandary over whom to select as Smith's replacement.

After his marriage, Rassam had retired from government service to spend his time "quietly in England." He had of course, ravenously followed the *Telegraph*'s accounts of Smith's adventures. The trustees turned to him as Smith's replacement, and the fifty-one-year-old Rassam leaped at the opportunity.

Money was still the Museum's principal bugaboo, however. As usual, the trustees explained, they were a bit short of funds. Like Layard before him, Rassam put them down gently, but firmly. "I offered to go out without a stipend," he said, "provided I should be allowed to carry on my excavations the way I deemed best."

But Rassam never got beyond Constantinople. The Sultan refused to issue a firman permitting him to excavate the mounds.

The notoriety attendant on Smith's discovery of the missing fragment and Heinrich Schliemann's discovery that same year, 1873, of mythical Troy and a hoard of gold at Hissarlik, Turkey, had shocked the Turks. They had been right: so-called archaeology was a cover for treasure hunters, gold seekers. As a result, the Turkish government summarily shut down all digs in the Ottoman empire.

For months, Rassam stagnated in Constantinople. Even the grand vizier was unable to help him. "The Sultan alone can give the permission and privileges asked for," Rassam was informed. Empty-handed, in disgust, Rassam returned to London.

At this critical stage, Layard rushed to the rescue of Rassam, the British Museum—and Assyrian archaeology.

Like Layard, Prime Minister Disraeli believed strongly that the collapse of the tottering Ottoman empire would be detrimental to Britain's imperial interests. Stratford Canning had long since retired— he died in 1880 at the age of ninety-four—and Layard argued that Britain needed a strong representative in Constantinople to put spine into a flabby Sultan.

"We want another Lord Stratford, if we can find him," Layard wrote a friend from Madrid. "To break up the Turkish Empire in its present state would be to run the risks of forming two great European powers—Russia and Germany."

Disraeli was precisely of the same opinion. "What we want is a man of the necessary experience and commanding mind at this moment in Constantinople—and one not too scrupulous," he said. "But such men are rare everywhere."

In the back of his mind, however, Disraeli had his man: Layard.

As 1876 drew to a close, the prime minister offered Layard the job. Layard snapped it up. As part of the arrangement, with Victoria's connivance—she had changed her mind about Layard and now viewed him favorably as a defender of the empire—Disraeli arranged for the Queen to bestow a knighthood upon him. For good measure, Layard also received the Grand Cross of the Bath. Shrewdly, Disraeli surmised that in Constantinople a Sir Austen Henry Layard would carry more weight than a Mr. Layard.

The Ninevite plot at this point is as incredible as Smith's discovery of the needle in the haystack. Who needs fiction with the following cast of characters?

Disraeli, who insisted more than thirty-five years earlier at Aunt Sara's brunches that he would one day occupy No. 10 Downing Street, and did.

Layard, who had cooled his heels in the cold reception room of the British embassy at Constantinople a generation earlier and, like a Cinderella pumpkin, was now miraculously transformed into the Great Elchi.

And *Ahmed Vefyk,* Layard's companion during his early escapades in the Turkish capital, who, at the age of seventeen, proclaimed that one day he would be grand vizier of the Ottoman empire, and shortly after Layard's appointment as ambassador emerged in that role!

Rassam was delighted by Layard's posting. "His appointment was naturally a harbinger of joy to me," he said. Rassam knew Layard perhaps better than any other man, and he said, "I knew that he still took a lively interest in all Assyrian discoveries." The British Museum was equally delighted. The secretary wrote Layard, "Do get a *firman* by hook or crook as ere long Mesopotamia will be lost to Turkey. . . . [and] if Aremenia and Assyria are lost, Russia will allow no excavations."

Neither Rassam nor the Museum was disappointed. With Enid on his arm, her eyes sparkling as she viewed the Golden Horn for the first time, Layard arrived in Constantinople on April 20, 1877. He no sooner unpacked than he brought his influence to bear directly on the Sultan and effortlessly extracted a firman for Rassam. This is all the more astonishing because Czar Alexander was about to declare war on Turkey, and a firman to dig up mounds should have been the farthest subject from the minds of the Sublime Porte and Her Britannic Majesty's new envoy at their first meeting.

Indeed, Layard was so confident of his success that he ordered Rassam forthwith from London to Mosul to organize the dig while the firman was being processed through the grand vizier.

On his arrival at Mosul, Rassam promptly called on the local pasha to find out if he had heard about the coveted firman.

"I was not a little relieved when he told me that he had received telegraphic orders from Constantinople to allow me to commence my explorations because, though the *firman* had been granted, it would take some time before it reached Mosul," Rassam said. "The British Ambassador, Sir Henry Layard, for the purpose of saving time, had begged this boon from the Porte, and it had been accorded him, though it was contrary to rule to allow any one to carry on excavations without possession of the royal mandate."

Coincidentally, Schliemann, who had smuggled Trojan gold out of Turkey, was in bad odor with Constantinople. He had no luck in acquiring a new firman to reopen his dig at Hissarlik, and turned to the British ambassador for help. Once again, Layard's diplomatic magic produced results. Thus, single-handedly, in a tour de force, Layard went to the rescue of not only Assyrian but also Greek archaeology. Indeed, Layard played so critical a role in Schliemann's work at Troy that Schliemann publicly attributed his later success there to "the aid of my honored friend . . . Layard . . . who smoothed away all my difficulties with the Turkish government."

Thus, as a direct result of Layard's influence at Nineveh and Troy, Rassam and Schliemann, respectively, resumed their historic missions. More than a generation after he had gazed in awe at the mysterious mounds of Mesopotamia and had brought to light the lost cities of Assyria, Layard's life was still inextricably interwoven with the worlds of the past.

Let the prince who comes after me,
when that temple shall fall to ruins,
restore it.
—ASHURBALLIT

CHAPTER 17

The British Museum's instructions to Rassam were ". . . to try to find as many fragments as possible from the libraries of Ashurbanipal and Sennacherib." But Rassam was in search of greater things—new palaces, lost cities, new art treasures. Like Layard and the Assyrian kings, he sought a place for himself in the sun.

Nearly twenty-four years had passed since Rassam had closed the excavations at Kouyunjik, and he attacked his new assignment with relish. "It was impossible for me to lose my interest in the old explorations," he said.

The first firman Layard secured for Rassam was good only for one year. It gave Rassam the right to explore any Assyrian ruin not occupied by a Moslem cemetery. The firman, however, reflected, for the first time, rising Turkish interest in archaeology. It allotted one-third of Rassam's discoveries to the British Museum, one-third to the newly established Archaeological Museum at Constantinople, and one-third to the owner of a given mound or piece of land on which excavations were conducted (if there was no owner, the one-third reverted to the Turkish government). Furthermore, the imperial decree provided that a representative of the Sultan must accompany Rassam at all times to ensure that the finds were properly reported to the authorities. The Turks had been burned by Schliemann when he smuggled the gold of Troy from Hissarlik to Athens, and they were determined not to be robbed again in the name of science by foreigners. Rassam considered this stipulation an impertinence and a nuisance, and Layard succeeded in having the odious condition withdrawn. (Schliemann had no such luck.)

Rassam's methods of excavation left much to be desired, however. It was physically impossible for him to supervise each dig simultaneously, and he delegated authority to a number of his Mosul cronies, including a nephew, Nimrud Rassam. The digs were conducted on a catch-as-catch-can basis. Rassam led a flying squad which galloped from mound to mound to sift evidence and collect material. No records were kept. Notes were haphazardly written up. Rassam's letters to Layard constitute the only regular flow of reports on his work.

Rassam lacked patience and discipline. The pressure on him, in his own mind, was very great. He suffered from an inferiority complex. He was a Chaldean, a Nestorian Christian, a native of Mosul, and inwardly, he felt he had to prove himself better than the natives of his adopted country, England.

In complete disregard of the trustees' order that he concentrate on the Ninevite libraries, Rassam's first dig was at Balawat, the ancient Assyrian fortress city of Imgur-enlil, 15 miles east of Mosul and 9 miles north of Nimrod. Through contacts, Rassam had learned of the discovery in the area of two pieces of bronze adorned with inscriptions and figures. The place, to his chagrin, turned out to have been converted into a Moslem graveyard, but Rassam was determined to dig there "even for one day."

"I thought that the prize was well worth the risk of a row," he said, "or even a riot."

Rassam no sooner put his spade to the soil than he uncovered seven magnificent strips of bronze, each 8 feet long, richly ornamented and inscribed. They bore the annals of Shalmaneser III, who reigned some 2,500 years earlier. It was a spectacular discovery—the famed Balawat Gates, among the greatest treasures of the British Museum.

But the discovery caused such an uproar at Balawat that Rassam was compelled to abandon further excavations. Orthodox religious leaders were enflamed over the desecration of an Islamic burial ground.

In March 1878, Rassam's firman expired and he was detained at Mosul with his treasures as a dispute erupted between him and the Turkish authorities over the disposition of one-third of the relics.

Layard arranged for the collection to be shipped to Constantinople and told Rassam to "leave it to me to settle about the division."

Rassam arrived in the Turkish capital with the treasure June 21, 1878. He spent the next twelve days as the personal house guest of Layard and Enid. Because he was one of her husband's closest friends, Enid was especially fond of him.

At Layard's suggestion, Rassam also brought with him some old bas-reliefs from Nimrod "as a present to the Sultan from the trustees of the British Museum." Such a gracious gesture had never entered the minds of the trustees—nor anyone else's, except Layard's. Although the Sultan considered the Assyrian trophies "old stones," Layard's thoughtfulness was warmly appreciated, and thereafter Rassam encountered no difficulty, not even with sticky Turkish customs officials, while loading his share of the treasures onto a Messageries Maritimes Company vessel for the journey to England via Marseilles (a rather roundabout way of getting to London).

By then, the first firman had expired and Layard again interceded directly with the Sultan on behalf of Rassam and the British Museum. This time Layard extracted an imperial decree for two years, 1878–80, with the option of extending it another two years, until 1882. The new firman was extraordinary. It invested in the holder the unprecedented power of conducting excavations anywhere in the Ottoman empire. But following the cemetery incident at Balawat and the dispute at Mosul over the finds, Rassam was suspect in Turkish eyes. Accordingly, instead of being issued in Rassam's name, the firman was made out in Layard's name, a tribute to the Great Elchi's unique relationship with the Turkish ruler, Abdul Hamid.

Rassam lost little time taking advantage of the new firman. In late 1878 he extended his excavations from Mosul south to ancient Babylon. His discoveries were truly spectacular, rivaled only by those of his mentor, Layard.

In addition to the Bronze Gates of Balawat, Rassam's major finds included 100,000 clay tablets and fragments of tablets, some containing new and important versions of the Creation and the Flood; the cylinder of Nabonidus, with its checklist of early Babylonian kings; Nebuchadnezzar's palace at Birs Nimrod; a new series of Ninevite lion-hunting scenes (surpassing those of Layard in beauty and execution); the discovery of ancient Kuthu at Tel-Ibrahim; and the identification of the Hanging Gardens of Babylon at the mound known as Babil.

Like many of Layard's discoveries, Rassam's finds were the gift of luck. At Kouyunjik, for example, the capricious goddess stood at his side as he discovered a hidden recess in a brick wall in Ashurbanipal's palace and within it the almost perfect, ten-sided terra-cotta cylinder inscribed with 1,300 lines of cuneiform, detailing the conquests of that Assyrian king. In a talk later before an archaeological group in London, Rassam recounted his discovery:

"Generally speaking, we do not waste our time and money in digging out thick solid brick walls to no purpose; but as I had given orders that when the workmen came to a broken wall they were to search it . . . I was asked by the overseer superintending the work in the palace of Ashurbanipal if he was to demolish a small remnant of a brick wall which was left in digging out two chambers or leave it to be covered over with the debris that came out of the excavations. On seeing that its removal would entail very little expense, I ordered it to be pulled down, and it appears that I had not gone two hours on my way to Nimroud [to inspect another mound], before they came upon this rare object, buried in the center of the solid wall."

Both Layard and Rassam were troubled, however, by the emergence in these years of a new species in archaeology—the antique dealer or broker. The excitement in Europe over the discoveries of Smith and Schliemann demonstrated that there was a market for "antiquities." Indeed, in this period, "on or about the 15th of June, 1877," Scotland Yard reported the first theft of Assyrian relics. A thief or band of thieves made off from the British Museum with a collection of Assyrian pieces, including a rectangular ivory panel from Nimrod (a drawing of which appeared on page 60 of Layard's *Monuments*), a lapis lazuli cylinder, several intaglios with cuneiform inscriptions, and several Assyrian seals decorated with figures. They were never recovered.

But the major marketplace for brokers was in Mesopotamia. Armenian and Jewish merchants there cornered the field. They bribed Arab diggers to sell them relics, especially those bearing inscriptions. This in turn stimulated independent treasure hunts among the Arabs.

The damage done by these sub-rosa operations was incalculable, far exceeding even Rassam's blunderbuss approach to archaeology. "In nine cases out of ten they [the brokers] break or lose a large part of their collection," Rassam wrote Layard, "and worse than all, they try to make a good bargain by breaking the inscribed objects, and dividing them among their customers."

But like latter-day archaeologists, however dissatisfied with this state of affairs, Rassam admitted he was not adverse to dealing with the brokers. "I myself bought, when I was at Baghdad, a most valuable Babylonian terra-cotta cylinder for the British Museum, which had met with the same fate," he said. "The discoverer had tried to saw it in two, and in doing so the upper part broke into fragments, some of which were lost altogether." The saw gnawed off nearly half an inch of inscriptions.

The pilfering of archaeological monuments by "antica dealers," as they are known in the Arab world, persists to this day wherever there are grounds for digging up the past.

Although Rassam was tight-fisted in money matters, he often rewarded his workers for important discoveries. The dealers, however, offered his workers double rewards. In truth, both Rassam and the Armenian and Jewish brokers cheated the ignorant Arabs. A wretched digger, living in a hovel, would be rewarded with twenty or forty cents for an object which later brought upwards of $50 in Baghdad. In one instance, a marble table from Khalah Sharghat was sold by a digger for $1.25 and resold by a broker to the late George Smith for $350. It is now in the British Museum's priceless collection.

In 1880 the Disraeli cabinet fell and Gladstone, the Turkophobe, returned to power. "One of the first things I expect is the return of Henry and Enid from Constantinople," Lady Charlotte Schreiber wrote in her diary. "He is sure to be superseded." Enid's mother astutely judged the political situation. Indeed, one of Gladstone's first acts was to order Layard back to England on home leave. "This is a great blow," Enid confided in her diary, "as I believe we shall never return."

They never did.

Rassam was stunned by the news of Layard's removal. So were the

Turks. Rassam raced to Constantinople to renew the two-year-option on Layard's firman. He just made it. The firman was renewed, and Rassam excavated unmolested for the next two years. In his last dig, on April 21, 1882, before the firman expired, he completed the recovery of the lost Biblical city of Sippara or Sepharavim in the Abu Habba mound, another of archaeology's greatest finds.

But when Rassam applied, on his own, for yet another firman, he was turned down. The new British ambassador was equally powerless. Without Layard, a firman was out of the question. On November 11, 1882, the fifty-six-year-old Rassam sailed for England and arrived in time for Christmas dinner with his family.

Ten years later, at the Ninth International Conference of Orientalists, Rassam publicly confirmed Layard's influence in promoting Assyrian archaeology as Great Elchi. "There are still very valuable records and monuments to be found in Assyria and Babylonia . . . ," Rassam told the Congress. "Had Sir Henry Layard remained a little longer at Constantinople, I should have been enabled to add more important acquisitions to my late discoveries."

Neither he nor Layard ever again dug in Mesopotamia. The heroic age of Assyrian archaeology had ended.

Thus, they took me and made me reside far away.
—GILGAMESH

CHAPTER 18

Layard's recall to London terminated his public career. Although he longed for the embassy in Rome, Gladstone offered him no other diplomatic assignment. For all practical purposes, the fiery and outspoken Layard was forced into early retirement. The word "retirement" is a misnomer, however. Layard was sixty-three, and still robust; Enid, a sparkling thirty-six. As she quickly learned, for Layard "retirement" was a full-time job, with overtime.

They tarried in England and soon withdrew to Venice where Layard acquired a fourteenth-century, three-story *palazzo*, Casa Capello or Ca Capello, as Italians referred to it. The ornate, stately building was perched astride the Grand Canal, boasted a lovely roof garden, and commanded a sweeping view of the canal and one of its tributaries, Rio di San Palao.

At Ca Capello, Layard devoted himself to the three great passions of his waning years—Enid, art, and writing.

The first four years he worked steadily on his two-volume *Early Adventures*, which John Murray brought out in 1887. Like *Nineveh and its Remains*, it was highly autobiographical and led him to resume work on his *Autobiography*, which he had ended abruptly in 1869, on the eve of his marriage and departure to Spain as ambassador. This uncompleted work was published posthumously in 1910.

During this period Layard also wrote extensively on art, and as a disciple of the revolutionary Giovanni Morelli, whom Layard considered the greatest living authority on Italian painting, the bull found himself in the familiar role of wrecking a china shop. Layard assailed the established art critics of the day and promoted a radical approach to the study of painting. Layard's views were contained in his revision of *Kugler's Handbook of Painting*. The latter was based on Morelli's theories and advanced the concept of analyzing paintings by a study of the original drawings and sketches of the artist in question—a commonly accepted method today but startling in Layard's time. Morelli also argued that in order to account for certain features and peculiarities which some schools of art and painters may have had in common, writers on art had attached too much importance to the influence which one school is supposed to have had over another.

In his introduction to the revised edition, entitled *The Italian Schools of Painting*, Layard observed, based on his experience among Assyria's mounds, that "hard and fast lines fixing periods of development are not to be drawn in the history of art." At best, he said, such lines are arbitrary and unscientific. If divisions are to be made, he argued, those of Morelli were preferable.

Layard also wrote regularly for *Quarterly Review* and, as a gourmet, contributed as late as 1891 a lengthy article on Renaissance cookery for *Murray's Magazine*. "A banquet of the time," the now portly, white-haired, and white-bearded seventy-four-year-old Layard concluded, "would probably be to us moderns more gratifying to the sight than to the taste." Obviously, despite his chronological age, inwardly he considered himself quite youthful and "modern."

Life was pleasant in these last years, as Layard happily acknowledged: "I am leading the life which, from my earliest days, I aspired to lead—what more can I want?"

He was also pleasantly surprised by the honors bestowed upon him as the winter of his life lengthened. "I thought I was well forgotten by the world," he remarked.

He was appointed a trustee of the prestigious National Gallery and played a major role in the Gallery's acquisition of Italian masters; he was named a corresponding member of the French Academy; elected president of the Huguenot Society; selected to fill the seat of Robert Browning in the Royal Academy upon the latter's death in Venice in 1889; and made "honorary member of I don't know how many learned societies," he joked in private.

He took the honors in stride, albeit a bit cynically. "I am too old to care for any honor that may be conferred upon me," he wrote in 1891. "Honors are only of use to those who still have the world before them, not to those who should be making their preparations for leaving it."

In 1894, at the age of seventy-seven, Layard participated in his last dig. He and Enid spent the early part of the year in southern Italy "in search of warmth." At Pompeii, in his honor, the Italian archaeological authorities put on a *scavo*, or excavation. "We discovered a dining room, with its table and triclinia, the bronze brazier on which meats were kept hot, various utensils and many small objects," he wrote a friend in England on February 23. "The owner of the house had been probably entertaining his friends when he was disturbed by the ashes from Vesuvius."

In the letter, Layard expressed the hope that he and Enid would return to Ca Capello in time to celebrate the twenty-fifth year of their life together. "How time flies!" he said. "Well, I have been very fortunate."

They did get back in time, and their Italian friends "overwhelmed us with flowers," and gave them a champagne dinner, although both of them would have preferred to have a quiet dinner together. In another letter, dated three days later, March 12, Layard reflected on his silver wedding anniversary.

"I can say what few married men can—that during twenty-five years I have not had a single holiday, or a single quarrel to relieve the monotony of wedded life!" he exclaimed. "It is perhaps too late to begin anew—so we may thus remain until the end—which in the nature of things cannot be far distant."

A fortnight later, April 3, he complained of terrible pains in the area of the groin. "On the advice of my doctor here," he recorded at Ca Capello, "I am leaving Venice for England tomorrow . . . to consult Sir

Henry Thompson on a matter which caused me some trouble four or five years ago, which cannot be neglected."

On April 9, six days later, he reported that "the case does not appear to be so serious as my Venice doctor feared." He had a tumor on the groin, but apparently the cancerous growth was not malignant, or so he was told.

He was immediately confined to bed, however, and thereafter deteriorated rapidly. Layard was shrewd enough to suspect something. "I am rather bad," he wrote May 3, less than a month later. "I cannot sit up without pain."

With Enid at his side, Layard lingered uncomfortably into July. Her diary is a poignant record of his journey into the Assyrian *arallu,* the vast land, the land of no return.

"This is the first day since his illness he has not asked for the newspaper," she wrote alarmingly on July 4. "I was terribly anxious."

That night the physician informed her that "there is no hope."

"After the first shock, I was more or less prepared by my own observation," she said. "I managed to pull myself together . . . but it was a terrible night, so restless and his breathing terrible."

On Thursday, July 5, 1894, the wild bull was stretched out on the ground. "This day, at 8:15 P.M., my husband died, and after twenty-five years that we had never been apart, he left me forever," Enid wrote in her diary.

Reserved and reticent to the end, a genuine Victorian, Enid rarely put her emotions on display—or paper. On the page of that last entry, in the lower left-hand corner of the diary, the lines of black ink ran together and turned into a gray blotch. The ink had been diluted by a teardrop.

Layard was buried at Canford, where he first met tiny Enid and bounced her on his knee.

Three years later Rassam wrote Layard's epitaph. He dedicated *Asshur and the Land of Nimrod* "to the loving memory of . . . Austen Henry Layard . . . the pioneer of Assyrian explorers. . . ."

THE BUNKER

A Condensation of the book by

JAMES P. O'DONNELL

Adolf Hitler, who caused the deaths of millions of people in World War II, spent the last 105 days of his life isolated underground in his Berlin bunker. Deserted by all but a few, Hitler in the end had but one friend, his German shepherd, Blondi.

PROLOGUE

Members of my own generation are my witnesses that 1945 was a breathless year, perhaps the most remarkable on the calendar of our turbulent century. I remember hearing of the sudden death of President Roosevelt on the same day, April 12, 1945, as we who were soldiers had reached the Elbe River and were preparing to cross. Events, tremendous events, were in the saddle; history was happening faster than it could be recorded or comprehended.

This report turns the clock back to that April 1945. It centers on the grisly death of one man only, Adolf Hitler. Most of the Allied world was waiting for news of his death as it paused to mourn the passing of that jaunty warrior, the stricken American President. Roosevelt and Hitler had both come to power in the same year, 1933, in the middle of a catastrophic world depression. Both left the stage of world history in that same April 1945. But there the parallel ends, abruptly. It was Hitler, not Roosevelt, who radically changed the lives of almost every member of my generation. Paltry as a human being, yet a mighty phenomenon. World War II was Hitler's war.

Berlin was Adolf Hitler's capital, the bunker his last abode and legal address; his suicide took place there on a horsehair blue-and-white velvet sofa. A decade ago, the Russians finally announced that they had cremated Hitler's charred body. They were vague about the exact place.

The city of Berlin is built on alluvial sand. It is located on a flat plain, or geologic end-moraine, formed by the departing glaciers of the last ice age; these left behind the confluence of two rivers, the Spree, which flows into the Havel, in an ancient river valley. Many men of power have built monuments to themselves on this sand. The monuments topple, the power-handlers vanish, the sand remains. The muse of history collects this shifting sand in her Berlin hourglass.

In German, an hourglass is called *eine Sanduhr*, a sand clock. An hourglass has no hands; that is its fascination. I have such a *Sanduhr* on my desk before me as I write. In the bright Berlin early morning hours, or again in the late evening when the great city falls deathly quiet, I can hear the sand flowing. I force my thoughts back to the year 1945. I reach for the hourglass, turn it bottom up, reverse the flow. The ghost of Adolf Hitler comes knocking at my door.

Our troops had been marking time on the Elbe River for more than ten weeks before they finally reached Berlin on July 4, 1945. On April 11, when the U.S. 2nd Armored Division reached and took Magdeburg on the Elbe, it was then less than ninety miles west-southwest of Berlin, with one last river to cross. Nothing else stood between us and the tottering capital of the Third Reich except an open and beckoning autobahn, a few Brandenburg lakes, scraggy Scotch pine and birch forests, and beaten sadsack German soldiers yearning to surrender. That Berlin autobahn became the road not taken, in our fateful hesitation.

On that Fourth of July 1945, the lingering exultation of Allied victory in the summer air was mingled with foreboding. Berlin was now supposed to become the revolving stage for an exercise in international harmony, Four Power government. But the stage was already set for what has since become the most durable confrontation in post-World War II history. Berlin is a city in suspense; here, 1945 never really ended. It simply repeats itself. In a city of three and a third million, which is still the largest metropolis and industrial city between Paris and Moscow, life goes on, the decades pass. For Berliners, life in Berlin is life in an hourglass.

Berlin is a great theater city, and the theater is in the tradition of Bertolt Brecht. Now and then, a shot rings out in the night. Some desperate soul has tried to cross the smooth-sanded death strip that today runs through the heart of the city. This death strip, parallel to the hideous Berlin Wall, was once a simple borough line, drawn up by municipal planners in 1920. Sometimes this imaginary line runs down the middle of a street or follows a sidewalk, a curbstone, a river bank, a canal, a house-fronting.

In 1945, this invisible borough line was adopted by the four victorious Allied commanders as a convenient, temporary demarcation line for the quartering of troops. Today, that old borough line is guarded by sentinels in green uniforms atop tall towers. One third of Berlin has become a roofless concentration camp.

As at least most Berliners are glumly aware, there is a perverse element of historical continuity from the brown bunker to the Red wall. If a visitor stands today on Potsdamer Platz, he can see how the lengthening shadows fall toward, and point to, the desolate plot where the Hitler bunker once was.

But the bunker was still there on that Fourth of July 1945, and it was very much on my mind. That day I also had reason for private celebration. On July 1, *Newsweek* magazine had secured my early release from military service. This involved a quick shift from the rank of captain to civilian correspondent, with no time to change uniform.

My assignment was to establish a German bureau in Berlin. In the morning hours of that Fourth, I was aloft aboard a U.S. Air Force C-47 as it headed toward Berlin's Tempelhof airport. Our pilot was flying a precise, narrow air corridor. He had even more precise instructions to keep that matter secret. Had I been more curious, or at least more persistent, I might have had my first exclusive before landing. Air corridors, corridor ceilings, air lift, autobahn checkpoints, confrontation—all words soon to become clichés of crisis; Berlin was already pregnant with alarming headlines of the future.

But the past, the immediate Armageddon past, was still omnipresent, overwhelming. We could now look down and see it in an apocalyptic panorama as our pilot circled the shattered city before landing. We were flying low over a stony ocean of monumental rubble, a desolation that resembled the vague ideas we Americans then had of the landscape of the moon. The stricken, prostrate capital city was no longer smoldering, but a pall of powdery yellow dust lay over it like malignant morning fog.

Still, from the air I could make out a few orienting landmarks announcing the old capital of Prussia—the Brandenburg Gate, the charred shell of the ponderous, gutted Reichstag, the marble-halled New Reich Chancellery. They stood out like derelict hulks that had refused to sink into that ocean of ruin. I had a cable in my pocket from *Newsweek*'s foreign editor in New York:

PLANNING COVER STORY UPCOMING POTSDAM CONFERENCE   STOP
MEANWHILE WANT FULLER DETAILS EVENTS IN HITLER BUNKER
STOP   RECONSTRUCT LAST DAY   STOP   WHO WAS EVA BRAUN?

Surely the Hitler bunker story was the first among many still-untold stories under all this appalling devastation. To my disappointment, the bunker had not been visible from the air. It was quite impossible to spot or identify it among several score bunkers, squat, like brown mushrooms, that still cluttered the flattened downtown area.

To get from the airport to the Reich Chancellery area as rapidly as possible, I flagged down a passing jeep. We were soon lost in the labyrinth of rubble, winding our way along the only street cleared for vehicular traffic.

To my surprise, the scene at the battered Brandenburg Gate was a lively, even colorful, spectacle, the first visible Berlin crowd. This, I soon discovered, was the already flourishing black market. The currency, cigarettes; the Berliners, mostly lean and hungry housewives. What furnished the dash of color was the motley display of Allied uniforms. The Four Power experiment, at least at the simple soldier level, seemed to be working out splendidly.

I moved over to the Reichstag, nearby. Here, a steady flow of Russian officers, in groups of twelve to twenty, were visiting the double ruins of this solid parliament building, gutted in 1933, stormed in April 1945. Like skilled acrobats, many were standing, shoeless, on each other's shoulders. They were inscribing in Cyrillic letters names, ranks, units, and other graffiti on the tall, chipped Corinthian columns.

I moved off quickly, heading down the Wilhelmstrasse, passing ruined embassies, toward the Old and New Reich Chancellery only some five blocks away. The Old Reich Chancellery had been the traditional residence since Bismarck's day. Hitler kept his apartment there even after he built the New Reich Chancellery in 1938. The old building remained as a wing of the much larger new one. In the long marble halls of the New Reich Chancellery itself, most of which, to my surprise, was still defiantly standing, I met up with perhaps a dozen uniformed visitors, Russian, British, American, French. Nobody seemed to know for sure just where the already half-legendary Hitler bunker was. In our imaginations, perhaps, we were all looking for something vaguely impressive, like Cairo tourists heading for the Giza pyramids.

On my own, in the far corner of the Old Chancellery garden, now an obscene junkyard, I finally located the obscure entry. I found there a rectangular, unsurfaced tawny-colored cement block, perhaps twenty feet high, with a narrow oblong entrance and indented vestibule. The whole garden round-about now looked as if it had been churned up by myriad giant moles. What had once been trees were now blasted, uprooted stumps. I saw the rusty tail of a dud bomb poking up from a crater; I treaded warily.

A single Russian soldier, armed but pleasant enough, stood on sentry duty. At first I feared he might have orders to turn sightseers away. I saluted him in the name of the common victory and offered him a pack of Camels. He handed me a yellow kerosene lantern.

I had already had enough experience with Russian soldiery to know they were seldom on duty alone. Sure enough, at the bottom of the staircase I met a second sentry, not quite so pleasant or, perhaps, just more bored. He had set up quarters in a room where the walls and ceiling were charred, the floor smeared with gray ash. He was armed with a submachine gun, but this lay on the table. He was also flourishing a long-barreled .22 caliber German target pistol. Another pack of cigarettes, my last, and the premises were open for inspection.

At first I thought I was alone; it was spooky. Soon I came on three Russian military visitors, officers, who were moving about silently with pocket flashlights. A few minutes later, we were all quite startled when a staccato shot rang out. The sentry had winged a rat. Other rats, some as fat as groundhogs, were scooting and slithering up and down the one long room, the main corridor. They had gnawed away much of the waterlogged red carpeting.

Worse than the darkness and the dankness was the odor. Although I could make out, in a separate power room, a quite modern ventilation machine, it had long since been closed down. The untended latrines were clogged but obviously still in use. From the sickening sweetness of the strongest stench, I guessed that an earlier rodent casualty had crept into the ventilation system to die. There had been suicides down here, but the smell was not the sweet-sour smell of decaying human flesh. War and rubble have their distinct malodors.

At some time, a bunker pipe or an emergency red-rubber garden hose had burst. There was thus a shallow, stagnant pool at the far end of the central corridor, some three or four inches of water, muck, and slime. I had to slosh through it to get to the farther reaches of the bunker. Soon I came to a large steel bank-vault door that opened onto an iron spiral staircase leading to what—as I was later to learn—was called the *Vorbunker*, the upper bunker.

I was wary. I still had that former soldier's instinct not to reach for or pick up any stray bric-a-brac or harmless-looking souvenirs. They just might be booby-trapped. The Germans were mean-minded, even sly, about such matters, and this had recently been a military headquarters.

However, trudging back through the water, I kicked up by accident what appeared to be a large map. I did pick this up and found it was a large parchment in faded purple-sepia, a blueprint for the postwar remodeling and enlarging of the Austrian city of Greater Linz (Grosslinz). I let the map and the matter drop.

My mind, at the moment, was on other things. I had now been underground perhaps twenty minutes. I noticed that one of the visiting Red Army officers, less booby trap-conscious than I, had picked up and donned an old German gas mask. That had solved for him the odor problem. As he left, he handed the mask to me. I too had been about to flee up those steep stairs, gasping for fresh air. Now I could move about, room by room. I counted more than thirty cubicles. I was astonished by how cramped and small they were—the largest three by four meters, many smaller.

The longer I dallied below deck, the more frankly puzzled I became. Something in this dungeon did not quite add up. Obviously, the original German occupants had fled in a hurry. They had left behind a mass of military impedimenta. It was equally obvious that the victorious Russian soldiery had ransacked the place. There was nothing of any intrinsic value, no full liquor bottles, no usable weapons, no blankets or articles of clothing, no dress daggers, radios, or cameras.

Still, the bunker looked like the Paris flea market after an auction sale, and this perplexed me. Everywhere the floors, corridors, and duckboards were littered with glass shards and bottles, rusty picture frames, German Army cheesecake photos, warped gramophone records, scattered sheet music, dented air-raid warden helmets, empty first aid kits, bloodied bandages, old knapsacks, tin cans, ammunition drums, empty pistol clips, scattered playing cards, film magazines, cigar and cigarette butts, slimy condoms.

But what most caught my eye was the sheer mass of printed and written material—military telephone books and telephone-number pads, looseleaf notebooks, business office files and dossiers, diaries, military manuals, scratch pads, letters. What was so wrong with that picture? Simply this: this Reich Chancellery bunker had been not only an air-raid shelter; it had also served as a military headquarters.

As I now know, one of the documents still lying in the bunker on that July 4 was Adolf Hitler's appointment book (crowded) and Martin Bormann's personal diary (boring). Another, most probably, was a daily battle log. This had been kept by Lieutenant Colonel Klingemeir, the chief of staff to SS Major General Wilhelm Mohnke, the bunker troop commandant. A fourth document may have been microfilm cassettes of the Goebbels diary, 1923-1945, as well as voluminous writing he had done in the last days.

What I had stumbled on was glaring evidence that the Russians, for reasons that were to dawn upon me only many years later, had committed an intelligence oversight of major importance. At least five Red Army search teams had been in the bunker the day it fell. They had been looking for one thing only, the body. Operating under instructions from Hitler's great antagonist, Stalin, these NKVD hearties fell over each other to locate it. But the bunker, from the first day of entry by the Russians, was already on its way to becoming a nonplace. Hence that steady crowd of sightseers at the Reichstag, the official bus tours. Always to the Reichstag, *never* to the Hitler bunker.

One of the few Soviet historians, even today, willing to talk on this matter, Lev Bezymenski, insists the original Soviet motive in playing down the Hitler bunker in 1945 was a very genuine fear that it might one day become "a German national shrine like Frederick the Great's summer place, Sans Souci."

None of these second thoughts were troubling me that July morning on my underground trip into the past, a ghastly, now already ghostly, past. I did linger some forty-five minutes, despite my fear of rats. I came up out of the bunker. Four flights. I counted forty-four steep steps. With fresh air in my lungs, back in the sunshine, I began to collect my addled thoughts. Suddenly, Grosslinz! I now recalled that Linz was the county seat of Braunau, Adolf Hitler's birthplace. Cursing my own dull reaction, I whipped back to the bunker, down the forty-four steps on the double. Too late. One of those British colonels one usually meets only in the pages of *Punch* had found and was rolling up the map of Grosslinz: "My only war souvenir. It won't look half bad over my fireplace in Kent."

The story of that blueprint does not end in 1945. Almost a quarter of a century later, in Heidelberg in 1969, I was sitting interviewing Albert Speer, Hitler's former architect, on the occasion of the German publication of his memoirs. I told him about the trivial incident, the blueprint and the colonel from Kent. He confirmed that my lost souvenir had belonged to Hitler: "Ah, yes. On my last day in the bunker, seven days before Hitler's suicide, the nostalgic Fuehrer hauled out that blueprint and began to reminisce."

I was at first astonished to hear that Adolf Hitler and Albert Speer, in the tumult of the last days in the bunker, had found time for auld lang syne. I asked about this. Speer replied, "Yes. Reminiscence, perhaps a more exact word would be sheer escapism, was a bunker leitmotif. My final visit lasted twelve hours. The only real event was the flap over a telegram from Goering and his instant dismissal. Almost all the rest of Hitler's time, at least while I was with him, was spent in recollection of things past."

So in fact was Speer's, as he made the rounds and said goodbye forever to Eva Braun, Magda Goebbels, Ambassador Walter Hewel, Colonel von Below, General Krebs, others. The place was utterly divorced from any objective reality. To preserve what was left of his own rationality, Speer fled.

What Speer said here we will later hear confirmed by more than fifty witnesses. It is the one point perhaps on which all agreed. Adolf Hitler told and retold the whole story of his life during the endless days and nights underground. Arrivals and departures, and there were many, always touched off some memory of things past.

Speer, of course, is a most exceptional man, able to articulate his experience. Most of the other bunker men and women are anything but exceptional. All, I found, performed remarkable feats of memory about certain bunker events, drew total blanks about others. This was seldom cover-up. Most spoke freely. Almost all were willing to talk about matters passed over in silence for many years. More than twenty of the bunker group were speaking for publication for the first time.

Just how close this composite account comes to historical truth, to the kind of documentation an academic historian insists on, I simply cannot say. Nor is it overly important to my purpose. I am a journalist, not a historian. I ring doorbells; I do not haunt archives. What I was looking for is what I believe most people look for, psychological truth. I am aware that many of the accounts here differ from the accounts—meager, in any case—given in some of the first interrogations back in 1945. Few of the interrogated Germans were then in any mood to volunteer answers that might prove embarrassing. Most were under arrest; all were under duress. It was like asking the shell-shocked to describe exactly the burst of artillery. These people needed time to collect their own thoughts.

Early in 1970, the editors of the *New York Times* magazine, who had just run my profile-interview with Albert Speer, queried me as to whether there were other major witnesses now willing to reconstruct their personal experience in the bunker. I set out and soon located Professor Ernst-Guenther Schenck, a practicing physician in Aachen.

He had recently published a moving account of the bedlam conditions in his own emergency operating room in the cellar of the Reich Chancellery. Schenck had performed more than 300 major operations on soldiers wounded defending the bunker.

In talking to Dr. Schenck, I found that his narrative alone raised mighty ghosts. It was impossible to handle in a single magazine article. Schenck, as our interviews proceeded, began mentioning several figures: General Mohnke, Professor Werner Haase, Ambassador Hewel, Gestapo chief Heinrich Mueller, all of whom he described as playing critical roles in the last days of the bunker. In earlier accounts, these names, when mentioned at all, were footnote names among those present. Haase, Hewel, and Mueller are all known to be dead. But whatever had happened to General Mohnke? The story of the bunker commandant had never been told. And yet on military matters, Mohnke clearly was the soldier charged with minding the shop.

Dr. Schenck had lost all contact with General Mohnke after their release from Russia in 1955. He mentioned that Mohnke's whereabouts were a bit of a mystery, then dropped the subject. He did, however, give me the names and addresses of three other bunker veterans, Major Otto Guensche, Captain Helmut Beermann, and Sergeant Rochus Misch. Sergeant Misch turned out to be my first real windfall. Not only was he in touch with some twenty old comrades; he also had an accurate, no-nonsense memory. Misch was both a switchboard operator and a valet. He was also a highly decorated soldier and the last military man to leave the Fuehrer-bunker, an escape at dawn.

Moreover, Misch was and still is a Berliner. Today he runs a paint-supply shop some two miles away from the old bunker and only five or six blocks from my office in downtown West Berlin. This was again most helpful. Misch, who had manned Adolf Hitler's switchboard for five years, became my message center for the five years I spent flushing out bunker witnesses.

In the summer of 1972, I began to compile a card-index file of bunker veterans. I called it my black box. The rock-bottom basis was Misch's handy list of twenty names. Seeking these people out—almost all were in West Germany—I found that most were both willing and able to come up with two, three, even four new names and addresses.

The timing turned out to be most propitious. From the beginning of my long journey down the autobahn into the past, I realized I was operating on the very outer fringes of time and human memory, including my own. Thirty years are a chunk of living in everyone's life.

In another decade, many of these witnesses will have reached what the computer registers as terminal status. Or their fading memories will be too clouded to be reliable.

Further, and for a variety of reasons not excluding human vanity, I found many of these witnesses far more willing to talk freely than they would have been three, two, or even one decade ago. This, I suppose, is the process of Hitler and the Berlin bunker becoming a part of history. All of these people did play a role, if sometimes only a walk-on role, in a historical event. They seemed to recognize that the opportunity to tell their story, in pretty much their own words, might never come again.

In that first year of basic research, which consisted of ringing doorbells, thumbing through provincial telephone books, cross-checking references, I had hopes of locating, at most, perhaps forty or fifty sources. At year's end, to my amazement, I needed a second black box. The first contained more than 250 names, all genuine, still-living witnesses who had been present in the bunker at some time during the last battle in Berlin. My surprise was based, of course, on my own memory of the cramped and limited topography of the bunker proper. What I had overlooked was the maze of tunnels leading into the New and Old Reich Chancellery and other nearby government buildings. The bunker was a small stage, a snakepit. But the comings and goings, in the desperate last days of April 1945, had a rush-hour atmosphere.

I pruned my list drastically. From the black box I dropped all mere spear-holder witnesses. With some reluctance, I also eliminated that half of the Reich Chancellery Group, some of whom had been with Hitler long years, who were flown to Berchtesgaden on April 22. This evacuation was called Operation Seraglio. I repeated, in short, the "hiving-off" process that was itself very much a part of the original bunker reality. There was a clutter of witnesses present when the last stand began, but only a relevant dozen at the end.

There were all those who had left with the major ministers, right after Hitler's birthday. That was April 20. Two days later, Operation Seraglio took place. One day later, Field Marshal Keitel and General Jodl departed, trooping off with large military staffs.

The hiving-off process, although interrupted now and again by spectacular arrivals (Goebbels, Speer, Eva Braun), is precisely why we have so many published accounts of the beginning of Hitler's Alamo stand, but so few of the very last days and last hours, practically nothing on those more than thirty hours that elapsed between Hitler's death and the dramatic breakout.

A word on method. This is an interview book. Although I located the names and addresses of more than 250 genuine bunkerees, and communicated with more than 100, I actually interviewed at length only about 50, concentrating on the Reich Chancellery Group itself. From Chapter 3 on, each chapter is as seen through the eyes of one or two major witnesses only. The exception is the breakout.

Technically, it was just not possible to have every witness read the final draft of every chapter in this revised and expanded American edition. But all have read any chapter in which they appear or are quoted. All have read the original German version, *Die Katakombe*. Many have made valuable corrections. To maintain credibility, I simply eliminated four or five overloquacious witnesses I knew or believed to be lying, or "spinning," as they say in German.

The others, while they often fall into palpable error or are victims of lapses of memory sometimes verging on amnesia, on the whole did their best to recapture historical truth, or the truth as seen through the Berlin hourglass. By mutual consent, we spared each other many valuable hours by not discussing whether Adolf Hitler was a great man. Some, above all the women, would sigh that the verdict should be left to history, and I went along with the banality of that.

Most of my witnesses talked so willingly for a simple reason. They are all getting long in the tooth. In their youth, these Germans all knew Adolf Hitler well. Most worshiped the man. One is young only once. But with luck one is old only once, too. These people are survivors, still clutching their survival kits. Many struck me as chastened, sobered survivors. The long years of secret interrogation lay behind them. So did the bunker. When they talked of present-day politics, as they sometimes did, it was like listening to a group of middle-aged fire-insurance salesmen who had all had a fling at arson in their youth.

From 1972 to 1976, cruising Hitler's old autobahns out of Berlin, I clocked more than 50,000 miles. Sixty months elapsed between my first interview with Professor Schenck and my last with Hitler's secretary Gerda Christian. She agreed to meet me in the home of a third party only after she had read several draft chapters. I had been warned that she might be hostile or at least haughty and difficult. She was, in fact, frank, intelligent, witty—a pleasant surprise.

According to my card-index record, at least 90 percent of those who were in the breakout survived. Ninety percent of these, in turn, managed to endure more than a decade of Soviet prison camps. And of these, more than 90 percent are still alive today. A hardy lot.

Let us go back now to January 1945. Berlin, chill and cheerless, was still Hitler's capital, the hub of the reeling, tottering Greater German Reich. It had become Hitler's hourglass, one he could not reverse. Every frail military front was now wobbling or collapsing. He had just lost his last desperate major offensive in the Ardennes. The American First and Third Armies had defeated and decimated his last two intact panzer armies, two elite armies his harrassed generals knew they had needed to defend the capital. Berlin was now being steadily pulverized by 1500-plane saturation-bombing raids. It was sinking into a molten mass. Firestorms made a maelstrom of its asphalt and agitated rubble. The groggy big-city citizenry were reduced to a troglodytic existence. During one bombardment stretch, death was falling from the air on twenty-one successive days and nights, by sunlight, by moonlight.

Standing silent amid their ruins, Berliners could also see the even more dismal shape of things to come. A steady parade of forlorn, bedraggled refugees plodded through the city day and night. But now, in mid-January, these derelicts of a lost war had to trudge through snowdrifts more than two feet high. A mighty blizzard had struck between air raids. For many thousands of these trekkers, often peasant families, it spelled the white death.

Even the rhythm of nature was disturbed. Berlin in peacetime has many remarkable bird colonies; one of the largest and most visible is the hooded crows. This migratory breed nests in Poland, summers in Russia, but always winters in Berlin. These winter Berliners had arrived in November 1944, as usual. Their favorite feeding stations were downtown in the heart of the city, in the many spacious parks, whereas the best overnight roosting perches were out in the tall pines, willows, and elders of the Havel lakes on the western outskirts. Of a Berlin winter midafternoon, as the sun fades rapidly toward the northwest horizon, these giant flocks of more than 40,000 birds can be seen, wheeling in the sky. Then slowly they head west in loose but very methodical formation. For one long hour, they blacken the darkening sky.

But this, the last fierce winter of the war, was otherwise. In the daytime, the morning hours, these startled Berlin crows found their familiar feeding plots under steady bombardment. They swarmed, enraged, about the sky, cawing at the larger, mechanical silver birds above them. At night, in their rookery roosts, phosphorous bombs set the trees aflame. When the blizzard hit, the exhausted and baffled birds, hungry and insomniac, deserted Berlin. They flew off in scattered, flapping flocks. In the Middle Ages, the mysterious and sudden departure of such large black birds would have been interpreted as a harbinger of death and pestilence, of the coming doom of a Godforsaken city. It was.

There was another harbinger. On January 16, 1945, Commander-in-Chief Adolf Hitler returned from the west, by train, unannounced, to set up his last field headquarters in an obscure and hidden midtown air-raid shelter. He knew it was a symbolic necropolitical move, the stage-managing of his own approaching death. Hitler had become German's underground leader.

CHAPTER 1

THE CAVEMEN

On the morning Adolf Hitler went underground in downtown Berlin there had been a thousand-plane raid by the U.S. Eighth Air Force. Now, in the bleak afternoon, a pall of smoke hung over the city. A few casual passersby may have noticed the Fuehrer's yellow and white standard, which he had himself designed, flying above the New Reich Chancellery. It announced his return to the German capital after several weeks' absence.

No curious passerby could have seen the Fuehrer descending into the safest bunker in Berlin. He moved through an underground tunnel that led from the New Reich Chancellery into and under the garden. The Chancellery garden was a kind of spacious interior court, in atrium style, discreetly shielded from public view. Few Berliners, and only a few hundred Hitler court retainers, knew of the bunker. Aboveground, there was not much to see, anyway—an emergency exit, about twenty feet high in the form of a square blockhouse, and a round pillbox-tower. The latter was unfinished; it was supposed to have been a watchtower. There was also a raised wooden water barrel, or cistern, used by air-raid wardens. Finally, there was a curious trench, designed as a moat, that ran around both the emergency exit and the tower. A part of the permanent outside décor of the bunker drama was a large, abandoned cement mixer; in the general confusion, nobody had bothered to trundle it away.

Adolf Hitler made his last move into the bunker quietly, without fuss, with the aid of a single soldier-valet, who lugged his personal belongings and his toilet kit. The move was from his luxury apartment, in the upper reaches of the Old Reich Chancellery, into a catacomb fifty-five feet below ground level. The buried roof of this bunker was sixteen feet thick; the exterior walls, six feet wide. The roof was covered with several tons of earth, to a depth of thirty feet. From the moment Hitler moved in, this cement cave became the Fuehrerbunker, a kind of Third Reich in miniature.

Down under, the interior was ghostlike and bleak. All ceilings were low. The corridors were like the narrow passages in a crypt. A few of the thirty-odd cramped rooms had been painted battleship gray. The rough corridor walls were a rusty brown. In places, the bare cement dripped moisture; the masons had never been able to finish their plastering work. Three rooms, only slightly larger than the rest, ten by fifteen feet, plus a toilet and shower, were Hitler's private quarters. Like monastic cells, they were furnished with a few sticks of furniture. The living room had a couch, a coffee table, and three chairs; the bedroom, a single bed, a night table, a dresser. This was now not only the Fuehrerbunker; it was also the Fuehrerhauptquartier (FHQ), the supreme military headquarters of the Third Reich, the last of the thirteen command posts from which Hitler had directed the war. Command posts from which, only three short years before, Hitler the conqueror had dominated Europe and beyond, from the North Cape of Norway to the Africa deserts, from the Pyrenees to the Caucasus.

The historic moment of Hitler's descent passed unnoticed. He preferred to make his moves unannounced. And the distance from his old to his new bedroom was only about 100 yards. Those who must have seen him, as he shuffled toward the tunnel leading out of the cellar of the Old Chancellery, would no doubt have assumed he was just making another of his inspection tours, minding the shop. Adolf Hitler was, after all, the most familiar sight in the dreary routine of their daily lives. Some were guarding his personal security as head of state; some simply waiting on him; all were serving in his intimate court in some capacity. Most had known him for years. For them, he was less Der Fuehrer than Der Chef, "The boss."

Adolf Hitler was destined to live another 105 days. But he had spent his last full day aboveground. "To the best of my memory," said Captain Beermann, one of the SS honor bodyguard (Fuehrerbegleitkommando, or FBK) who attended him during this time, "Hitler never saw another sunrise or sunset after January sixteenth." He worked, slept, took meals and tea, bathed, made his toilet, and finally married and died—all underground. In a world where day and night blended into a continuous glare of artificial light, the departure from reality became more evident with each passing week.

There were, though, several breaks, for at least a few hours, in this marathon underground endurance contest. Like a submarine commander coming up for air, Hitler surfaced from time to time, to re-enter and prowl his familiar haunts in the New Reich Chancellery. When there was no air-raid alarm, he would risk a military conference around the great marble table in his old spacious office on the ground floor; only its tall windows had been shattered. In a corner of the old dining room, where he once held daily noontime table for from forty to fifty guests, he sometimes took a snack alone, or with his dietary cook, Fräulein Constanze Manzialy, a fellow Austrian. Or he would take tea and crumpets with one of the four female secretaries who had accompanied him to the bunker. Most of Hitler's meals were now with women— the secretaries, the cook, and, in the last stages, Eva Braun.

Apparently Hitler did make two brief sorties out of Berlin. On February 25, he was chauffeured by his old stalwart behind the wheel, SS Colonel Erich Kempka, to address a secret meeting of Gauleiters (the brown-shirted guardians of the Nazi state) just outside the city. This was one of his last political acts, although he was still chief of state and head of the Nazi Party. And on March 15, he emerged from his bunker lair around noon, to make a quick overland drive to the east front. According to Kempka, the Fuehrer was back in about four hours, before sundown.

The last formal exception to the underground monotony was his own last birthday party. On April 20, Adolf Hitler was fifty-six. With the Battle for Berlin already on—it had begun four days before—with the city all but surrounded by the Red Army, Hitler still insisted on this last appearance of all the major power-handlers of the Third Reich. Although the party was held in the Court of Honor of the Chancellery, it lasted less than an hour. No champagne was served. The participants then adjourned back to the bunker for a listless military briefing.

That birthday party was a spectral performance, the guests trying to act as they had in the giddy years of power now so clearly over. This cheerless *Fest* was the last time Hitler ever saw Heinrich Himmler or Hermann Goering or most of his more than twenty ministers. Himmler and Goering vanished from Berlin, Himmler to the north, Goering south. Most of the ministers packed up to join ministries which had already left.

On this day the newsreel cameramen also captured a second scene, a melancholy vignette with a touch of realism. In the garden, just outside the bunker, Hitler decorated twenty Hitler Youth turned soldiers, all orphans who had come to Berlin from Breslau and Dresden. He was patting the cheeks of one of them, a forlorn gesture. Photos of Hitler in the last weeks are rare. None was ever taken in the bunker proper. That was *verboten*.

From time to time, for a few nighttime minutes, Hitler would venture outside the bunker to walk his German shepherd, Blondi. For long weeks on end, this was Hitler's one desultory gesture toward getting some fresh air and exercise. The fact that these short strolls were nocturnal lends credence to the belief, held by many of his intimates, that Hitler's fast-fading eyesight was irritated by sunlight.

Hitler always walked alone with his dog. But alert eyes constantly watched his halting steps, his shambling gait. The fear that Hitler might collapse on one of these rare excursions to the surface, or that Blondi could pull him off balance, was a genuine worry. For months, he had been complaining of a sudden loss of his sense of balance, and he had a tendency to lurch to the right.

One of these pairs of eyes belonged to Captain Beermann, who remembered the Fuehrer "painfully negotiating those forty-four steps, four steep flights of concrete steps, up to the emergency exit." Beermann and the rest of the SS honor bodyguard were rugged young bucks. But their customary twelve-hour shift made even them groggy and intensely weary. "We would murmur about this batlike routine among ourselves, part-time prisoners of this cave life. The old life at Berchtesgaden was a perennial topic of conversation. We were all silently hoping that Der Chef would take off. Better to face death in the sunlight, and in the Alps, than to perish like miserable rats in a musty cement tomb in Berlin. None of us ever expected to survive."

At the end of their long tours of duty, they would come up, literally gasping for air. Beermann recalled:

> The whole atmosphere down there was debilitating. It was like being stranded in a cement submarine or buried alive in some abandoned charnel house. People who work in diving bells probably feel less cramped. It was both dank and dusty, for some of the cement was old, some new.
>
> In the long hours of the night, it could be deathly silent, except for the hum of the generator. When you came upon flesh-and-blood people, their faces seemed blanched in the artificial light. The ventilation could be now warm and sultry, now cold and clammy.

Then there was the fetid odor of boots, sweaty woolen uniforms, acrid coal-tar disinfectants. At times toward the end, when the drainage backed up, it was as pleasant as working in a public urinal.

In the pages to come, we shall see scores of actors entering and leaving the bunker. Some are there but briefly, on purely military missions. Some stay for a few hours only, very important hours in the case of Albert Speer, quite unimportant ones in the case of Joachim von Ribbentrop. Some, like Eva Braun and the whole Goebbels family, arrive quite late but are with Hitler underground for several days and nights running. Yet none endured the subterranean endurance test Hitler imposed on himself.

Eva Braun, for example, in the middle of the Battle for Berlin, went casually strolling in the Tiergarten, the large public park just west of the bunker and the green lung of the city. Eva and several of the young secretaries took daily pistol-practice on an emergency range set up in the yard of the Goebbels' Propaganda Ministry.

Even Hitler's personal secretaries, and such important assistants as Martin Bormann and Major Otto Guensche, Hitler's senior SS adjutant, left the lower bunker at least twice daily for meals. They ate in the upper bunker, in the Old Chancellery dining room, or in the large military mess, operating after April 16 on the ground floor of the New Reich Chancellery. Smokers nipped up from time to time for a cigarette break. Smoking was forbidden in the bunker proper, on orders of Hitler.

Very few, even of the Hitler inner circle, actually slept in the Fuehrerbunker. The only exceptions to this bunking-down rule were the chief valet, Heinz Linge, who moved out when Dr. Goebbels finally moved in; Hitler's personal physician, Dr. Theodor Morell, who was succeeded in the last stages by the surgeon SS Colonel Ludwig Stumpfegger; and Fräulein Manzialy. These were all people Hitler might need in a hurry—the valet, the doctor, the cook. Eva Braun, when she arrived in mid-April, had a small suite next to Hitler's. And finally there was Blondi. Blondi even whelped in March.

The presence of Hitler at this very center of things, for all that he is more than fifty feet underground, determined to run his own show to the bitter end, lends to the action a theatrical effect. The leading actor has withdrawn as far away from objective non-Hitlerian reality as his own wish fulfillment can take him, short of that death itself which will close the Hitler book forever. But random actors and messengers entering the bunker from the outside world—and some come from hundreds of miles away—have the dust, grime, and blood of a different reality on their uniforms and faces. Always, when we listen to testimony, we must make quite clear whether the witness is outside or inside the bunker.

More than a quarter of a century later, so I discovered, many otherwise rational men and women had trouble explaining their own bizarre actions in the bunker—just as victims of a shipwreck, a train crash, or an earthquake can never quite reconstruct in tranquillity the moments of panic and trauma.

Back on that January 16, 1945, Hitler had been in Berlin only about twenty-four hours before he decided to make his permanent descent into the bunker. He had come, via his night train, from the field headquarters known as Adlerhorst, or Eagle's Eyrie, not far from Frankfurt on the Main. From here the Fuehrer had masterminded the last desperate, lunging German offensive in the west, now known in the annals of the U.S. Army as the Battle of the Bulge.

There was a direct connection between the Battle of the Bulge and the Battle for Berlin. It was this shattering setback in the Ardennes that had brought Hitler, posthaste, back to Berlin in mid-January 1945. As the then Chief of the General Staff, Colonel General Heinz Guderian, had repeatedly, if vainly, tried to warn him, the two crack panzer armies Hitler had thrown at the Allied armies in the west might have been more wisely employed in stemming the Red Army offensive in the east. The Russians were advancing from the Vistula to the Oder rivers. The Oder is only sixty miles east of Berlin, and the Red Army reached it in mid-February.

Hitler's descent into the Berlin bunker, for all its symbolic Wagnerian overtones, was thus dictated by the realities of a disastrous military situation, including that war in the air over Berlin so often forgotten in accounts of the fall of the city. Like the avenging furies, U.S. and British strategic bombers were now engaged in round-the-clock saturation bombing. Targets in the west, Cologne, Hamburg, Frankfurt, had long since been reduced to rubbled ruins, in a systematic overkill.

Now, for long months, Berlin had been the prime target of the air fleets, which often numbered more than 1500 four-engine bombers. Two thirds of the total bomb load dropped on Berlin was unloaded in the last three months of the war. Sixty-two percent of Berlin housing was destroyed or badly damaged. In the downtown heart of the city, where the bunker was located, destruction was closer to 85 percent.

The phrase "round-the-clock bombing" now took on a terrifying literalness for the average Berliner. Based in the United Kingdom, American daylight bombers, the Flying Fortresses and Liberators, protected by long-range fighter escorts (P-51s), would take off at break of dawn. They could be expected over Berlin by the middle of the morning. They were back in England in the afternoon. The RAF, relying more on saturation techniques, took to the air at dusk. They were usually over Berlin around midnight. More than 1.5 million Berliners had already been evacuated, but three million still remained in the city.

The groggy Berliners had learned to snatch what sleep they could, in heatless, often windowless, bedrooms, during afternoon and early evening hours. From midnight to noontime, many of these hollow-eyed, sleepless citizens burrowed into their cellars or fled to the larger neighborhood shelters. Most Berliners were not even aware that Hitler was back in the capital. The Fuehrer never visited a Berlin public shelter. Nor did he ever tour the ruined city, as Churchill had done so gallantly at the height of the London Blitz.

Perhaps nothing better symbolized Hitler's complete isolation from the great municipality, the capital of his Third Reich, then the bunker's self-contained utilities and facilities. Water was piped from a nearby artesian well. The sixty-kilowatt generator supplied electricity for lighting, heating, the switchboard, and the water pump. Food, drink, medicine, candles—all were in plentiful supply in the vast storerooms of the New Reich Chancellery and in the narrow corridor that served as the bunker butler's pantry, known as "Kannenberg Alley," after the fat chief steward, Artur Kannenberg. Only the air was Berlin air, and even this passed through a filter system.

Hitler's life would obviously have been endangered had he stubbornly remained aboveground. He was not a physical coward. His Iron Cross first class, which he had won as a front-line regimental courier in World War I, counted as a high decoration indeed for a man of humble origins and low rank. It was earned, and he wore it proudly to his dying day, one of the few authentic touches in his elaborate act. What Adolf Hitler really dreaded was not death, but that fate might deprive him of the chance to stage-manage his own departure.

It had been SS General Johann Rattenhuber, chief of the Fuehrer's detective squad, who had urgently advised the Fuehrer to vacate the Reich Chancellery and move both his office and his residence underground. The target of the saturation bombing was now clearly the center of the city.

American and British pilots flying into Berlin from the northwest or west soon learned to orient themselves easily by the great wide artery called the East-West Axis, which Hitler had constructed in 1938. This grand avenue ran almost as straight as an arrow, for fifteen miles, directly to the Brandenburg Gate.

The gate is the true center of the city. It is rather small—much smaller than the Arc de Triomphe in Paris. But its conspicuous position made it visible from the air. Traffic flowing eastward through this gate then entered Unter den Linden, Berlin's most famous boulevard, which had become an extension of the East-West Axis.

For a pilot, the last two critical miles of his flight toward the gate would be over the heart of the Tiergarten, which extended along on both sides of the axis. The Tiergarten is clearly bounded to the north by another topographical landmark easily identifiable from the air—the meandering, darkling Spree River. And there was still a third familiar landmark. In the narrow bit of space between the Spree River and the Brandenburg Gate stood a large, isolated square building, the Reichstag. Although gutted since the fire of 1933, this squat edifice was so conspicuous that no attempt was ever made to camouflage it.

The pilot's trained eye would, however, have been even more interested in what he saw just at the edge of the Tiergarten, due south of the Brandenburg Gate. Here lay a huge wedged-shaped block bounded by the Unter den Linden in the north, the Wilhelmstrasse in the east, the Hermann Goering Strasse to the west and Voss Strasse in the south. Here the Reich Chancellery stood.

When the 1945 Battle for Berlin began, this governmental area became known as Zitadelle. From the air, the New Reich Chancellery, which Albert Speer had built in 1938, was even easier to identify than the Reichstag, though it was camouflaged. To maximize available space, Speer had designed an extremely long, rather narrow building with a facade running the whole length of the northern side of Voss Strasse, the equivalent of four normal city blocks. The Chancellery somewhat resembled an art museum, although it mounted a good deal more concentrated antiaircraft batteries than any art museum. The building had already received several direct bomb hits, at least a dozen, most of them through the roof. The windows were shattered from blast effect and flying mortar. But on the lower levels, the ground floor and the shelter-cellar, the solid building was still habitable.

For security reasons, all who entered the bunker had to pass through a bewildering maze of controls set up in the New Reich Chancellery. And those working in the bunker during the day ate and slept in the much larger Chancellery bunker at night. Some were in a second bunker, also large, under the barracks of the SS honor guard nearby. This was at the corner of the Hermann Goering Strasse, at right angles to the Chancellery. The whole area was honeycombed with at least six large bunkers and as many smaller ones. All were interconnected, underground, in what was probably the most elaborate labyrinth built since the cult of the Minotaur in ancient Crete.

Photographs of the only part of the Hitler bunker that was aboveground, the emergency exit and that curious round tower, sometimes convey the impression that visitors entered or left here, but only the security guards themselves were allowed to do this, when they were mounting watch. Even the high-ranking generals could enter the bunker only by passing through three separate checkpoints and by showing passes and identity papers. At night, the watch was doubled. They were armed with machine pistols and hand grenades.

It was not only security, and the pressuring plea of General Rattenhuber, that led to Hitler's decision to go underground. His personal physicians had become increasingly worried, in these last months, about the state of his health. Although he doped himself with sedatives, sleepless nights exhausted him. But Hitler knew, from earlier nocturnal sojourns there in 1943 and 1944, that he could at least snatch some sleep in the bunker. Here the shattering roar of aerial bombardment was muffled and remote. "It felt like a distant artillery barrage on the World War One front," Hitler once said. Only when a two-ton blockbuster landed really close by would the bunker shimmy and shake. The soft alluvial sand on which Berlin is built had a kind of cushioning, shock-absorber effect. Thus, the bunker was even safer than if it had been built on rock or more solid earth foundations, though the trembling made its denizens queasy. The lamps would swing as if moved by a silent underground wind.

The bunker really did not solve Hitler's sleep problem. At best, he seems to have managed about four hours of sleep a day, and that was fitful. He seldom retired before 4:00 or 5:00 A.M., or rose before 10:00 or 11:00 in the morning. We know that he spent some of this time reading, with special magnifying reading glasses for his fast-fading eyesight.

"We all knew the man was only fifty-five," said a young officer in the FBK, "and those of us who had known him in the earlier years before the war, when he was a human dynamo often bursting with restless energy, now noted, from about 1942 on, that he seemed to be aging at least five full years for every calendar year. Near the very end, on the day he celebrated his last birthday, he seemed closer to seventy than to fifty-six. He looked senile. The man was living on nerves, dubious medicaments, and driving will power. Sometimes, even the will power seemed to slacken. Then suddenly it would flash again, with all the old drive and fury."

To what extent did this unnatural bunker life—Adolf Hitler's "speological hang-up," as one medical man put it—directly affect, or accelerate, the German leader's failing health? There is an obvious cause-and-effect at play here, although it was probably never as simple as that. Hitler was a notorious hypochondriac from the days of his youth. Even during the peacetime years of his chancellorship, when he was, in fact, in quite robust health, he was constantly changing his diet, experimenting with pills, worrying about his pulse beat, his vocal cords, his potency.

One of the odd reasons he sometimes gave for his wartime retreats into various cavernous headquarters was that he could work better there, "free from fresh-air poisoning." Daylight, fresh air, the morning hours, these had never been his working ambience. "It is always late in the night that I get my most creative ideas," he liked to say.

Part of the riddle was whether Hitler's worries about his health drove him underground or whether, as many suspected, what finally shattered it was his unnatural regimen. It was the classic vicious circle, where psychosomatic, sometimes hysterical, symptoms began, in fact, to erode the hypochondriac's once-vigorous constitution. By the end of his life, Hitler was also suffering from real organic ailments.

If there is disagreement as to what those ailments actually were, it is perhaps due to the Byzantine atmosphere of his court and the rivalry among his doctors. Many among the courtiers strongly suspected Dr. Theodor Morell, Hitler's private physician, of quackery and misuse of drugs. But Hitler regarded Morell as a miracle worker and brooked no criticism of him. Four other doctors were also present in the last fortnight. They were Dr. Werner Haase, Dr. Ernst-Guenther Schenck, Dr. Karl Gebhardt (all three professors), and Dr. Ludwig Stumpfegger. Dr. Morell left the bunker forever on April 22. Haase, who had first been Hitler's doctor in 1933 and who returned just before the end in 1945, was both Hitler's first and last personal physician in the Chancellery.

Haase was in attendance on Hitler every day until the end. He sometimes came over to the operating room in the New Reich Chancellery cellar to chat with troop doctor Professor Schenck, and often gave him surgical advice. Schenck, by profession an internist, was performing frantic emergency operations on wounded soldiers. Stumpfegger, a real surgeon, spent most of his time drinking with Martin Bormann and was to die with him; his views are not known. But the three professors all made diagnoses. Haase was convinced that Hitler was suffering from Parkinson's disease. Schenck, though he did not see Hitler up close until April 30, took one long look and came up with the same diagnosis. Both Haase and Schenck also suspected that Dr. Morell, himself a morphine addict, had been injecting Hitler with morphine and other detrimental potions. Professor Gebhardt, in a postwar affidavit, did not accept the Parkinson's diagnosis; he tended to defend Dr. Morell, *his* protégé.

Hitler's eyes, once iceberg blue and lustrous, were now often glazed, the eyeballs sunken and bloodshot. His brown hair had turned suddenly gray. He no longer stood erect. His walk was more of a shuffle; he dragged one leg behind. His head was bowed, his body bent forward, with a list to portside. He often seemed in danger of losing his balance. Both hands trembled, and he used the right hand to hold the left up close to his body. While standing, he often leaned his left leg against a table for support. When he lay down on his bunker couch, his senior valet, Linge, had to lift his feet from the floor to the couch. In the very last days, there was often spittle on his lips, and at times he simply drooled or whistled through his teeth. His complexion was sallow. Soup-slop and mustard spots now stained his once spotless jacket.

Now, in his last bunker in Berlin, Hitler was reduced to one switchboard, one radio, and one radio-telephone to the OKW, the German Supreme Command of the Armed Forces. The telephone depended on a swaying antenna, hanging aloft from a toylike aluminum balloon. And yet with this puny signals setup, almost a parody of the spider-like network he had once spun out across Europe, Hitler remained in command, underground, to the last day, the last hour.

CHAPTER 2

THE THIRTEENTH BUNKER

The Berlin bunker had now become the final FHQ, the last of the command posts from which Adolf Hitler had personally directed every aspect of the war. The Allied wartime propaganda picture of the tyrant of Berlin, sitting in his Chancellery in the capital of the Greater German Reich, was absurdly wide of the mark.

Strange as it may seem, even in retrospect, Hitler had seldom been in Berlin, after 1941, for any lengthy period. The capital had become for him a mere place to visit. Most of the summer of 1942 the Fuehrer was not even inside Germany. He was deep in the Ukraine. Most of the years 1943 and 1944 he spent in East Prussia. East Prussia was the remotest corner of the Reich—both historically and geographically. Rastenburg, the FHQ in the East Prussian lake country, was as close to Leningrad as it was to Munich. Now, from mid-January 1945, the Fuehrer was leading the embattled nation from *underneath* his capital, at a level twenty feet lower than that of the municipal sewage system.

This lifestyle was not, however, anything new. This was Adolf Hitler's thirteenth FHQ. Almost all of these had been giant bunkers, and at least half were underground. The Fuehrer's staff, although they grumbled or suffered in silence, had slowly inured themselves to this troglodytic life. As early as 1940, we hear Fräulein Christa Schroeder, Hitler's bright, pert speed-typist, complaining about the clamminess of Felsennest (Rocky Nest), the Hitler hideaway in the remote Eifel Mountains. From here the Fuehrer had conducted the opening stages of the *Blitzkrieg* into the Lowlands and France. Felsennest was, in fact, the first of his long line of underground headquarters; the embattled bunker in Berlin, the last.

The patent absurdity of much of the action that follows, the turgid atmosphere and snapping nerves of most of the actors, came, in part anyway, from the paradox that this last "field headquarters" was located in the middle of Berlin. By returning to Berlin so late in the game, Hitler found that he had painted himself into a corner.

For hitherto, Hitler had always managed to remain linked with Berlin, with the ministries, for example, by a superb communications system. Now, in the Berlin bunker, from January 1945 on, there was no such elaborate communications system. This irony is explained by the fact that, with the Fuehrer back in his capital city, the builders of the bunker had assumed he would no longer need extensive electronic communications. He could simply tie in with the great grid of large signal centers, military and civilian, already within Berlin or just on the outskirts.

At Zossen, for example, only fifteen miles due south of Berlin, there was Central 500, the largest long-distance central board in Germany and, most probably, in all of Europe. Central 500 was directly linked to, and serviced the army, navy, and air force headquarters, all of which had duplicating, if smaller, signal centers inside the city—as did most of the major ministries. Central 500 handled long-distance calls, military and civilian. It had a direct line into the New Reich Chancellery, but *not* into the bunker.

In mid-January 1945, when they first heard that Hitler was descending into the bunker, both Field Marshal Keitel and General Jodl, Hitler's senior military advisers, who, of course, knew the Zossen layout well, tried in vain to induce Hitler to move there. He would, they reasoned, be safer, away from the constant Berlin air raids and at the very center of a giant communications war room. But here Hitler's political instincts prevailed, evidence that he was thinking beyond the purely military situation. He was already planning his own death—as a symbolic act.

In a single room of the bunker, which was also shared by the guards on duty, a new, modern switchboard had been hastily wired up in November 1944. It even had a scrambling device, used for Hitler's private calls to Munich and Berchtesgaden and for highly classified military messages. But this switchboard was not large, and the single operator was not even a professional. He was Sergeant Rochus Misch, who had learned to handle a similar small board in earlier years at Berchtesgaden.

In the last fortnight in the bunker, the normal Berlin municipal telephone system began to falter. In the last days, it went dead silent in several Berlin borough exchanges as these fell into Red Army hands. Harassed staff officers would often use Misch's board, just before briefing Hitler, to call up old friends around town, asking if the Russians had already arrived and, if so, with how many tanks.

In this same room in the middle of the lower bunker, where Sergeant Misch had his switchboard, there was also a German Army medium- and long-wave radio transmitter, but it had no short wave. For the radio-telephone linked up to it, it needed an outside antenna. This was hastily improvised by signalmen dangling a wire suspended above the bunker. Before the end, this emergency antenna was twice knocked out by artillery fire. When the land line leading to the switchboard was also hit by shellfire, as it finally was on Friday, April 27, the switchboard, too, was out for critical hours until new wire could be laid.

Here we have the reason why, in the climactic days of the Battle for Berlin, military couriers, with their hectic arrivals and departures, played such an important role. It is also why—a minor but delightful irony—Adolf Hitler, in the last days of his life, was getting his world news roundup from BBC broadcasts.

With twelve abandoned FHQs stretched across Europe, from Soissons in France, across the Black Forest to Silesia, to Vinnitsa in the Ukraine, finally we find Adolf Hitler, at bay, in a ridiculously small cement command post designed neither for permanent living nor as a proper FHQ. The lower bunker looked like an air-raid shelter designed as a place for perhaps a dozen people to spend a not too comfortable night, or day, in a city under steady bombardment. There were several score larger bunkers in Berlin.

Johannes Hentschel was the chief electrician in the Reich Chancellery. He is the man who was in charge of the engine room with its Diesel motor, which powered most of the bunker utilities during the hectic last stand—air, electricity, water.

Hentschel is the best eyewitness authority on the successive stages in which the Berlin bunker had been built. This is, in part, because he himself attended to all the wiring, and also because he was able to watch the progress of the bunker work from a window in his own nearby flat.

According to Hentschel, the first bunker air-raid shelter was a rather modest affair, with walls less than a meter thick. It was about thirty feet underground and was dug early in 1936. This was the same year German rearmament began—officially. This bunker was to serve the Old Reich Chancellery, since the New Chancellery was yet to be built. This is why, even at the end, one finds the Hitler bunker, above all the so-called upper bunker, or "foreshelter," so close to the surface, just under the Old Chancellery garden.

This distinction also helps to orient us on the difference in location between the Old and the New Reich Chancellery, which pops up so often in this narrative. Basically, these two key buildings stood at right angles to each other. The old building faced the Wilhelmstrasse and the Wilhelmplatz. The new building, however, was around the corner. It ran the entire length of the Voss Strasse. However, they met—and were internally connected—at the Wilhelmplatz corner.

According to Hentschel, the place where he saw the first digging back in 1936 was, naturally enough, the garden—before it was so greatly enlarged in 1938. This, too, helps explain what must be a puzzle to many—namely, why the Hitler bunker seems so off-center, almost in a corner of the vast complex. It is because of the special relationship of the two buildings, erected at different times. The Old Reich Chancellery was a baroque building in the shape of an H—that is, the original eighteenth-century building plus four later wings. A part of the west wing of this structure was originally directly over a part of the upper bunker (until this west wing collapsed into rubble in 1943). One originally entered the first bunker not through any tunnel, but simply by way of a staircase in the cellar of the west wing of the Old Chancellery. This first bunker, later to be called the *Vorbunker,* was only about fifteen feet below cellar level.

The New Reich Chancellery was built in 1938. In itself, it had no bunker, but Albert Speer had designed the cellar in such a fashion that it could easily be converted into bunkers. (This is just what happened in the middle of the war.) A tunnel, more than ninety feet long, but only five feet underground, was bored to connect the New Reich Chancellery to the upper bunker of the Old Reich Chancellery.

As the war progressed, tunneling toward the Fuehrer became a kind of government game. Soon both Ribbentrop's Foreign Ministry and Goebbels' Propaganda Ministry had tunnels into the Old Reich Chancellery, hence underground access to Hitler. What grew up was a kind of downtown governmental labyrinth. Officials and messengers could pass for whole city blocks, always underground, to arrive, ultimately, at one of the underground entrances to the Fuehrerbunker.

Hentschel went on with the story of the building of the bunker.

> In 1943, a Berlin private-construction firm was called in to reinforce the upper bunker as larger bombs began to fall. But it was not until late in 1944 that the same people came back again to build, this time much deeper and with solider walls, what now became known as the lower bunker, the Fuehrerbunker proper. Its roof was more than sixteen feet thick, the walls at least six feet. Tons of earth were piled on top of it all. The lower bunker never was completed, as far as permanent facilities were concerned.

This lower bunker was safer, of course. When we hear bunkerees speaking of bunker events involving Hitler, we can be sure they are always talking of this lower bunker, for Hitler seldom changed levels, as all others did, even Eva Braun, Bormann, and Goebbels. One of the reasons for this is that there was a convivial mess, operating around the clock in the last days. It was in the corridor of the upper bunker. The only description we ever get of Hitler just outside the lower bunker is on the last night, when he said goodbye to a group of nurses. He had emerged from his study and come to the vestibule entrance. But he did not change levels.

These two bunker levels were connected by a wrought-iron staircase, ten to twelve steep spiral steps. A bulkhead and a steel door on the lower level separated the two areas. There were always two armed sentries posted just before the bulkhead. With Hitler always in the lower bunker, the upper bunker became a kind of servants' quarters, with storage space for provisions. The kitchen was here, the pantry, the oak-table communal mess, the refrigerator, the wine cellar.

Before I met Johannes Hentschel, I had already heard so many complaints about the ventilation that although I accepted this technical explanation, I did query him, yet once again, about the filter system. Was he sure that it was always functioning? I had my reason for this question, but did not let Hentschel know it at the time. He thought it over, then replied:

> Yes, there just may have been some malfunction with the filters—although they were quite new. Back in February 1945, in that long lull before the storm, Hitler had come to me and asked how often the filters had to be changed, and whether I could check and see that they had been properly installed. Then, the next day, or maybe it was the day after, Minister Speer spoke to me about this same matter.

Together, Speer and Hentschel went to take a look at the air-intake. It was half-concealed behind an iron grill, which was itself obscured by a low juniper bush. Speer casually suggested that Hentschel remove the old filter for the time being and look around for a replacement, and this Hentschel agreed to do.

A trivial, routine happening. Except that it set up the last of at least nine serious assassination attempts.

CHAPTER 3

THE BUNKER BRUTUS

A late winter lull prevailed through February. Along the Oder, an unexpected thaw slowed all movement by the Red Army. The Yalta Conference was meeting. Every evening, a triumvirate of old Hitler cronies—Martin Bormann, Dr. Joseph Goebbels, and Robert Ley, boss of the Nazi Labor Front—met for a regular parley in the bunker, from 7:00 to 9:00 P.M. Later, at a midnight conference, a glum Hitler would listen in silence to news of how the British and American armies, though still west of the Rhine, were slogging forward on a broad front. It had become increasingly clear that nothing could stop them.

As is perhaps too often forgotten, in February 1945 the most active front was the vertical "third front," the air war over the Reich. Hitler and those in the bunker at least could not forget this. Spring was announcing itself early, by mid-February. The clear skies now meant that Berlin would be bombarded for twenty-one consecutive days and nights, often daytime and nighttime. This is why these early evening Nazi bull sessions were always in the bunker, in the hours after the U.S. Air Force had left and before the RAF arrived.

March came. For the Russians, now on the Oder, it was a month of thaw and steady buildup. German Army counterintelligence gave Hitler a quite accurate estimate of the extent of this Red Army buildup—2.5 million men, 6250 tanks, 7500 tactical aircraft. This meant a superiority of at least 3 to 1 in manpower, 4 to 1 in airpower, 5 to 1 in tanks, and probably at least 10 to 1 in artillery, the Russian specialty.

On the east, Hitler had but one army group to meet this onslaught. This was Army Group Vistula. It consisted of two infantry armies, the Ninth and the Twelfth, both undermanned, and only remnants of the German Third and Fourth Panzer Armies.

Most of the month of March, events again directed Hitler's attentions westward. General Eisenhower's three army groups, comprising seven armies, were now advancing rapidly to and across the Rhine on an extremely broad front. It now extended from Holland to Alsace and the Swiss border. Cologne fell, after a hard fight, on March 6. The first American troops crossed the Rhine on March 7. In the third week of March, Field Marshal Montgomery's whole Twenty-first Army Group, aided by an airborne operation, crossed the Lower Rhine at Wesel.

The one intact German army group still in this area, General Model's Army Group B, now received orders from Hitler to hole up in the Ruhr Pocket. Here they were later double-enveloped. Now, for two of Montgomery's armies, the British Second and the American Ninth, the way to Berlin was a 300-mile open road. One armored corps, given preferential logistic support and supplied by air, could have barreled into Berlin in less than a fortnight.

A rather special authority for this statement is General Guderian. As he later put it, almost diplomatically, "I was then Hitler's senior briefing officer in the bunker. When he asked me why the British and Americans had opted for such a slow, broad-front strategy, I could give no valid, purely military answer."

General Guderian gave a graphic description of the doubletalk atmosphere of those March 1945 bunker briefings:

> In our army briefings, almost every day we too had to announce the fall of some major German city, now Cologne, now Mainz, or Muenster, Frankfurt, Mannheim, Aschaffenburg. We often did this simply by dropping them from the previous day's situation map. We were using large-scale grid-coordinate maps. As a city disappeared, so would a map.

By the end of March, Guderian had had enough of these spectral war games. His abrupt departure is memorable as one of those very rare occasions when somebody really did talk back to Hitler.

The date was March 28. Hitler, in a vile mood, started out to blackguard his generals. The object of his wrath was General Busse, commander of the hard-pressed Ninth Army, the one that was doing most of the fighting outside Berlin. Guderian vehemently came to the younger general's defense. The slanging match got so hot that Guderian's aide, cavalry Captain Berndt von Boldt, had to hold his general back by the tunic. Guderian, to everyone's amazement, was shaking his fist in the Fuehrer's face. Hitler was, of course, astonished. When he recovered, he played the affair very coolly. The Fuehrer adjourned the briefing. An hour later, he quietly suggested to General Guderian that he take a six-week vacation—"after which time your services may be even more urgently needed."

In these waning days of March, Hitler dispensed with the services not only of Guderian, but of the only other voice in the bunker courageous enough to tell him to his face that the war was lost. That second voice belonged to his minister for war production, Albert Speer, the architect who had once been the Fuehrer's most trusted confidant.

Speer was the one prominent member of the old entourage who had deliberately distanced himself from the court—though in terms of Berlin municipal geography, he was only four blocks from the bunker. He was working and living in the last surviving corner wing of his own bomb-shattered ministry on the Pariser Platz, next to the Brandenburg Gate.

Like Hitler, Speer was still operating from the same building that had been the scene of his earlier triumphs. As minister for war production from 1942 to 1944, Speer had doubled, and in some instances tripled, German arms production. September 1944 had been the peak month, but also the month in which the graphs of Speer's team of 300 crack technocrats spelled out the doom to come. The production of fighter planes had reached 3000 a month; Tiger and Panther tanks, 900 a month; construction of submarines had been narrowed from nine months to less than two. The production of synthetic gasoline, however, had plummeted by 70 percent. U.S. Air Force strategic bombers had, finally, got to the great Leuna and I. G. Farben hydrogeneration plants.

As a young and ambitious architect in quest of a patron, Albert Speer eagerly bartered his soul to the devil. His mundane motive was decent enough; he wanted to build. In his one brilliantly intuitive appointment, Hitler put Speer in charge of armaments, early in 1942.

Once Speer became minister, the sheer pressure of work and the realities of the war estranged him from the court, and thus from his youthtime idol, Adolf Hitler. As architect, Speer had always been treated by Hitler as an equal; as a minister, only as one among several, a subordinate. Hitler himself, once war began, became the prisoner of his own court. Speer did not. His job now brought him back into daily contact with one of Germany's true elites, the industrial managers, the technocrats, and the more intelligent and rational among the military.

Speer, moreover, had always had a deep streak of patriotism in him, less the tub-thumping chauvinism of the National Socialists than the more old-fashioned, almost poetic devotion to the hills and valleys, the rivers and streams, the forests and heaths of his native land. As an architect, Speer could describe the nave and transept of every cathedral in Germany. But as a technocrat, he knew that the romantic fatherland of the past, the Germany of cathedrals and lyric poets, now lived in the highly industrial present. Postwar Germany, whatever the military decision, would have to export or perish.

During the earlier years of the war, Speer had managed to convince himself that the fate of Germany, for better or for worse, was linked with the person of the Fuehrer. But, this also implied that Hitler would have the same feeling of responsibility. Now, however, in the last months of 1944 and early 1945, Speer had filed memorandum after memorandum on the mounting hopelessness of the supply situation. He had constantly stressed the imperative of making peace. Hitler filed these in his safe; some he even refused to read.

Neither before he met Hitler, nor after, had Albert Speer ever read *Mein Kampf*. Once, on a quiet weekend above Berchtesgaden, he had started to wade through it, but the author told him that "it is quite outdated." Then, in his office in Berlin in mid-February 1945, Minister Speer received a visit from one of his close friends, Dr. Friedrich

Lueschen, a senior industrial manager of Siemens and the spokesman for the German electrical industry. Dr. Lueschen *had* read *Mein Kampf*, and he now quizzically asked Speer, "Are you aware of the passage in *Mein Kampf* that is most often quoted by the public nowadays?" With this, he handed Speer a slip of paper with the following quote:

> The task of diplomacy is to ensure that a nation does not heroically go to its destruction but is practically preserved. Every way that leads to this end is expedient, and a failure to follow it must be called criminal neglect of duty.

No sooner had Speer read and absorbed this than his friend presented a second similar slip.

> State authority as an end in itself cannot exist, since in that case every tyranny on this earth would be sacred and unassailable. If a racial entity is being led to its doom by means of governmental power, then the rebellion of every single member of such a folk is not only a right, but a duty.

The elderly man then departed, without saying a word.

Nation . . . Tyranny . . . Folk . . . Duty. Seldom had the pages of *Mein Kampf* been quoted with better effect. This, after all, was precisely what Speer had been brooding about for months, what he had been iterating and reiterating in his oral and written reports to the Fuehrer.

For long hours of the rapidly fading Berlin afternoon, Speer paced the floor of his bleak office. Finally, he was triggered into action. The time was shortly after 7:00 P.M. At this hour, Speer knew, Hitler would be palavering in the bunker with Goebbels, Bormann, and Ley.

Clad in the warm long overcoat he had been wearing in the office, Speer now put on the visored cap he wore when driving and went down into the underground garage. As a minister, he was entitled to a limousine, chauffeur, and bodyguard. Instead, and as usual, he preferred to take the wheel alone.

The guards at the Reich Chancellery recognized the familiar figure; "*Guten Abend,*" they said, and waved him on. Adolf Hitler had given his protégé many privileges; one of these was that he could park in the courtyard, as he had been doing ever since the days when he was building the place.

It was now perhaps seven-thirty, and the winter evening was dark; the moon had not yet risen. Speer did not enter the underground tunnel, as he normally would have done had he been reporting to Hitler in the bunker. Instead, he sauntered out into the Old Reich Chancellery garden, which now looked less like a garden than a dump. He headed straight for the blockhouse that served as an emergency exit, passing the water barrel and the cement mixer. Soon he was strolling along the narrow gravel path where Hitler, when he did emerge from his catacomb, walked Blondi. Speer's mission, on this particular evening, was to inspect the air-intake of the bunker ventilation system. He had designed and built almost everything else in this area, but *not* the bunker.

If anyone had stopped him at this point—a most unlikely prospect, since he was an old familiar on the premises—Speer would simply have answered that Hitler had been complaining about a possible malfunction in the ventilation system, which was true enough, and had asked Speer to talk to Cheftechniker Johannes Hentschel about the possibility of changing or cleaning the filter. But what Speer really had in his thumping heart this evening was the decision he had taken that same afternoon. He was preparing to murder Adolf Hitler and his three bunker cronies by filtering poison gas into the bunker.

The architect found the air-intake pretty much where he had expected it—at ground level, within easy reach, only partly hidden by a scrawny evergreen, and covered by a removable iron grill. Examining it more closely with the help of his flashlight, Speer could make out the filter. No problem, really. The gas he had in mind was a deadly new nerve gas called Tabun.

Speer remained at the bunker only about ten minutes. He did not enter it, nor did he intend to be present at the second staff conference scheduled, as usual, for midnight. Instead, he drove back to his office, ate a snack alone, and went to sleep. The problem was how to procure the gas without arousing suspicion.

Then in the course of a technical discussion with an assistant, Speer discovered to his consternation that Tabun became effective only after it had been exploded in a shell or a hand grenade. But such a grenade, introduced into the bunker, would, of course, have shattered the thin wall air ducts. Speer continued his search for one of the conventional gases, such as mustard. February was fading into March.

While awaiting the Tabun, Speer had, on at least three other occasions, repeated his nocturnal prowling of the bunker area. He found Hitler, Goebbels, Bormann, and Ley meeting, as usual, and at the same hours. On one of these lonely clandestine strolls, he met Hentschel.

Realizing now that he would have to use mustard gas, he casually spoke about removing the filter of the ventilation system. Hentschel did this, a bit too promptly, for two nights later Speer found that the filter had been replaced. This was a minor obstacle. When the mustard gas arrived, he would simply have Hentschel repeat the performance.

Considerable time had, however, now elapsed. It was March 7 before Speer got the news that mustard gas was on the way and would arrive the next day. Yet once more, Speer made the short journey at 7:00 P.M., from the Brandenburg Gate to the Reich Chancellery. Once again he parked in his special corner lot and headed, on foot, through the short passageway directly toward the bunker.

Now, as he entered the Chancellery garden, Speer found, to his astonished dismay, that he was walking directly into a garish glare of searchlights. They were mounted atop the bunker and were serviced by four armed SS guards of the FBK. In the light he could make out that the searchlights were playing on a round metallic chimney, about ten feet tall, that rose from the ventilator air-intake that was his destination. Speer froze in sheer terror. At this moment he was convinced that somewhere along the line his plot must have been discovered. "I stood there, flat-footed, feeling guilty, as all conspirators do. I thought I must have been betrayed. There was cold sweat on my brow and running down my spine. At this moment, I half-expected a tap on the shoulder. . . ."

But all was silence. Nothing happened. Even the mounted guards took no notice of the nighttime lone intruder. They were about forty feet away and higher up, and could not see him in the darkness. They themselves were in the glare of the lights, whereas Speer had stepped back into the shadow. When he finally did turn around, nobody was there. Slowly, Speer began to recover his composure. He soon surmised the triviality of what had happened. Since January, Hitler had been complaining not only about the ventilator, but also about the fact that the bunker was unfinished when he had first moved in. Hitler himself, one of the mustard-gas victims of World War I, knew that this gas was heavier than air. Therefore, he must have ordered the chimney as a routine antigas precaution.

"On that evening, as I left the Reich Chancellery," Speer remembered, "I felt like one of those desperate gamblers who had just played Russian roulette—and won. I was completely frustrated in my poison-gas scheme, for there was, now, no practical way to bring gas into the bunker. Inwardly, I was also—strangely—relieved. My mind quickly shook off all brooding ideas of assassination. I now began to feel it was better, on balance, to attempt to frustrate Hitler's 'scorched-earth' plans."

The end was not yet. By the time Albert Speer had pushed from his mind the thought of killing Hitler—and had canceled the mustard-gas order—it was already the second week in March. The U.S. 9th Infantry Division was now across the Rhine, and the Red Army might cross the Oder at any moment. Budapest had fallen; Vienna was besieged. Hitler was preparing to execute his scorched-earth or so-called Nero orders.

On March 15, 1945, Albert Speer sat down to draft the most courageous memorandum ever penned in the Third Reich, and the most important historical document ever to be delivered to Hitler in his Berlin bunker. Speer wrote:

> In four to eight weeks the final collapse of the German economy must be expected with certainty . . . After that collapse the war cannot be continued . . . We must do everything to maintain, even if only in the most primitive manner, a basis for the existence of the nation to the last . . . We have no right, at this stage of the war, to carry out demolitions which would affect the life of the people. If our enemies wish to destroy this nation, which has fought with unique bravery, then this historical shame should rest exclusively on them. We have the duty of leaving to the nation every possibility of enduring its reconstruction in the distant future.

In the last fortnight of March 1945, Albert Speer was to use every ruse, invoke every friendship, manipulate every string he had learned to pull in his once high-riding days as the fair-haired prince of the Hitler court. If the technocrat had been living all too casually among born intriguers, toadying yes-men, all the doubletalkers and doublethinkers of the Third Reich, he now employed their methods to play off one satrap against another. For he still held one of the very highest of court cards in his hand—his sophisticated knowledge of the complicated psyche of Adolf Hitler.

He knew that if Hitler read the memorandum of March 15 in one of his black moods, the Fuehrer would, at the very least, fire Speer and probably have him placed under house arrest. Speer's "eyes and ears" in the bunker, with orders to stick as close as possible to the Fuehrer, was Luftwaffe Colonel Nikolaus von Below. Von Below was given a typed copy of the memorandum by Speer and was told to give Hitler a verbal briefing. He was advised to choose a moment of relative calm. An experienced courtier, he carried out this risky assignment with the utmost skill.

Strange is the role of sheer chance in what follows. Albert Speer's birthday was March 19. The Germans make a great thing of birthdays, and seldom had any man approached the threshold of forty with less assurance that he had a fair chance to live to be forty-one. Within the inner circle of the Reich Chancellery Group, Hitler always remembered birthdays. One of the most prized gifts was an autographed photograph of the Fuehrer, framed in solid silver with a gold-inlaid swastika, mounted in a red leather case. Speer had always been too proud to ask for one—above all because, since the bunker, Hitler had taken to handing them out like Crackerjack tokens. Now, however, Speer approached Hitler's adjutant, SS Major General Julius Schaub, to drop the hint that he would not mind being given such a framed photograph.

Thus, on March 18, the eve of his birthday, Speer headed once again for the bunker, less than a fortnight since he had abandoned his poison-gas mission. He had the original of the twenty-two-page memorandum under his arm. Before the routine midnight conference, Hitler, in a fairly cordial and relaxed mood, came into the conference room to greet him. "Ah, you know, Speer, your beautiful architecture is no longer the proper frame for the situation conferences."

During the conference itself, however, Hitler's mood darkened. The chief topic was General George S. Patton's Third Army, its armor now rampaging through the Saar and the Palatinate. Hitler turned to his armaments minister and said, "Speer, explain what the loss of the Saar means to our production."

"It will speed the inevitable collapse."

Most of the conference participants were startled at the bluntness of Speer's answer. There was a shattering silence. But Hitler let it pass. Before the conference broke up, however, the Fuehrer unleashed one of his Nero-like orders: all Germans west of the Rhine River were to be evacuated forthwith. This involved a population of some eight million.

The conference broke up around 2:00 A.M. It was now March 19, Speer's fortieth birthday. Partly to deliver his March 15 memorandum personally, partly to receive his birthday present, but mostly to say goodbye to the Fuehrer, Speer requested a private audience. For many reasons, it might be the last. A scant two weeks before, this same Albert Speer had been standing outside the bunker, preparing to play a mustard-gas Brutus to this most malignant of the world's long line of Caesars. Now he was asking for an autographed picture.

Hitler rang for his valet to fetch the framed picture, as requested. His hand trembled as he handed it over. Tears were welling in his glassy blue eyes. He mumbled a friendly felicitation. Since the gift was enclosed within a leather case, Speer first put it casually aside, laying it down on the Fuehrer's desk; he intended to open it later. Hitler began to fumble with his nickel-rimmed spectacles, murmuring apologetically, "Lately it has been hard for me to write even a few words in my own hand. You know how it shakes. Often I can hardly complete my signature. What I have written for you came out almost illegible."

At this hint that he should open his present, Speer did so, and, as Hitler had warned, he was barely able to decipher the scrawled handwriting, as familiar as it must have been to him. The dedication was, however, warm and friendly, thanking the architect and minister for his past work, and pledging enduring friendship. Nothing catches the ambivalent nature of the relationship between these two antithetical men better than this nostalgic moment. Hitler was touched by the corny request for the autographed photo, from the same man who had come to tell him officially that his Third Reich was tumbling down. Hitler was sincere; but he was also, still and as always, the inveterate actor. He was hoping to soften Speer's resolve. At this moment, Speer recently admitted, "I almost flinched." Except that he knew Adolf Hitler far too well. He also had in his mind's eye a harrowing vision of the world of catastrophe outside the bunker.

He therefore now handed Hitler the memorandum. To break, somehow, the long and ugly silence that ensued, as casually as possible Speer informed the Fuehrer that he had changed his mind about his own plans. Instead of flying to Koenigsberg, as he had announced earlier, he would be leaving by car for western Germany. Discreetly, he then left the Fuehrer's office.

But while Speer was still in the bunker, telephoning for his car and driver, Hitler summoned him back. "I have thought it over. It will be better if you take my car and have my chauffeur, Kempka, drive you."

Hitler had thus not taken long to fathom Speer's mind and purpose. The military conference just held had made clear to him that Speer had switched plans and was heading west for the Rhineland and the Palatinate to block industrial destruction. This sinister little matter about the car and chauffeur meant that Hitler wanted to control Speer's activities, outside the bunker and outside Berlin. He was using Erich Kempka as a personal spy on his own minister. Speer at first protested. A compromise was reached. Speer could take off in his own car, Hitler said, provided he took Kempka along as chauffeur. The atmosphere in the bunker had become icy. The friendly birthday warmth had dissipated.

Even Erich Kempka, for all the sliminess of his stool-pigeon mission, was happy at this moment to leave the fetid atmosphere of the bunker and to come up into the early spring air of nighttime Berlin. Like his chum, Chief Pilot Hans Baur, Kempka belonged to the higher ranks of the coterie of cronies in the inner circle of the Reich Chancellery Group, which Speer derisively called the "Chauffeureska." Like Baur, he had been faced, for long weeks now, with technological unemployment. In the past three months, he had driven the Fuehrer perhaps five or six times.

Speer and Kempka had only two things in common—their personal relationship with the Fuehrer, and a mutual, almost boyish, fascination with fast automobiles. Auto buff Speer insisted on keeping the wheel of his own car—it was, after all, now his birthday. For the next forty-eight hours, most of them spent without sleep, Speer covered a fair amount of German geography. He was now in the Rhineland area that had become the western front—the Palatinate, his native North Baden, and the Westerwald, which is just across the river from Bonn. He even managed—still on his birthday—to visit his parents in Heidelberg, just before it was to fall to the rapidly advancing Americans. Otherwise, he was zooming about, talking to generals, plant managers, mayors, anybody and everybody in a position to block or forestall the scorched-earth decrees soon to come from the Berlin bunker.

Because the Fuehrer had isolated himself in Berlin, he was utterly out of touch with public opinion. The prevailing mood was now of galloping defeatism. Millions of chastened Germans, going down in a sea of white flags, were already snugly behind the ever-advancing American lines. Millions more—not least the three million Berliners—were quietly hoping for a similar beneficent fate. Even several Gauleiters, once the brown-granite pillars of the Nazi state-within-a-state, were now wobbling. In the Palatinate, General Patton was a lot closer to the local Germans than was Martin Bormann in Berlin.

True, Bormann still had formal control of the Gauleiters. His problem was he now had no henchmen in the field to discipline reluctant Gauleiters. Speer, who still had the nimbus and power of a minister, was also a well-known, still-respected figure, as Bormann was not. Only the Gauleiters knew how powerful Bormann really was in the Hitler court. Speer's effective power was outside the bunker, out where reality was.

In both cases, the power was derivative—from Hitler. If Speer stayed out of the bunker one day too long, the ultimate in disaster loomed. So he cagily returned to Berlin, every second or third day, to protect his own shoulder blades. Bormann's problem, in this den of court intrigue, was even more thorny. He knew very well what Speer was doing, for Bormann was getting daily reports.

Roving around the Palatinate, Speer discovered, happily, that the mass-evacuation order was being ignored. The three Palatinate Gauleiters whom he met in Mainz all assured him it was not too late to carry out any demolition orders. Because he knew the people on the spot and they knew him, because he was there so close to the collapsing front, Speer's communications net and his authority were thus able to trump Bormann's.

On March 20, however, Speer received the telegraphed answer to his memorandum. Hitler was replying with a written text, as promised. The long and short of the message was that Speer was stripped of all power to advise or interfere in the destruction program. The power was handed over directly to the Gauleiters, under Bormann.

Hitler, in the most savage of his decrees, now ordered "the destruction of all military, transportation, communications, industrial and supply facilities, as well as all resources within the Reich." Every previous Speer order—for example, the one for crippling rather than destroying the industrial infrastructure—was thus explicitly revoked. Speer received this Hitler directive while sitting in an army headquarters in the Ruhr Valley, the most concentrated industrial complex in Europe or, for that matter, the world. The literal carrying-out of Hitler's order meant that within less than a year's time, even as peace came, the life of the Ruhr miners would be thrown back to the anthropological level that once prevailed here along one of the Ruhr tributaries, the Neander. The Ruhr miner would become a modern, more wretched version of his museum-piece ancestor, the Neanderthal man.

Seven hours on the road, and Speer was back in Berlin. It was the afternoon of March 21, the first day of spring, when Speer reported back to the bunker. Hitler asked for a briefing, not from Speer but from Kempka. Technically, Speer was still minister, but he had been stripped of all effective power in the only field that really mattered. Hitler invited him to the briefing that evening, but Speer decided not to show up.

On March 24, Speer again left Berlin for the great industrial basin, once the first arsenal of the Reich. Although badly bombed, Ruhr factories were still functioning at 91 percent capacity. Militarily, the

Ruhr was now about to be cut off from the rest of Germany by a classic double-envelopment operation. The encirclement and by-passing of the Ruhr Pocket was about to put the Ruhr and Germany out of the war.

As minister, Speer had been stripped of his power to forbid scorched-earth measures. Despite this handicap, Speer was still able to softsoap the hesitant Ruhr Gauleiters into waiting at least for "implementation orders."

Before returning to Berlin, Speer took a last quick swing south, to Baden. He was in Heidelberg when the Berlin order came through to blow up every waterworks and public utility in Baden. He suggested that all these orders be dropped into a mailbox about to be overrun by American troops. On at least two occasions, Speer was driving and weaving his car *between* the advancing Americans and the retreating Germans. Only his knowledge of the backroads of the Odenwald, his childhood tramping grounds behind Heidelberg, saved him from capture.

Speer was back in Berlin the next day, March 26, having arrived around midnight after a strenuous drive. He was physically and nervously exhausted as he approached the inevitable confrontation and showdown in the bunker. Hitler, after the midnight conference, now received Speer alone and came directly to the point. "Bormann has given me a report of your conferences with the Ruhr Gauleiters. You pressured them not to carry out my orders and declared that the war is lost. Are you aware of what must follow from that?"

Had the culprit been anyone else but Speer, the choice might well have been between shooting and hanging. But the tension soon seemed to lessen. Hitler merely said, calmly and rather matter-of-factly, "If you were not my architect, I would take the measures called for in such a case."

Speer refused to flinch. "Take the measures you deem necessary and grant no consideration to me as an individual."

Hitler countered, solicitously, "Speer, you are overworked and ill. I have therefore decided that you are to go on leave at once."

"No, I am perfectly well," Speer replied. "If you no longer want me as your minister, dismiss me. I cannot keep the responsibility of a minister while another is acting in my place."

The Fuehrer sat down. So did Speer, unasked, a real breach of established court etiquette. Now Hitler began again, this time almost pleading. "Speer, if you can convince yourself that the war is not lost, you can continue running your shop. You have twenty-four hours to think over your answer. Tomorrow let me know whether you *hope* the war can still be won." There was no handshake. Speer was dismissed.

Standing up to Adolf Hitler had exhausted Speer, as it had the very few others who ever did so and lived to tell about it. He emerged from the bunker like a frogman surfacing for fresh air. It was the middle of the silent Berlin night. There was a bright moon overhead. He wondered idly why the RAF had failed to put in an appearance.

Speer drove again down the deserted Wilhelmstrasse, to his bachelor's flat in the ministry. He tried to sleep, but sleep came only fitfully. Sitting on the edge of his cot, he began drafting a handwritten letter to Hitler. It was twenty-four pages long, a mixture of honey and vinegar, a long philosophic review of how, why, and when the war had been lost. It ended with an earnest plea to Hitler to end the insensate destruction. Some time in the early morning hours Speer must have fallen asleep, for it was late afternoon before he sent the letter over by courier.

Once again it was close to midnight as Speer drove toward the bunker. The twenty-four-hour deadline was lapsing. All the trenchant points he had so neatly rehearsed in the personal letter suddenly became a vast blur in his mind. He entered the Fuehrer's study unsure of what he was going to say. Hitler greeted him with one terse word: "Well?"

"Mein Fuehrer," Speer said, "I stand unreservedly behind you!"

For the moment, the Fuehrer did not even answer. Then, slowly, he shook hands, his own hand trembling. His eyes welled up with tears of gratitude. "Then all is well." It was a mellow moment and a melancholy reminder of the old days now vanished forever. Hitler had what he wanted and apparently needed, a lachrymose profession of mouth loyalty. Now Speer moved deftly to nail down what he in turn needed, like a poker player asking the dealer for one card. "Since I stand unreservedly behind you, then you must once again entrust me, instead of the Gauleiters, with the implementation of your decree."

The operative word here is "implementation." Hitler authorized Speer to draw up a document that, he said, he would sign at once. He did not really budge an inch in principle, but he allowed Speer to smuggle in the loophole clause that "the same effect can be achieved with industrial installations by crippling them." Speer had retreated upstairs into an empty room of the New Chancellery to work up this draft. When he came back, Hitler initialed it in pencil.

These initials—A.H.—spelled restored power. As dawn broke over Berlin, Speer, with his revived ministerial authority, was out to restore the situation as it had existed before the Hitler decree dated March 19.

Each of the printed orders that he now sent out, posthaste, stressed that "precise implementation orders will follow."

As Speer said recently:

> I had no intention of ever sending out any such orders, and the key people at the receiving end all knew this. They were, so to speak, in the position of carrying out my orders *not* to carry out my orders.

To end the account of this amazing period—all that was at stake was at least $200 billion worth of industrial plant—Speer also managed to wring from Hitler, when he caught him a few days later in a relaxed mood, the common-sense admission, "Perhaps, after all, the scorched-earth idea has no point in a country of such compact topography as Germany. It can fulfill its purpose only in vast spaces, such as Russia."

CHAPTER 4

THE MOUNTAIN PEOPLE

For Berlin in 1945, April was indeed the cruelest month. On April 23, the ultimate military alert was proclaimed for the city under siege. Operation Clausewitz, a hasty, ill-prepared plan for a last stand within the city, went into effect. Around noontime on that day, a Monday, SS General Mohnke and his battle group of some 2000 combat troops marched seven miles from their barracks into the cellar of the New Reich Chancellery.

The 1st Ukrainian Army Front under Marshal Georgi Zhukov had begun storming across the Oder River in force. The Oder, which flows south to north, is only sixty miles east of Berlin. The Russians, who had come from the Volga and the Don, across the Dnieper and the Vistula, had now bridged the last river barrier on their 2500-mile march to Berlin.

Thus another forlorn hope, to which most of the three million Berlin civilians had still been clinging, was about to be dashed. For weeks, Berliners had been eagerly following reports of the extremely rapid advance east of the U.S. and British armies after their Rhine crossing in March. Twelve days earlier, on Wednesday, April 11, advance units of the spearhead U.S. Ninth Army had reached and crossed the Elbe River at Madgeburg, which is only ninety miles west southwest of Berlin.

Military men in the bunker, who knew that the autobahn from

Madgeburg to Berlin was now free of any large German combat units, also calculated that elements of the U.S. 2nd Armored Division and the U.S. 83rd Infantry Division would be arriving in Berlin within twenty-four to forty-eight hours; that is, at least two full days before the Russians stormed across the Oder. Americans now had an open road to Berlin.

Although it is not directly the theme of this book, this historical event—more strictly speaking this historical nonevent—is still a matter of much dispute today. What was the real reason for this strange American halt, in effect a pull-back order by General Eisenhower to allow the Russians to become sole conquerors of Berlin?

This writer and several thousand other American soldiers were eyewitnesses not of events in Berlin, but of just what was happening on the Elbe River. Sometime before noon on Thursday, April 12, we were all set to cross the Elbe River. There was no visible opposition as combat engineers strung out a pontoon bridge and brought up amphibious "ducks." We heard that ten miles to the south of us units of the 83rd Infantry Division were also preparing a crossing.

Just before noon—it was a warm, cloudy day—we received from on high sudden countermanding orders. This baffled us. By radio we were told that no American soldiers were to cross the Elbe; if any were already across, they were to return immediately to the west bank of the Elbe.

Orders, as they say, are orders. To clear up part of the popular mythology relating to this vignette of world history, it is just not true that any American soldiers, at least any whom I knew or met, were particularly eager to roar into Berlin as conquering heroes. Three-day passes for Paris were much more in demand.

Moreover, as far as daily military tasks were concerned, my own operation could function almost as well from the west bank of the Elbe River. Our radio mission then was to establish, by wireless intercept and direction-finding devices, the precise German OB (order of battle)—or what was now left of it. For we were now no longer able, by the usual means, to identify German Army units we had been tracing and tailing since the Normandy beachhead. On the other side of the Elbe, between us and Berlin, the German front seemed to be disintegrating into battle groups. Most of these battle-group units were at first heading west, that is, in our direction, then east, and then, like phantoms, they vanished from the air waves.

It was only during my research for this book that I finally established to my own satisfaction what was really happening in that chaotic military situation around Berlin in mid-April 1945. The answer is simple enough. While Hitler in the bunker was girding for Armageddon, determined to defend his capital to the last man, last building, and last cartridge, cooler heads among the German General Staff, above all Colonel General Gotthardt Heinrici, the last commander of Army Group Vistula, had other, saner ideas.

German generals and other senior officers active in the field, at long last able to ignore or fudge orders coming from Hitler, were out to help their troops—plus the gigantic flow of German civilian refugees—elude Russian captivity. General Heinrici was able to do this by clever maneuvering—and by poker-faced doubletalk whenever he had to report to the Fuehrerbunker. This took courage. The two battered German armies now trapped between the Oder and the Elbe were the Ninth Army under General Busse, east of Berlin, and the Twelfth German Army under General Wenck, west of the city and east of the Elbe. Heinrici so maneuvered these two armies that while creating the appearance of falling back to defend Berlin—Hitler's persistent order—he was, in fact, quietly telling General Wenck to collapse the front in the west; to move east to support General Busse's disengaging efforts, and then to head west again.

Heinrici thus created a corridor through which both the battered German units and the civilian refugee flood could by-pass Berlin, both to the north and to the south. In the final stages, they could make a dash for the Elbe, to surrender to the British and the Americans. Under the circumstances, it was an eminently sensible decision. By these delaying tactics, General Heinrici also quietly hoped that American armor would use this corridor for a quick dash into Berlin. But here foxy General Heinrici had outsmarted himself.

Another quite unexpected event on this same fateful Thursday, April 12, was the sudden death of President Franklin D. Roosevelt in Warm Springs, Georgia. Death struck around noon, Eastern Standard Time. The startling news, picked up by radio-monitoring of a BBC Reuters flash, reached the Berlin bunker around 11:00 P.M., Middle European Time. This was just before Hitler's second, or midnight, situation-briefing. Any urge in the bunker to celebrate was more than slightly dampened by a mighty RAF raid then in progress.

Just after midnight, Joseph Goebbels, en route by motorcar from a visit to the Oder front, arrived at his residence, to get the news at the door. According to one witness, "his face lit up—partly from the news, partly from the reflection from the burning city." The propaganda minister was soon on the phone to the Fuehrer, some five blocks away.

Sergeant Misch, who was at the switchboard, recalled Hitler's reaction. "He said something to the effect that, with this remarkable turn of events, the U.S. Army and the Red Army might soon be exchanging artillery barrages over the roof of the Reich Chancellery. I didn't quite fathom just how he meant that." Misch was not really a political animal. What Hitler obviously meant—or at least yearned for—was the sudden breakup of the alliance between the western powers and Stalin. He knew it was in the cards; he was simply a few critical months off in his timing.

The appearance and actions of Goebbels in this macabre, flaming midnight scene—the telephone call was followed by a champagne party celebrated in his study—helps us locate one of the major actors in the developing bunker scenario. The little doctor was not, as yet, holed up in the Fuehrerbunker, nor would he be for another ten days. As Gauleiter of Berlin, he was always where the action was—now visiting the battle front, now giving bitter-end speeches, still writing his weekly column, still holding daily press conferences.

By mid-April, just one day before the Battle for Berlin was to begin, who was present in the bunker? We meet several members of the Hitler court already mentioned, as well as others soon destined to play major roles in the developing action. Johannes Hentschel is at his post in the machine room. Sergeant Misch is at the switchboard. Some thirty members of the FBK, under Lieutenant Colonel Franz Schaedle, are mounting guard. Major General Rattenhuber, chief of the security squad, is present with at least a dozen of his detectives, all of them in their SS uniforms. The military proper have not yet moved in to take up battle stations. They first file in on Monday, April 23.

The busiest retainer at this moment is pilot Hans Baur. Der Chefpilot has not flown the Fuehrer for long months, not since December 1944. But he is still in charge of considerable air activity in and around Berlin. He spends about half his working time in the bunker. He is also often out in the city, straw-bossing construction of an emergency air strip near the Brandenburg Gate, or inspecting the small fleet of planes he still has in the underground hangar at Tempelhof airport.

One of Baur's aides, copilot Colonel Beetz, is already moving about the bunker, compiling a list for the flight called Operation Seraglio. On this list are the names of all those of Hitler's staff who have been chosen to fly to Berchtesgaden as soon as the Fuehrer gives the word. Whether Der Chef will fly with them or not is still a moot question. The list contains the names of half of the permanent personnel present.

"I think," said Bauer in retrospect, "that this whole flight idea was much more Martin Bormann's than Hitler's. Anyway, it was always Bormann, not Hitler, who kept nagging me about that list, about the condition of my planes, and progress on the emergency airstrip."

Martin Bormann is not only present; he is omnipresent. Stocky, bullish, drinking heavily when off duty, Bormann is literally at the Fuehrer's elbow, wheeling and dealing madly in what is left of the Nazi power game. In terms of physical proximity, although not of course of power or influence, there is, however, one man who is often to be found even closer to Hitler. This is Major Otto Guensche, the tall rugged soldier of twenty-seven who is the Fuehrer's senior SS adjutant. Guensche is a kind of bunker Man Friday.

There are some dozen women present in the Fuehrerbunker, and more in the Reich Chancellery and the barracks. Fräulein Else Krueger is secretary to Martin Bormann, and there are three or four German Army signal corps women running messages back and forth from the bunker to the Reich Chancellery.

All four of Hitler's permanent women secretaries are also still with him. The eldest is Fräulein Johanna Wolf. In her mid-forties, "Wolfie" has been with Hitler since 1924. The second unmarried secretary is Fräulein Christa Schroeder, thirty. The two youngest—and best-looking—are in their mid-twenties, both married. Frau Gerda Christian, once engaged to Erich Kempka, is now married to Luftwaffe Major General Eckard Christian. Frau Gertrud Junge is a recent widow. She married a corporal in Hitler's honor bodygurad, the FBK; he fell in 1944 on the Russian front.

Ambassador Walter Hewel, the liaison officer from the Foreign Office, is an old friend of Hitler's from the 1923 Munich beer hall *Putsch* days. Kempka, now in charge of the Chancellery garage, is usually in or about the bunker—as are chief valet Heinz Linge and some half-dozen other minor charges. Heinrich Mueller, chief of the Gestapo, moves in and out of the bunker frequently, but is not stationed there.

Finally, there is SS Lieutenant General Hermann Fegelein, Eva Braun's brother-in-law. Liaison man between Himmler and Hitler, Fegelein usually appears in the bunker at least twice every day at briefing time. But he is spending most of his hours in a bachelor-style flat in the Bleibtreustrasse, just off the once-fashionable Kurfuersten-damm. He is keeping a lady friend there—a naughty liaison that will have some wildly dramatic consequences.

Thus, the men and women known today to historians as the Reich Chancellery Group are pretty much the old familiar court, or rather the remnant of it still with Adolf Hitler in his last bunker. When interviewing various members of the Reich Chancellery Group, I noted that while they often used this term to describe themselves to me, it was not, in fact, the way they spoke of themselves at the time these bunker events were happening. They then called themselves *"die von dem Berg"* (the mountain people). Those, that is, who had also served Hitler in Berchtesgaden.

This cozy, familiar phrase also accounts, I believe, for the extraordinary amount of otherwise listless bunker hours, day and night, spent in reminiscence. Whenever I was checking out just exactly what this or that witness was doing on a specific day, at a given hour—or, for that matter, what Hitler himself was doing—I invariably ran into evidence of these marathon talk-sessions about the happy, happy days on the Obersalzberg.

The Reich Chancellery Group in 1945 included two ministers, Speer and Goebbels, though rarely in their official capacities. Speer enters the inner circle as an architect; Goebbels, as prophet and raconteur. The group also includes Bormann, who may not have been a minister but who was as powerful as any. But it did not include von Ribbentrop, the foreign minister; he was represented by his subordinate, Walter Hewel. Neither Goering nor Himmler belonged; they were off running their own courts. Goering's man at the Hitler court until 1944 was Colonel Nikolaus von Below. General Fegelein was Himmler's liaison man. Although we meet them often enough in the bunker, neither Field Marshal Wilhelm Keitel nor Colonel General Alfred Jodl really "belonged to" the Reich Chancellery Group. Present twice every day to conduct briefings, they always leave and go to their own headquarters just outside Berlin. But Generals Hans Krebs and Wilhelm Burgdorf, destined to remain in the bunker until the end, *did* become late members of the group. As did Major General Mohnke, the two doctors, Professor Werner Haase and Colonel Ernst-Guenther Schenck, and Reich Youth leader Artur Axmann.

At the time the New Reich Chancellery was built, in 1938, Albert Speer also threw up, in nonornamental, strictly utilitarian style, two large barrackslike structures at right angles to the showpiece Chancellery, on the Hermann Goering Strasse. This helped to close off the whole Chancellery site from the nearby Tiergarten. The architect thus also betrayed his knowledge that Hitler was not only running a court, but that this court was, by now, a far cry from the relatively small, chummy group of personal retainers with whom Adolf Hitler had first entered the Old Reich Chancellery, in 1933. These two military-style *Kasernen* could have housed a regiment. They were the occasional quarters for the military members of the Reich Chancellery Group, Hitler's Praetorian Guard.

Its official military designation was Leibstandarte Adolf Hitler. (Leibstandarte means "lifeguards.") The LAH had begun as an honor guard about the size of a platoon. The recruits were all tall, all young, all volunteers. By 1941 the LAH had become the first of the elite divisions of the Waffen SS. Major General Wilhelm Mohnke, its last commanding general, had begun the war as a captain and company commander.

Although the Leibstandarte, like so much in the Third Reich, had vastly outgrown its original function, it still retained its bodyguard role and its personal link to the Fuehrer. It was the only division that bore his name. From its members were recruited the Fuehrerbegleitkommahdo, the FBK. This consisted of a detachment of some forty men, ten officers and thirty enlisted men, most of them handsome and strapping SS stalwarts, many highly decorated. Hitler used the enlisted men not only for normal guard duty, but also as orderlies, valets, waiters, couriers.

The FBK, however, never did have charge of Hitler's personal security. This was a job for professionals drawn from the Reich Security Service (RSD) under SS Major General Johann Rattenhuber. They were professional police officers and plainclothes detectives. Friction between the two groups was, of course, constant. The detectives tended to be "dick" types, older and more experienced hands, and they regarded the FBK as "parade soldiers and skirt-chasers." This is perhaps just another way of saying that the younger FBK men were more successful with the ladies of the Fuehrer's entourage.

Hitler was aware of most, if not all, of the hanky-panky in the Reich Chancellery Group. He rather encouraged it. Hitler was part panderer, part avuncular father-confessor—boys will be boys and girls will be girls, he said. The bachelor Fuehrer, in his more mellow, less lonely moments, regarded these personal retainers as part of his family. He seldom fired anyone, security from gossip about goings-on in his own shop being one of his pragmatic motives.

Hitler was also a great tease. He spent several years actively trying to promote a match for his old friend Walter Hewel, the shy bachelor. Hewel was one of his several candidates for the hand of Eva Braun's promiscuous sister Gretl, a matter of some urgency when Gretl became pregnant. This problem was solved, to the Fuehrer's relief, by SS Lieutenant General Hermann Fegelein, always a fellow for the main chance. Hitler's special interest in marrying off his mistress's sister was, of course, to make Eva Braun socially acceptable. When, in June 1944, Eva became the sister-in-law of General Fegelein, Hitler could present her at parties and diplomatic receptions—except that the time for parties and diplomatic receptions was, by 1944, fading fast.

In addition to the FBK and the RSD detectives, there was a third mixed bag of uniformed men in the Fuehrer cortège. This was a group that was expanding steadily even before war came: the personal adjutants, aides-de-camp, and a cluster of liaison officers. They were attached either to Hitler personally, or assigned to the Reich Chancellery Group by the armed services and the ministries. This, too, is another infallible sign of court government. Not even the ministers, the heads of the armed services, or the major party functionaries really knew what Hitler, the chief of the government, was thinking, saying, or plotting to do next. Thus, all insisted on having at least one set of eyes and ears as close to the center of omnipotence as possible. A sharp liaison man, of course, would keep his ears tuned to the frequency that most concerned his boss. A disapproving word or phrase from the Fuehrer could rock a ministry. It also helped the ambitious to keep book on just who was who in the murderous Nazi pecking order.

Once the war began, there came an interesting alien penetration into the Hitler inner circle. Until 1939, it is safe to say that anyone within the Reich Chancellery Group was an ardent National Socialist, although not everyone was a party member. The few who may have been genuinely nonpolitical were, nonetheless, admirers of the Fuehrer. But this was not true of some of the younger military adjutants and field officers who now began to appear. Several of them were aristocrats. Most were decorated front-line officers. Some had admired the earlier Hitler, some not. Suddenly assigned, by chance, to the FHQ, they found themselves caught up in the swirling intrigue and sordid selfishness of the whole Hitler crowd. Most were appalled.

In the years of ascendancy, there was a kind of pattern of court ritual, and every member was well advised to adjust his personal routine to that of Hitler. As we have seen, he invariably arose late, around 10:00 or 11:00 A.M. It was often noon before he first looked into his office, usually a brief visit to chat with the secretaries, glance at the fan mail, peruse the press summaries. By 2:00 P.M. some forty or fifty guests were gathering for luncheon in "The Merry Chancellor's Restaurant." This sitting seldom broke up before 4:00 P.M., often later. Hitler then might or might not whip back to his office, depending on his interview schedule, or on whether Speer had brought along another rolled-up set of enticing blueprints.

Shortly after 5:00 P.M. came the tea ceremony, sometimes with the secretaries, sometimes with two or three guests. The Fuehrer's work-style was unorganized, lackadaisical. Except during real crises, Hitler had a Bohemian flair for avoiding routine. By constitution, or perhaps by early habit, he had become definitely a man who first really came alive after the sun went down. German suppers are cold, rather tasteless affairs, and supper in the Reich Chancellery was no great splash. The evening guests tended to be more from the Berlin entertainment milieu than from the political or governmental world. Every night, two movies were shown.

Then, around midnight, when most of the guests had already departed, Hitler would gather around the fireplace, usually with old cronies—Ley, Dr. Morell, Hewel, Baur, sometimes Goebbels. These were, invariably, reminiscence sessions, less about the topics of the day than about the exhilaration of the early days of struggle in the 1920s. Except when Goebbels came, these fireside sessions tended to be monologues. But Goebbels had the raconteur's knack of relaxing the Fuehrer, getting him to listen. Goebbels could always be counted on to come up with the latest gossip, a tidbit of Berlin scandal, now and then a good political joke—against Goering, for example. Except in the deep of winter, dawn comes early to Berlin, announced by a shrill, chattering chorus of black thrushes. This serenade was long over before Hitler, reluctantly, said good night to the last lingering, weary guest, around four or five in the morning.

It was a highly idiosyncratic style of government. Such satraps as Hermann Goering, Heinrich Himmler, Joachim von Ribbentrop were notably absent. They were all off running their own satellite courts, as was Goebbels, in his own way. Hitler was able to parcel out vast domains of power precisely because he had no real rivals as Fuehrer. The rivalry, and it was intense among the paladins, was *always* for Number Two, or crown prince, slot. Hitler encouraged this rivalry. The whole preposterous wrangle over the succession reached its dizzy climax in the last days in the Berlin bunker. It was won, if won is the word, by Martin Bormann and Joseph Goebbels at the expense of Goering and Himmler.

Hitler had, without doubt, a fair amount of executive ability. He reserved all the big decisions for himself, often retiring to Berchtesgaden to brood before making one. But he certainly was no organization man. It was not until the arrival of Bormann, in 1938, that the amorphous Reich Chancellery Group was whipped into shape. Bormann was the bureaucrat personified, with a yen for administrative paperwork, and he gave scrupulous attention to detail. His very appointment as Hitler's private secretary was a court maneuver. Bormann for years had been secretary to the rather hapless Rudolf Hess, whose title, Secretary and Deputy to the Fuehrer, was imposing but hollow. By 1938, Hess realized he had fallen from grace in the Hitler court. He sent Bormann to the Fuehrer to represent his interests.

Bormann had a real gut instinct for the realities as distinct from the trappings of power. More intelligent than Himmler, more hard-working than Goering, more stolid than the too-clever Goebbels, Bormann also was well aware that he had all the necessary humdrum qualities the Fuehrer himself so conspicuously lacked. Hitler loathed anything with the inartistic odor of routine—administration, paperwork, filing, programming. Until the arrival of Bormann, the Reich Chancellery Group was anything but a disciplined outfit. Anybody could go directly to Der Chef and, if he caught him in a soft mood, get pretty much what he wanted—a raise, a vacation, an autograph for the kiddies. To this inner circle, Hitler was no ogre.

Martin Bormann, the take-charge man, changed all that. He was universally hated and feared by almost all in the Reich Chancellery Group. By placing his own desk in the anteroom to Hitler's office and by processing all nonmilitary papers before they crossed the Fuehrer's desk, Bormann could control access to Hitler.

There was one person in the court who made no bones about her loathing for Bormann. This was Eva Braun. The rest of the Reich Chancellery Group often counted on her to get their message through to Number One. She told Hitler about Bormann's sycophancy in pretending, in the Fuehrer's presence, to be a nondrinker, a nonsmoker, even a vegetarian. "And besides," as Eva put it, "the girls all tell me he is an oversexed toad." For Eva Braun, in a cloistered lifetime loaded with humiliations, not the least embarrassing moment was when she had to go to Martin Bormann to beg for pin money. Bormann's takeover operation included his handling of the Fuehrer's personal finances.

Little Eva was no du Barry, no Pompadour, not even a Lola Montez. Perhaps for this very reason she fitted rather snugly into the screamingly petit-bourgeois atmosphere of the Hitler court. Hitler fondly called her "Tschapperl," a Bavarian dialect word for "honey bun" and a trifle belittling. When Goebbels once penned a pompously long article stressing that Adolf Hitler, the Fuehrer of all the Germans, had "no private life," Eva came up perkily with a great anti-Goebbels line: "Just call me Fräulein No-Private-Life."

There is perhaps no better definition of the loose Reich Chancellery Group, a most banal elite, than Erich Kempka's: "Those of us who were really in the know about Eva Braun." The number, all told, of those who were privy to this rather harmless, yet best-kept, secret of the Third Reich must have been at least 200, and probably closer to 300. Whole books have been written about Hitler's allegedly bizarre sex life. These books usually throw more light on their authors than on the humdrum private life of Adolf Hitler. All courtiers testify that his relationship to his mistress was normal, almost respectable. The affair was about as exciting as the mating of fireflies in a wet summer.

The Berlin weekend that began on Friday, April 13, was still one of anxious anticipation—manic hope, depressive fear—just before the battle. This was the day of that obscene champagne party in the small hours at which Goebbels and company celebrated the death of President Roosevelt. On Saturday, in the Reich Chancellery, Colonel Stump-fegger's medical corpsmen could be seen setting up the emergency field hospital.

Sunday, April 15, also brought a new VIP arrival as resident in the lower bunker—Eva Braun. Eva had been in Berlin since mid-March, living in her private apartment in the Reich Chancellery, which was, miraculously, still undamaged. Now several people saw her supervising soldier-valets as they trundled her bed and dresser down from the apartment into the lower bunker.

Gerda Christian described the scene. "Her arrival was greeted in silence. We all knew what it meant. The day before we were still wondering whether the Fuehrer would leave for Berchtesgaden. I was now convinced Der Chef would never fly off to the Obersalzberg. Berchtesgaden, in the person of Eva Braun, had come to Berlin."

An SS enlisted man in the canteen put it more bluntly. "*Der Todesengel* has arrived." *Todesengel.* The angel of death.

Albert Speer, in those early April days, kept up his shuttle visits from the front to the bunker and back. With the front moving closer and closer, this was easier to do. He could be in Hamburg at noontime, and back for the bunker séance at midnight.

With General Guderian gone, General Hans Krebs took over as briefing officer. Krebs, the last Chief of the General Staff, was a fairly decent man and no fool. Yet night after night, Speer listened in utter astonishment as he moved the German armies, corps, and divisions that simply no longer existed. He was playing phantom wargames on the Fuehrer's bunker briefing map. And every night the Fuehrer, as of old, would give orders for this or that division not to yield an inch, or for this or that city to be defended to the bitter end.

In the second week of April—it must have been on or about April 18—Baur was shaving in his heatless, windowless, unfurnished emergency flat. He heard a loud explosion nearby, somewhere in the already ravaged trees of the Tiergarten. At first he took it for a delayed-reaction bomb—he had heard no planes in the air. The sound was new to the pilot, yet somehow familiar. A second followed, and now Baur recognized it for what it was—Russian field artillery, the 17.5 centimeter gun. When, around noon, he nervously reported this news to the Fuehrer, Hitler was instantly convinced that the Soviets must have had a railroad gun on or near the Oder. They were, in fact, a good deal closer.

Friday, April 20, brought a strange interlude. It was the Fuehrer's birthday, since 1933 a national holiday. It was celebrated, as in former years, in the New Reich Chancellery. Speer drove to Berlin for what he believed would be the last time. This was also the last appearance of such other major figures as Hermann Goering and Heinrich Himmler. Most ministries had already been evacuated, and their moving vans were clogging the arterial roads. Luftwaffe Colonel von Below told Speer by phone that most of the court, sparked by Martin Bormann, was still trying desperately to convince Hitler that he must leave for Berchtesgaden. Hitler had, to this point, kept this option open; but he had agreed to send half of his staff there, just in case. They would fly out sometime on Monday. Von Below himself now told Speer he believed "Hitler will never leave the capital."

CHAPTER 5

FAREWELLS

All through the war, Goebbels had been trying to get Hitler back to Berlin, away from the remote bunkers. Now, on Sunday, April 22, 1945, he himself finally moved into the Berlin bunker, with his wife,

Magda, and their six children. To bunker veterans, the sudden arrival of the whole Goebbels clan could have only one meaning. Like the arrival of Eva Braun just a week before, it meant that the end was near.

In the week just passed, the Red Army had swept from the Oder to the outskirts of the city. On this day, it had entered the boroughs of Koepenick and Spandau. Some advance tank elements were reported *west* of Berlin. The city was closed on three sides; only one road to the south and one to the west were still open. On the Elbe, neither the British nor the Americans had budged. So ended another forlorn hope.

The day before, Hitler had ordered a counterattack by SS General Steiner's Panzer Corps just northwest of Berlin. This battered force had fewer than 11,000 men and less than fifty tanks, at least half of which had run out of gas. Steiner could not possibly attack; even his last chance to retreat was rapidly vanishing. As reports reached the bunker of Steiner's utter inability to attack—a whole Red Army group was moving in on him the Fuehrer's anger mounted. By the midday conference on the 22nd, Hitler had lost all control. He blurted out, "The war is lost!"

This was not only his first open admission of the obvious. It was also the signal for his first serious crackup. Even when he had exploded at Guderian, Hitler had managed to keep relatively cool. Now he turned chalk white, then blue in the face. He was silent for long minutes. Flopping back into his chair, trembling, he ordered the startled conference room cleared of all save his four senior generals (Keitel, Jodl, Krebs, Burgdorf) and Martin Bormann.

The whole flock of adjutants and aides retreated in a hushed flutter. Some felt that Hitler had had a stroke or a heart attack; others, that he was simply suffering from exhaustion. All were convinced that this time the man was definitely not play-acting. As the senior generals stumbled out, a half hour later, the adjutants buttonholed them and managed to piece together a garbled story of what had happened.

The gist of what Hitler had said, before dismissing his generals, was this: the war was lost; he would give up the supreme command, sending both Keitel and Jodl to direct resistance in the south; he would remain to conduct the Battle for Berlin; he would not surrender, could not physically fight, and hence he would commit suicide; anybody who now wanted to leave the bunker could do so; all the women would be flown to Berchtesgaden. He asked everybody to clear the room and leave him alone.

Twenty minutes later, Hitler emerged and asked Major Otto Guensche to fetch his senior adjutant, SS Major General Julius Schaub.

Together, they began sorting out Hitler's private papers. A few he kept and entrusted to Schaub. The rest, Schaub, with two valets, began lugging up the steps of the emergency exit into the Chancellery garden, where they were burned in an incinerator. When Schaub returned, he found Hitler fondling his large Walther pistol. Schaub retreated, feeling this might be the moment. But soon Eva Braun appeared, stayed for ten minutes, and left. Hitler—it was now almost 5:00 P.M.—put in a call to Goebbels.

It was the familiar baritone voice of his old friend that seemed to calm Hitler completely. Either Hitler had abandoned all idea of immediate suicide, or Goebbels talked him out of it—probably both. Instead, Hitler gave his propaganda minister the order Goebbels had long been waiting for, even pleading for. He was to announce over the Berlin radio that "the Fuehrer is in Berlin and will die fighting with his troops defending the capital city." This was the first news Berliners had had that Hitler was in their midst.

In the bunker it was now tea time, in Hitler's life a ritual hour. Fed up with the men around him, above all the generals, he tried to find as much time as possible for the women in his entourage. This Sunday afternoon he was joined by the two younger secretaries on duty, Gerda Christian and Gertrud Junge, and by Eva Braun. At first he repeated the order that all three were to fly away—"Girls, the situation is hopeless." But he was not unhappy when the trio pleaded to stay. There was no more talk of suicide.

Goebbels, meanwhile, spent all afternoon in his residence near the Brandenburg Gate, for his office was now in his residence. At five-thirty, the minister called his staff together and dismissed them abruptly, telling them they would have to join in the coming battle or fend for themselves. His aides had already helped him burn his own papers; one had been busy for days microfilming his diaries. Two Mercedes limousines, one Goebbels' official bulletproof model, had been standing for the last hour before the entrance. He packed his wife and the children into the unarmored limousine and stepped into his special vehicle. The two cars headed toward the Chancellery; they moved slowly, like a funeral cortège.

Not even toilet articles had been packed for the children. Each was clutching a single toy. Magda Goebbels had but a small valise and one extra dress; Goebbels, two pearl white shirts. This seems evidence that Goebbels had some reason to expect the Russian breakthrough to come much more quickly than it actually did. By persuading Hitler to postpone his suicide, Goebbels had extended the bunker melodrama by eight days.

The arrival of the Goebbels family on this hectic Sunday coincided with a mass departure just about to begin. Hans Baur was waiting for nightfall to launch Operation Seraglio, the mass escape to Berchtesgaden. Goebbels himself moved into the lower-bunker room just deserted by Dr. Morell, one of those scheduled to leave. Magda was assigned a separate room in the upper bunker, with three small rooms for the children. The corridors were crowded wtih some forty members of the Reich Chancellery Group and their luggage. Departures began at sundown and lasted until midnight. Hitler spent much of this time seeing them off: it was clear to everyone that they would never meet again.

The departure of so many familiar faces changed the mood of the bunker, from a hectic one to a new stillness after midnight. Captain Helmut Beermann of the FBK explained how this affected his duties.

> We veterans of the bunker called this day Blue Monday because, with the departure of half of our comrades and the arrival of the whole Goebbels family and Eva Braun, everyone could now read the handwriting on the wall. The last act was about to begin. Previously, I had had enough officers and men to be able to work out shifts, twelve hours on, twelve off. Now, every hand was assigned to his task for the duration, which might be for two days or for two weeks. I issued sleeping bags, so that some of my key men could sleep at or near their stations. The old spit-and-polish discipline was all shot to hell. Many soldiers were not even saluting anymore.

Back on the Elbe River, Albert Speer made a snap decision to head east again to Berlin. There were personal reasons for his sudden return. "The driving motive," he admitted, "was to say goodbye to Adolf Hitler. I had left his birthday party, only three days before, like most of the other ministers, without even shaking hands, without a formal goodbye. We all just faded away. It nagged my conscience, and I wanted to make amends."

At Rechlin, while waiting to be flown with fighter escort to Gatow airport on the western rim of the city, Speer encountered Major General Eckard Christian, the senior Luftwaffe liaison man in the FHQ. The general had left the bunker shortly before noontime. He was now waiting to take off for Berchtesgaden to join his chief, Hermann Goering. General Christian filled Speer in on the exodus of the military high rank from the bunker. Admiral Doenitz, he said, had headed north to Schleswig-Holstein on Friday. Field Marshal Keitel and General Jodl had both checked out of the bunker that morning. These two old familiars never saw Hitler again. The Fuehrer had created a Northern Command under Admiral Doenitz. He wanted the Southern Command to be under Jodl and Keitel, *not* under Hermann Goering—even though the Reichsmarschall was already on location in the south.

There is a bit of bunker gossip connected with the departure of General Christian, the former ace who was also the husband of Hitler's best-looking secretary, Gerda Christian. Now the husband was leaving, though he knew his wife had opted to stay with Hitler. True, Hitler had told Christian that he could leave to join Goering, but it was apparently the kind of permission he hoped would be rejected. At this point, however, survival apparently meant more to Christian than his wife.

After his chat with General Christian, Speer was flown from Rechlin to Gatow. The fighter planes that had escorted him then peeled off to attack the Russian tanks already on the outskirts of Potsdam. At this time, the highway from Gatow to downtown Berlin was still open; Speer could easily have driven to the bunker. Instead, sparked by the curious spirit of adventure that had inspired his whole junket, he accepted a lift in a small artillery-observation craft to the Brandenburg Gate.

As he entered the Reich Chancellery on Monday, April 23, Speer saw that it was being hit here and there by long-range Red Army artillery, but was not much damaged. The earlier bomb damage had been far more extensive. Speer clambered over a hurdle of burned beams as he headed for the adjutant's office to announce himself. Here he stumbled into the middle of a drinking party. In these elegant rooms once inhabited by Bismarck, where Speer himself had spent many evening hours with Hitler in the early years of his chancellorship, disarray now reigned. Beer and wine bottles, messkits, stale sandwiches, littered the marble floor. The whole Chancellery atmosphere had suddenly changed over the weekend.

Speer was happy to see the florid, smiling features of one of Hitler's senior adjutants, Schaub. Although Speer had made a point of telephoning ahead, it was obvious that Schaub was surprised at his turning up. Schaub left, returning five minutes later to say the Fuehrer was ready to receive Speer.

Speer went alone through the upper bunker and down the spiral iron staircase to the lower chambers. At the bottom of the staircase he met Martin Bormann. Bormann, too, was all smiles. In fact, he was oozing cordiality and bonhomie. Nor did it take Speer long to discover why.

"Speer," Borman said, "when you talk with the Fuehrer, he is certainly bound to raise the question of whether we should stay here in the bunker or leave for the Obersalzberg. It is my feeling that it is high time he now took charge of things in South Germany. These are the last hours in which such a necessary move is still possible . . . Please use all your powers of persuasion to induce the Fuehrer to fly out and away."

This was a moment of minor personal triumph for Speer over a man he had always feared and hated. He had no intention whatever of telling Hitler this. But Speer rather enjoyed having the born bully at long last reduced to wheedling.

Speer entered Hitler's study. There was no warm greeting, no handshake, nor was he even asked to take a chair. The last meeting between Adolf Hitler and Albert Speer, in marked contrast to their previous long discussion on the eve of Speer's birthday, was neither emotional nor particularly cordial. Hitler did not seem to be impressed or flattered that his old friend had returned.

Speer, still standing, studied Hitler's face and demeanor. He seemed strangely empty, burned out, more shadow than substance. The first businesslike question Hitler asked of Speer was his opinion about the leadership qualities of Grand Admiral Doenitz. From this, Speer deduced correctly that Hitler was at long last about to name his successor. Speer spoke well of the admiral, but was careful not to lay praise on too thick. From long experience with Hitler's suspicions and whims, he knew that overpraise could have an effect opposite that intended.

Soon Hitler abruptly changed the subject. "What's your opinion, Speer? Should I stay here in Berlin or fly to Berchtesgaden? General Jodl has told me I now have, at the most, twenty-four hours to make my final decision."

"My Fuehrer, it seems to me much more advisable, if it must be, that you end your life here in the German capital as the Fuehrer, rather than in your weekend vacation chalet," Speer replied.

Hitler's response seemed both sincere and in character. "I, too, have resolved to stay here in Berlin. I only wanted to hear your view once more."

With two old friends and senior ministers as different as Albert Speer and Joseph Goebbels strongly urging him to stay and die in Berlin, with only lesser personalities like Bormann still touting the flight to the Alps, the issue was already a foregone conclusion—if, indeed, it had ever been an issue. Willful and erratic as he now was, Hitler never completely lost sight of his historical image. Speer, still closeted with Hitler, noted how listless, how subdued his manner had become. His glaucous eyes were glazed; his left hand trembled as if he were an old man with palsy; his face was puffed, part yellow, part gray. The man seemed to have aged in what had been only weeks. His voice was now soft, low-pitched, clear but a monotone.

"I shall not join the battle personally," Hitler announced. "There is always the dangerous prospect that I might merely be wounded, and thus fall into Russian hands while still alive. I do not want to give my enemies any chance to mutilate my corpse. I have already given orders that my body be burned. Fräulein Braun has expressed her desire to end her life with mine."

Then, in an almost stoic mood, Hitler added, "Believe me, Speer, it is easy for me to put an end to my life. One brief moment, and I am freed of everything, liberated from this painful existence."

He had, seemingly, given up again. Not, as on the day before, after a violent emotional explosion, but calmly, with the plaintive overtones of resignation and self-pity. At this point Speer, his own emotions frayed, blurted out how he had been frustrating the demolition orders since mid-March. This was something Hitler surely knew, anyway. Hitler just stared at him morosely and vacantly. Speer, stammering, uttered words to the effect that he was willing to stay in the bunker with the Fuehrer "to the bitter end." A merciful interruption came at this point, giving Speer time to recover his emotional balance. General Krebs appeared to announce that he was ready to give the military-situation report.

Speer is not the only bunker witness who observed that Hitler, on this Monday afternoon and early evening, was in a relaxed, almost philosophic mood. There may, however, be a simple medical explanation for these placid hours. Among the some fifty who departed during Operation Seraglio was Dr. Morell. Everybody in the court knew that Morell had been treating Hitler with frequent injections and mysterious pills. The suspicion of some was that, at best, these were very strong tranquilizers; at worst, morphine. Before departure, realizing he would not be attending his star patient for at least several days, Dr. Morell might well have given him "farewell booster shots" and a supply of pills. This could account for the period of calm—and for the emotional outbursts, symptomatic of withdrawal, which followed.

Speer noted how Hitler, in the military conference that followed hard on the melancholy soliloquy about his own suicide and cremation, was once again all aglow, exuding sheer optimism about the military situation. Yet there was nothing in the military situation on this day calling for any optimism. Every soldier in the conference room was aware of this. But this is the kind of rapid shift of mood, from low to high, often induced by drugs.

This military conference was brief; it ended around five-thirty. Outside the door, in the long reception lobby, Speer next met Dr. Goebbels. In Goebbels, too, Speer noted that flight-from-realism that so soon overtook all bunker residents. Goebbels told Speer, "Yesterday the Fuehrer stopped the fighting in the west so that British and American troops can now enter Berlin unopposed." There was no truth to this. Hitler had never given such an order.

Speer also saw the three older Goebbels children romping up and down the corridor, playing with a ball and a hoop. The three younger ones were already in bed. Although he knew them all by name and liked them, Speer did not interrupt the game to say goodbye. He simply nodded to them quickly and passed on. The father of six children, all born into the Third Reich, Speer could not face any of these six, whom he knew would die in the bunker.

Eight in the evening. The calm of Monday afternoon had been broken. From Berchtesgaden, a telegram had just arrived from Reichsmarschall Hermann Goering. It was addressed to Hitler, inquiring whether, in line with the 1941 law of succession, he, Goering, should not take over the leadership of the Reich "if you my Fuehrer are now hindered in your freedom of action or decide to remain in Fortress Berlin." Given the grim situation, it was a sensible if somewhat fatuous request. Martin Bormann, however, roared into Hitler's office, accusing Goering of treason. Speer followed Bormann, more out of curiosity than any active interest in the dwindling power game. He thus became the only eye-and-ear witness of just how Bormann did, finally, succeed in knifing Goering.

Bormann had two obvious motives for eliminating Goering. The first was to induce Hitler himself to take off for Berchtesgaden. That, after all, was exactly what had been on his mind when he pleaded with Speer just a few hours earlier. Bormann had not yet given up. His second motive was even more personal. It really had less to do with the truly mad "succession problem" than with Bormann's own status. Despite the high-sounding title of "Reichsleiter," his only real job was secretary to the Fuehrer. He was not a minister, not a general, not even a Gauleiter, although he controlled the Gauleiters, in Hitler's name. If Hitler were to die intestate, if he did not draft a political last will and testament before his suicide, then Bormann would suddenly have no status—and no powerful friends. Even the fifty-odd Gauleiters would switch loyalty either to Heinrich Himmler or, possibly, Goebbels, who was the senior Gauleiter. Had Hitler, as threatened, in fact committed suicide twenty-four hours previously, by law Hermann Goering would already be Fuehrer and chancellor. One of his first acts would have been to order the arrest of Bormann.

Goering's fatal blunder, according to Speer, was not his first telegram, which was addressed, properly enough, to Hitler, but a second one to Foreign Minister von Ribbentrop:

> I have asked the Fuehrer to provide me with instructions by 10:00 P.M., April 23. If by this time it is apparent that the Fuehrer has lost his freedom of action to conduct the affairs of the Reich, his decree of June 29, 1941, goes into effect, according to which I inherit all his offices as his deputy. If by twelve midnight, April 23, 1945, you receive no other word either from the Fuehrer directly or from me, you are to report to me in Berchtesgaden by air.

Despite the meticulous legalities in which this telegram is phrased and hedged, and the care we can be sure went into the drafting of it, Goering had badly blundered. Bormann was able to convince Hitler that Goering was now dealing in "ultimata" and was thus guilty of "treason." Goering's double mistake was to have set time limits; above all, such short ones. Worse still, he had communicated directly with Hitler's top official rather than with the Fuehrer himself. That did it.

Martin Bormann was out for blood. He suggested that Goering be shot forthwith. Hitler was not willing to go quite that far. But, whipped into high fury by Bormann, the Fuehrer now stripped Hermann Goering of all rank and office and demanded that he resign instantly for "reasons of health." Meekly, before midnight, Goering complied with Hitler's orders, proof positive that he was engaging in no conspiracy, no usurpation.

Speer discreetly refrained from intervening, as he well might have done, had this power struggle had any real meaning. As he looked on, Hitler had an outburst remarkably similar to the explosion of the previous day. He began to rage in a wild fury, with manic expressions of bitterness, betrayal, self-pity, and despair. His face was flushed crimson, his gray-blue eyes glaring, and his mustache, now white, was twitching.

If the dramatic and sudden downfall of Hermann Goering this day in the bunker was a real historical moment, the arrival and departure of senior minister Joachim von Ribbentrop, had elements of farce in it.

It happened shortly after the Goering episode. Speer was back in Hitler's study. The Fuehrer, he noticed, had again dropped back into his listless, weary-with-it-all mood. Speer, therefore, took advantage of the occasion to request Hitler's approval for a flight west of Czech industrial managers still in the Skoda works in Prague. The Czechs wanted to escape the Russians and establish contact with the Americans in Munich. A short fortnight ago, Speer would not have dared to sponsor such a plan. Now Hitler voiced no objection, initialing the flight permission.

At this point, there was another interruption. Bormann bustled in to remind Hitler that von Ribbentrop had been waiting several hours for an audience. "Bormann," Hitler said, "how many times do I have to repeat that I just don't want to see that man?"

"Ribbentrop says that he won't move away from your doorstep. He will wait there like a faithful old hound dog until you relent, mein Fuehrer."

As Bormann knew, the dog ploy was always a good one with Hitler, who now relented. Speer left, and Ribbentrop waddled in. During their short talk of ten minutes or so, Hitler must have told the foreign minister about the Speer scheme to airlift the Czech managers. For later, as he left Hitler's office, Ribbentrop buttonholed Speer. He began to insist, querulously, that such a project needed *his* approval. Speer reminded him that it was the Speer ministry, not the Foreign Office, which had the available plane. "Well," said Ribbentrop, "I shall be satisfied if the document says 'Approved by the Fuehrer at the suggestion of the foreign minister.'"

Speer yielded to this absurd point of bureaucratic punctilio. Ribbentrop left the bunker around 11:00 P.M. and was driven by his chauffeur to Hamburg, where he intended to go into hiding in the apartment of his mistress. Thus, he departed from the bunker and Berlin forever.

As one reconstructs this last appearance of Albert Speer in the Fuehrerbunker, one continually notes a distinct change in the atmosphere on this day. The lower bunker was no longer crowded; there was much less hustle and bustle. The corridor lounge, where Speer met Bormann and Ribbentrop, was empty. Just a few days before, it had been crowded. This is explained by the departure, the day before, of most of the high military.

Hitler had, in fact, abandoned the Supreme Command of the Armed Forces to Keitel, Jodl, and Doenitz. He was now concentrating his attentions on the area around Berlin. The other senior military man in the bunker, in addition to General Krebs, was General Wilhelm Burgdorf. Others who came and went were the city commandants, Generals Reimann and Weidling. In command in the Reich Chancellery area itself, reporting only to Hitler, was Major General Wilhelm Mohnke.

Women had been in the bunker from the beginning, but now their presence became more apparent and of increased importance. Although Johanna Wolf and Christa Schroeder had left, Eva Braun and Frau Goebbels had arrived. The active and excited Goebbels children created a problem the women were best able to handle. Frau Goebbels herself was in no condition to attend to her children and this gave both Gerda Christian and Gertrud Junge something to do. They were soon joined in their task by Eva Braun. These three childless women did their best to mother the youngsters. Among them, the fate of the children was often talked about, if only in whispers.

Adolf Hitler—it was part of his general withdrawal from political reality—was spending more and more of his time in female company. Many of his meals he took alone, from a tray. But at tea time he usually invited Gerda Christian and Gertrud Junge to join him. Since January, in fact, he had seldom dined with men, nor had them to tea. In this last week, even Constanze Manzialy was invited to join the tea group. Frau Goebbels was not invited, probably for reasons of protocol. Neither was Eva Braun. Hitler preferred to keep his female admirers in distinct categories.

But for the most part, Frau Christian recalled, Hitler would drink his tea and eat in silence. It was "a silence broken by reminiscence, recriminations, or some bleak comment on the events of the day. The general themes were all too familiar—Berchtesgaden days, the loyalty of women, the disloyalty of Prussian generals, the breeding of dogs. We just listened glumly. We had heard it all before."

It was now after midnight in the bunker. Once the busiest of hours, there were few souls about now in the lower bunker. But Eva Braun had not retired. She sent an orderly to invite Speer to join her in her combination bed-and-sitting room. Speer had been waiting for this invitation. He braced himself for still another farewell meeting. It was already Tuesday, April 24; he had been up and about since 4:00 A.M. the previous day.

As Speer entered Eva Braun's cramped quarters, he saw how bulky the familiar dresser now looked. He had designed it, back in 1938, for a much larger apartment. The young woman's first words were casual, spontaneous, quite in character. "Albert, you must be hungry!"

In the general orgy of selfishness and self-pity in the bunker, no one had yet offered Speer so much as a sandwich. He himself had been too busy, perhaps too distraught, to take time out for a meal. Eva now managed to hustle up a postmidnight snack, cookies and sweets. And, for old times' sake, she opened up a bottle of Moët et Chandon champagne.

Speer was soon aware that, however incongruous, Eva Braun at this moment was perhaps the only bunker inmate who seemed even remotely happy. She radiated a quiet serenity that was not merely play-acting. It was a serenity, Speer felt, not unmixed with exultation on the part of a woman who, if only in a morbid pact, like that of Tristan and Isolde, complete with poison potion, was finally going to get her way with the man she loved.

Eva told Speer, with obvious pride, about how Hitler in an avuncular way had tried to induce her, only the week before, to leave for Munich; how she had categorically refused; and how this stubborn show of loyalty had so pleased him. Then she let drop a remark that, however casual, Speer instinctively sensed was loaded. It was a shuddering reminder that as long as Hitler was still alive, neither Albert Speer nor any other human being was completely safe in this concrete shelter.

"How glad I am, Albert, that you have managed to find your way back here to the bunker. The Fuehrer had come to believe that you were working against him . . . Ah well, now that you are here it proves just the opposite, doesn't it?"

Speer, stunned, made no reply. He knew that his presence in the bunker this night proved nothing of the sort. A naïve Eva Braun might, touchingly, believe so, but Adolf Hitler was no naïf. It was now 3:00 A.M. Hitler, in the next room, was up and stirring, so Speer sent in word that he would like to come over to say goodbye. He had now been in the bunker for twelve hours. The pilot, still waiting for him at the Brandenburg Gate, was naturally anxious to fly before dawn, now only ninety minutes away.

The final parting of Adolf Hitler and Albert Speer was a masterpiece of anticlimax.

"So, Speer, you're leaving? Good. *Auf Wiedersehen.*"

No thanks, no handshake, no present, no good wishes, no greetings to the family, no nice-having-known-you. Speer, dog-tired and overwrought, again mumbled some banality about his willingness to stay until the end. Hitler simply turned away. Speer had risked his life to come to the bunker. He got this curt, rude put-down. On this tawdry, unworthy note ended one of the strangest friendships of the twentieth century.

It was still pitch black outside the bunker. The new moon had long since set with the evening star. The desultory nighttime rumble of the battle building up was now ominous, now still, a quiet broken by random shell bursts. Speer walked alone to the Brandenburg Gate and was soon airborne.

CHAPTER 6

CASUALTY STATION

Even when outside the bunker—and he is one of the few of its inhabitants who was, every day—Hans Baur did not see much of Berlin in its death throes since he always went directly to the Brandenburg Gate, only a half-mile away. In normal times, this was a lively area, the very center of the city, but now 92 percent of it was bombed. Few Berliners lived here anymore. Fewer and fewer had to report to work; the ministries had been evacuated. The great department stores were closed; most had been bombed and looted. No restaurants, no theaters, no movie houses. Buses, street cars, the subway, were no longer running.

A strange oasis still in operation was the cellar bar of the once-posh Adlon Hotel, most of which was still standing, in the shadow of the Brandenburg Gate. Now it was the exclusive preserve of the few diplomats still accredited to the Third Reich—those from Mussolini's rump Italian Republic, the Japanese, Eastern European satellite governments-in-exile, like Tiso's Slovakia, and some French Vichyites, who had discreetly not gone back to France. These derelicts of diplomacy were not only drinking at the Adlon; when the bar closed at midnight, many slept there. Their embassies had been bombed.

Baur talked very little about what he saw aboveground. This is symptomatic of the bunker mentality, which he shared with all of the mountain people. They knew little if anything of what was happening in the big city above them. The Berliners, though they had now heard that Hitler was in town, did not know where he was; the bunker was not visible from the street. Nor did very many care. Baur was moving between two utterly different worlds. The Berlin he had once known well had vanished. There was, however, a second man who emerged often from the subterranean depths. This was Professor Dr. Ernst-Guenther Schenck.

He was operating in the emergency casualty station in the cellar of the New Reich Chancellery. Schenck spent the first week of the siege aboveground in Berlin, the last seven at the operating table.

The doctor described the scene there: "Casualties were now tumbling in from the fierce street fighting just three blocks away at the Potsdamer Platz, and from the larger battle now raging for the Reichstag. This was only four or five blocks from us. From time to time, soldiers who were still conscious and could talk told me of their hopeless battle. The younger ones, many under sixteen, were terrified, bawling."

The Red Army had by now reached the Berlin inner ring, the Zitadelle. Most of the German casualties had been inflicted by artillery-fire shrapnel. Now, more were from rifle and small-arms fire, grenades. This meant there was close combat by tank and infantry forces. Russian planes and artillery were now hitting the area of the Chancellery and the bunker. The battery lamp over Dr. Schenck's operating table swung like a jerky pendulum.

The Russians captured Tempelhof airport on Wednesday, April 25. The next day, they turned the captured guns on the Germans. Because Berlin is built on alluvial sand, every shell burst had a crunching side effect. As Professor Schenck put it: "Sometimes, I felt as if I were standing in a shot-put pit."

The Russians were not firing directly at the Fuehrerbunker, which they could not see, and the precise location of which they did not know. Still, the noise of exploding shells gave the inhabitants of the bunker, including Hitler, once again the grand illusion that they were at the epicenter of things, that the whole vast capital city was under similar bombardment. It was on this night, according to Colonel von Below, that Goebbels made the most grandiloquent of his bunker pronouncements: "When we leave this stage, then will the planet tremble."

Professor Schenck himself knew better. When he went in desperate search of medical supplies now in such short supply—bandages, splints, iodine, morphine, plasma—he found that while many boroughs of Berlin had been occupied with little or no fighting, others had simply been bypassed by the Russians. He became acutely aware of the appalling human tragedy all around him.

More than ten square miles in the center of the city were flattened; less than one third of all private dwellings escaped destruction or were classified as even half-habitable. Intact windows were a rarity. More bombed-out Berliners were living with relatives, friends, or strangers than were living under their own roofs. Kitchens had become communal, mostly those with old-fashioned wood-burning ranges. There was no gas; electricity was available only at odd hours.

Yet almost to the end, life staggered on with a ludicrous facade of normality. Six hundred thousand Berliners still had essential wartime jobs; they could be fined for being late. The factories, even in mid-April 1945, were producing at 74 percent of top capacity. Absenteeism was negligible. All Berliners were groggy. No one had had enough sleep for long weeks. Most beds were slept in in relays around the clock. Managers and shop stewards moved cots into their offices. Nerves were frazzled, not only from constant loss of sleep, but from lack of fresh vegetables or vitamins, meat or fresh fish, real coffee or tea. What served as coffee was made from acorns; cigarettes were made of dried dandelions.

Dr. Schenck, on his forays outside the bunker, also shuddered at the familiar stream of silent refugees passing through Berlin in the dark. From January 1 to April 15, 1945, 672,000 had already trooped through the city. They had permission to linger but one night and one day. It was a somber parade: 80 percent were women of all ages; the rest, either men over sixty-five or children. None had autos or buses. A lucky few had bicycles, wagons, carts, horses, cows, poultry, pigs.

Dr. Schenck recalled, "All of us were now living a waking nightmare. We had lost any sense of clock or calendar time. Even today I often remember, in turbulent dreams, a kind of spectral hourglass: the sand in the upper glass never empties; the bottom glass never fills. Life and death were then the only grim realities, not transient and deceptive time. Many a wounded soldier died, in horrible anguish, on the blood-smeared table as I operated. I was up to my elbows in entrails, arteries, gore."

Dr. Schenck was not a surgeon but an internist and a nutrition expert. He was almost as groggy at times as a punch-drunk boxer, keeping going on nerves and reflexes, with little more than his general knowledge of anatomy, and some field experience he had had at the front. Toward the end, the last two or three days, the casualty station ran out of bandages. The staff had to rip blood-soaked rags and casts off the unburied dead.

The operating room itself, very primitive, was equipped with no more than basic surgical instruments. Nearby, on the same level in the cellar of the New Reich Chancellery, General Mohnke had already set up his command post and had stored several tons of bulk provisions, adequate supply for a six weeks' siege.

These stores had been rounded up in the city by Dr. Schenck, on General Mohnke's orders, during the third week in April. It was this food-requisitioning mission that had, in fact, brought Dr. Schenck to the Reich Chancellery, on Monday, April 23, 1945. Since Dr. Schenck arrived on the scene just as Speer was departing forever, in a sense he picks up the story were Speer left off—a civilized man's comment on the final descent into barbarism.

There were two other doctors present and on duty. One was Colonel Stumpfegger. He had been called in, a fortnight before, to replace Dr. Brandt as Hitler's attending private physician. But as soon as Professor Werner Haase arrived, on April 21, he in turn replaced Stumpfegger. Hitler knew Haase was a far better doctor, and it was Haase, not Stumpfegger, who was closest to Hitler in the last days.

In the Reich Chancellery, more than 2000 Germans were now crowded into the Chancellery cellar—the fighting soldiers, the wounded, the Nazi Party "*Bonzen*," many Berlin women who had either fled thither for safety or had been brought in by their boy friends in the FBK. Although the word "orgy" is perhaps a bit too lurid, the combination of free-flowing liquor, distraught, terrified women, the impending doom of the great city, and the Nazi Goetterdaemmerung mood was having its effect. I had already heard several accounts of the wild parties building up, which were to climax in a *Hexensabbath* on the day the Fuehrer finally committed suicide. Since Professor Schenck had proved a most sober and meticulous witness, I felt that his version would be the most reliable, so I asked him about this.

> There was a kind of contagious mass hysteria seeking a group outlet. Many of the same wild, red-eyed women who had fled their Berlin apartments, in terror of rape by Red Army soldiers, now threw themselves into the arms, and bed rolls, of the nearest German soldiers they could find. And the soldiers were not unwilling. Still, it came as a bit of a shock to me to see a German general chasing some half-naked signalwoman between and over the cots. The more discreet retired to Dr. Kunz's dentist chair upstairs in the Chancellery. That chair seemed to have had a special erotic attraction. The wilder women enjoyed being strapped in and made love to in a variety of novel positions.

It was also in this saturnalian atmosphere that the morbid talk of

Nazi propaganda minister Joseph Goebbels and his wife, Magda with three of their six children. A fanatical Nazi, Magda committed the horror of horrors: she killed all her children with cyanide capsules and then committed suicide.

Sgt. Rochus Misch, the bunker's telephone operator, told the author valuable details about Hitler's last days. Hitler did not even say goodbye to him before his suicide. One of the few bunker survivors, Misch now manages a paint-supply shop in West Berlin.

Gertrud "Trudl" Junge witnessed Hitler's last-minute marriage to Eva Braun. Gertrud and two other secretaries escaped from the bunker but were caught and raped by Russian soldiers. Later, she managed to flee to West Germany.

"A kind of bunker Man Friday," SS Major Otto Guensche did odd jobs for Hitler, his last the burning of Hitler's and Eva Braun's bodies. He escaped from the bunker but was arrested by the Red Army and imprisoned for ten years in Russia.

Hitler's personal pilot, Hans Baur, wished to fly the Fuehrer to his Berchtesgaden retreat, but in the end Hitler refused to leave.

Bullish, ruthless Martin Bormann was the most powerful Nazi after Hitler—and the most hated man in the bunker. Postwar rumors that he had fled to South America are false. Bormann poisoned himself when his escape from Berlin was blocked by Russian soldiers; his body was found in 1972 and identified by police.

Eva Braun at her sister's wedding party in 1944. Her role as Hitler's mistress was "the best-kept secret of the Third Reich." She hastily wed Hitler in the bunker just a day before their deaths, and reportedly shed "tears of radiant joy." By all accounts Eva was a petite-bourgeois, and her relationship with Hitler was normal—even dull. Loyal to the Fuehrer to the end, she bit into a cyanide capsule at the instant that Hitler shot himself in the temple with a Walther 7.65 pistol.

The Fuehrer and SS chief Himmler greet Lt. Gen. Hermann Fegelein in better days. The SS general was an opportunist who tried to advance his career by marrying Eva Braun's sister, Gretl. While serving as SS liaison in the bunker, Fegelein secretly planned to escape to Switzerland with his foreign mistress. He was caught at the last moment and executed by the SS for treason.

"A most exceptional man, able to articulate his experience," Albert Speer, minister of war production, was the only real intellectual in Hitler's circle. His memoirs told how "a young and ambitious architect . . . bartered his soul to the devil." The sole Nazi leader to express remorse at the Nuremberg trials, Speer served twenty years in prison for his war crimes.

Erich Kempka, Hitler's chauffeur, claimed he had heard Hitler's suicide shot, but he later admitted this was not true. A "vainglorious blackguard" as well as an unreliable witness, Kempka escaped to the West; he died in 1975.

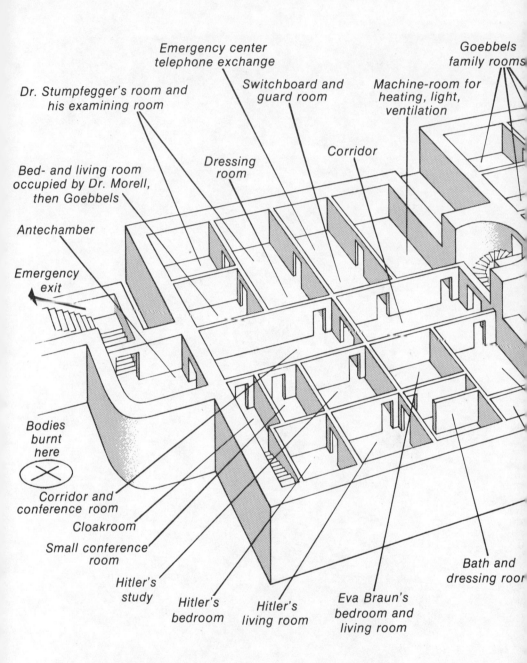

Emergency center
telephone exchange

Switchboard and
guard room

Goebbels
family rooms

Dr. Stumpfegger's room and
his examining room

Machine-room for
heating, light,
ventilation

Corridor

Dressing
room

Bed- and living room
occupied by Dr. Morell,
then Goebbels

Antechamber

Emergency
exit

Bodies
burnt
here

Corridor and
conference room

Cloakroom

Small conference
room

Hitler's
study

Hitler's
bedroom

Hitler's
living room

Eva Braun's
bedroom and
living room

Bath and
dressing room

Plan of the Fuehrerbunker, Hitler's thirteenth and final command post. The
entrance at top was through a rectangular cement building about twenty feet high.
The bunker itself was sunk twenty feet below Berlin's sewage system. Its concrete
roof was sixteen feet thick; the walls, six feet thick. A self-contained unit, the bunker

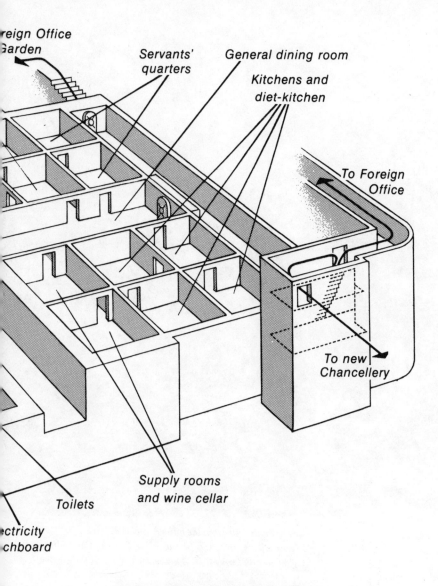

reign Office
Garden

Servants'
quarters

General dining room

Kitchens and
diet-kitchen

To Foreign
Office

To new
Chancellery

Supply rooms
and wine cellar

Toilets

ctricity
chboard

The Fuehrerbunker

had an electric generator, water supply and ventilation system. Once he took refuge in the bunker on January 16, 1945, Hitler never left. His hasty marriage to Eva Braun was held in the small conference room at lower left; their suicides occurred in Hitler's living room.

*Emergency exit from the bunker into the Reich
Chancellery garden, after the fall of Berlin. The bodies
of Hitler and his mistress had been burned in the garden.*

*Map of downtown Berlin showing the escape routes of
the Reich Chancellory Group from the Hitler bunker.
Some escapees walked through the subway and the
rubble-strewn streets as far as the
Schultheiss-Patzenhofer Brewery, at top of map. Here
they learned of the German Army's surrender to Soviet
troops on May 2, 1945. Some managed to escape to the
West; others surrendered to the Russians; a few were
killed or committed suicide.*

Schultheiss-Patzenhofer Brewery

Prinzenallee

Flaktower

Humboldtshain

Brunnen Strasse

Museum of Natural History

Stettiner R.Y. Station

Lehrter S-Bahn Station

Bridge

Humboldt Hafen

Charite Hospital

Invalidenstrasse

Lehrter R.Y. Station

Schiffbauer

Damm

Weidendamm Bridge

Friedrichstrasse Subway and S-Bahn Stations

River

Reichstag

Spree

Brandenburg Gate

Unter den Linden

Tiergarten

East-West Axis

Französische Subway Sta.

Gendarmen-Markt

Reich Chancellery and Hitler Bunker

Stadtmitte Subway Sta.

Voss Str.

Kaiserhof Subway Sta.

Wilhelmstrasse

Friedrich Strasse

Central Berlin

———— Group I route
- - - - Group III route

Belle-Alliance-Place

suicide kept mounting. This was once again a clear case of infectious group hysteria. Liquor, profligacy, fear, despair, the handiness of weapons and poison vials, all played their suggestive role among lost souls. All were now waiting for Hitler, still the center of the bunker melodrama, to shoot himself. This, too, made suicide the foremost topic in almost every group conversation. It became an obsession.

Late Saturday, April 28, it was Goebbels who, in his capacity as Gauleiter of Berlin, had to hustle up a minor official with notary and registrar powers to preside at the Hitler marriage ceremony. He quickly managed to locate one Walter Wagner, a fiftyish, quite bewildered municipal bureaucrat who now makes a very brief appearance on the stage of world history, a spear-holder with a ludicrous walk-on role.

Wagner had been told to hustle through the ceremony, and no nonsense. Hitler and Eva Braun were actually married as a "war couple." But Wagner could not legally by-pass the formality of asking the bride and the bridegroom whether each was a third-generation Aryan. At the close of the zip-zip ceremony, with a glance at his watch, Wagner also noted that it was just after midnight. So, with a pedantic scribble, he changed the date on the marriage certificate from April 28 to April 29, 1945.

Walter Wagner, a born Berliner, lingered for some twenty minutes at the reception, meeting his Fuehrer for the first time in his life. He munched a liverwurst sandwich, had one or two glasses of champagne, chatted with the bride. He then was ushered out of the bunker and back into the night. Walter Wagner was dead a half hour later, shot on the Wilhelmstrasse.

The wedding formalities had taken place in the small conference room. Because this was one of the smaller rooms in the lower bunker, only Joseph Goebbels and Martin Bormann were present to sign as witnesses. The bunker bride wore black, appropriate enough in the funereal atmosphere. It was a short-skirted silk taffeta afternoon dress with two gold clasps at the shoulder straps, Hitler's favorite in her wardrobe. Afterward, at the reception in Hitler's study, a larger room, a dozen bunker veterans moved in and out—Magda Goebbels, Gerda Christian, Gertrud Junge, Ambassador Walter Hewel, Generals Krebs and Burgdorf.

It was the next day, Monday, April 30 that Dr. Schenck entered the Fuehrerbunker proper. He describes his first bunker meeting with Hitler in this way:

I had retired around midnight. It had been a very exhausting day; more wounded than ever coming in. I soon fell into a deep sleep. But less than two hours later I felt a hand on my shoulder, shaking me. It was Professor Haase who said that Hitler wanted to see me and my two attendant nurses. I looked at my uniform, which I had not taken off for two or three days. It was torn, crumpled, and caked with dry, brownish blood—not mine.

We wound, Indian file, through the underground passage into the upper bunker, a distance of about a hundred and fifty meters. Professor Haase, puffing painfully while he walked, led the way, since it was very familiar to him by now. The two nurses followed. We passed through the central gangway of the upper bunker, which was still crowded at this hour with some twelve to fifteen bunker night owls. There was a long oak table here, laden with ample food from the pantry, cognac, wine, and beer.

Hardly had the small party entered the lower bunker than they saw Adolf Hitler standing before them alone, just outside his quarters. Haase made the formal introductions. Schenck remembered, "My first reaction on meeting Adolf Hitler face to face, although the man was relaxed and friendly enough, was to snap to attention and salute. I was a mere colonel in a not very presentable uniform; he was still Fuehrer, chancellor and Supreme Commander-in-Chief of the Armed Forces. My whole body seemed to freeze. A chill went up and down my upper spine. I imagine it was my uniform—and his—that made me snap to attention."

Soon, however, Professor Schenck was looking at Hitler with a doctor's clinical eye. He was a bit shaken himself, since he had never seen his Fuehrer before, except from an admiring distance. Schenck was standing within three feet of Hitler. The pathetic man he saw bore little resemblance to the old, mesmerizing idol of the masses.

He observed:

Hatless, he was still wearing the familiar, once-spotless, natty pearl gray tunic with green shirt and long black trousers, the simple uniform he had donned on the first day of the war. He wore his golden party badge and his World War One Iron Cross on his left breast pocket. But the human being buried in these sloppy, food-stained clothes had completely withdrawn into himself. I was still standing erect, on a kind of concrete step above him. As I glanced down, I could see Hitler's hunched spine, the curved shoulders that seemed to twitch and suddenly to tremble. Somehow his head seemed withdrawn into his shoulders, turtlelike. He struck me as an agonizing Atlas with a mountain on his back. All of these thoughts must have raced through my mind in thirty seconds or so, not more. This pause came because Hitler seemed hardly able to shuffle the two paces forward to greet us. Which he now did.

Professor Schenck's description is not only graphic; it is also precisely clinical and is leading up to a diagnosis. Professor Schenck is here describing Adolf Hitler less than fifteen hours before his death.

> His eyes, although he was looking directly at me, said nothing. They did not seem to be focusing. They were like wet pale-blue porcelain, glazed, actually more gray than blue. They were filmy, like the skin of a soft, ripe grape. The whites were bloodshot. I could detect no expression on his vapid, immobile face. Drooping black sacks under his eyes betrayed loss of sleep, although Hitler was not the only one suffering from this bunker malaise.
>
> Today I can see him there still, although the whole scene lasted only about four, maybe five minutes. Deep folds ran down his rather large, pulpy nose to the corners of his mouth. This mouth was set firmly, his lips nervously pressing each other. The cold-fish, flapping gesture with which he shook my hand was listless. It was really only a jerky reflex, although it was meant to be amiable enough. As he mumbled his thanks, perfunctorily, I was at a loss to make any coherent reply.
>
> I was profoundly shocked, and reacted, I suppose, as any doctor would have, not without sympathy. And yet it was far too late, in more ways than one, for any mortal doctor. At fifty-six the Fuehrer was a palsied, physical wreck, his face wrinkled like a mask, all yellow and gray. The man, I am sure, was senile, without the dignity of silver hairs.

After Hitler and Professor Haase, two sick men, shuffled off, Dr. Schenck was invited to join the party in the upper bunker. He sat there for a long while, dumbfounded; they were talking about old, happy, far-off things, the piping days of peace before 1939. They compared notes on the beauty of various Bavarian lakes, reminisced about the luminous, ocher light of Munich in autumn, the Rhine waterfall at Schaffhausen, the Romanesque loveliness of Worms cathedral, a kind of nostalgic Baedeker trip far, far from the Berlin bunker.

> After a half hour or so, just as I was moving to leave, three quite good-looking young women joined us, coming up the staircase from the lower bunker. One was Frau Junge, one was Fräulein Else Krueger, Bormann's secretary, and the third, a lithe, well-dressed strawberry blonde. Someone leaned over and whispered to me that this was Frau Adolf Hitler, the bride of the day. I had never heard of the lady or of her special relationship to our Fuehrer.

I must say, I felt an awkward outsider in this chummy group, once the exalted Obersalzberg circle. I was a little fish, wriggling in the same big net, and I knew it was closing on us all. But they kept talking on and on about life in Berchtesgaden, of how they had lived up there, enthroned like Wagnerian gods, above the clouds that encircled the foothills and cut them off utterly from other Germans, all other lesser mortals. Eva Braun, now Frau Hitler, came from this world. It was probably her only world. I began observing her as if from afar. If this young woman knew the desperate situation she was in—and one can hardly doubt that—she gave no visible sign of it. Once in a while, I thought I detected a slight tremor in her lisping voice, but that may have been only alcohol. She was not drunk, but was well on the way, tossing her glass back regularly. She was seated at the head of the long oak table in the gangway and was the real life of the party—like a Rhineland carnival queen.

A small social note in this woman's sad life. With the exception of the champagne wedding breakfast, just twenty-four hours before, this seems to have been the only table at which Eva ever presided as Frau Adolf Hitler. But without the bridegroom.

The Fuehrer's bride talked away, in a chirpy, rather pleasant Bavarian accent, to this audience of some fifteen or sixteen men and women. It was all small talk, gossip, rather pointless anecdotes. What she looked like, today I only dimly recall. But what I do remember vividly is that she did not seem to share one bit in the general demoralization that had overcome almost everyone else and was now seeping into the bunker from every corner. My impression was that she was fighting back hysteria, and this exaltation was, in a clinical sense, a prolonged manic phase. She was deeply neurotic.

Just how many goblets of hock Dr. Schenck tossed back, he does not say, but it did lead to one pressing human problem. Although there were normally two toilets in the bunker, the upper one was now clogged, and these party people were using the john at the other end of the lower bunker. This meant they had to descend and march past Hitler's quarters, an unthinkable intrusion at any earlier time.
Schenck went on:

Now I had a better chance to look around. I was amazed at how small Hitler's private quarters were. Doors led off left and right from the central corridor. In a kind of vestibule before his bedroom, sitting at a small round table, were Hitler and Professor Haase. They were engaged in an intense conversation. Luckily, they did not even notice me.

The ghostly scene fascinated him. The two men were talking, or rather whispering, so intensely that they took no notice of the intruder.

> For the second time within two hours I could observe Hitler, this time *without* his observing me. It was pitiful. His flabby left hand, in which he was clasping his steel-rimmed spectacles, was also clutching the table. His whole left arm, up to the shoulder, was trembling and, now and then, shuddering. This arm kept tapping the table rhythmically. To brace himself, he had wrapped both his left calf and foot around one leg of the table. This leg was throbbing. He could not control it.
>
> Now, most doctors would agree with me, I think, that these are the classic symptoms of Parkinson's disease. If my quick diagnosis was correct [and it was later confirmed by Dr. Haase], this meant that Hitler, even had he lived, would in a very few years have been a hopeless cripple.

Dr Schenck added, "It was now obvious to me, on this second meeting, that Adolf Hitler had found his last physician. It was with him and him alone that the Fuehrer discussed the manner and method of his own suicide. I know this because Professor Haase told me, later that day—after the suicide. They were also discussing the problem of how to destroy the bodies."

It was now about 4:00 A.M. Outside, the first streaks of predawn April light fell on Berlin. Professor Schenck, when answering the call of nature, had just missed, probably by a matter of minutes, an event described by Major Otto Guensche, who reported the following:

> When I entered and headed for the familiar toilet, I found it occupied by Professor Haase and Sergeant Tornow, Hitler's veterinarian and dog trainer. Haase was holding in his hands an ampule, or vial, and a pair of pliers. I had heard Hitler say, earlier that evening, that he wanted to test the poison because it had been given to him by Himmler, "and one could no longer be sure of Himmler." Blondi, Hitler's dog, was poisoned in the toilet. I saw it happening. Tornow forced her mouth open and Haase reached into it, crushing the ampule with his pliers. The cyanide poison acted almost instantly. Soon after, Hitler showed up and went into the toilet to make sure Blondi was dead. He did not say a word or betray any emotion. A moment later, he disappeared into his study.

Sergeant Tornow now shot Blondi's four puppies, who had been born in the bunker in March, plus the dogs of Eva and Gerda Christian, and his own dachshund.

To backtrack for a moment: on Sunday, April 22, before the noontime conference, Hitler had formally placed the government area, including the Reich Chancellery and the bunker, under the command of SS Major General Wilhelm Mohnke.

Hitler told him, "General Mohnke, you are a professional soldier. Frankly, I had hoped to be able to remain alive and in Berlin at least until May fifth. There are historical reasons . . ." A pause. May 5 sounded still an eternity away. Mohnke wondered. Hitler did not elaborate.

"However, General, under no circumstances can I risk being captured alive. Whenever you feel the military situation to be such that you can no longer hold for more than twenty-four hours, you must report this to me, in person. I shall take the consequences. This is a personal request. It is also an order."

Mohnke, a man not given to loquacity, said nothing. He simply saluted. Hitler returned the salute and shook hands. Here again we hear a calm Hitler, resigned to his fate, in a meeting only a very few hours *before* his nervous explosion and crackup that same Sunday midafternoon. He was already relaying to Mohnke the suicide-in-Berlin decision he did not give his senior generals until that afternoon. It is added proof that this resolve was no snap decision or a result of the crackup.

Unlike other German general officers who were outside the city, and thus able to operate pretty much on their own, Mohnke was the last general in direct command of troops who was still at Hitler's immediate beck and call. On the Potsdamer Platz, he went into classic hedgehog position with his remaining 100 or so veteran soldiers. Sweating out the inevitable end, he gave orders of the day that were very simple: dig in, take cover, hunker down, don't draw fire.

It was now a long week since General Mohnke had taken over his battle post; Sunday, April 29. The artillery cannonading of the two previous evenings had suddenly been cut off. Hitler's midnight briefing had been short, desultory, uninformative. General Mohnke had returned to his command post in the cellar of the New Reich Chancellery, which was also his sleeping quarters. He had turned in around 1:00 A.M. Now, at 6:00 A.M.—April 30, 1945—the jangling field telephone beside his cot rudely awakened him.

Sleepily, Mohnke recognized the familiar voice of Sergeant Rochus Misch. "General," Misch said, "the Fuehrer wishes to see you alone in his quarters. Please come over immediately."

General Mohnke asked, "What temper is the Fuehrer in? Is he as down in the dumps as he was last evening? Who else is there?"

Misch replied, "No problem, General. Der Chef is now in a calm and relaxed mood. No one else is with him. I don't think he has been able to sleep at all this whole long night. Twice within the last hour he has come out to chat with me. Just a moment ago he said he wanted to have a talk with his old friend Mohnke. He told me to ring you."

The general was now fully awake and much relieved. Mohnke gulped a quick cup of coffee, combed his hair, buttoned up his uniform collar, and left on the double.

Passing through the tunnel from the Chancellery to the Fuehrerbunker, the general noticed for the first time that either shrapnel or a bomb had pierced the roof, which was only five feet underground. He examined it more closely. Shrapnel. He had not noticed this break the night before, but now bright shafts of the dawn sunlight pierced the jagged aperture. He made a note to have this repaired.

As he strode briskly the some 1600 yards, General Mohnke recalled the standing order the Fuehrer had given him a week back—the twenty-four-hour notice, the man-to-man request that was "also an order." True, his battered troops were still clinging, surprisingly well, to their positions on the Potsdamer Platz. The Reichstag had not yet fallen. But tomorrow was May 1, the great Soviet political holiday. One last Red Army assault, and that would be it. Today was the day Mohnke finally had to give Commander-in-Chief Adolf Hitler the bad news. *Der Tag.* His word of honor as an officer, soldier to soldier. This must be what Hitler's otherwise quite unusual summons was about.

There was, too, that curious matter about May 5. A date that meant something to Hitler, obviously. Mohnke had been curious, but he had not asked.

Now the general had arrived in the lower bunker. Hitler usually received Mohnke formally, either in the small conference or map room, or, in more recent days, in his private study. These rooms were now empty in the early morning hours. Mohnke had noticed a few retainers sleeping in the upper bunker. But there was nobody in the lower bunker except for Sergeant Misch at the switchboard and two snoozing guards. Sergeant Misch saluted snappily and said, "Der Chef told me he wants to receive you informally in his bedroom."

Highly unusual. As Mohnke entered, he found Hitler sitting on the edge of his bed. He was wearing a black satin morning robe over his pajamas. Hitler rose politely to greet Mohnke. He moved himself from the bed to the only chair in the room, then motioned to Mohnke to take a seat on the bed. The general now noticed that the bed, a single cot, had not been slept in.

The two men were within three or four feet of each other, in half-profile. Hitler's chair was near the head of the bed and the night table. For most of the time, he gazed straight ahead, past Mohnke toward the wall. Mohnke, in turn, looked past Hitler, his eyes on the door. He recalled that Hitler had made the quick move without clumsy effort. The Fuehrer's left arm was trembling now and then, but only slightly. He was grasping the arm of the chair and used his right arm freely to gesture.

As usual, Mohnke began with a brief situation report. Hitler listened for five minutes or so in silence. The Russians had reached the Wilhelmstrasse, in the area of the Adlon Hotel, about four blocks away . . . Red infantrymen had penetrated into the subway tubes under both the Friedrichstrasse and the Voss Strasse . . . Most of the vast, wooded Tiergarten was now in enemy hands . . . Russian assault troops had all but encircled the German positions on the Potsdamer Platz. Here they were only 300 meters from the Reich Chancellery. Mohnke droned on, listlessly. Hitler took it all in, intently, calmly. He posed no questions.

The silence, according to the usually taciturn Mohnke, "was palpable. You could reach out and touch it." To break the extreme awkwardness of the moment, the general raised the matter of his pledge. "My Fuehrer, as soldier to soldier, true to my oath to you, I no longer can guarantee that my exhausted, battle-weary troops can hold for more than one more day. I now expect a frontal, massed-tank attack tomorrow at dawn, May first. You know what May first means to Russians."

Hitler said, "I know. Let me say that your troops have fought splendidly, and I have no complaints. I had sincerely hoped to make it until May fifth. Beyond that date, I have no desire to live."

General Mohnke was still curious about this seemingly minor Fuehrer obsession. Hitler apparently sensed this puzzlement, and answered the riddle himself, with a trace of a wan smile. "General Mohnke, May fifth is a red-letter day all soldiers should remember and circle in their diaries. Napoleon died on St. Helena on May fifth, eighteen twenty-one. Another great career that ended in total disappointment, disillusion, betrayal, despair. The fickle Europeans did not really understand the French emperor and his great plans, as they have not understood me and mine. We were both men born before our times. Well, so much the worse for Europe. History will be my only judge."

Mohnke, at this peculiar moment, was less interested in collecting historical phrases than he was in keeping the Fuehrer in as calm a mood as the one now prevailing. And it did prevail, for most of what turned out to be a long sitting. It soon became clear that Hitler had called Mohnke over for no particular reason.

At 4:00 A.M., so Schenck reported, Hitler had been trembling so badly that he had to wrap his left leg around the table to support himself, to keep his balance. Now, only a short time later, and without having slept more than a wink, Hitler was sitting fairly calmly by the bed with Mohnke. The general noticed only an occasional twitch. One suspects that Haase had given Hitler a shot of morphine. Or at least a very strong tranquilizer to face the end.

Years later Mohnke commented:

> Obviously Hitler was in very bad health, and had been for months. We all knew this. But on this last day, my memory is that his control over his nerves and emotions was far better than just eight days before, the Sunday of the blue-faced explosion at the noontime briefing. Nor did he look quite so sallow, so pasty-faced, as he had on many occasions in the past year.
>
> Throughout the whole talk I was seated almost at his side, perhaps three or four feet away. But he was either gazing at the wall or looking down at the floor. After the first ten minutes, our talk ceased to be a conversation. It became a monologue.
>
> The monologue began with a bitter denunciation of the west. "The western democracies are all decadent, feeble. They will all fall one day to the more virile, vigorous people of the east, who have shown themselves to be the stronger, and for whom the rigid system of Communism is the proper one!"
>
> Then he began a review of his whole career, what he called his dream of National Socialism and how and why it had failed. The German people had, in the end, proved unworthy, just not up to the supreme challenge. His spirit lifted when he reminded me of his old triumphs, like the tumultuous victory parades.
>
> When he spoke of the war, he insisted that it had been forced on him by Anglo-American plutocracy, the Marxist-Bolshevik world conspiracy, Jewish international finance, the Freemasons, the Jesuits, all the familiar enemies and scapegoats from "the days of the struggle." Finally—and now Hitler's gorge was rising—he went on to complain woefully that he had not been spared even the humiliation of treason and betrayal within his inner circle. Enemy espionage, he insisted, seemed to know every secret order he gave—twenty-four to forty-eight hours after he gave it. His own FHQ, he could prove, was not secure. It leaked vital information like a sieve. There was a spy somewhere, either in the bunker or the Reich Chancellery. As he

said this his voice rose, his fists clenched, his face turned white. It was obvious to me that the thought or reality of treachery almost drove him up the wall. When he used the word *das Leck* [the leak], he was almost screaming. Hitler had begun to suspect every face he saw about him.

CHAPTER 7

THE LADY VANISHED

Das Leck! The leak! It was a woman. The story is as old as that of Samson and Delilah. This bunker report is not a detective story, but the matter of *das Leck,* the security leak in the bunker itself, suddenly took on great significance. General Mohnke was at least the fourth of my present-in-the-last-days bunker witnesses to stress this.

I had first heard the leak story from Albert Speer, but did not then tumble to its import. Speer, after all, had left the bunker forever in the early hours of Tuesday, April 24; much had occurred thereafter. How, I asked myself, could Hitler be worried about some annoying security breach when his whole world was crashing about him?

I was wrong. Later, several other witnesses, ones who were there until the end, confirmed what Speer had said. Hans Baur, Kempka, Guensche, even Misch, returned to the theme often. They insisted that Hitler, surrounded by what he kept calling the phenomenon of general treachery, was also nagged by a specific security leak, something he was aware of but could not locate.

As Speer first put it:

> In that last fortnight, when Hitler mentioned *das Leck* he knew what he was talking about, a steady flow of information out of his own shop. For example, he told me of an order—I believe it was a rather routine promotion list—that he had for some reason pulled back and *not* sent to the Armed Forces and Wehrmacht Supreme Commands [OKH and OKW]. Yet within forty-eight hours, he complained, the news of these "promotions" was on the British radio. Hitler could thus no longer blame this kind of security breach on either the OKW or the OKH. It utterly exasperated him.
>
> During my last visit to the Fuehrerbunker, on April 23 and 24, I recall Hitler mentioning that he had at last called in Gestapo Chief Heinrich Mueller to make a thorough probe of bunker internal security. Mueller was in the bunker until the very end. He was not normally a member of the Hitler inner circle. He was there because he had one specific job to do.

Hans Baur made the same point. "In his last talk with me, mid-morning of April thirtieth, Hitler said, 'My God, even my own HQ has been penetrated.'" Again Baur, quoting Hitler, used the word *das Leck*.

From Sergeant Rochus Misch, certainly no high-level source but often close to Hitler, I heard, "During that last fortnight, when Hitler talked to me, he would sometimes ask, 'Misch, what do you think of so-and-so? Can we be sure he is secure?'"

How does all of this connect with the mysterious Fegelein affair?

Hermann Fegelein had been blessed by good fortune in his career. When he was a young man, his skill as a jockey had attracted the attention of Christian Weber, the Nazi boss of Munich, who thereafter helped him to advance. Fegelein joined the Waffen SS, rose to the command of a cavalry division, and enjoyed several military successes on the eastern front. In 1944, he was assigned as Himmler's liaison officer with Hitler and, as noted previously, made his opportunistic marriage with Eva Braun's sister Gretl. He was definitely a part of the favored inner circle in the bunker.

On Wednesday, April 25, Fegelein left Berlin by car to visit Himmler's headquarters at Hohenlychen. Late that same day, with the roads cut by advancing Russian troops, he made his way back to Berlin by air. He did not report in at the bunker and his absence was finally noticed on the 27th. On the night of the 27th he was found in his flat, brought to the bunker, court-martialed, and executed within twenty-four hours. The charge, according to Hans Baur, had been desertion. These are the bare bones of the Fegelein case. But as I started to investigate, that case began to take on some astonishing features.

General Mohnke hotly denied to me that such a court-martial for desertion ever took place. If Mohnke was right, then logic dictated that the man must have been executed for some other reason. (That Fegelein was killed almost twenty-four hours after his return is generally agreed, though there are no eyewitnesses—or, at least, none willing to talk.)

Here is General Mohnke's surprising version:

> We set up the court-martial in a room next to my command post. But no sooner were we seated than defendant Fegelein began acting up in such an outrageous manner that the trial could not even commence.
>
> Roaring drunk, with wild, rolling eyes, Fegelein first brazenly challenged the competence of the court. He kept blubbering that he was responsible to Himmler and Himmler alone, not Hitler. Fegelein had a right to defense counsel but rejected it. He

refused to defend himself. The man was in wretched shape—bawling, whining, vomiting, shaking like an aspen leaf. He took out his penis and began urinating on the floor. He really was drunk; he was not acting.

The German Army *Manual* states clearly that no German soldier can be tried unless he is clearly of sound mind and body, in a condition to hear the evidence against him, and able to aid and understand his own defense. I felt I had no alternative but to adjourn and dismiss the court. In my opinion and that of my fellow officers, Hermann Fegelein was in no condition to stand trial, or for that matter even to stand. I closed the proceedings and turned Fegelein over to General Rattenhuber and his security squad. I never saw the man again.

Fegelein before the court was still in custody of the Waffen SS, a branch of the military. The martinet Mohnke, so otherwise meticulous, even hair-splitting about legal procedure, would not normally have turned any soldier over to Rattenhuber. It wasn't done. Rattenhuber, though he held the same rank as Mohnke—each was a major general—was not really a soldier, least of all in the eyes of a professional military man like Mohnke. Rattenhuber, as head of Dienststelle I in the Reich Chancellery, was responsible for the personal safety of the Fuehrer. He was now also reporting to his superior, Gestapo Chief Mueller.

Mohnke, I believe, was telling the truth; he did hand over Fegelein to Rattenhuber. But, once again, not the whole truth; he had concealed something. Why did he turn a soldier-prisoner over to the security spooks?

"Yes, that was unusual, I admit. Fegelein was my prisoner. But you see, General Rattenhuber had just hotfooted it over from the Fuehrerbunker and demanded custody. I gladly yielded it. Rattenhuber later was to tell me that the fate of Fegelein was decided and handled internally in the hour before the Hitler-Eva Braun marriage."

In plain language, "handled internally" is a euphemism for "executed." It happened more than twenty-two hours after Mohnke turned him over. This is thus a midnight-to-midnight black melodrama, from about midnight on Friday, April 27, to nearly midnight on Saturday, April 28. Around midnight on Friday, Hitler, by giving the court-martial order to Mohnke, had wanted Fegelein to pay the supreme penalty for desertion, clearly a military offense. One hour later, however, Hitler must have changed his mind, for he now brought in General Rattenhuber. This has to mean that in this short interim Fegelein, in Hitler's eyes, had become a security problem. He was not only a deserter, which was glaringly obvious, but a suspected traitor in the bargain. Something important had been uncovered in this critical hour that put an even grimmer face on the matter.

There was now, almost surely, a link between Fegelein's military desertion and the security-leak matter. It was *das Leck* that had brought Gestapo Chief Mueller into the Fuehrerbunker one week back and that now brought him into the Fegelein affair.

As we know, on Wednesday, April 25, three days before, Fegelein had left Berlin at dawn that morning for Hohenlychen, Heinrich Himmler's last headquarters, about ninety miles northwest of Berlin. After the short visit in Hohenlychen, he set out for SS headquarters at Fuerstenberg. Some time during that afternoon, the road back to Berlin was cut off by Red Army tank patrols. Fegelein had to take to the air.

Here a common-sense point arises. If, by Wednesday, April 25, Fegelein's simple and only motive had been to escape from the Fuehrerbunker and thus avoid the doom awaiting the other members of the Hitler court, the man, on this busy day, most obviously had it made. Instead of flying back to encircled Berlin, he could have motored in the opposite direction—back to Hohenlychen. Here he could have joined the well-armed entourage of his chief, Heinrich Himmler.

Himmler was longing for Hitler's demise any day, expecting it perhaps at any moment. He thought this would secure for him the "succession," now that Goering was out of the running. Himmler had not been back in Berlin since the Fuehrer's birthday, April 20. On April 22 he had, cagily, come back *halfway* to Berlin. He had had a roadside rendezvous at noontime, near Nauen, with his liaison man, General Fegelein. Himmler had then disappeared into North Germany, up to the Baltic coast, to begin his secret peace-feeler negotiations with the British and Americans, through a Swedish intermediary.

Hence something—or a rendezvous with someone—made Hermann Fegelein's flying return to Berlin most urgent. Flying into and out of Berlin was most hazardous—if not downright foolhardy. In his ever-calculating mind, his rendezvous in Berlin must have been stern necessity.

It was certainly no sense of devotion to the utterly lost cause of his Fuehrer that compelled this return. Around noontime, in the officers' mess at Fuerstenberg, nervous SS fellow officers had asked their visitor just what was happening in the bunker. Fegelein replied: "I have no intention of joining those bunker maniacs in any mass-suicide ceremonies. The Valhalla stuff is for the Bayreuth Festival, but not for me."

Fegelein was a lifelong climber. He had married plump Gretl Braun at Hitler's suggestion, if not insistence. Gretl was known in the FBK as the "nymphomaniac of the Obersalzberg." It was strictly a marriage of convenience, for Hitler as well as for Fegelein. Now, less than a year later, this connection so close to the toppling throne was a distinct embarrassment for Fegelein.

He was by no means the only outspoken "survivalist" in the Reich Chancellery Group. For all his blatant cowardice, the man was at least rational, and the special nature of his liaison job had given him a much clearer topside view of reality.

Fegelein knew that the chances for survival outside the bunker catacomb were far better than inside. A quick discarding of the uniform, a disappearance into the universal chaos of the collapse, a quiet rustication to await better days. Maybe in Switzerland. These must have been his thoughts as he flew to Berlin, late in the evening of Wednesday, April 25. Fegelein arrived in time to make the midnight bunker conference, but he did not attend. This was not too unusual, nor was it even remarked by others. As liaison man, he had often of necessity missed the regular conferences in the past hectic fortnight, since he was en route between Himmler and Hitler. All day Thursday, April 26, Fegelein again did not show. Yet still no one missed him, officially.

It was not until the next day, Friday, April 27, around noon, that Hitler finally missed Fegelein and noted that his SS liaison man had played truant from six briefings running.

Major Guensche related, "The routine matter Hitler wanted to check out with Fegelein was some trifle, so minor that I forget just what it was. However, when Fegelein was not immediately available, Hitler's suspicion flared like a sudden flame. Hitler and I now recalled that we had not seen brother Fegelein around the bunker for two full days. Hitler, livid with anger, rang for General Rattenhuber."

Nobody present in the bunker at this moment had a clue as to where Fegelein could be located. He had not called in, had left no covering message, no Berlin address, no telephone number. Only Guensche, who was a tippling companion of Fegelein's, quietly nursed a vague hunch, but he said nothing. Several weeks back, after one of their wassailing evenings out on the town, Fegelein, with a wink, had given Guensche a phone number where he could be reached "in a real emergency."

At this point in our narrative, sex rears its lovely head. For the past year, man-about-Berlin Fegelein had been keeping a very good-looking, tall, classy mistress in a modest furnished flat at Number 10-11

Bleibtreustrasse, only about four miles from the Reich Chancellery. By a freak, this was one of the few large downtown houses that had escaped serious bomb damage. To this convenient and inconspicuous hideaway, far from the madding bunker crowd, Fegelein had now retreated.

The sands in the Berlin Hourglass were running out, rapidly. The Russians were already much closer to Fegelein than to Hitler and company. They were, in fact, only four blocks away—an immediate problem. General Fegelein had already changed into mufti. He was drinking regularly. It was obviously high time to take it on the lam. Equally obvious, something was delaying him.

The scene shifts back to the Fuehrerbunker, four miles to the east. The short briefing was over. It was now about 2:00 P.M. on Friday, April 27. Hitler had had Rattenhuber on the mat and had been chewing him out unmercifully. No Fegelein for more than forty-eight hours, and Rattenhuber, fine security man, had not even noticed this defection. Nor had he the foggiest idea where Fegelein might be.

Rattenhuber emerged from Hitler's study wringing his hands. He appealed to Guensche for help. It was only now that Guensche mentioned the telephone number, located the notebook, and gave the number to Rattenhuber. The chief detective at once asked Sergeant Rochus Misch at the switchboard to trace the number to locate the exact street address. Misch promptly did. The Berlin telephone central was still functioning with its usual Prussian efficiency.

Around two-thirty, General Rattenhuber got through. Fegelein himself answered, blearily. After the initial surprise, foxy Fegelein played it cool. He told Rattenhuber that he had been drinking and still had a terrible hangover. This was certainly true enough. He went on to say that he had not yet shaved but would report within two hours. Rattenhuber ordered Fegelein to shave and leave immediately. If he did not have transport, Rattenhuber said, he would send a car. Fegelein again gave his "word of honor as a German officer" that he would appear "within two hours."

At first sight, in reconstruction, it seems that the usually canny Fegelein had made the first of several appalling blunders. Why did the man answer the phone at all? A fair surmise is that he must have been waiting for an urgent call. He could, for example, have been waiting for a woman or a plane—or both. He needed a plane, for there was now no other way to leave Berlin—and decamping was now his obvious intention. A plane would not be able to land at the Brandenburg Gate before nightfall. Fegelein clearly was playing for time. Had his female companion been present, she most certainly would have been the one to answer the phone. So we can assume he was, in fact, alone.

Liquor, too, was playing its role. Fegelein must have been reeling, for his astonishing next move was to call Eva Braun. To her, he had already made his escape intentions crystal clear. He simply wanted to disappear from world history, and he now brazenly invited her to do the same. Fegelein apparently did not know very well the deep death wish of his sister-in-law. She was naturally indignant and tartly reminded Fegelein of the Fuehrer's seething wrath, the obvious danger to his life, and the fact that his wife, far away in Bavaria, was expecting a baby any week now. At this point—the source here is Sergeant Misch—Fegelein, that good Bavarian family man, got off one of his deathless lines: "The proper place for an expectant father is at the bedside of his spouse."

There is no evidence that Eva Braun, caught up in a deep conflict of loyalties, reported this highly indiscreet conversation to Hitler. She did not know it, nor did Sergeant Misch at the switchboard—but Hitler most probably heard every word. There was a concealed microphone in the switchboard piping directly into Hitler's study.

Five o'clock came and went. No Fegelein. It was still late afternoon, spring sunlight. Rattenhuber sent out a posse of four men in a German jeep to contact Fegelein. This detail was commanded by SS Captain Helmut Frick. A decorated soldier with battle experience, Frick was chosen because this was clearly a military situation, a risky trip to the front, which had now reached the streets of Berlin.

Usually, in peacetime, a drive from the Reich Chancellery to Bleibtreustrasse would have taken ten to fifteen minutes, depending on traffic. Now, because of a long detour to loop around the street fighting, it took Frick more than an hour. Thrice, he and his men had to dismount to take cover. A brisk exchange of fire with Russian snipers near the Savigny Platz led to the severe wounding of one of the party.

Captain Frick did not have orders to arrest Fegelein. A captain does not arrest a general officer. He was simply to use "friendly persuasion" to induce Fegelein to come along quietly for his rendezvous with the Fuehrer. When Frick arrived, he found Fegelein alone, still not in uniform, still unshaven, still drinking. There were three cognac bottles on the table. Fegelein brashly tried to induce this young captain to decamp while the decamping was good. Even had he been alone, Frick, a loyal soldier, would hardly have deserted. After a half hour of heated, fruitless parley, Frick and his party drove back to the Reich Chancellery.

Martin Bormann had appeared on the scene. He ranked General

Rattenhuber, of course, and proceeded to bawl him out for having sent such a low-ranking officer on so important a mission. Another long lower bunker parley was held. Finally, it was decided to send a full colonel, SS Standartenfuehrer Hoegl, with a larger "commando of six." They took off in an armored weapons carrier. It was now dark in Berlin, around 10:00 P.M. Apparently Hoegl's orders were ambivalent. He was not to arrest Fegelein. But he was also aware that it would be most unwise to return without his man.

Once again, it took almost a full hour just to reach the Bleibtreustrasse. In the ghostlike streets of Berlin, the party had to weave its way through fresh, fuming rubble. They were driving with dimmed blue headlights, under a clouded three-quarter moon. Without any battle incidents, they arrived at around 11:00 P.M.

It all reads like a movie scenario. The script now called for a man of Hoegl's experience to approach his target from the rear, to ring the building, to place at least two guards outside. Anyone who goes to the movies knows that. Instead, these Nazi Keystone cops tramped en masse up to the second story. Hoegl and a husky adjutant rushed the door. It flew open.

The posse found Fegelein inside, now back in uniform, his collar open, his face clean-shaven. He was standing at a round mahogany table together with a young woman. She was tall and blond, with a tint of red in her shoulder-length hair. Both were busily engaged in packing a hand valise, much smaller than a normal suitcase. Hoegl saluted snappily. He then politely but firmly reminded Fegelein of the long-standing order that he return to the Reich Chancellery immediately. Fegelein, still in his cups, first pulled his rank, protesting the brusque manner of the breaking and entering. But after some woozy palaver and the lighting of two or three cigarettes, Fegelein did agree to come along. To Hoegl's relief, the problem of a formal arrest thus never arose.

The arrest protocol made Colonel Hoegl very nervous. Hoegl was well aware of Fegelein's high standing in the Nazi pecking order because of his family relationship to Eva Braun. This nervous hesitancy must account for a whole chain of blunders that not even a German provincial detective should ever make. Not only had Hoegl forgotten to post guards around the house, but he paid scant attention to the young woman who quietly slipped out of the living room during the talk. Carrying a tray of empty glasses toward the kitchen, she seemed to be fetching water for the cognac that Fegelein had graciously offered his guests. Hoegl was concentrating his powers of persuasion on Fegelein.

The others were simply listening. All were highly relieved when Fegelein agreed to go.

By this time, one of the other detectives did notice that the unknown woman had not returned, though he could hear water running in the kitchen. Thirsty, perhaps, he went to have a look. The lady had vanished; the window was open. He closed it—a delightfully German touch. On a night like this, anything could happen. It might rain. He also turned off the tap.

That the woman had walked out so impolitely on the SS party disconcerted Hoegl. So he confiscated the valise. He next went to the telephone to call Rattenhuber and set him at his ease. Hoegl reported that he was en route with Fegelein. He made no mention of the woman. He had not even asked Fegelein who she was.

The rocky ride back to the Chancellery was uneventful, if not particularly jolly. Fegelein, who does not always seem to have realized what a jam he was in, alternated between loud singing and profanity.

Hoegl felt he had a good night's job behind him. He had carried out the precise orders of his mission; he was bringing back his man and that valise. The thought of opening it to examine and list the contents did not cross his serene mind. Hoegl, one feels, had not read many thrillers, though at the moment he was right in the middle of one.

Around midnight on Friday, April 27, Hoegl and his group, with Fegelein, reached the Chancellery. Hoegl's nighttime mission seemed all but completed, though he had to report to his boss, Rattenhuber, before turning in. Still clutching the valise, the colonel walked through the long tunnel from the Reich Chancellery to the Fuehrerbunker. He was startled to be confronted in the lower bunker by a group that included not only General Rattenhuber and Major Guensche, as expected, but also Martin Bormann and Gestapo Chief Heinrich Mueller. A powerful reception committee.

Colonel Hoegl saluted, reporting successful completion of mission. Neither Bormann nor Rattenhuber was at this moment in the mood for official congratulations. Obviously, they had talked with at least one other member of the Hoegl party and thus already knew what had taken place in the Bleibtreustrasse apartment. When Hoegl, giving his account, came to the seizure of the valise, Bormann quickly grabbed it and tumbled the contents on the old map-room conference table.

The valise contained a chamois bag that, when opened, spilled out several diamonds, amethysts, rubies, an opal, a diamond brooch, several rings, a pearl necklace, three gold watches (including one Eva Braun had given Fegelein to have repaired), 105,725 Reichsmarks (around $40,000), 3186 Swiss francs (around $800), two passports, both made out to the same woman (that is, they bore the same picture although they had different names) and some road maps.

The least common denominator of these sundry items was glaringly obvious. It was just what any well-fixed Berlin couple would scrape together before trekking west as the capital was about to fall. Martin Bormann, who had an instinct for the jugular, spotted something else. One of those two passports was British. It implied that Fegelein, a lieutenant general in the Waffen SS, was scheming to skip off with a woman who was not even a German. She was probably an enemy national. Not only in the feverish mind of Bormann, but also on the material evidence before the eyes of all Germans present, the case of desertion at this moment became something more: treason.

Bormann, roaring like a wounded bull, pounding the table with both fists, now exploded in Hoegl's face. "The woman! Why did you not grab her and escort *her* back here, instead of this damned valise? Fegelein is a traitor; this woman is British, an enemy agent. Fegelein went to bed with this spy and blabbered everything. *She* was *das Leck*."

The great clichés of life often have a way of coming true. Bormann had just invoked one—*cherchez la femme!* Further recrimination could wait. Bormann now took charge and mounted two more motor cavalcades to roar through the night. Hoegl was sent back posthaste over the same rubbly streets he had traversed just one hour before. Bormann also dispatched Heinrich Mueller by a different route. The flat was empty. What had they expected to find on this double wild-goose chase? The real wild goose had flown the coop.

Mueller did not return with the others to the bunker. He went directly to his own cellar to begin the intensive interrogation of Hermann Fegelein. One can assume that his first and leading question was precisely the one that most concerns us here: Just who was this woman, and what was her real mission in Berlin?

I have talked to four witnesses—Guensche, Baur, Mohnke, and Misch—all of whom had met the lady in question at least once. Guensche—one remembers here the little matter of the telephone number—recalled her best. While by no means a close friend of Fegelein's, and of far lower rank, Guensche had joined him on several occasions at a popular Berlin nightspot that had been allowed to remain open because it also served as a convenient air-raid shelter.

Guensche's description was this. "Fegelein's mistress was classier than most of his other women. I can remember only that she was good-looking, tall, well groomed. Her hair was blond with a reddish tint. She was thirtyish. She spoke German, with an accent, and at least two or three other languages. I heard that she had a husband, some foreign diplomat, conveniently out of town. She and Fegelein came for a quick drink and then left. One talk was about horses."

Not much, but something. As Guensche spoke, I thought I was at least about to clinch the nationality point. An Irishwoman, out with a cavalryman, might quite likely chat about horses. Sergeant Misch, however, who had also met the woman, said he thought she was Scots and "married to a Hungarian." Mohnke, too, was aware that the woman was of another tribe, but he said Danish. All three agreed that she was working in broadcasting.

Where had Fegelein met this woman, his *femme fatale*? Hans Baur, who let drop the information perhaps without realizing its significance, said the meeting had taken place at a 1944 summer party in the swank Goebbels villa. And just what was the Irish lady doing there? A fair guess, I believe, was that her first affair—affair in the sense of her penetration of high Nazi circles—was not with Hermann Fegelein. It was, I now suspect, with Goebbels, the most notorious wolf in town and the man who had just become her boss.

This was the connection. The lady we will call Mata O'Hara because she was thought to be Irish—and on this Baur, Mohnke, and Guensche are all agreed—was the wife of a fairly senior Hungarian career diplomat. The couple had arrived in Berlin some time in 1943, at precisely the time when German-Hungarian relations, never really warm, were getting cooler. Events were building up to a major showdown between the Nazi regime and the nominally pro-Axis government of the Hungarian regent, Admiral Horthy. Horthy had never really believed in an Axis victory; he hated Hitler. By 1944 the desperate Hungarian statesman was pro-West, but trapped by geography. The Hungarian game was, by hook or by crook, to extricate the nation from the war and pull its east-front army back to Hungary.

The crisis mounted all summer. In the autumn, with the Red Army already approaching Budapest, the military situation was truly desperate. Admiral Horthy, sensibly, wanted to sue for peace. Hitler countered by ordering Horthy's arrest. Some dozen of his followers in the Berlin embassy were also arrested by Himmler and sent to keep Horthy company.

This bizarre situation explains why Mata O'Hara was so suddenly stranded in Berlin, unable to get to Ireland, Hungary, or even Switzerland. It also suggests that she was an amateur rather than a professional agent. Whatever funds she might normally have had access to were outside Germany. With her husband interned, the woman needed a job, some source of income.

Goebbels, who always had a keen eye for a good-looking woman, had found work for her in the logical place, his own shop. The Berlin-based Deutschlandsender broadcast round the clock in several of the languages in which we know Mata O'Hara was fluent—she knew English and French and possibly Hungarian. Her routine job was not voice broadcasting; it was simply translating. In addition, as everyone in Berlin social circles knew, when Goebbels lined up a job for a woman, she was expected to go to bed with him.

Her later switch to Hermann Fegelein is easy to explain: she had found a better source of information. Goebbels was not so stupid as to babble military secrets in the boudoir, and he was no drinker. Fegelein was both.

Her chance came in late 1944, when Hitler pulled his elite Sixth SS Panzer Army out of action on the eastern front to spearhead the Ardennes offensive. This was Fegelein's old outfit, and when General Sepp Dietrich and most of his staff officers passed through Berlin in November, nothing was more natural than a get-together between Fegelein—with his elegant new mistress—and his old comrades. The lady soon flashed the news of the coming attack to London. And there, some clod in Intelligence refused to believe it.

However, there is other evidence that Mata O'Hara was successful in leaking information to the British. It concerns Soldatensender Calais. As its name was meant to imply, this was a secret, or "black," radio station supposedly run by an SS opposition group but in fact operated by the British. Beginning in 1943, the shortwave broadcasts were beamed from England. The name "Calais" was chosen to confuse German Army listeners with access to direction-finding devices.

Soldatensender Calais had a phenomenal success with its German Army audience. So clever was the dissimulation, so German the voices, so attractive the programs, that only the most sophisticated of listeners recognized this new art of black propaganda in the British bag of dirty tricks. Goebbels had been gone one better. As he noted in his diary, the propaganda minister himself was too clever to expose the station. He knew that even in wartime, indeed especially in wartime, the prestige of the BBC was so high in Germany that to unmask the operation as British would only enhance its appeal.

The British psychological-warfare stratagem was ingeniously simple. The station's programs captured a mass audience of German soldiers in the first weeks on the air simply by the playing of traditional German military tunes and the reading of Wehrmacht bulletins. Only slowly did experts begin to put in the propaganda needle, many weeks later, and only in the evening programs, which came in prime listening time. A man called "Der Chef," pretending to be a loyal but disgruntled SS man, began to expose the goings-on in the Fuehrerhauptquartier. Adolf Hitler was never criticized directly—that would have scared off Nazi listeners—but everybody around him was.

In fact, and in retrospect, the British psy-warriors were successful beyond their wildest dreams. Some of their solid information, of course, came from prisoners of war or genuine anti-Nazi sources; some from a careful perusal of captured German Army newspapers and magazines; some from the usual agent, underground, or intelligence sources. The special SS angle was always played up. News from the Fuehrer's HQ—most Germans were news-starved on that score—was always stressed, in terms of promotions, decorations earned and otherwise, anecdotes, and randy tidbits about who was sleeping with whom. Goebbels' mistresses, and those of Himmler and Bormann, got steady coverage. The soldier audience slowly got the sly message: "These, comrades, are the rogues who are leading you while you fight and bleed for your fatherland. If the Fuehrer only knew."

None of this leering chatter, with its high porn content, was world-shattering news. But that is precisely the point. To Hitler and Bormann, if the perfidious British had a source that close to the FHQ, obviously they must also be getting more important information that they were *not* broadcasting. Hence the loaded sarcasm of such Hitler remarks as the one he often threw at Keitel and Jodl: "I wonder if we can get this order to the troops at the front before we hear all about it over the BBC."

Many pieces of the puzzle begin to fall into place. Here, I believe, is the explanation of why this pesky matter of the leak, which had been going on for more than a year, concerned Hitler more than ever in these last days in the bunker. His security barrier had been penetrated, and he knew it; this was no imaginary obsession. The Fuehrer was terrified that his body might fall into enemy hands, a prospect that worried him far more than death itself. It was imperative for him to locate the leak before his suicide could safely take place. Time was running out.

An emerging picture, but a faint one, a tantalizing phantom. For a few weeks, and with these random clues, I had hoped that it might not be too difficult to locate this mystery woman if she was alive, or to identify her if she was dead. On both counts, I was too sanguine. The leads trailed off to Budapest, London, Dublin, Galway, Salzburg, well out of the framework of this book. But I still hope to find her. At least we know enough about her to realize why she could well have been what cost Hermann Fegelein his neck.

One hour after Fegelein's execution—the timing here is blood-curdling—Adolf Hitler married Eva Braun. Another deed of black midnight, murder, followed by marriage. The bridegroom clearly saw to it that Fegelein did not live to become his brother-in-law, a traitor in the bosom of the family. The bride knew this. She did not hesitate or balk or even bat an eyelash. As Gerda Christian reported, "There were tears in her blue eyes, but they were tears of radiant joy."

Up to this point in the bunker narrative, including Hans Baur's account of his talk with Eva Braun this same morning, the picture we have always had of Hitler's mistress, although sentimental and dripping with treacle, has been rather positive. I have dutifully recorded it. But this marriage scene is what really gave the bride away. Her character, too, was suddenly "isolated by a single deed."

CHAPTER 8

THE SHOT NOBODY HEARD

Hitler's last day began in total quiet. He had retired just before sunrise at four-thirty. He was up and about one hour later. It was Monday morning, April 30, 1945, *dies irae*. The artillery barrage had again fallen off. All hands still on duty in the Fuehrerbunker had welcomed this chance to snatch at least a few hours sleep.

Except for the lonely Fuehrer himself. Reversing his usual bunker behavior pattern, Hitler was up betimes and was pacing about the bunker, alone. At 6:00 A.M. the Fuehrer, as related, had suddenly summoned General Mohnke to report to the lower bunker.

After the Mohnke interview, until 8:15 A.M., Sergeant Misch and one lonely guard were the only souls on duty as Hitler wandered listlessly about the lower bunker. He shuffled hither and yon in the cramped quarters, his eyes usually cast to the floor, his hands clasped behind his back. He paced from his quarters to the corridor, from the corridor to the staircase, like a frustrated zoo animal. Two other staffers were present, but both were fast asleep in bed rolls spread on the concrete floor—Gerda Christian, now Hitler's senior secretary, and General Hans Krebs, the Acting Chief of the General Staff.

Misch noted, "I knew this was the end, or very close to it. To me and most of the other old hands it had long been clear, at least since the stormy Hitler explosion of April 22, that our Fuehrer had no realistic choice except suicide. We were all nervously waiting for just that to happen, the sooner the better. At the same time, we were trying to conceal our nervousness with frantic little flurries and shows of activity. So I just crouched over my switchboard, fiddling about with the plugs, though few calls were now still coming in."

"The Fuehrer is still alive and is conducting the defense of Berlin . . ." So ran the telegram Martin Bormann had dispatched to Admiral Doenitz earlier the same morning, around three-thirty. Admiral Doenitz was already installed in his new command post 270 miles away in Schleswig-Holstein. In this same telegram, Bormann also relayed a Fuehrerbefehl that the admiral "must move quickly and strictly against all traitors." The special traitor Bormann here had in mind was Heinrich Himmler, who at this same moment was holed up in a red-brick police barracks about thirty miles southeast of Admiral Doenitz. In between his "momentous, historical sessions" with the Swedish intermediary, Himmler was now blithely working on his own "governmental and cabinet list." Himmler's serene belief that he could play the role of a *grand gendarme* for liberated Europe was preposterous, and everyone present except Himmler knew it.

Around 8:30 A.M. in the bunker, as Hitler was still at breakfast, the several hours' respite from Russian artillery fire ended abruptly. This ninety-minute barrage was to prepare for the upcoming final assault on the Reichstag. The Red Army infantry attack kicked off at 10:00 A.M.

General Krebs now came up with a situation report even more alarming than that given the Fuehrer by General Mohnke only three hours before. Krebs reported how—slowly, remorselessly—the Red Army generals were closing the iron ring. According to those present, Hitler listened "in apathetic silence" as Krebs droned on. He did not even pose any questions. At the end of this briefing, the last, he turned to one of his military aides and dictated a Fuehrerbefehl, the last written order Hitler was to give.

In case there is a shortage of either ammunition or provisions in the Reichshauptstadt, I herewith give my permission for our troops to make a breakout attempt. This operation should be organized in battle units as small as possible. Every effort must be made to link up with German troops still carrying on the fight outside the city of Berlin. If such cannot be located, then the Berlin force must take to the woods and continue resistance there.

A document, in short, expressly forbidding even the thought of capitulation. No surrender. An SS captain was sent to hand this order to the city commandant, General Weidling, in person. It took the courier almost two hours to traverse the distance of less than one mile. He returned wounded, mission completed.

According to those who were still present with him, General Weidling, during midmorning of this Monday, April 30, had already called together his five or six division commanders and told them he intended to order this breakout attempt on his own authority. The H-Hour he then gave was ten o'clock that same evening.

Even on this last day, it is still easy enough to reconstruct, pretty much, just what Hitler was doing. General Mohnke has covered us well for the period of 6:00 A.M. to 7:00 A.M.; Sergeant Misch, for 7:00 A.M. to 8:15 A.M. As a hungry Misch then left for the canteen, Gerda Christian was again at Hitler's side, ready for work, such as it might be. Major Otto Guensche was on deck by 9:00 A.M.

Frau Gerda Christian spoke of this last morning.

I soon gathered, from the general, glum mood, that this was to be our last bunker day. But nobody yet dared say or even hint as much. And yet, all things considered, it was routine enough, taken up with the usual rounds of conferences, parleys, dictation. Goebbels was closeted with Hitler, although only for a short while, perhaps twenty minutes. This was around noontime. I suppose it was around twelve-thirty when my relief, Trudl Junge, arrived. This was the usual time—we were still working in shifts—and it was also, again as usual, the familiar signal for lunch. Hitler, "for old times' sake," now invited both of us secretaries, along with Fräulein Manzialy, to join him for lunch at one o'clock.

We ate at the small table in Hitler's study, the so-called map room. It was a melancholy and rather tasteless repast, spaghetti and a tossed salad. Very little was said, certainly nothing new. One topic was the proper mating of dogs; another, that French lipstick was made from grease gathered in the Paris sewers. We had often eaten alone with Hitler before, of course, but this was the very last lunch, and everybody knew it.

It seems strange that Eva Braun Hitler was not at her husband's side in this cozy little luncheon group. Frau Christian observed, "Perhaps a simple explanation is that the Fuehrer really felt, now that E.B. was legally Frau Hitler, that she was no longer on the same quite humble social level she had been as his mistress. He was rather persnickity, in his Austrian way, about just such minor table formalities. Or perhaps poor Eva just wasn't hungry."

The final goodbyes came shortly after three o'clock, when the newlywed Hitlers, so seldom together since the bleak midnight wedding some forty hours before, now made their last appearance in the main corridor of the lowest bunker. It was *ave atque vale* to what was left of the bedraggled Reich Chancellery Group. Present were Goebbels, alone; Bormann; Generals Krebs and Burgdorf; Ambassador Walter Hewel; Vice Admiral Voss; Professor Werner Haase; Major General Rattenhuber; Colonel Hoegl; the senior valet, Heinz Linge; Major Otto Guensche; the three secretaries, Frau Christian, Frau Junge, and Fräulein Kreuger (Bormann's secretary). This is close to the complete final cast. Missing were only Chefpilot Hans Baur, Artur Axmann, the chauffeur Erich Kempka—and Magda Goebbels.

This formal bunker leave-taking was brief; it lasted less than three minutes. No one later recalled any last, immortal words. In the awkward silence, it was finally Linge, who, after a cue from the Fuehrer, opened the door leading to Hitler's private apartment. Hitler, with a courtly gesture, directed his doomed spouse to precede him.

Then, just before disappearing forever, Adolf Hitler turned to Heinz Linge, shook hands with him, and said, "Linge, old friend, I want you now to join the breakout group."

Linge, taken aback, asked, "Why, my Fuehrer?"

Hitler said, "To serve the man who will come after me."

Whatever that may have meant. These were Hitler's last words in the presence of the court. The silence was almost tangible.

Now Hitler, moving slowly but steadily, passed through and closed the door. At this point Linge lost his composure completely. For no apparent reason, he ran up all forty-four steep steps of the four-flight emergency-exit staircase. Soon he came running back, speechless, wild-eyed. Yet Linge still had one more important assigned role to play. All the others, stupefied, simply watched Linge's antic activity.

Major Otto Guensche was the next to make a move. He left to round up several young officers of the FBK and post them in the upper bunker. Their imminent chore was to lug the two Hitler corpses out of the lower bunker. Guensche soon returned and stationed himself directly before the door to the Hitler apartment. His legs were spread, and he was clasping his machine pistol at port arms, before his breast. All present expected the end at any minute. All ears were cocked for the sound of a revolver shot, possibly two. As a soldier, Guensche himself began to wonder, as the minutes ticked by, whether anyone would really be able to hear a shot through the heavy, vaultlike steel door. Two doors, in fact, because there was also the small vestibule before the Hitler living room.

Action outside the door, however, was not quite over. Two important latecomers who had missed the corridor farewell ceremony now suddenly appeared. The first was Magda Goebbels, who bolted toward Guensche. Surprised and perplexed, Guensche, flourishing his weapon, tried to wave her back. But the frantic Magda persisted. She was determined to see Adolf Hitler, and Guensche relented. He entered the room to relay Magda's request to the Fuehrer. At this unguarded moment, Frau Goebbels burst past him and lunged into the Fuehrer's study. This unplanned interlude lasted perhaps three minutes. Hitler gruffly refused to talk to Magda Goebbels or even listen to her plea that "there is still a chance to take off for Berchtesgaden."

The second VIP late arrival—he appeared on the scene while Frau Goebbels was still closeted with Hitler—was Artur Axmann. He had been delayed because he had had to come from his battle post across the street, crossing the Wilhelmplatz under fire. When he approached Guensche, who was again at his post before the door, this time the irritated major was adamant. He told Axmann bluntly, "Too late; too late for anyone."

It was one, possibly two, minutes later that "a single shot was heard." So ran the version as the world first heard it in 1945. It has since been recorded in most historical accounts of Hitler's last moment. That version was based on the original testimony of Erich Kempka (and that of Linge as well), one of the few key witnesses destined to evade the Red Army dragnet and to surface in the west. However, as he sheepishly admitted in 1974 to this reporter, Kempka was not even among those present in the corridor at this critical moment.

Back in 1945 the contrary evidence of Artur Axmann—his testimony became available late in December 1945—was dismissed or ignored. Axmann then said simply, "I was standing right there, as close to the door as possible, but I certainly heard no shot." This was the truth. The Fuehrer was exchanging his last blunt words with Magda Goebbels.

Guensche was the one man who was really centerstage at this critical moment. Wherever I could check him out, I found Guensche to have, like Axmann, a very high veracity ratio.

Nobody, among those who were really present, did hear any shot. This, as they later reported, is what increased the tension. Guensche corroborated, saying,

> Nobody was standing closer to that door than I, that is for sure. I have good ears, and I was listening intently. The 1945 testimony of both Linge and Kempka just does not stand up; they must have been confused or were under interrogation pressure. Linge, for example, was really beside himself, running up and down those stairs like the King of Spain, and Kempka was not present. Kempka, as I recall, was not even present when we first entered the death chamber. I first met him at the bottom of the stairs, when we were carrying the bodies away. That was ten or even fifteen minutes after Hitler's suicide.

Otto Guensche then returned to his narrative of what really did happen that mid-Monday afternoon in Berlin, April 20, 1945.

> There were, as I now recall, at least six people almost as near that door as I was. These were Goebbels, Bormann, Linge, Generals Krebs and Burgdorf, Axmann, maybe one or two others. None of us heard a shot. I believe this was because of the sealed double doors. Both these doors were fireproof, gasproof, hence soundproof. The last instruction both Linge and I had—directly from the Fuehrer—was to wait ten minutes and then, and only then, to enter the room. This is just what we did. I kept glancing at my watch. I thought it must have stopped; they were the longest ten minutes in my life.

I sent Kempka a copy of Guensche's testimony and pointed out the obvious conflict. Kempka told me in 1974,

> Yes, Major Guensche is right. I was on my way back to the Fuehrerbunker when I met up with the funeral cortège. That lout Bormann was carrying the body of Eva Braun, clutching her breast with his apelike paw. Somehow this maddened me. He was carrying her as if she were a sack of potatoes. Just as they all started to ascend the staircase, I reached the bottom. So I grabbed the body of Eva Braun from Bormann and began to carry her up the stairs myself. I think if Bormann had resisted my effort, I would have hauled off and clobbered him, but he made no protest.

To reconstruct what really did happen behind those closed doors—for there can be no question of any direct eyewitnesses, any third person in the room—is not difficult. We have the testimony of at least three of the five bunker witnesses who were the first to enter that room, around 3:40 P.M.: Kempka and the much more reliable Axmann and Guensche.

For the hour of Hitler's death, we also have, albeit secondhand, the very important contemporary account of Professor Haase, as recalled by Dr. Schenck.

Shortly after 4:00 P.M., less than one half hour after Hitler's death, the now breathless Professor Haase gave Schenck a quite precise account of his last, long consultation with Adolf Hitler. This had taken place, Haase said, in the lower bunker at around 3:00 or maybe 4:00 A.M., Monday, the same day. Hitler had once again queried Haase on the foolproof or pistol-and-poison method recommended by the latter. If Hitler followed Haase's clinical instructions to the letter—and all later circumstantial evidence indicates that he most certainly did—then what follows is a fair reconstruction of what probably happened.

Hitler had in his possession two pistols. The larger and far more potent was a standard Walther 7.65 caliber. The Fuehrer had been carrying this gun in his tunic pocket since April 22, possibly earlier. The smaller pistol was another Walther, a 6.35. This was the weapon Hitler had been carrying for many years, concealed in the leather holster sewn inside his trousers near the right pocket. This smaller gun he now placed on the table before him in front of the sofa. One assumes this was simply a precaution in case the heavier pistol, with which Hitler was far less familiar, should jam.

Then Hitler sat down on the left-hand corner of the narrow sofa (left, as viewed from the door). Next, he took out of his tunic pocket two poison vials. One he placed on the table between the pistol and a vase. This was a reserve. The other he put into his mouth.

His bride, Eva, was seated in the other corner of the blue-and-white sofa. They were only about two feet apart. Eva had kicked off her buckskin spectator pumps and pulled her feet up snugly under her lithe body. She had two similar capsules. One of these she placed on the same small round table. Beside it she put her own small pistol, also a Walther 6.35. Next to it was a raspberry-colored silk scarf. She put the second capsule into her mouth. Eva was not holding any pistol in her hand.

Hitler was. She must have been watching him. On the matter of timing, Hitler had told Haase that it was his last wish that the double deaths be simultaneous—"We both want to go together when we go."

After his last conference with Hitler, to make doubly sure, Professor Haase had visited Eva Braun Hitler in her chambers and told her, "Simply bite quickly into your capsule the moment you hear a shot." The girl apparently did just that; she had some reason to fear that the sight of her dead lover might shatter her resolution. Eva Braun Hitler was thus almost surely the only person to hear the single shot many millions in this world would have been most delighted to hear.

Adolf Hitler—again assuming he had followed the last advice not only of Professor Haase but also of his senior military men, Krebs and Burgdorf—must have put the muzzle of his black Walther directly to his graying right temple, right-angled at eyebrow level. He then squeezed the trigger and simultaneously bit into his capsule. Given his physical condition, this called for one last, vehement act of concentrated will power. We know Hitler had that quality right to the end. Bang! The pistol slipped from the tyrant's right hand. It fell to the carpet at his feet. This is a sign that the poison, potassium cyanide, had done its job quickly. Most pistol-only suicides are usually found clutching the weapon with clawlike tenacity.

For Eva Hitler, too, death must have come quickly, if not painlessly. Her frail body was found in the same position she had assumed when she kicked off her pumps. The double odor from the pistol shot and the cyanide, a mixture of acrid cordite and bitter almond, now filled the small, stuffy death room. But it did not seep into the vestibule or into the corridor outside from the room proofed against poison gas.

Bormann and Guensche were standing together near the door to the vestibule. Four others were present: Goebbels, General Krebs, General Burgdorf, and Artur Axmann. All hands had been told by Hitler just how he wanted them to go about the disposal of his body and that of his wife. He had made each of them swear to see to it that his instructions were carried out meticulously, for all in the bunker had heard by this time some of the sordid details of what had just happened down in Italy to the corpses of Benito Mussolini and his mistress, Clara Petacci.

Somebody had to be first to enter that sinister room. In the end it was poor Linge, who was the second lowest-ranking member in this small group (like Kempka, he was a colonel in the SS). As he slowly opened the door, he was taken aback. The strong fumes from the pistol shot and the poison made his eyes smart. He turned back to summon Bormann. "Frankly, I was trembling," Linge says, "and I simply did not have the gumption to go in there by myself. It was too eerie."

With Bormann leading, the small group finally entered, gasping from the toxic fumes. Three of the witnesses to this grim yet fascinating moment—Linge, Guensche, Axmann—are still alive, and I have talked with them. All three agree pretty much on the horrible historical tableau.

Eva Braun Hitler was in the snug schoolgirl position. Her small pistol was next to her brightly colored scarf. Hitler was more slumped-over, but was still on the blue-and-white velvet sofa. Blood was oozing in steady drips from his right temple.

"At least two minutes—two very long minutes—passed before any of us said or did anything," Guensche related. Guensche finally snapped out of the trance and directed Linge to move aside the two chairs and the table, in order to spread two woolen military blankets onto the floor. He then left the room to summon three young officers who were waiting nearby in the guards' room. At this moment another witness arrived. It was Colonel Ludwig Stumpfegger, the surgeon. He examined both bodies and pronounced Adolf and Eva Hitler dead.

To my mind what really clinches the circumstantial evidence about Hitler's death is what I heard from Dr. Schenck. He not only told me about the long conversation he had had with Haase within less than an hour after Hitler's death, he also added a final, psychological sidebar. "Many people tend to forget that Adolf Hitler was not alone when he shot himself. He was in the presence of a brave woman who was very much in love with him. Why, therefore, should he arrange a coup de grace for himself but not for her? One can despise Hitler, but he was not a coward. Moreover, he was a great actor and a born show-off, above all before women. For him to have flinched at this last moment, before Eva Braun, *that* would have been quite out of character."

Three of the tallest young SS bucks from the FBK were now lugging Hitler's corpse. They had no stretcher or portable bier, not even a plank. Hitler's blood-stained cranium was hidden from the view of pallbearers and mourners. Visible were only the familiar black trousers of the simple uniform Hitler had donned back in September 1939. Hitler weighed about 180 pounds, so it was a somewhat awkward task to get him up those steep, narrow stairs. They hauled him up head first, two stalwarts clutching the still-warm corpse near the shoulders, the third pushing from below with a firm grip on both ankles.

Carrying the smaller, lighter body of Eva Braun was an easier task. Kempka, after grabbing her body from Bormann, found that he could make it only halfway up the stairs. Here he was relieved of his burden by Major Guensche. Guensche in turn handed the body over to SS officers as he reached the top of the stairs. This otherwise trivial pantomine underscores the almost instant collapse of Bormann as a figure of any real authority, pushed aside by a chauffeur and a mere major.

Once the group was out in the Berlin fresh air, the stage was set for a kind of instant state funeral, probably the shortest such requiem in world history. The three SS officers lowered the corpses into a long, rather shallow makeshift ditch. It was less than ten meters from the bunker exit. Two of the officers emptied several jerry cans over the corpses, probably something less than fifty gallons of gasoline. They then stepped back and tried to ignite the two splashed cadavers in the soggy blankets by tossing lighted matches toward the trench. Nothing happened; there was too much wind.

Too much wind and also, now, a good deal of metal flying about in the form of shrapnel. This accounts for much of this hectic, anarchic, if sometimes intrepid dramaturgy. The Soviets, although at the time they could not know this, were supplying non-Wagnerian funeral music.

Thus it was that the action was interrupted three or four times as the agitated principals waited for those few pauses which meant that the Red Army artillery men were reloading. They would move out on the double from the bunker entrance for a few seconds only; then duck back to take cover in a kind of vestibule to the bunker exit, which had a cement canopy.

Heinz Linge had a bright idea. To light the emergency butane lamp in the bunker, Linge had been in the habit of carrying slips of paper tucked into the broad lapels of his fancy butler's uniform. These, when needed, he would twist into a fidibus, a kind of pipesmoker's paper spill. Linge now twisted one of these to make a flare, lighted it with his pocket lighter, and then handed it ceremoniously to Bormann, who tossed the fidibus through the air like a schoolboy's paper dart. His first attempt fell short. On the next try, a lighted flare landed directly in the trench, close to the two bodies. A second later, both cadavers burst into sudden blue flame.

Without anybody having been given an order, the participants, as one man, stood at rigid attention at the graveside to give the Hitler salute. There was no music, no flag, no swastika banner, no funeral oration.

With Adolf Hitler gone, only one figure moving about the Hitlerless bunker can, by any stretch of the imagination, be called a major historical personality, a man of a certain character, formation, intellectual depth. This was Joseph Goebbels.

Although Goebbels at this moment was Hitler's successor as Reich chancellor, only a few bunker insiders—and nobody outside—yet knew this. It was not known even to Grand Admiral Doenitz, now Reich President Doenitz, who was up north in Schleswig-Holstein. Bormann, still trying to manipulate the power that was flowing through his fingers like sand, failed to inform the admiral—or anyone else—either of the death of Adolf Hitler or of the clauses of his testament. Goebbels, however, in no mood to take any nonsense from Bormann, sent a telegram to Doenitz that evening, telling him what had happened in Berlin and informing him, correctly, of the new power situation, such as it was. This was one of Goebbels' few official acts as German chancellor.

The new chancellor and his wife spent almost all of that long evening in the conference room of the lower bunker, reminiscing. He was called away two or three times by pressing business, but he always soon returned. Those who had gathered about him were either his few very close personal friends or some of the old mountain people.

What is astonishing is that no one in this elite Nazi group, not even Goebbels, showed the least interest in what had happened—or in what was still happening—to the Hitler remains.

Cremation is not a process to be carried out by novices. Novices, moreover, acting under shock and quasi-battle conditions. In order for any human body to be burned to ash, both intense heat and proper fuel, on a prepared site, are necessary. Otherwise, as in this case, the product is bound to be a charred torso. The casual trench into which the two Hitler bodies had been thrown did not allow for any real combustion; there was no draft of air from below. Moreover, it is probable that most of the gasoline, splashed onto the bodies in such a wild hurry, sank quickly into the sandy Berlin soil. Hitler's bones, teeth, and skull were only charred. Identification was thus easily possible.

On Rattenhuber's orders, some time after midnight—it was already May Day—three of his soldiers placed the two charred bodies on a tent shelter-half and dragged the load to a second nearby and deeper trench. It had been dug out of a pothole made earlier by artillery.

One of these soldiers, with a certain sense of awe and even dignity, came back into the lower bunker and politely asked for a flag. A short frantic search ensued. But there was no flag, not even a last swastika banner. So the disconsolate soldier returned to his grave-digging detail and helped toss the bodies into the second trench. The three soldiers filled it with earth and rubble, pounded the grave firm with a wooden pestle, and that was that. It was almost dawn.

CHAPTER 9

DEATH OF THE MYTHMAKER

In my interviews with bunker survivors, even the most hardboiled, I found no theme quite so hushed, so wrapped in signs, as the fate of the six Goebbels children. The oldest was Helga, twelve, her father's favorite—intelligent, tall, mature for her age; she had her father's walnut eyes and dark hair. Then came Hilde, eleven, the prettiest, also a brunette; Helmut, ten, the only boy, a dreamy youngster with bad grades in school; Holde, eight, blond, the one the others always teased; Hedde, six, blond; Heidi, not yet five, the family pet.

Many men and women came to know these children well in these eight long days the youngsters were scampering blithely about the upper bunker. For adults it had become a chamber of horror. For these innocents, bunker life was an exciting diversion, a sport, fun and games with the grownups in an upside-down, night-is-day world.

Several plans were afoot to whisk the children away. Albert Speer had worked out a scheme, and General Mohnke, on one late occasion, offered to put a tank at the disposal of Goebbels to evacuate the children. But any scheme to save the children would have involved direct action against both parents—such as putting them into straitjackets.

Those in the bunker who most detested Goebbels are guilty of sentimentality when they place sole blame on him as father. Magda Goebbels dazzled men with her charm and beauty, women with her eternal maternal histrionics. She was able, at the end, to evoke a good deal more sympathy than the hard facts in her case warrant. Frustrated Magda was a natural actress, as theater-minded as her husband. And she knew how to forge for herself a bogus martyr's crown.

What many people in the bunker did not know was that there had been several occasions when Goebbels had shied from the idea of slaughtering his own offspring. It was precisely on these occasions that the female of the Goebbels kind proved deadlier than the male. Magda Goebbels' death wish had lurid sexual overtones. For her, it was just not dramatic enough to die with Adolf Hitler. Her cerebral propagandist-husband might have been interested in the death of Hitler as a historical mystical event. Magda's hopelessly warped emotions were far more personal, visceral. She was determined to pile up the corpses of her own children on the underground cement altar. Those offspring, as she had said so many times, she had borne "for the Third Reich"—though she would have preferred to have had them by "Him." Eva Braun may have become Frau Hitler, but too late to offer him children. Only by her children could Magda achieve a morbid, Medea-like triumph over her childless, younger blond rival.

Late one wintry weekend in January 1945, around a crackling beechwood fire at their country estate, Magda calmly broke the news to a small gathering that when the end came, she and her husband planned suicide with the Fuehrer. There was a long, solemn silence. It was broken by Goebbels' quoting, with his one-volume copy of Thomas Carlyle's *History of Frederick the Great* in his hand, the passage wherein the Prussian king scoffed at "the events of our little planet which, as important as they seem to us, are of no significance."

To which Magda replied, "You may be right. Still, Frederick the Great had no children." The woman was an actress, and this was one of her better, more lucid lines.

On another occasion, after the family had returned to Berlin in early March, she said that she was determined to die with the Fuehrer and take her children with her "because my darlings are simply too good for this bad world." But the problem still nagging Goebbels was to make sure that the Fuehrer stuck to his decision to end his life in the German capital. For several long weeks, the minister's had been the sole voice resolutely holding out for this last stand in Berlin. The vast majority in the bunker favored the Alpine Redoubt alternative and yearned to decamp to Berchtesgaden.

Just after Easter weekend, on March 29, the strong Berchtesgaden clique in the bunker, led by Bormann, had caught the Fuehrer in a moment when he seemed to be suddenly overcome by a yen for the air of the Obersalzberg. Goebbels got wind of this and came bustling over. Major Guensche described this tense scene. "Goebbels, clutching his Fuehrer by both lapels, implored him to remember the solemn oath that he had once sworn, with Goebbels, toward midnight on January 30, 1933, the day Hitler had become chancellor and entered the Old Reich Chancellery: 'We shall never abandon this building voluntarily. No power in this world can ever drive us out.' "

There was at least one side of Goebbels' sophisticated mind that was always coldly rational. He did not, for a single instant, doubt the validity of the Hitler myth. The messiah must die. This was the whole purpose of the exercise. To be meaningful, death must be in Berlin, in the historic governmental area, at the last possible moment.

Goebbels appeared often enough in the bunker, but he never tarried long. As Gauleiter of Berlin he was visible every day aboveground. As propaganda minister, he kept his mill turning over at full turn. It was still the most active ministry in Berlin, and—after April 16—the only one.

The weekend of the Fuehrer's birthday, Friday, April 20, saw the last parade of the familiar VIPs of the Third Reich, limping in from the provinces to say farewell to their Fuehrer. All were most anxious to leave quickly—Goering, Himmler, Ribbentrop, Ley. Goebbels saw these crestfallen peacocks strut in and out. He watched with haughty disdain. He had often predicted they would all leave before the end, as they were now doing. This, too, fitted the script just as the prophet wanted it. It strengthened his own bond with the Fuehrer. Although Goebbels showed up briefly at the bleak birthday festivities, he soon left.

Sunday, April 22, was a momentous day in the bunker. Shortly after noontime, Hitler cracked up, dismissed his generals, and ordered Julius Schaub to burn his private papers. He confided to Eva Braun that he intended to commit suicide. In the afternoon, Goebbels dissuaded him and wrung from Hitler permission to announce that "the Fuehrer was in Berlin and would die fighting with his troops." Around 6:00 P.M. the whole Goebbels family moved into the bunker.

Goebbels, in the following days, was left with much time on his hands. Bunker inmates reported that he spent long hours, in his office next to Hitler's, simply reading and writing. He was still making diary entries. He was also working over his last testament, to be appended to Hitler's. It seems probable that he worked on the rough draft of Hitler's own political testament. Much of the phrasing has the Goebbels touch. And he attended the military briefings.

Goebbels, as father, found he now had abundant time for his children, time he had never quite found before. He read to them, told stories, played games, sang songs. This was not just an act—Goebbels was most fond of his children—but it added to the stupefying unreality, as Liesl Ostertag, Eva Braun's maid, reported. "You simply could not watch those touching family scenes and still believe this doting father had multiple murder in his heart."

Though there was now a distinct cooling-off of the old friendship between Goebbels and Hitler, they met for at least an hour every day during the last week when Goebbels apparently was drafting notes for Hitler's last testament. Yet while he was busy with the hollow eloquence of this curtain speech, Goebbels was being undermined. And as he lost influence with Hitler, he was replaced as chief adviser and intimate by Martin Bormann. How did this come about? The fact seemed to puzzle most of my bunker witnesses as they recollected the scene.

Thus, I asked myself what had been the major new development in the bunker during the forty-eight hours preceding the drafting of Hitler's last will?

As we now know, it was the Fegelein affair. And where had Fegelein first met his *femme fatale*, Mata O'Hara? At a party given by Goebbels. Is there any circumstantial evidence to support my surmise? An interesting bit of evidence comes from Sergeant Misch.

> For years, in all thirteen of the wartime FHQs, my standing orders [at the switchboard] were to put Dr. Goebbels through directly to Der Chef when he called. But, around April 27, Reichsleiter Bormann came to me and insisted that all calls be routed through him. He told me that this had the weight of a Fuehrerbefehl. I, of course, had to obey.
>
> It was a ridiculous situation, in view of our cramped geography. Although Hitler and Goebbels were in adjoining rooms and I was seated just outside in the corridor, I now had to reroute Goebbels' calls to Hitler through Bormann's phone.

This is a historical footnote of some importance. As late as April 20, Hitler's birthday, there were still seven Nazi VIPs who could get through directly on what we would now call the "hot line." In order of precedence, they were Goering, Goebbels, Himmler, Speer, Doenitz, Keitel, and Bormann. Now, near the end, Bormann had overleaped every rival, and the only direct line of power left in the crumbling Third Reich was Hitler-Bormann.

Magda Goebbels was not insane in the legal or clinical sense of the word, but she was Hitler-crazed—a madness of a different order. (About her, Kempka made one of his typically crude—but pertinent— observations: "Whenever she was in the presence of the Fuehrer, I could hear her ovaries rattling.") In the grip of this obsession, she was to commit the act that all bunker witnesses agreed was the most perverse in this cave of horrors.

How does a mother go about killing her six children? It seems most probable that one of the doctors supplied her with sleeping potions and poison. But the fact is that it was Magda Goebbels who killed her own children, and the evidence is damning. It rests on three points:

1. In a letter to Harald Quandt, her son by an earlier marriage, she wrote, "God will forgive me as a mother provided I have the courage to carry out this deed myself and do not leave it to others. When the time

comes, I shall give my darlings sleeping potions and then poison, a soft and painless death."

2. Werner Naumann, Goebbels' secretary, testified, "I could not talk this willful woman out of her deed. Her husband was not present nor was I. We absented ourselves from the hour of five to six P.M. When I returned, around six-fifteen, I found Dr. Goebbels with his wife. She then told us what she had done. There were no eyewitnesses.

As Naumann got the story, partly from Magda Goebbels and partly from her husband's reiteration of what she had told him, this is how she had proceeded. First, she had gathered her brood together in one room. She told them the whole family would soon be leaving for Berchtesgaden with "Uncle Fuehrer." She then prepared all for bed. She fed each child chocolates, "to prevent air sickness." These bonbons had been doped with a soporific drug. These preliminaries over, she next led them back to their beds. They soon fell asleep.

The mother had in her possession six of the familiar cyanide capsules, the blue plastic vials with the brass rings. They were the kind Dr. Stumpfegger had been distributing all week in the Fuehrerbunker.

3. Sergeant Misch, not an eyewitness but very close to the scene of action, reported, "I had come on duty at the switchboard that day at two o'clock. The three younger Goebbels children were romping about in the lower bunker, playing with a ball. I gave them some soda. With the Fuehrer dead, most of the lower bunker was now empty, and the youngsters were using it as a playground. After a while, they left."

Then, around five o'clock, the three rompers reappeared. Five minutes later Frau Goebbels arrived, bringing with her the three older children. She was wearing a long-skirted navy blue dress with white collar, cuffs, and piping. Her face was ashen. She took all the children into the room just opposite Misch. This usually served as an off-duty room for the guards.

Misch went on:

> All of the children were now clad in white nightgowns; this was their usual bedtime hour. Frau Goebbels, as usual, was playing her attentive-mother role to the very hilt. Carefully, she combed the long hair of the five girls; she then brushed down Helmut's cowlick. Next, she kissed each of them, very affectionately, as she had done every evening during the last week.
>
> I watched all of this with apprehension; I was appalled. I still have on my conscience that I did nothing though I sensed what was about to happen. At the time, watching the mother, I just could not believe it. I suppose I did not *want* to believe it.

Now, without saying goodbye, Frau Goebbels, like a mother duck with six ducklings, headed for the door, up the spiral staircase into the upper bunker. Heidi, the youngest and a little flirt, turned back to the sergeant, giggling. But her eldest sister Helga was morosely dragging her feet. The mother had to push her on her way.

Misch continued:

> At least an hour must have passed. It was now as quiet as a tomb in the lower bunker. Only one or two calls came in. Finally, Frau Goebbels reappeared. This time she was alone. There was no expression on her face. Her blue eyes were ringed with red. At first she stood there, just wringing her hands. Then she pulled herself together and lit a cigarette.
>
> There was a small champagne bottle which someone had left on the long table in the main corridor. She took it and proceeded into the room next to the watchroom, the one Dr. Goebbels had been using all week as his study. She had left his door open. I got up, walked past, and could see that she had taken out a pack of small cards and had begun to lay down a solitaire hand. Instinctively, I knew that her children were no more of this world.

Misch, during this long hour, remained on duty in the lower bunker. From time to time, apparently after each separate child murder, Magda Goebbels had emerged into the corridor of the upper bunker for a break. She was seen there, between five and six o'clock, by at least three people—Professor Schenck, Gerda Christian, and Captain Helmut Beermann of the FBK.

Nor did this coldly calculated, multiple infanticide go off quite as smoothly as planned. There is evidence that the oldest daughter, Helga, apparently awoke in fright as her mother approached her bedside. The autopsy report signed by several Soviet doctors one week later records, laconically, that Helga Goebbels had "several black-and-blue bruises." These were almost surely sustained as the terrified girl struggled for her life.

I never did discover where Goebbels betook himself during the awful hour of five to six on Tuesday, May 1, 1945. Nobody seems to know. Apparently, Goebbels was either walking about in the garden outside the bunker or had gone into one of the many empty rooms in the New Reich Chancellery. Quite possibly he was writing in his diary, on the meaning of sacrifice.

Wherever Goebbels had been, he reappeared shortly afterward, in the glimpse we get through the eyes of Artur Axmann. He said:

I came over from my command post in the Wilhelmstrasse and into the lower bunker around 6:30, Tuesday, May 1. I wanted to say goodbye to both the Goebbelses. I found the couple sitting at the long conference table with Werner Naumann, Hans Baur, Walter Hewel, General Krebs, three or four others. Goebbels soon launched into lively memories of our old street-fighting days in Berlin from 1928 to '33. But there was not a word about his family. Magda Goebbels just sat there, saying little, head high. She was chain-smoking and sipping champagne. I did not ask about the children because someone, either Baur or Hewel, had whispered to me that they were already dead.

Axmann says the reminiscence session ended around 7:00 P.M. This was about the time Sergeant Misch left his switchboard to go out of the bunker for air and a cigarette break. Except for Johannes Hentschel, in the machine room, and one FBK guard, the lower and upper bunkers were both empty.

Misch again picked up the account:

It was a strange sunset, the sun's rays trying to shine on a dense, overhanging cloud of choking yellow dust and black smoke that was blanketing the city. I was beginning to wonder how long I was supposed to remain at the switchboard. The Fuehrer was dead; all day there had been but three or four calls.

I heard over the grapevine that the breakout was being planned for later this same evening. But I wasn't sure even of that, because I had heard the same rumor the night before.

When I got up to the Chancellery garden, the only person I saw was Dr. Goebbels. He was now Reich chancellor and in this sense, I suppose, my new Chef. He was alone, without his usual aides, just strolling about. He was smoking a cigarette. I decided to tell him about my small problem and seek his advice. He told me he did not see sense in my manning the switchboard any longer. He suggested that I join the breakout. He spoke without any show of nerves. As I was talking with him, I guessed that his children were already dead, but he spoke no word about this. Hentschel, horrified, confirmed the deaths after I was back in the bunker. He said the cadavers had been left sprawled in a single room covered with winding sheets. We first thought of burying them, but to tell the truth, neither of us had the gumption to enter the death room.

The Goebbels whom Misch had bumped into so casually must have been prospecting for the spot where he intended to commit suicide. At 8:15 P.M. Goebbels, who had re-entered the upper bunker, went to his wife's chamber. Together, they descended into the lower bunker. Only three people were still present—General Mohnke, SS Captain Schwae-germann, and Olds, Goebbels' junior aide. All had been told the precise details of the ceremony about to come. Goebbels gave Schwaegermann his autographed picture of the Fuehrer, an unconscious touch of black humor. His last words were rather thoughtful, or perhaps a lame attempt at irony. "At least you good people will not have to lug our bodies up that long flight of stairs."

General Mohnke gave us the last, crisp, eyewitness account we have of the living Goebbels. "Going over to the coatrack in the small room that had served as his study, he donned his hat, his scarf, his long uniform overcoat. Slowly, he drew on his kid gloves, making each finger snug. Then, like a cavalier, he offered his right arm to his wife. They were wordless now. So were we three spectators. Slowly but steadily, leaning a bit toward each other, they headed up the stairs to the courtyard."

Night had fallen in Berlin; it was 8:30. The waning lemon moon was riding high. At the bottom of the cement stairs the couple passed, in silence, six jerry cans of gasoline standing ready. Forty-four long steps. At the head of the stairs husband and wife met one FBK officer, an SS captain. Briefed to give the coup-de-grace, this officer was standing by, just in case. He remained in the shadows, in the door frame of the emergency exit. He was the only eyewitness. His special service was not needed.

For both Joseph and Magda Goebbels had carefully rehearsed Professor Haase's approved bunker method, pistol and poison. The wife went first. She bit into her capsule, sank slowly to the ground, lay prone on the soft spring earth. She was wearing for a brooch Adolf Hitler's golden party badge, which the Fuehrer had given her as a parting present the day before his own death. Her husband fired a bullet into the back of her blond head. Goebbels then bit into his own capsule, squeezed off the trigger of his Walther P-38 pistol, and put a bullet through his right temple.

CHAPTER 10

THE BREAKOUT

With Adolf Hitler dead, a change in atmosphere pervaded the bunker. The situation was still grim, but at least it was no longer heroic-hopeless. The breakout offered hope, however perilous.

The breakout was indeed the only military operation that had been fairly well planned in the bunker, and, at least in its initial stages, it was rather shrewdly executed. Yet it was to fall apart in the middle of a long, twelve-hour operation. Only a lucky handful of this Reich Chancellery Group was destined to get out and away from Berlin forever.

The breakout had originally been planned to begin in the late hours of Monday, April 30, when the bodies of Adolf Hitler and Eva Braun had not been buried. It was postponed, less out of respect for the Fuehrer and his consort than because of the rapidly disintegrating military situation in Berlin. By now, the Soviets had closed off the only major escape route through the Tiergarten. A second reason for the delay was the utterly exhausted state of most of the Reich Chancellery Group. All hands were advised to spend Tuesday, May 1, sleeping; most did so.

On Tuesday, toward sundown, General Mohnke summoned a staff conference in his cellar command post. In his double capacity as bunker military commandant and also commander of all troops still defending the Zitadelle, Mohnke was the logical man to take charge, since he was also the most experienced front-line soldier.

Mohnke launched into a matter-of-fact account of the major bunker events of the thirty-six hours just past, events still unknown to most of these troop officers, who had been fighting outside the bunker. Mohnke told of the Hitler wedding, the execution of General Fegelein, the Hitler suicides, the death of the Goebbels family. He then noted the breakoff in the desultory negotiations between Russian General Chuikov and General Krebs. All rumors of a falling-out between the British and the Americans and the Russians, he said, were premature at best. Most of this news came as some shock to these medium-rank officers.

Mohnke continued his report.

> General Weidling has ordered that active position fighting shall cease at eleven o'clock, whereupon all German troops must be prepared to try to break through the Red Army iron ring now closing around Berlin. We must attempt this in small battle groups, probing for weak links wherever we can find them. Our first goal inside the city will be Gesundbrunnen in Wedding, near the *Flak* tower. Once outside Berlin, our general compass direction will be northwest. This is a general order; there are no more specific details. No provision can be made for any rear guard. We *are* the rear guard.

This briefing was over in twenty minutes. Like gray ghosts, the parade of officers vanished into the night.

In this first account of the breakout, which now follows, there was no dearth of informed witnesses. I relied therefore on the major surviving marchers with whom readers will already be familiar—General Mohnke, Chefpilot Baur, Dr. Schenck, Artur Axmann, Erich Kempka, Heinz Linge, Gerda Christian, Gertrud Junge, Else Krueger—as well as some dozen others.

The number of unwounded Germans still left in the Reich Chancellery was fewer than 800. About 700 of these were SS soldiers who had been fighting outside the Chancellery. About eighty were men of the FBK or General Rattenhuber's RSD, the security people. The members of the Hitler court proper had by now dwindled to fewer than twenty. All were scheduled to take part in the breakout, except for three who had opted for suicide (Generals Krebs and Burgdorf, Colonel Schaedle). A majority of the people still in the Chancellery were destined to survive. My estimate is that somewhat fewer than 100 were killed in action during this long evening, though no exact figure exists.

Mohnke told me:

> I spent the whole long afternoon working out the details of the breakout with my staff. We established the march route, organized the separate groups, calculated and synchronized the timing. Then we went over to consult with Generals Krebs and Burgdorf, who approved our plan. On this occasion both of these senior military men confided to me that they were resolved not to leave the Fuehrerbunker but would commit suicide after the last soldiers had departed. Finally, I informed my one remaining acting superior, General Weidling, who was a mile away in the Bendlerstrasse. My agreement with General Weidling was that he would not sign any capitulation document before daybreak on Wednesday, May 2. This would give us more than five nighttime hours to make our getaway.
>
> Our plan called for ten breakout groups, some large, some small. I took command of Group I. General Rattenhuber, I named to lead Group II. Group III, I put under the command of a responsible civilian, Werner Naumann. Bormann was in Group III at his own request. Each group was to vacate the Reich Chancellery in twenty-minute intervals, so that the initial takeoff itself was to last a bit more than three hours.
>
> As long as the coast remained clear, each group was to bolt as quickly as possible across the Wilhelmplatz and head for the protective shelter of the Kaiserhof subway station. The march was then to head due east to the next subway station, Stadtmitte. The planned route then turned north, still through the subway tube where it runs right under the Friedrichstrasse, until we were to come to the central Friedrichstrasse subway station.

From there, we intended to head under the Spree River to the Stettiner Bahnhof subway station, which is in the borough of Wedding, in north Berlin. Our hope was to surface outside the Russian ring. From this point, general direction northwest, each group was to be on its own.

General Mohnke had about thirty experienced field officers still under his command. At that staff briefing on May 1, he had told them that Adolf Hitler's last order to him had been to deliver copies of the Hitler testament to Admiral Doenitz. Then, Mohnke had sonorously read the document aloud, asking all officers to memorize as many of the details as they possibly could.

The breakout rendezvous point General Mohnke had specified in his briefing was in one of the underground garages, beneath the Ehrenhof, facing the Wilhelmstrasse. The action was scheduled to begin at 11:00 P.M. Dr. Schenck described the scene:

> Now, from the dark gangways, there kept arriving, in small groups, both the fighting troops being pulled in from the outside, then the officers and men of the Reich Chancellery Group. The troops, many of them very young, were already street-fighting veterans. Other soldiers had stubble beards, blackened faces; they wore sweaty, torn, field-gray uniforms, which most had worn and slept in, without change, for almost a fortnight. The situation was heroic; the mood was not. The official announcement of Hitler's suicide had not yet reached the lower ranks. But they guessed as much—from the silence of their officers. There was little talk now of "Fuehrer, Folk, and Fatherland." To a man, each German soldier was silently calculating his own chance of survival. For all the discipline, what was building up was less a military operation in the classic sense than what I imagine happens at sea when the cry goes out to man the lifeboats.

Punctually, ten minutes before eleven, General Mohnke arrived in the garage. He began to chat in whispered tones with the special group that had been in the Fuehrerbunker. Most of these would leave with General Mohnke's Group I. They were Major Guensche; Ambassador Hewel; Vice Admiral Voss; Hitler's last two secretaries, Gerda Christian and Gertrud Junge; the cook Constanze Manzialy; and Bormann's secretary, Else Krueger.

General Mohnke began to give last instructions. He turned to the doctor, Colonel Schenck, and formally placed the four women in his special care. They were all clad in masculine uniforms—jackets, trousers, heavy marching boots, coal-scuttle helmets. At eleven o'clock sharp, Mohnke gave the order to his lead group to line up and prepare for departure. It numbered twenty men, four women. Mohnke next ordered that the bricked-up cellar window be broken through with crowbars. Then he himself quickly clambered up and out, cocked pistol in hand.

The first obstacle course to be traversed, from the Chancellery cellar to the subway entrance, was only 120 meters, down the Wilhelmstrasse and across the Wilhelmplatz. But it might have been the most dangerous stretch of all, a shooting gallery, had anything alerted the Russians. Although it was long after dark, the darkness was broken by a crimson glow from several raging fires. For a full two minutes or so, Mohnke warily cased the lay of the land. He heard sporadic small-arms fire. But it did not seem to be aimed at him, so he signaled a go-ahead to the others. The dash was made, without incident, in groups of four to six. This meant that the Russians had as yet not discovered the operation.

In these last days, Red Army artillery had blasted away most of the granite steps that led down into the Kaiserhof subway station. It was now less a staircase than a rough granite chute. Most simply slid and bumped down. They dared not use flashlights, for they could not know just who might be inside this station. Undercover now, it was dark, deathly still. The soldiers in the lead crawled cautiously on hands and knees until they came close to the station platform. Here they sensed, in the total darkness, the presence of other humans, for they heard low murmurs. A raspy cough. A long minute passed before Mohnke dared shine his flashlight. To everyone's relief, the whole station platform was crowded with Berlin civilians, men, women, and children.

This station platform, 100 meters long, pitch dark and crowded, also housed several stretchers and cots. Some of the civilians had been here as long as a week; most had arrived in the last two days. Now the Mohnke group, with sharp elbows, had to force their way through to get down onto the rocky railroad-track bed and head east.

Group communication, even with the immediate follow-up Group II, under General Rattenhuber, was already nonexistent. There was no provision for radio contact. Those bringing up the rear of Mohnke's group were too far ahead of Group II for voice or courier contact, or even for simple Morse signals with a flashlight. As it happened, on this 1500-meter march through the subway system, Group II, having taken off after a twenty-minute interval, was now following Group I on the agreed route. Naumann's Group III, as we shall learn, missed the critical turn north, at the Stadtmitte station, and emerged into the street.

Most of the military were equipped with flashlights, and some now started to use them, but Mohnke gave a sharp order to extinguish them, pronto. They made a too-obvious target. Stumbling along, again in total darkness, on the crossties, the group slowly began to lose cohesion. Mohnke was still in the lead, with Guensche. They were followed, at an interval, by Schenck, with his four female charges. The others followed, in groups of three or four, strung out over perhaps 100 meters. They had no visual and little voice contact. Mohnke made frequent pauses to stop, look, listen; above all, when there was any strange noise. This allowed stragglers to do some catching up.

Dr. Schenck recounted:

> It must have been at least midnight as we plodded into the next station. This was Stadtmitte, the familiar transfer station. Here, on upper and lower levels, the tracks cross at right angles. This was our first and very welcome break in the long march. A breather for some, a cigarette break for smokers. We all clambered up like squirrels onto the station platform.

The next lap was a very short one, only 250 meters, on to the Franzoesische Strasse station. General Mohnke's group now had a chance to re-form and count heads. Although they were by now much more accustomed to the dark, contact remained difficult, and the number still marching in Group I had dwindled to fifteen. Instead of holding up for the others, Mohnke impatiently opted to push on to the Friedrichstrasse station.

The new worry was caused by the sudden loud sound of renewed artillery action. The tunnel and even the tracks began to tremble, as if in an earthquake. Mohnke concluded that the Red Army, at long last alerted to the breakout, was counterattacking. He calculated that the loudest explosions were less than a mile away, in the general direction of the Chancellery. This led him, in turn, to fear that the last four or five groups might now be unable to depart. In fact, however, at least six groups had taken off by this time, which was around 1:00 A.M. on Wednesday, May 2. The other four were to push off later, for, despite Mohnke's fear, the Russians were not yet aware that the breakout was in progress.

Now came a truly farcical touch that, somehow, could happen only in Germany. General Mohnke is something less than droll, but he did manage a smile as he told me of this incident.

We were dog-weary but still tensed up, for we feared that we might meet up with Russians at any turn in the winding track. We were coming ever closer to where I assumed their lines must be. The one organization we were not braced for was the BVG. That's the Berlin Municipal Transport Company.

Less than a hundred meters after we had passed the Friedrichstrasse station platform, we came on a huge steel bulkhead. Waterproof, it was designed to seal this tunnel at the point where the subway tube starts to run under the Spree River.

Here—and I could not believe my own eyes and ears—we spotted two stalwart, uniformed BVG guards. They were surrounded by angry civilians imploring them to swing open the bulkhead. They kept refusing. One clutched a giant key. When I saw this ridiculous situation, I ordered them to open the bulkhead forthwith, both for my group and for the civilians. The guards categorically refused.

Not only were these stubborn fellows going by the book; each had a copy of the book and began reading from it. The regulation, dating from 1923, *did* clearly state that the bulkhead was to be closed every evening after the passage of the last train. It had been their job for years to see that just this happened. I was flabbergasted. No trains had been running here for at least a full week, but these two dutiful characters had their orders, and that was that.

Even today, though I admit the situation was ludicrous on a night of such galloping chaos, I harbor a lingering respect for this eccentric devotion to duty of those two stubborn guardians of the bulkhead. I suppose it was my own ingrained sense of duty that led me to respect theirs.

My group retraced our steps to the Friedrichstrasse station and went aboveground. Just ahead was the dark Spree, which we had to pass over. We could see dimly that Russians already controlled the upper Friedrichstrasse, three or four blocks away. A tank trap in the middle of the Weidendamm Bridge had been erected by German defenders; it marked the perimeter of the Zitadelle. After some reconnoitering we located a narrow catwalk or swinging bridge over the Spree River.

Once safely across the Spree, the fugitives clambered down an iron staircase and made for the nearest rubbled cellar. They were now on the Schiffbauerdamm. The time was around 2:00 A.M. It was cold and damp. Now and then the waning, slowly setting May moon floated into view between the clouds.

After a pause of ten to fifteen minutes, Group I spent almost an hour following an unmapped, winding, narrow path. This fresh path had been beaten through whole alps of rubble in a northerly direction from the Spree River to the Invalidenstrasse. It led through old cellars, through walls or tenement courts, through ruined buildings where combat engineers had blasted away walls and partitions in the recent fighting. Again and again Mohnke's group stumbled on clusters of terrified civilians, huddled around lighted candles, in cellars or impromptu air-raid shelters. These civilians seldom knew whether the people coming toward them in the night were the last of the Germans or the first of the Russians.

General Mohnke, aware that the Russians had already stormed the Charité Hospital, decided to give it a wide berth. The group next emerged near another recognizable Berlin landmark, the ruins of the monumental Museum of Natural History. This meant that they were now across the Invalidenstrasse. On their way, they had been joined by at least a score of military stragglers.

For a long hour, from 1:30 to 2:30, there had been no sound of nearby artillery. Now it flared up again, suddenly and violently. It seemed to be mounted in the Tiergarten, centering fire on the Friedrichstrasse, which lay about one mile back. The target was, in fact, the Weidendamm Bridge and the streets leading to the west bank of the Spree. Now the Berlin battlefield was lit up with giant searchlights, in addition to the familiar rockets and flares.

The group took cover again, this time on a low garage roof. From here, with night glasses, they could look back and observe the brisk skirmish that was building up on and near the Weidendamm Bridge. Both Russian and German tanks were finally in action. Although General Mohnke had no way of knowing it at the time, the Germans who had triggered this brisk Russian reaction were those of Group III, which included Martin Bormann, Chefpilot Baur, Werner Naumann, Kempka, and Artur Axmann. Axmann had originally taken off with another group, under his lead. This group had also come all the way overland, suffering very heavy casualties, so Axmann had attached his remnant to Group III, which had been joined by General Gustav Krukenberg with five Tiger tanks—all lost at the bridge.

While this battle was still in progress, General Mohnke wisely decided to head north again and finally entered the Chausseestrasse, an extension of the Friedrichstrasse and the main artery leading northwest toward Wedding. Moving now in Indian file along a wall, Mohnke's people suddenly spotted a Red Army T-34 tank. Luckily for them, the tank did not move or fire. The Germans were able to retreat discreetly. Four terrified women were still in the company.

What one notes here—and the phenomenon keeps popping up in all other accounts—is how wary, on this eventful evening, both the German and the Russian soldiers were. Nobody was particularly eager to fight; soldiers seldom fired unless fired on. The Germans simply wanted to fade away with a minimum of fuss. Moscow epic films to the contrary, the Russian soldiers, sensing that Berlin had all but fallen, were not looking for any extra medals. Again and again, small German battle groups moved through or around larger Russian units like ships passing in the night, under total blackout conditions.

Russian artillery shells, most of them coming from the Tiergarten, whistled over their heads. Suddenly, one exploded in the middle of Group I, killing Major General Juergen Ziegler.

Dr. Schenck, when he told me about the artillery burst that had killed General Ziegler, had then gone on to say, "It was at this time that I lost sight of and contact with Fräulein Manzialy. Hitler's cook had gone along without a murmur up to this point. When we pulled ourselves together in the dark she was among those missing. Somebody came up and told me that she too had been hit and killed."

The time of this incident was close to 3:30 A.M. Shaken by the explosion so near them, the women announced that they were utterly exhausted and could no longer keep up with the group.

Fatigue, in fact, was overcoming everybody. The group was just about to reach the Stettiner Bahnhof, the trunkline terminal for trains coming from the north. General Mohnke realized that it had taken more than four hours to move less than four miles. There were still two long miles to go before Gesundbrunnen, the second major goal of this night march, could possibly be reached, so he called for a halt. Dawn might bring a bit more warmth and cheer. It would also bring heightened danger.

The men gathered a few charred beams and used them as a fire for warming their hands. Sentries were posted. The famished marchers opened their rations of tinned meat and hard bread, but they found the food difficult to eat; all canteens had long been empty and there was no water. Cold, exhaustion, and fear made sleep impossible.

It struck me as curious, in interviewing these survivors, how often they mentioned not so much the noise of war as its sudden still moments. Many told me how silently this slow dawn came on Wednesday, May 2, 1945. I suspect that they remember and describe it so vividly because this was the last dawn they were destined to enjoy before a captivity that lasted, for most of them, ten years. Around an impromptu campfire, though there was not much to talk about, the one-hour break Mohnke had originally announced finally lasted three hours.

It was now almost 7:00 A.M. In the broad daylight, General Mohnke's small group discovered they were not the only derelicts to have sought shelter in this immediate area. At least a half-dozen other motley units, with no particular goal other than to keep out of the hands of Russians for as long as possible, had joined them. As General Mohnke gave the signal to break camp and take off once again, the column behind him had become much longer, 150 to 200 people. The course was still north, along the Brunnenstrasse.

Elsewhere, the sound trucks were getting ready to move out to announce General Weidling's official capitulation of Berlin and a general cease-fire. But none of these marchers heard this news en route.

With the Berlin spring sun now high and the morning warming up, the long march ended, around nine o'clock. The exhausted Mohnke group had finally come to the Humboldthain, a heathlike, spacious municipal park in the heart of Wedding. It was also the site of a fourteen-story *Flak* tower, one of the largest and tallest in Berlin. This was right next to Gesundbrunnen, the old spa site that had been mentioned in the briefing in the Reich Chancellery cellar ten very long hours back. All hope of any further progress had now been quietly forgotten.

Moments of sheer astonishment were not quite over. As the utterly bushed Reich Chancellery Group staggered out of the night, it came to the Humboldthain in bright, streaming spring sunshine, and the marchers rubbed their eyes in disbelief. Before them stood what looked like a new German Army host, banners still flapping in the breeze, as if it had come out of nowhere. The *Flak* tower and huge bunker was ringed with some twenty German Tiger tanks, all stripped for action. Heavy field artillery, with crews, was drawn up into position. There were weapons carriers and armored personnel wagons, bristling with soldiers behind mounted heavy machine guns. Several companies of tank and infantry troops, in fairly fresh battle dress, were being briefed by their officers.

General Mohnke related, "We who had been trudging all through the Berlin night were astounded. A crazy new hope rose briefly."

A heated discussion was in progress about a massive breakout north and west. Finally, cooler heads among the senior officers prevailed, for somebody who had a functioning radio had now picked up General Weidling's capitulation order. The order went out to destroy or dismantle quickly all weapons.

No one can recall just who came up with the eminently sensible idea of moving on a bit to still another fairly well-known, popular Berlin institution, the Schultheiss-Patzenhofer brewery, only a few blocks away. By this time practically all the survivors from the ten Chancellery groups had managed to get this far. It was already high noon before the short trek to the brewery began, a march of perhaps twenty minutes.

There were several hundred other Germans, military and civilian, who had also taken refuge in this convenient Berlin hideaway on the last day of the dwindling battle, and morale and discipline began rapidly to disintegrate. In some of the upper rooms, drinking parties were already in progress. Somebody had located the reserve of kegs. Several hysterical women who were fleeing the invading Russians now threw themselves into the arms of impromptu—and startled—German lovers. Group sex took over on the top floor of the brewery. "It might have been a lot more fun if we were not so utterly exhausted," one of those men told me.

Some time around 2:30 P.M., General Mohnke went with Colonel Clausen to seek out the Russian general commanding in the Wedding sector. He soon returned, leaving Clausen to parley. He then convoked his senior officers for a last staff meeting. They discussed how, when, and if they should surrender. Most were of the opinion that the Red Army would simply storm the brewery after nightfall. There was no way as yet to know. Clausen had not returned, was indeed gone for several hours; many assumed he was gone forever.

General Mohnke next advised the survivors to try to escape capture when and if the chance should ever come, even by changing into civilian clothes. Many eagerly took the chance, that afternoon, of slipping out of the brewery and heading north and west. It was still about ten miles to the outskirts of Berlin. A Luftwaffe sergeant who was a Berliner, and thus knew the way, volunteered to escort the three secretaries—Gerda Christian, Gertrud Junge, Else Krueger. The small group did reach the outskirts of Berlin that evening and hid overnight in the forest. They eventually all made it to the west—but not before encountering a roving party of Russian soldiers, on the nighttime prowl. The Russians captured and dispatched the sergeant and then lined the women up for the usual. From the account I finally got, indirectly, it was a boisterous and unchivalrous performance, hectic while it lasted—and it lasted two long hours. Gertrud Junge, Hitler's youngest secretary, resisted like a tigress and was cruelly beaten up, her skull fractured. She was finally rescued and taken to a doctor by a Russian major, who then kept her for a year in Berlin as war booty.

CHAPTER 11

THE FLIGHT THAT NEVER WAS

Having followed General Mohnke's group, we now return to the Reich Chancellery at the hour of 11:40 P.M., when Group III was about to depart on the prearranged route. The four escapees we shall be shadowing in this group are Artur Axmann, Werner Naumann, Hans Baur and, most important, Martin Bormann. The events compel careful examination because nothing in this story—not even the death of Hitler—has received such vivid attention as the fate of Bormann. And as we shall see, his fate was closely linked with that of Hans Baur, Hitler's pilot. Their relationship is the key to the whole puzzle, and it explains every move the rattled, drunken Bormann made during that wild Berlin night.

Martin Bormann became famous only in death. Before that, he had been virtually unknown in Germany, a colorless, faceless, toad-like bureaucrat who had been Hitler's secretary.

A case can be made that Hitler's first descent into the bunkers of wartime was the beginning of his decline and fall. As Goebbels, Speer, and others have observed, the isolation of the Fuehrer was the making of Bormann. The cramped geography of bunkers was ideal for his slow takeover operation, and by 1943 Bormann controlled all access to Hitler except that of the high military. For different reasons, Bormann and Eva Braun were two of the best-kept secrets of the Third Reich, which probably explains the morbid public interest in them after 1945. At the Nuremberg trials, Bormann was sentenced to death *in absentia*. Could the truth about his fate have been even then established and the furor over this mystery laid to rest? I believe so. That, however, would have involved bringing together four key witnesses: Artur Axmann; his aide, Major Weltzin; Goebbels' aide, Werner Naumann; and Hans Baur.

Axmann and Naumann escaped to the west; Weltzin and Baur were captured by the Soviets. But in 1945, the story that Bormann had escaped and was living high on the hog in South America made many headlines. And, in the emotional postwar era, millions of readers had visceral reasons for wanting Bormann to be captured alive. Hitler, Goebbels, and Himmler had cheated the hangman, and Goering and Robert Ley were to do the same. Also, it seemed somehow credible that the mystery man in the bunker power structure should escape to become a mystery man elsewhere.

Before the breakout Bormann already had inherited the shadowy eminence of Reichsleiter and was now the highest Nazi Party official in the new government Hitler had so pedantically spelled out before dying. In the bunker after April 20, however, with General Mohnke in clear command, Bormann had no influence. His only hope for a role in the future came from the curious legacy Adolf Hitler had left him. And that legacy involved much more than the nomination to high rank.

Those details were not to be revealed until Hans Baur finally returned from Soviet imprisonment ten years after the fall of Berlin. They came out partly in my long talks with him, partly in interviews he gave to the press and partly in a bouncy book of memoirs he later wrote.

In October 1955, he related this account.

> On the evening of Sunday, April 29, Hitler said, "Baur, I would like to bid you farewell. It is drawing to an end."
>
> He thanked me several times for my services, and said that he had two final orders: "You must take the responsibility," he said, "that the bodies of my wife and myself are burned so that my enemies do not do the same mischief with me as was done with Mussolini.
>
> "My second order: Doenitz will be my natural successor. I have given Bormann several messages for Doenitz. See to it that you get Bormann out of Berlin and to Doenitz."

Nothing could be more explicit. Then came a last handshake with both hands, a characteristic gesture of Hitler when saying goodbye to a close friend.

Hitler was to commit suicide a little less than six hours afterward, but Baur, never informed of the timing, failed to carry out the first order. Instead, Baur went about the business of preparation for the breakout, which was then planned for the night of Monday, April 30. The next day, Baur reported, he had a last conversation with Goebbels, who wished him luck and, echoing Hitler, said, "See to it that you make it. Bormann has been given important matters to take up with Doenitz."

When the postponed breakout was finally ready late on May 1, Baur was assigned to the fifteen-man Group III. This is significant. The only men of rank in it were Bormann, Baur, Dr. Stumpfegger, and State Secretary Werner Naumann. Thus, Bormann had gathered around him a pilot, a surgeon, a high bureaucrat, and a small body of battle-trained soldiers. I submit that this is strong circumstantial evidence of "an operation within an operation."

Baur recalled:

> Around eleven P.M. we were lined up for the breakout. I stuck close

to Reichsleiter Bormann, as I had been ordered to do. I watched the first group take off, five or six at a time, through a window in the Chancellery cellar wall. They drew only occasional fire, as did the second group.

Our group decided to chance it together. We all ran pell-mell out of the huge main portal where, for years, the tall, white-gloved, black-uniformed SS guards had stood their silent watch. Less than two minutes later, I was sliding down into the Kaiserhof subway station like a kid on a playground chute. Now it was pitch dark—stupidly, few of us had brought pocket flashlights—and, like blind mice, we began to probe our way along the tracks.

Halfway along the prescribed route to the Friedrichstrasse subway station, Group III lost contact with the group ahead and so missed a critical left turn to the north. As a result, this third group decided to surface from the Stadtmitte station. They emerged into the Gendarmenmarkt, once a lovely Baroque square in the center of the old city, now a blazing chaos.

They regrouped and began to make their way, Indian file, northward up the Friedrichstrasse. They crossed Unter den Linden and approached the Weidendamm Bridge; in the flickering firelight, they saw that it was blocked by a tank barrier. There was no artillery at the moment, but Russian mortars were beginning to zero in just south of the bridge—a sign that the Soviet troops had finally been alerted to the German movement.

As we have seen, General Mohnke and at least some of his group had already crossed the Spree on the catwalk bridge. Now all three groups had arrived at roughly the same point, but in the general confusion and lack of communication few were aware of it.

Some time within the hour, General Krukenberg's five Tiger tanks arrived at the bridge, blasted the barrier, and rumbled across. The escapees followed, amid the sulphurous clouds that now and again blotted out the moon.

Baur had been separated from Bormann for the past twenty minutes, but, once across the bridge, he caught sight of him again. "I found Martin Bormann sitting on the stone steps of a bombed-out house. It was the corner house where the Schiffbauerdamm meets the Friedrichstrasse."

The Schiffbauerdamm runs along the north bank of the Spree in a generally westerly direction. From the Weidendamm Bridge to the Lehrter railway station is roughly a mile. This was the course Group III ultimately took.

It was now around 2:30 A.M. Group III was no longer a cohesive body of fifteen, but Bormann, Baur, Stumpfegger, and Naumann were still with it. Moving along a still-standing yellow-brick wall, they suddenly blundered into a fierce tank battle.

Erich Kempka told me that he suddenly saw Martin Bormann "blown up" (though he also confessed that he himself was blinded by the flash). Others told of seeing Bormann in one of the tanks—by which they must have meant that he was riding aboard one. Here, part of the bogus postwar Martin Bormann legend was born. This, according to the story, could have been that last tank left in the Reich Chancellery garage, now coming at a prearranged time to pick up Martin Bormann and vanish into the smoke.

All that is absurd. As we know from General Krukenberg's account, these were *his* Nordland tanks that had begun to leave the Zitadelle and move north as soon as the word was passed that Mohnke had decamped. If Bormann had had any such deus ex machina available, he surely would not have exposed himself to that perilous march from the bunker to the Schiffbauerdamm.

After this episode, Baur was able to rejoin Bormann and the two others in the entrance hall of a ruined tenement. In the courtyard to the rear, they could hear staccato small-arms fire and so, like an Indian scout, Baur crawled cautiously up the stairs to a window. He counted twenty Russian soldiers in the courtyard and reported to Bormann, "They have only to come in the back door to grab us. In an hour it will be daylight; we must get a move on."

At last they moved out again, single file and about twenty meters apart, following the course of the Spree. There was now a lull in the fighting, and they moved quickly along to a spot opposite the Reichstag, where Russian snipers were on the lookout. Coming under fire, the Germans took separate cover in the shelter of the railroad embankment—and this was the last Baur ever saw of the other three.

He looked up and saw the first streaks of dawn. Soon he moved out alone for the agreed-on rendezvous point, the Lehrter S-Bahn station. He came to a wide bridge over the Humboldt Harbor, crawled across it, jumped into the street, and ran for the station entrance. And here the pilot's luck ran out.

He was gunned down by machine-pistol fire. Severely wounded in both legs, his chest, and one arm, Baur managed to crawl to a burning house. As the flames licked closer, he prepared to kill himself with his service pistol. Then the flames receded, and he changed his mind. After four more hours of anguish, he was picked up by German stretcher bearers who, under Russian orders, had begun to clear the battlefield of wounded.

We now must pick up the story of Artur Axmann and return to his Wilhelmstrasse starting point on this night.

That story was well known to the judges sitting at Nuremberg in 1945-1946. After more than thirty years of critical examination, it still stands up. Axmann's testimony about Bormann's eventual fate might have been corroborated by Guenther Weltzin, who accompanied him in the escape. But Weltzin later died in Russian imprisonment.

An hour before jump-off time, Axmann had consulted with General Mohnke, but the briefing must have been sketchy. Axmann told me that he never knew of Mohnke's *Flak* tower destination and was aware only of the immediate downtown goal, the Weidendamm Bridge. Axmann, who had lost his right forearm in his first action on the Russian front, in 1941, was no real soldier; he also chose to take his group into the city aboveground. This blunder was to cost him seven of the ranking members of his group—including two women from his staff—in the next two hours.

Here is his story, as he told it to me thirty years later.

> Our compass reading was north, straight up the Wilhelmstrasse toward the Brandenburg Gate. At this stage, we did not run into any fighting. Just before we turned right and east, into Unter den Linden, we suddenly saw the giant hulk of the old Reichstag, which was still smoldering. Even closer, we could now spot Russian infantrymen and tankers in bivouac, directly around—and under— the Brandenburg Gate. The Russians simply did not see us. Many of them were singing. We were not . . .
>
> There was still no fighting as we moved now, as fast as possible, down the once-fashionable Unter den Linden. It was only after we turned north again, entering the Friedrichstrasse, that we landed plumb in the middle of a very brisk skirmish.

Axmann estimated that an hour had passed since he had started out, but actually two hours had gone by. He saw the Tiger tanks burst through the barriers on the Weidendamm Bridge.

Thus, at this point, the Axmann group had now nearly caught up with the lead element because, as we know, Mohnke and his men and women were already across the Spree, lying in the rubble and watching the progress of the follow-up groups. The groups that now had to cross were Axmann's and, nearby, Group III with Martin Bormann.

Axmann continued, "What happened now was that suddenly, in the pitch dark, one of our Tiger tanks exploded. I was blown through the air. I was not knocked unconscious and was only slightly wounded by a sliver of shrapnel in the calf of my leg. Five minutes later, when I recovered my bearings, I crawled into the nearest shellhole. It was here that I first met up with Bormann. This was between two and three A.M." Thus, Bormann had come out of the skirmish alive—and he was definitely *not* riding in a tank.

Axmann went on to describe how this augmented party chose to proceed along the raised railway embankment from the Friedrichstrasse station to the Lehrter Bahnhof—the Spree River route already described by Baur.

Axmann also related another bizarre, theatrical incident—one in which his artificial right arm was the central prop.

> We reached the bridge over the Friedrich-List-Ufer just west of the Humboldt Harbor. This bridge leads to the Lehrter S-Bahn station. Several of us jumped down from the bridge and found, to our chagrin, that there was a whole Russian infantry platoon in bivouac under it. They promptly surrounded us. But to our amazement and joy they simply kept announcing in a boisterous chorus, *"Hitler kaputt, Krieg aus!"*
>
> Next, they engaged us in a very pleasant chat in broken German. All seemed to be fascinated by my artificial arm, and I kept showing it to them as if it were the latest product of some Nuremberg toy factory. What spoiled this bit of fraternization was a psychologically false move by the tipsy Bormann and Dr. Stumpfegger. They began to edge away and finally broke out running. This made the Russians suddenly suspicious, but Weltzin and I were now able to shuffle off as casually as possible without being noticed.

Axmann and Weltzin proceeded west along the Invalidenstrasse. After about four or five city blocks, they ran into a sudden explosion of Russian tank fire and had to hide in the rubble until the tanks lumbered past. They decided to retrace their steps along the street. About 150 meters from the spot where they had talked with the Russians, they reached the bridge that passes over the great trunk lines into the Lehrter Bahnhof.

Axmann recalled, "We now came across the bodies of Martin Bormann and Dr. Stumpfegger, lying very close together. I leaned over and could see the moonlight playing on their faces. There was no visible sign that they had been shot or struck by shellfire. At first, they looked like men who were unconscious or asleep. But they were not breathing. I assumed then, and I am sure today, that both had taken poison. Weltzin and I did not linger to take pulses. We were in danger and hardly interested in historical moments. Axmann then went to the house of a former sweetheart and there found a hiding place. Weltzin continued on and was captured that morning.

All that is now missing from the story are two bodies. But Berlin was filled with dead bodies on the morning of May 2, 1945. Thousands were shoved into unmarked graves, and others were cremated as a health measure. It is true that some search was made for identity cards, but Bormann and Stumpfegger, on the run, would have destroyed theirs. No trace was turned up for twenty-seven years.

Then, on a snowy morning in 1972, workers constructing an exhibition park just opposite the site of the vanished Lehrter railway station—that is, within fifty feet of the street-level bridge—uncovered two skeletons, side by side. One was that of an extremely tall man (Stumpfegger was six foot six) and the other was that of a short man. Splinters of plastic cyanide capsules were lodged in the jawbones of both. The hardhats called for the police, and subsequently the police were able to make a positive identification from dental records.

CHAPTER 12

DINNER WITH THE RUSSIANS

It was at the Schultheiss-Patzenhofer brewery, in which Mohnke's group had sought refuge on May 2, that Dr. Schenck met Walter Hewel; the two had known each other casually back in the Fuehrerbunker. Schenck came upon him in the brewery cellar, sitting on the lower tier of a wooden double bunk. He was wearing the tailored but tattered blue ambassador's uniform. With the toe of his boot, Hewel was idly nudging some spilled coffee beans into neat, pyramidal piles.

Hewel could have left the bunker, as Ribbentrop did on April 23. But his old friend the Fuehrer asked him to stay, and like a loyal liegeman he remained to the end.

In a parting monologue Hitler displayed a characteristic spirit of malignity—but this time toward an old comrade, who had served him loyally and selflessly. "Hewel, they will torture and kill you and mount you in a waxworks," he said. At this point, Hewel told Schenck in the final moments of that afternoon's long story, the diplomat raised his right hand and swore to take his own life rather than fall into Red Army hands. His old friend now made him a present of a pistol and a cyanide capsule.

Walter Hewel was the only one of his retainers Hitler ever pressed to commit suicide.

Schenck, playing the role of priest, tried desperately to dissuade Hewel from suicide. The time was now about 7:00 P.M. on May 2. General Mohnke, sitting nearby, was still in command but saying little. Around 2:00 P.M. he had left with Colonel Clausen to negotiate with the Russians, and he returned at three o'clock, having left Clausen to continue the parley. From time to time he dispatched single scouts to snoop down the corridor, checking on Russian progress. These scouts reported back that Red Army soldiers were approaching warily, room by room, softly now, in no great hurry.

There was compelling reason for this Russian supercaution. Red Army soldiers knew the SS, from long, bitter battle experience. This last cellar-retreat was half-concealed behind brewery boilers and coiling steam pipes. It could be defended. Finally, hearing approaching footsteps, Mohnke and the other twelve field-grade officers arose and came to attention as one man. They all cocked their weapons.

The padding footsteps, however, in the best thriller tradition, proved to be those of Colonel Clausen. Clausen brought news of the capitulation, signed by General Weidling that morning, some eight hours back. All German officers, Clausen reported, would be allowed to keep their sidearms—a symbol, to field officers, of honorable surrender. There was a silence of long seconds. Then, after a nod from General Mohnke, came the unanimous, metallic click of uncocking pistols. Battle Group Mohnke had surrendered.

Unanimous, that is, except for a staccato shot, almost simultaneous, which now sounded as the desolate group had begun to file out. A pistol shot fired in a closed room sounds as loud as a hand grenade. Startled, Schneck and the others spun around, to discover that Ambassador Hewel had blown his brains out.

At 8:00 P.M., a half hour after the surrender, three olive green Red Army jeeps pulled into the dark courtyard of the brewery. As the twelve German SS officers walked out, however, garish searchlights played on them. A young, stocky, blond Red Army second lieutenant ordered his prisoners into the three waiting jeeps.

The Russian drivers drove very fast. Skirting the rubble dexterously but not always missing the craters and potholes, they roared on through the streets now quite empty of pedestrians or bystanders.

The twelve officers of Kampfgruppe Mohnke, bouncing about in the jeeps, gazed out now and then on the same city they had made their way through from midnight to dawn of this same tumultuous Wednesday. It still resembled a churned-up battlefield—abandoned artillery pieces, charred wrecks of tanks and armored vehicles, discarded bazookas, burned autos and jeeps, crashed planes, spiked ack-ack guns, dead horses and dogs, soldier and civilian corpses.

The ride lasted some twenty minutes. The small convoy came to a section of the city much less bomb-and battle-damaged and pulled to a halt before a large, four-story, gray-stucco building. Military guards posted at the entrance showed that it had become a Red Army headquarters. The day had been warm and sunny until noontime, but rainfall and the east wind had brought another chill evening. Ordered out of the jeeps, the Germans stood about, shivering.

These German SS officers, all at least of field grade, had every reason to expect the worst. General Mohnke remembered:

> What happened next was this: we were led into what appeared to be an officers' club, up four flights of stairs. At the head of the stairs we were met and greeted by a German-speaking staff officer, a major in a formal, well-pressed uniform. He opened the door and cordially invited us to step into a combination living-reception room.

As described by General Mohnke and others of the party, this room, not very large, was rather crowded. Several upholstered and leather chairs were available, supplemented by a large sofa that probably had been hauled in from another room. This, too, helped give the crowded effect. The dozen SS officers remained standing, nonplussed, embarrassed. The half-dozen Red Army officers present were soon joined by an equal number, all officers of field-grade rank. An atmosphere of military punctilio dominated the scene. The obvious difference between victors and vanquished was evident from the condition of their uniforms. The Germans were in tattered, torn, dusty field gray. Most of the Russians had already changed into brand-new, olive tan dress uniforms, with battle medals and campaign ribbons.

Soon a Russian full colonel entered the room. He invited the still-astonished, still-apprehensive Germans to be seated. "We are all aware that it has been a long and active day, and now is a good time to relax. Would the German officers and gentlemen like to remove their pistol belts? If so, here is a small table reserved for that purpose. It has been a long war."

General Mohnke and his fellows demurred, afraid of some trick. They had been promised, in terms of their formal surrender in the brewery a short time back, that they would be allowed to keep their sidearms. In any case, the very polite colonel did not press the point.

For the next fifteen minutes or so nothing happened, the Germans conversing with each other in German, the Russians in Russian. An odor of cooking wafted over from the next room.

Now a second Russian full colonel entered the room and came to the table in the center. The seated Germans promptly arose and stood at attention. At the colonel's side stood a tall, erect man in his late forties, very correct in manner and bearing. On his epaulets were three stars, indicating that he was a lieutenant general. This was their host, Lieutenant General Vladimir Alexei Belyavski, chief of staff of Chuikov's elite Eighth Guards Army, the tank army that had defeated von Paulus at Stalingrad and spearheaded the long drive to Berlin.

Now a young interpreter moved forward to translate an official welcome speech.

> Gentlemen, we pride ourselves on having fought in the field against such valiant opponents. We congratulate you on the soldierly valor your troops often displayed. The Battle for Berlin was a bitter encounter while it lasted, and this has been a long and cruel war.
>
> We Soviet officers are sure that a lasting peace will follow this terrible war, and that there will be a real rebirth of that once-traditional friendship that, over generations, has allied the German and the Russian peoples.

The gracious host went on, "May I herewith invite you to be our guests for supper this evening, to enjoy what hospitality we can offer?" A Russian orderly now swung open the door to the adjoining room. It was a much larger room, a long dining room, in the middle of which was a banquet table groaning with plentiful supplies of bread, lashings of butter, hams, cold cuts, sausages, chicken and fish, red caviar. The table was set formally. Before each plate stood a full bottle of vodka with a tumbler.

Anyone who has ever attended such a show of Russian hospitality knows how embarrassing it can be if one does not drink the vodka, usually proffered in successive toasts. Abstinence may be interpreted as weakness, even as an insult to the host and the traditions of his country.

A guest is supposed to down the vodka, chug-a-lug and bottoms up, in one shot, along with the hosts. I asked General Mohnke just how General Belyavski and his fellow Russian officers reacted to the cautious, still quite wary Germans.

> Our hosts, however genial, most certainly had the mission to get us to drink so that they could acquire information that might be helpful in later military interrogations. We did not do them this favor.

The jolly mood of German-Russian military confraternity began to wane the same evening, as the second round of vodka bottles appeared. The Russian toasts grew louder and louder, the German abstinence more painful. The cultivation of harmony and appeals to historical friendship with which this improvised gala had begun now slowly soured. General Belyavski, who had not quaffed as much vodka as his fellow officers, glanced at his watch and suddenly ended the festivities. It was ten-thirty.

Now another door was opened by one of the Red Army orderlies. The Germans, without further ado, were shoved vigorously through the door by their rollicking hosts. The door was slammed, the bolt slid loudly into place. A double watch was posted outside the door. The honored officers were again simple prisoners.

What, more than thirty years later, should one make of that 1945 Russo-German dinner party? Two points, I believe.

The first is that the speech of friendship given by General Belyavski, though perhaps nothing more than a curious fossil today, was, in fact, one of the last serious echoes of what *might* have been Moscow's 1945 policy in Germany—had the Red Army General Staff had more to say. The tempting idea of a postwar alliance with a nationalist, united, Soviet-oriented but not necessarily Communist or even Socialist Germany had a rather natural attraction to the Russian military mind.

By 1945, however, the opposite political decision had already been taken in the Politburo. Stalin decided to opt for the communizing of his zone of defeated Germany.

A second point: readers with any experience in intelligence work, at least as it is practiced in the western world, have probably already spotted the egregious blunder perpetrated by Soviet Intelligence on this very day and evening in Berlin, Wednesday, May 2, 1945. In fact, one can even mark the hour. It was that moment, just before midnight, when Mohnke and his companions passed out of the hands of the Eighth Guards Army to come under the *Politruks* of the NKVD. This was the symbolic meaning of that brusque push through the door at the end of the *Gastmahl.* It was a handover at midnight.

With the fighting over on this day, the some nine Berlin "search groups" of Russian Intelligence, which had been attached to the fighting armies, now began operating independently, beyond military control. This led to the dispersal of the Reich Chancellery Group. For the next days and weeks, key witnesses were scattered in a whole series of camps strung out on the long route from Berlin to Poland to Moscow.

In retrospect, it is easy to fathom what happened. On May 2, the Red Army dragnet had captured almost all of the leading members of the Reich Chancellery Group. Of those few still present in the bunker on the day Adolf Hitler died, only six of this inner circle had successfully eluded Russian capture—Artur Axmann, Werner Naumann, Erich Kempka, Gerda Christian, Gertrud Junge, Else Krueger. A few FBK officers and enlisted men also made it underground to the west. Otherwise, the whole bunker cast, minus suicides, was present, now prisoners, still in Berlin. All told, there were more than fifty officers and men.

Why were they ever moved away from the scene of action? Most obviously, there could have been no better place to reconstruct their story than the Fuehrerbunker itself—while memories were fresh, the survivors exhausted yet most willing to talk, all the props and artifacts still in place. In other words, there should have been a re-enactment on the scene, the standard police procedure in the reconstruction of any crime. The whole story could have been cleared up in a week, at most a fortnight. It was by scattering the witnesses that the NKVD vastly complicated its own sleuthing task.

CHAPTER 13

LAST MAN OUT

The last man on duty in the Berlin bunker was Johannes Hentschel in the machine room. He had a job to do, and he stuck to it above and beyond the call of duty. In his cramped machine room, he sat, most of the time, on a high stool, tending the Diesel engine that powered the ventilation system. This Diesel, which also supplied power to run the smaller generator, kept the water pump functioning.

The pump, installed back in 1943, had originally been no more than an emergency device for use during air raids. Now, at the end, the pump was serving an unforeseen, vital function. Hentschel was maintaining a flow of pure water through a makeshift pipeline to the casualty station, where Dr. Haase and a few orderlies and nurses were struggling to tend the many wounded.

In several interviews, Johannes Hentschel kept insisting that he had been much too busy during the last stand to appreciate the irony of his position. Amid the collapsing physical monuments of the older Prussia that Hitler and his National Socialist Wagnerians had now destroyed forever, one Prussian virtue survived. Hentschel quietly embodied it. For Prussia, in its better moments, was more than a state. It was also an ideal—the Protestant idea of duty. Hentschel's quiet gallantry in action managed, through one harrowing Berlin night, to help keep alive more than 300 wounded young soldiers, Colonel Schenck's patients, who lay in anguish on their cots in the nearby Reich Chancellery cellar.

The precise historical time, for those who like to read the sands sifting so remorselessly in the hourglass of world history, was now 11:59 P.M., one minute before midnight, Tuesday, May 1, 1945. The place, the now all but deserted Fuehrerbunker.

There were now only two characters still on stage, underground, two old lower bunker familiars: Sergeant Misch at his silent telephone switchboard and Hentschel in the machine room. Our narrative is reduced, at last, to a single, yet reliable, witness who managed to see it all through to the surprising end. For Sergeant Misch was blissfully asleep.

Crouched at his lonely command post, Hentschel glanced up nervously now and then at the large brass marine clock. The victorious Russians were coming and the only operative question was "When?" Tick, tick, tick . . . midnight. Tock.

One minute after midnight. A new day was born in bleak silence. Hentschel took a glass of cold pump-water for his parched, burning throat. He was dog-tired. He had been awake now for more than fifty-five hours. He knew that he could not afford to doze off without first waking Misch.

The clock moved on slowly to two-thirty. Still black outside. Black and silent. Hentschel, a technician, was a methodical man. He liked to make his round-the-bunker checkup tours exactly once an hour, on the half hour.

> I was scared, believe you me, and, curiously, it wasn't only the threat
> of the Red Army arrival that frightened me. I knew that there were

at least nine unburied corpses about—either inside the bunker or nearby. Earlier in the evening, I had seen the stiff bodies of the six Goebbels children piled, two by two, on three old air-raid shelter cots, the kind that fold into the wall. Rigor mortis. White sheets covered their faces. I saw only their nightgowns, bare legs.

Johannes Hentschel wished that he could at least talk with the Russians in their own language when they came. He also began to speculate about how much ideological ice his genuine workingman's status might cut with the uniformed sons of the world proletarian revolution—the overalls, the monkey wrench, the grease gun.

With more realism, he began to play his own little wargame, contemplating just *how* the Red Army would arrive. Storming infantry, with flame-throwers? Point-blank artillery? He neatly calculated the relative merits of being in the upper or the lower bunker when Zero-Hour came. The lower bunker was safer against explosives because of the triple bulkheads. But the upper bunker had certain advantages, too. It could not, for example, be fired on directly. The bunker had held up against scores of British and American air raids.

There was one other critical factor in the whole complex equation that Hentschel had going for him. Like a fox in his own burrow, he knew his way around. He knew which corridor led just where. As they approached, the Russians would be bound to be wary. He was unarmed, but they did not know that. The SS men had decamped four long hours ago—but the oncoming Russians might not know that, either. The place could be mined. Therefore, so reasoned der Cheftechniker, they would first approach with sappers, carrying portable mine-detectors, flayers, or other antimine techniques.

Finally, another factor on the plus side of Hentschel's calculation: the Russians, unless they were to storm the bunker from both approaches simultaneously, would have to make a choice of entry. This would allow Hentschel to choose his path for a quiet exit. He felt it was more likely the Russians would come through the Reich Chancellery garden emergency exit. This, after all, was the only visible approach. Or, somewhat less likely, the Russians might come the longer way, which was through the Reich Chancellery cellar and tunnel.

It was now 3:00 A.M., Wednesday, May 2. Sergeant Misch, still at his post, was dead to the world, which created a tricky problem. Misch was armed. He was also SS. Much as Johannes Hentschel liked Misch personally, he now decided that it would be more discreet to face the music alone. The last thing Hentschel needed, against the whole Red

Army, was a one-man SS bodyguard. It was high time to wake Misch and send him on his way.

Hentschel began to help Misch put on full field kit for his departure.

> Just before Misch left, we exchanged letters we had composed earlier that evening. He had a letter for my wife Greta, in case I did not survive, and I had a letter from him addressed to his wife, Maria.

(Neither of these letters was ever to be posted; this same day both men became prisoners of war. It was months before either wife knew that her husband had survived this evening.)

Misch left the bunker by the tunnel route into the New Reich Chancellery, turned left, and crossed the Ehrenhof to enter the Old Reich Chancellery. He crawled out warily. It was only about 200 meters to his first goal, the Kaiserhof subway station entrance. Despite his full field equipment, Sergeant Misch said, he made it "in something close to Olympic time." The hour was about 3:50 A.M.

Hentschel went on with his story. "No sooner had Misch left than a feeling of desperate isolation overwhelmed me. It was like being left alone in a crypt. So, almost in panic, I took a quick nip up out through the emergency exit, just to relieve the tomblike atmosphere and get a whiff of fresh air. The sun was not yet up, but it was daybreak. The eastern sky was already a kind of pastel, pea soup green, streaked with yellow and orange. Black smoke was rising from burning buildings. It didn't look real. It looked like a stage set."

Since the Fuehrer's last birthday, less than a fortnight back, Hentschel had seen two Reich chancellors, a Reichsfuehrer SS, a Reichsleiter, a Reichsmarschall, one grand admiral, three field marshals, some fifteen ministers, and a dozen generals depart. Then Kampfgruppe Mohnke. Now, the last sergeant.

At five o'clock, Hentschel cautiously ventured out of the bunker for a second time. The whole landscape was brighter but hardly more picturesque. At five-thirty der Cheftechniker made the next of his every-hour-on-the-half-hour rounds. Even tension, he now noted, can become routine and verge on monotony when one is dog-tired. Another long half hour came and went. At six o'clock, with the Berlin sun now up and trying to announce a glorious day, Hentschel surfaced again.

At 7:45, his usual breakfast time, Hentschel slowly scrambled three eggs, with bacon. He found slices of liverwurst, marmalade, black bread, and powdered coffee, of which he drank four or five cups. He then washed the dishes, another delightful German touch.

He listened to the eight o'clock news in a German-language broadcast from London. Hentschel thought he heard a short item about the Red flag flying from the Reichstag. But he wasn't sure. The broadcast faded. Otherwise, not much news from Berlin. Odd.

Nine o'clock came—and went. Then, just a few minutes later, while he was in the upper bunker making his wearying routine rounds, der Cheftechniker thought he heard voices, and they certainly weren't German. They were not masculine voices, either. Pleasant surprise. He quickly turned up the lights.

He could dimly make out, coming through the tunnel from the Chancellery, a group of twelve uniformed Russians moving toward him. To his astonishment, they were all women. Whispering, giggling, laughing—until they spotted Hentschel, who promptly raised both hands high in the air to show convincingly that he was not armed.

He saw that most of these women were carrying large satchels or duffel bags. They were Red Army Medical Corps personnel. Not nurses, as Hentschel at first guessed, rather young women doctors or internes. The leader of the group came straight up to Hentschel; she asked him who he was and what his duties were. He noted that her German was not only fluent but that she spoke with an educated, pronounced Berlin accent. Her next question was very much to the point. "Where is Adolf Hitler?" Hentschel told her of his death, the circumstances, the burning in the yard. She listened intently. Then a second doctor, who also spoke German, cut in. "Where is Hitler's *Frau?*"

> Now it dawned on me what these Russian females were really up to. To the victor belongs the spoils. After a long, bitter war in the field, they were simply out to liberate some proper civilian clothes. With a sigh of relief that our meeting was passing off so well, I took the women down and escorted them into Eva Braun's boudoir. E.B. had a dresser there half the size of the room. The other German women had said it was loaded with all sorts of frilly stuff. Changing her wardrobe at least five times a day had been that woman's major bunker activity.
>
> Shortly afterward, around nine-thirty, I suddenly saw two male officers with drawn pistols. They had come the same way the women had. Once again, I raised both hands. Then something unexpected happened, thank God, which really helped to relieve the tension. Six of the Russian women rushed past, whooping, like Indian squaws in one of your Western movies. Above their heads, one in each hand, they were gaily waving at least a dozen brassieres, all black satin trimmed with lace.

And thus the bunker story ends on this piquant note of the sheer absurd—not with a bang but with twelve brassieres.

*Sophia Loren scored her first dramatic film success as
the sensuous heroine of* Woman of the River *in
1954. Her discoverer, Carlo Ponti, became the only
man in her life. On the last day of the film's shooting
Carlo presented her with a small diamond ring.*

SOPHIA
LIVING AND LOVING
HER OWN STORY

A Condensation of the book by

A. E. HOTCHNER

THERE WAS ONCE A LITTLE GIRL with very thin legs, huge eyes, and a worried mouth. She disliked herself so much that she feared that fairies did not like her. But she loved every blade of grass and flower on the land, and she believed that those who seek a treasure must never mention it. She had been born in a knot of bitter roots, in the flower of which she eventually discovered the world: mountains to climb, streets to run.

She embraced the whole universe; everything was to be seen and experienced. But she feared the role that life gave to her, feared having to walk straight toward a faraway destination; feared weakness and love. But she persevered. And she overcame her fears.

This book is dedicated to her, and to all little girls with big eyes and spindly legs who are born in a knot of bitter roots.

PROLOGUE

I am in a small room in a hospital in Rome where my father lies dying. I sit on the bed beside him, holding his cold hand. In this room are four other people whose eyes are fixed upon the agony of his slow death: my mother, whom he seduced and abandoned; my sister, who suffered terribly because of his refusal to give her his name; a young man, Giuseppe, one of my father's legitimate sons from his marriage to a woman who is not present; Carol, a small blond German woman with whom my father lived for the last ten years of his life.

As he lies dying, I think: for so much of my life he has been a source of pain and rejection and humiliation, yet whatever negative feelings I have had about him have been erased by a wash of pity; and a glow of love has somehow managed to penetrate the grim events of our past relationship.

Pity and love.

As I look back now, I realize that the story of my life must begin and end with my father. I sought him everywhere. I married him. I made my best films with him. I curried his favor. I sat on his lap and snuggled him.

Yet I saw him only a few times in my life. Once when he came to Pozzuoli and brought me a little blue car. Once in a courtroom. Once toward the end of his life when I visited him in his home. A few isolated meetings, that's all, yet he dominated my life.

And now, as he breathes his last, I feel that he has been a father to me. It may be that in thinking about my life, in recalling old events and emotions for this book, I can come upon the truth about him.

And about myself.

We were only ten minutes out of Paris when the plane hit a stone wall, rocked violently, and fell interminably before righting itself. The movie screen, wrenched from its invisible moorings, shot out of the ceiling and down to the floor; then, as the Caravelle nosed up to break the fall, the screen snapped back up into the ceiling as if manipulated by the same giant hand that was assaulting the aircraft.

I screamed as the plane was rammed from the left side, the force hurling it up and rocking it, a chip on violent waves. The closet doors in front of me popped open and an avalanche of blankets spewed out. A woman across the aisle was now also screaming, and behind me I could hear the commotion of panic.

I had left my Paris apartment early that morning for the hour flight to Nice. Carlo was already there. The car was waiting in the garage basement and I would leave from there because the lobby was under siege by photographers who had been keeping a vigil for two days because they knew that I was going to Cannes for the film festival. But they are often in the lobby, film festival or not. How often I long for a few days' respite, somewhere beyond the reach of the long lens.

How could I have anticipated that on May 19, a lovely spring morning, my life would end like this, in this doomed airplane? I think of my two little sons and what will happen to them if I die this miserable death; all the trouble, the pain, the agony I went through to bear them and then to throw away my life with them, just for vanity, because I was summoned to Cannes for my film—and what will their life be without me? And what about Carlo? Glimpses of my life roll across my eyes, like film being edited: my mother, who vicariously lives my life; my sister, our lifetime of intimacy and interdependence; flashes of moments from forgotten memory, glorious, painful, wistful, interrupted by the violently lurching plane; I am certain now that death is imminent, since the airplane (which I fear even in normal flight) is unable to evade the vise of this frightening, destructive barrage.

When I was a child, fear was common to my life—fear of having nothing to eat, fear of the other children taunting me at school because I was illegitimate, and particularly fear of the big bombers appearing overhead and dropping their lethal bursts from the sky. But that was a child's fear and a child's fear is not the same as that of an adult.

Carlo holds my arm securely and steers me across the tarmac of the airport. Someone has handed me a bouquet of red roses. I am still violently airborne but I smile fixedly for the phalanx of photographers backpedaling in front of us in a clicking, flashing arc. I have not been able to tell Carlo about the flight but he knows how upset I am. Carlo. His instincts. His strength. The haven of his arm wrapped around mine. His strong smile. Never have I needed him more than at this moment. I met him at fifteen, got seriously involved with him at nineteen, and now at forty-four he means as much to me as he ever did. We endured terrible years together, when the church pilloried us and the Italian government prosecuted us for bigamy, but it was a fire of calumny that tempered the steel of our relationship and made it all the stronger.

Carlo tightens his grip on my arm and whispers, "We are almost there. See, there's our car." Carlo—lover, protector, friend, sensitive and creative; a father image for me? Yes, I suppose he's the father I never had, the father I needed in my life. The little, shy, illegitimate, fatherless girl of Pozzuoli is still very much inside me, and I need the fathering of Carlo as much today as I ever did.

In ten minutes I will be leaving my hotel for the premiere of my film *A Special Day*. This film represents a new and important and risky involvement for me. Performing without makeup, I play a drab, forlorn fortyish housewife during the days of Mussolini's Rome. But now, for the premiere, I am wearing a new gown, gay, colorful, gypsy-inspired, all the more to heighten the contrast between what I play on the screen and the glamour role I am playing tonight. The gown suits me, it fits the occasion, and it makes me feel especially good—my criteria for being well dressed.

Two plainclothes detectives are here with the walkie-talkies, keeping in touch with special police in the lobby and outside the hotel. They tell me that in all the years of the Cannes Film Festival, they have never had a situation like the one they face tonight. The lobby is packed solid with hundreds of spectators, photographers, and reporters. Outside the hotel, a mob has jammed itself around the entrance, and all along the five-minute route to the theater, dense crowds have gathered.

Mastroianni is now in the room, black tie, handsome, and smiling. He kisses my neck and smiles upon me. This is our eighth film together; there's no doubt by now that our marriage will last. We respect each other and love each other and on the set we have wonderful rapport. Many laughs. Marcello can be mercilessly funny.

But we rarely see each other away from the movie set. Marcello is a man beset with problems he cannot solve but which torment him, and for twenty years they have always been the same. The people in his life have changed but the problems remain the same, and Marcello has steadfastly refused to change his life in order to ease those problems. I figure that he must like the problems, and the torment. But on those rare occasions when we have gone out to dinner and he has permitted his spirits to soar above his problems, he has been the funniest, gayest man I ever encountered.

He adores the little daughter he had during his love relationship with Catherine Deneuve, but he lives in Italy and she is in Paris and he rarely sees her. Things like that depress him, and he can see no way out of the morass of these problems which fill the well of his private life.

Marcello and I step from the elevator into the lobby as an enormous burst of light from hundreds of flashbulbs goes off in our faces. There is a roar of welcome from the mass of spectators. A wedge of sweating special police, their arms locked, with Marcello and me in the pocket of the wedge, starts to move toward the doors, the crowd not giving way until forced to, pressing in on us, striving to touch us, pushing in the sides of the moving wedge.

Somehow, despite little flares of violence, despite moments when the police wedge is in danger of collapsing and crushing us, we reach the car, where other special police are trying to maintain a path to the open door of the car. Miraculously we land inside the car, but now the crowds in the street impede the car, rocking it, banging on the windows, chanting, "Sophia! Sophia! Marcello! Marcello!" only giving ground as police around the car physically move them out of the way.

This is the fifth time I have been to Cannes for a film of mine in competition, but I have never before experienced anything even approaching this. It is even worse when we get to the Palace, where the picture is to be shown. The crowd is bigger, denser, and noisier. This time there is a double wedge of police to move us up the long, steep steps into the crowd which is pressing down on us from above. I stumble but hands grab me and keep me from falling down the steps. I hear the sounds of my dress as it rips and tears. At times like this I honestly don't know whether to be frightened or to be elated, because these people are communicating something to me that makes this moment unique, a moment perhaps never to be repeated in my lifetime.

When this kind of thing happens to me, I feel that I am in a dream, and I seem to step outside of myself and look at Sophia struggling inside a police wedge, trying to reach the doors at the top of the steps. I see myself as if I were watching myself on television. This phenomenon of viewing myself from outside myself is something I've been doing all my life. It helps me keep my balance.

Now in the hushed presence of obligatory black ties and the glitter of Van Cleef & Arpels, I wait for the verdict of the audience. A film is shot in isolation, as a book is written, and there is no way to predetermine how the mass audience for whom the film is intended will react. The terrifying moment comes when the end titles start to appear and the audience responds. Will they applaud? Will it be perfunctory applause or will it be a wholehearted outpouring of approval? It is quite easy to tell. I am not one who with my imagination magnifies audience reaction, or who quickly stands up to provoke a heartier applause.

But on this night, I do not have any doubt. The audience has been involved and enthralled and their applause is deafening. They shout approval and finally, at their insistence, Marcello and I rise and acknowledge their acclaim.

For me it is a moment of sweet fulfillment, as gratifying as any moment in my career. This was an extremely difficult movie to make and the most difficult role I ever performed. Thus, this day that started so terribly has ended wonderfully well.

Which, it seems to me, is as good a starting point as any for what I have to tell you about my life, which also started terribly.

CHAPTER 2

In the Clinica Regina Margherita in Rome, there was a charity ward for unmarried women, and it was there that I was born in 1934, the year before Mussolini bombed Ethiopia. My name was entered in the hospital records as "Sofia Scicolone" by virtue of the fact that my father, whose name was Riccardo Scicolone, made an affidavit that affirmed that I was his issue. He had refused to marry my mother, or even to see her during the months she was pregnant, but strangely he did come to the hospital and give me his name.

My mother, though, had to keep her maiden name, Romilda Villani. She had brought terrible disgrace and humiliation to her family in the little seaport town of Pozzuoli, which is about twenty-five kilometers from Naples, but painful as it must have been for my grandmother, she nevertheless came to Rome to be with her daughter when I was born.

I was a skinny, pale, ugly little thing but my mother tells me that despite my unattractiveness and her humiliating and precarious condition, it never crossed her mind to put me in the orphanage which was run by a nearby convent for the accommodation of babies from my mother's ward. She was and is a fiercely determined woman and she had determined that I was going to be a part of her life.

In the Italy of 1934, the prospects facing my mother were certainly not good. The strict Catholic tenets which governed life in Italy gave no comfort to those who sinned against the church's precepts, and having an illegitimate baby was one of the severest sins. In the small town of Pozzuoli illegitimate childbearing was virtually unheard of.

But, temporarily at least, my mother was able to avoid facing the moral hostility of Pozzuoli. My father, who had little money and no job, asked his mother whether he and his new family could stay at her house while he looked for work, but his mother turned him down. He found a tiny room in a boardinghouse and that was where my mother and I went to live with him on leaving the hospital. Although he had studied to be an engineer, my father had never followed it up and remained without any trade or profession.

As soon as my mother could, she too went out every day to look for work, leaving me in the care of the woman who ran the boardinghouse. But Italy in the thirties had virtually no job opportunities for women. Mussolini had ordered them to stay at home and bear children. The little money my father had quickly dwindled to nothing. The landlady was aware of my parents' plight and tried to convince my mother to get rid of me. "Why don't you let this ugly thing die?" she asked. "Just look what you're going through—and for what? It's ridiculous. I can't keep you on here if you can't pay rent. His mother won't have anything to do with you. Your breasts are dry and the baby sucks on you without getting anything to eat—look at her . . . she's all skin and bones. Just let her die. No one will blame you. I'll take care of everything."

My mother's answer was to redouble her job-seeking efforts, but with no better results. Finally, one day when I was alone with the landlady she took matters into her own hands. She decided to put some food in me; the food which she forced down my throat was a mixture of lentils and stewed tomatoes. I was about six weeks old. Of course I became violently ill and developed severe colitis. When my mother found out what the landlady had done she furiously railed at her, but the landlady replied that my demise would be the best thing that could happen for my mother's well-being.

My mother tried to contact my father but he had disappeared. In desperation, she took me to the clinic but they said there was nothing they could do for a condition as severe as mine. There was no medicine to prescribe for it. They did say that a baby afflicted as I was must subsist entirely on natural milk from the mother. But my mother's breasts were dry. Riccardo Scicolone had departed for good without leaving her so much as a lira, the landlady was demanding her rent, now considerably in arrears, and I was dying.

It was a situation made to order for her natural defiance of life's darker forces. Actually, my mother had been born much too soon. At a time when women were docile and obedient to the strictures of a male-dominated society, she was a vehement iconoclast—fiery, eccentric, beautiful, uninhibited, stubborn. She still is. My mother had no interest in school but a great affinity for the piano; somehow my grandmother, that remarkable woman, contrived to get a piano, which she crammed into the small living room.

My mother quickly established her talent for playing the piano, and was given a scholarship for lessons at the conservatory in Naples. By the time she was sixteen, she was already so accomplished that the conservatory awarded her a professorship and authorized her to give lessons.

But more remarkable than my mother's ability at the keyboard was her resemblance to Greta Garbo, who at that time was one of Hollywood's great stars. People would stop my mother on the streets of Naples and ask for her autograph. As luck would have it, when my mother was seventeen, MGM announced a Greta Garbo look-alike contest that would be held throughout Italy, the winner to go on an all-expenses-paid trip to Hollywood, a first-class steamship ticket included, and be given a screen test in MGM's Culver City studios.

From the moment she read about the contest, my mother never had a moment's doubt that she would win. She took a bus to Naples, paraded before the judges, and was ultimately crowned the winner over three hundred and fifty other entrants. Her ecstasy was boundless and she rushed back from Naples to tell the good news to my grandmother and grandfather. My grandmother, however, didn't regard it as good news at all. I adored my grandmother, who was destined to be one of the most important persons in my young life, but she was a totally provincial person, devout, hardworking, suspicious. Very Neapolitan. "No," she said to my mother, "you cannot go." My mother was stunned.

MGM officials came to Pozzuoli to see my grandmother but she stood her ground. No amount of assurance or persuasion would budge my grandmother, and since her permission was necessary, because my mother was only seventeen, the movie people eventually left and switched the award to the runner-up.

It was a bitter and infuriating frustration for my mother. To have gotten so close to her dream and then been thwarted was not something that her volatile disposition could easily deal with. Thus, it was in the wake of these events that she had, without my grandmother's permission, gone to Rome to try to get into the movies, which were then being made in quantity at Cinecittà, the vast cinema complex that Mussolini intended as his answer to Hollywood.

I don't know how much ambition my mother really had. I think she was more piqued at being denied the Hollywood trip than she was ambitious for a career. At any rate, it was while she was in Rome in this frame of mind that she met Riccardo Scicolone, and as her pregnant belly grew, her dreams of ever becoming a concert pianist, which perhaps she could have done, or a movie star, receded.

Now on that day in Rome when she was alone with me, faced with the reality that the father of her child had abandoned her, that the child itself was near death, that she had no money, no food, no job, and was about to be evicted, she did the only sensible thing she could do to survive: she somehow managed to acquire a bus ticket to Pozzuoli.

CHAPTER 3

Pozzuoli is an ancient town with some well-preserved Roman remains, especially an amphitheater, which was located directly behind our flat. From the kitchen window we could look out on the beautifully formed and preserved arena, with the blue of the Tyrrhenian Sea behind it. Unlike big-city slums, like those of Naples, which are adjacent to luxurious sections of the cities, we children of Pozzuoli were not very aware of being underprivileged since everyone was poor and there were no rich kids to envy.

The Villani family lived over a vinegar factory in a compact flat that consisted of a small living room, a narrow dining room, two modest bedrooms, and a small kitchen. There was a toilet but no bath. We were seven in all (grandfather, grandmother, two uncles, an aunt, my mother, and I)—eight after my sister was born; we slept four to a bed. Until I left

Pozzuoli I never slept in a bed with fewer than three people in it. In true Neapolitan fashion, the living room existed only to receive company; since we never had any company, we rarely set foot in it. Except for Sunday, we ate most of our meals on a wooden table in the kitchen.

My grandfather was a foreman at the munitions factory, and we considered him quite an important man, but his title was more impressive than his pay. My grandmother carried the burden of the family on her shoulders. She was the wellspring, the spirit, the evaluator, the prodder, the comforter. I patterned some of the middle-aged housewife I depicted in *A Special Day* after my grandmother.

It was Grandma Luisa who opened the door that evening when my fearful mother, fatigued from the long bus ride from Rome, stood there with her sick baby, desperately wondering if she would be received or turned away. The Villanis had no telephone, of course, and there had been no way to inform my grandmother that she was arriving.

Without a momen't hesitation my grandmother opened her arms and pulled her daughter and granddaughter against her breast. A bottle of liquor, preserved for important occasions, was taken from the cupboard in the dining room, and all the family drank a toast to me, the new addition. Then my grandmother turned her attention to the grave condition of her granddaughter. "The clean sea air will help her," she said, "but she must have milk. It's the only hope. We will immediately put her to feed with the wet nurse Zaranella, who is the most prolific fountain of milk in all Campania."

Not only did my grandmother pay the prodigious Zaranella fifty lire a month to enable me to join the dozen or so babies who suckled her bountiful breasts, but my grandmother also decreed that for however long it took me to recover, all meat that she normally bought for the family table would go to Zaranella to nourish and improve the quality of her milk. None of the Villanis protested the meatless months that followed. That is the kind of love which, to this day, I especially prize. Giving like that without expectation of anything in return. Giving out of love, and love alone.

CHAPTER 4

I was either the first one in the schoolyard, at eight o'clock, or the last, arriving just as the last girl was filing into class at eight fifty-five. Only by being inconspicuous could I avoid the whispers, derisive glances, snickers, and taunts that my schoolmates directed at me because I was the illegitimate offspring of an unmarried mother. Every morning of my childhood I dreaded having to go to school. I felt that the stigma of my illegitimacy was tattooed on my forehead.

I suffered doubly from the fact that my mother was tall and beautiful and didn't look like any of the other mothers. She sometimes picked me up after school and my classmates reacted with the same derisiveness that greeted me in the morning. I tried to avoid being picked up by leaving school as quickly as I could. I would always go home very fast.

My mother earned what money she could by playing piano in the little cafés and trattorias. Sometimes she went to Naples and to Rome. One evening, pale and fearful, she got up her courage and confessed to my grandmother that she had seen my father a few times in Rome, hoping to persuade him to marry her. But in the process, she had become pregnant again. My grandmother bowed her head and put her hand over her eyes. But she had a forgiving heart and she accepted my sister, Maria, into the family, as she had accepted me. I was four years old when Maria was born.

I was five years old when I met my father for the first time. As a ruse to get him to Pozzuoli, my mother had sent him a telegram that I was very sick and he should come as quickly as possible. She had not told me he was coming, but I sensed that something special was happening from the way she fussed over my hair and dress, trying to make her skinny, sallow, homely daughter look as attractive as she could.

She brought me into the rarely used living room, where a tall, handsome man was standing with his back to the window. He was considerably taller than any of the men in the Villani family, and he was much more elegantly dressed. On the floor in front of him was a blue pedal car, fashioned after one of the Italian roadsters. No child in Pozzuoli had a car like that, and certainly I had never seen anything like it. Painted on the car was my nickname, Lella. My father bent down and extended his hand to me. He had a charming smile. "I brought you this little present," he said.

This much I remember, but curiously I'm fuzzy about what followed. My mother says I recoiled from him and refused to believe he was my father; that I told him to go away, told him that I had a father and that he was not at all my father and that I didn't want to see him. Whereupon, in tears, I ran from the room.

My mother should have prepared me for this confrontation. It was simply too big an event for an outcast five-year-old to handle. I suppose my father was hurt by my rejection of him, but the fact was that I had never considered him my father, or even a member of my family. How can a child have affection and feeling for someone who should be with her but isn't? This man called father never came to see us, didn't care about us. My grandfather and grandmother did. They were warm and loving and gentle, and until my grandfather's death a few years ago, I continued to call him "Papa" and thought of him as such.

As for Grandmother, when I came home from school in the afternoon and we were alone in the kitchen, her whole personality changed. She used to cast off her cares for an hour or two and be gay and funny with me. While a big pot of *pasta e fagiole* was bubbling on the stove, she sang songs to me that she made up, about how life would be for me when I grew up—a wonderful life filled with Pozzuoli dream objects such as automobiles and fur coats and diamond rings. She would be sitting there sewing me a garment she was making out of an old blanket and singing to me of this sumptuous life in the fairyland of tomorrow. At the same time I was making shoes for myself from two flats of leather to which I'd affix strings to bind around my andles.

How I loved Grandma Luisa! The first success I had in the movies, *The Gold of Naples,* I took what little money I earned and bought a ring with a tiny diamond in it. By then, my grandmother was sick and bedridden. I went all the way to Pozzuoli on the bus from Rome to surprise her with my diamond ring. "Look, Mamma," I told her, holding up my hand in front of her face, "your dreams for me have come true." You would have thought it was twenty carats of the finest stone. Grandma Luisa died six months later but her voice lives on inside me.

After that first time in Pozzuoli, my mother often sent telegrams to my father urging him to come immediately because of my grave illness, but he never again fell for that hoax. A few years after my sister was born, he got in touch with my mother and told her that he had met a girl whom he had made pregnant, and he threatened to marry this girl unless my mother came to Rome and asserted her prior rights. "She's a good deal younger than you and quite pretty," my father had said, "and I'm going to marry her unless you show up and stop me." My mother was angry and disgusted with him by then and told him to do whatever he wanted, that she was through with him. So he married this girl and had two sons with her. But some years later, he left her and went back to live for a while with my mother.

While my father was alive, my mother often denounced him in violent terms and said she hated him, but it always seemed to me that what my mother had for my father was not hate but enormous love. She conceived two children with him, she never married nor had any other true lover, and until the day he died Riccardo Scicolone aroused her deepest emotions. I know I never really hated my father—oh, a momentary flash of hatred when he did something outrageous—but as I got older I think I developed a pretty good understanding of my father and his failures. Even though absent, he was a very important element in my life, a long shadow of influence.

CHAPTER 5

In 1940, when I was six, war came to Pozzuoli. It seemed that overnight German soldiers were everywhere. They were our allies then, and friendly, and my earliest memories are of delightedly watching the young, handsome soldiers in their beautiful uniforms, playing war games in the backyards of the houses on our street. I don't think I had ever seen a blond, blue-eyed man before the German soldiers arrived. After the war began, everything in Pozzuoli gradually shut down and finally there was nothing at all for a child to do, so that all we had as a diversion was the war itself. Since the tracks through Pozzuoli joined the important Naples-Rome line, German soldiers were always in our area, patrolling the railroad station on one side of us and the harbor on the other.

It wasn't long, however, before the twin magnets of the munitions factory and the harbor began to draw the attention of the Allied planes. As the bombing intensified, food and water began to disappear; the food, because transportation was cut off, and the water, because the bombs destroyed the water mains. For safety, the people of the town had to crowd into the railroad tunnel every night after the last train left for Naples. In the morning, everyone had to get out of the tunnel by four-thirty, when the first train from Naples came roaring into the tunnel.

The tunnel became the focal point of our lives. Every night we dragged our mattresses and, in the winter, our blankets, into its pitch-black interior—no light, not even a candle, was permitted. No one was allowed near the entrance, where there was some air, because of the possibility that fragments of a bomb could penetrate into the interior of the tunnel. The central part of the tunnel, where we were all squeezed together, was very dark and humid, a hot, stinking atmosphere, putrid with the smell of unwashed bodies, overripe, half-rotten food, urine, feces, and garbage. Cockroaches were everywhere and enormous tunnel rats scurried around and over us to get to the food. Night after night after night, for unending months.

Running for the shelter when the alarm sounded became an exciting event for me. But one devastating raid caught us by surprise. The air-raid alarm had failed to sound, and we were asleep in our beds when tons of bombs began exploding all around us, shaking the walls, shattering windows. We ran for cover but a shard of shrapnel caught me in the chin, and by the time we got to the air-raid shelter my face was all bloody. The following morning, when we returned to our rooms, the streets were covered with blood and with badly injured people and with devastation. My sister had lost her shoes and her feet were badly cut by broken glass. When we got back to our house, it was half ruined.

In the winter the tunnel became freezing cold and we never had enough warm clothes and blankets. Crying babies, husbands and wives screaming at each other, couples making love, snorers, teeth-grinders, lost children, people bitten by the rats, sickness, laughter, drunkenness, death, and childbirth were all part of the interminable nights in the tunnel. To this day, as a result of those terrible black nights, I have a phobia about the dark.

Under the pressure of the shortages of food and water, and of the bomb hits on the munitions factory, the marginal existence of the Villanis collapsed. The specter of starvation was omnipresent. My mother devoted herself to foraging for enough food to feed me and my sister but she often didn't succeed. More days than not, we didn't have a crust of bread nor a swallow of milk. Our hunger was constant and numbing.

Bread was very scarce and it was distributed by the town on the basis of coupons which were allotted to each family. But there is a confession I have to make about the bread, something I did which troubles my conscience to this day. It was my duty to take our coupons to the bakery each week and get our allotment. We were given the number of grams allotted for eight people, and this always came out to a large loaf plus an extra little piece. On the way home, I always ate that little extra piece and I never told my family about it, although my grandmother used to weigh the bread and I think she suspected my pilferage.

I had one other secret source of food, but this was my mother's secret, not mine. Some mornings at dawn, when the wake-up cries resounded through the tunnel, my mother would take me by the hand and, making sure she wasn't followed, hurry me along into the open country. We followed a path that led to a series of small caves, from one of which emanated smoke from a wood fire. In this cave there was a goatherd who was a friend of one of my uncles. He had an empathy for me as he would have had for one of his little goats that was undernourished. The goatherd would milk one of his goats, filling a big mug with frothy, warm milk which he would hand to me. I cannot possibly describe the exquisite taste of that fresh milk as I felt its warm little river run down my insides and settle in my empty stomach. That cup of milk lifted me physically and spiritually; on those mornings when my mother took me to the goatherd, it really didn't matter if there was no food for the rest of that day.

My mother's sacrifices were boundless. Her most cherished possession, and she didn't have many, was a camel's-hair coat that seemed to heighten her Greta Garbo resemblance. She adored that coat. But that first freezing winter in the tunnel, when I had nothing to wear to keep warm, she unhesitatingly took a scissors to her coat, recut it and sewed it into a dress for me. She did the same thing to one of her two dresses for my sister.

A proclamation, signed by the mayor, appeared on all the bulletin boards of Pozzuoli and on the radio. All citizens of Pozzuoli were to evacuate the town within forty-eight hours. The bombing raids had become intolerable.

There was no organized evacuation. Everyone had to leave but where we went and how we got there had to be our own concern. My grandparents' only relatives, outside of Pozzuoli, were a family named Mattia that lived in Naples. Signora Mattia was the cousin of my grandmother. Unfortunately, they had not seen each other for years, nor kept in touch; my grandmother warned us that her cousin had a rather selfish personality and that we were not to expect a warm welcome, or, in fact, any welcome at all.

As my grandmother had predicted, the Mattias were certainly not hospitable, but they didn't turn us away. My mother, my sister, and I shared a tiny room which fortunately had a balcony. For the five months we stayed in Naples, that balcony was my only contact with the outside world; my mother and grandmother feared that if we left the room the

Mattias might not let us back in, so my sister and I acted as room insurance. The Mattias had tins of biscuits and a cache of other food which they had put aside for themselves, but which they never shared with us. We never got so much as a crumb of bread or a glass of water from them; as a matter of fact, they went to great pains to hide their food and water. I understood this. It was a desperate time when people were dying of starvation and dehydration and my grandmother's cousin had to insure the survival of her own family.

The survival of ours was something else again. Conditions in Naples were even worse than they had been in Pozzuoli. There was no water at all, not even spring water. Apart from a virtually inedible black bread that was severely rationed, there was absolutely no food, except on the black market. In the house, we could feel the hatred of the Mattias. Naples was the most bombed city in Italy, and when the air-raid sirens started wailing it really sounded as if the world were ending.

My mother had a terrible time those months in Naples. Her nerves were always on or over the edge. When the mass of sirens sent up their wail, my mother would scream at the top of her lungs, scream right along with the screaming sirens. She used to scare me to death. My mother still screams at life.

My sister was ill all during our stay in Naples, and this added immeasurably to my mother's nervousness. Maria had measles and then, barely over them, she developed typhoid. Luckily, I didn't catch any of Maria's diseases, but I was a skeleton. Sometimes my mother or my grandmother would bring home a sack of rice or potatoes, which would be our entire diet for a week or ten days, but more often than not, all that Maria and I had to eat was a hunk of that gooey black bread. This bread was rock-hard on the outside and gummy within. My sister and I would eat the thin hard crust and then mold little animals out of the inside dough and put them in the window to dry. But usually we were so hungry the following morning that somehow we managed to eat those indigestible objects, which dropped into our stomachs like paper weights.

As the war worsened for the Nazis, they became uglier toward the Italians, whose sentiments were now staunchly with the Americans. Toward the end of their occupation of Naples the Nazis began to kill the Neapolitans indiscriminately, and then, seeing it for myself, I really understood the appalling viciousness of war. I saw men grabbed on the streets below me, beaten, thrown into German army trucks and hauled away. People were shot in the streets without warning. My young eyes saw one appalling, gruesome spectacle after another.

And then came the worst bloodbath of all—what became known as the Four Days of Naples, when ragged little boys from the slums finally rebelled against the German oppression and took matters into their own hands. Armed with bottles filled with gasoline they had stolen from the Germans, these boys ignited rags they had stuffed into the bottles to serve as wicks, and then darted from side streets and swarmed over the huge German tanks, stuffing the bottles into the gun slits in the tanks just before the gasoline exploded. These were ragamuffin little boys, mind you, ranging from five to ten years of age, whose courage was unbelievable. I couldn't believe my eyes. Many of these boys were shot and killed by the Germans, their bloody little bodies dotting the streets, but nothing daunted their attacks.

After four days, incredible as it may seem, the boys of Naples had brought the German army to its knees; to our amazement, the entire German military establishment withdrew from Naples. By the end of the fifth day, there wasn't a Nazi soldier left on the streets. But the fury of the Nazis was still to be reckoned with. They had taken all the food and water with them, and as they left they had blown up sewer mains and what remained of the water system. They then stationed snipers in the hills and mountains to the north. Directly above our house was Monte Santo. And directly below us was a food store which constantly had a long queue of people in front of it, patiently waiting to buy some black bread and what little other food was available. Almost all the people on line were women, children, and old persons. The Nazi snipers on Monte Santo would fire on these bread queues, wounding and killing people indiscriminately. When the snipers scored a hit, the wounded or dead would be taken away, but the people did not give up their places in the line.

Two days after the German retreat, the Allies came marching in. We knew they were on their way and there was great anticipatory excitement. The Americans came in jeeps and trucks and right away started to hand out candies and biscuits and other forgotten delicacies. A soldier threw me a piece of chocolate but I didn't know what it was. I had never tasted any. I tried to catch some of the marvelous boxes and cans and packages that were flying through the air but all I snared was a little can of concentrated coffee. I gave it to my grandmother but we couldn't figure out what to do with it. My grandmother knew from the smell that it was coffee but it obviously wouldn't work in her espresso machine. Eventually she discovered the miracle of adding hot water.

We had to leave Naples as precipitously as we had arrived. The Allied military requisitioned our building and we were forced to depart on a few hours' notice. The train tracks to Pozzuoli had been destroyed, and no other transportation existed (penniless, we couldn't have bought tickets anyway), so we were obliged to travel the twenty-five kilometers on foot, with our possessions on our backs.

The road to Pozzuoli was choked with refugees, lugging their possessions on their backs, and in carts and wagons and all manner of wheeled contrivances. The road itself was in terrible condition, covered with bomb craters. People got in each other's way, carts broke down and blocked the road, some people tumbled into the craters, there was yelling and screaming and joyful reunions and fistfights and exhausted people sitting on the roadside, but withal, I felt elated because we were going home.

As we neared Pozzuoli in the late afternoon, the throngs of refugees became even denser and we began to run into friends and neighbors. That day on the road stays in my memory like flashes of a well-cut film. (In fact, the refugee road that de Sica created in *Two Women* was very much like what happened that day going back to Pozzuoli. Much of *Two Women* corresponded to this childhood period of my life.) As we trudged through the outskirts of the town, my apprehension grew because the desolation was terrible. We were climbing up and down huge mounds of rubble and twisted girders—the unrecognizable remains of stores and paved streets and houses.

Then, suddenly, there was our house, badly damaged but still standing. All the windows had been blown out, the roof sagged, the walls were cracked, but it was standing.

But our two old nemeses of no water and no food were as much of a problem as ever, and there was a new tribulation—lice. We were covered with them—in our hair, all over our bodies and thick in our clothing. They had swept through Naples like a virus, and everyone had them. The problem was that there was no way to kill the eggs, which hatched as soon as we took the clothes out of the water.

We were desperate. My scalp and skin were bleeding from all the scratching. I couldn't sleep. And besides, I had a second affliction that none of the others had: scabies, which is a disease caused by a certain kind of mite that burrows under the skin and deposits its eggs there. As the eggs hatch in ever increasing numbers, the itching they cause becomes more and more unbearable. So I had the double plague of the mites and the strange white lice. I would sometimes weep from the intensity of the itching. I kept moving around as much as I could, because I scratched more when I was quiet.

The shape of those lice, the way they felt when I plucked one from my hair, the satisfaction I got from squeezing one between my fingers and feeling it pop—a horrible memory that I'll never forget. Those bugs seemed to sum up all the suffering and horror and injustice of the war.

I don't know what would have happened to me if the United States Army had not come to our rescue with its miracle powder, DDT. The army set up aid stations in the town, and after one application of DDT we were miraculously free of this pestilence. But I still had the mites to contend with. DDT helped, but not until an American doctor gave me a sulfa compound was I entirely rid of them. The disappearance of the lice was a sign, for me, that the war was really over.

We began to get some food from the army, even *white* bread, which was considered a great delicacy, but our biggest problem that first winter back in Pozzuoli was the cold. We had no fuel and woefully inadequate clothes. The kitchen was the only room we tried to heat by burning scraps of wood in the old iron range. When it was time for bed, my grandmother would fill a long-handled receptacle with some of the hot coals from the stove and warm the sheets of the bed with them.

But as I said, this part of my life was not much different from what it had been. The important thing was that despite all the problems and privations, I had the love and protection of my mamma and my mammina, and I was surrounded by a big family, which gave me a sense of security; and for a kid it was fun to race from the kitchen through the ice-cold rooms and jump into a bed with a nice warm sheet on the bottom and an ice-cold one on the top.

Day by day, a little at a time, the mystery of self-restoration began to be solved. But for us a source of some concern was the contingent of Moroccan soldiers that had been billeted in the ground-floor quarters of our building. They were commanded by a French officer, but he didn't exercise much control over them. They were always drinking and playing cards and dancing to the rhythms of cymbals. To get to our flat on the top floor, we had to pass by the Moroccans and it was always frightening. Actually they never molested us, but a couple of times in the dead of night, when they had had much too much to drink, they had come pounding on our door to frighten us. But finally my grandmother marched down to the Moroccans' quarters and had a good, tough talk with the French lieutenant. After that, we were never again bothered in the night.

My mother began to earn a little money by playing piano in the little café and restaurant across the road from us which had just reopened with mostly American GIs as clientele. After my sister recovered her health, she often joined my mother in the cafés. For a six-year-old, she had a remarkable voice and she loved having an audience to hear her sing. I yearned to join in the singing, although my voice wasn't as good as Maria's, but I was much too shy even to go to listen to them.

These entertainments by my mother and sister gave my grandmother an idea of how to bring in some badly needed revenue. Aside from a few bare cafés and a couple of shabby restaurants, there was virtually nothing to do for the large numbers of GIs who were bivouacked around Pozzuoli. So my grandmother hit on the notion of turning our unused living room into a kind of home café, where soldiers could have a few drinks, listen to music, sing, have some laughs, and, above all, feel that they were spending a few hours with a family group inside an Italian house. The big problem for my grandmother was how to provide drinks. She solved that by using the little money my mother had earned to buy pure alcohol (on the black market), to which she added essence of cherry Strega, a liqueur. It was a sweet-tasting drink but my mother had discovered, from observing the GIs in the cafés, that they liked sweet drinks. Some of them even put sugar in their wine.

My grandmother's home café caught on immediately. The GIs loved to pass a few hours there, and we were like a foster family to them. They often brought records to put on our old hand-wound Victrola, and some of the regulars brought PX food such as biscuits, pasta, flour, coffee, and cans of fruit. I helped serve and wash dishes but my shyness prevented me from singing or taking part in the festivities. At ten, I was still stunted in growth, terribly thin, and quite ugly.

Sometimes when they got a little drunk, the GIs would start to think of home and get very sad. My grandmother would keep an eye on them, and when she saw them getting into this condition she began to water their drinks. These boys were very young, not more than twenty, twenty-two, and sometimes, under the release of a few drinks, they would break down and weep. Then my grandmother and my mother would console them. Of course, my mother and grandmother neither spoke nor understood English but it didn't seem to matter.

At six o'clock Grandmother would announce closing. We never entertained at night. Hearing about my grandmother's success, many other families on the block opened their houses to the soldiers in the same way, serving drinks and providing entertainment. After a while there was a spirited competition for GI customers.

One of those American GIs arranged for my mother and me to visit the American army base, where, even though it was against the rules, a doctor performed a minor operation on the shrapnel scar on my chin and succeeded in making it virtually disappear.

CHAPTER 6

I did not start to develop physically until I was fourteen, which is quite late for a Neapolitan girl. My friends were all bigger than I was in every way. They had breasts and were menstruating and discussed sexual intercourse and conception. I pretended that I too had become a woman, lying about everything, but in the process I got a pretty good education. In those days it was unheard of to discuss anything that related to the body or to sex with one's family, so that my grandmother and mother never mentioned such things to me. My skinny, breastless body, plus the fact that I had not yet begun to menstruate, made my inferiority complex even worse.

When I was eleven I started to play the piano, which I adored. I think I could have been a very good pianist, but we couldn't afford to pay for lessons and my mother was my teacher. Parents rarely make good teachers for their children, and my mother was certainly no exception. She was terribly impatient with me, and every time I made a mistake she banged me on the head. I loved everything about the piano, even practicing, but my headaches from being knocked on the head by Mother became so severe that I had to stop.

When Pozzuoli's only movie theater reopened, it offered Hollywood movies for the first time. Before the war only drab Italian films had been shown. The Hollywood films took me into a world far removed from the desolate years of my childhood. But it was not the opulence I saw on the screen that overwhelmed me; it was the stars themselves and the roles they played. Fred Astaire dancing with Ginger Rogers was a fairy-tale dream. Gable, Cary Grant, Rita Hayworth, Sinatra, and, above all, Tyrone Power. He was the god of my adolescence. When he appeared in the melodramatic epic *Blood and Sand,* I went to see him twelve times.

I felt a real physical pain each time I had to leave the theater, no matter how many times I saw the film. After I saw Rita Hayworth in

Gilda, I started to comb my hair the way she wore hers; later I switched to Veronica Lake's hairstyle when one of her pictures captivated me. But I had no desire to be a star, to be glamorous, to have cars and furs and a castle in Beverly Hills, and not because of the impossibility of attaining them. What these movies set off in me was the intangible of emoting, of *acting* itself. I was not interested in what I could bring *to* myself by being an actress, but in what I could bring *out* of myself.

I have no way of accounting for this reaction. There had been no plays or entertainments at the strict Catholic school I attended. But even if there had been plays, I would have been much too shy to appear in them. Nor did we have any books in the house, so that part of my development, the world of imagination, I guess you'd say, was totally neglected. I had never heard of Shakespeare or Shaw. My family simply had too many problems just keeping all of us alive to pay any attention to books and reading. They were church people who went along with the church's notion that strict adherence to basic studies was all that a girl should concern herself with. My grandmother and my aunt were devout Catholics but my mother was not.

My aunt and my sister are still devoutly religious and go to mass regularly, but I am not. I never go to mass. Not necessarily because I am against the church but because I think you can pray anywhere, and I don't need a church to commune with God. I must confess, however, that the attitude of the church toward Carlo and me has contributed to this feeling.

Every time I entered the hallowed darkness of the Teatro Sacchino I could feel a change in my whole person. The Teatro had been a legitimate theater before it turned to films, and it had a proscenium arch, velour seats, and elaborate friezes in its baroque interior. When the lights went down and I was alone with Rita or Tyrone, I was suffused with the feeling that that's what I was put on earth to do. Although there was a far, far distance between the desire of a ten-year-old poor kid and the realization of that desire, curiously I felt a confidence in myself. Naturally, I have never confided any of this to anyone, but deep down inside me I felt a conviction that I had been put on earth to be a movie actress.

At fourteen my body miraculously came to life, virtually overnight, and by fourteen and a half the ugly duckling had bloomed into a long-legged, full-breasted swan. It was as if I had burst from an egg and was born. For the first time in my life, when I walked down the street, I heard the mellifluous sound of male whistles. And I definitely knew I had finally and fully matured the day our physical education teacher, a handsome young man who used to supervise calisthenics in the amphitheater, came to see my mother to request permission to marry me. She told him to go home and soak in a cold tub.

A friend of my mother's, who lived across the street, brought us a Naples newspaper that gave details about an impending beauty contest that promised lavish prizes to the girl crowned Queen of the Sea, and to the twelve girls chosen as her princesses. The rules stipulated a minimum age of fifteen, but my mother said that now that I had filled out I looked at least fifteen and she was going to enter me. My shyness being what it was, I tried to protest, but my mother shut me off. "Lella, you are going to enter this contest," she said forcefully, "and you are going to win."

The contest was sponsored by the newspaper *Il Mattino* and contestants were required to appear in Naples with an afternoon dress and a gown for the evening. My mother saw in this contest possible vicarious revenge for the Greta Garbo prize she had been denied, and the fact that I didn't have the requisite evening gown was not going to stop her. She enlisted the help of my grandmother, who was a genius with needle and thread. She had just made a brown-and-beige dress for me out of scraps of material she had in her sewing bag, so that would do for the afternoon, but the evening gown was a problem since, as usual, there wasn't a lira in the house.

"I'll tell you what we'll do, Lella," she said, after long reflection. "We will just take down one of the drapes in the living room and I will make you an evening gown out of that." And so she did. And it did look nice, at least to my fourteen-year-old eyes. But I didn't have white shoes to go with the dress. In fact, the only shoes I had were black, and worn, but my mother solved that problem by getting some white paint, and by applying two thick coats, created my white shoes. We prayed it wouldn't rain.

The contest was held at night; my mother and I went to Naples by train, traveling in a crowded third-class compartment. I wore my new pink drapery dress, with my old school coat over it, and I was very careful not to scuff my shoes and let the black show through. I had my hair up, to look older, and my mother let me use some makeup.

We had to walk quite a far distance from the train station to where the contest was being held in a villa called Circolo della Stampa near the sea. It was a rather exclusive press club, and I felt, as my mother led me to it, as if I were the proverbial lamb being led to its execution.

There were upwards of two hundred girls with their mothers there, primping, combing, powdering, nervously waiting their turn. The girls wore beautiful gowns which quite obviously had not previously hung in their living room windows, and many of them were wearing jewels and flowers. I sat quietly in a corner and tried to pull myself into the wall.

When my time came to appear before the jury, I found, to my astonishment, that when I entered the room where the fourteen jury members were sitting at a long table, my nervousness seemed to fly off me. Before entering, I had been scared to death. I am always frightened before I do anything that requires me to perform. To this day, before the camera turns, I am still frightened of the scenes I must play. I have no arrogance, not even confidence. I never expect anything. Then when it happens, I am doubly happy, but if it doesn't, I am not so badly disappointed. But there is this: once I put myself into a thing, I do my utmost, my very, very best. I never take for granted any demand I put on myself. My attitude is that nothing is going to come of my exertions, and I prepare myself mentally for rejection. But this attitude does not affect my performance: I still perform at the top of my talent—a positive performance, but a negative attitude.

That night in Naples, I was scared to death. It was very late when the last girl had paraded and the judges announced their verdict. I was prepared to console my mother. As it turned out, my name was called as one of the twelve princesses, and I felt a bubble of joy rise inside me such as I had never felt before. Photographers took our pictures, reporters asked me for the spelling of my name, and we were each given a bouquet of flowers. It was my first bouquet.

Then I received my prize: a railroad ticket to Rome, several rolls of wallpaper, a tablecloth with twelve matching napkins, and twenty-three thousand lire (about thirty-five dollars), which to us was a very impressive sum of money.

The wallpaper was immediately pasted over our cracked, peeling walls of the living room, the tablecloth and napkins became fixtures of our Sunday lunch, and I hid the Rome ticket and the lire in a secret place behind a bureau drawer.

In seeing her daughter crowned a Princess of the Sea, my mother had received all the encouragement she needed to concentrate on my future as an actress. Her next step was to enroll me in a drama school in Naples, which she paid for out of money she had started to earn giving piano lessons.

The faculty of the drama school consisted of a single professor, a former actor, who had his own approach to acting—a method that he called "shaping an actor out of stone." What he taught us, pure and simple, was how to make faces. He gave us a printed list and we were expected to make faces precisely as they were described on the list. Horror, joy, despair, ecstasy, love, anger, whatever—the professor had a specific face for each and every emotion. Joy—both eyebrows up; surprise—both eyebrows up with the mouth formed in an *O*; skepticism—one eyebrow up; horror—big eyes; pain—little eyes. The professor obviously had never accepted the passing of silent movies.

My lessons at the acting school were only incidental to my main schooling, which I now pursued in the Pozzuoli public school; my goal was to be a teacher. But one day at the acting school, the professor made an announcement which changed the course of my life. He told us that a colossal American production moving into Cinecittà, called *Quo Vadis*, had put out a call for hundreds of extras. "Those of you who can get to Rome will probably get your chance in the movies," the professor said.

I carried this news to my mother, who made an immediate decision that I should quit school; she decided that we would set out for Rome and really devote ourselves to trying to make me a movie actress.

As for me, I had no ambition as such to become a movie actress in Rome. I would have been happy being a teacher in Pozzuoli, marrying a good local fellow, and raising a family, although I did feel in my heart that I had a force in me, a talent, for acting. But without my mother's ambition, her drive, I doubt that on my own I would have pushed myself out of Pozzuoli and into the frightening world that was faraway Rome.

CHAPTER 7

I didn't realize, until we got off the train, that my mother knew no more about big-city life than I did. She didn't even know how to use the telephone. Finally we had to go into a bar at the railroad station and ask someone to make the call for us. It was my father she was calling.

He was astonished to hear from her. "What are you doing in Rome?" he asked.

"We wanted to see you. Sofia is here with me and she would like to see you very much because she is quite sick." Countless times my mother had failed to lure him with my imaginary illnesses; this time it worked.

"All right," my father said, "I'll meet you at my mother's house."

The first thing he said when he came in was, "You can't sleep here." Then he said, "I haven't any money, you know." Finally, he looked at me and said, "She doesn't look sick to me."

My mother told him why we had really come. My father jumped to his feet. "The movies!" he shouted. "Why, you're crazy! You're absolutely insane—you have no idea how tough things are in Rome! The movies? Why, is she such a beauty? Well, do what you like but leave me out of it."

"I just thought, since it's your own daughter," my mother said, "that you might want to see her get ahead."

"How, by making a ridiculous ass out of herself?" my father said. "You do what you want but leave me out of it!" He walked us firmly to the door and ushered us out.

My mother's only other Rome contact was a cousin I had never met. She used the same word as my father, "crazy," and tried to induce my mother to take the next train back to Pozzuoli. After much wrangling, my mother wrung out of her a concession that we could sleep on the couches in the living room for one week without paying, but that if we stayed after that we would have to pay a weekly rate.

They did everything they could to make us feel unwelcome. Since we had very few belongings, our presence was scarcely noticeable. The only thing I wore, night and day, was a black skirt and a black shirt because my mother said that if I was dressed in black I would always look elegant.

Quo Vadis was indeed hiring a horde of extras, and Cinecittà was packed with thousands of people seeking to be hired. The director, Mervyn Le Roy, had all of them parade by him, choosing for interviews those who looked promising. My mother and I were called forward. My mother had primed me to answer any question I was asked in English with one word, yes. So that's what I did, answered all of Mr. Le Roy's questions with a pleasant yes. But he finally got wise to me when, in response to his question, "What is your name and address?" I answered yes. Although I didn't get the little speaking part he had in mind, he did hire both my mother and me as extras.

We reported to the vast sound stage where all the extras were being processed. An assistant director was summoning each extra by name. He called out, "Villani," and my mother stepped forward. "Scicolone" was next, but when I walked up to the production table, so did another woman. "Which one of you is Scicolone?" the man asked. "I am!" this woman said to me. "The man said Scicolone—that's me!"

I was stunned. We were standing in front of several hundred extras, and they were all listening to this confrontation. Then it dawned on me who she was. My stepmother. I had never seen her before but obviously this was the woman my father had married when my mother had refused to come to Rome and bail him out of his predicament. Now here she was screaming at me in front of all these people. She was like a fury.

I was rescued by the assistant director: "Scicolone, Sofia," he said, emphasizing the Sofia.

It was an unnerving way to get introduced to one's stepmother.

My mother and I worked on *Quo Vadis* for several days. We earned a total of fifty thousand lire (seventy-six dollars) and were exultant, but that was the beginning and the end of easy times in Rome.

Word reached us that my sister was gravely ill. My mother immediately packed up and left for Pozzuoli. For weeks we had been tramping from one movie office to another, but there were no calls for extras or bit players.

My mother was deeply concerned about leaving me alone in Rome, and I was scared to death. I had never been alone anywhere and, despite the fact that we paid them something out of our *Quo Vadis* money, our cousins were no friendlier. But I had found work at the *fumetti*. That was the primary reason my mother left me in Rome. I earned enough from the *fumetti* to keep all of us going.

As a movie actress my future was bleak, but not so in the *fumetti*. It's hard to explain the *fumetti*, which were panels of soap-opera photos that used small puffs coming out of the characters' mouths in which dialogue appeared. The *fumetti* were peculiarly Italian; they ran in the newspapers daily and were very popular. It was my training at the Naples acting school that got me the job, for what the *fumetti* people wanted by way of expressions was exactly what the professor had taught us. "What! You love another woman, John?" would appear in a balloon above my head while my expression—eyes wide, eyebrows arched, mouth in an *O*—was pure Naples acting school. At night I practiced my grotesque expressions in front of a mirror.

I was usually cast as the villainous girl of the strip, conventionally a gypsy or an Arab. When I began to receive a little publicity for my *fumetti* roles, the director decided that Scicolone was a rather comic and difficult name so he changed it to Sofia Lazzaro.

Without the *fumetti* I'm sure I could not have stuck it out in Rome. The *fumetti* put me in contact with other young actors and in this way I developed a few friends. And it was on an evening when I went out with several of these friends that I entered my second beauty contest.

On this particular evening, my friends had taken me to a big outdoor restaurant-nightclub overlooking the Colosseum. When we got there we discovered that a beauty contest to crown Miss Roma was scheduled as part of the evening's festivities. At that time, beauty contests sponsored by movie companies were commonplace, ostensibly to find new girls for the movies. Later in the evening, when the jury had assembled, one of the officials came to our table and invited me to enter the contest. I said no. I was, as usual, much too shy for that kind of spontaneous behavior.

A few moments later the official returned. He said that the members of the jury were all movie people and that one of them, a producer named Carlo Ponti, had noticed me and had specifically requested that I join the contest. My friends urged me to enter. You already start with his vote, they said, and anyway these are all people in the movie business.

So I entered. And after the usual rigmarole of parading around and answering questions, the results were announced: second place, Sofia Lazzaro. Always a bridesmaid. Afterward, Carlo Ponti came over to our table and introduced himself. He invited me to go for a walk in the little garden in back of the restaurant. I said to myself, Oh-oh, here comes the proposition. We walked around the garden and Carlo said, "I think I have a pretty good eye for talent. I have made a career for Gina Lollobrigida, Alida Valli, and many, many others. You have an interesting face. I suggest you come to my office tomorrow and we run a test. Have you ever had a test? No? Good, we will see how you look on the screen." He gave me his address and bade me good-night. He couldn't have been more businesslike.

The following morning, nervous and apprehensive, I went to the address he had given me and found myself in a police station. I was so angry to have been duped like that that tears came to my eyes. One of the policemen came over to me and I showed him the address. The policeman smiled. The address I was looking for was next door.

Carlo's office was on the first floor and he received me immediately. He took me to a nearby theater where his company (he was in partnership with Dino de Laurentiis) was making a movie. A set had been built on the stage. Carlo turned me over to the director and cameraman, and left. My first screen test. I was so nervous I could feel the blood pounding in my temples and I seriously thought I might faint. I was given a bathing suit to put on and told to make myself up.

Once I was ready, it took an enormous effort on my part to force myself to go back on that set wearing that bathing suit, to face the camera. The director handed me a cigarette and told me that the test would consist of my lighting the cigarette and then walking back and forth in front of the camera while smoking. A battery of blinding lights was turned on. I had never before in my life held a cigarette in my hand, much less smoked one. The camera started. Action. I was terrible. All thumbs. Ruinously nervous. Mercifully, it was over very quickly. Lights out. Disaster.

Carlo Ponti

When I first laid eyes on Sophia, I was struck more by her personality than by her looks. Something played off her that gave her a kind of illumination. I couldn't believe she was a teen-ager. She was so mature, so focused in her desire to be an actress, so professional, yet at the same time timid and unsure of herself. It was an entrancing mix. I knew immediately she was someone remarkable. Shortly after our first meeting at the beauty contest, she came to talk to me in my office; after I got her to tell me about her struggles during and after the war, and how poor she was, I began to understand about her. She was the man of the family, the provider, and everyone was dependent upon her. She spoke with deep feeling about her mother, deep love and gratitude.

I honestly admit that I was first interested in Sophia as a woman, and only afterward as an artist. I use the word artist instead of actress because Sophia is not an actress, she is an artist. An actress is something you become, an artist is born that way. By the time I met Sophia, I had given many actresses their start, but I had rarely found an actress who was a woman. An artist is always a woman, an actress rarely is.

Sophia understood where and how she thrived and what she wanted. Her screen tests didn't succeed because the men who made them were conditioned only to look for physical beauty, not inner beauty. They complained about the size of her nose but they never bothered to consider the quality that was inside her. I did. I sensed her potential: I was impressed with her serious nature and the fact that she wasn't on the make like most of the other young girls who were willing to pay any price to get into the movies. Sophia was determined to be an actress, but she made it clear that she did not regard the casting couch as a stepping-stone.

Over the course of the following year, Carlo gave me a number of screen tests, each time with a different cameraman, but each time there was the same negative reaction. The cameramen complained that there was no way to make my face attractive, because my nose was too long—also, I was too hippy.

But Carlo continued to stay in touch with me to find out what I was doing, to give me words of encouragement. I told him some things about my life, about my family in Pozzuoli, about the problems of struggling alone in Rome. He always asked if I had enough money to get by, and when I did not, he sent me small amounts to tide me over. But there was nothing serious between us. I had just turned sixteen; Carlo was thirty-eight, married, with two children, and although we played around, we did not have intercourse, not until later.

One day he asked me to come up to his office. We had just completed a third or fourth screen test, I can't remember which. He was tentative about what he had to tell me. "I've just had a meeting with the camerman," he began, "and he says the same as all the rest. It's, ah, about your nose."

"What about my nose?" I knew what was coming.

"Well, ah, if you are to have a career in films, then, you see, you should perhaps consider a little bit of modification."

"You mean get my nose fixed?"

"Yes, and another thing: perhaps you could lose a bit around your hips. You see, I am just suggesting this from what all the cameramen say."

I realized, of course, that I looked different from established movie actresses. They were all beautiful with perfect features and I was not. My face is full of irregularities, but put all together they somehow work. If I had had a bump on the bridge of my nose, I wouldn't have hesitated to get it fixed. But that my nose was too long, no, because I knew that the face is commanded by the nose, that it gives the face its character, and I liked my nose and my face just the way they were. It's true, I told Carlo, that my face doesn't resemble anyone else's, but why should I look like everybody else?

"I understand," Carlo said, "I too would like to keep your face as it is, but the cameramen—"

"I want to keep myself just as I am. I won't change anything."

"Well, we'll see," Carlo said, sorry he had brought up the subject.

"And about my hips," I said, "I do have rather robust hips, but that's part of who I am. I want to keep myself just as I am."

It seems rather remarkable to me now, looking back on it, that I was so boldly confident about myself. But I guess you could say that I was blessed with a sense of my own destiny. I have never sold myself short. I have never judged myself by other people's standards. I have always expected a great deal of myself, and if I fail, I fail myself. At sixteen I already knew certain self-truths: I was a survivor; I relied on myself and no one else; I would get to wherever I was destined to go and it was futile to try to alter my fate.

Carlo never again mentioned my nose or my hips.

After my sister recovered her health, my mother brought her to Rome and we all three lived together in a cramped furnished room. Very difficult living conditions, but I was happy to be liberated from my cousins and reunited with my family. From morning till night my mother and I were out looking for work, but without much reward. Without my mother, I don't think I would have had the drive. But my mother was a fury of ambition. It was, in effect, her career and she was determined to make amends for all that had been denied her when she was my age. But despite her perpetual efforts, all I got was a few bit appearances in low-budget Italian movies bearing such titles as *Bluebeard's Six Wives*, *Hearts upon the Sea*, *It's Him, Yes! Yes!*, *The White Slave Trade*, and *The Dream of Zorro*.

But these bits and pieces of movie appearances, banal though they were, kept us going. The popularity of the *fumetti* was waning, and aside from an occasional modeling job, there was no other work to be had. We were having a hard time in our tiny furnished room. My sister refused to go to school because she did not have a legitimate name to put on her certificate, and technically, the rules being what they were then, she could not take exams. So she simply stayed in our room all day while my mother and I were out.

Early one morning during this bleak period, we were awakened by the police, who requested that we accompany them to police headquarters. We were taken to the office of a police official who started to interrogate us. What kind of work did we do? Where did we get our money? How much did we earn?

"We have a formal complaint," the official said, "filed by a Signor Riccardo Scicolone, questioning the legality of your status."

My mother was aghast. I looked at my sister. Her face showed the pain of this stab to her heart. I simply couldn't believe what I was hearing.

"If you cannot prove satisfactorily to us that you are making your living by legitimate means, then we must give you papers and send you back in police custody to Pozzuoli."

Of course, I was able to prove how I earned my money, and, after much anxiety, the charges were dropped; but the humiliation was terrible. I have never in my life felt so degraded as I did that day. I was sixteen, my sister was eleven. Just imagine the life that our own father had tried to inflict upon us.

My only other brush with the law was caused by a photograph which appeared on the cover of a magazine. It had been taken near the sea, and it showed me wrapped in a big beach towel with one bare leg pointed forward. The pose gave the impression that I was naked underneath the towel, but of course that was a matter for the imagination. It was a sensual picture, but in a healthy, outdoor way. Nevertheless, it was considered risqué by the guardian of Rome's public morals, and all copies of the magazine were confiscated and the publisher was hauled into court. I was fined a few lire for not appearing, as required, as a witness for the defense.

Much more revealing than that photo was a scene I played in one of my bit pictures, *It's Him, Yes! Yes!* In those days scenes were often shot specifically for the French version of a picture being made. During the shooting of the scene in which I appeared with several girls like myself in harem costume, the director asked that we do one take topless for the French version. The other girls obliged him, and after a moment's hesitation, I did too. It was a quick take, and that was that, but I learned something about myself from that incident. I don't feel seductive or sexy when I expose myself to the camera. I feel awkward and childish. I think exposure is a debasement of the acting process because it removes the element of mystery. Clothes are much more seductive than the naked body. That is not to say that I am opposed to eroticism, which can be beautiful and effective when it is natural and free of vulgarity.

Sex for me is an exalted act. It is private and mysterious and precious, and I have never denigrated its role in my life. Back when I was struggling for parts and recognition, it would have been unthinkable for me to go to bed with someone in order to further my career. Many girls did, thinking they could get parts that way, but I never believed in that. I believed only in myself.

CHAPTER 8

In 1952, when I was eighteen, I finally got my first good part in a film, but I lost my name and almost lost my life in the process. My mother had heard about a low-budget film, *Africa Under the Seas*, that had a role for a young lady who was required to do most of her acting underwater in the seas around Rome.

"But, Mammina," I protested, "you know I can't swim a stroke."

"You'll learn. Just get the part and then we'll worry."

Even though Pozzuoli was on the sea, it was common for Neapolitans not to know how to swim. However, when the producer asked me if I could swim, my answer would have made my mother proud. "Like a champion," I said.

"All right," the producer said, "you've got the part, but I don't like your name. Sofia Lazzaro is like too many other names, and besides, it connects you with those dreadful *fumetti*. We've got to change it." He had just finished a picture with the Swedish actress Marta Toren, and there was a large poster on the wall with her picture and her name on it. His face lit up. "That's it, Toren!" and he started down the alphabet—Boren, Coren, Doren—until he got to Loren, which struck him just right. Sofia Loren. "No," he said, "I don't like the spelling of Sofia. Outside of Italy they will think it's a misspelling of Sophia, so we'll change it to Sophia. All right with you?"

I readily agreed, but in Italian, *ph* is not pronounced *f* but *p*, so for a long time the people I knew in Pozzuoli wondered why I wanted to be called Sopia.

Bravado in an office on the Via Veneto is one thing, but quite another on the bow of a rocking ship on the Tyrrhenian Sea. The director explained the first scene to me. I was to jump from the ship into the water. It was a sizable vessel, and as I leaned over the side to have a look, I panicked.

"I don't know how to swim," I blurted out, drawing back. "Send me back—please, send me back to Rome."

"Now don't you worry," said the director. "We have a man in the water who's an expert swimmer, and the minute you go under he'll be there to fish you out. When the cameras turn and I say jump, just jump. All right, everybody—places, we're ready to roll!"

The director was obviously a student of psychology, for he knew that if I had had two minutes to straighten out my sanity I would never have jumped. But there's a little animal in me that occasionally goads me to take risks, and this time he gave me a shove. I hit the water a few feet away from the churning propellers. Down under I went, my ears popping, but as promised, strong hands immediately grabbed me and guided me up to the surface. I took a deep breath. On the deck high above me, the crew was applauding. The man holding me in the water was angry. "Are you crazy? They made you jump where the propellers were. You almost got chewed up."

This was the man who taught me to swim. He gave me lessons every spare moment we had. By the time the movie was over I was quite a good swimmer, and I thanked my inner animal who had given me the shove.

I've heard it said that it was Gina Lollobrigida who, in 1953, without knowing it, presented me with my first starring role. An Italian film company had mounted a lavish version of Verdi's opera *Aida* and wanted Lollobrigida as the star. The part was to be sung by the great diva Renata Tebaldi, with Lollobrigida mouthing the lyrics, but at the last moment, I'm told, Gina reneged because she felt that serving as a stand-in for a singer was beneath her star status. Since the production was ready to roll, the studio desperately needed a last-minute replacement, and that's how I got the part.

The first thing I did was to get a recording of Tebaldi singing *Aida*; I listened to it for countless hours of countless days, becoming so familiar with the lyrics and with Tebaldi's phrasing and delivery that her voice, and my miming of it, blended perfectly. By the time we went into production, Tebaldi and I sang as one person.

The movie was shot in an unheated studio in the middle of winter. Every time I opened my mouth to sing, puffs of steam would fill the air. To correct this, I chewed ice before each take, frosting my mouth, and an assistant stood just out of camera range with a powerful hair dryer which he aimed at my lips. In my scanty costumes, I was often blue with cold underneath my dark makeup, but the result was good and I received the kind of notices and publicity for my portrayal of *Aida* that I had secretly hoped for (but had prepared myself not to expect). The movie was widely distributed, and for the first time I was seen in England and the United States.

The salary I received for *Aida* was the first substantial amount of money we had ever seen. There were so many uses to put it to but I felt that the most pressing need was to rescue my sister, Maria, from her withdrawal of shame. There was only one thing that would send her back to school, and that was her father's name.

No words could move my father, because as a result of having given me his name, it had cost him money, and he was not going to repeat that mistake. My father had steadfastly refused to give my mother anything for my support, so at some point she had gone into court and succeeded in getting a decree requiring him to pay me a monthly stipend. I still have in my possession a receipt which I gave him:

> *Rome, 3 October, 1950*
> This note is a receipt for the amount of six thousand lire (6000), which my father gives me for: three thousand lire as legal allowance for the past month of September 1950, and three thousand lire legal monthly allowance for the current month of October 1950.
> *Sofia Scicolone*

In those days, three thousand lire amounted to $4.60, which was hardly a financial burden, but nevertheless my father resented paying it to me, and was determined not to fall into the same trap with my sister.

But when my mother spoke to him after I had made *Aida*, he had a proposition: he would sell his name to Maria for the one million lire which he had found out I had been paid for *Aida*. My mother was furious. "He blackmails his own daughter for money! He is an animal! An absolute animal! "

I didn't hesitate. As far as I was concerned, Maria must have her name, whatever the price. I gave my mother the one million lire (about $1500 in those days), and she arranged to meet my father at a notary where he signed the necessary papers in exchange for the money.

When my mother came back to our room we did not mention my father but only felt happy that my sister, who joyfully clutched the notarized papers to her bosom, had been given what in those days was generally regarded as her dignity.

After *Aida* was released, Carlo Ponti suggested that I sign a personal contract with him. That meant that my contract would be with him individually, and not with the Ponti–de Laurentiis Company. My mother didn't like the idea. "You should not be tied down to a contract. You are just starting your career."

"That may be true, Mammina," I said, "but why don't I sign a contract for just one year and see what happens?" So I signed with Carlo, but my mother was right. Time passed and all the good parts went to established "names." Whenever I discussed this with Carlo, at my mother's insistence, he urged patience. "Wait five minutes," he always said.

During this period I worked constantly in a series of quickly made, forgettable pictures, ten films within those twelve months. My spirits were lifted momentarily by the prospect of an interview with the great film director Michelangelo Antonioni, but our meeting wasn't fruitful. I also had a meeting with Vittorio de Sica, who was charming and complimented me for *Aida* and said he was sure that someday we would work together; but he did not bring up any of the projects he was then working on.

I went from one inconsequential film to another, but it was a period of important learning for me. I was busy working in films, I was learning, I was earning enough money for us to live in a decent apartment and eat well. I was the head of the family, the husband, going out to work every day, my mother was the wife, and my sister, now back in school, was the child.

Carlo and I began to see each other in a quiet, rather secret way. I was very much attracted to him—his open smile, the quality of his eyes, his diffident but forceful manner, and I trusted him right away—but it is difficult to explain the nature of our relationship then. At eighteen, I still had the mentality of a Pozzuoli girl; none of the sophistication of Rome had rubbed off on me and my behavior was still influenced by the primitive mores of Pozzuoli. Respect for the family was deeply imbedded in me, and for a Pozzuoli girl, an affair with a married man was unthinkable. And, of course, my mother's early transgressions in Rome were a severe deterrent to any premarital involvement with a man. This does not mean that I did not "pet" with Carlo, but there is a vast difference between petting and real sex involvement.

Carlo was aware of all this, of my fears and reticence, aware that I wasn't just another accessible starlet (how I despise that word!) and he never tried to go very far with me. From what I gathered, Carlo had always had little affairs with actresses, and his wife didn't seem to mind as long as he didn't see the same girl very often and there was no threat of a serious relationship. That's why we saw each other secretly, so that his wife wouldn't become aware of me.

But when we did see each other, it was as if I were Carlo's fiancée in the Pozzuoli manner. I had family taboos and religious taboos to overcome before I could have an affair with Carlo. Eventually it was to happen, but not then, not until I felt the strength of his love and my deep need for him as my father figure. In the meantime, this was our period of courtship, very private, explorative, growing steadily in intensity.

To my surprise, Vittorio de Sica had not forgotten me. He phoned to say he had a project that he would like to talk about: *Gold of Naples,* an episodic film based on a novel by the Neapolitan author Marotta, that de Sica would direct. The real surprise for me was that this was a Ponti-de Laurentiis film that Carlo had not even mentioned.

I had a very enjoyable interview with de Sica but we didn't discuss the film nor did he offer me a screen test, so when I left I knew there was nothing doing. De Sica was one of the glamour names of Italian moviemaking, a man I greatly admired, and this would obviously be the kind of quality film that had proved so elusive for me. What's more, it was a part made to order for me: an explosive, earthy Neapolitan woman, a type I knew so well; she was even called Sofia.

One week after our interview, de Sica called and said, "Can you leave for Naples tomorrow?" What had happened in the intervening week was this: de Sica had gone to de Laurentiis and Ponti and told them that he wanted me for the part. He said that I had a quality of spontaneity, an outgoing impulsiveness, typically Neapolitan, that he wanted to capture in this part. He said that since he and I were both Neapolitan, and quite alike in temperament, he knew he would be able to work with me very well. De Laurentiis wanted de Sica to make a screen test, but de Sica refused. Neapolitans go by instinct, they *live* by instinct, he told de Laurentiis, and he said that his instincts about Sophia Loren were better than any screen test.

De Laurentiis still objected. He wanted a bigger name. But de Sica was very blunt. What was needed was a wildcat with fire inside and Loren was it.

Through all of this, Carlo wisely said nothing. Finally, de Laurentiis gave in, but grudgingly. "You have always had good judgment, Vittorio, and I hope that you're right."

That first day in Naples, I came on the set congealed with apprehension, but by the end of the day de Sica had freed me of all my apprehensions and we were two free Neapolitan spirits, improvising, communicating, and enjoying ourselves. "You have juices running in you," he told me, "that have the force to carry you anywhere you want to go. Stay away from acting schools. You will teach yourself." By the time our episode was over, de Sica had become a force in my life. I liked him, I loved him, I admired him, and our "love affair" was to last for twenty years. We were destined to make fourteen films together, and our method remained the same as it was in that first film: de Sica standing behind the camera, directly in my line of vision, showing me with his expression, his gestures, his whole being, what he wanted me to do; we rarely talked; words were superfluous. He was a superb actor and he understood my shallows and my depths, but also he understood how to make me go beyond myself, beyond where I thought I could go, or dared go, into dramatic or comedic waters where the risk of overplaying is great and the percentage for succeeding is small. C above high C. That was de Sica's great gift to me, his profoundest talent.

In *Gold of Naples,* he helped me create an explosive, sexy, blowsy Neapolitan pizza girl who sprang from a part of me I never knew existed. I trusted him completely and that is the key to what I require to function well, whether in movies or in daily life. Trust. I must. If I don't, I become insecure and I withdraw and revert to my shy self.

De Sica

In making this film with Sophia, I discovered some basic truths about her personality. She had built a thick protective wall around herself and was reasonably content there. But her true nature was dramatic and temperamental, typically Neapolitan, and her reactions—joy, sorrow, anger, impatience, whatever—were excessive. So she kept them well contained behind that wall. But when she acted, she could leap over that wall and free her true inner feelings. She could scream, laugh, have hysterics, seduce, remonstrate, and reach the most emotional heights. Acting in an emotional movie scene does for her what lying down on the couch at the psychiatrist's does for other people.

The most memorable scene in *Gold of Naples* was pure de Sica. A slow, long walk through the streets of Naples in a teeming rain, my soaked dress clinging to my body while the eyes of the men whom I passed followed me in carnal wonderment and approval. I caught pneumonia from the deluges of the rain machines and had to stay in bed for a month, but it was well worth it. I had found myself as an actress. The dream of that skinny girl, sitting in the dark in the Pozzuoli movie house, had finally come true.

CHAPTER 9

After my success in *Gold of Naples,* Carlo, for the first time, took me seriously. The "five-minute wait" was up. He created a picture especially for me, a film called *Woman of the River*, which was directed by Mario Soldati, one of the best directors in Italy. The story was co-authored by Alberto Moravia and no fewer than six screenwriters worked on the script; one of them was Basilio Franchina, who would become one of my dearest lifelong friends.

This was Carlo's personal picture, not a co-production with de Laurentiis, and that fact, plus the fact that the script called for an enormous range of emotions, culminating in a melodramatic scene when I find my baby drowned in the river, put enormous pressure on me.

I previously mentioned that I had caught pneumonia from the rain machines in *Gold of Naples*. By the time *Woman of the River* started I was entirely over the pneumonia, but on the first day of shooting I developed a condition which I thought indicated a relapse. At night, I had trouble breathing. My breath came in strident wheezes, thirty violins sawing away, and I couldn't sleep. In fact, I couldn't lie down because it worsened my condition. My doctor said I was suffering from asthma. He was baffled as to its cause or how to treat it, but pooh-poohed the suggestion that it was psychological. In the mornings, however, the minute I set foot on the set and got busy, the asthma disappeared.

During this time, Basilio Franchina, who was also the producer, became aware of my insecurity about the script's demands and my battle with the nocturnal violins, and he started to work with me on the script. Basilio had an empathy, a warmth, a sweet sense of humor, and a plain honesty that endeared him to me. I have a rather infallible instinct for choosing the right people to help me in my life, and who, in turn, I can help and trust. There have not been many of them, sad to say, but surely Basilio is one of them.

Some nights Carlo would sit up with me all night to keep me company while I battled for each breath. We had grown very close, Carlo and I—we were father-daughter, man-woman, producer-actress, friends and conspirators.

So intensely had I prepared myself for the big river scene that, complicated though it was, I did it in one take, with an exhilarated feeling of great accomplishment. And two important things happened on the last day of shooting. The first was that my asthma completely disappeared, and it has never recurred.

The second thing that happened was that Carlo came on the set, and taking me aside, handed me a small box. In it was a ring with a small diamond. We had never spoken a word about where our relationship was heading and now, still without a word, Carlo had told me. I went off by myself and wept with joy. He was the only man who had entered my life and now I felt I could give myself to him completely. Of course, he was still living with his wife and children but my feelings were too strong now to be deterred by Pozzuoli's morals or anyone else's. I needed love.

It is not easy to tell if you are successful in a particular movie. Film performance is not the same as the theater, where the audience's immediate reaction and the next day's reviews give you a verdict. When the shooting is over, the actress has no way of knowing how it will all turn out. Months later, the finished product will be released at different times in different parts of the world, and even then it takes considerable time before a verdict is rendered—primarily in box office receipts.

So, especially as a beginner, all you have as a measure of how you are doing is the fact that you are or are not hired for other pictures, and if you are, for how much increase in salary. Using those criteria, I was tasting success. I could not keep up with the demand for my services, and I went from one movie to another, finishing on a Friday and starting a new one the following Monday, as if I were starving and needed the employment to eat. Security was work. Security was money. Security was a big, sunny apartment with a balcony, a luxury car, and other such trappings. I was far away from this level of affluence but I had made a start. When the time would come that I acquired these trappings, I would eventually discover that they were meaningless and divest myself of most of them. Success, I would find out, is interior. It has to do with self-fulfillment and the joy of living. But at nineteen, I was a light-year from such wisdom. I was a conformist.

In the flurry of pictures I made in 1955, the year after *Woman of the River*, there was one called *Too Bad She's Bad*, which was directed by the very talented Alessandro Blasetti, and which brought me together for the first time with the two men who would figure so importantly in my life—de Sica, this time as an actor, and Marcello Mastroianni, who at that time was not a very well-known screen actor.

The rapport among de Sica, Marcello, and me was immediate. We all three came from the Naples area—Mastroianni was born in a little town a few miles from de Sica's birthplace—and we shared a conspiratorial bond reserved for Neapolitans. We shared a sense of humor, a rhythm, a philosophy of living, a cynicism that lurked behind our lines of dialogue and interplay. We played scenes with a kind of flair and fire that I had never experienced before. Freer. Nearer to life—in fact, magnifying life to the point of making a comment about it. De Sica created a style which Marcello and I picked up, and we three performed together with a subtlety and verve that set the tone for the many films we were to make together.

I showed Mammina the ring Carlo had given me, holding my hand up in the sunlight, expressing my happiness, but knowing that she would not approve. She didn't.

"He's a married man with two children, he's twenty years older than you, and you will have nothing but heartache. You want heartache? That's what you'll get. You are a baby."

"I am in love with him, Mammina. He is so intelligent and cares so much about me. He's a doctor of law—did you know that?"

"Never mind law—it's a doctor of babies you will need. Don't you think I know what I'm talking about? Now is the time—before it starts—before it gets serious."

"Well, it *has* started and it *is* serious, but don't worry, I can take care of myself."

"Has he told his wife—is he leaving her?"

"No."

"You are a fool. Mark my words—*he never will*. Wait around for him and you will wind up an old maid lighting candles."

"No, Mammina, I don't think so. I love him, but I love myself, too."

Carlo was very concentrated on my career now and his eyes were on the future. He said that I had to learn English if he was to get me parts in international films, and eventually a deal with Hollywood. He also gave me a list of books to read—just left the list with me because it was not Carlo's style to demand, only to suggest.

I do not recall how Sarah Spain came into my life, but she was a linguistic angel with a soft Irish face who by prodding, wheedling, and bullying taught me to speak English. Total immersion, and she taught me not as a parrot, but with an emphasis on grammar and comprehension. Happily, I discovered that I had a good ear and an aptitude for language. But while I was still trying to make phrases like "Please pass the butter" and "November is a month for overcoats" sound more like English than like broken Italian, Carlo informed me that I was to co-star in a huge period film, *The Pride and the Passion,* that was about to start shooting in Spain. When I heard the names of my co-stars I almost passed out—Cary Grant and Frank Sinatra.

I, little Sofia Scicolone, was to play opposite two of those romantic figures of my Pozzuoli dreams, in an English-speaking, multi-million-dollar spectacle film!—but (alas, reality!) at the same time, here was Sarah Spain berating me, scolding me, warning me that my English couldn't even be understood by sympathetic Italians on Mulberry Street.

It was a bursting time for me. I was simultaneously learning English, learning to read literature, learning the intricacies and refinements of being a good movie actress, and learning how to relate to a man.

What I didn't know at the time was that Carlo and Stanley Kramer, the producer and director, were faced with large obstacles to overcome before I could join the cast. First of all, the producing company, United Artists, wanted a star name for the part, not me, and secondly, Cary Grant, who had contractual cast approval, also was not in favor of playing opposite an unknown Italian girl who was still wet behind the ears. United Artists made an attempt to get Ava Gardner but she was committed to another film. So were the other stars whom they sought. But Kramer had seen *Woman of the River* and he kept the pressure on United Artists to let him have his way. Finally, they gave in.

Stanley Kramer gave an elaborate cocktail party to commemorate the start of the film, and that's where Cary and I first met. I can't recall ever being as nervous. The very thought of having to face the judgment of Cary Grant—*Cary Grant,* for God's sake!—who had performed with most of the world's most glamorous screen actresses—well, the thought itself was paralyzing.

Cary Grant arrived late, and Sinatra even later. When Cary and I were introduced by Stanley Kramer, Cary joked around with my name. "How do you do, Miss Lolloloren, or is it Lorenigida? Ah, you Italian actresses, I can never get your names straight." He exuded charm, and he was even more handsome and debonair than he appeared on the screen. I immediately felt at ease with him and after a few minutes of lively banter, I could tell from the look in his eyes that I had passed muster.

While we were talking, Sinatra arrived and Kramer brought him over. Standing there with Cary Grant on one side of me and Frank Sinatra on the other, I said to myself, it's not possible that this is happening. Again, as always, I was looking at myself from the outside, my nose pressed against the glass.

The Pride and the Passion was a long and arduous movie, plagued with problems and delays. We were in remote parts of Spain for a good six months, during which time I got to know Cary and Frank quite well. Especially Cary. We liked each other from the very first, and in that remote setting we were constantly in each other's company. And such wonderful company Cary was! I was fascinated with him, with his warmth, affection, intelligence, and his wonderfully dry, mischievous sense of humor. I had never met a man remotely like Cary before, and for him, I was a Neapolitan first.

In the beginning he was very reserved with me, and if our talk turned to something sad or introspective he would try to make a joke out of it, to keep it from touching him. But more and more he confided in me and trusted me. There were patches of self-doubt in him which he disclosed—with reluctance, but needfully. He was deeply disturbed over the fact that he had never had a really sustained relationship in his life. He talked about his early life in London, his struggles, and the three women he had been married to, but when he got too close to his center, he would put up the mask he hid behind and turn to joking.

As I got to know him, I began to realize that he had an inner conflict of wanting to be open and honest and direct, and yet not make himself vulnerable. Of course, one cannot have it both ways. And slowly, as our relationship grew and his trust in me grew, he came to realize that trust and vulnerability went hand in hand; when his trust was strong enough, he no longer bothered with his mask. And I was just as open and trusting with him. He told me about his early life, and I told him about mine, and we found a bond in their emotional similarites. We saw each other every night; we dined in romantic little restaurants on craggy hilltops to the accompaniment of flamenco guitars, drank the good Spanish wine and laughed and were serious and confessional and conspiratorial.

And we fell in love.

But I was also in love with Carlo. How could it be possible? Well, it was, and I was very confused. Carlo was an enigma. He was still as solidly entrenched in his marriage and there was no sign that he intended to give up his wife and children for me. I empathized with Carlo, but my sympathy was intellectual, not visceral. In my heart, I wanted him to discard everything for me. I did not want to be an undeclared mistress, or any kind of mistress, no matter how much he meant to me.

And now here was Cary Grant, ready to renounce everything for me. Wanting me with no strings attached.

Although Cary was my main concern, I managed to find time to work on the movie. Mercifully, I did not have a great deal of dialogue in the picture.

Frank and I got along fine. That we were both Italian was a factor, I guess, but Frank doesn't speak Italian (or pretends not to) outside of a

Sofia Scicolone at her first communion, long before she became the famous film star, Sophia Loren. Life was hard for this illegitimate child in the small Neapolitan village of Pozzuoli, but she loved living with her Grandmother and Grandfather Villiani.

She was taught piano and steered into films by her mother, a frustrated actress. After being crowned a Princess of the Sea in a Naples beauty contest, Sophia was taken to Rome by her mother to be a movie extra, as at the right. She first appeared as a slave girl in the epic Quo Vadis *(1950).*

At eighteen, Sophia landed a starring role in a low-budget Italian film, Africa Under the Seas. The role required her to swim like a champion—and she could not swim a stroke! In the first scene, Sophia jumped blindly from a boat into the water, nearly colliding with the churning propellers. An expert swimmer hired by the director pulled her to the surface. "By the time the movie was over," she writes, "I was quite a good swimmer." Five years after her first sea epic, Sophia was all wet again—as Alan Ladd's co-star in Boy on a Dolphin. Although she described the film as a "disenchantment," this movie still of the dripping, clinging actress brought her loads of publicity and offers of Hollywood starring roles.

In Rome she met film producer Carlo Ponti, who
encouraged her despite the fact she failed her screen tests.
The cameramen said her nose was too long and her hips
too big, but Sophia flatly refused to have her nose fixed. She
played bit parts in low-budget Italian movies and made
cheesecake publicity photos, such as the swirling one at left.
Below, Sophia as a newcomer in Hollywood—jewelless
—with Yvonne di Carlo and Gina Lollobrigida.
Although this was the only time that Gina and Sophia
met, the press created a "breast war" between the two
Italian beauties.

"She's the mostest," Frank Sinatra, above, said of Sophia while they filmed The Pride and the Passion in Spain in 1956. Later, she nearly died of asphyxiation while making Legend of the Lost in the Sahara with John Wayne.

*Sophia married Cary Grant in
Houseboat (1958)—and she might
have married him in real life were it
not for Carlo Ponti. She adored
Cary's marvelous charm and
spontaneity from the moment they
met when filming* The Pride and
the Passion *in Spain. He proposed
to her there and then pursued her
ardently in Hollywood. In the end,
though, she chose Carlo.*

Although Sophia opposed her sister Maria's marriage to Romano Mussolini, son of the late Italian dictator, she adored Mussolini's widow, above with Maria, Sophia, and their mother. Maria's marriage to Romano produced two children but did not last. Sophia writes that Romano, like most Italian men, was "a married bachelor."

Opposite, Sophia played a princess with regal splendor in A Breath of Scandal.

Sophia's favorite leading man is Marcello Mastroianni, with whom she has appeared in eleven films. Above, she played his mistress in Marriage, Italian Style. At left, she performed a striptease for him in Yesterday, Today and Tomorrow. Perhaps her least favorite co-star is Marlon Brando, below, whom she found hard to take while filming A Countess from Hong Kong.

Sophia and Carlo have found it impossible to live as man and wife in Italy because the Roman Catholic Church has not recognized his Mexican divorce from his first wife or their proxy marriage in Mexico. They live in Paris but hope someday to return to their beloved villa near Rome, shown opposite. She has found it difficult to bear children, and years ago suffered two miscarriages. But by staying in bed for nine months and undergoing extensive medical care during two later pregnancies, she succeeded in giving birth to two sons, Carlo, Jr. and Edoardo.

"When I am an old woman of eighty (as I portray her here in Lady L), I see myself surrounded by my two sons, daughters-in-law and grandchildren, my sister and her husband and children, but best of all, my husband, stealing the show from me because he will have turned one hundred just a few months before."

few words like *pasta e fagiole*. On days when he was in a good mood, Frank told engaging stories about his early life, his mother's involvement in politics, his father's exploits.

One day our location was visited by an American reporter who was doing a story about the film. He asked Frank how he would define the new girl who was on the picture. "Sohpia?" Frank said. "She's the mostest." One of the nicest compliments I ever got.

During those perfect days in Spain, Cary and I shared much. He taught me many things quite wise, he opened my mind in many ways, and I learned a great deal just by observing his attitude toward life. And in some ways he learned from me. Aside from him, only Carlo has had this effect on me, no other man, before or since.

One day, while we were having lunch, a waiter approached Cary, who was deep in conversation with me, and timorously asked for his autograph. "Don't bother me," Cary said, and waved him away. The poor man recoiled and hurriedly withdrew.

I said, "Don't do that, Cary. Look how upset he is."

Cary looked at the man and called him back and apologetically gave him an autograph. "How nice you are," Cary said to me after the waiter had gone. "You really care about that man, don't you? I didn't mean to offend him, I just wanted my privacy with you . . . "

"But your autograph meant a great deal to that waiter," I said.

My reaction was a revelation to Cary. I do not know whether his reformation stuck, but from then on, when he was with me, he gave autographs. He used to kid around about it, but he had learned something from me, young as I was, about simple humanity.

Late that night we dined alone in a little restaurant on a hilltop outside Avila. Cary talked about getting married. With every passing day, he said, he was more sure that we belonged together, that finally he had found in me someone to whom he could totally relate. Finally, someone to whom he could commit himself and to hell with being vulnerable. I trust you and love you and want to marry you, he said.

I never doubted for a second that Cary loved me as much as I could hope to be loved by a man. What he had said to me struck me like a jolt and took my breath away; I couldn't answer him. How could I explain to him the conflict between his image and Carlo's image? I told him that I didn't dare give an answer yet, that I still needed time and I needed to go back to my own environment and to be able to make up my mind away from the magic of those Spanish nights.

Besides, I was committed to a film, *Boy on a Dolphin,* in Greece and Cary was due to start work on a picture in Los Angeles.

The windup on *The Pride and the Passion* was hectic. The last night, Cary and I had dinner together. This was our last time together. We had been joking and laughing, but over coffee the talk turned serious. "Sophia," Cary asked, "what is going to happen to us?"

"I don't know, Cary. I really don't. And I wish I weren't so mixed up and confused. I don't know what's going to happen."

Cary's face brightened with a mock idea. "Why don't we just get married and discuss all this afterwards?"

I was so grateful to him for having released the tension and for having made a joke out of the serious turmoil of our souls.

CHAPTER 10

After the enchantment of Cary Grant and what turned out to be the disenchantment of Alan Ladd and *Boy on a Dolphin,* I didn't know what to expect of John Wayne. My destination now was the oasis village of Ghadames, located in the Sahara near Timbuktu, where Tunis and Libya conjoin. Remote, primitive, completely isolated, scorching days, freezing nights. The picture: *Legend of the Lost.*

I was relieved to find that John Wayne was exactly as advertised. Big, authoritative, gruff but polite, and a pro through and through. He showed up right on the minute, knew all his lines and moves, worked hard all day long without letup, and quit right on the minute. There was no doubt that he was in command, the captain on the bridge of the ship. But he never abused his powerful position. With me, he was polite and pleasant, but distant.

Physically, it was one of the most difficult pictures I ever made, and in the course of it I almost died. The only living accommodation in Ghadames was a flimsy, primitive, unheated motel. At night the cold was intolerable, and the only heat I had in my room was a gas space heater installed by the crew. On the night about which I am telling you, I began to have ghastly nightmares, unlike anything I had ever experienced in my sleep before. I would half wake from a nightmare, try to rouse myself but then lapse into sleep again, only to have another horrible nightmare. I fought desperately to wake up. I was also aware that I was gasping desperately for air, as if I were having a suffocation dream.

Then, suddenly, a violent thump, and a sharp pain in my shoulder as my body fell from the bed and hit the tiled floor. I was awake, but still gasping, as in the nightmare. I tried to get up but I couldn't. All my strength was gone and my head was fogged with panic. The space heater had exhausted all the oxygen in the room and there was nothing for me to breathe but deadly fumes of carbon monoxide. I was asphyxiating.

I began to inch myself along the floor toward the door, constantly passing out and reviving. I knew I was dying, strangling from lack of air, but instead of succumbing, from deep inside me there arose a pocket of strength. The enormous determination to live—my God, what it can achieve! Slowly, slowly, slowly, little by little, I forced myself up until I could reach the knob and open the door. I pitched forward and fell into the corridor, unconscious. Luckily, Rossano Brazzi, coming in late, found me and frantically called the doctor. Mouth-to-mouth resuscitation, injections, frantic first aid. I had severe headaches for a week. The doctor said I had been just seconds away from death.

Rossano Brazzi was the personification of the bigger-than-life Latin lover. Perfectly coiffed, impeccably dressed, he was a welcome relief, always performing, prancing about, giving seductive looks in every direction, and *always* singing "Some Enchanted Evening"—he had just completed the film version of *South Pacific*. He was a splendid partner to work with.

By the time I had finished *Legend of the Lost,* I had made three American films in succession, in which I played a Spanish camp follower, a Greek peasant, and an Arab street girl. None of the parts or movies was memorable, but Carlo had adroitly used them as stepping-stones toward his coveted goal, a Hollywood contract. It worked. Columbia Pictures made a deal with him for four films. The year, 1957—I was twenty-two years old.

Almost three years had passed since that euphoric moment (it was my birthday) during the shooting of *Woman of the River,* when Carlo came to our location and presented me with that diamond ring. Until then, we had only seen each other secretly, but during the location shooting of *Woman of the River* Carlo stayed with me at my hotel. I didn't care. I loved him and wanted him.

My mother continued to lecture me about Carlo. She didn't like him. "Italian men do not leave their children," she warned. "They will play around but they will always go back to their children." The fact that Carlo had two young children did upset me. And that he was married

433

continued to bother me, but how can I explain that I had the feeling that Carlo was someone I had known all my life, that I had as much right to him as anyone else, and that he had been my father and my husband for a long time? The thing I found most attractive about Carlo was his gentleness. I have my own peculiar yardstick for measuring a man: does he have the courage to cry in a moment of grief? Does he have the compassion not to hunt an animal? In his relationship with a woman, is he gentle? Real manliness is nurtured in kindness and gentleness, which I associate with intelligence, comprehension, tolerance, justice, education, and high morality. If only men realized how easy it is to open a woman's heart with kindness, and how many women close their hearts to the assaults of the Don Juans.

I have another way to measure a man: with his bad qualities. Of these, I'd say that stinginess, arrogance, and cruelty are fatal.

From what Carlo told me about his relationship with his wife I knew that something vital had gone out of their marriage and that they had settled for a *modus vivendi*—living in the same house but not really as man and wife any more.

I had never met Carlo's wife—Giuliana Fiastri was her name, daughter of a general—but the dignity and maturity which she exhibited all through this long, trying period elicited my profound admiration. Having accepted the fact that her marriage was over, she tried to make the transition as easy on herself and her children and on Carlo as she possibly could.

But since Italy did not recognize divorce, even with his wife's cooperation there was little Carlo could do to dissolve the marriage. He did apply for an annulment on the grounds that when he married Giuliana he had not believed in the sacrament of marriage, but the action was flimsy and the annulment quickly denied. But no matter how much I needed Carlo in my life, how desperately I wanted to furnish a home with him and have children with him and mingle my life with his, I nonetheless was determined that I was not going to get strung out as his mistress.

This was the state of affairs when we flew to Beverly Hills, where Cary Grant eagerly awaited my arrival.

Hollywood. *La patria del cinema.* That long-ago shy dream come to reality. Triumphal entrance. Glittering reception. A posh suite at the Beverly Hills Hotel, a stack of invitations, publicity men by the dozens, limousine at the ready, couturiers dancing attendance, a cabana at poolside, the telephone operator saying, "Good morning, Miss Loren, what can I do for you, Miss Loren?" waved through at the studio gate, a queen-size dressing room newly decorated in royal colors—Hollywood.

Homage from the aristocracy—the stars, the unreal images on the screen of the Teatro Sacchino come to life, smiling, calling me by name, but it is not me, for I am sitting shyly and invisibly in the corner watching Sophia Loren in her moment of glory, letting the other Sophia bask in the starlight. A grand party in her honor at Romanoff's. And at Romanoff's, my first taste of Hollywood mores, in the person of Jayne Mansfield. As photographers surrounded my table, the precipitous arrival of Jayne Mansfield, whom I had never heard of, in a *very* low cut dress; she joined my table, and just by chance one of her ample breasts tumbled out of her dress as the photographers clicked away. Welcome to Hollywood.

Hollywood's bright promise, but the films not so bright. *Desire Under the Elms,* Eugene O'Neill's great searing drama, diminished and tepid because it was shot on an unrealistic sound stage instead of on location, and because as passionate lovers, Tony Perkins and I lack chemistry. *Black Orchid* with Tony Quinn, same problem. Paramount tried us again a year later in *Heller in Pink Tights,* but the chemistry between Tony and me was no better.

The movie I made with Cary Grant, *Houseboat,* was the only one of my Hollywood endeavors that came off well. But looking back on that Hollywood period—I have not made a movie there since then—I feel it was not Hollywood's fault that they didn't know what to do with me. American films at that time limited Italians to being gangsters and waiters. And they had never been able to accept a foreign actress for what she was. They felt they had to change her. That's what happened to me.

Carlo Ponti

As for leading men, Sophia's problem is that she comes across as a very strong personality on the screen and consequently she is not easily partnered. (*Time* magazine commented that she could have swallowed her Hollywood leading men with half a glass of water.) There are only a few men who can compete with Sophia on the screen, who can exert domination when it's needed. Cary was one of them, and Mastroianni, Richard Burton, Peter O'Toole, Brando, Clark Gable, and Gregory Peck. Not many, considering that she's done over sixty films.

"Who invented the heart? Just tell me and show me the spot where he has been hanged." Often my sentiment, because my doubts and conflicts over Cary and Carlo had come to a boil again in Hollywood. When I first arrived I had to do some pickup shots for *The Pride and the Passion* with Cary, and we saw each other quite often. His warmth and appeal were as strong as ever. Then after our work was finished, he called every day and sent flowers and it didn't matter to him or me that Carlo was staying with me. It must have mattered a great deal to Carlo, but he didn't discuss it. Nor did he discuss his marital impasse. He had separated from his wife. But after his halfhearted try for an annulment, I was not aware that Carlo had any further plans for our future together.

But that did not mean that Carlo was able to take me for granted. Certainly the situation with Cary, which Carlo was fully aware of, was exerting pressure on him. And so was I. I know a woman can become very boring when she's pressuring a man, but I had come to realize that if I did not reach a point of crisis with Carlo, nothing was ever going to happen. A married man wants to string along with the status quo—let's wait and see, have a little patience, dear—and if pressure isn't brought to bear on him nothing is ever going to happen. I instinctively knew that pressure mounting to a crisis was the only way to get a response, but knowing that, I also knew that such a move generated the risk that Carlo might jump back into his old marriage rather than into my arms.

That was a risk I was willing to take. If I lost out, then his feelings for me weren't as strong as I had thought they were. So I told him, "Carlo, I love you, I have committed myself to you, but this is no life for me. I want children and a house we can call our own and I'm tired of hearing my mother's lectures. I want to feel pride when I'm with you and feel a nice wedding band on my finger. I met you when I was sixteen. I have lived with you, off and on, since I was nineteen. I am now twenty-three. That is long enough. I am tired of being badgered by the press about you—of being coy with them and evasive. And sometimes dishonest. That's not for me; I hate having to do that and the time has come to put a stop to it. I know it's not easy. But your whole way of life is overcoming obstacles and you could overcome this one if you *really* wanted to."

Now Carlo had a sharp, unequivocal crisis.

And so did I. Now that I was living in Hollywood and experiencing the everyday life there, it was having an effect on my attitude toward Cary.

From the start of our film *Houseboat*, Cary sensed the change in me. We were not quite as easygoing with each other. Although we often had lunch together, and as always it was enjoyable, I suppose something had gone out of me, and Cary, who is very perceptive, sensed it.

My first impression of Hollywood was precisely as I had imagined it to be. Beautiful scenery, expensive cars of dazzling colors, and obligatory swimming pools rarely swum in. It was all brand new to me, a unique *ambiance,* a different kind of living. A very appealing life-style, I thought—at first. But then I began to discover something else about life in Hollywood: it only ran on one track, and that track was the motion picture. Any and everyone was obsessed with movies.

But my working experience in Hollywood was valuable. I learned about American movie technique and I was able to perfect my English. But I had also learned that in Hollywood I could not achieve for myself those goals as an actress which I aspired to. If my career was to move forward, I knew that I would have to return to Europe, where I was more at home, and eventually to Italian productions in my own language.

It was not a pleasant time for me. All I had established were my negatives: I would not go on indefinitely in that awkward situation with Carlo; I would not give up my European roots and make a permanent home in Hollywood. But what *would* I do?

Toward the end of *Houseboat* the situation was finally resolved by a totally unexpected event. Carlo and I were staying in a bungalow on the grounds of the Bel-Air Hotel. We were at breakfast. I picked up the newspaper, which had been brought with the breakfast, and there, the lead item in Louella Parsons' column, was the news that changed my life. On the previous day, Louella reported, two Mexican lawyers had appeared in a courtroom in Juárez, and within ten minutes had obtained a decree, officially divorcing Carlo from his wife, and, immediately afterward, with one lawyer standing in for me and the other for Carlo, they had exchanged marriage vows in a proxy ceremony performed by the judge. A marriage certificate had been issued. Sofia Scicolone of Pozzuoli was officially and finally married to Dr. Carlo Ponti of Milan.

I was stunned. It was scarcely the wedding I had dreamed of, but it was legal. Mr. and Mrs. Carlo Ponti, not a fabrication for a hotel register, but the truth. We were. We really were.

Carlo came over and took the newspaper from me. He was as surprised at the announcement as I was. Of course, he had initiated the proceedings (after I had created our "crisis") but he had not expected anything so swift and final. He sat down beside me and took my hands in his, and he looked in my eyes and smiled at me—like a husband.

I wanted to share my moment of happiness, shout with joy, but we had no friends and there was no one to call. The grandest, happiest moment of my life and no one to tell.

That evening, we celebrated alone. We had dinner in our bungalow, by candlelight, and later I discovered that my secretary had put rice in our bed.

When I came on the set the following day, one look told me that Cary had read Louella's column. "I hope you will be very happy, Sophia," he said. Bravely, he kissed my cheeks. That's all he ever said about it, but finishing the picture with him was trying and upsetting.

One important scene remained to be filmed. Ironically, it was the climax of the film—my marriage to Cary—and it was precisely the wedding I had always dreamed of.

Seeing myself in a long white gown, a radiant bride, was a vision that went back to the darkest days of my girlhood in Pozzuoli. I used to cut bride pictures out of old magazines and paste them in my scrapbook. And now I was having that dreamed-of wedding with Cary, only a few days after my marriage to Carlo. A long white gown of antique lace, high at the throat, trim buttoned bodice, a sheer veil held in place with a sprig of white flowers, a bouquet of white roses, Mendelssohn's wedding music, a flower girl and bridesmaids, and Cary Grant waiting at the altar with a white carnation in his buttonhole. It is at a moment like this that playacting and real life touch each other and mingle.

I was so concerned about Cary, and about my own wedding emotions, that I could scarcely keep my mind on the business of the film. I cared very much about Cary, as I do to this day, and I was aware of how painful it was for him to have the minister pronounce us man and wife, to take me in his arms and kiss me. It was painful for me, too, his make-believe bride. I could not help thinking of all those lovely times in Spain, of all the souvenirs I had in my memory. I am very romantic and vulnerable and I will cherish forever what Cary brought into my life.

CHAPTER 11

My marital bliss was short-lived. Scarcely a month after our marriage a thunderous pronouncement appeared in *L'Osservatore della Domenica,* the official paper of the Vatican. Although I was not mentioned by name, the article identified the person involved as "a young, beautiful, Italian film actress." It stated:

"Civil divorce and successive civil marriage are gravely illicit acts and have no judicial effect whatever before God and the Church. Those responsible are public sinners and may no longer receive the sacraments.

"The code of canon law regards as bigamists those who contract a new marriage—even if only a civil one—although they are bound by a valid marriage. It punishes both parties with the penalty of infamy (a stigma attaching, in canon law, to the character of a person). If they set up life in common, this is termed concubinage and may be punished even with interdict and excommunication."

Reading those words, my insides turned to ice. Even though I no longer went to mass or confession or communion, emotionally Catholicism was my heritage and excommunication was a chilling threat. Of course, from the Vatican point of view, the article was absolutely correct; what we had done was indeed contrary to the strict canons of the church. But many Italian Catholics had procured divorces in Mexico and had remarried and were living their new lives in Italy without the church's molestation. But Carlo and I were the celebrity scapegoats whom they decided to hold up as examples. I hurled the Vatican newspaper to the floor and wept bitter tears. Why persecute me for wanting to be married to the man I love, to have children with him, a home with him, a normal, fruitful life with him? Does that make me a public sinner? For that do I deserve to be subjected to the church's scorn? The more anger and hopelessness overcame me, the more I wept. That was the saddest day of my life.

Others quickly jumped on the Vatican doomwagon. The Italian Men's Catholic Action organization demanded that all Catholics avoid going to Sophia Loren movies—and asked that they pray for my soul. Newspapers all over Italy took up the hue and cry against us. A magazine ran an article that recalled, with some regret, that if Carlo and I had been living in the Middle Ages we would have been burned alive in the public square.

When Carlo returned to our Bel-Air bungalow and found me in tears, he reacted forcefully. This is Carlo's way; when strength is required, he is strong. "Now listen to me, Sophia," he said. "We are married, and we are going to stay married. If this Mexican marriage falls through, we'll find some other way. This is all just a dust storm that will blow over. It is the ones who are denouncing us who lack morals. We are the moral ones. Whatever has to be done, we will do. You are my wife and nobody will ever change that, and that's all there is to it."

Carlo's words were great comfort but the situation was destined to get far worse.

Carlo and I were on an airplane, leaving Hollywood. I don't recall just what triggered it, but suddenly Carlo turned in his seat and slapped me. It hurt. It was a powerful slap, full force, and my head was wrenched by it and I burst out crying. I was so humiliated and incensed. I wanted to get off the plane. Of course the slap had nothing to do with the moment. Maybe it was because of Cary Grant. Maybe all those unspoken gnawings of jealousy that Carlo had endured so long.

Carlo didn't say a word, he just turned away and looked out the window. I bent my head into my hands and wept.

It was the only time in our twenty-seven years together that Carlo ever struck me. Or lost his temper, really. But even now I can feel the pain and the humiliation. My cheek was sore for several days.

CHAPTER 12

My father had suddenly materialized in my life. My mother informed me that he had decided to leave his wife and children and come back to live with her, who I had established in a fine apartment in Rome. And he started to make suggestions for investments for me.

I made it clear to my mother that Carlo was handling all my business affairs, because I had trust in Carlo, but no trust in my father. I didn't want any more disillusionment, any more heartache because of my father. Of course, there was the possibility that he meant well, but the fact is that I don't care about money, I never have; what upsets me are the emotions that are involved when people are corrupted because of it.

After a combative three years with my mother, my father deserted her for a young, attractive German woman. I never heard anything more from him about investments.

But a few years later, he again came into my life, this time through a lawsuit. I had stated in an interview with a German magazine something to the effect that when I was a child I had not received so much as a pair of shoes from my father. For this, my father sued for libel. Even though the case was eventually dismissed by the court before coming to trial, it received considerable publicity which was painfully embarrassing for me. I suppose my father thought I would pay him some money to drop the suit. I don't know.

Criminal law in Italy allows any citizen, even anonymously, to charge any other citizen with a crime. Thus, when the public prosecutor received a letter from a Milanese woman whom I had never met nor heard of charging Carlo with the crime of bigamy and me with being a *concubina,* the prosecutor was obliged to proceed against us. The condemnation of the Catholic Church had now escalated itself into a crime.

Once the newspapers got hold of the story, Carlo and I were assailed from all sides. I was particularly upset by a letter, condemning me, sent by a group of Pozzuoli women. I was not aware that a single letter was received by the prosecutor which defended us.

At a preliminary hearing before a magistrate, none of these accusers showed up in the courtroom, but Italian law did not compel them to. The magistrate signed the prosecutor's warrants, which meant that if we set foot in Italy we were subject to arrest and jail. The basis for the bigamy charge was simple: the church had declared the Mexican divorce illegal. Our homeland had now shut its doors to us. We were exiles.

My reaction was a defiance of all of them. When I know deep down that I am doing something that is right, I do not brood about what is appearing in the papers or try to analyze why they are persecuting us or even try to justify myself. I am right and that's all there is to it. The courage of my conviction is what sustains me. I have no capacity for self-doubt.

During this time, I received an official invitation to attend the Venice Film Festival. *Black Orchid* was in competition and I was a candidate for best actress award. But Carlo and I were wary of the possible consequences of entering Italy while under indictment as criminals. The festival invitation could have been a lure to capture us, confiscate our passports, and throw us into jail. Italian law did not permit a writ of habeas corpus, which meant that a prisoner could be held indefinitely without hearing or trial.

Carlo got in touch with the festival people and made a bargain: as the alleged bigamist, Carlo was the major criminal, and I, the alleged concubine, was the minor criminal; therefore only I, the minor criminal, would attend but with the assurance that the police would grant me free passage into and out of Italy. The festival officials gave us that assurance, but I half expected *carabinieri* to seize me and whisk me away.

My fears were groundless. Instead of *carabinieri*, there was a festive crowd of shouting, laughing, waving Italians to greet me, and a welcoming fleet of gondolas and motorboats in the Grand Canal, tooting boat horns and calling my name. It was altogether a triumphal return to Italy after an absence of four years—and my indictment as a public sinner did not seem to have dampened the ardor of the Venetians.

That evening, I was thrilled to hear my name called as best actress. As I stood on the stage in front of my applauding, cheering countrymen and received the Volpi Best Actress plaque, I had a difficult time containing my jangled emotions.

But when I left Italy that night, the criminal charges against us had in no way been altered and Rome was as inaccessible to Carlo and me as it had been before.

The sad fact was that Carlo and I had no place to live. We were without home and country. A rented villa on the French Riviera, a rented chalet in Switzerland, but our minds always on Italy, an incessant yearning to go back. In Switzerland, when my homesickness became unbearable, Carlo would drive all the way to the top of the Furka Pass or the pass at San Gottardo, where we had a magnificent sweep of the Italian countryside in the distance. There was not much to see, but it was Italy, and that in itself was gratifying.

Carlo constantly badgered his lawyers in Rome to find a way to invalidate his crime—that Mexican marriage—and finally, after five years of legal jousting and hearings, they did. But it was a matter more of luck than of astuteness.

Mexican law requires that the marriage vows must be exchanged before a notary, and the certificate signed by the bride, the groom, and two witnesses. In our case, however, the proxy lawyers who handled our marriage had neglected to provide the required two witnesses. By Mexican law, this oversight invalidated the marriage, which meant that Carlo and I had not legally married in Mexico, and thus Carlo was married only to his first wife and not a bigamist.

Before the Roman magistrate would consider this plea, he asked that the Mexican marriage certificate be presented in court. But when the court clerk in Juárez went to the files, he discovered that the Ponti-Scicolone document had been removed. Through some astute detective work, the missing paper was finally traced to an Italian newspaperman who had stolen it from the Juárez courthouse. After studying the certificate, the magistrate would only go so far as to say that he was taking the matter under advisement.

"The time has come," Carlo said to me, "for us to be bold. Let us go back to Rome and take our chances. I don't think they'll bother us now, as long as we don't live together."

"Not live together!"

"I mean openly. We may have to do some sneaking around, but it will be nice to end our exile."

CHAPTER 13

Carlo Ponti

My original plan was to do *Two Women* with Paramount, with George Cukor to direct. It was Cukor's notion to have Anna Magnani play the mother and Sophia the daughter. Cukor flew to Rome to talk to Magnani. She had read the Alberto Moravia book but under no circumstances would she play the mother if Sophia played her daughter. "She's too tall," she told Cukor. "How can I perform with a daughter I have to look up to?" I had known Magnani for many years and I tried to make her change her mind, but she was the most stubborn woman who ever lived. Without Magnani, Cukor had no interest in doing the film, and withdrew. That's when I bought the rights from Paramount and brought in de Sica to direct.

I don't think Magnani ever got over her mistake in rejecting *Two Women*. "Sophia Loren makes all of my films," she once complained bitterly. If only I could have convinced her to act in *Two Women*, how different the end part of her life might have been.

De Sica had not approved of my English-speaking film odyssey, but now Carlo had brought him a project which would reunite us, Alberto Moravia's novel *Two Women*. Set in wartime Italy, it was a re-creation of some of the life and events I had endured in Pozzuoli and Naples during the war.

Although George Cukor had failed, de Sica believed he could induce Magnani to play the part of the fifty-year-old widow. But when de Sica went to see her to discuss the film, she again rejected me as her daughter. De Sica held his ground, trying to cajole Magnani into accepting me, but the more he insisted, the more she hardened in her resolve not to have me in the part. Finally, intending only to needle him, Magnani said, "Listen, Vittorio, if you are so enamored to have Sophia in the film, why not let her play the mother?"

The idea had not occurred to de Sica until that moment, but once he heard it, he was intrigued with the possibility. As he said his goodbyes at the door, he said to Magnani, "Have you given me your final word on playing with Sophia? "

"Yes. Final—*final*! "

"Well, then," de Sica said, "I just may follow your suggestion and cast her as the mother. Thanks for the idea."

De Sica sent me a telegram: How about you playing the mother with a daughter of thirteen? I consented immediately. So it was Anna Magnani who gave me the role of my life and turned my whole career around.

After all the confectionary roles I had been playing, I knew I would have to work terribly hard in order to prepare myself mentally to get inside the earthy woman I would have to portray. "It won't be easy," de Sica warned. "You are not yet twenty-six and you will have to be convincing as a woman ten years older than that. You have a daughter of thirteen. You are a poor woman who has worked hard all her life but lived honorably and devoted herself to raising this young girl. Your whole attitude toward life is primitive, simple, direct. The war has been brutal and it has aged you even beyond your years. So we will shoot this with no makeup, and we will dress you as a peasant woman really dresses. If you can become this woman, without any thought as to how you look, without trying to restrain your emotions, letting everything flow into this character, I guarantee you, you will have the role of your life."

To prepare for the part, I opened the sluices of my memory, letting the bombing raids, the nights in the tunnel, the killings, the rapes and starvation and inhumanity wash back over me. I particulary concentrated on my mother as I remembered her during the war, her fears, connivances, and sacrifices, and especially the way she fiercely protected us against the scourges of the war.

The climax of *Two Women* occurred in a deserted, bombed-out hull of a church where I had taken my daughter for refuge during our harrowing flight from the Allied bombers attacking our native village. Suddenly a group of Moroccan soldiers emerged from the shadows of the church and in a frenzied orgy savagely raped us. My agony on picking up my ravaged thirteen-year-old daughter whom I had fought so hard to protect during the preceding months, the loss of the last thing left to me in life that had value and meaning—I knew this would be the most difficult scene in the film for me.

The night before we shot the scene, I stirred up my emotions with my sharp recollection of the band of Moroccan soldiers who had been quartered on the ground floor of our place in Pozzuoli. I relived the terror that had seized me on those nights when they drunkenly pounded on our door, their gruff, unintelligible voices echoing through the flat.

It was the most difficult role of my life. In memory, I still looked at my experiences with the eyes and emotions of a girl, but the role demanded that I see them with the eyes of a tortured woman. In large part, I was portraying my mother, reacting as I imagined she would have reacted if, on one of those frightening nights in Pozzuoli, the Moroccan soldiers had succeeded in breaking down the door and raping me.

As the movie progressed, I drew constantly upon the storehouse of those war-years emotions. Behind the camera, de Sica's compassionate face and sharp eyes followed my every gesture, every word. Without de Sica, I could not possibly have performed that part as I did. He gave me the confidence to go far beyond where I had ever gone before, into an area where I would not have dreamed to venture. Thanks to his support, I even dared to play certain key moments out of control, as a skier will throw all restraint to the winds in order to achieve a new mark.

Before I made *Two Women,* I had been a performer. Afterward, I was an actress.

Carlo and I lived a strange life in Rome. We were constantly under surveillance and we had to invent an absurd existence in order to avoid being clapped in jail as public sinners. Some nights we stayed in my mother's apartment. We regularly changed the apartments we rented, often renting them under assumed names. Sometimes we stayed overnight with friends. Of course, we never appeared together in public. It was a silly and strenuous way of life, but I must confess that the cops-and-robbers aspect of it made it rather exciting. We were like two lovers trying to avoid a murderously jealous husband. Whatever the cost, it was worth it, for we were back in Rome, exiles no longer, and I loved the city and being among my friends more than ever before.

However, the prospects for a marriage with Carlo were still bleak. Six years had passed since Carlo had given me that fateful diamond ring during the filming of *Woman of the River.* It was a riddle without solution.

When I first heard that I had been nominated for an Oscar for my role in *Two Women,* I ecstatically announced that I would attend the Academy Awards ceremony in Hollywood. But then, upon reflection, I changed my mind. My competition was formidable: Audrey Hepburn in *Breakfast at Tiffany's;* Piper Laurie in *The Hustler;* Geraldine Page in *Summer and Smoke;* Natalie Wood in *Splendor in the Grass.* Besides the formidable opposition, the plain fact was that in its long history an Academy Award had never been given to an actor or actress in a foreign-language film. Anna Magnani had won it, but for *The Rose Tattoo,* an American production in English.

So I decided that I could not bear the ordeal of sitting in plain view of millions of viewers while my fate was being judged. If I lost, I might faint from disappointment; if I won, I would also very likely faint with joy. Instead of spreading my fainting all over the world, I decided it was better that I faint at home.

I honestly had no real expectation of winning. But nevertheless, hope being the eternal rogue that it is, on the night of the awards I was too nervous to sleep. At three o'clock in the morning (6 P.M. Hollywood time) I tried going to bed, but my eyes would not close and my heart would not stop pounding. There was no coverage of the awards on Italian television or radio. By six o'clock I knew that the ceremony was over and I had not won. I went to bed. At six forty-five the phone rang. It was Cary Grant.

"Darling," he said, "do you know?"

"Know what?"

"You won! You won the Oscar for best actress! I'm so glad I'm the first to tell you."

I didn't faint, but I went rather giddy. It was incontestably the greatest thrill of my life.

I know that some actors have recently deprecated the value and purpose of an Academy Award, but I'm certainly not one of them. As far as I am concerned, if you are a professional actor who has pride in his work, then the judgment of your peers should be important to you. I treasure each and every award I have ever received—and my Oscar is in a place of honor. It was stolen several years ago from the Villa Marino by thieves who must have thought it was solid gold. I sent the Academy sixty dollars and they mailed me a replacement.

My mother is tormented with the thought that she lost out on a movie career because she was not allowed to go to Hollywood when she won the

Greta Garbo contest. I doubt, though, that she would have had the patience, the concentration, the passion for being a movie actress that one must have to succeed. Nor would she have loved acting the way I do. So she has lived her movie career through me, and I owe her a great deal. She was my mouth when I was too shy to speak, my legs when I was too withdrawn to step forward, and my courage all those times when I was turned away without hope.

I have inherited some of her characteristics—especially her frequent changes of mood—but the difference between us is that she lets everyone know exactly how she feels at any particular moment, whereas I have come to realize that if I showed all my moods the way she does the people I work with and live with would go crazy.

My mother and Carlo are about the same age, which, when I think about it, does make me feel a little strange. I don't really know how they feel about each other because they don't exchange two words when they are together; they seem a little uncomfortable with each other. But I do know, from their comments to me, that they respect one another, and that's what counts.

CHAPTER 14

For the comedy *Yesterday, Today and Tomorrow*, de Sica wanted me to do a striptease, so sexy, so arousing, so provocative, it would make a man howl.

"But, Vittorio, I've never even *seen* a striptease."

"Don't worry. First, I will get you a professor of striptease, then we will create a routine that will melt Mastroianni into a puddle of hot flesh."

De Sica's professor turned out to be the man who staged the numbers for the exotic ladies of Paris's Crazy Horse Saloon. I had several sessions with him to learn the basic moves, struts, and teases. But then, using these routines, I had to mold them, with de Sica's help, into a striptease dance that was my own personal interpretation of how to excite my male audience of one.

The scene was my bedroom. My audience was a fully clothed Mastroianni stretched out on the bed. I asked de Sica to clear the set (a rare request on my part) except for the two cameramen. Rhythmic music flooded the set. And then I let him have it. Slowly, sensuously, tantalizingly, I removed my clothes, letting each article dangle provocatively in front of his eyes while my body undulated to the throbbing music. When I got down to my silk stockings, which I peeled off my legs in a graceful, languid manner, Marcello began to howl, braying at the ceiling like a lovesick coyote.

De Sica caught it all—the interplay, the timing, the sexiness, the carnal thunder my tease set off in Marcello. No scene ever gave me more pleasure. Marcello and I had finally found a script that let us open up, with insouciant, Neapolitan give-and-take. And Carlo had another script lined up for us that would give us even more opportunity to strut our stuff—*Marriage, Italian Style*—but abruptly the euphoria of the film was snatched away from me. God knows I wasn't prepared for it.

Yesterday, Today and Tomorrow was composed of three segments, the first of which we shot in Rome, the second in Naples, the third in Milan. While I was doing the Naples section, I began to feel strange, and it finally occurred to me that I might be pregnant. I consulted a local doctor, who took tests which he said were negative. But my feeling persisted so I asked a physician to come down from Rome. He came to my apartment in Naples bearing a frog he had brought with him from Rome. He injected my urine into the frog and we both watched anxiously for the results. If the frog dropped dead, I was pregnant—at least that's what the doctor said—and if the injection didn't faze the frog, then I was not.

After a little while, the frog began to act a bit strange. When he jumped, he lost his equilibrium. But he did not die. After a few hours of frog observation, with the frog getting no nearer to the grave, the doctor announced that I might be pregnant—and then again I might not.

I thanked him and bade him good-bye. Afterward I took a walk and released the poor frog into a little pond.

That night I prayed that I was pregnant. My prayers were answered. Shortly before our shooting schedule ended in Naples, it was officially confirmed that I was indeed pregnant. It was a moment of great joy for me. The fact that Carlo and I were not married didn't bother me at all. All that mattered to me was that I had Carlo's child in my belly.

At twenty-nine, I had become obsessive about turning thirty without having produced a child. I think thirty is the big turning point in a woman's life. Every woman I've known has experienced a certain fear at turning thirty. If she is not married, then on her birthday she is a self-ordained spinster. If she is childless, she fears that she will be forever barren. I had never known a woman who happily greeted her thirtieth year, but it looked as if I was going to be the exception.

Curiously, even when I was reveling in my pregnancy, I felt something was not quite right. I didn't mention anything to Carlo, who shared my happiness, but by the time we were finished with the Naples segment I knew it was not normal for a pregnant woman to have the symptoms that I was experiencing. So I went to Rome by car and saw my gynecologist. After examining me, he said I should spend two or three days in bed, after which I would be all right and could go to Milan to film the third and last segment of the film. But he cautioned me to be careful, to go to Milan by train so as to avoid the bumpiness of an automobile ride.

But my pregnancy didn't even survive the start of the filming. The first night in Milan, I experienced great pain. Carlo wanted to keep my pregnancy a secret, because the press would have made so much out of it, so he called a local doctor to our hotel. The doctor gave me an injection, said that everything was going to be all right but that I must stay in bed and not work for the time being.

That night the pain suddenly intensified and I told the nurse, whom Carlo had hired to stay with me, that I had to go to the hospital immediately. She started to call an ambulance; although I could barely stand up, I insisted that we go by car so as not to attract attention. At the hospital I was rushed to an emergency room, but I knew that my situation was hopeless; the baby was gone and nothing could be done.

The doctor came the following day and performed a curettage, and the day after that I went back to work. Carlo, as shaken and depressed as I was, asked me to keep the whole thing a secret. I felt as if I had been physically beaten.

I worked every day, full days, and we finished the film on schedule. I had constant pain, but my physical pain was nothing compared to the pain in my heart. In all my years, I had never doubted myself. But now, facing the fact that for no apparent reason I had lost a baby that was three and a half months old, I felt a twinge of doubt about myself. What if I could not bear a child? What then?

CHAPTER 15

There are certain moments which sparkle in memory.

"You are wanted on the telephone, Miss Loren. Mr. Charles Chaplin is calling." Charlie Chaplin? Me? The patron saint of laughter from my girlhood wants me?

Now he stands at the door of my rented cottage near Ascot, and rings the bell. I am so nervous my throat is dry and the muscles of my face are frozen. He bears flowers in one hand and a script in the other. He is as shy as I am. And just about as nervous. He reads the script to me, performing all the parts. I do not hear a word of it. I am captivated by his performance. I would do this film if what he was reading were the London telephone directory.

A Countess from Hong Kong had been in his desk drawer for twenty years. I heard that he had originally written it for Paulette Goddard, and that he had updated it after he saw me in *Yesterday, Today and Tomorrow*. To be directed by Charlie Chaplin—I would never have even dreamed it.

When Charlie had a finished script he invited me and Marlon Brando, whom he had cast in the male lead, to his house in Vevey, Switzerland, for a reading. His wife, Oona, daughter of Eugene O'Neill, an exquisite woman, gracious and beatific, was there, as was Charlie's son, Sydney, who also had a part in the film. Charlie seated us comfortably and read the script in its entirety, again acting all the parts, playing my role coquettishly, then switching abruptly to the stern, befuddled American consul whom Brando was to play. Charlie even went to the piano and played a song he had composed for the film.

I adored Charlie. I truly loved him. We saw each other often, even after the film was finished. He spent long evenings reminiscing wonderfully, especially about his boyhood in London. He knew about my beginnings; the slums of London and the slums of Pozzuoli had a lot in common. "I wouldn't want to go through all that suffering and unhappiness again," he once told me, "yet I wouldn't want it to have been any other way. I think of going back to the smell of cabbages and beans, and I could weep with nostalgia." When he said that, I could smell my own girlhood aromas of cheap white beans and pasta, and I shared his nostalgia.

He told me about his young years spent in a London workhouse, his head shaved for ringworm, his mother in an insane asylum; about his boyhood dreams. "Be careful what you wish for," he said, "because you are sure to get it." Then, speaking of his ambition, "It is desire that creates something desirable. But if the world and I don't get along together, then the world must change." I don't think he was being egotistical; I think he meant that conformity is undesirable for the artist, who must be true to himself and only himself. "Every art," he said, "contributes to the biggest art of all—the art of living."

I was often stimulated by his homespun wisdom. "Do not fear a confrontation," he told me at dinner one evening. "Even when planets collide, out of the chaos comes the birth of a star."

During one of our discussions, I confessed to him that I enjoyed solitude. "Well," he said, "when you are alone you are in good company." I told him how much I admired the love that he and Oona had for each other. So unselfish. So deep. "One of the things I have found out, Sophia," he said, "is that you have to have had meaningful experiences in life before you can truly love." He also said, "As I get older, the more I see, the more I don't want to see."

The last time I saw him, he had some gentle advice for me. "You have one thing you must learn if you are to be a completely happy woman, maybe the most important lesson in living: you must learn to say no. You do not know how to say no, Sophia, and that is a serious deficiency. It was very difficult for me, too, but once I learned to say no, life became much easier."

He was right of course. It is certainly a serious failing on my part. But I don't want to upset people. I don't like to disappoint. If I were to force myself to say no, it would be harsh and unnatural. As it is, I only say no when I have turned a thing over and over and have developed a strong feeling that has swept away all doubt. Then nothing can deter my decision. If only I could make those decisions sooner. If only no came easier to me. That's what Charlie was saying.

The movie didn't do very well. The critics called it old-fashioned, the box office was poor, and the movie's failure was heartbreaking for Charlie. It was his last film. Perhaps if it had succeeded, he would have made more. As far as I was concerned, what I learned from him as a director, and as a man, made the experience, for me, a triumph.

And now he is gone. There will never be another like him. I carry his words of wisdom in me, and often listen to them, as a miser takes out his gold and counts it.

CHAPTER 16

O f all people, it was Carlo's wife who at last found a solution for our troubles over the Mexican divorce and marriage. The bigamy prosecution was still active, but nevertheless, Carlo and I had risked a resumption of living together in Rome; there was no hope, however, that in the face of the Vatican's condemnation we could ever find a solution in Italy. For eight years we had been bigamist and concubine, and it looked as if we were going to be eternally condemned to that fate.

Carlo's wife, Giuliana, proved to be a better lawyer than all of Carlo's high-powered attorneys. Her solution was simple: move to France and apply for French citizenship. Once that was achieved, then as French citizens she and Carlo could be divorced, thereby enabling Carlo to marry me (a Frenchwoman) without fear of political or religious persecution.

We did just that. And with a flourish. By government decree, Carlo and I were invested with French citizenship as a way to honor us for our contributions to the cinema art of France. Giuliana Fiastri, who had automatically become a French citizen by virtue of her marriage to Carlo, was granted a divorce on the grounds of adultery, and Carlo and I set our wedding day in April, 1966. We were determined to make the wedding ceremony as private as possible. Despite the fact that we had an apartment on the Avenue George V, Carlo engaged a large suite in the Lancaster Hotel and stayed there by himself on the night before the wedding. He had arranged for the ceremony to be performed by the mayor of Sèvres, a Paris suburb. The mayor had been sworn to secrecy.

I was in London doing *A Countess from Hong Kong* at the time: I spent the eve of my wedding at a friend's house in Paris. We were confident that our subterfuge was succeeding, but the next morning I looked out the window and saw a photographer outside the front entrance. My friend was as tall as I, so I suggested that she put on my coat, scarf, and dark glasses, and rush out to the chauffeured car that was waiting. I would leave five minutes later with my friend's husband, who would drive me to Sèvres in his car.

The ruse worked. The photographer dashed after my friend, and the only outsider present at our wedding was a photographer friend whom I had invited to take pictures for our family album. It was not the wedding of my dreams but I felt quite all right in the yellow dress and coat I wore, set off by a small bouquet of lilies of the valley.

The ceremony was simple and brief. Strangely, it was both meaningful and meaningless. To be finally married after eight years of struggle and abuse certainly had importance, but standing there, as the bride, I couldn't help but feel that Carlo and I had been married a long time.

I phoned my mother in Rome to tell her the good news (she wasn't at the wedding because she refused to go up in an airplane).

"Well, Mammina, you were always pessimistic but it's happened. We are Mr. and Mrs. Carlo Ponti."

"Ah, yes," she replied, "but not in white, and not in the church."
My mother only sees the dark side of the moon.

Moscow Film Festival. Best actress award for *Marriage, Italian Style*.
Our film was presented in a theater that seated six thousand people, the
biggest movie audience I had ever seen anywhere. The film was
presented in Italian but without subtitles. The sound track was kept low
and an interpreter, standing beside the screen, spoke all the dialogue in
Russian.

I had anticipated little or no recognition on the Moscow streets; movie
stars, I had thought, were deprecated and ridiculed as figments of the
sick Western culture. To my surprise, though, I found Moscow fans just
as ardent, as star-struck, as movie-oriented as they are anywhere else.

It seems to me that adoration of a hero figure is universally as basic as
hunger. As I always do, I tried very hard to keep my feet on the ground.
I think people who meet me feel that, feel that I am one of them, a
member of their family who has returned after a long absence. I
personally answer all my fan mail, and not with a form. I get hundreds
of letters a week; it sometimes takes an entire weekend just to autograph
and send off photographs which have been requested. But I accept that
as part of my existence. Just as I accept the fact that I am a prisoner of
press photographers.

However, I do not share the sentiments of celebrities who proclaim
that the price of fame is too high, and publicly yearn for their days as
unknowns. They are either lying or pretending modesty. For is not
recognition, fame, success—call it what you will—what we strive for
when we begin a cinema career? Loss of privacy is a painful price to pay
for our success, but it would be more painful if an appearance in public
did not arouse a response from the people who come in contact with us.

So publicity is a tiger, as they say, easy to jump on but very hard to
ride; a loss of privacy is the price of the ride. But if you have a giving
nature, as I have, there are many compensations in being a public figure.

CHAPTER 17

While making a fairy tale called *Happily Ever After*, a title which
should have augured well for me, I discovered I was pregnant for
the second time.

After my first miscarriage, my doctor had said that my trouble was that I had been working too hard, that I was fatigued and filled with the anxieties that filming generates, and that that was what had caused me to abort. I went to another doctor, my sister's gynecologist. Then pregnant with her second child, she swore by him.

He looked at the test results and said, "I want you to go right home, get into bed, and stay there."

"I haven't finished the picture I'm making."

"Do you want this baby? Then do as I say. You are not to get out of bed. I don't want you to move at all. The more quiet you are, the better your chances."

I went striaght home and got into bed. I was not going to make the same mistake I had made with my first pregnancy. I phoned Carlo, who was producing the film.

"Carlo, guess what. I'm pregnant."

"Oh, my God, no!"

"I feel rather strange, sort of the way I did the first time, but the doctor says I have a good chance if I stay in bed. So even though I have only three days left to complete the film, I can't finish it. *I am going to have this baby.*"

Carlo was not upset over the unfinished picture, but he said he had no confidence in that doctor and wanted me to get someone else. I said I felt I could trust this doctor.

I stayed in that bed for three months, absolutely immobile. I didn't even risk sitting up to eat my meals, and taught myself a technique for eating flat on my back. I focused my mind on one thing and one thing alone: having this child. I didn't read, I didn't look at television or listen to the radio, I tried to talk as little as possible, I kept plugs in my ears to shut out any noise that might disturb me, I didn't take phone calls or read my mail. I thought about my insides constantly, about what was happening to me. I didn't even dare touch my stomach for fear I would disturb something. I have never been in prison but surely no prison confinement could have been worse than those months in bed. I felt a constant uneasiness, an anxiety about my condition, despite my efforts to be tranquil. The doctor was giving me hormonal injections and telling me that everything was going along fine, but that inner voice of mine kept saying, "No, Sophia, it isn't. Look out."

The night it happened, Carlo was in London. I was at our place outside Rome. It was snowing. Basilio Franchina was keeping me company. We were talking when abrupt, stabbing pains assailed my stomach. Basilio immediately called the doctor, and urged him to hurry out to see me. The doctor said not to worry, a visit wasn't necessary, nothing unusual was happening, but I knew better. Basilio wanted to call an ambulance but I didn't want to attract attention. A makeshift bed was arranged for me in the back of our car and somehow I managed to get down the stairs and to the hospital. I was having contractions every ten minutes, as if I were in labor. The pain was intense. Ines, my faithful Ines, was at my side. She is my secretary, but she is my sister, too.

When I arrived at the hospital I was rushed into the emergency room. My face had drained to a yellow color. My mother and the doctor were already there and Carlo was on his way. The doctor examined me and said, "It's just a little crisis, it will pass, you have nothing to worry about."

My mother was furious. "Don't say she has nothing to worry about because I know she is in trouble and you must do something!"

"Now, now, my good woman, calm down," the doctor said. "I have given her something for the pain and something strong to sleep and we will see what is going to happen."

As the night wore on, the pains became unbearable, but suddenly, around 4 A.M., they ceased, and I could feel the life drain out of me. Ines called the doctor. She told him to come right away and not to say everything was all right because I had already had a miscarriage and I was hemorrhaging. The doctor eventually arrived and around six in the morning I was taken to the operating room and a curettage was performed on me for the second time.

Carlo had returned and was with me. My three and a half months of inactivity had left my legs so thin and weak I could barely stand. This was surely the lowest point of my life. And to make matters worse, while I was still on the operating table, a Rome newspaper already had a detailed account on their front page of how I lost my baby. This terrible moment of private grief, spread luridly before the eyes of the world.

"Well," I said to Carlo, trying to sound bright, "now I can finish those three scenes for *Happily Ever After*." Then I broke down and wept as despairingly as I had ever in my life wept before, and Carlo wept with me. We had lost something precious, a fatal irreplaceable loss, and we felt diminished by it.

Sophia's Secretary, Ines Bruscia

I have worked for Carlo Ponti for twenty-eight years. At first, I was the script girl on the films he made in Rome, and I was there when Sophia, who was then fourteen or fifteen, came to make her first screen tests. She was serious, very grown-up, really not much different from what she is today. She had never before faced a camera but she had very good instincts about what to do, how to move, where the chalk marks were. She made an impression on me.

Then, in 1958, when Sophia was making *That Kind of Woman* in New York (I had left Ponti's employ temporarily and was living in New York), Ponti asked me to become Sophia's secretary. That was twenty years ago. I have devoted my life to Sophia and her family since then, and she has brought love and caring into mine; I consider it an even exchange. When she has suffered, I suffered, when she has triumphed, I was exalted. The worst times, by far, were the miscarriages. Her whole philosophy of living was damaged. After the second miscarriage, the light in her eyes extinguished and I feared for her. I think it hit Ponti just as hard. It was the only time in all those years I saw him depressed, but a deep depression so that for some time he could not properly work or eat or live his everyday life. We Italians have an affinity for *bambini* that consumes us.

It is my opinion that if Sophia had not been able to get pregnant again, it might have destroyed her. She was obsessed with those miscarriages. It was the only time she had failed in life, and she didn't know what to do about failure, certainly not as final and tragic a failure as the loss of those two babies.

I threw myself back into work, trying to keep my mind off what had happened. Up to that point in my life, despite formidable obstacles, indomitable will and self-belief had never failed me. Now I grew more and more obsessive over the fact that apparently I could not carry a child for more than three months.

It took a good five or six months for the pain and defeat of the miscarriage to fade far enough away to allow my strong natural feelings to return. A friend of mine, who had had a great deal of trouble getting pregnant, had been telling me about a wonder doctor in Switzerland who had solved her problems. He was Professor Hubert de Watteville. He told me to come to Geneva for a thorough examination, bringing all my medical records with me.

Dr. de Watteville was a very thin, tall man in his early sixties, with a face like an aristocratic bird—a pronounced nose. On first meeting he was rather distant, and I felt disappointed that I wouldn't be able to talk to him easily, as a friend. But later, when we got to know each other, he emerged as one of the most understanding, generous, caring people I have ever known. His own marriage was childless and he seemed to compensate for his lack of children with the babies he helped his patients bring into the world.

Dr. de Watteville injected me with Pentothal, which put me out, and thoroughly examined me, testing my tubes to make sure they were open, giving me another D and C to be sure I was perfectly clean, testing my uterus, but finding nothing that could account for the fact that I lost my babies around the third month. He said there were several factors to consider that might have caused the miscarriages. But under the circumstances, he could do nothing until and if I got pregnant again. I was by then thirty-two years old, and after two miscarriages pregnancy might be difficult. I found Dr. de Watteville's prescription for my getting pregnant rather peculiar, to say the least. He gave me a four-month supply of birth-control pills. "When they are used up," he said, "we will see what happens."

What happened was that when I started to take the pill, which I had never taken before, my entire body seemed to go into hibernation. I had never felt less capable of having a baby.

I could not lift myself from the valley of my depression. There was nothing around me that offered even a thread of hope or uplift—except my strong belief in God. My alienation from the Catholic Church did not at all affect my allegiance to the Almighty. I feel that a pure religious feeling has very little to do with the machinery of the church—going to mass, taking communion, blindly obeying its stringent do's and don'ts. I have always believed in the existence of a supernatural force that I could reach through prayer. But not normal prayers, by rote out of a prayer book. My prayers are inward, silent, directed to God, who dwells within me. I do not ask for miracles or even overt assistance. I firmly believe we can make our own miracles if we believe strongly enough in ourselves, and our mission on earth. So I spoke fervently to the God within me, the God who is within all of us, and my spirits rose.

I also spoke to my grandmother. When she died, I am convinced her spirit entered my body. When I need her, she is there to succor me. She is my guardian angel. So my thoughts turned to her and I spoke to her, and her words further strengthened my forlorn spirit. Although I don't believe in the traditional rigmarole of church ritual, the quiet sanctity of a church is welcome to my meditations, and often when I am near a church I find time to visit its peaceful interior if there is no service in progress, and feel comforted by its spiritual silence. But I don't get on my knees and pray. I don't cross myself or anoint myself with holy water. I relate to God directly instead of through the intermediaries of church and priests. I suppose this makes me a failed Catholic, but I feel I am a religious person, and for me that is all that counts.

When my four-month supply of pills ran out, I went to Geneva to see de Watteville and spent several days undergoing tests and getting hormonal injections to induce ovulation. I worried constantly. Obsessively. Finally, Dr. de Watteville said, "Now, listen, this is not the way to have a child. I want you to go back to Rome and get your mind off your problems. We've done all we can to prepare you, now nature must take its course. But nature will better take its course if you put yourself at ease."

Exactly one month after I returned to Rome, I got pregnant.

First I called Carlo, who was in London. "Oh, no!" he exclaimed and I could see him slapping his palm against his forehead. I knew he was apprehensive of the terrible effect a third miscarriage would have on me. Then I phoned Dr. de Watteville, who took the next plane to Rome.

I immediately went to Geneva and settled down in a little hotel on the lake, close to Dr. de Watteville's office. He ran a twenty-four-hour urological test; from detailed analyses he discovered that I was suffering from an imbalance of hormones. He said the imbalance was primarily caused by a shortage of estrogen, with which he planned to inject me regularly. Twenty-four-hour urine tests would be run every week to monitor my hormonal balance.

"Would the shortage of estrogen be the reason I lost my first two babies?"

"I think so. But let's not dwell on the past. Let's get this little fellow through his nine months and out into the world. Unfortunately, because of your history, I am going to have to ask you to remain in bed, in as quiet a state as possible."

"For the entire nine months?"

"I think it's best. We're going to produce this baby, you and I, and we want to give him every possible break."

That is precisely what I did. I wrapped myself in the cocoon of motherhood and hibernated. Dr. de Watteville gave me tranquilizers, primarily Valium, and since I had never taken tranquilizers before, they had a strong effect on me. I slept a great deal of the time. Only Ines stayed with me, although Carlo visited regularly. During the third month, I experienced a recurrence of the strange, light-headed, drained feeling that I had had prior to my previous miscarriages. But Dr. de Watteville gave me a special injection that contained, among other things, an extra-strong dosage of estrogen, and within twenty-four hours the crisis miraculously passed and I felt all right again.

During the fourth month, I changed to more spacious quarters on the eighteenth floor of the Intercontinental Hotel, but it really didn't affect the monotony of my existence, which was spent flat on my back.

The most emotional moment for me occurred in my thirteenth week, when Dr. de Watteville brought a machine to my room with which to listen to the baby's heartbeat. The machine had an amplifier on it, so that I would also be able to hear the heart. It was a terribly exciting moment for me, the first concrete evidence that a living thing actually existed in my belly. Dr. de Watteville rigged up the machine and then, with a sounding cup, started to probe around on my stomach. Five minutes passed. Ten. Nothing but silence. Another five minutes passed with no response. My breathing became difficult. I was prepared for the worst. The sounding cup had by now covered my entire stomach and picked up nothing. Panic words like "false pregnancy" and "breech birth" filled my mind. Then, suddenly, there it was. A miracle of sound. The steady, rhythmic, beautiful music of my baby's beating heart. I cried with joy as little involuntary chirps of relief came out of me. It was one of the grandest moments of my life.

Dr. de Watteville took me secretly to the hospital at five in the morning to avoid the hundreds of journalists from all over the world who were staked out in the lobby. He accomplished his subterfuge by having an automobile driven directly into the ballroom of the hotel through a large rear door. The baby was to be delivered by Caesarean section; thus the time of delivery was set by the doctor rather than by nature.

I had never seen Carlo, ordinarily the calmest of men, as nervous as he was before the operation. The night before, he paced the room and carried on a nonstop, disjointed conversation. At one point he went down to the lobby, where there was an exhibition of primitive paintings; he returned shortly afterward, lugging canvases into the room, having bought *all* the pictures in the exhibition. At the moment, Carlo was only thinking of my need to have that baby, with no thought given to what fatherhood, at age fifty-three, would mean to him. He had had two children, but at a time when he was young and distracted by the demands of his career. Often men don't seem to realize that they have just as great a need to have children as women do. Usually a man discovers this only after the child's birth. Thus it was with Carlo, who for the first time would find deep joy in fatherhood.

A Caesarean, I discovered, is a terrifying operation. In the operating room, with needles in my arms, all prepped, my stomach covered with tape except for the part to be cut, the blinding lights above, all surgery conversation clearly heard and adding to my anxiety, no anesthetic given until the very last second for the sake of the baby. Dr. de Watteville was already leaning over me with his scalpel, and I thought, My God, are they never going to put me to sleep? My body contracted in anticipation of the cut of his knife, but mercifully I went under the anesthetic at that very moment.

But not far enough under. The anesthetic was too mild, and I felt everything toward the end of the operation when I was being stitched up. The pain was ghastly, and I tried to scream out but I couldn't. I was gripped by a nightmare in which I kept hearing, over and over, "Your baby is dead, your baby is dead," the voice a series of echoes. "It was a girl, a nice baby girl, but your baby is dead, your baby is dead."

The first person I saw when I came to was de Watteville, who said, his face all smiles, "You have a fine baby boy." I embraced him, this man who had helped give me this most precious gift. Then there was Carlo embracing me and whispering joyful things in my ear. The baby was in the incubator, but a few hours later he was brought to me and placed in my arms. He had a little bandage on his bottom where de Watteville nicked him with the scalpel (he must have been as nervous as the rest of us). The baby had the beautiful round face of an apple, an apple inset with perfectly round blue eyes. What a strange moment that was, that first moment with the baby. A stranger put in my arms, feeling not at all that he had come from my body, a moment of bewilderment for me, until he turned his pink mouth to my nipple and put his tiny hands on my breast and sucked his first milk. Then we were joined as mother and child, and that special happiness, so long postponed, was mine forever.

The day after my delivery, four hundred and fifty reporters and photographers packed into the hospital amphitheater where normally students watched operations. My bed was wheeled into the room, with the baby beside me, and I had the unpleasant feeling that I was playing a scene in a movie. I was too weak to talk. Carlo and the doctors answered the barrage of questions and I managed wan smiles for the photographers. "This child," Carlo told the assembly rather grandly, "is a triumph for women all over the world." Carlo Ponti, Jr., the baby was named, with middle names of Hubert, in honor of de Watteville, and Leone, after Carlo's father.

Now comes the embarrassing part: my postpartum nuttiness. When the time came, I refused to leave the hospital. It was January, cold and snowy, and I was afraid to expose the baby to the outside world. Ten days had passed, but no, I wouldn't go home. The baby stayed in the room with me and I looked after his every need—much too well. Anytime he cried, night or day, I picked him up and walked him. During the night I diapered him repeatedly, whether he needed it or not. And I constantly fed him, even though the doctor asked me not to. I had very little milk because of the Caesarean, but I fed the baby as much and as often as I could. I had the windows of the room taped shut, so that no fresh outside air could possibly find its way into the room. Whenever anyone entered the room, even the nurses, I made them put on antiseptic masks.

For a month and a half little Carlo and I stayed snug in our hospital room. I spent much of my time answering the hundreds upon hundreds of letters I received from women everywhere, congratulating me, asking advice. I discovered that thousands of women shared my problem and some of them wrote so movingly about how much joy my own triumph brought to them that it made me weep. I answered every one of them.

Finally, on my fiftieth postpartum day, the hospital threw me out.

Four years later, when I had my second son, Edoardo, I couldn't wait to leave the hospital. I had again spent almost eight months in bed, but as an accomplished mother. As a consequence, motherhood was much more enjoyable. In that respect, motherhood and film acting had much in common: sound instincts are essential but are made all the better by experience.

CHAPTER 18

I am a witch with visions that affect all my senses. I have acute extrasensory perception. Eerie premonitions. Haunting superstitions. I always have something red on me, even though it may be out of sight. Ever since I was a little girl—witch's red. Never a day of my life, without something red on my body. I have always believed that red would bring me good luck and ward off negative, evil forces.

Just last year I had an eerie fire premonition. In the evening, I often light a candle in the living room, which my secretary routinely extinguishes before she goes to bed. On this particular night, after I had gone to bed, I felt impelled to go to the living room. The candle was still burning, my secretary (for the first and only time) having forgotten to put it out. As I snuffed out the flame, I had a terrifying vision of a raging fire. I put it out of my mind and went to bed. In the predawn hours of the following morning, I was awakened by cries of "Fire!" The lower floors of the building where we live in Paris were in flames, and dense smoke was pouring into our apartment. It was terrifying. Carlo was out of town. Since descent was impossible, the governess and I wrapped the children in blankets and climbed the smoke-filled stairs to the roof. I broke a window with my shoe and we somehow managed to get out on the roof, where later we were rescued by firemen. I had to spend the day in the hospital, where I was treated for smoke intoxication—smoke from the fire I had clearly seen seven hours before it broke out.

Somewhat later, I had a dramatic extrasensory warning about a robbery, a premonition I also ignored with disastrous consequences.

We were staying at our apartment in the Hampshire House in New York when Carlo received word from Milan that his father had died. Carlo was deeply attached to his father and he was terribly shaken by the news of his death. I drove him to the airport to take the next available plane to Italy.

When I returned, I sat in our living room for a while, talking to Ines and Carlo's son Alex, who had come to our apartment upon hearing of his grandfather's death. Carlo, Jr., then four years old, was in his room with his governess. Around nine o'clock I excused myself and went to my room to go to bed. Immediately upon entering my room, I was aware of a "presence," a distinct feeling that someone was in my room. Then a sinister black moving shadow cast its length across the room, causing me to gasp and rush back to the living room.

Alex and Ines laughed at my upset over the "sinister black shadow," but good-humoredly went back with me to my room and gave it a thorough search. Needless to say, no sinister presence revealed itself.

Early the next morning, I heard distant muffled screams in my sleep. I woke, wondering if the screams were in a dream or real. I took out my earplugs, which I always sleep with, and again I heard the scream, immediately followed by a pounding on my door. Before I could respond, the door opened and in came a man carrying a large brass ring with keys on it; he was the concierge from the hotel desk.

Right in back of the concierge was a second man who had a gun in his hand. "This is a holdup," he said.

I pretended not to understand. "What do you mean?" I asked.

This irritated the bandit. He put the muzzle of the gun against my forehead. It had a silencer on it. "Don't kid around," the man said. By now I was trembling with fear. The man was wearing a wig and a false mustache. He had olive skin and wore dark-tinted glasses. He resembled Ringo Starr. His face was close to mine now, and I could see that he was as scared as I was. I could also see that his eyes, beautiful, piercing blue, were precisely Paul Newman's eyes. He ordered me to get out of bed and get my jewelry. I hesitated, primarily because I sleep in a very short nightgown that stops at the top of my thighs.

The thug was at my dressing table, ransacking it. He rifled through my wallet and took the two thousand dollars he found there. He also pocketed a ruby ring that was beside the wallet. In the other part of the apartment, I could hear Ines crying. I realized that it was she who had been screaming. What I found out later was that three men with guns had held up the desk and bound up the five or six people they found there, with the exception of the concierge and the manager. They had demanded a list of the hotel's safety-deposit boxes, which the manager had given them. Not finding my name there, they knew that what they wanted was in my suite and demanded to be taken there. The concierge and the manager could have easily taken the thugs to an unoccupied suite, but instead they brought these three armed men directly to us.

When Ines saw them enter with their guns drawn she immediately started to scream. One of the men pistol-whipped her across the head and face and told her to shut up. The governess picked up the phone and told the operator to call the police. The hotel operator said, "Now, take it easy, don't panic, honey."

As far as I know, the operator did not call the police.

The two holdup men in my bedroom were getting tougher and more nervous by the minute. I had gotten out of bed, as ordered, not caring any longer about my shorty nightgown. The thug with the blue eyes demanded the "real" stuff. I had asked the jewelry house of Van Cleef & Arpels to lend me some jewelry to wear to a big Rockefeller party I was going to attend that night—an exquisite diamond-and-ruby bracelet, with matching necklace and earrings; I told the bandit the jewelry was in a bag in the lowest drawer of the dressing table. Instead of being satisfied, the leader got more angry and more irritable as he examined the jewelry and then stuffed it into his pocket.

"This is junk," he said. "We want the ring, not this junk. We want the ring you wore on TV with the David Frost guy."

Not until then did I realize what had been the magnet for this robbery.

I had been interviewed on television by David Frost, a ninety-minute interview during which I had worn a fantastic diamond ring which, again, had been loaned to me by Van Cleef expressly for the telecast. The ring's value was around a half million dollars.

"That wasn't my ring," I said. "That was loaned to me by Van Cleef and I've already returned it to them." Which was the truth. The thug grabbed me by the hair and hurled me to the floor.

"Goddamnit, I told you not to look at me. Now give me the ring, not this junk!" Now that he was getting physical with me, my fear intensified. I would certainly have given him the ring if I had had it. Then he said, "Where's your baby?"

I panicked. The second thug, who had been in the living room guarding Ines, now came to the door and said, "Let's go!" All I could think of was my baby's welfare. I ran to a hall closet and grabbed a bag off the shelf. It contained every piece of jewelry I owned. I thrust the bag at the thugs as they were moving by me and out the front door.

I learned my lesson. From that day to this I have not owned a serious piece of jewelry, an expensive fur, or anything else for which someone might pull a gun or threaten my family.

The second those thugs disappeared, I ran to my son and squeezed him to my breast. At that moment I realized that the most exquisite strand of diamonds or emeralds around your neck is as nothing compared to the loving arms of a child. The police had me look through books of mug shots, but I didn't see Ringo Starr with Paul Newman's eyes. If only I had heeded more of my premonitions, I could have avoided robberies, fires, and assorted disasters. But I suppose I never shall, and so, you see, I shall never amount to much as a witch.

CHAPTER 19

Richard Burton came to Rome in the summer of 1973. Carlo had signed him to co-star with me in *The Journey*, which de Sica was to direct. Richard and I had never met before, but he telephoned me from Hollywood and asked if he could come to stay with us in Marino a month early, in order "to get in shape" for the film. From newspaper accounts, I knew all about the troubles he was having with Elizabeth Taylor, to whom he was then married but estranged. I told Richard we would be delighted to have him come and stay in the guesthouse.

He arrived with an entourage that consisted of a doctor, a nurse, a secretary, and two bodyguards. What I didn't know was that Richard had started a detoxification program to cure his drinking habits, and that that was what he had meant when he had talked about getting into shape for the film.

We got along fine. He was still very much in love with Elizabeth, and when he wanted to talk about her, which was frequently, I was glad to listen. He was witty and vibrant, and dazzling words and quotations tumbled from him as from a literary cornucopia.

Just before the film was to start, Carlo came to me with the sad news that de Sica would have to have an operation (he suffered severely from emphysema but refused to stop smoking), and that our film would be delayed at least a month. It upset Richard very much, but he said he would like to stay on at Marino and continue with his cure if that was all right with me. In our talks, Richard always took full blame for his troubles with Elizabeth.

Elizabeth was also scheduled to start a film in Rome, and when she arrived, Richard met her at the airport with high hopes of reconciliation. She came out to Marino for lunch. Richard was tense, she was amusing and charming, but it was apparent that she was tentative and ambivalent about Richard. All of us, except Richard, could see it was going to end. His personality underwent a disheartening change; he became much more aggressive, and sometimes rather violent in his reactions.

In the middle of one night my telephone rang, waking me from my sleep. It was Richard. He had just had a long talk with Elizabeth and she had made it clear that it was finally, completely, irretrievably finished between them. "She talked about divorce, Sophie," he said, his speech a bit slurred, "and she means it, it's over. I am all alone here and I don't know what to do. I need help, Sophie, I really need help." I said that I was in bed and alone with the children, that Carlo was away, but that he should take a sleeping pill and try to get through the night as best he could and we would talk in the morning. I looked for him the following morning but he slept all day and did not show up at the pool. I tried to think of how I could help him, but what could one say or do?

Richard was appreciative of his sojourn at Marino and the relationship we established. A year later, he and I did *Brief Encounter* as a television special.

I have not seen Richard since then, but he seems finally to have triumphed over himself. I certainly hope so. I have great fondness and admiration for him, and consider myself his friend. During the sad period when I knew him, however, he was a tragic figure, the way kings in Shakespeare, once grand, are broken upon the wheel of preordained tragedy.

CHAPTER 20

The last time I saw de Sica was on the final day's shooting for *The Journey*, which he was directing. Unfortunately, he had had his ups and downs during the picture, having not fully recovered from his operation. On this final day of photography, however, shooting a scene between Burton and me in a cabaret, de Sica was his happy self. After Richard and I had completed our scene, we all said fond good-byes. De Sica had to stay on the set to complete some shots of the dancers on the stage of the cabaret. I embraced him and he said, "I'll see you in Paris." I walked off the set, but inexplicably I felt impelled to turn around and have a last look at de Sica.

He was sitting on the apron of the stage in a characteristic pose: legs apart, smiling, joking with the girls on the stage while he waited for the camera setup. Then he threw back his head and laughed at something one of the girls had said, as only de Sica could laugh—and that's my last vision of him, sitting there on the stage, roaring with laughter.

One evening a month or two later, Carlo called me from Rome, and I immediately knew from the tone of his voice that he was trying to break bad news to me gently.

"Did you know that de Sica is in Paris?" he asked.

"No."

"Yes, and he was very sick. They took him to the American Hospital yesterday—"

"Then I must go right out and see him."

"—and this morning, today, you see, he is . . . oh . . . dead."

I had no reaction. My mind could not comprehend that de Sica, *Vittorio de Sica*, was dead. I did not cry. I went to my bedroom and locked the door. I sat down on a chair at the window and looked far across the Paris housetops to the white gleaming towers of Sacre-Coeur. Then in my mind, like a reel of film, a cavalcade of our relationship over the years began: our first meeting in Rome when I was fifteen, and then our first film, *The Gold of Naples*, which really started me on my way; de Sica going through my part with me from behind the camera . . . The tears began to come and great sobs rose from within me as we relived our film adventures, from *Two Women* to *Marriage, Italian Style*. "How the years can fly away, and how little one forgets."

The following night I went to the American Hospital, accompanied by Ines. I was taken to the end of a long, dark corridor in the basement of the hospital, where a door was unlocked for me. I went in by myself. It was a tiny low-ceilinged room, illuminated by a single candle that burned beside the coffin, which was already closed. Next to the coffin was a cot on which remained the impression left by de Sica's body when it had lain there, prior to being transferred to the coffin. On the pillow was the indentation left by his head, and a little smudge from where his hair had been. I put my arms on the coffin and bowed my head on them and meditated about him. A painful sense of loss swept over me, loss of this man I loved, and loss of a part of myself that would be buried with him. I thought about many things, and I prayed for his beautiful soul. Some of my tears fell on his coffin.

I went to Rome for the funeral, which was an agonizing experience. Photographers were everywhere. When de Sica's coffin was carried into the huge cathedral, the crowd applauded, as they had applauded my entrance. (There had also been applause at Magnani's funeral, a tribute to the artist.)

I had a terrible time keeping my grief from the photographers. How awful it is, at times like that, not to be left alone. No respect for grief, or for the church. No respect even for the dead. Not to be granted a private moment to say a proper farewell to a man I loved.

CHAPTER 21

I don't believe I ever went into a project with higher expectations than I did with *Man of La Mancha*, my first and only musical, but it ran into trouble right from the start. First of all, the indecision of the producer as to just who would direct the film, and then the indecision as to whether it would be shot on Spanish location or on sets in Rome. It was ultimately decided to shoot everything in Rome, thereby losing that realistic quality that the magnificent Spanish countryside could have brought to the story.

But the film did have its compensations for me, the chief of which was the advent of Peter O'Toole into my life. Gay, witty, ribald, outrageous, and crazy—but crazy in a lovely way. A nocturnal carouser, he was always punctual and sober on the set. We played poker incessantly and I was amazed to discover that he cheated more than I did. He is awesomely educated and literate and always stimulating. I loved to talk with Peter, whose conversation was constantly elevating. We really *talked*. We really communicated, exchanging ideas, touching on feelings, laughing at silly, wise, cockeyed observations.

At the very end of the picture, I found out I was pregnant with Edoardo-to-be, and immediately took to my maternity bed. Peter still had scenes to shoot, but he called every day with a warmth and affection that only a true friend could display. When the movie was over he brought me an enormous ostrich egg on which he had written, "With all my love, Peter." I truly love Peter, and whenever we see each other, no matter how much time has elapsed, our conversation picks up from yesterday. I must confess how delighted I was with the statement Peter gave an interviewer about me: "The more I was with Sophia, the more edible she looked."

I love to be considered a dish; I suppose it's the cook in me.

Long after *Man of La Mancha* had been completed, and I was in bed in Geneva awaiting the debut of Edoardo, I received the record album made from the sound track of the film. I had not seen the picture but I knew that it had not been very well received and would not be a commercial success. I put the disc on the record player; what I heard made me burst out in tears. What I heard sounded so good to my ears, so full of life and entertainment, and I cried for the unrewarded efforts of Peter and Jimmy Coco as well as for my own. A professional actress really shouldn't cry over a spilt film, but as I said before, I am not a professional. I am an amateur and always will be, and when I hurt, I cry.

I always seem to be working as if I were starving. I learn all my lines weeks before the film starts, to enable the dialogue to marinate in me and become a part of me. I could never do what Marcello does. He doesn't look at his lines until he comes on the set in the morning. No matter how difficult the dialogue, he memorizes it just before doing the scene. He is always scared to death when the scene begins, but this is his way of acting and certainly, for him, it is very effective. I could no more do a scene like that than fly.

When I make a film I really live what I do. I am not acting, in the sense of pretending. In the theater, gestures, voice, mannerisms are more effective than they are in films. When the camera comes in on the actor for a close-up, it is totally revelatory, and if the actor doesn't truly feel what he is performing, if real emotions are not there, but only technique, nothing will come off that screen that will touch the emotions of the audience.

That's why I suffer so much before doing difficult scenes. I am totally insecure; I have enormous self-doubts. It is harder for me to do a difficult role now than it was ten years ago because I am more critical, I expect more of myself, and I want to give more of myself. But the danger in going so close to the line is in losing control. No matter how much emotion I give—anger, grief, passion, hysteria—I must neverthe-less keep a firm grip on the throttle so that I control what I am doing, rather than the other way around. Intimate sexual moments must be played with the imagination, not real sexual response, or I could not possibly adhere to the technical demands of the scene. Also, the nature of film acting is such that scenes have to be repeated several times from different angles, in close-ups, in a master shot, and the performance must each time be identical to the previous rendition or the shots won't match. This is one of the most difficult aspects of film acting—to control emotions that look out of control.

Comedy scenes thrive on a flip, jovial set, and I am grateful when the atmostphere contributes to the performing—although playing Ameri-can comedy is totally different from playing Italian comedy. American comedies are written to be funny, funny lines and situations that are played for laughs, whereas Italian comedies are serious, and the laughs come from a tragic or dramatic moment that points up some funny foible of the characters, the locale, or, with great good luck, of the human race itself. *Marriage, Italian Style,* with Mastroianni, was a perfect example of the seriously funny Italian comedy.

Marcello and I share an Italian point of view, of course, but there's much more to our partnership than that. Our impulses are on the same frequency. We first met in Pompeii in 10 A.D. when he was a chariot driver and I was selling statuettes on the Via Dei. When we act together, our souls join hands. When I perform with Marcello, I am the full moon. And he is the ring around me.

We also share an outspoken honesty. Neither Marcello nor I have any artifice, which, by the way, isn't always a blessing. We recently went to the United States to help promote *A Special Day*. We made an appearance together on the Dick Cavett show, in the course of which Cavett began asking Marcello questions about the reputation of Italian men as great Latin lovers. After several such questions, designed to identify Marcello as one of those great Latin lovers, Marcello said to Dick Cavett in his heavily accented English, "Well, to tell you the truth, Dick, I'm not a great fucker."

The studio audience gasped. I said, "You must excuse him, Dick, because he doesn't know the language very well and he thinks he can say anything in America. What he really wants to say is that he's not a love machine. That he's fallible like everyone else."

Marcello gave me a look. "No," he insisted, "I said what I wanted to say: I'm not a great fucker."

There was a long pause, then Cavett said brightly, a rather sick smile on his face, "Do either of you have any hobbies?"

And that's how the program ended.

CHAPTER 22

How long is it going to last, this love? I don't know—three weeks, three years, three decades. You are like everyone else, wanting to shorten eternity by using numbers."

This is my answer to those who question my relationship with Carlo. I admire Carlo's intellect, his tenderness, the way he kneads himself into my problems. He is, above all else, a helpmate, not just a mate.

The foundation that Carlo and I have built, on which we have based our life together, was firm and it has admirably supported our life. I do not ever think of Carlo as older or in any way except as the man I need in my life.

That doesn't mean that Carlo doesn't have his shortcomings. He doesn't talk much, so that I have to guess most of the time what he's thinking about. I have to take words from his mouth with a pliers. Also, he works too much, but this is intrinsic to people from the north of Italy; if they don't work, they die, so I have learned to accept this as a fact of life. And I have learned to accept the telephone. Life for Carlo without a telephone is intolerable.

I have also adjusted to the fact that Carlo is antisocial. He doesn't like theater or music. He is just as bored in a nightclub, and every place he is bored, he sleeps. Actually, Carlo's napping doesn't annoy me; it's been a fact of life for such a long time I'm amused by it. Long ago I decided to protect him from his boredom, which is easily achieved simply by avoiding social events.

It really isn't much of a sacrifice for me since I myself am anything but a social butterfly. In the six years we have lived in our Paris apartment, we have rarely had a dinner party or any other social event. At the most, I enjoy having dinner with two friends in my own dining room. But sometimes when I am forced to go to some social event, despite my protests I have a good time.

Carlo is terribly impatient, volcanic inside, although outwardly calm. His face appears expressionless, but I know just by looking at him when he's bored or irritated, although other people haven't a clue. Perhaps he sees the same things in me, for he knows me as well as I know him. But the only thing he can't really deal with is boredom. He deals with me adroitly. When, for instance, he notes that I am a bit depressed, if he thinks it is for something that he has done he never mentions it; but if he thinks I'm depressed for something that doesn't concern him, then he brings it up and discusses it helpfully.

But I rarely bring to Carlo my problems about the children or my family or anything else. I like to solve my own problems because he spends his day solving problems. I don't know anything about our money or our investments or the nature of contracts or any of that, not because Carlo wants to keep these things to himself, but because I am totally uninterested in any of this and prefer it to be Carlo's exclusive domain. He tries to insulate me from all bad news; he is my shock absorber.

Carlo rarely displays his emotions. Only a few times have I known him to weep. A couple of years ago, while he was away, his sister called with the sad news that their mother had died. When I told him, Carlo broke down and wept over the phone. Another time he wept was when news reached him in New York that his father had died. He adored his father and held him in great respect; Carlo wept then, letting the sadness seep quietly out of his soul.

And then there was the time that Carlo wept with joy, that precious moment when he walked into my hospital room and I handed him the little blanket that contained his son. The tears sprang from his eyes and his cry of pure joy filled the room as he took his new little son in his arms. This is a side of Carlo that he shows to no one but me. People who don't know him very well think he's a cold, aggressive businessman. But actually Carlo is a very emotional man, as sweet and empathic a person as one could hope to know, generous to a fault, involved, and anxious to please. But his personality is such that he never makes a show of these qualities.

Carlo travels a lot and is away from the children and me more than I would like, but this is the nature of his business and it has been like this since I first knew him. In the beginning, when I was very young, I used to resent his absences, but once my own career got under way I was away on films for extended periods myself, and we both adjusted to absenteeism as a facet of our lives. Then, too, I found out something important about solitude.

I need solitude in my life as I need food and drink and the laughter of little children. It nourishes me, and rejuvenates me. In solitude, I read and experience what I read. And in solitude, I deal honestly with my feelings, and with myself. I test new ideas. I redress any missteps I have taken; solitude for me is a house of undistorted mirrors. When I am alone, I am never lonely.

We quarrel infrequently. We do not raise our voices or throw objects or slam doors. What upsets me most are the times that Carlo won't respond. But when Carlo decides to sit out a quarrel and say nothing, I finally get upset and go to my room. Sometimes we don't talk for several days. That constitutes a major quarrel.

When I am upset like that, I get in bed. I am a firm believer that the bed generates only good. When I am upset I can descend into sleep with ease, like a deer or a baby. All my life, from early girlhood on, I have taken refuge in sleep. Misery and hunger never found my dreams.

But sleep does not cure my suffering, only postpones it. When I suffer, I lose my ability to think and reason, so I stay mute until my suffering abates and I can again coordinate my thoughts. The silence between us is broken when one of us speaks to the other, not about the quarrel itself, which we never again discuss, but when one of us just resumes talking—about children, house, help, work—husband-wife small talk. Sometimes, if Carlo is the one who decides to make up, he phones me long distance. Of course I never refuse the call; he is away and whenever he is away, quarrel or not, I miss him.

For as long as I can remember, the press has been writing lurid obituaries for our marriage. On the rare occasion when I go to dinner or a nightclub with a friend while Carlo is out of town, I'm cheating. If I stay home and confine myself to family life, I'm fighting to save my failing marriage. If I don't perform in one of Carlo's pictures and he hires another actress I suddenly read that I'm crying myself to sleep because my husband is having a red-hot affair with this actress.

This is what I most resent about being in the public eye. I cannot have any life of my own. Their constant harassment occasionally does get to us, although we never respond to anything they print. The very continuance of our marriage is the best answer to all these cheap stories, which die aborning because they are baseless.

I am a free woman, a *liberated* woman on my own terms. I have an independent career. I make more than enough money to be self-supporting. I could leave my marriage at any time without fear of being alone. So you see, I freely choose to preserve the life I have.

But this does not diminish my approval of the main objectives of the women's lib movement. I have never joined a women's lib group, although many times invited to, but I agree that women should be as free to deal with their lives as men are with theirs. Being female should not limit employment, earnings, or opportunity for advancement. Young mothers must have a chance to prepare themselves for their later lives. I personally think there should be a provision in the marriage contract that gives her twenty-five percent of her husband's annual net income.

I approve of this goal and others for which women's lib groups are fighting, but I think that lately these groups are getting.too aggressive, too bullying in their tactics, and that is a grave mistake. No matter how hard they fight for these rights, women should never forsake their natural qualities, not in their actions, nor in the concepts they are fighting for.

I do not sympathize with those women who want to fully emancipate the young mother from the home. I recognize that it is extremely difficult to run a house and take care of little children while at the same time trying to prepare for a future, but we must never overlook the deep need that a young child has for its mother. Nor should we forget that the love of a little child is a greater reward for a woman than any job can bring her. Of course, I am speaking from the snug perspective of a woman with young children who leads a very privileged and special life.

But even mothers who don't have my privileged life could begin to prepare themselves for later careers if they were provided with an income from their husband's earnings. And this, I think, is the most important of the goals which the women's liberation movement has set for itself, one that I heartily approve of. But one goal that I do not approve of is that of free-will abortion. My struggle to have children, and the emotional scars left by my miscarriages, caused prejudices that I cannot overcome. To my mind, abortion kills a fetus-child as surely as does an automobile that might run over him in the street.

But I must confess that I just as strongly believe that women must not be forced back into the dark ages of illegal abortions performed in dirty back rooms by charlatans who hack out their insides. Certainly women who are impregnated as a result of rape should be afforded legal abortions. And young, unmarried girls who do not want their babies and who are not able to care for them either financially or emotionally should have the right to eliminate that child. But emotionally I cannot countenance the life-ending aspect of abortion.

The pill and other modern contraceptive devices are an effective means of preventing unwanted babies, and I am all for such methods. But I certainly don't approve of birth-control pills being given to thirteen-year-olds, even though I am aware of how difficult it is for the parents of these girls, who are, in effect, given the choice between nonpregnant and pregnant promiscuity.

When I was a teen-ager, my family and I lived as an entity, and I faced them and their morals, their wisdom, their strictures, their approvals and disapprovals, every day. They cared about me and it would have been unthinkable for me to have done anything that would have brought disgrace upon them. I pity these young girls today who do not have such a positive family force in their lives. Neither the pill nor abortion can help them. Only their parents.

CHAPTER 23

There comes a time in life when it appears that all possible goals have been achieved, universal fame has been achieved, a number of pretigious awards have been amassed, married happily, two enchanting sons—there would seem to be no further challenge. Where, then, is the motivation to continue acting? Has not striving lost its cutting edge, and complacency subdued wonderment? Not with me. I am as insecure about my acting as I ever was. I do not feel that as an actress I have achieved all that I think I can achieve. So I am still driven by my insecurity into the mist that shrouds potential. After all these years, I am still involved in the process of self-discovery, still subject to an inner force that makes me seek even deeper satisfactions than those I've experienced. The dream beyond the dream.

But that does not mean that my ambition, as such, hasn't slacked; it has. When I gave up two years of my professional career to have my sons, I realized for the first time in my life that I could live happily without working. Before that, work was a total way of life. Now, I still adore my profession and love to act, but I will not perform just for the sake of working.

But no matter whether exciting parts come along or don't, I would never announce my retirement. How can an actor honestly retire? How does he know when the greatest part of his life might come along? No, I think an actor who doesn't "feel" his profession any more should simply stop acting. That's what I will do if I ever get to feel that way. I was sad to read that Garbo, who is in her seventies, said that she now regrets having cut off her career when she did. That kind of regret, unfortunately, is irreversible.

I myself have few regrets. If I had my choice, I would relive the past twenty-eight years of my life exactly as they were. That doesn't mean that I haven't made mistakes, but I'm even glad of that because that's the way I learned about people and the quality of life. I have learned much from those mistakes, and I have tried never to repeat them. I don't think I've made any really big mistakes but plenty of small ones. They are mostly mistakes in behavior, in judging people, and as I've pointed out, my inability to say no has sometimes made my life miserable. I have been corrupted by selfish people's persistence, and that has been the biggest mistake of my life. But my philosophy is that it's better to explore life and make mistakes than to play it safe and not to explore at all.

Another regret is two movie roles which I was dying to do but couldn't: the wife in *Who's Afraid of Virginia Woolf?*, and *Anna Karenina*. I first saw *Virginia Woolf* on the stage with a German actress in the part, and I was so moved by the powerful role that before the curtain went down I was urging Carlo to buy the movie rights. Alas, they had already been sold, and I do think that Elizabeth Taylor was splendid in the part, but not being able to play that role is a haunting regret.

Of course, *Anna Karenina* was very well done by Garbo, but nevertheless I wanted to perform it again. I identify with Anna and I think my interpretation would have a quality of its own. But Carlo thinks this is the wrong time to attempt a romantic movie, especially one as costly as this would be, and, regretfully, I am inclined to agree with him.

But there are other projects in view, which shine like distant lighthouses. I am particularly intrigued by the possibilities in a novel about an Italian immigrant woman who comes to New York and raises a large family. At the rate I'm going, I will probably still be before the cameras when I'm eighty. In *Lady L,* I played a woman of eighty—

amusing, well-groomed, bright-eyed, a little shaky, but filled with good humor and warm memories, with her children and her nephews all around her.

I hope that's how I'll actually be at eighty (although it won't take me four hours to get made up, as it did in *Lady L*). I see myself surrounded by my two sons, daughters-in-law and grandchildren, my sister and her husband and children, but best of all, my husband, stealing the show from me because he will have turned one hundred just a few months before.

CHAPTER 24

I was on a sound stage in Rome making *A Special Day* when my sister unexpectely came to tell me that our father was in serious condition in the hospital. I immediately left with her. My father was in a room with three other patients. He looked gaunt and wasted, and at first I feared that we had come too late.

"We are here, Papa," Maria said, "Sophia and me."

On hearing our voices, he opened his eyes and managed a slight smile. "*Sono felice*," he said, which means, I am happy. He closed his eyes. Before I left, I managed to have a talk with the woman whom my father had lived with for the past ten years, a very nice German woman named Carol, who had been quietly sitting in the corner. She was taking my father's condition very hard. She had been completely devoted to him and he was the only life she had.

In a way, strange to say, my father was the most important man in my life. I had spent my life seeking surrogates for him—in Carlo, the husband who fathers me, in de Sica, who fathered me as a director, and so forth.

My sister, who has a much more forgiving heart than I, told me about his illness and about how, when he felt well enough to leave his flat, he would go to movie houses that were showing my films and sit for endless hours watching me. I wondered what went through his mind as he sat alone in the dark observing me on the screen. Whether he ever recalled the early days of our existence when he had not only turned his back on us but in a curious way tried to punish us. Did he have any memory of, or guilt about, all the times my mother asked for his help when we were starving?

I did not expect him to understand the pain of a young girl branded as illegitimate, nor even the raw shame of his wife screaming at me in front of all those *Quo Vadis* people. "You're not a Scicolone! I am! I'm the only Scicolone here!" But surely he must have recalled with some contrition the libel suit. Surely some guilt that he sued his own daughter for libeling his reputation when he himself had branded her reputation with the stigma of illegitimacy. That lawsuit had roused anger in me, and for a time I hated my father for what he had done. But as I got older and learned more about people, I came to realize that hate is an acid that eats away—not the person hated but the one who hates.

I had also faced reality about my father: he was what he was, and festering criminations about him was pointless. As my viewpoint about him changed, so did my emotions. I no longer had any hate or scorn for him—only pity. He could have had a rewarding and fruitful life, and instead he spurned the people who wanted to love him, who cared about him, and he seemed always to be living against himself.

Not long before he went to the hospital, at his request my sister arranged for me to visit him in his apartment in Rome. I had not see him for many years, and I had never been to a place he lived in. I found him much older than his years. I believe he was suffering from cancer. He was very pleased to see me and took me all around the flat showing me his possessions and mementos.

We did not have much to talk about, but it mattered a great deal to him that I see everything in his home. When it was time to leave, and we stood in the doorway saying good-bye, he took one of my hands in his and said, "Lella, I am very proud of you."

That was the only affectionate thing he ever said to me.

A short time after my first visit to the hospital, Maria again came to fetch me. "Come quickly," she said, "Papa is dying. Quickly!"

My father had been moved to a private room. And to my amazement, my mother was present. She has a terrible fear of death. She never goes to hospitals or funerals. She had not seen my father for years, but the fatal fascination he had for her had held true even to his death. Also present was the Carol woman.

My father had an oxygen mask on his face, and an attendant stood beside the bed, monitoring the breathing apparatus. Seated on one side of the bed was a handsome young man, thirty years or so of age, who was holding one of my father's hands in both of his. The young man looked familiar, like someone I had known well a long time ago. Carol led me to the bed and introduced us. Giuseppe was his name, the younger of my father's two sons. He shyly acknowledged the introduction. I felt strange, meeting my brother for the first time at my father's deathbed.

I sat down down on the opposite side of the bed and took my father's other hand. My father's hand felt cold and inert in mine. Life was running out of him. I looked across at Giuseppe, joined as we were by my father's hands. There was a soft, gentle quality to his face. I had an illusion that we were old friends. There was a shyness about him with which I identified.

I turned my attention to my father's anguished breathing. Giuseppe had shifted around to look at the monitor beside the bed. It was going erratically.

My mother never took her eyes off my father. Carol sat in the corner, her face covered with her hands. My sister stood beside my mother, watching the breathing machine.

And then the attendant turned off the oxygen and my father was dead. I had never seen anyone die before. The attendant took the mask off my father's face, and placing both his hands on my father's chest, he gave a mighty shove, pushing the last of the oxygen from my father's body.

Carol started to weep. Giuseppe released my father's hand and walked over to the window. I looked at my father's face, now free of the oxygen mask, and I felt compelled to touch his cheek with my fingertips.

"*Ciao, Papa,*" I said, and welcome into my heart forever.

My mother had started to cry, not covering her face, letting the tears run freely. My sister, too, was weeping, but she had turned her back to the bed and was weeping against the wall.

I went over to the window where Giuseppe was standing, looking up at the sky. He was striving to hold back his tears. And so was I. Unlike me, as a child Giuseppe had lived with my father, so I guess he felt his loss more keenly. He turned and looked at me; it was a look of distress, of need. I reached out to him and he collapsed against me, releasing his tears. As did I. I put my arms around him and comforted him and felt very much his sister.

United in our sorrow, embraced, shedding common tears, I felt a surge of love for this new brother of mine who wept in my arms. How ironic that at his death, my father, who had given me so little in life, had left me a priceless legacy—a brother. I felt an eerie exultation, as if this young man had risen from the corpse of my father, his flesh and blood, to bring to me the kind of kinship that I had never had with my father.

So there in his death room, I both grieved for my father's demise and experienced the throb of encountering new life. It was a moment of great meaning for me, which will endure for the rest of my life.

Peter Townsend, who loved—and lost—a princess, yet found personal happiness.

TIME AND CHANCE
AN AUTOBIOGRAPHY

A Condensation of the book by

PETER TOWNSEND

PROLOGUE

I still marvel, sixty-odd years after I came into this world, at the way it has so strangely reshaped my life. Many have been the strokes of fortune—and misfortune—to which I owe this change. The key one, since it was curiously related to subsequent events, occurred on July 11, 1940. That day I woke up just after first light and, rolling off the bed where I had lain sprawled in a shallow and all too short sleep, lifted the tent flap and peered out: low fog and drizzle. It was my turn for the dawn patrol.

An hour later, suspended on the end of my parachute, I was being wafted down toward the sea half a mile below. My aircraft had been badly hit, but by some miracle the blinding orange-colored explosion in the cockpit had not blown my guts out. I had jumped for my life, counted one—two—three, and pulled the ripcord.

Hanging there between sky and sea, I still clutched the ripcord in my right hand. I carefully tied the ripcord to the cable of my microphone; I would keep it as a souvenir when I got home. But perhaps after all I never should get home, for I still had to fall into the sea and I had no inflatable dinghy, only my "Mae West" to keep me afloat. I might never be picked up. "One of our pilots is missing," the BBC bulletin would say, leaving a last vestige of hope. However, in all that watery desert, there happened to be one small ship in sight—incidentally, miles off course. It was the second stroke of luck of that morning. The ship was some distance away when I splashed down into the sea, but it lowered a boat and not long afterwards I was hauled aboard.

The ripcord which opened my parachute that morning opened also the way to a life which no man in my boots would normally have dreamed of. The destiny that was reserved for me was marked by three main events, all of which occurred also in July, on dates close to my escape that morning of the 11th.

A year later, on July 17, 1941, I married a girl whom I had known but a few weeks, a tragic mistake for us both, for it ended like thousands of wartime marriages, in the divorce courts.

Then, on July 14, thirteen years after that combat in which I had been trying, not very successfully, to defend England, I was expelled from the country. The reason for my exile was a pressing one: the world was speculating on whether the Queen of England's sister and I would marry.

The third event would eventually mean more to me than both the others: eight days before my early morning escape in 1940, an infant girl had celebrated her first birthday in Brussels, on the other side of the sea into which I had just fallen. Nineteen years later, she became my second wife, and, with her help, I have been able to build a new life on the ruins left by those two other shattering events.

What strikes me when I look at that ripcord today is that this totally undistinguished object, a squarish, chromium-plated ring attached to a short length of steel cable, could have had such a bearing on my future. But for it, my life would have ended there and then and I should have disappeared unnoticed to join my ancestors.

CHAPTER 1

BURMESE BEGINNINGS

My ancestors, if they happened to be looking as their descendant was descending into the narrow sea off the east coast of England, might have found the episode inappropriate. For they were men of the West, worthies of Devon whose shores and granite cliffs resound with the thunder of the long Atlantic swell. Westward Ho! and across the oceans to the ends of the earth. That is the Devon tradition. Yet it was not until the mid-nineteenth century, when my grandfather married a girl from a seafaring family, that my own family began to venture forth across the seas. Until then my ancestors had lived out their lives as squires or parsons in sleepy places with strange, sweet-sounding names like Whitestone and Farway, Tedburn St. Mary and St. Mary Down,

Ottery St. Mary, Mohun's Ottery, Buckland Toussaints and Bovey Tracey.

My father was born in 1864, at a time when Britain was the richest country in the world. New public schools were springing up everywhere and it was not surprising that my father should be sent to one which bore the stamp of the East India Company, Haileybury. He was a quiet, likeable person. Though not made for greatness, he lacked neither brains nor character and played as hard as he worked. His name is enshrined as a member of the 1881 rugby team in a gallery in the chapel precincts—sport and religion enjoyed, of course, equal status in an English public school, producing between them the muscular Christianity needed of the men who ruled the Empire.

The Royal Military College, Sandhurst, taught my father the elements of soldiering, but he was never destined for a military career. He shared, however, his father's taste for adventure east of Suez and it was to India that he headed in the mid-eighties.

Hardly had he joined the Bengal Staff Corps than there occurred an event which changed his life. The Bombay-Burma Corporation had been caught poaching teak from the royal reserves of Thibaw, King of Burma. Thibaw imposed a fine and, encouraged by the French, made it hefty enough to ruin the Bombay-Burma. Queen Victoria despatched General Harry Prendergast and ten thousand of her soldiers to invest Thibaw's immense, moated palace at Mandalay. Thibaw wisely gave in without a serious fight; Victoria, Queen of foggy, faraway England, became overnight Queen of the Golden Land, a few degrees north of the equator. My father was one of the men sent to Burma to exercise the Queen's writ. He was not yet twenty-three.

Men like my father lived lonely lives in outlandish places. They were forbidden to marry until they reached their thirties. They administered vast territories practically from the back of a horse; their power, within its limits, was absolute but rarely abused. They were picked men, devoted to improving the lot of the "natives," often too zealously for the latters' liking. With very little in the way of naked force at their disposal they relied on tact and persuasion.

My father moved rapidly up the ladder. He loved the Burmese; more, he realized than some of them loved the British. It was nearly twenty years after he arrived there that he married. He was by then forty-two. My mother had come all the way from her home, Hartford Hall, in Cheshire. It is today a three-star hotel where, in the oak-beamed 16th century stateroom, one may dance to "live music." I am sure that she would have been philosophical about this, for she lived with the times and never grew old. She was a great romantic, as ready for a walk in the woods as to sail or fly to the other side of the world in search of something new, unexpected, exciting.

This is what she found when, at the age of twenty-two and the end of a four weeks' sea voyage, she arrived in the Golden Land. Notwithstanding the strict surveillance of her uncle, Harry Todd-Taylor, she was swept off her feet by my father, twenty years her senior, and led to the altar. As she once told me, she knew nothing, not even how babies were made. She herself made six, all of whom adored and admired her. So did it matter all that much that her sexual education was nil? I believe that the fact that she had learned the basic values, how to "behave" as the English say, was in the end what mattered most.

My parents were married in Meiktila, near Mandalay. My father gave of his best to Burma, I nothing. Rather, Burma has given to me. I never knew my motherland as a child except through the tales my parents told, the household souvenirs and pictures in the family album that my father showed me as I sat on his knee. It was twenty-one years before I returned to the Golden Land. The Burmese, be they wizened, sun-dried old ladies or lovely maidens; silent, saffron-robed monks or enchanting sloe-eyed children; are gentle, unhurried and smiling people. They treat you as if you were one of them—which in a mysterious, unchangeable way I am.

Of this I was quite ignorant when, with my mother and my three year-old sister Juliet, I sailed for England. On a previous return voyage my mother had taken Audrey, my eldest sister, and Philip, my second brother; Michael, the eldest, was born at Hartford. Her odyssey finally ended at Tavistock, in Devon. There she left her five children in the care of our redoubtable aunt Edith, and a dragon of a nanny, Miss Knowles. Then she returned for the third time to join my father in Burma. Such was the lot of Britain's empire-builders and their wives. Two years passed before my parents saw their family again; then, in 1917, my father retired and returned to England, at that time half-starved and on the verge of defeat.

My parents must have found the change a hard one. Burma, despite the responsibilities, the separations, the lack of modern amenities, had after all been bliss: a climate of sun and warm, torrential rain, glowing sunsets, purple, starry nights and dew on the lawn at dawn; a prodigious vegetation, an easygoing people full of color and laughter; faithful servants, kind with children. Then, the day ended, there was polo and drinks in the velvet twilight on the verandah. And of course my father was a man of authority. Now at Tavistock he was nobody—except to us, his children.

For us he was a father whom we respected, because his age and his quietness filled us with a certain awe, yet one whom we genuinely loved because of his goodness and his unconcealed affection for us. My mother, so much younger, was more approachable; yet she inspired a healthy fear in a way my father never did. With her blue and piercing eyes she could drill the life out of you.

So there at Whitchurch, near Tavistock, with the Golden Land behind them, my parents turned to the arduous task of educating their six children. They never failed us. Our education, though it impoverished them, brought us great riches.

CHAPTER 2

A DEVON CHILDHOOD: WESTWARD HO!

Cross House was our home at Whitchurch; its stone walls, washed a light pink as is often the way in Devon, harmonized pleasantly with the gray slates of its long gabled roof. A charming house, already a century or so old, it was solid, mature and comfortably contained our large family.

During my parents' absence our aunt Edith, or Edie, took over as mistress of the house.

My nanny, Caroline Knowles, was a great walker. When I went back over the old ground at Tavistock I was amazed at the distances I had walked as a very small boy. On one of these walks we were trudging up the steep, short hill leading to the church when a coal wagon laden with bulging black sacks and drawn by an emaciated horse began the climb. The coalman, mouthing a torrent of oaths, lashed the wretched animal with the leather thong of his whip and I watched in horror as the old horse heaved and strained against its impossible load, faltered and then fell.

That coalman, red-rimmed eyes glaring out of his lean, black face, was the first fiend I had ever set eyes on. His cruelty shattered my cosy little world of jam and honey and cake and kisses. In time I was to discover that there were brutes like him the world over, riding or driving jaded, half-starved animals with flanks beaten into raw, festering flesh.

Miss Knowles's favorite walk was to Tavistock, the best part of two miles. She only went there on Sundays—for the good reason that her young man blew the trumpet there in the Salvation Army band.

Sometimes we arrived before the appointed hour and then we would loiter on the iron bridge across the Tavy, a singing, swift-flowing little river which provided yet another source of terror. Standing on my toes, I could just peer over the iron railing into the dark, peat-stained waters gliding swiftly below, swirling among rocks, whirling into pools and plunging headlong and foaming over the weir. Looking down from the bridge, I felt hypnotized by the power of that torrent, as I did later when first I saw the Victoria Falls and the rapids on the Congo River, downstream from Kinshasa.

Come three o'clock, Miss Knowles, with my small hand in hers, would be watching, entranced, as her young man stood round with the somber-uniformed soldiers and the snooded ladies of the Salvation Army, bravely blowing the chords of a few happy hymns. Then, after a polite exchange of greetings between the two, the time would come to plod home. Invariably, long before we reached Cross House, I began to feel the pressure, but never could there be any question of relieving myself, however discreetly, by the roadside. "You must hold on," commanded Miss Knowles. "Only another half mile"—a long way for my short legs. I did not always make it, but I tried, for the command was "Hold on." Thus at a tender age I was impressed with the essential secret of life—and more, of survival: *Hold on.*

One day, my second brother Philip was involved in a drama. A marvelously handsome boy with a fine head of golden hair, he came crying to my mother with marks of violence on his fair young face. My mother confronted Miss Knowles, who responded fiercely: "I swear by Almighty God I never touched the child," and left next day. Philip at this time developed a stammer which hampered him cruelly all his life.

I was about five when we moved from Tavistock to Bideford, on Devon's Atlantic coast, spending a summer holiday on the way at Trebarwith, Cornwall—known of old, I suppose, to King Arthur at nearby Tintagel. At Trebarwith, for the first time, I came face to face with the ocean. I was terrified by that first confrontation with such an immense mass of swollen, angry water, by the incessant roar of the Atlantic swell as it did battle with the red granite cliffs, invaded their dark caves and retreated in a disarray of spume and spray. And when I walked on Trebarwith strand and the huge green rollers uncoiled in an explosion of foam, I shrank back, afraid to let the sea touch me.

From the high cliff top, where I sometimes sat with my brothers, the sea below, though still immense and brooding, lost some of its terror. Watching there, I marveled at the seagulls gliding effortlessly on the invisible air currents. How different was the element in which those sleek white birds were floating, impervious to the forces at play below. From my bird's-eye view, below all looked dark and dreary and dangerous, but up above there was light and boundless space. I longed to be a bird.

One day about this time a small airplane appeared in the Cornish sky, the first I had ever seen. I envied the birds, but infinitely more I envied the man in that flying machine.

Our new home, Glen Garth, was a roomy house at the end of a cobbled lane at Northam, near Bideford in Devon. Glen Garth had not the charm and the clean lines of Cross House, but its solid gray stone walls and spacious rooms gave it a friendly, reassuring feel. The garden was the answer to a child's prayer, with its croquet lawn and tennis court and yet another lawn, where shrubs and trees and flowers grew in abundance, which sloped down into a little copse we called the wilderness. Birds nested in the tree tops. Five giant cedars rose out of that great garden—each one of us had our own to climb. Bunches of fat grapes hung in the vinery close to the house, too close to make surreptitious tasting an operation entirely without risk.

That garden was paradise for us children and for my father too, who tended it lovingly with the help of Padden the gardener, a warm-hearted old rascal. One day, as I toiled beside Padden, a wasp stung me on the leg and I gave a howl of pain. The old man did his best to calm me. Pulling up an onion, he cut it in half with his curved knife and rubbed it on my pink, swollen flesh. There is no antidote better than an onion for wasp stings. One day, at my home in France, a wasp got into my mouth and before I could spit it out stung me on the tongue. I remembered Padden and sucked an onion. His remedy again saved me.

Michael, my elder brother, began to take me under his wing. He was a rather naughty boy with a fierce and sometimes perverse defiance of authority; doing evil not for evil's sake, but because he enjoyed the risks involved. I needed Michael and have always needed people like him; I lacked his cool courage, mine only coming with the heat of action. Michael sharpened my appetite for adventure and taught me how to handle risks. I found in him a loyal and daring ally; I in turn became his willing accomplice.

We were a close-knit, happy family; our distractions were of the simplest; our visitors rare. One visit I appreciated was the one made, all too rarely for my liking, by "Cousin Addie," my godmother and my mother's cousin. My mother would thoughtfully warn me in time so that I could pen a note to Cousin Addie, discreetly hinting that I needed money or coveted a particular toy. Cousin Addie responded generously; an extremely vivacious lady, she always put new heart into my mother when the strain of her large family got her down.

Addie Gaitskell's two sons, Arthur and Hugh, were favorites with our family and not least with me, who was not too young to appreciate their charm and the indulgence they showed for one so small. One or other would take me, standing on the step of his bicycle and clinging on to his shoulders, shuddering across the cobbles of Durrant Lane and down the hill beyond. It gave me my first sensation of speed and I was thrilled. Hugh's penchant for high-speed pedaling cost him a broken arm; he was in any case less gifted for sport than as an intellectual, which is not surprising in one who became the leader of the British Labor Party. Arthur's gifts lay in other directions. He was a great romantic, too. Though he failed in turn to conquer the hearts of my two elder sisters, he carried the day with my sister Stephanie, whom he married.

I first went to school at Northam, a simple little school run by Miss Simmons. I learnt to read and write—and recite. Miss Simmons taught me my first lines of verse and I have never forgotten them—who could?

> All things bright and beautiful,
> All creatures great and small,
> All things wise and wonderful,
> The Lord God made them all.

Simple, but basic. Miss Simmons did not stop at our reciting those lines. We lifted up our small voices and sang them. That song of praise made us feel good, and I still feel good when I hum it. Besides, it makes me think of Miss Simmons who was a very kind and dear old lady.

On the Northam road a child risked nothing, either from those afoot or driving. I had only one apprehension: a walk to the village meant running the gauntlet of the "village boys." Not that I feared that they would hurt me, but they teased me and sometimes asked me to play. This I could not dream of doing—for the unarguable reason that it was not "done." My family belonged to the "gentry," a part—now almost extinct—of the English middle class. Though only six, I knew exactly where I stood in relation to the adjacent layers of society, the "lower class" and the *nouveaux riches*. With the former I must be neither familiar nor condescending, but courteous, respectful of their sterling qualities. They were the backbone of England, the archers of Agincourt, the "tars" of Trafalgar, the Tommies who stuck it out in the trenches. The second category, the *nouveaux riches*, though far better off than us, were what my mother called "another sort." Their unforgivable failing was to be "common."

This is how in my family the division was made between the sheep and the goats: on the one side people who were "common"; on the other, those who were "ladies" or "gentlemen," to be found mostly among the "gentry" and the upper classes. A "nature's gentleman," though rare, was accepted as a possibility. The English may be the greatest snobs on earth, but this aspect of their snobbery is unique and laudable because it is based not on material but on moral values, on the importance of proper behavior (no matter how eccentric).

I was made to believe that the village boys were beneath me because of their lack of manners and education. It took me many years before I began to feel free of the inhibitions planted in me from my earliest youth and to acknowledge that "village boys" could turn out to be far better men than the highest born in the land.

My father, true to the family tradition, was a religious man; no doubt more so because his long years of loneliness in Burma had inclined him to live, like an oriental sage, a life of contemplation. Not that for him, a father who had to provide for his six children, it was all that simple. He took care personally of our religious education. We gathered about him in his study every Sunday morning, when he read the Bible to us and rehearsed us in the catechism and the Ten Commandments. Mine was no more than a listening brief—I was too young to understand the Bible's wisdom or the Church's dogma. But the atmosphere impressed me.

The Sunday morning session over, we would troop off with my father to Northam Church. I loved those walks to church with the air full of the joyful peal of bells. Today those who seek the Lord in Northam Church are turned away with an apology: "We are sorry, this church has to be kept locked." Mr. Hookway, who was mowing the graveyard, told me why: "Vandalism." He unlocked the door for me; it was over half a century since I had been inside. There was our pew and opposite the legend, "This yele (aisle) was made in anno 1593." One thing struck me: the vergers' long staffs, which had used to be topped with a golden cross, now looked like billiard cues. I asked Mr. Hookway what had happened to those crosses. He repeated sadly: "Vandalism."

The time came—I was about seven—when we left our garden of Eden and moved east, halfway to London, to settle in the prim purlieus of bourgeois Bournemouth. My father's sole reason was to find better schooling for his large family. To turn his back on the West, where he belonged, was a wrench for him, as it was for us. Michael was the only one of us to continue in the tradition of the West, at the Royal Naval College, Dartmouth. Philip was soon to go Londonwards, to my father's old school, Haileybury. The girls and I were despatched to local schools.

We were heartbroken to leave the house, and worse, the garden we had loved so much. In the garden at Glen Garth my father left something of himself, something that he had created. In vain; for of all his love and labor there remains no trace today.

CHAPTER 3

EASTWARD HO:
BOURNEMOUTH AND TO SCHOOL

The Moors, Spur Hill Avenue, at Parkstone, a suburb of Bournemouth, was our new home. Bournemouth, with its tearooms and Winter Gardens, its piers and its municipal orchestra, struck a very different note to that of Bideford and Westward Ho! We had come to settle in a bourgeois stronghold, an environment with which we were not familiar, but to which we quickly adapted. The house was hideous, too high for the ground it stood on, with walls of bright red brick, lavishly adorned with drainpipes; a roof of asymmetric slopes and equally bright red tiles completed the disharmony.

After the richly planted acres of Glen Garth, our new garden was but a narrow plot, from whose mean, gravelly soil my father somehow managed to coax a harvest of fruit and flowers.

I was sent to a kindergarten run by Miss Lawrence, a middle-aged lady whose dark brown eyes looked at you straight out of a finely molded face; her sallow skin had the luminous quality of wax and her hair, combed back from a high forehead, was raven black. But behind her somber features there abounded warmth and comprehension.

My religious education and that of my brothers and sisters continued under the aegis of my father. Daily, he said prayers with all of us kneeling on the floor around the breakfast table, our elbows leaning on the soft leather seat of our mahogany chairs. Whatever our feelings, we submitted unquestioningly to this ritual—all except Michael, whose dissident spirit burned ever more fiercely. Heaven help me if he were kneeling next to me. With his devilish green eyes and deadpan smile, he would shoot me a glance which sent me into a fit of giggles and it was always I and never he who caught the resultant packet from my father.

We trekked a mile to St. Luke's church, all of us dressed in our Sunday best and well washed behind the ears. I could not wish to see a man dress better than did my father; in his perfectly tailored blue suit and his bowler hat, a rose bud in his buttonhole and his gold watch chain making a graceful double-U across his waistcoat front, he looked extremely handsome. A light tap on the barometer before leaving would tell him whether to take his fine Malacca cane or silk umbrella, tightly rolled in the superstitious belief that it would stay the bottles of heaven. Church was as much a social as a religious occasion and my parents carefully controlled the pace of their little platoon, according to whether they wished to meet or avoid other families churchward bound.

A Hindu prince I got to know years later told me that he pitied Christians because their religion was so dreary and morbid. In many ways it is; yet at St. Luke's, Christianity, and particularly the songs that I heard Christians singing, came across to me in a way that filled my young heart with gladness.

My parents nurtured in their home the sunny nostalgia of the East. The drawing room, whose bay window admitted, when available, the maximum of sunlight, was the natural repository for their simple souvenirs: a few aquatints of the Irrawaddy and Mandalay and the Shan Hills; a teak, ivory-tusked elephant and another of shining ebony; a river boat with eyes in the prow, and a glass-fronted cupboard filled with Chinese objects; tiny blue silk shoes, delicately embroidered, which had once contained the bound, stumbling feet of some elderly Chinese lady; porcelain bowls and spoons painted by hand.

Then there were friends, "old Burma hands" as my parents called them, who talked of the old days and sipped tea, a fragrant blend from Assam, and glanced, maybe, at the family album with its shiny sepia prints of scenes which were forever gone: picturesque landscapes and pagodas and my father's polo ponies, their bridles held by respectful *syces;* the proud-faced polo team and groups of bald, bewhiskered *sahibs* with their *memsahibs* sporting flowery and immensely broad-brimmed hats, and here and there a senior Burmese official, small and slim in national costume, tucked in between those bony, broad-framed white men who ruled the Golden Land.

I kept on good terms with the cook and the kitchen maid. While the kitchen was out of bounds, they could be persuaded to become the clandestine purveyors of the good things which came out of it. Kindness went a long way with these often lonely, bleak-faced ladies who spent most of their lives in other people's houses and seldom had one of their own. I was a keen if not particularly gifted cook myself, though my culinary creations were chiefly limited to toffee, shortbread and jam, for my personal consumption. At the same time, I made so light of laundering that my mother nicknamed me the Chinese washerman. It is proper that a man be able to cope alone with his personal chores, when so many saints—notably, in my time, Mahatma Gandhi—have done the same. Besides, the staff who performed these tasks was already a fast disappearing race; the more so in my parents' case since the time came when they could no longer afford domestic help.

For the decline, not to speak of the fall, of the British Empire was preceded by the decline of the humble and obedient servants who had so faithfully served it. The causes of their decline—as with the Empire—were largely economic. People like my father, having served the Empire, felt bound, through loyalty and pride, to raise their sons in the same tradition of imperial service. This meant giving them a costly education, paid for from their own pockets, which often impoverished the unfortunate parents. My parents saw us through. It cost them dearly, though in the end it was not they who fell into ruin, but the ugly house in which they had raised my brothers and me.

CHAPTER 4

WYCHWOOD

Every little bird must leave the nest; but not all little birds, nor, for that matter, little boys, are pushed out of it at such an early age as English boys who are sent to preparatory boarding schools. I was eight when I was weaned from my family and sent to swell the bevy of boys who formed the stock-in-trade of Mr. Insley, headmaster of Wychwood School. To be honest, I would say of most of my teachers that they gave us more of themselves than they ever got out of us in terms of income. I still owe much to Wychwood; it was a sort of nursery garden where the seeds of manhood were planted in us.

But the start was difficult. The impression of being abandoned—surely the most miserable that exists—made me feel like Oliver Twist; I cried in my bed at night. Wychwood stood up proudly among the pines and heather and rhododendrons on the high ground north of Bournemouth. Wychwood once had a headmaster who had an illicit love affair with the school matron, a liaison which led to tragic consequences. Matron was not above the temptations of the flesh. While nursing a little boy gravely ill with pneumonia, she left the bedside of her young patient for the bed of her lover. During the moments of ecstasy that she enjoyed in the headmaster's bed her little patient was agonizing in his. He died, alone and uncomforted. Not long after, Matron, full of shame, died too. Thereafter her ghost came to haunt Wychwood, sitting on the stairs in the corridor just outside the little boy's death chamber, weeping. It was eventually exorcised by a Roman Catholic priest.

Our own headmaster, Mr. Insley, was kind but severe. We feared him. A massive man, he had a rubbery nose and invariably wore rubber-soled shoes. So when, after lights out, Mr. Insley came striding down the corridor, we were warned of his approach by the squeaking of his soles on the linoleum. I suspect now that he purposely wore rubber soles to warn us of the approach of Nemesis.

Another who walked on rubber was Mr. H. He was fat and swarthy and suave, from his slimy smile down to the squishy crepe soles of his shiny brown shoes. Mr. H. was a pederast; not that it worried us, for we had not the faintest idea what a pederast was. Nor did it strike us as unusual that Mr. H. should always turn up, a willing helper, at our bi-weekly bathtime, when Matron scrubbed us from head to foot.

One evening, I was washed by Mr. H.; he massaged the more inviting curves of my small body with his soapy hand, sliding it up deftly between my thighs until, in a slippery lather of soap suds, he was fondling my private parts. It never occurred to me what Mr. H. was up to. Nor to any of us; all we noticed was that he disappeared abruptly one day, soon after, and was never seen again.

Yes, pure and innocent we were. To us *sex* was Latin for *six* or, at a stretch, a word to differentiate male from female. TV did not exist; only radio programs of unquestionable propriety were broadcast from London. We were forbidden to read the daily newspapers. Of sex and homosex we neither knew nor cared. None of us disliked Mr. H. He was our history master and taught us well. It was a pity that he liked us the way he did and, at bath time, came clean off the rails. For little boys, with their heads full of dreams and inventions, with their exploring and their experimenting, their hurts and disappointments, need the sympathy of a man they can trust.

Wychwood did not lack such men. One was Mr. Williams, a rather special brew of Mr. Chips. Brew was the word—Mr. Williams liked his beer and often reeked of it. He was our Latin master. His blue eyes, blood-shot and short-sighted, looked out, over-large, from behind the thick lenses of his gold-rimmed pince-nez, which he removed in order to read, bending down to within nose-length of the paper. A white, tobacco-stained moustache and ill-fitting false teeth added to his forlorn expression. Despite it, Mr. Williams often laughed, in a loud guffaw, and then his upper teeth would detach themselves and crash down on to the lower ones, leaving the bare gums of his upper jaw exposed.

Mr. Williams was not to be judged by his forbidding appearance. His heart was of gold and, though he frightened us with his sudden outbursts of temper, we found no fault in him. "You fool, you!" he would shout when infuriated by our ignorance. When he shouted at me, I often felt frustrated and helpless, not because I did not know the answers—for I was one of his best pupils—but because I could not say them for shyness. I panicked at the sound of my own voice and remained tongue-tied. That was how I got to know the agony of being a stammerer.

When he was not teaching us Latin, Mr. Williams would coach us at cricket, his major passion. It became mine, too. On Wychwood's cricket field I learnt the most civilized and testing game in the world. Cricket is not a trial of strength; it is a test of character and a key, incidentally, to the English character. People who do not understand cricket will never understand the English.

An Englishman's life pattern is largely based on cricket; it provides him with a code of behavior, a technique for survival and the ability to remain detached when all about him is tumult. The Championship Test score takes priority over the most world-shattering political event. The greatest moments in cricket take place in silence, not to the frenzied shouting of the crowd. There is melody in cricket: one of the most beautiful books I ever read about it was written by Neville Cardus, music correspondent of the *Manchester Guardian.* It is a game for the gods, which is why the English pay it godlike reference. Fly low over England any Saturday afternoon in summer: on every village green you look down on white-clad cricketers. Before them, centuries ago, it was the archers who besported themselves on that same green.

I lived for cricket, I went off alone to the county ground at Bournemouth, timidly paying a few pennies to enter, and then sitting in the crowd, a small, inconspicuous figure in gray shirt, flannel shorts and felt hat with silken cord of red and green, the Wychwood colors. I sat there, basking in the glory of my heroes. Inspired by these great cricketer stars, I won my cricket colors at Wychwood.

We said our daily prayers every morning at nine, we acted plays and we sang, under the baton of the Reverend Mr. Batley, who took Mr. Insley's place as headmaster a year or so after I arrived. Under Mr. Batley's inspiration, singing became part of our life. Gladly we lifted up our voices and sang—psalms and hymns and songs of praise, as well as the rollicking, sentimental and patriotic kind which we took from the Harrow songbook, *Gaudeamus.* The Reverend Mr. Batley M.C. took care that our repertoire included songs like *The British Grenadiers, Hearts of Oak* and *Rule Britannia,* that stirred our hearts and prepared us subtly but surely to answer, if need be, the message: "England expects . . ."

Mr. Batley brought along with him a second-in-command, Mr. Calkin, a younger man with a fine brain, dynamic and enterprising. Mr. Calkin spent hours reading to us in his rich, expressive voice. He opened our eyes to the beauty of the English Bible, preferring the Old Testament to the New. We were not mere listeners to the prose and verse that Mr. Calkin read to us, but learnt much of it by heart, so that today it remains graven in my memory. Mr. Calkin's reading went far beyond the Bible; his feeling for fantasy was contagious. We rattled off "The Jabberwocky" and other rhymes from *Alice,* and revelled in the *Bab Ballads.* For fun, Mr. Calkin read to us Edward Lear; for romance, adventure and heroics, Conrad and Robert Louis Stevenson and Rider Haggard with, for good measure, the *Iliad,* the *Lays of Ancient Rome* and old ballads like the *Inchcape Rock.* The *Adventures of Sherlock Holmes* and the *Innocence of Father Brown* allowed us to savor different techniques in the detection of crime; Edgar Allan Poe provided all we needed, and sometimes more, of the supernatural and the macabre.

But of all this wide diversity I enjoyed the Bible most. Not that I was particularly religious; it was the melody and rhythm of the language, the marvelous stories, the poetry and the imagery and, above all, the wisdom. In it there was a message which no other book succeeded in conveying so wholly, so convincingly, even to one so young. I felt that I could trust the Bible and ever since have felt that until you have got its message you have no inkling, whoever you are, of what life is really about.

CHAPTER 5

HAILEYBURY

Wychwood had molded me, rather than knocked me, into shape and filled me with ardent dreams for the future. Haileybury was to provide the toughening process, the technique of survival. It was a hard school.

I was still only twelve when I passed the entrance exam, taking second place. This put me in a class with boys much older than myself. They adopted me as a kind of mascot and were kind to me—which was not the case with my housemates in Lawrence, my father's old house.

With his hand gently clasping the nape of my neck, my father propelled me towards the dormitory where he, in his time, and my brother Philip, in his, had slept for five years. My own five-year spell was beginning. I was a "new guv'nor" and wore the prescribed dress: a blue suit and bowler hat. My father bid me goodbye—it would be three months before I saw him and my family again. I felt no desire to cry, only to steel myself for worse times which, I knew from Philip, were yet to come.

Lawrence was one of eleven houses, each of fifty boys who slept in one long dormitory. My pied-à-terre for the next five years would be a cubicle separated from the next one by a low, white partition. In half of this narrow space a modicum of privacy was possible when we dressed or undressed and the surrounding red curtains were drawn. The other half contained a bed covered with a red blanket.

At seven o'clock each morning, the school bell tolled, a dreadful, compelling sound which dragged us out of our sleep and sent us leaping out of bed to undress and run, half asleep and totally naked, at top speed, to the bathroom. Any hesitation or loitering on the way, and you were punished. Many were the boys who, waking with the most flamboyant symbol of their puberty arrogantly refusing to subside, rushed to the bathroom praying that it would do so before they arrived there. This enforced exhibitionism was an offense to our *amour propre*.

If we accepted this embarrassment, we felt differently about the treatment meted out by the senior boys of the Dormitory Classroom. The "D.C." was the home of a dozen and a half first-year boys. Its floor was of bare boards. On one side of a large rectangular table, chipped and mutilated by preceding generations, was an upholstered bench, the "soft-arse," reserved for the privileged bottoms of all but us new guv'nors, who were relegated to the "hard-arse," a wooden bench opposite. Extra seating was provided by a few dilapidated Windsor chairs, most of them with spokes of their backrest missing. In one corner stood a chest of drawers where various cooking utensils were stored. At the far end of the room, rows of lockers, one for each of us, completed the rudimentary furnishings.

In these uncongenial surroundings, we were tortured with diabolical thoroughness. The first trial came three days after our arrival, with the "new guv'nors" exam. Each candidate was required to recite Kipling's poem *If*, from beginning to end. Well might it admonish you to

> . . . keep your head when all about you
> Are losing theirs and blaming it on you.

Blows rained down on us at each mistake we made. They were struck with tennis shoes on the hand. It hurt. Trick questions followed: "How many masters are there?" Few of us knew that there was only one "Master," the headmaster; the rest were "beaks." More blows. "How many plots of grass are there in 'quad'?" Four, you would have said, but you were wrong; there was another slender strip, making five. Again more blows. From the start I resolved to submit without resistance; the humiliation would harden, not diminish my own pride and my contempt for my torturers.

I was beaten for trivial offenses on six occasions. Once, realizing my number was up, and to minimize the pain, I slipped a silk handkerchief—the recognized specific—into the seat of my trousers. After an interview with the head of the house, which ended with the command: "Prepare for D.C.," I had to run down the length of the dormitory to do so. As I ran, I noticed my silk handkerchief fluttering like a pennant from the bottom of one of my trouser legs. That earned me an extra stroke.

The condemned prepared the D.C. It was like digging your own grave. You cleared all the furniture to one side—except two wooden chairs which you placed back to back, so as to allow your executioners a clear run at you of three or four paces. For the victim, a beating was a test of behavior. You awaited your executioners; when they arrived and you received the command "Bend over," you climbed the scaffold, in the noble tradition of the courageous host of martyrs, kneeling on one chair and bending over, so that your head touched the seat of the other. You gripped that seat with your hands and waited for the first of the executioners to come running in, then the second, the third and the fourth—the maximum allowed for a house prefects' beating. Then came the command: "You may go," and you rose with all the dignity you could summon and, head held high, left the room—with the certainty, if you had not flinched, that you had successfully accomplished yet another exercise in survival.

At Haileybury, where life for us young ones was hard and sometimes cruel, there was no one to help us but ourselves. Yet, for all the cruelty, the callousness and the unloveliness, it did no good to cry out for pity. On the contrary, the grim conditions made me clench my teeth; I felt within me a growing determination to resist. Without knowing it I was being inoculated with the serum of survival. Survive your first two years at Haileybury and you could survive anything.

I had been warned, of course, about "older boys," but it never occurred to me that I should run into trouble in that area. I was innocent to the point of naiveté, uncorrupted with every intention of remaining so. Yet, one day, Ashcroft, my housemaster, called me to his study. "Sit down," he said. "I have something very serious to say to you. It has been reported to me that you have been consorting with older boys."

I was stunned. All the boys in my form were much older than me, anyway, and it seemed idiotic to make insinuations about their or my conduct. I burst into tears of anger and despair. It appeared that our drawing master was the author of this sinister report. I had taken him for a friend, he had helped me with the problems of perspective involved in drawing airplanes and ships. Perhaps he meant to do me a good turn, but I took him for a traitor and a purveyor of lies. I went on crying bitterly, screwing my handkerchief up in a ball, while Ashcroft continued, quite kindly, to lecture me. Then he let me go.

I wrote immediately to my father to tell him of my woe and that I could no longer stay at Haileybury. "My life is ruined," I concluded, and that is exactly what I felt.

There was no reason why my father, now well into his sixties, should suddenly take an interest in airplanes: on the contrary, if they were not exactly anathema to him, they represented a break with tradition. So it was, I believe, entirely because of his goodness to me—because he meant to prove to me that my life was not, as I thought, ruined, and because he must have noticed that I always looked up at the sound of a motor in the sky—that he took me to an air meeting at Bournemouth: a kind of aerial Derby Day, with its atmosphere of the fairground and the crowd pressing to the edge of the paddocklike enclosure, where the shining little thoroughbreds, all biplanes, waited to taxi to the start.

My father propelled me, his hand as usual on the nape of my neck, to one of the turning points. From there, I witnessed a spectacle which itself was a turning point in my life. I watched, spellbound, as those little airplanes came boring down at full throttle on the checkered pylon, banking vertically so that I could see the pilot crouched behind the windscreen, his scarf trailing in the slipstream. That sealed my passion for the air.

And it so happened that the pilot who turned lower and faster than any of that day, was my future commander-in-chief, Sholto Douglas.

About this time, when I was thirteen, we moved from Bournemouth back to the West Country. Our new home was a 400 year-old cottage, once the village blacksmith's and his forge, now knocked into one. Crowcombe was our village, a tiny one beneath the rolling Quantock Hills in Somerset. We all breathed more freely now that we were back in the West, though my father was rather piqued that it was Somerset and not his native Devon.

For me the horizon widened. I loved the hills. I climbed to Hurley Beacon and lay there in the heather, listening to the coming and going of the bees in the warm air. Where I lay, I imagined that I was in an airplane looking down on the patchwork of fields and woods in the valley below.

Back at school, I began gradually to emerge from hell. Moving on from the Dormitory Classroom to the "house room" was a release from one ghetto to another, where conditions were less sordid and sadism was not on the daily menu. Moreover, our house room, being wedged between the Master's house on the one side and the library and the chapel on the other, was in a kind of silent zone, and that tended to restrain its senior inmates.

We congregated twice every day in "chapel." Under its high-domed roof we prayed briefly in the morning, and went back for more prayers and singing in the evening. At Haileybury, as at Wychwood, singing was part of our life, an uplifting and dynamic influence. It was in chapel that the school motto *Sursum Corda*—Lift up your hearts—came alive. We lifted up our hearts and our voices and sang, the five hundred of us, with all our youthful verve.

I, who would not dare utter a note in public, and would only sing in my bath with the tap running, found myself singing with full-throated, almost reckless assurance. Our faith was pretty formal, our theology practically nil. It was not the religious theme, but the mood that got us going. The praise-and-glory hymns are unfailing morale-raisers; the emotional ones stir you to the depths; and the crusading ones made you feel you could conquer the world. Christmas would be dull without carols; the triumphant Easter hymns justify the preceding tragedy. And at the end of a long summer's day we sang:

> The day thou gavest Lord is ended
> The darkness falls at thy behest

and went to bed with the surge of its words and music in our ears.

The din of the world can never, in my mind, muffle the words or silence the music of those hymns. They penetrated into the depths of my soul and there will they remain until I depart from this life.

My housemaster, Ashcroft, who had been gassed in World War I, was understandably a lover of fresh air. He inhaled the largest possible quantities of it when he went flying. Ashcroft loved flying. He knew too that I was longing to fly and, being a good and understanding man, he fixed it for me one day, during my fourteenth summer.

He drove me to the R.A.F. base at Old Sarum, near Salisbury, where I presented my father's written permission for the venture. And venture it really was: flying was practically unknown to the general public, and to small schoolboys in particular. I signed a "blood-chit" absolving the R.A.F. from responsibility in case of an accident. The blood-chit gave me the fleeting thought that I might die; if so, it would be a hero's death.

From Old Sarum's grass field, I soared off the ground for the first time. Standing in the back cockpit of the Bristol Fighter—a World War I biplane—I watched the green grass and the golden fields of corn slipping away below, until we rose to a height where we seemed to be poised motionless. Looking out along the wings, I could not believe that we were flying through the air, were it not for the slipstream pressing like a cold, strong hand against my face, exhilarating me and taking my breath away.

That flight decided me: I would become a pilot.

The squadron-commander, Leigh Mallory, wished me luck "if ever you think of joining the R.A.F." He did not know that my mind was made up, and I did not know that, eleven years later, I myself would be a squadron commander under Leigh Mallory's command.

Ashcroft took me under his wing and I began to feel more secure. He fanned my enthusiasm for flying. He took me to North Weald, a nearby R.A.F. base, where I watched the little Siskin fighters gamboling in the sky. Then I met the pilots; they seemed to me like gods descended from heaven to earth. I flew again, thanks to Ashcroft, and yet again. It sounds banal, but in those days it was very rare for earthbound creatures to fly.

Along with my growing passion for flying came a consolation on other fronts; I became captain of swimming, won a place in the rugby XV; and Ashcroft made me head of Lawrence house. The statutory exams passed, I became early entrenched in the VI Form, the top one, waiting until I was old enough to pass into the R.A.F. College. Maths and higher maths being essential subjects and my weakest, they caused me long and uneasy hours of sweated labor. I enjoyed writing and worshiped Shakespeare.

I was no intellectual yet I was admitted to the Guild of Pallas Athenae, the select and secret society composed of VI Form intellectuals. When I read them my thesis on the history of aviation, they hung on every word, so little was known of the subject outside aviation circles. Finally, I ascended to Elysium, the club restricted to a dozen of the elite. Elysium, the sunny paradise which had seemed so remote when contemplated from the sordid, sadistic hell of the Dormitory Classroom. It was good that I had held both ends of the stick. I could sympathize with those who now held the dirty end.

I passed fifth in the written exam for the Royal Air Force College, gaining a cadetship which spared my father the fees—an important contribution to his sorely strained budget. However, it was a blow to him to learn that I had failed the medical exam. A kick on the head at rugger had apparently damaged a blood vessel in my head. Today I am not so sure. There was no doubt about the kick, but the diagnosis depended much on my own testimony. And, at this moment, there came to be a premonition—I am at a loss to explain it—that this was not the moment to leave Haileybury. It influenced my answers to the doctors' questions.

My rejection left me, on account of my father, with an uneasy conscience. I would have to resit the written exam. Could I again win a cadetship? No one was more surprised than I when, at the next attempt, six months later, I passed fourth into the Royal Air Force College. The doctors cleared me; so did my conscience. But the delay involved was to change the subsequent course of my life.

CHAPTER 6

CRANWELL: FLEDGLING PILOT

I was bound apprentice, as a pilot, in that famous county—at the R.A.F. College, Cranwell. It was autumn 1933. The Royal Air Force was just fifteen years old. The Royal Navy—since the Armada, the sure shield of Britain and her pride—and the crack regiments of the Army could boast of centuries of hard-won glory. The Royal Air Force, short of money and modern equipment—it had been contemptuously nicknamed the Royal Ground Force and the Cinderella Service—could boast of nothing, save a belief in its destiny.

The R.A.F.'s impudent claim that priority should be given to air defense rocked the sea dogs and the Colonel Blimps. It was unbearable that the old country should have to look for protection to pilots of the R.A.F., whom the old guard tended to despise as the ragtag and bobtail of the country's youth, beyond the fringe of respectable society, with their pub-crawling and their noisy sports cars. Insurance companies exacted an extra premium from these accident-prone young men.

As far as I was concerned, the R.A.F.'s role in a future war could not have interested me less. Though Hitler had already begun to build his secret Luftwaffe, war, on our side of the Channel, seemed too remote even to consider. All I yearned for was to fly, and the R.A.F. enjoyed, deservedly, the reputation of being the best flying club in the world.

Flying had not yet emerged from the pioneering stage. It offered the highest form of adventure; it was dangerous. "I see in *The Times* there has been another R.A.F. crash," my father would say—all too often, but with just enough indifference to avoid upsetting me.

There was, however—and this is what fired me—a positive side to flying. It was still a new thing, unfamiliar, thrilling, and out of this world and it attracted young people, like myself, who thirsted for adventure along new and untrodden paths. Flying meant breaking with the slothful pace and the safety of *terra firma*. It meant risking your neck. Precise data was too scanty and technology too imperfect to exclude all reasonable risk of engine or structural failure. Radio and meteorology and the aids to navigation were rudimentary and unreliable. To make up for these shortcomings, a pilot needed to possess a powerful mixture of faith and enthusiasm and senses keen enough to enable him to fly by the seat of his pants. Thus provided, we felt in us an immense urge to rise up into the sky in the wake of the pioneers, to free ourselves from the confines of earth and discover the exaltation of flying through the boundless realms of the air.

Early in September 1933, my instructor, Flight Lieutenant Poyntz Roberts, introduced me to the Avro Tutor, a little open-cockpit biplane powered with a 250 h.p. engine. My initiation in the art of flying had begun. Poyntz was a small, irascible man with a face as pink as a rose and an inexhaustible vocabulary of swearwords. The advice he gave me, laced with oaths, came straight out of the R.A.F. Training Manual. But he left me with two of his own dicta: Treat everybody else in the air as a bloody fool; handle your airplane as if she were your favorite girl.

After six hours of takeoffs and landings, of diving, climbing, banking, gliding, side-slipping, spinning, rolling and looping we landed one afternoon in the middle of the vast sward of Cranwell's airfield. Poyntz climbed out of his cockpit and onto the wing below mine. "She's all yours," he shouted. "Off you go."

That day, September 15, 1933, I made my first solo. It was less than thirty years before that Orville Wright, the first man to fly, had made his—that is, the first powered, controlled, sustained flight. Not many more years after my first solo, men would be landing and taking off from the moon.

I was eighteen. For the next two years I submitted, gladly for the most part, to the intensive and variegated process which was to mold me as a pilot, an officer and a gentleman. Our education, largely academic, was generously dosed with sport and parade ground drill and spiced, all too slightly for our liking, with flying.

Our routine consisted of a relentless sequence of lectures, flying, sport, and drill. We paraded every morning at 8 o'clock with rifle and bayonet. Outside the seriocomic atmosphere of drill and physical training, we were nurtured in a discipline which was stringent and just.

As my first year of training ended, there came bad news about my father. He was seriously ill. I hurried back to Crowcombe and found myself, at nineteen, acting head of the family, my brother Michael being on the high seas and Philip with his regiment, the Gurkhas, on India's North-West Frontier. My father was sinking steadily, while my mother kept watch by his side. She asked me if I would like to see him, but I refused. I knew he was dying and I could not raise the courage to look a dying man in the face, be he even my own father. I wanted to cherish the image of him alive, smiling, gardening, reading his *Times* or walking, debonair, to church on Sundays. Had he asked for me I should, of course, have gone to him, but he never did.

I would not put it beyond my father voluntarily to have spared me the sight of him sinking toward the grave. He knew me well, my childhood terrors, my fearful thoughts and fancies, and he understood, I am sure, how I, a stripling pilot, shrank from looking death in the face. For an airman, death was always round the corner, and might show up at any moment. Until then, we preferred not to look its way.

With my father at rest in the bosom of his beloved West Country, I again took to the air. At nineteen, I was fatherless—deeply saddened, but without a feeling of irreparable loss. I felt passionately alive, absorbed by my longing to fly.

Now in the second year, my training on "service type" aircraft began, and I was overjoyed at being designated as a fighter pilot. The single-seater fighter mentality suited my temperament of a "loner." Some eighteen months had passed since my first solo and I was beginning to feel bored with the conventional ways of a collegian and the dullness of life as a groundling pilot. I longed to fly more. So did we all, but some hid their impatience better. Try as I did to lend an attentive ear to our esteemed professors, my thoughts always wandered beyond the classroom to the sky. My apprenticeship in Lincolnshire culminated with a posting to No. 1 Fighter Squadron, one of the R.A.F.'s three crack interceptor units.

CHAPTER 7

FIGHTER PILOT

A month's leave gave me time to get used to the fact that I was now an officer in His Majesty's Royal Air Force. I felt proud, yet when the day came, late in August 1935, for me to assume my duties with No. 1

Fighter Squadron at Tangmere in Sussex, I was so overcome with shyness that I waited till dusk before slipping into the camp unnoticed and creeping into bed. I had never worn my wings nor my thin pilot officer's stripes in public. Next morning, feeling awkward in my new uniform, I braved the breakfast table. Immediately the hospitality of the "best flying club in the world"—the R.A.F.—was mine. "Why didn't you let us know last night?" those pilots of the R.A.F.'s crack squadron asked me, the stripling in their midst. "We'd have given you a party."

In October 1935, the shadow of war fell, if ever so lightly, on Tangmere. Mussolini launched his invasion of Abyssinia (Ethiopia); his son Bruno returned exultant from a raid against tribesmen armed with bows and arrows to describe how his bombs had exploded amidst that mass of black-skinned flesh, like scarlet flowers bursting into bloom. Reading this account, I felt sick, never imagining that it would one day fall to me to slay men.

The Ethiopian crisis made Britain stir from her pipe dream of peace eternal. The bases along her lifeline to the Far East—Gibraltar, Malta, Suez, Aden, Colombo, Singapore—had to be reinforced, and this meant depriving her fighter defense of pilots. Half of 1 Squadron's Furies were sent, with their pilots, to Suez. I begged Philip Babington, now Director of Postings, to let me join them, only to be reminded that my training as a fighter pilot was not yet complete. It eventually culminated at the Air Firing Range of Catfoss, in Lincolnshire. There, in what seemed to me to be the dreariest outpost of the British Empire, I spent my twenty-first birthday in a dingy hut, before a foully smoking stove, waiting for the chilly North Sea mist to clear.

CHAPTER 8

ASIAN ADVENTURE

At the outset of her marriage, my mother, with thousands of miles between her husband's post in Burma and her young family in England, had been torn alternately from one and the other. Now that my father's death had separated him from her forever, the careers of her sons were to take them too from her. One after the other, the Empire claimed them. Michael was away for years at a time on the high seas or in some distant naval base; Philip on the North-West Frontier of

India. Now my summons came to leave. The long awaited telegram from the Air Ministry stated curtly: *Posted to 36 Squadron Singapore.* It was farther than I had bargained for and 36 Squadron was a torpedo bomber not a fighter squadron. No matter, there was a threat of war and anyway I had had enough of the cozy life, kicking my heels at home, and of the cold and clammy mists of England. I was headed for adventure beyond the seas and I could not wait to be off.

At Southampton, the troopship *Neuralia* was alongside. My mother came with me to the foot of the gangway. She showed not a trace of emotion, though I knew it was there and for a moment felt uncomfortable. But so eager was I to be away that I gave it no thought—until years later, when I realized the pains that mothers bear for their children. My mother kissed me, warmly but without fuss, and said: "Well, off you go."

The *Neuralia*, a rickety old coal burner, steamed slowly eastward. The great mass of Gibraltar loomed out of the rain and gloomy tidings came from the Spanish warship anchored alongside us: a dozen men had been executed on her quarterdeck that morning. Spain was on the verge of civil war; it was to claim a million Spanish lives, and provide an arena in which Hitler and Mussolini could practice for total war. Junkers 52's of the German Luftwaffe circled us as we set course for Malta.

We coaled at Port Said. We came to Colombo, Ceylon, and coaled again. Five days later, we were steaming through glassy waters, picking our way through the archipelago at the approach to Singapore.

Life at Singapore was serene and enjoyable. Day in, day out, the sun set at six, rose again at six the following morning. All of Singapore, ourselves included, rose with it. The mynahs began their chatter and Suan Kye, my Chinese boy, came shuffling down the corridor in his wooden sandals, slipping them off before sliding silently through the lattice door of my room. "Morning," was all he would say, as he laid down a tray of tea and fruit and arranged my clothes.

Singapore's population was a mélange of races. The Chinese, numerically superior by far, provided the mind and the muscle. The English, a tiny minority, were the masters. Their social and business clubs—cricket, golf, yachting, racing, and swimming clubs—were exclusively English. Asians and Eurasians were barred from English life, not with ill-feeling, but simply because it wasn't done to mix with "the natives." This was the secret of the British Raj, wherever it might be installed; how a handful of British held sway over the hundreds of millions of subjects. The British simply did not mix with the natives, however rich or influential they may have been, however beautiful their wives and daughters.

In many ways it was a pity, because we missed so much by not mixing. Many of us wanted to; I often felt far more inclined to mix with the natives than with the British; but such conduct would have been considered unbecoming to an officer and a gentleman. So my contacts were limited to simple people like Suan Kye.

Spy scares were not infrequent, and almost invariably the Japanese were involved. They were a tight, retiring community, for the most part masseurs, tailors, barbers, and photographers, trades in which they were well placed to listen, record and report. My hair was cut by a Japanese, who massaged my head with cool, astringent bay rum, ending up with a little tap of his hand on the nape of my neck. A harder one, karate-fashion, and he could have broken it. It was a Japanese photographer who took our annual squadron photograph. Doubtless he took others, if only mental ones, on his way through the base, and sent them back to General Headquarters in Tokyo.

What incredible naïveté the British display before their enemies. In Singapore we took the whole subject of Japanese spies as a huge joke. Yet Singapore was riddled with them and, within five years or so, the Japanese would be the masters in Singapore.

Those days at Singapore, spiced though they were with the danger of flying, were sweet and easy days. Our duties held us from 7 A.M. till 1:30, when our working day was ended. After lunch came the siesta, officially recommended "because the climate thinned your blood."

We seldom went out with girls, because there were very few girls— white ones—to go out with.

One day a boatload of young Germans came steaming into Singapore in the training cruiser *Emden*. The first German I ever met in my life was stark naked. We confronted each other under a shower in the Tanglin Club, alike as two peas in a pod—in our birthday suits. But back in uniform we were each in a different camp. That evening the Germans, our guests at dinner, raised their hands in the Nazi salute as the band played *Deutschland Über Alles*. They looked quite comic. Later, a toast was drunk: "Germany and England will beat the world!"

Outside my ground-floor bedroom was an asphalt space where I parked my beautiful, blue, long-nosed M.G. One afternoon I was changing the right, rear tire when something made me stop and walk over to my bedroom, ten yards away, to look for a rag. During the few seconds I was there I heard an airplane pass over the mess, approaching to land. A moment later I was back beside my car; the right rear mudguard was deeply gashed and on the ground beside it lay a string of lead beads, the kind that were attached to the end of a trailing aerial. The weighted aerial would have cut me in half like a piece of cheese, had not that kindly unseen hand pushed me out of the way just in time.

CHAPTER 9

PREPARING FOR WAR

Early in 1937, Singapore's defenses, considered impregnable, were put to the test in a full-scale exercise. Flying boat squadrons scouted the sea for the imaginary enemy (which no one now doubted would be the Japanese). We, in 36 Squadron, were despatched to torpedo imaginary enemy warships and transports, while the long-range batteries pounded them in an imaginary bombardment. As everyone now knows, the pundits were imagining all the wrong things. The enemy, when he came early in 1942, overran the defenses from the rear. My old squadron was wiped out.

Possibly I would have perished with them, but for the plague which had afflicted me off and on for four years and was reducing me to a physical and mental wreck. No doctor had yet found a remedy, but after a year in Singapore, I found, quite by accident, a doctor wiser than them all: Professor Young, head of the School of Tropical Medicine. We met at a dinner party; afterwards, in the warm Singaporean night, I unburdened myself to him. He examined me next day; yet all his tests and treatments were unavailing. Then, one morning he said to me, in his quiet voice: "Stop thinking that you have the plague. The origin of your trouble is entirely nervous. Without your realizing it, flying gets you over-strung, hence the skin lesions. There is only one thing for it: you must give up flying, go home and live like a cabbage for several months."

I nearly cried. Give up flying, the one thing that I lived for! "It's your only chance," said this kind, wise doctor. I departed, heavy-hearted, on the next homeward bound P & O liner, shutting myself in my cabin and playing Rossini's *Barber of Seville* most of the day—it lightened my sorrow. Within a few days, my skin was once again as smooth as a baby's bottom. A month later, I faced the R.A.F. doctors in London and showed them Professor Young's report. They gaped at it, then at me. "But you are perfectly well," they chorused, and rated me fit for flying duties.

It was incredible. I had been sent home, over 10,000 miles, to be cured of a four-year-old illness provoked by flying. And here was the medical grand jury pronouncing that flying was just the thing to set me right. Why in heaven's name, then, had I been sent home?

My sole consolation, short-lived as it happened, was to be sent back to Tangmere, this time to 43 Squadron. It was a joy to be back in my home-away-from-home. A plague on the doctors and on the plague itself! I threw myself into flying and, in no time, it was again on me.

I soon realized another depressing thing as I tried, not very successfully, to settle down at Tangmere during the summer of 1937. Dramatic changes had taken place since I left. The R.A.F., faced with the growing menace of the German Luftwaffe, was expanding fast. Gone were the halcyon days of the best flying club in the world. Tangmere was now peopled by strange faces, different people with a different style. I resented this new generation of pilots who had answered the R.A.F.'s urgent appeal and found heaven-sent relief from boring civilian jobs.

Having served temporarily in a torpedo bomber squadron, Coastal Command now claimed me as theirs, and the Air Ministry, forgetting that I had been trained and had served as a fighter pilot, treacherously posted me to an air navigation course at Manston, on the eastern tip of Kent. It could have been in Siberia, for all I cared; this was the crowning disaster—being deported, for life it seemed, from fighters.

The Air Ministry finally sent me back to Tangmere, to the Coastal Command squadron at the end of the tarmac. It was the ultimate humiliation. Condemned to these lumbering twin-motored aircraft which staggered off the ground with a crew of four, I watched bitterly, enviously, as my friends in 43 Squadron gamboled in their Furies. I determined to escape. I still had the plague on me and, for once, I was glad. I wrote to the Air Ministry an incredibly naïve but categorical letter. I said that, flying as a passenger in a multi-place aircraft, I became so nervous that it made me ill; my skin complaint was still there to prove it. Unless I could return to single-seaters and receive proper medical treatment, I would resign.

That letter did the trick. Within a week I was transferred from the Coastal Squadron at one end of the tarmac to 43 Squadron at the other. At the touch of the wand, I was changed from a navigator back into a fighter pilot. And the doctors, apparently impressed by my threat to resign, sent me away on six months' leave. Thus, a year after Professor Young had advised me to live like a cabbage, I was at last allowed to do so. I vegetated in the Quantock Hills.

In September 1938 I went back to 43 Squadron, back to flying, and never again was my skin marred by another sore. The cure had worked. So glad was I to be delivered, as if by the Almighty, from my satanic affliction, that I felt like crying aloud with friend Job: "I know that my Redeemer liveth."

The signs of war were growing daily. In the Sudetenland province of Czechoslovakia, people were clamoring: *"Ein Volk, Ein Reich, Ein Fuehrer."* And the Fuehrer turned his rage and threats against Czechoslovakia. Hardly had I taken to the air again with 43 Squadron, in September 1938, when the Munich crisis brought England to the verge of war.

At Tangmere, all was gloom. We were less depressed by Hitler's threats than by the fact that we were so poorly armed to meet them. The R.A.F.'s proud claim to be England's first line of defense now made us look, and feel, ridiculous. Our Furies were obsolete. The German Heinkel and Dornier bombers (not to speak of their Messerschmitt fighters) could easily outstrip us—which was of academic interest anyhow, for if by some miracle we managed to get within range of them, our two puny Vickers guns would merely act as pinpricks.

On September 28, Londoners were being issued gasmasks and were digging trenches, a passive form of resistance against the Luftwaffe's expected "knockout blow." We, in 43 Squadron, spent all that night in the hangar, making up ammunition bands for our guns and daubing our shining silver Furies with warpaint, brown and green. The added weight and skin friction of the camouflage made them drag their heels even more.

With the departure to Munich of the British and French premiers, Chamberlain and Daladier, the suspense eased somewhat. Within 48 hours they had agreed to sacrifice Czechoslovakia to the Teutonic war god. Chamberlain returned to Croydon airport, waved a little white paper signed by Hitler, and talked in his frail voice of "peace in our time." He was hailed as a savior. War was averted and the nation cheered gratefully.

At Tangmere we stood down. We did not cheer, but just heaved a sigh of relief.

The Air Ministry lost no time in administering the tonic needed to revive us—Hurricanes, the new "300 m.p.h.-plus" monoplane fighters. By mid-December we were fully equipped. We felt better, and braver. The Fury had been a lovely plaything; the Hurricane, with its powerful motor and its battery of eight machine guns, was an engine of war.

A complete change of mind and heart had by now come over me. I relished every moment of flying, now that it no longer afflicted me with the plague. My pacifism of the previous year had evaporated; I was becoming rather bellicose—at least as bloody-minded as every other Englishman felt toward the swaggering, bullying Germans. And, in the growingly tense atmosphere, I was discovering that those parvenue pilots I had once so resented were really the warmest, most generous friends. They were, after all, genuine "fighter boys," who lived for the shining hour, who did not take themselves seriously.

Our training increased in tempo, became more warlike. Battle climbs took us to 30,000 feet, where the Hurricane wallowed, barely afloat in the thin air. We fired our guns at a splash target in the sea, where the bullets kicked up jagged white plumes and churned the water into foam. Nothing, it seemed, could survive in that hail of metal.

Two things were happening: we were drifting inexorably toward a conflict and, at the same time, perfecting ourselves as aerial killers. We were on the warpath, and by mid-March 1939, when Hitler, from Prague, yelled: "Czechoslovakia has ceased to exist," we felt ready and armed, anxious almost, for the fight—a rather naïve attitude, it is true, for we were David against Goliath, refusing to acknowledge the Luftwaffe's enormous superiority in weight and numbers.

The hour struck—for Poland on September 1, for England and France on the 3rd. That morning, I lay on the grass beside my Hurricane with the rest of my flight. We were at "readiness"—five minutes notice to take-off, but still there was no word of war. Then we were informed: "The balloon goes up at 11:45."

We walked over to the mess, that sprawling building, now covered with autumn-pink creeper, where I had lived on and off for the last four years. Now all was grim and solemn, as we waited in the mess for Chamberlain to speak on the radio.

Suddenly Chamberlain's voice, heavy with disaster, broke the silence: "It is a sad day for all of us. All the aims I have tried so hard to attain, all the principles in which I believed . . . have come to nought. I hope to live long enough to see the day when, with the end of Hitlerism, a free Europe will be born."

The tension suddenly broke. The fatal step had been taken; we were at war. Caesar Hull, a South African and a superb pilot, was the first to rejoice. "Wizard," he kept repeating and, turning to John Simpson, he laughed: "Don't worry, John, you'll be one of the first to be killed!"

John, like me, would survive, but not Caesar, nor Woods-Scawen, nor

Wilkinson in A flight, nor Tiger Folkes, Eddy Edmonds, Pat Christie or Joe Sullivan in B flight. By the time another year was out, they would all be dead. With one chance in five of survival—not counting the burnt and the wounded—only a handful of us would come through.

When the lot of my generation is compared to succeeding ones, I believe that we had it as hard as any. True, we had known a carefree youth and tasted copiously of the joy of living. But six years of war compelled us to live with the horror of dying, day after day; it took from us all we had, our friends included, and left us empty-handed and disillusioned.

I was twenty-four—quite old for a fighter pilot. Not all that long ago, I had sat on my father's knee, while he told me about Queen Boadicea and King Alfred, Drake and Nelson and all the great company who had fought against the invaders of England. Now it was my turn to be numbered among them, and my brothers too: Michael, a destroyer captain, and Philip, guarding a distant outpost. I believe my father would have felt proud, in his quiet way, that his three sons were in the front line. My mother no doubt felt the same. But now, with my father gone, it was alone that she would have to do the waiting and the praying.

From the beginning, the war in England was a strangely domestic affair. We were all in it; it was everybody's war. We fighter pilots were confined within the base, lived and slept beside our aircraft, in a tense state of alert. But families and friends came to wish their men well, waiting for them by the surrounding barbed wire fence. My mother came too, with my brother Francis, then fourteen, to talk to me. She was very calm; that was her great quality—she never showed fear nor distress, only joy.

A few alarms and excursions stirred us from our increasing inertia. We waited and waited and became bored and fretful, longing to escape from our barbed wire enclosure. Months were to pass before England was threatened with invasion. Meanwhile, the Phoney War was on.

CHAPTER 10

WAR: THE AIR BATTLES

The exigencies of war soon changed the pastoral atmosphere of Tangmere. Mechanical diggers came, clawing up the green turf, to clear the way for asphalt runways, and the green itself was camouflaged with soot. Repeated flaps kept us on the alert; but "bandits" and "bogies" (code for, respectively, enemy and unidentified aircraft) always turned out to be one of ours. Only once did I shoot—at a stray barrage balloon which flopped down into a field, like a tired elephant, with the local villagers in pursuit.

With ground control still in a rudimentary stage, many fighter pilots, blinded and confused in the unaccustomed obscurity of the blackout, crashed to death. Though for months the enemy never showed up, we kept our senses sharpened with wild aerial escapades. In tight formation we dived those Spitfires low over 152's hangar, pulled them up into a loop, dived again, rolled and gamboled. It looked like terrible exhibitionism, but was really only an expression of *joie de vivre*, which the whole squadron shared. No one, we believed, least of all the Germans, could ever beat us.

Our role being the protection of coastal convoys, we patroled above them from dawn to dusk, in fair weather and foul. The sea was our one dread. Our single Merlin engine kept us flying; if it stopped we would inevitably fall into the drink where, with nothing but our kapok-filled Mae Wests to keep us afloat, we stood less chance than the mariners below.

Caesar was the first to score: his victim, a Heinkel bomber, crashed into the sea. A few days later, I drew level with him. It was February 3, 1940. At the head of Blue section, I was skidding low over the sea, Tiger Folkes and Sergeant Hallowes in my wake. The crew of the Heinkel I spotted that morning never saw us until the bullets began tearing into their bomber. Only then did red tracer come spurting from their rear guns. In the first foolish rapture of combat I believed myself, like Achilles, invulnerable. The Heinkel scraped over the cliffs at Whitby and crashlanded in the snow behind the town—the first German bomber down on English soil since World War I.

I felt elated as I watched the enemy bomber crash. Then the full implication struck me. Someone heard me murmur, as I climbed out of the cockpit: "Poor devils, I don't think they're all dead." Two of them were. Remorse, rather than curiosity, impelled me to visit the survivors in the hospital. One of them, Karl Missy, the rear gunner, had tried to kill me; he was prevented when the bullets from my guns sawed through his leg and felled him. Despite the harm I had done him, he clasped my hand, but, in his steady brown eyes, was the reproachful look of a wounded animal.

A few days later, I killed four more men. "Did you really have to kill them?" asked my 12 year-old Pierre when, many years later, I told him of that morning. I never had the slightest wish to kill anybody, least of all young people like myself, with the same passion for flying. It was not them but their bomber, invading our sky, that filled my sights after I had stalked it, with all my cunning, four miles up in a deserted sky. There I did it to death in cold blood. Only later did I picture the crew, with one more mission accomplished, chatting on the intercom, perhaps munching a sandwich or drinking ersatz coffee, as they headed for home and safety, where their comrades and their loved ones waited. How could I escape a feeling of remorse when it was I who put an end to all that, I who struck them down? I, the one, ever unsure of myself, afraid of death and darkness, who shunned a fight, of whom it had always been said "Needs encouragement." Now I needed none. A terrible change had come over me.

The squadron moved north, to Wick, to defend the naval base of Scapa Flow. There, at the extreme tip of Scotland, we stood guard throughout the long northern days and, during the bitter cold of the night, slept briefly, fitfully, under rough blankets and newspapers. Not that the hard lying was a bad thing—it made it easier to go out, face the weather and the enemy and, if need be, die. One morning, Tiger Folkes, patroling with me, low above the tumultuous waters, disappeared.

The Luftwaffe men faced the double hazard of our fighters from the sea. We sat, strapped into our cockpits, waiting to sally forth against them. With the approach of the enemy, the radio jamming grew louder and louder, and the tension became so unbearable that it sometimes drove us from our cockpits to vomit. When at last the code word SCRAMBLE unleashed us, we surged forward, throttle wide open, tails up like baying hounds. Only a kill could satisfy our lust for the chase. But the scent, thanks to imperfect radar coverage, was sometimes false.

One night, after searching vainly, high among the A.A. bursts over Scapa, and low, where bombs and unspent shells were plopping into the Pentland Firth, the controller called me in to land. I switched off my radio and continued to search. Then, high up in the glow of the departed day, a speck materialized. With my radio still mute, I began to stalk, silently, stealthily, my eyes glued on the speck in the sky. But when I closed in on my prey, he resisted desperately.

In aerial combat, you usually only hear the enemy's fire if you stop a close one. But there in the darkness, far out to sea, Heinkel and Hurricane were fighting a terrible gun battle at point blank range, so that when I came in for the coup de grace I would actually hear the Heinkel's guns, in their last dying fury, firing just above my head. I was now seized with an irresistible desire to destroy. Down went the bomber into the sea, and with it four more dead men. I all but died with them, as I realized when, next morning, I examined my Hurricane. It was riddled with bullets.

That fight made me think. The killing game was increasing in pace, and this time I had barely escaped death. It was a sobering thought. But a more awful one was that I myself had become an implacable agent of death. Next day, when a small horde of us pounced on another Heinkel, I did not bother to fire—the machine was already floundering. I flew in close beside it. The young pilot and his companions regarded me helplessly as their flying tumbrel bore them on, down to the sea. I would have given anything to save them; instead, I found myself escorting them to their grave. A few minutes later they were swallowed up by the sea.

By now, the first carefree rapture of victory had faded. No longer was I an amateur, but a hard-bitten professional. The medal recently pinned on my breast by the King confirmed the fact. But so far the air war had consisted of skirmishes: violent hand-to-hand fighting over the sea. The real air war started, on May 10, 1940, with the German offensive in the west.

A week later, I took command of 85 Squadron at Debden, north of London, where they had repaired after escaping, barely, from the military disaster in France. At our forward airfields, Castle Camps and Martlesham, near the North Sea coast, camping under canvas, in an atmosphere scented with mown hay, heather and wildflowers, and sweetened by the song of birds, I rediscovered the sublime peace of the pastoral life. For a month or so war was not for us an urgent preoccupation. It merely involved us in patrolling from dawn to dusk over the east coast convoys. Occasionally we picked up scraps of talk from the squadrons over Dunkirk; we ourselves were well beyond range of that titanic operation. Then, suddenly, I was ordered to concentrate my entire squadron at Martlesham. The Battle of Britain had begun.

I myself was lucky to survive the first twenty-four hours of the battle. During a sharp fight, miles out to sea, my aircraft was disabled by enemy bullets. One exploded in the cockpit. For some minutes, as I searched vainly for a ship, it looked as if I were going to die, rather slowly, by drowning. But first I had to jump into the sea, three thousand feet below. Faced with the prospect of death, I was astonished to find myself so calm and lucid. I jumped, and my parachute deposited me in the sea, which would have claimed another victim, but for the minesweeper *Finisterre*. She seemed to have appeared from nowhere, and was miles off her course.

Back on dry land I telephoned my mother, who feigned indifference and advised me to be more careful in future. That evening I was back again in the air.

The Luftwaffe's increasing offensive against our coastal convoys kept us patrolling ceaselessly during the day and—those few of us who were qualified—during the night as well. In June, July and August I flew as many hours as in a normal year. I learned not to sleep and, when I did, it was with one eye open and both ears cocked. Gradually, insidiously, fatigue began to weigh down on us, and our nerves tensed more and more to resist it. The south-coast squadrons were having it far worse while we, on the left wing of the battle, waited impatiently to be thrown into the fray.

Our turn came soon after Goering, on August 13, launched his *Adlerangriff*, Eagles' Attack, which, he promised Hitler, would wipe out the R.A.F.'s fighter defenses within a week. 85 Squadron were moved back to Debden where the Luftwaffe were attacking in mass.

My frightening childhood impressions of Germans were as vivid as ever; there still echoed in my ears nanny's terrifying threat: "Master Peter, if you're naughty, I shall give you over to the Germans." I was still frightened of Germans. The fierce individual combats I had so far fought with them had not made me feel any braver. Quite recently, I had dived slapdash into a formation of thirty Messerschmitts, hoping to pick one off. The storm of lead which followed my hasty withdrawal into a nearby cloud confirmed my fears that the Germans, en masse, were redoubtable. And now I had to lead my squadron of twelve against hundreds of German bombers and fighters. I dreaded the idea and tossed sleeplessly in my bed thinking about it—luckily for no more than a few nights, for the test came on August 18, the day after our move to Debden. When I received the order: "Patrol Canterbury, two hundred plus approaching," I felt not the slightest qualm, even less when I sighted the massed enemy formations, stepped up over thousands of feet like a giant moving staircase, as one fighter pilot put it.

By the end of the day, the Luftwaffe had suffered a shattering defeat. Goering's boast of victory within a week evaporated in the English air, and it was Churchill, two days later, who had the next word to say, when he paid his immortal tribute to the British fighters: "Never in the field of human conflict was so much owed by so many to so few."

The enemy's initial onslaught had been repulsed, but the hardest fighting was yet to come. My squadron was now moved up to Croydon, in the forefront of the battle. Of the twenty pilots I led to Croydon on August 19, fourteen, including me, were shot down within the next two weeks, two of them twice. The number in itself looks insignificant; never, in fact, did the R.A.F. lose more than a few dozen fighter pilots in a day. Yet, during these crucial weeks such losses, especially in experienced pilots, began to spell defeat. As reinforcements, came pilots from other commands, from the Navy, too, and the flying schools—the latter, boys hardly past their teens, brave as lions but tenderfeet. Our battle was a small one but on its outcome depended the fate of the western world.

No such thoughts ever bothered us. Obviously, we knew we had to win; but, more than that, we were somehow certain that we could not lose. I think it had something to do with England. Miles up in the sky, we fighter pilots could see more of England than any other of England's defenders had ever seen before. Beneath us stretched our beloved country, with its green hills and valleys, lush pastures and villages clustering round an ancient church. Yes, it was a help to have England there below.

She was behind us, too. When, at the end of the day, we touched down for a beer at the local, people were warm and wonderfully encouraging. They were for us, the fighter boys, who had once been the bad boys, who supposedly drank too much and drove too fast. Now people realized that, on the job, we were professionals. They rooted for us as if we were the home team, and we knew we had to win, if only for them.

Those days of battle were the most stirring and the most wonderful I have ever lived, all the more so that they were lived in the midst of death. Death was never far away, a few minutes maybe, or a few inches, so it was all the more exalting to be alive. Though our numbers dwindled steadily, no one ever believed that he would be the next to die.

The Luftwaffe's massed formations, laying waste our bases, were smashing their way inland, nearer and nearer to London. Day by day, hour by hour, we took off to battle with them. When possible, I led the squadron in a head-on charge against the enemy bombers. Often, though, we would have to duel single-handed with their escorting fighters.

By the end of August, the Luftwaffe, by sheer weight of numbers— four to one in their favor—was wearing us down; we were weary beyond caring, our nerves tautened to breaking-point. On August 31, the British fighters suffered their heaviest losses. I was among them. The Germans attacked in the middle of our hasty lunch. Their bombs all but hit us as we roared, full-throttle, off the ground. The blast made our engines falter. I never felt any particular hatred for the German airmen, only anger. This time, though, I was so blind with fury that I felt things must end badly for me. But I was too weary and too strung-up to care. For a few thrilling moments, I fenced with a crowd of Messerschmitts. Then, inevitably, one of them got me. Down I went, muttering: "Christ!"—then jumped for it. I fetched up in a mass of brambles, feeling rather foolish, as if I had been unhorsed in the midst of a jousting tournament. That evening, at Croydon hospital, the surgeon pulled a heavy caliber bullet out of my foot.

Two weeks in the hospital gave me an idea of the courage of people on the ground. Night after night, the raiders were overhead. Our nurses, charming and serene, pulled our beds away from the windows, which were regularly blown in, occasionally admitting a few bomb splinters. Supposedly a hero of the air battle, I was now terrified, and abjectly ashamed, too, before the resolution of those nurses.

With me wounded, our two flight commanders killed and more of our pilots dead or wounded, 85 Squadron was, early in September, withdrawn from the front line and sent north. I had to rejoin them within three weeks, or I should be replaced. My wound prevented me from walking, but not from flying, so, when I arrived at our new base, Church Fenton, in Yorkshire, I took the precaution of going straight to the hangars, where I was helped into a Hurricane. Then I took off. When I reported to the doctor, he told me gravely: "It will be some time before you can fly again." "But I've just been flying," I replied, and he said no more.

Early in October, Goering gave orders for what he called "the complete annihilation" of London. The massive night raids on the capital had started a month earlier and the meager British night fighter force, practically powerless to stop them, was now strengthened. My squadron was one of the day squadrons assigned to night fighting. All through the winter months, we were to grope blindly after the enemy, invisible in the English sky.

Only half a dozen pilots in the squadron were night operational; the others had a month to learn the basic elements. These were imparted to them at Kirton Lindsey, in Lincolnshire. The Luftwaffe took a lively interest: a Dornier machine-gunned the flare path where I was directing operations—which ended abruptly with my diving under the mobile floodlight. One morning, a few days later, as I talked to Jim Marshall at the dispersal point, he suddenly leapt at me and knocked me flat. "What the hell . . ." I began, indignantly, then saw tracer whipping past just above us, as a marauding Heinkel slipped low across the airfield.

We moved to Gravesend, at the eastern approaches to London; the very name reflected the dreary atmosphere of the place. A quagmire surrounded our damp dispersal huts, lit by paraffin lamps. There we waited through the night for our turn to patrol, surrounded by the artificial gloom created by our dark glasses, which kept our eyes in a state of night vision. (It takes about twenty minutes for the eyes to become fully adapted from day to night vision.)

Our Hurricanes lacked the proper means for all-weather night-fighting: radar, cockpit heating, de-icing equipment. The ground control, for all their concern for our safety, were seriously handicapped by the rudimentary nature of navigational and landing aids. Fighting by night in these conditions, experience counted more than anything; the weather, not the enemy, proved the greater hazard and killed more pilots. For this reason, it was normal that I, the oldest hand, should do the trickier weather tests. One ended badly for me, when I crashed while landing in a dense fog which had obliterated everything at the airfield, except the red light on the hangar.

Meanwhile London burned, while we, searching blindly in the dark, were impotent, without radar, to find the German bombers. On the airfield at Gravesend, we listened in frustration to the ceaseless rumble of engines overhead, as they came streaming up the Thames estuary on their way to stoke the fires raging in the city. Ironically, it was the sea of flames below which offered us fighters, stacked up in layers above it, our only chance of discerning the silhouette of an enemy bomber. This crude method occasionally succeeded, but not with us. We continued groping in the dark while below us London was a tumult of explosions and fire.

We moved back to Debden. To the south, London's fiery skyline looked like a flamboyant sunset. Yet still, for all our desperate searching, we remained powerless to come to grips with the enemy.

For interception and navigation, we relied solely on radio, directions being transmitted by the controller. One dirty night, a generator failure left me erring like a lost sheep. The controller's voice grew dim and disappeared, the cockpit lights faded into obscurity, the signalling lamp was useless. There remained only one way out—to jump.

For some moments I circled, contemplating this hazardous prospect. Then, suddenly, far below in the murk, a light came on, went out and, a little later, came on again, to be extinguished once more. I dived down to investigate. Aircraft, invisible save for their navigation lights, were circling and landing, so I slipped in behind one and landed in its wake. A man climbed up on the wing and I shouted to him: "I'm the commanding officer of 85 Squadron." "We'll see about that," he yelled and pressed a revolver into my back, where it remained until I had taxied in and proved my identity.

The enemy continued to elude us—even when he landed on our own airfield, as a Heinkel did one night. Realizing his error, the pilot took off and escaped in the dark. However, I caught another erring German. His aircraft was held in the searchlights and, incredibly, his navigation lights were burning. Error or ruse? Or was it, after all, one of ours? I got close enough to see the black crosses, then fired. Three parachutes streamed into the dazzling blue searchlight cone and the bomber, a Dornier, its navigation lights still on, dived into the ground. It was the only enemy aircraft to fall to our Hurricanes in six months of futile searching.

Meanwhile, the scientists were foisting on us the strangest lethal devices: aerial mines, trailing hundreds of feet of wire and parachuted across the incoming bomber stream; aerial hand grenades, to scatter in the enemy's path; and an aerial searchlight, the turbinlite, guided by radar and powered by a ton of batteries, which would illuminate the target for thirty seconds, during which a "satellite" fighter was supposed to make a lightning kill. But we, who had to experiment with these odd contraptions, were convinced that the only solution was airborne radar, electronic eyes to replace our own, and heavy caliber guns. Thus armed, as at last we were, we went forth into the dark and became a scourge to the enemy.

By early 1941, the night-fighter force was inflicting such losses that, after the devastating fire attack on London on May 10, the Luftwaffe's mass night raids ended.

By now, twenty months of day and night operations had reduced me to a nerve-racked, sleep-starved wreck. I was flying more like a tired chicken than an avenging angel. In my last night combat, a Junkers 88 riddled my aircraft and continued blithely on its way. The fight had gone out of me. I had flown myself to a standstill. The doctors grounded me and put me on barbituates. In June 1941, I was sent to a staff job with the title "Wing-commander, night operations"—one that provoked smiles, for it was at this time that I married.

Rosemary lived with her parents hard by our airfield at Hundson, in Hertfordshire. She was twenty, tall and lovely—never more so than that evening we met at a local country house. I could not wait to make her my wife, for life in those dangerous days seemed a brief, precarious thing. So, true to that wartime phenomenon, the urge to reproduce, we rushed hand-in-hand to the altar. In the ancient church at Much Hadham, we vowed—alas, all too hastily—to be one another's forever. Exactly nine months later, our first child was born.

But, before that, the stresses and strains of the past months had produced in me the inevitable breakdown. Sleep was the gnawing problem. I had learned to do without it, now it evaded me altogether. Unprotesting, I was led before doctors and psychologists, then sent away for three months. Rosemary found herself with an invalid, half-demented husband on her hands, and a baby on the way.

One event which helped, more than any other, to settle my disarray, was the birth, in April 1942, of our son Giles. There was more to it than just becoming a father. Giles's birth had a deeper meaning for me, for while during all those months of fighting I had been living in an environment of death and destroying life with my own hands, I now found before my eyes a life that I had actually created. It was a welcome compensation, if only a symbolic one, for the lives I had taken.

I was sent to command the fighter station at Drem, near Edinburgh. With the Spitfires of 611 Squadron, I began to regain my verve for flying. I flew again, as of old, with daring—fast, hard and low. Regrettably, I once flew, with a Polish officer as passenger, through the local telephone wires. On landing, the Pole, crazy with joy, threw his arms round me: he had never had such a thrill.

Yet for all the newfound thrill of flying, I knew in my bones that I should never again be the pilot I once had been. I had gone too far down the hill ever to get to the top again. The thought haunted me. Hoping to exorcise it, I begged to return to operations. My wish was granted, but my comeback, as commander of 605 Night-fighter Squadron, was brief and inconspicuous. It was also morbidly reminiscent of the past. Once again, I felt death breathing down my neck. I even got the feeling that I was a harbinger of death. Our new pilots, keen and brave, were babies. Nine were killed within a few weeks. Our aircraft were "clapped-out" rejects from other units; it was most probably through mechanical failure that our best crew was lost one night over the Channel.

Fear had come to dwell within me. It had become my constant companion by day, my terrifying bedfellow by night. In my thoughts and visions I saw myself crashing, over and over again, to a horrible death. I was convinced I was going to die—an abject state of mind, exactly the reverse to what I had felt during the heroic days of 1940, when I was convinced that I was going to live!

The more I flew (and there could be no relenting), the more fear, stark, degrading fear, possessed me. Each time I took off, I felt sure it would be the last. I found myself reacting to the smallest shudder of my aircraft and telling myself "This is it!"

And so my unbearable liaison with fear dragged on. It ended at last when, in October 1942, I entered that seminary for the chosen few, the Staff College. There, I was taught how, at a desk, to destroy on a scale which made my efforts in the cockpit look derisive. But I had no ambition to become a mastermind behind the air war. The course over, I was happy enough to be given command, in January 1943, of the fighter station at West Malling, Kent. It was there, one night, that I was once more "at home" to the Luftwaffe.

It was mid-summer 1943 and already the Second Front, the invasion of Nazi-held Europe, was in the air. I was counting on going to France with the 2nd Tactical Air Force. Instead, I was despatched in the opposite direction, to Yorkshire, to command a French training wing.

And then, out of the blue, a telegram arrived. It said curtly: "You are requested to report to the Chief of the Air Staff . . ." What on earth, I wondered anxiously, had I done to deserve this peremptory summons?

CHAPTER 11

THE PALACE

On an upper floor in the Air Ministry building in Whitehall, I was led into the presence of Air Chief Marshal Sir Charles Portal, Chief of the Air Staff. His office, with its blue carpet and pleasant furnishings, might have been that of the chairman of a prosperous company, and he himself, the chairman—charming, soft-spoken and with strikingly Semitic looks. Dressed in *khaffkir* and *burnous* and mounted on a camel, this remarkable Englishman would have been salaamed as an Arab sheik.

I listened, amazed, as "Peter" Portal explained to me that the King, whose equerries were traditionally chosen on a personal basis, had decided to widen the net and appoint temporary equerries, who would be picked not for their family or regimental connections, but for their fighting record. The C.A.S., in his soft voice, concluded: "If you don't find the idea particularly revolting I propose to recommend you for the job of equerry to His Majesty. The appointment will be for three months."

Rosemary was waiting for me in the street below. In the taxi I told her what had happened and she threw her arms around me and exclaimed rather indecently I thought, "We're made." It was natural, I suppose, for her to be glad—but how tragically mistaken she was. For from now on we were destined, as a married couple, to be unmade.

On February 16, 1944, after a casual briefing by Sir Piers Legh, Master of the Household, I found myself in the green-carpeted Regency Room at Buckingham Palace, alone with His Majesty King George VI. Outside, there raged a black, violent storm. The King did not try, or even need, to put me at my ease. King though he was, Defender of the Faith and Emperor of India, the humanity of the man and his striking simplicity came across warmly, unmistakably. Despite his easy manner I felt impressed and so kept well within myself. But sometimes he hesitated in his speech, and then I felt drawn toward him, to help keep up the flow of words. I knew myself the agonies of a stammerer.

The King, and everybody else I had seen so far, had been unbelievably nice to me. My interview over, I was thanking Sir Piers Legh when he stiffened slightly. Down the corridor came two adorable-looking girls, all smiles. "Hullo, Joey," they chorused, and "Joey" introduced me to Princess Elizabeth and her sister Margaret. Our meeting might have been a coincidence, but thinking back, I would not have put it beyond the King to have buzzed them on the interphone and told them, "If you want to see him, he's just left my study." Elizabeth, then seventeen, and Margaret, fourteen, spent, in those dangerous days, a sequestered life at Windsor Castle; the faintest curiosity, like myself, could brighten it.

A couple of weeks later a taxi deposited me at Buckingham Palace to take up my duties. I went straight to my room, as I had done at Tangmere years ago, and crept into bed.

Buckingham Palace, solid, square-shaped and built around an interior courtyard, is a gray, unlovely edifice. Above the steady hum of London's traffic comes, intermittently, the clatter of sentries' rifle butts on the paving and the thump of boots as they turn at the end of their beat— it would be hard to say which suffers most, their feet or the paving.

After graduating from the Royal Air Force College, Cranwell, Peter was posted in 1936 to the 36th R.A.F. Squadron in Singapore; above, he is in front row, 10th from the right. The biplanes in background are Vildebeestes. During the Battle of Britain, he flew Hurricane fighter planes against the invading Luftwaffe. Below, he carries a cane after being wounded in the foot.

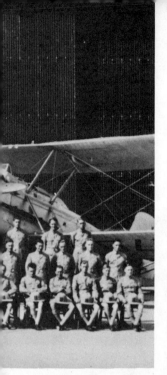

Squadron leaders Townsend, left, and Caesar Hull, "a superb and fearless pilot," in April 1940. Like so many brave R.A.F. pilots who served with Peter, Hull was killed in action within a year of this photograph. "I was convinced I was going to die," Peter writes; but he was one of the fortunate few who survived the air war. Below, he is shown at the controls of a Hurricane.

THE LAST OF THE MANY

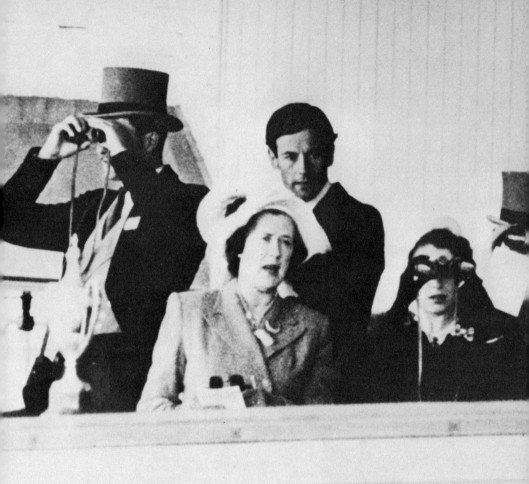

Above, Peter Townsend, at the back, steals a glance at Princess Margaret, at right, during the running of the 1952 Ascot races. Looking through the binoculars is her sister, Queen Elizabeth II. The captain and the princess were often thrown together at these social functions, and soon fell in love. The photograph at right, a closeup from a larger picture, enabled the press to link the two together romantically. The Royal Family took the news, Peter says, "with perfect calm."

Peter found happiness after his marriage to Marie-Luce Jamagne in Brussels in 1959. They are shown together, at left, on their engagement day. Above, they drive through Belgium to Switzerland for the honeymoon. The following year, Princess Margaret married Anthony Armstrong-Jones; the marriage eventually ended in divorce, which, Peter writes, is "infinitely sad." Below, Peter and Marie-Luce (in polka-dot dress) picnic with friends.

The use of "Buck House's" several entrances was determined basically by the rank and station of the user. All normal comers entered by the Privy Purse Door at the right side of the facade; the King's visitors were set down, in wartime, at the equerry's door, within the interior courtyard. When peace came, the Grand Entrance, a little further on, was used for ceremonial visitors who drove up in style, in their own cars or the King's horse-drawn carriages, and stopped under the portico from which, in 1897, Queen Victoria had departed for her Diamond Jubilee drive through London. In the time of her great grandson, King George VI, the Grand Entrance was the starting point for ceremonial drives, like the opening of Parliament. For their personal comings and goings, the King and Queen used the Garden Door, a private entrance on the north facade.

It was vital for the equerry, who had to receive the King's visitors, that the latter be directed to the right door. Once, as I waited for Queen Eugénie of Spain at the Privy Purse Door, her car shot past and disappeared into the interior courtyard, heading for the Grand Entrance—whither I sprinted, down the long corridor, sidestepping startled footmen, until turning into the straight with but a few yards to go, I collided head-on with Her Majesty, who had beaten me to it and was backtracking in my direction towards the King's study. Grinding to a halt, I lowered my head in the customary bow, like a charging bull (nothing new to a Spanish Queen) and, with my hand outstretched in humble greeting, was just in time to grip that of this spirited royal lady, no lightweight, and prevent her collapsing backward onto the floor.

The Palace Staff were loyal, willing and efficient. They never let you down and expected in return the same of you. In a house as big as Buckingham Palace, internal communications, whether vehicular, pedestrian or telephonic, were vital. The gentlemen who operated the telephone exchange were invariably courteous, patient and painstaking. Very rarely was there a slipup, but the King himself related a famous one to me: Mr. George King, who looked after His Majesty's bank account, called the Palace one morning. The lines got crossed and after some delay the banker heard a voice: "Hullo?" "Hullo," he replied somewhat testily, "This is George King." And the voice, unruffled, replied, "Well, this is King George."

The Palace Staff was headed by the Palace Steward, Ainslie. Mr. Ainslie was a man of high professional capacity, but a man, too, with a twinkle in his eye, who, in moments of crisis, seemed to be laughing behind a perfectly straight face. When lightly admonished one day by the Master of the Household, "Joey" Legh, Ainslie's reply was a classic of its kind: "Let me assure you, Sir Piers, that my sole object is to obey the orders of the Master of the Household and give pleasure to the Ladies in Waiting."

Most Englishmen have the soul of a butler in them—it is after all only a desire to serve. Butlers are a breed which has enriched English literature and theater. They have provided the grist for many good stories, one of which was told to me by the Queen, who had a delicious and highly imaginative sense of the ridiculous.

The butler in question was in the service of a celebrated London hostess. Unfortunately, he had a weakness for the bottle and at one glittering dinner party—the Queen was present—he was tottering so unsteadily round the table that his mistress decided to act. She wrote out a message on the little pad beside her. "Get out, you are drunk," and beckoned to the tipsy butler, who read it gravely then, unperturbed, placed it on a slaver and delivered it, with a reproachful glance, to one of the distinguished lady guests.

The "King's Page," an ex-serviceman, who rejoiced in the offical but archaic title of "Page of the Back Stairs," was in close and constant attendance on the King. He possessed up-to-the-minute information on what was going on in the royal presence and was an indispensable link between the King and the equerry-in-waiting. The Queen also had a page, "the Queen's Page" who, as often as not, was to be seen in the corridor, dragging, or dragged by, the Queen's three dogs. There were pages of this and pages of that, of the presence, of the pantry and so on—all conscientious, professional men who worked as a team and kept the royal machinery running smoothly. I admired those men; they were the ground troops. I often wondered what they were thinking behind their impassive features.

Beyond the circle of the Palace Staff were men who could be, had to be, slightly more demonstrative. They were more like the storm troops, in action in the melee of an outside royal function. There was Hawes, the King's chauffeur. Alongside Hawes sat Superintendent Cameron, the King's detective, tall, lean and spare of words. Cameron was the King's sole bodyguard, bowler-hatted and, as far as I know, unarmed—except with prevision and persuasion, weapons which invariably proved effective. Hurle, the Queen's chauffeur, was retained, I suspect, more for his sensitive, human qualities—a factor which always weighed heavily with the Queen—than for his driving.

That corridor, not much less than a hundred yards of it, along which I had sometimes to hurry in such unseemly fashion, was the main business artery of Buckingham Palace. Its red-carpeted floorboards creaked under the incessant passage of those on the way to do business with the King; private secretaries bearing trays of correspondence, pages with red boxes, leather-covered, locked and containing secrets of state from one or another ministry; or ministers themselves and other persons, the high and the mighty, the modest also, who had been summoned to an audience with His Majesty. It was the equerry's job to meet them at the door and usher them into the royal presence with a stiff, formal bow of the head, announcing their name.

They were of all sorts and conditions, these men and women who were received by the King. The most redoubtable, of course, was Prime Minister Winston Churchill. He came every Tuesday to discuss business, over lunch, with the King, who paid him the singular compliment of himself coming to the door and waiting at the top of a short flight of stairs to receive him. Sometimes, Churchill was very tired; in the Government offices in Whitehall he had to be carried upstairs. When, dressed in a black coat, stiff collar and striped trousers, he came to see the King, he shuffled, head bowed, shoulders hunched, crushed by the cares of state and five years of wartime premiership. Mounting those few steps towards the King, he dragged one foot after the other, barely making it to the top.

When, on these occasions, I met Mr. Churchill, there was rarely enough time for anything but the briefest and most banal conversation. One morning, while I waited to take him to the King, he lamented how, because of an electricity cut during the early hours, the water in his aquarium had begun to cool off. The entire Churchill household was routed out of bed to go down to the kitchen and heat up reserves of warm water. The Prime Minister, in dressing gown and slippers, personally took charge of the operation, pouring kettles full of warm water into the aquarium. Now he waited, at Buckingham Palace, to discuss state business with the King.

Burdened as he was with affairs of state, the Prime Minister must have found the formal receptions irksome. Once, however, there came a welcome interruption: Mr. Churchill was called urgently to the telephone to learn from his private secretary the news of some hard-won success. Replacing the receiver, he walked back, singing "Roll out the barrel . . ." and joined the other guests.

Another time, when Britain's prospects in the Middle East looked far from promising, I listened to Churchill, as he waited for his audience with the King, discussing the situation. Suddenly, he turned towards me, fixing me with his bulldog regard, and growled "We must hold Suez!"—as if assigning that vital task to me.

During my eight years with the King, I led into his presence all sorts of people—British, Commonwealth and foreign. Among them were statesmen and politicians, judges, generals, admirals and air marshals, ambassadors and governors of His Majesty's territories beyond the seas, heroes and heroines, venerable ecclesiastics and men of letters and of learning. Few of them remained unaffected by their meeting. General Eisenhower, in uniform, and treating me as if I were his favorite nephew, arrived fifteen minutes too soon and during that time talked pleasantly, if a little nervously, without drawing breath. American Secretary of State Edward Stettinius seemed in a tearing hurry. On entering the King's study with me, he straightened up his coat lapels, switched on a broad, American smile, and before I could announce him, charged past me, and began warmly to pump-handle the King's hand.

After Labor's sweeping victory in the first postwar election, the socialist ministers—particularly those who had made it the hard way, from mine and meadow, dockland and railway yard—who came for audiences with the King, at first seemed ill at ease in the capitalistic atmosphere of Buckingham Palace. They lacked the assurance, the polished manners and the well-tailored appearance of their Tory rivals. Clement Attlee, the Labor Prime Minister, despite his three years as Deputy Prime Minister in the wartime coalition government, was no exception. Attlee was the very antithesis of his predecessor Churchill— one of the most striking contrasts is his 250-page autobiography which reads like a schoolboy's essay beside Churchill's majestic prose.

Attlee's looks were not impressive. His bald pate and ugly moustache, his flat, unimaginative speech, his timid manner and short, uncertain step, all suggested a rather uninspiring schoolmaster. But his appearance did not do him justice, for there was fire in his soul and when he spoke to you, if only briefly (he never wasted words), you felt immediately the goodness and sincerity of the man. In politics he possessed the integrity of a judge and on certain problems (like decolonization) his tenacity and wisdom exceeded Churchill's. What he lacked was the personality and the oratory that made Churchill such an inspiring figure.

The equerry, after meeting the ministers at the "equerry's entrance," would install them, pending the King's summons, in the nearby Chinese

Room amidst whose oriental trappings they looked like a bunch of visiting mandarins. I watched this parade of ministers, Labor and Tory, the most powerful men in the land, of potentates and eminent personages, with some detachment. Their business was not mine; and it seemed to me that their passing, individual glory faded before the mystic, enduring splendor of the throne, so that they appeared like an actor held in a spotlight—the man alone was visible, the decor excluded. Thus I regarded each one as a man—like myself, who had been fashioned on another anvil, perhaps, but tempered, all the same, in a fierce fire—fiercer than some of them had ever known. Some of them made me wonder how they had ever made it to the heights of fame and power.

The King and Queen—I would not exclude the princesses, either—exercised, quite involuntarily, an extraordinary and entirely benign levelling effect on people. They somehow brought them out of their official selves back to what they really, humanly and ordinarily were.

That is how I came to regard the people, so famous and powerful, who presented themselves to the King—as men who had left their arms and armor at the door of Buckingham Palace, and walked on stripped of their ego and importance, down the corridor and into the royal presence. On leaving, they picked up their arms again, clothed themselves once more in armor, and returned to their well-entrenched positions in the Establishment.

These men were the pillars of the British nation, they supported the Establishment and powered its mills which, like the mills of God, grind slow, but exceeding small.

Lending distinction to the pageant of politicians and important people who crossed the threshold of Buckingham Palace, came Kings, Princes and Princesses, and Presidents. Among them was King Haakon of Norway, a kindly and cadaverous-looking giant who, defying the Nazis, had escaped with Prince Olav, his cheerful, plumpish heir. Another royal Scandinavian giant, King Frederick of Denmark, with his beautiful Queen, Ingrid, paid a state visit. King Frederick had the breezy manner of a sailor, which he was—as well as an accomplished conductor. Towards the end of his stay, I was summoned to his room. The Danish equerry announced me and I entered. There he stood, the King of Denmark, in shirtsleeves. With a casual "I thought you might like to have this" he handed me a small red leather case. In it was the insignia of a Knight of the Order of Dannebrog.

During the visit of the French President and Madame Auriol, I did nothing in particular, but presumably did it very well, for I was made an *Officier de la Légion d'Honneur*. This time I received the insignia by post, in a brown envelope.

That indomitable lady, Queen Wilhelmina of the Netherlands, in a cloche hat and a coat-and-skirt, had tried to lead her troops in a counterattack against the invading Germans in 1940. Failing to contact her army, she had escaped, with nothing but what she stood up in, to England. The war over, the brave Wilhelmina returned, still dressed countrystyle, and, in gratitude for the sanctuary she had received, presented at Buckingham Palace a squadron of big-boned, jet-black chargers to the Household Cavalry.

I was standing quite close to the Queen, watching the ceremony, when something sent me off into a terrible and ill-concealed fit of laughter, in which the Queen immediately joined, skillfully dissimulating her amusement behind a radiant smile. It was the first time (but by no means the last) that I was seized with laughter "in the presence." I never mastered the Queen's technique—I had no business to be laughing in public anyway—so my only hope was to bury my face in my handkerchief and feign a fit of sneezing.

When the Shah of Iran paid a state visit, I was attached to his imperial person. Cutting quite a different figure then—thin, strained, unsure of himself, with an absent look—he was in the throes of divorcing his first wife, the Egyptian princess, Fawzieh. When, by bus, underground and taxi, I took his Imperial Majesty round London, he relaxed and apparently enjoyed it. Back in official circles, however, he once more became taut and uneasy. The Queen, who, as I have mentioned, had a most enjoyable sense of the ridiculous, told me that once when she said to him, "We are taking you to a show, *Annie Get Your Gun*," the Shah shot her a nervous glance and enquired, "An' you get your gun? I am so sorry, I left it in my room. I send my aide-de-camp."

The next story I can vouch for myself. During dinner one evening at the Savoy with the Shah-an-Shah and his A.D.C., who spoke good French but poor English, the latter asked me, "Were you in the war?" "Yes," I replied, "I was a pilot." "So you were a big arse!" he exclaimed. I thought the man was insulting me, then realized that, after all, he was complimenting me on being a big ace—*as* in French sounds more or less like "arse."

Before the Shah departed, I was summoned to his presence at the Iranian Embassy. Charmingly, he thanked me, adding, "I want to give you a present to remember me—you are standing on it." Horrified, I looked down, expecting to find the crushed fragments of some priceless Persian antique. Instead, I saw that I was standing on a magnificent rug.

Such was a cross section of the famous, the high and mighty, whom I met at the entrance to Buckingham Palace and led into the presence of the King, after walking them down that blessed corridor or up a wide staircase which wound up from it to the floor above, where, after the war, the King had his study. Most of the time I dreaded this ritual. The family stammer got hold of me and, after writing out the names on the King's engagement card for the following day, I spent a sleepless night rehearsing them. My apprehension increased as the moment approached for the visitor's arrival. I knew that the chances were that his name would stick at the back of my throat, at least for a few agonizing seconds. I was incapable (as I still am) of reciting a word or a line "to order." So with my heart pounding, I tried to keep up a light conversation all the way down the corridor right up to the door of the King's study. It was a stammerer's trick, to help me into a smooth liaison with the dreaded word, Mister, Sir, General or Lord So-and-so.

The King, to whom I had spoken of my problem—which was his—was most sympathetic and helpful. Once I announced the ambassador-designate to Paris, Mr. Oliver Harvey, as "Mr. Oliver Hardy." The King shot me an enquiring glance, as if expecting me to add "and Mr. Stan Laurel, Your Majesty."

CHAPTER 12

THE COURTIERS

Onto that creaking, red-floored corridor gave the main offices, one after the other: those of the Keeper of the Privy Purse, the King's private secretaries, the Queen's private secretary, the press secretary and the equerry, each at a respectful but easy distance from the King's study. Everyone in that warren was assiduously engaged in the King's or Queen's business. The only one to whom any form of intellectual activity was denied was the equerry-in-waiting. He was not called that for nothing. His job was to WAIT, which he did uninterruptedly during the King's waking hours. It could happen that the equerry could make the King wait for him, if he drifted out of earshot of the King's bell, which occasionally shattered the silence of the equerry's room.

Facing north, as it did, not a ray of sunlight, summer or winter, ever penetrated the french windows of this gloomy room, with its lofty ceiling and its drab walls lined with shelves of books, massive historical and religious tomes, hardly the kind to provide light reading for whiling away the interminable hours. People dropped in, of course, now and then—members of the Household for a cup of tea or a scotch in the evening. Occasionally the King himself would put his head round the door with a charming "May I come in?" or during a long summer evening there might come a tap at the window and there would be the King and Queen and perhaps their daughters on their way for a stroll round the garden. They were most welcome visitors.

The dreariest period of waiting was the one that dragged on through the long winter evenings, after the other members of the Household had returned to their home and their family. It was then that I thought most of mine, far away. Then between 11 P.M. and midnight would come a knock at the door: Frederick, the King's page, was there to announce "His Majesty has retired."

The King and Queen lived in peacetime on the first floor, in the northwest corner of the building. There at least they could enjoy the afternoon sun and a view of the garden and the lake, where ducks nested and raised their young until they were old enough to join higher duck society; then the family would waddle off ceremoniously through the gates of the palace to the more animated surroundings of St. James's Park. As they crossed the Mall, a policeman would hold up the traffic. The whole thing was very civilized.

Opposite the Bow Room, one of the state rooms, the Grand Entrance gave on to the inner courtyard and between the two stretched a long, wide, red-carpeted gallery, practically empty, except on the days when the King held investitures. It was in this gallery that, week after week, he awarded honors to those who had won distinction in the firing line and behind it. For two hours he would stand on a raised dais with a ramp on each side, along which the recipients would approach and withdraw. While the Lord Chamberlain read out each name, some three hundred of them, "gentlemen ushers" stood motionless to each side of the King. The equerry stood close behind him, to hand the King a sword when a knight came to kneel for the accolade, and to pass each medal, which reposed on a velvet cushion.

The King's technique was so faultless that he could lay his hand on that medal each time without looking for it. If ever he failed, it was your fault and you had to juggle the cushion, like trying to find the right gear.

Very much at ease, he pinned on each medal, spoke briefly to the recipient, and shook hands. At times you could hear him humming the tune being played by the string orchestra, in a gallery opposite. Or he might turn round to you and say, rather too loudly, "For God's sake tell them not to make such a ghastly noise."

There was seldom a hitch, though they did occasionally occur. An Indian sepoy, up for the Victoria Cross, marched smartly up the ramp, eyes to the front, straight past the King and down the other side. He made it the second time around.

The King was tolerant of human failings. As he shook hands with a stout elderly lady she dropped her oft-rehearsed curtsey and lost her balance. Luckily, the King still had her by the hand and helped her to rise, if a little unsteadily, to her feet. When Laurence Olivier came to receive his knighthood, his hair was an outrageous blond. He pulled me aside. "For heaven's sake," he begged, "tell the King that I haven't gone queer. I'm just playing in *Hamlet*."

Joey, Sir Piers Legh, Master of the Household, was my immediate chief in the Household hierarchy. A man in his sixties, of average height, frail, myopic, his glasses permanently balanced on the high bridge of his nose; his speech was vague, his walk aimless. But despite appearances Joey was far from gaga. His judgment was unerring, his reflexes lightning-fast. He was moreover, a most lovable character.

As equerry to the Prince of Wales he had once attended an official reception in Australia. As the evening wore on Joey, resplendent in his household coat (dark blue tails, brass buttons, and velvet collar) and medals, slipped out to relieve himself. On returning to the room, he had difficulty opening the door, until it suddenly gave and he found himself confronting a giant, liveried Australian who rasped at him, "How many more times must I say: WAITERS OUTSIDE!"

The man with the most difficult and delicate job was the King's private secretary, Sir Alan Lascelles. In his own words, "Life in that office is not by any means beer and skittles." Professor Laski amplified this earthy phrase: "The private secretary," he wrote, "is the confidant of all ministers . . . Receiving a thousand secrets, he must discriminate between what may emerge and what may remain obscure . . . It is a life passed amid circumstances in which the most trifling incident may lead to major disaster . . . He must move serenely amid all the events which move other men to passionate statements."

There was a mutual affection between us. I admired his dry, pungent wit, though less when it turned to pitiless sarcasm. "Tommy" Lascelles' character was written all over him: spare of frame, his steel-rimmed spectacles and World War I moustache were the main features of his thin, pallid face. He still dressed in the fashion of the 'twenties, in dreary, outmoded gray or brown suits, with waistcoat and watchchain and narrow trousers. The points of his stiff collars were rounded, his ties were somber and colorless. There was great kindness in him, but in purely human affairs, affairs of the heart, to be more precise, he had an archaic, uncomfortable outlook which irked me. Perhaps it was just as well, when the monarchy was like an island in a world evolving at a frightening speed around it. Tommy did not adapt himself to the changing times nearly as well as the monarch himself.

Table talk in the Household dining room taught me much—it helped me to avoid many pitfalls and it sharpened my wits. Quick repartee was appreciated. Once everyone was discussing Princess Margaret, who was suffering from a torticolis, a stiff neck. What kind of specialist should be called in? they wondered. A masseur, a chiropractor, an osteopath? Who could cure the stiff neck? I suggested a necromancer.

CHAPTER 13

THE ROYAL HOMES

Before I had time to adjust myself to the fusty, august atmosphere of Buckingham Palace, Easter brought a dramatic change of scene. I found myself alone, except for the lady-in-waiting, with the King and Queen and their daughters, in a small house, Appleton Lodge, on the King's estate at Sandringham. It was my first opportunity to see them out of their royal context, thinking and acting for themselves, behaving and looking more or less like anybody else. It was then that they were at their best and most enjoyable.

The King was a man of medium build, lean and athletic. His head, rather small, was statuesque, so finely chiseled were his features; his hair and his skin had the look and the luminosity of bronze. The steady regard in his blue eyes only changed—and then, to an alarming glare—when he was irked or rattled. Then, he would start to rant, noisily, and the Queen would mollify him with a soothing word or gesture; once she held his pulse and, with a wistful smile, began to count—tick, tick, tick—which made him laugh, and the storm subsided. In those moments he was like a small boy, very lovable. "The most marvelous person in the world," the King called his wife. Although I hardly knew her as yet, I came, within my limits, to think so, too.

At your first (and every subsequent) meeting with Queen Elizabeth, you did not notice her small stature, her *embonpoint* (chubbiness). You were simply swept off your feet by her warm and totally captivating charm. It radiated from her smile; you felt it as you took, but never shook, her small, soft hand—which members of her Household were privileged to kiss. In her quiet, enquiring voice, she would first invariably ask a stranger about *himself*. That was the secret of her charm; she gave people the feeling that she was interested primarily in them; that she knew them, almost. And when she laughed, her very blue eyes laughed, too. The Queen enjoyed laughing. Only rarely did she betray anger—and then it was in her eyes, which blazed, bluer than ever.

The two princesses had the same colored eyes as their parents. Those of Elizabeth were the porcelain blue of her father, of her German ancestors; Margaret's were of a darker blue, like that of a deep tropical sea. Both had inherited their parents' flawless, luminous complexion and their shortish stature, too. Elizabeth, the sturdier built, had not yet attained the full allure of an adult. She was shy, occasionally to the point of gaucheness, and this tended to hide her charm. When it showed through, it was with a touching, spontaneous sincerity. Her younger sister was as unremarkable as one would expect of a fourteen-year-old girl—except when she came out with some shattering wisecrack; then, to her unconcealed delight, all eyes were upon her.

So charming and thoughtful was this family, whom I hardly knew, that they made me feel more of a guest than an aide, showing me over the "Big House" at Sandringham (closed for the duration of the war), where daffodils bloomed, a mass of gold, on the lawns; driving me—the King at the wheel—to the Royal Stud, where the stallions were paraded, and to the museum, guarded by the vigorous bronze statue of the Derby-winning Persimmon.

The Princesses led me in a hair-raising bicycle race, pedaling headlong down the switchback slopes of the lawn, round the pond and down the narrow paths between the flower beds. Then through the woods, now coming alive with springtime, we walked—and talked.

Talking of Kings, Princess Elizabeth told me of her grandfather King George V: "His manner was very abrupt; some people thought he was being rude." "I rather like people like that," said I, unwittingly putting my foot into it, "because if they are rude to you, you can be rude back at them." "Yes, but you can't very well be rude to the King of England," retorted the heir to England's throne. I took note to be more wary in future of what I said.

Easter, I think, is the most soul-shattering of all church feasts; after humiliation and disaster—triumph, to which the Easter hymns give full vent. The Royal Family attended matins as usual. The King was deeply religious; he knew the Bible well. Some of his favorite quotations were the ones with a double meaning that crop up here and there in the Bible and the hymns. He laughed when I told him that Mr. Williams, at Wynchwood, had found two mentions of cricket in the Bible: when Peter stood up with the eleven and was bold, and when Rachel came out with a full pitcher. That Easter morning we sang the traditional Easter hymn, No. 140: "Jesus lives!" We came to the lines

> This shall calm our trembling breath
> When we pass its gloomy portal

Portal. I glanced across at the King, wondering whether the same thing has struck him. It had. Our eyes met and he grinned broadly at this unexpected and quite undeserved allusion to the Chief of the Air Staff, Sir Charles Portal.

What struck me during those few days *en famille* with the King and Queen and their daughters was the astonishing affection generated by that small family. Perpetual currents of it flowed between them, between father and mother, sister and sister, between the parents and their daughters and back again. Then it radiated outwards to the ends of the world, touching thousands of millions of hearts who sent, rolling back, a massive wave of loyalty and love to the Royal Family.

The King and Queen were good and upright people who had inherited a gigantic burden to which they were selflessly devoted. Everybody knew that. But now I saw them not as King and Queen, but as the father and mother of two rather adorable and quite unsophisticated girls, as affectionate, understanding parents who had succeeded in creating a family atmosphere which every other family could admire, even envy.

The disputes, the sulking, the voices raised in protest or disapproval, that were to be found in the households of his subjects, never—at least, so that you could notice it—occurred in the King's home. People talk about royal training; well, this was a part, a very basic part, of it. "Our family, us four," the King once wrote, "the 'Royal Family' must remain together . . ." All was subordinated to that heartfelt sentiment.

In that small house, Appleton Lodge, as in all the King's private residences, we, the Household in Waiting, shared the recreational hours of the day with "the Family," lunching and dining with them and remaining with them until the evening was spent.

The Easter holidays over, the King returned to London, there to pick up his burden once more, to live again the anxious days—now more anxious than ever with the preparations for "Overlord," the invasion of Europe, nearing completion and D-Day at hand.

I was, at this time, living with Rosemary and Giles among the Kentish orchards and hop gardens. Rosemary's unhappy lot, like all courtiers' wives, was to become a "court-widow" during my spell of waiting—two weeks. Then for four weeks she had me more or less on her hands, an unbalancing routine. But who were we to grumble? Many men in the forces, including my two brothers, had it much worse. Yet, in our case the imbalance proved more upsetting than the absence.

Exactly one week after D-Day, at 5 A.M. on June 13, we were awoken by a shattering explosion. Believing it must have been a stray bomb dropped by a German raider, we thought no more of it. Two nights later, the sky was overcast, the ceiling low. Some time before midnight, approaching from the south-east, there came an unaccustomed droning which rapidly crescendoed into an ear-splitting thunder until we could see, against the clouds, the silhouette of a small and villainous-looking winged projectile darting overhead, trailing a jet of red, roaring flame.

Hitler's V-1's (vengeance weapons) had arrived. One of the first of them had shattered our sleep two days earlier. But that night they kept coming in a continuous stream. Totally indiscriminate weapons, they were aimed at London, but hundreds fell all along "bomb alley," between the Kentish coast and the capital.

At Buckingham Palace, waiting in the equerry's room, I would listen to the V-1's as they came roaring into London. As long as that pulsating noise continued, all was well for those below; but as soon as the ram-jet engine spluttered to a stop it was time to get your head down, thrust your fingers in your ears, open your mouth and wait for the shattering blast.

The King showed remarkable phlegm under fire, as he had done when, as a nineteen-year-old midshipman, he had manned A-turret in the *Collingwood* at the Battle of Jutland. He was inclined to fuss when "ordered" below to the underground shelter; the royal quarters were tiny and the rest of us had to make do.

The V-1's died away in September, but not before one had blown a gaping hole in the garden wall at Buckingham Palace—its ninth hit. The V-2's then took up the bombardment of London. Being supersonic, they hit before they were heard, so the possibility of running for cover did not arise. Bomb for bomb, they killed three times more people than the V-1's.

During those empty, endless hours in the equerry's room I was all too conscious that my next breath might be my last. One evening, the lady in waiting and I were invited to dine with the King and Queen; perhaps it was a gesture of solidarity under the V-2 bombardment. During dinner a terrific explosion rocked the palace. The King asked me to find out where the V-2 had fallen; it had hit a pub off Oxford Street, killing over a hundred people. In ten months, they killed over 10,000 civilians in Britain.

In Autumn 1944, Rosemary and I moved from Kent to a house in Windsor, which we shared with two young and attractive newlyweds, Lord and Lady Rupert Nevill.

In the spring of 1945, with our second child on the way, the King proposed that we should move our abode to a small house, Adelaide Cottage, in the Home Park of Windsor Castle. It was a generous gesture for which I felt deeply grateful, despite the limited amenities of the house.

By early spring 1945, the Allied armies were across the Rhine. But the Germans, holding out in the Hague, were able to bombard Antwerp, now an Allied port, with many thousand V-1's and V-2's. They killed over 3,000 Belgians.

One little Belgian girl, not yet six, had a narrow escape from death when she was riding on the back of her nine-year-old brother's bicycle through Antwerp's Nouveau Parc. Suddenly the bicycle and the children on it were knocked flat by the completely unheralded explosion of a V-2; it fell just the other side of a grassy bank which deflected some of the blast. The little boy led his sister home; she was badly cut and shaken. Her name was Marie-Luce; today she is the mother of three of my children. Marie-Luce's parents moved with their children to Brussels. The following day a flying bomb demolished their house.

The last V-2 I heard rocked Adelaide Cottage early one spring morning. About a month later, on May 8, deliverance came, at last, from the European war. VE-Day was, as Churchill said, the signal for the greatest outburst of joy in the history of mankind. It brought welcome release, too, for the young princesses imprisoned, more or less, in a tower in Windsor Castle. The King's thought for them was, "Poor darlings. They have never had any fun yet." That day they did. They broke out into the crazy, rejoicing world which was London and I stood near them in the dense crowds in front of Buckingham Palace as they cheered, with everybody else, each time their parents, the King and Queen, came out onto the balcony.

Six weeks later, Hugo, our second son, was born. He was christened in St. George's Chapel, where his godfather, the late King, now sleeps. For reasons doubtless valid, but best known to himself, Hugo would later abandon the church of his fathers—and godfather. Today he is a brother in the Roman order of Carmel.

Slowly, England began to come alive again, though rationing and restrictions, which lasted another few years, kept the pace slow. The King holidayed, for the first time in six years, at Balmoral, his Dee-side residence in Scotland, built by Queen Victoria in the mid-nineteenth century. "This dear Paradise" she called it and her feelings found an echo in my own heart. Of all the King's estates, I loved Balmoral best. I liked it less for the house itself, a solid pile of dour gray granite, with its interior of tartan-clad walls and emotional Landseer engravings; I loved Balmoral first and foremost for "the hill."

Beyond the Dee valley, wooded with fir and birch, the "low ground" was all rounded, heather-covered hills. Further, beyond the Gelder Burn, the "high ground" rose up and culminated in the rugged peak of Lochnagar. You could go to the hill and be very close to yourself and to the earth. I loved the hill, open to heaven and horizons, unlike the forest, closed and mysterious, dark and menacing in its silence.

At Balmoral, more than anywhere, the King and Queen were on holiday, the house full of guests. The equerry's duties were not onerous, but were generally enjoyable. He acted unobtrusively as a kind of general handyman, with eyes and ears alert, wary even to the wishes of the royal hosts and the needs and foibles of their guests—a shy girl arriving, late and blushing, for dinner; a young blood with a drop too much inside him; a cabinet minister, still wearing the pallor of Whitehall, and often ill-at-ease in this highland lair; a reverend minister, distractedly contemplating the sermon he was to preach on the morrow; and finally, their Majesties' old and intimate friends who knew the form better than the equerry himself—and consequently needed the most delicate attention.

The days at Balmoral passed pleasantly, energetically. The King and the rest of the shooters, dressed if the King had favored them, in the green-gray tweed of the royal estate, left for the hill, at 9:30, to shoot grouse. After seeing them off, I would discuss with that dear man Ainslie (the palace steward), or his deputy, the immediate commitments on the domestic front.

One day I told Ainslie, "Please note: Tomorrow King Faisal of Iraq and the Regent will be staying. They are Moslems, forbidden to eat pork. So for heaven's sake, no bacon and sausages." This was a serious break with tradition.

Next morning, at breakfast, I led the King's Moslem guests to the sideboard and, raising the lid of a silver dish, invited them: "Please help yourselves; you have a choice of haddock, kippers or scrambled eggs." But there was nothing of the kind; the dish was full of bacon and sausages, upon which those royal sons of the Prophet fell with unconcealed relish. Ainslie, in the background, smiled approvingly.

While the guns were at the morning drive, there would gather back at the ranch a small posse of riders, headed by the princesses. Elizabeth, on a horse, was competent and classic, Margaret pretty and dashing. I often rode with them on the hill.

The sporting day ended, sportsmen and spectators foregathered in the drawing room. Its bay windows gave on the distant hill; its pictures, furniture and bibelots exuded so strongly the intensely romantic personality of Queen Victoria that you almost felt that you were in her august presence. Which did not dispel the pleasure of downing a well-earned drink, chatting animatedly about the day's sport, or getting drawn into the wiles of canasta.

Then, invariably too late, everyone would hurry to their room, hurriedly change, and hurry back, just in time for dinner—to learn that the Queen had returned only a few moments earlier from fishing and would not be down for half an hour.

Dinner at Balmoral was a joyous feast which capped the day's sport. The Scottish gentlemen, resplendent in kilt, jacket and jabot, far outshone the sassenachs like me, in our dowdy black dinner jackets. Grouse was on the menu each night during the six weeks' stay. For one half of the meal, conversation was directed to one neighbor, then switched (following the Queen's cue) to the other.

Towards the end of the dinner, the King's pipers, numbering up to a dozen, entered and blew their way round the table, to the stirring, moving but deafening wail of airs like *Scotland the Brave*, *My Home* or *Flowers of the Forest*. Those inimitable, nostalgic airs, better heard from the other side of the hill, penetrated, at point blank range, to the depths of my heart. I often asked the pipe major for a repeat on the following evening.

Dinner over, the ladies retired and the King passed the port to the gentlemen. It could happen (and often did) that the Queen, half an hour later, had a message passed to the King, telling him that the ladies were getting impatient. So the gentlemen then joined the ladies and the reunion led to crazy games, or canasta, or, most enchanting of all, Princess Margaret singing and playing at the piano. Her repertoire was varied; she was brilliant as she swung, in her rich, supple voice, into the American musical hits, like "Buttons and Bows," "I'm as corny as Kansas in August . . . ," droll when, in a very false falsetto, she bounced between the stool and the keyboard in "I'm looking over a four-leaf clover, which I'd overlooked before . . . ," and lovable when she lisped some lilting old ballad: "I gave my love a cherry, it had no stone. . . ." No one remained unmoved.

Quite another kind of evening was the Ghillies' Ball, held in the castle ballroom and attended by all the braw lads and the bonnie lasses of the Balmoral estate.

Time was given for pipers and dancers to warm up; then, when the air was vibrating with the wail of pipes and the measured beat of feet, the King, the Queen and the princesses, followed by their guests, joined the reels—the sassenachs, including myself, rather reluctantly. I much preferred to remain a wallflower and simply watch the handsome, kilted, screeching Scots pirouetting on tiptoe about their ravishing, tartan-sashed ladies, rather than cut a ridiculous figure, in black dinner jacket, trying vainly to emulate them.

About mid-September the King would go south, via London, to Sandringham, for the partridge and pheasant shooting. The Queen and the princesses stayed on at Balmoral till early October, when the hill echoed with the melancholy roar of rutting stags. I often stayed on, too, and day after day went to the hill to shoot.

At this time skeins of wild geese, silhouetted against a cold blue sky, began flying south. Then the Queen and the princesses departed in the same direction and the family was reunited in London for the winter season.

In London I was making a number of enjoyable, interesting and occasionally distinguished friends, though, unfortunately for Rosemary, I was never able to match her enthusiasm for the social life. I enjoyed dining out: a dinner party, particularly a small one, is a pleasant and civilized pretext for intelligent—and audible—conversation. For precisely the opposite reason, balls, to my mind, are a bore, cocktail parties an unspeakable curse and nightclubs the nadir as a form of social intercourse.

Weekend parties in the country are another enjoyable feature of English life. It is there that major business or political matters are often discussed and decisions made. Though this aspect did not as yet interest me, I enjoyed them for the opportunity they gave to meet people and their possibilities for fun and civilized conversation in pleasant surroundings.

For the first time since the war started, the King spent Christmas in the "Big House" at Sandringham. The interior of Sandringham House, for all its labyrinthine passages and staircases which seemed to lead nowhere, exuded warmth and a genial sort of comfort. It had the feel of an ancestral, a family home; it smelt of winter and log fires and still gave off a strong aroma of its first royal owner, King Edward VII, and the elegance of his times.

Not surprisingly, considering the Royal Family's Continental affiliations, the royal Christmas smacked somewhat of a Continental *réveillon*. The Christmas parade began the evening before. In the tinsel-hung ballroom the King's family and his closest relations gathered about the Christmas tree to open their presents. Within a few minutes they were standing amidst a debris of paper wrappings and colored string, embracing one another with thanks and kisses—a simple, heartwarming scene which, on the morrow, would be repeated throughout the land. For once, in the whole year, the Royal Family and their nearest kith and kin would be together in private.

The principal guest was Queen Mary, a grand and most gracious lady; if there was a certain stiffness about her manner it was because she was (like her son, the King) shy. When first placed next to her at dinner I said to myself "Speak before you are spoken to" (exactly the opposite to what nanny used to say) "otherwise you may never speak at all." Queen Mary's first responses were monosyllabic, but I talked on and was soon enjoying the warmth of her conversation. At the end of dinner she took a cigarette and puffed away at it gently, but contentedly.

Queen Mary was the most admirable of all the old ladies I have met. I was moved by her dignity, the straightness of her carriage, her flawless porcelain complexion, her majesty and her touching simplicity. One evening, after dinner, the party warmed up and people began to dance. Queen Mary, now in her 80's, did not hesitate. I found my arm linked with hers as we danced around, singing the Hokey Cokey:

> You put your left foot in,
> Your left foot out,
> In out, in out,
> Shake it all about,
> You do the hokey cokey and you turn around
> And that's what it's all about.

CHAPTER 14

PRESSURES ON MARRIAGE

I had now been with the King not, as originally intended, for three months, but for two years. As I came more and more to know the King and his family, my affection for them grew. I desired to serve them to my utmost, yet I felt restless and frustrated. The simple if rather special duties I performed were difficult to reconcile with the responsibilities, the stress and the danger I had known when commanding a squadron and a station, or the functions I was trained for at the Staff College. My job, to some extent exacting, if only because of the empty, interminable hours of waiting, was far from taxing my energies, either mental or physical, to the full. I longed to be more actively, more usefully employed.

The chance came with the Royal Tour of South Africa and Rhodesia. The King and Queen and the princesses were to leave England on February 1, 1947; they would be away for three months. Peter Ashmore and I were to go along as equerries. I had also to act as master of His Majesty's reduced Household, a kind of chief of personnel-cum-purser-cum-social secretary.

Britain's six-year war—longer than any of her allies or indeed of her enemies—had left her bankrupt and half-starving. Now she was hit by the cruelest winter in living memory. The country was still living on a basic ration of ½d worth of meat a week (a niggardly portion), one egg and a two-pound loaf. Shortages of clothes, equipment and houses made life a drab and difficult affair. And now the fury of the elements descended on Britain; gales and floods, frost and snow paralyzed communications. Power cuts left Britons shivering in their homes; factories were shut down and two-and-a-half million were thrown out of work. British agriculture was devastated in its worst crisis in three centuries. And, on top of all these calamities at home, the King faced immense and pressing problems in his Empire: India, Burma and Palestine—two-thirds of its population—were in turmoil, demanding independence from the British crown.

Such was the situation as the King prepared to leave, in the battleship *Vanguard,* his forlorn and frostbound United Kingdom for the midsummer of South Africa. He was loath to leave and would rather have stuck it out at home with his people. But the King of England was also King of South Africa, and South Africa claimed him.

The next three months were to be a key period in my life, with thoughts, frustrations and desires erupting in my mind and horizons widening before my eyes. Not since I went to Singapore, eleven years earlier, had I traveled so far from England. The effect on me was similar. It liberated me and altered my outlook. I instinctively felt that the South Africa tour would open up new horizons. It did, but sadly enough, some were darker than I imagined.

Snow lay thick on the ground as the royal procession left Buckingham Palace. At Waterloo there was time for a few words with Rosemary and Giles, a fond farewell, yet it marked the first stage of a parting which would eventually separate us forever. The *Vanguard* sailed from Portsmouth early next morning.

The Navy and the R.A.F. escorted the *Vanguard* down-channel; then, after some delay the splendid French battleship *Richelieu* took up station alongside. The King, on the *Vanguard*'s bridge, fretted at the delay. Despite the heavy seas, the *Richelieu*'s decks were manned and her brave sailors were getting a soaking.

For several days the *Vanguard* pitched and rolled through stormy violent seas. The King, a seasoned sailor if, at present, a weary one, stayed in his cabin and slept, though he became impatient as the days passed and the storm showed no signs of abating.

At last we sailed into calm waters; a warm wind blew and the Queen remarked "It's like being stroked." At night, sitting on deck, as the *Vanguard* rolled gently through the swell under a full moon, I felt great peace of soul and at close quarters with the Infinite.

As we sailed on into the limpid blue waters of the Southern Hemisphere, the sun began to warm out the discontent that had eaten into my soul. I poured out my feelings in my diary. I felt frustrated and unsettled in England. Though I felt for her and desired no better than to stay with her during her postwar struggle, I began, as the voyage

551

continued and my thoughts grew clearer, to doubt whether the England that I had been brought up to love and to serve would ever turn out to be the promised land that I had so passionately believed in.

As I sailed on toward South Africa, I looked back at England's horizons, and thought how narrow they were. Yet how could my English soul ever find an outlet from my English body, chilled, neurotic and overwrought as it was, after six years of war and privations? My soul was bursting for an outlet and if I could not find it in England, I would remove it elsewhere. I thought a lot about myself, it is true. But, quite truthfully, I thought as much about my beloved wife and family, intending that they, above all, should benefit from my adventurous projects.

When I returned to England, in May 1947, I hurried back to Adelaide Cottage, eager to see my wife and family. Within a few moments I gathered that something had come between Rosemary and me.

Ours had been a typical wartime marriage. After nearly two years of nonstop operations I had stepped out of my cockpit, succumbed to the charms of the first pretty girl I met and, within a few weeks, married her. We might have loved each other and left it at that, but that was not a solution to my craving for a rock and an anchor. I was determined to have and to hold her—till death did us part, and that, we knew—like every other young couple who married in wartime—might be all too soon. The wartime consciousness of impending death spurs people on to urgent, reckless marriage.

On the surface, we had everything going for us. I had a steady job and, thanks to the King's kindness, my family was installed in a most charming, if chilly, house. Yet it was at Adelaide Cottage that our marriage finally broke up. But not before we had held on for another five years, while our incompatibility weighed more and more heavily and our paths separated. We did our best to avoid hurting one another, but hurt one another we did.

In the autumn of 1947 I was attached to Princess Margaret's small entourage when she went to Belfast to launch the liner *Edinburgh Castle*. With the *Edinburgh Castle* launching, the Princess also launched herself on her career of public service. Though only seventeen, she stepped up to fulfill some of the tasks previously left to her elder sister, who, in the immediate future, had more pressing and personal things on her mind. Princess Elizabeth was shortly to be married to the Duke of Edinburgh.

Princess Margaret was getting into her stride as a public figure. In the autumn of 1948, she attended Queen Juliana's inauguration at Amsterdam. Once again, I was attached to the Princess's entourage, a larger and more distinguished one this time. Without realizing it, I was being carried a little further from home, a little nearer to the Princess.

CHAPTER 15

DEATH OF A KING

I n August 1950 there came a pleasant surprise in the form of my appointment as assistant Master of the Household—a position which, while it tended to confirm me as a permanent fixture in the King's Household, tended also to dislodge me further from the insecure place I occupied in my own.

Now that I had a fulltime job, Rosemary and I drifted even further apart, each of us going more and more our own way. It was a difficult and sometimes heart-rending time, with the conviction growing on us that a breakup was inevitable. Ours was the classical divorce story; there still remained between us vestiges of real affection, yet conjugal life, practically, emotionally and sentimentally, had come to a standstill. Both of us, in our own way, continued our sterile, uneasy existence.

As usefully and as energetically as I could, I went about my new duties. The health of the King was to become a growing problem. By May 1951, people noticed that he was looking very tired. In mid-May he and the Queen managed to get away to Balmoral, taking Princess Margaret with them. A lady-in-waiting and I accompanied them.

His elder daughter, Princess Elizabeth, was the King's pride; she was his heir, his understudy, his affectionate admirer, and played her role, as he did his, dutifully, punctiliously, charmingly.

Princess Margaret was the King's joy. She amused and delighted him and appealed to the lighter side of his nature—he had as a boy, after all, been something of a devil himself. The young Princess gave him a lot of fun. She enchanted him.

The King was not the only one to fall beneath the spell of Princess Margaret. If her extravagant vivacity sometimes outraged the elder members of the household and of London society, it was contagious to those who still felt young—whether they were or not. She was a girl of unusual, intense beauty, confined as it was in her short, slender figure and centered about her large purple-blue eyes, generous, sensitive lips and complexion as smooth as a peach. She was capable, in her face and in her whole being, of an astonishing power of expression. It could change in an instant from saintly, almost melancholic, composure to hilarious, uncontrollable joy. She was, by nature, generous, volatile. She was a comedienne at heart, playing the piano with ease and verve, singing in her rich, supple voice the latest hits, imitating the favorite stars. She was coquettish, sophisticated.

But what ultimately made Princess Margaret so attractive and lovable was that behind the dazzling facade, the apparent self-assurance, you could find, if you looked for it, a rare softness and sincerity. She could make you bend double with laughing; she could also touch you deeply.

I was but one among many to be so moved. There were dozens of others; their names were in the papers, which vied with each other, frantically but futilely, in their forecasts of the one whom she would marry.

Yet I dare say that there was not one among them more touched by the Princess's *joie de vivre* than I, for, in my present marital predicament, it gave me what I most lacked—joy. More, it created a sympathy between us and I began to sense that, in her life too, there was something lacking.

That spring of 1951, Balmoral was never more lovely. The sun warmed the scent from the pines and the crisp nights were full of stars. His short holiday in the Highlands gave the King a much-needed rest. But it was not long enough. He needed not a week, but months, to get him over his weariness. Instead, he returned to his endless days of work. Before May was out he was down with flu. His doctors found that his left lung was inflamed; they gave him penicillin, but his recovery was slow. He spent June and July convalescing.

One evening he rang for me. I entered his room and found him standing there, a lonely, forlorn figure. In his eyes was that glaring, distressed look which he always had when it seemed that the tribulations of the world had overcome him. Above the rhythm of the music and the dancing coming up from below, he almost shouted at me: "Won't those bloody people ever go to bed?"

It was the Queen who, suspecting that the King was suffering from something worse than a catarrhal inflammation, made him send to London for his doctors. They examined him at Balmoral on September 1, only some ten days after the rejoicings of Princess Margaret's twenty-first birthday. Their suspicions concerning the King's health were confirmed by a bronchoscopy made on him in London on the 15th, when they identified a malign growth in his left lung. The King made light of his infection, but on September 18 the doctors informed him that his left lung would have to be removed.

The operation was performed on September 23 in the Buhl Room at Buckingham Palace. During it, the doctors saw that the other lung was also affected. The King could not be expected to live for more than two years.

But the King surprised everyone by his rapid recovery. Less than a month after his operation he was writing to his mother, "I must now start to get up and do more to get stronger." From Dr. Malan, now Prime Minister of South Africa, the antimonarchist who had snubbed the King during his visit to that country, there came a warm invitation to His Majesty to spend his convalescence in the prime minister's official residence in Natal. The King sent me to look at the house. I reported to the King at Sandringham at the end of January. He seemed well and cheerful and was looking forward to his holiday in South Africa. On January 30, on the eve of Princess Elizabeth's and Prince Philip's departure on their tour of Africa, Australia and New Zealand, he came to London for a family reunion. That evening he took his family to Drury Lane Theatre to see *South Pacific* and I had the good fortune to accompany them.

Next day, at London Airport, he stood, hatless, in a bitingly cold wind and waved his daughter farewell. His face, haggard and drawn, bore the signs of all that he had been through. Both the King and his daughter knew that they might be parted forever. If that were to be, Princess Elizabeth would always remember that last sight of her father, upright, fearless, his face turned towards the future which, sooner than either imagined, would pass from his hands to hers.

The King returned to Sandringham, there to throw himself into his work and his favorite sport. On Tuesday, February 5, he enjoyed a great day's shooting. He spent the evening quietly with the Queen and Princess Margaret. At 10:30 he kissed them goodnight and retired to bed. A few hours later he died, very peacefully, in his sleep.

CHAPTER 16

PRINCESS MARGARET

During 1952, Princess Margaret and I found increasing solace in one another's company. The year began with the Princess's grief, caused by the sudden death of her father; it continued with the change in her own family situation—living alone with her mother (whom she adored)—and the steady deterioration of mine; it ended in the breakup of my family. Not that there would normally have been the slightest connection between her private affairs and mine but for the sympathy which had grown up between us in our particular and purely fortuitous circumstances: the King's death had left a greater void than ever in Princess Margaret's life, while my own was clouded by the failure of my marriage.

In the reshuffle of the late King's and the new Queen's households, I left my post as deputy Master of the Household to become, at the request of Queen Elizabeth, now the Queen Mother, the Comptroller of her household—which meant supervising its internal organization.

My admiration and affection for Queen Elizabeth was, like everybody's, boundless—all the more so because beneath her graciousness, her gaiety, and her unfailing thoughtfulness for others she possessed a steely will. For some months, Queen Elizabeth and Princess Margaret lived on at Buckingham Palace, while Clarence House, in the Mall, was being redecorated. White, square and solid, Clarence House had only acquired central heating when it was renovated, in 1947, for Princess Elizabeth and Prince Philip. They, on the Princess's accession to the throne, moved, of course, to Buckingham Palace.

This was a busy time for me; my preoccupation with the work going on at Clarence House helped me to keep my mind off my own troubled home, which was now in the last stages of disintegration. Yet we kept up the pretense of conjugal unity. In June, the Queen, the Duke of Edinburgh and Princess Margaret were our guests at Adelaide Cottage. Six months later, to the day, I was awarded a decree *nisi* against Rosemary with the legal custody of our two boys, who were left in the care of their mother. Two months later, she married John de Lazslo. His father, Philip de Lazslo, the celebrated painter, had done portraits long ago of both the King and Queen Elizabeth.

A spell of duty took me to Sandringham, where I found Princess Margaret. It was there, one winter's evening, that she had kissed her father goodnight, only to receive the cruel news next morning that he was dead. A year had passed since then and now, too, my own ordeal was over. We rediscovered one another, and in a new frame of mind.

We had known each other for nine years, during which time she had grown up from a school girl into a young woman whose beauty, charm and talent had attracted scores of admiring and faithful personal friends. Yet among none of them had she found the man of her choice. That—incredibly—was the lot that destiny had reserved for me. Completely in love with life as she was and surrounded by friends who were both eligible and available—which could not be said of me—I saw little of her as she grew to womanhood, nor was I in the least concerned with her private life. Yet, as the daughter of her father, I had come to know her so well that we could confide in one another.

One afternoon, at Windsor Castle, when everyone had gone to London for some ceremony, we talked, in the red drawing room, for hours—about ourselves. It was then that we made the mutual discovery of how much we meant to one another. She listened, without uttering a word, as I told her, very quietly, of my feelings. Then she simply said: "That is exactly how I feel, too." It was, to us both, an immensely gladdening disclosure, but one which sorely troubled us.

The times that we could share each other's company were infrequent. When they did occur, it was at no social function, nor dinner, nor dance, nor nightclub, but on a terrain which was to me, the stranger who had walked into her life, as dear and familiar after all these years, as it was to her, who had always belonged there. It was in her own home that we met, among her own people, surrounded by her memories, which she loved to recount. For Princess Margaret, if she was sophisticated and enjoyed the high life, loved, more passionately than anything else, her home and her family.

So, with due allowances, did I. Ever since that first visit, in 1944, to Appleton Lodge, I had felt most happy and at ease with them in the atmosphere of their own homes: Royal Lodge, their private house near Windsor, Sandringham and, dearest of all, Balmoral. It was in these places, more than anywhere, that I had come to know and to love this family, and appreciate their kindness, their affection and the feeling of permanence—which, for years, had been so lacking in my own life.

My relationship with them was a simple one, with none of the gloss that some people have put on it: that I was the "King's adviser," "closest confidant," etc. That is rubbish. The King's closest confidant was, obviously, his wife, Queen Elizabeth, and, on political matters, his private secretary, Tommy Lascelles. Nor was there any question of my "advising" the King. He was just about old enough to be my father and had no reason, on important matters, to ask my advice, nor had I any to give him. The relationship, I repeat, was a simple one, motivated as it was by sympathy.

So it was in the midst of her family, in those familiar, well-loved surroundings, that I came to discover Princess Margaret—the person she really was. At Balmoral, dressed in tartan skirt and green tweed jacket, she would sometimes walk with me between drives, a discreet but adequate distance from the rest of the party, so that we could have a tête-à-tête.

People usually do that in a quiet corner of a bar or bistro, over coffee or a bottle of wine. We talked while walking on the hill, among the heather, with the breeze in our faces; or riding, in the Great Park at Windsor, along drives flanked with rhododendron and venerable oaks and beeches; or through the pinewoods and across the stubble at Sandringham.

We talked. Her understanding, far beyond her years, touched me and helped me; with her wit she, more than anyone else, knew how to make me laugh—and laughter, between boy and girl, often lands them in each other's arms.

Her individual world and mine may have been widely separated, but we had discovered another world which belonged jointly and exclusively to us. In it there grew up between us a warm, profound affection. Absence, distance and our difference of station only tended to deepen it. Now that, at Sandringham, we were together again, we longed, as never before, to remain so—God alone knew how—and never be parted.

Our love, for such it was, took no heed of wealth and rank and all the other worldly, conventional barriers which separated us. We really hardly noticed them; all we saw was one another, man and woman, and what we saw pleased us. How to consummate this mutual pleasure was the problem. Marriage, at this moment, seemed the least likely solution; and anyway, at the prospect of my becoming a member of the Royal Family the imagination boggled, most of all my own. Neither the Princess nor I had the faintest idea how it might be possible for us to share our lives. That depended finally on the British constitution and the Church. But we were not there yet; all we could hope was that, with time and patience, some solution might evolve.

At all events, we wished the Queen to know of our feelings, and these Princess Margaret confided privately to her sister. A few days later, at Buckingham Palace, Her Majesty invited us both to spend the evening with her and Prince Philip. Both were in good spirits and the evening passed off most agreeably. From it there stands out in my memory one unforgettable impression: the Queen's movingly simple and sympathetic acceptance of the disturbing fact of her sister's love for me. Prince

Philip, as was his way, may have tended to look for a funny side of this poignant situation. I did not blame him. A laugh here and there did not come amiss. That evening we had several. But, as I sat there with them, the thought occurred to me that the Queen, behind all her warm goodwill, must have harbored not a little anxiety.

Princess Margaret also told her mother, who listened with characteristic understanding. I imagine that Queen Elizabeth's immediate—and natural—reaction was "this simply cannot be." But thoughtful as ever for the feelings of others, for her daughter's above all and for mine as well, she did not hurt us by saying so. Without a sign that she felt angered or outraged—or, on the other hand, that she acquiesced—the Queen Mother was never anything but considerate in her attitude to me. Indeed she never once hurt either of us throughout the whole difficult affair, behaving always with a regard for us both, for which I felt all the more grateful because of my own responsibility in the crisis.

Princess Margaret had broken the news to her family: if disconcerted, as they had every reason to be, they did not flinch, but faced it and us with perfect calm and, it must be said, considerable charity.

This was hardly the attitude of the Establishment to which, in the person of Tommy Lascelles (now the Queen's private secretary), I undertook to broach the news. I entered his somber but spacious office. When first Air Chief Marshal "Peter" Portal and then the King had initiated me to my job of equerry, both had received me, at my own level, standing. Now that I was on the point of leaving it, Tommy remained seated, regarding me darkly while I stood before him and told him, very quietly, the facts: Princess Margaret and I were in love. Visibly shaken, all that Tommy could say was: "You must be either mad or bad." I confess that I had hoped for a more helpful reaction.

I was, I told Tommy, quite ready to face the immediate consequences and leave the Queen Mother's household.

Tommy consulted the Queen, of course, doubtless reminding her that under the Royal Marriages Act of 1772, Princess Margaret would have to obtain Her Majesty's consent to her marriage—at least before her twenty-fifth birthday. Thereafter she would be exempt from the Queen's veto, but would still need the consent of Parliament, and of the Dominions' parliaments as well.

The crucial point, when it came to the Queen's consent for her sister to marry me, was that I was divorced. The Queen, as titular head of the Church of England, whose canon No. 107 of 1603 forbids divorce, could not constitutionally give her consent, unless her prime minister saw fit to advise her otherwise. When the Queen put the matter to Sir Winston Churchill, the prime minister replied, with good reason, that it would be disastrous for the Queen were she to consent, during coronation year of all times, to the marriage of her sister with a divorced man. There was an ironic twist to the premier's counsel, for Churchill's own son, Randolph, was divorced and remarried.

That, then, was that. Princess Margaret would have to wait another two years, until she was twenty-five, before she could hope to contract a legal marriage with me.

Tommy Lascelles (not that I was aware of it) also consulted the prime minister. Both agreed that I should leave the Queen Mother's household. Lascelles wanted more—to banish me, forthwith, abroad. However, the Queen, characteristically, would not hear of such drastic measures to separate me from her sister. She insisted, and the Queen Mother agreed, that I be allowed to stay on at Clarence House.

Incredibly, neither the Queen's nor the prime minister's advisers seemed to be paying sufficient attention to reports already circulating in the U.S. and the Continental press, not to speak of the rumors flying around London (but not yet in the British papers) about Princess Margaret and myself, and of which we ourselves were ignorant. We two had innocently confided our secret to the inner circles of the Royal Family and, by extension, to the competent authorities—notably the Queen's private secretary, press secretary and prime minister, who were secretly discussing it while the press of America and Europe were openly informing their readers about it. Yet neither of us knew, nobody told us: our secret was out.

The Queen's press secretary, Commander Richard Colville R.N., a thin man with a thin face, straight black hair, black-rimmed spectacles and dressed (invariably, it seemed) in formal black clothes, was a naval paymaster who had distinguished himself gallantly during the war. Richard came to his post, a delicate one and the object of constant, worldwide attention, without any professional experience. After six years of it, he was still being criticized for his handling of press problems, of which, from now on, he was to have more than his fair share.

Whether Colville, the press secretary, or Lascelles, his immediate chief, knew anything about the rumors in the foreign press, I do not know. It seems incredible that they did not; in which case, they might have whispered a word in my ear. We were, after all, colleagues. Had they only taken me into their confidence and alerted me to the danger, I would have got out of the way fast, on my own initiative—dutifully, for the sake of the Royal Family, and selfishly, for my own sake. I should have got well clear of the target area, Clarence House and Buckingham Palace—withdrawn, resigned, done anything reasonable to avoid the attention of the press, which at this moment was concentrated on the Queen's approaching coronation. Now was the time. But the Queen and the Queen Mother, apparently, were not fully aware, while the Princess and I were not aware at all, of a situation which was bound, very shortly, to explode.

Explode it did, on Coronation Day. That morning of Tuesday, June 2, after the splendid and moving service in Westminster Abbey, a great crowd of crowned heads, of nobles and commons—and newspapermen, British and foreign—were gathered in the Great Hall. Princess Margaret came up to me; she looked superb, sparkling, ravishing. As we chatted she brushed a bit of fluff off my uniform. We laughed and thought no more of it. But American reporters, not to say British, had apparently been observing us almost as closely as the coronation itself. Next day, that charming little gesture made the headlines in the New York press.

Even now, Colville did not react, at least towards me, to the reports circulating abroad. I never read the foreign press, and neither he nor anyone else breathed a word to me about the sensation that the Princess and I were providing in the U.S. Had they done so, there would still have been just time for me to fade out before the storm burst, for twelve more days passed before it did so.

Then, on June 14 the news hit the British public. The Sunday newspaper, *The People,* spoke out first: *It is high time,* it said under a banner headline, *for the British public to be made aware of the fact that newspapers in Europe and America are openly asserting that the Princess is in love with a divorced man and that she wishes to marry him . . . Every newspaper names the man as Group Captain Townsend.*

Next day, Monday, June 15, Lascelles and Colville could only tell the Queen what was very obvious, that it was now too late to stop the British press from discussing the case of Princess Margaret and myself. Things had been left too late for a denial; what they now proposed was instead virtually a confirmation. They advised the Queen that I should quit my post forthwith and leave the country. The prime minister concurred and insisted on a period of one year's separation.

Mr. Churchill told the Air Minister, Lord De L'Isle, to find me a job abroad without delay. A choice of three air attaché posts were communicated to Lascelles, who summoned me to decide my place of exile: Brussels, Johannesburg, or Singapore.

At first I thought he was joking. A few months earlier, as he well knew, I had been awarded the legal custody of my two sons, eleven and eight years old. How did Tommy expect me to exercise legal custody, let alone keep in touch with my young sons, from Johannesburg or Singapore? I chose Brussels—it was Hobson's choice.

Princess Margaret and I were prepared for this sentence of exile, harsh as it was. The Queen, however, was not to be rushed. She was due to visit Northern Ireland on June 30 and, in a most gracious and touching gesture, asked me to accompany her as equerry-in-waiting. The Royal Family, despite the embarrassing circumstances, showed me every possible consideration.

Sunshine warmed the Queen Mother's sitting room at Clarence House when, towards midday on June 29, I took leave of Her Majesty and Princess Margaret. The Princess was very calm, for we felt certain of each other and, though it was hard to part, we were reassured by the promise, emanating from I know not where, but official, that my departure would be held over until her return on July 17. We talked less, I think, of her forthcoming journey than of our next meeting, in about three weeks' time. Her mother—I blessed her for her exquisite tact—left us alone for a few precious moments. Then the Princess was gone. We were next to meet, not in three weeks, but in over a year.

Next day, I accompanied the Queen and Prince Philip to Belfast. It was my last duty for the Queen and a most agreeable one—until, in the middle of the civic luncheon, attended by the Queen, in the Ulster capital, Coleville's press office announced my appointment as air attaché to the British Embassy at Brussels.

That put the cat among the pigeons. For the rest of the Belfast visit, the public were treated to the embarrassing spectacle of photographers concentraing almost as much on me as on the Queen. It was when she alighted from the aircraft at London airport that they got their final scoop. There on the tarmac, for all to see, the Queen, smiling and charming as always, chatted with me for a few moments. I never admired her more, above all for publicly defying the cries of scandal which were resounding about her sister and me. She was truly Elizabethan. She and Prince Philip shook my hand and wished me good luck, as I bowed and took my final leave.

The sensation caused by the announcement of my transfer to Brussels caused the wheels of Whitehall, closely geared as they were to the secretariat at Buckingham Palace, to accelerate to full speed. Summoned by Tommy Lascelles, I was informed that the final date for my departure was now July 15—two days before Princess Margaret's return. Instead of our expected farewell, we were to be torn apart.

The parting with my sons was particularly harrowing. Those two little boys were boarders at a prep school in Kent, far from their mother, to whose good care they had been entrusted. Giles was brave, but Hugo, then only eight, cried a lot. He had seen a newspaper headline saying that I, his father, was to be banished and taken it in its literal, medieval sense. I hugged him and promised to come back. But Hugo, I believe, has never quite recovered from that brutal separation.

There was indeed a medieval atmosphere about my impending departure. I was being despatched, willy-nilly, to a virtually sinecure post in a foreign capital—a hefty come-down after the commands I had previously held in the R.A.F. and my nine years in the Royal Household. I felt rather like a political deportee. I was never consulted, only informed, on occasions, by Tommy.

To add to my discomfort, false statements were being made publicly and in high quarters about me. At this point a wave of disgust and disillusionment hit me. The R.A.F. had thought well enough of me to recommend me for my post with the King. I had been with the Royal Family for nine years. Now I was being booted out of England. But I quickly got over these feelings; self-pity was no remedy in the present crisis. I had no right to complain. I had offended the Establishment by falling in love with the Queen's sister, for whose heart, let alone hand, I was, by Establishment rules, quite ineligible. Now I was getting my deserts.

I put away rancor and bitterness as a waste of effort. So I reconciled myself to my exile. It was obviously my duty to accept—anyway, there was, by Establishment rules, quite ineligible. Now I was getting my desserts.

my exile to break up our relationship. It did not. It led, on the other hand, to a lamentable crisis in which Crown, Government, and Church were all embarrassed.

CHAPTER 17

EXILE IN BRUSSELS

At daybreak on July 15, 1953, I drove out of London. I felt no regret at leaving—what had to be, had to be. What sickened me was the manner of my leaving—hustled out of the country so swiftly that my future Ambassador, Sir Christopher Warner, had no warning of my arrival. He was away, touring the Belgian Congo; when he returned he was naturally embarrassed to find that his quiet embassy in the Rue de Spa, Brussels, had become a hotbed of world speculation.

Though I longed for nothing more than to fade out, pick up the threads of a normal life and go about my business like anybody else, it was at first not possible. I was still hot news and as I drove into Brussels, in shirt-sleeves and looking like anything but a diplomat, let alone a pretender for the Princess's hand, I was surrounded, every time I stopped to ask the way, by an animated little crowd. At last I found the embassy. Even there a crowd had collected.

Once inside the courtyard I mopped my brow; it was going to need tact and patience to settle down in my new surroundings. The counsellor, Joe Parrott, came to the rescue, taking me off to his home where he and his wife protected me, aided by a police guard outside, and helped me to make my first steps into the diplomatic milieu of Brussels.

In the quiet of Joe Parrott's house I was at last able to think over recent events. The inescapable fact was that Princess Margaret and I, much as we loved each other, could not, if ever we married, do so for another two years, because of the Royal Marriages Act. It was an insurmountable bar, unless or until Parliament abolished it. The act did indeed, at this moment, come in for much indignant criticism and there was a clamor for its abolition. But in a country like Britain, where the monarchy owes much of its stability to the hereditary principle, the act was a safeguard, if an unjust one on legal and humane grounds, to this principle, a safeguard not lightly to be set aside.

The Royal Marriages Act was conceived by the Queen's ancestor George III who believed that royalty should marry royalty. George's brothers, the Dukes of Cumberland and Gloucester, had thought otherwise—they married commoners. So did George's son (later George IV) who—heinous crime—wed a Catholic lady, Mrs. Fitzherbert. The Royal Marriages Act was intended to clear up the mess and, above all, protect the succession from undesirable pretenders.

Broadly, the Act stated that no descendant of George III could marry, before the age of twenty-five, without the sovereign's consent. Beyond that age, if the sovereign still disapproved, the consent of the British (and Dominions') Parliament would be required. The wretched royal lover was caught either way. The Act was presented to Parliament in 1772. Walpole, presaging Winston Churchill in another context, said of it, "Never was an act passed against which so much, and for which so little was said." Nevertheless, in 1953 the Act was still law. Not all the conjugal extravagances of the Princess's forbears provided a pretext for contravening it—the contrary, rather. Princess Margaret was bound by it until her twenty-fifth birthday, two years hence, on August 21, 1955.

The Queen was Head of the State, which permitted divorce; she was also Head of the State Church, which did not. The Queen then, constitutionally, was contradicting herself. The Church formally opposed an eventual marriage, yet its right to do so was not incontestable. Its Canon 107 (unchanged since 1603) forbade divorce, but the Church had always been divided on the question, as well as on the remarriage of divorced persons whose former spouses were living. At that moment there were hundreds of such people, many of them well known, whom the Church had remarried. One of the most recent was a first cousin of the Queen.

The Cabinet, for political reasons, was against a marriage; morally, however, they were on shaky ground. Mr. Eden (later, the Earl of Avon), soon to become prime minister in place of the aging Mr. Churchill, had recently divorced and remarried. Four members of the government had been through the divorce courts; three had remarried. Many people objected that it was pure hypocrisy for ministers to uphold the law of the state church in public and to ignore it in their private lives.

A pertinent answer to this objection was that the private life of Mr. Eden and the other ministers—indeed of every citizen—was his own affair; Princess Margaret's private life was the concern of the nation and of the Commonwealth. Against which, it was argued that it would be unjust to deny to the Princess, if the sister were still a subject of the Queen, the right to marry a divorced man when every other of the Queen's subjects was allowed by the law of the land to do so. A cry went up, "If they want to marry, why shouldn't they?" No doubt there were many who heartily sympathized with our predicament.

A fortnight or so after my arrival in Brussels, Sir Christopher Warner returned from his Congo trip. I was beginning to integrate myself into his embassy. He quickly got over his umbrage at my unheralded arrival and became, with his sister, Miss Warner (who ran his bachelor household), the warmest and surest of friends.

Briskly, amiably and most effectively, Miss Warner organized Her Britannic Majesty's ambassador in Brussels and, when she got the chance, the rest of us on his staff, as well. He himself was always imperturbable; his speech, however serious the subject, was flavored with humor. He was the classical diplomat.

I warmed quickly to the Belgians, whose small country is full of generous-hearted people who welcome the foreigner with open arms. There is a Bruegelian side to every Belgian; they are earthy and fun-loving and, like the English, have an instinct for maintenance and order which they apply to their gardens, their artistic treasures, their folklore and their friendship. I soon felt at home there.

By the end of 1953 I was settling down quietly in Brussels. A British newspaper, looking back over the events of that year, recalled the "rumors which had linked" me with Princess Margaret. "Handsome and reassured at the Coronation, harassed and distraught" during my precipitate departure in July, It now depicted me as "faded from the limelight—lapsing into slow oblivion." This was fine. I wanted to retire into the shadows and find peace in which to think clearly.

How much more profitable could it have been, had I been able, to discuss these pressing problems face to face with Princess Margaret. We wrote almost every day, but that was not the same. Audibly, visually and tangibly we were separated. Our own world was a vacuum which had to be endured day in, day out, and during the yearning hours of the night.

If I was "the loneliest man in Brussels," I had found a welcome port of call in Antwerp. Pure chance took me there. One autumn afternoon shortly after my arrival, friends took me to a horse show in Brussels. I was watching, spellbound, like everyone else, a young girl, Marie-Luce Jamagne, as she flew over the jumps with astonishing grace and dash. Suddenly, with a timber-shivering crash, her horse fell. Its young rider lay senseless, practically at my feet. I immediately left my seat and went to where she lay. My friend Didi van Derton, one of the judges, was already there. "She'll be all right," he said. Later he introduced me to her parents.

Early in 1954 the Jamagne family invited me to their home in Antwerp. They had not forgotten the days when the Canadians had liberated Antwerp and they had welcomed them to their home. I was no liberator; rather, I needed liberating from myself. They showered me with kindness; their home, far from the guessing and gossip which surrounded me in Brussels, was a safe and blessed haven. It was always open to me and in time I became one of the family. That is what I still am today. Marie-Luce, the girl who fell at my feet, has been my wife for the last eighteen years.

In July I flew to England. Unknown to me, the official in the British European Airways office in Brussels booked my ticket in his name. So, quite innocently, I traveled as "Mr. Carter." When the *Sunday Pictorial* found out, it asked on the following sabbath with grinding irony: *Are we to understand that this comparatively junior diplomat has a private life to justify a device normally used by people high in the affairs of state?*

What the *Sunday Pictorial* had not, fortunately, discovered is that when I reached London I went straight to Harrods, to the bookshop, where, as arranged with Princess Margaret (who had of course told the Queen), I met Brigadier Norman Gwatkin of the Lord Chamberlain's office. His rubicund face shone like a friendly beacon among all those books. Norman led me to a waiting car and we drove to Clarence House, straight in through the main gates. The press had no idea that I was in England.

Princess Margaret and I had not met for a year. Our joy at being together again was indescribable. The long year of waiting, of penance and solitude, seemed to have passed in a twinkling. We were together for a couple of hours and talked as if we had left off only yesterday. We did not discuss the future; all we knew was that for the present our feelings for one another had not changed. Another year's wait remained, until the Princess's twenty-fifth birthday, when she would be free of the Queen's official veto on her marriage. Until then, there was nothing for it but to hold on and wait. Until then . . . But events were not to turn out so simply as that.

It was a joy, too, to be reunited with Giles and Hugo. I had been forcibly separated from my sons for a year; now they were reassured that their father had not been banished for life.

CHAPTER 18

THE END OF THE AFFAIR

Early in March 1955, I took ten days leave. For the first two I enjoyed perfect peace, walking alone in the Forest of Soignes, listening to the urgent chatter of migrating birds. Nature was stirring to the call of spring. So, unfortunately, was the press.

Princess Margaret returned from a Caribbean tour—and suddenly I was pitched out of my placid retreat back into world headlines. A New York paper, hearing that the chapel in Saint James's Palace was to be restored, immediately deduced that the Princess and I were to be married in it. Some London newspapers (which I did not read) were loudly proclaiming that now the "Dolly Princess," as they called her, was back from the West Indies, she must make up her mind—about me, of course.

On Monday, March 2, I walked out of my apartment and was immediately surrounded by a posse of newspapermen. They took me completely by surprise. Howard Johnson of the *Daily Mirror* thrust a copy of the *Sunday Pictorial* under my nose. "Please read it," he said. I could have done so from a mile away. A huge headline screamed PRINCESS MARGARET MARRIAGE SENSATION.

Then the questions began. I could have replied curtly (but for how long?) "no comment." But I decided there and then to answer the reporters. It was a question of honesty, logic and courtesy. It was illogical to run away from the press. I had my life to live, my job to do. It was not possible to remain locked up in my apartment and withstand a siege of dozens of international reporters camped, twenty-four hours a day, on my doorstep. Besides, their presence caused considerable annoyance to my neighbors.

In that little Square Louise, facing the world's press, I badly needed professional advice. I should have welcomed a word from Richard Colville. He was the one person who might have helped. I have not the impudence to claim that I had any right to Colville's advice; only that, since I was so closely bound up with Princess Margaret's future, it might have been better if Richard Colville, instead of leaving me to cope alone, had cooperated with me. But not once, during the whole affair, right up to its bitter end, did he contact me or attempt to evolve a joint front with me toward the press.

Colville and the Queen's advisers, including Lascelles' successor, Michael Adeane, apparently believed that the feverish speculation about Princess Margaret and myself which, after two years, had suddenly flared up more intensely than ever, could be quietened by their own silence. I agree, silence is a most powerful weapon, but it was not, in this case, effective. The clamor over the next six months increased to a deafening crescendo while the "Margaret-Townsend" affair sank deeper and deeper into a morass of frantic, popular sensationalism. Today, twenty-two years later, that is really the only bitter memory that still lingers with me.

With the press in ferment, I did not feel that I could endure to wait much longer for a decision on our future. What we needed to know—urgently—was whether marriage was feasible—and this, only the Princess could ascertain. In five months' time, on her twenty-fifth birthday, the Princess would be free of the Queen's veto under the Royal Marriages Act—but not of her formal disapproval as Head of the Church.

Princess Margaret's twenty-fifth birthday, on August 21, 1955, was approaching. The press—newspapers, TV and radio—were converging on Balmoral in expectation. The Princess was immensely and deservedly popular; she personified the young and the unconventional, the go-ahead side of England. She won admiration, too, by the way she performed her royal duties. She was serene and dignified, as befitted the occasion, but once it was over, radiated warmth and gaiety. People liked her judicious mixture of the formal and the lighthearted. The public felt her happiness was very much their concern and wished her well. They believed that her twenty-fifth birthday would be the turning-point.

But nothing unusual happened. The Princess worshiped as usual at the Kirk at Crathie. I, too, went to worship that morning in the English church in Londonstraat at Ostende. I said a small prayer for us both in that dingy little church, with the plaster falling off its walls, and a congregation of five.

My plea to the Princess, to find out whether marriage was feasible, had been answered. At Balmoral the clans were gathering. The Queen and Princess Margaret had arrived there. On October 1, Sir Anthony Eden, now prime minister, arrived.

Eden could not fail to sympathize with the Princess, all the more so that while his own second marriage had incurred no penalty, either for him or his wife, he had to warn the Princess that my second marriage—to her—would bring her the most grievous penalties: she would have to renounce her royal rights, functions and income.

The Princess now had confirmation for the first time of the consequences of a marriage with me. If only she had known before, the approaching drama might have been avoided. But now it was too late.

We had arranged to meet in London on October 13. Everything was set; I should once more have to enter the arena; I knew that I was going like a sheep to the slaughter. But I went willingly, for her.

Despite the continuing public clamor, neither Michael Adeane nor Richard Colville invited me to discuss with them how to face a situation which had the entire world watching and waiting. I was given no up-to-date information about the political or religious issues, nor about the views of Eden and his cabinet colleagues. I knew nothing. I braced myself for the ordeal.

On October 12 I crossed the Channel, with my car, on the air ferry. Followed by a cortege of reporters in their cars, with others on motorcycles in close escort, I drove on into London. A two weeks' siege now began.

Princess Margaret arrived in London early on the morning of the 13th. We spoke on the telephone and fixed a meeting for that evening at Clarence House.

At last we found ourselves once more in our own, exclusive world, which had remained so empty since our separation two years earlier. As we rediscovered one another, we realized that nothing had changed. Time had not staled our accustomed, sweet familiarity.

Our meeting was the signal for the world's press to take off. There was not a civilized capital in the world where Princess Margaret and myself were not being discussed, often surrounded by the wildest travesties of fact. The Queen's press secretary, Commander Colville, asked three simple questions about that dramatic meeting, replied "No comment" to each of them. Next day he issued a tight-lipped, delphic statement: ". . . the Press Secretary to the Queen is authorized to say that no announcement concerning Princess Margaret's personal future is at present contemplated. The Princess has asked the Press Secretary to express the hope that the press and public will extend to Her Royal Highness their customary courtesy and cooperation in respecting her privacy."

The press secretary was asking a lot. The reporters followed me everywhere; they were decent to me, full of apologies and not a little ashamed for making my life nearly unbearable.

The Princess and I met on every day except two. As the hubbub intensified, we tried to keep our heads. As a private citizen, besieged, or pursued, by the press every minute of the day and night, I did not find it easy. Behind my polite and placid countenance, I was being demolished by the physical and mental strain.

On Friday, October 14, Princess Margaret and I headed separately for Allanbay Park, a Georgian residence near Binfield in a tranquil, rustic corner of Berkshire. Together we spent the weekend in virtual custody, surrounded by the press, to whose numbers were added police guards and dogs and motorized patrols—conditions which did not make for romance.

During the following week, the world was kept on tenterhooks. Each time the Princess and I saw one another or dined with friends, the suspense and the speculation mounted. Some said kindly, "They have not seen each other for two years; give them time to consider the problems and make up their minds." Others remarked less kindly, perhaps, but more logically: "The problems have been known for the last two years. Why, then, can't they decide?"

The answer was that Mr. Eden had only recently brought home fully to the Princess the consequences of her marrying me. The brave Princess had a huge load on her mind.

Adding to the suspense came the Queen's return from Scotland; then, on Tuesday, October 18, a cabinet meeting at which the Princess's eventual marriage was discussed. Eden went on from the meeting with his cabinet colleagues to Buckingham Palace for an audience with the Queen. It lasted ninety minutes instead of the usual thirty. The Queen and her prime minister dwelt long on the problem of her sister.

Meanwhile, that afternoon, at Clarence House, the Princess and I, more personally, were weighing the pros and cons. Queen Elizabeth joined us for tea and, in the midst of this appallingly serious situation, an American headline next day gave us a welcome laugh: "Meg sips tea with Peter. Mom makes it a crowd."

On Wednesday the 19th, for the first time the Princess and I did not meet. I kept my distance before the important engagement she had that evening: dinner with the archbishop and bishops at Lambeth Palace.

When I saw her next day at Clarence House she was in fine form, quite unperturbed after junketing with the bishops who, admirably it must be said, refrained from allowing the rigors of the canon law to spoil the party. Some observers commented, somewhat irrelevantly, that the Princess could not now flout the archbishop after dining at his table.

The day after the party, Thursday the 20th, world excitement reached its peak. That morning the cabinet met at Downing Street with the clear impression that nothing, not even the episcopal feast the night before, had dissuaded the Princess from her intention to marry me. The cabinet meeting had hardly started when the Attorney General, Sir Reginald Manningham-Buller, was sent for. He was in the middle of pleading a case in the Queen's Bench Division and, excusing himself to the Lord Chief Justice, left the court and hurried to Downing Street.

I have not the faintest idea what those eminent gentlemen discussed, any more than I had of anything else that was going on behind the scenes. My place was down in the street, among the crowd, while the Government and Buckingham Palace palavered. But it is likely that the cabinet, that morning, came to terms on a Bill of Renunciation, to be placed before Parliament, freeing the Princess of her responsibilities under the Royal Marriages Act, and thus—at crushing cost to herself—enabling her to marry me. It was contended by observers that, while abdication was as old as the monarchy itself, renunciation of royal rights was unknown.

For the past week, the world around us had loudly and passionately discussed two concrete questions, one posed by the law, the other by the Church. The legal situation could be solved, but only by exacting big sacrifices from the Princess. Being twenty-five years old, she was free of the Queen's absolute veto under the Royal Marriages Act. But the act did not leave her free to marry whom and when she liked. It required her to give notice of her intentions to the Privy Council, whose three hundred-odd members were drawn from the political, aristocratic, and military leaders of the land.

The Privy Council was the hardcore of the Establishment. It could not prevent the Princess's marriage, but its members could strongly influence Parliament to whom the veto, relinquished by the sovereign, had now passed. The Princess would have to wait up to twelve months more before the British Parliament and those of the seven dominions—Canada, Australia, New Zealand, South Africa, India, Pakistan, and Ceylon—gave their consent.

If they did not, her last chance was to contract a marriage abroad. It would be illegal, and its offspring considered, in Britain and the Commonwealth, illegitimate.

However, it was practically certain that the British and Dominions' parliaments would agree—but on condition that Princess Margaret was stripped of her royal rights and prerogatives, which included accession to the throne, her royal functions and a £15,000 government stipend due on marriage—conditions which, frankly, would have ruined her.

There would be nothing left—except me, and I hardly possessed the weight to compensate for the loss of her privy purse and prestige. It was too much to ask of her, too much for her to give. We should be left with nothing but our devotion to face the world.

Besides, there was an important political aspect to the situation. It was difficult for the prime minister, Anthony Eden, to oppose the marriage, because of his own position as a divorced husband, remarried. But the Marquis of Salisbury, an influential member of Eden's government and leader of the House of Lords, was, as a high Anglican, flatly opposed—to the point where, rather than introduce into the upper house a bill enabling the marriage, he would probably resign.

Salisbury's resignation might have seriously weakened Eden's government. Even if it did not, it would come as a bombshell. "Bobbety" Salisbury was a close friend of the Royal Family. His ancestor, the first Lord Burghley, had served Elizabeth I as Chief Minister; it was he who sent Mary Queen of Scots to the block. His descendant could well send Margaret, Princess of England, virtually in the same direction.

Some of the Church's most devout and erudite prelates had contested the validity of the laws on divorce and remarriage. In this atmosphere of doubt, the Church of England had frequently remarried the "innocent" or "wronged" party of a divorce. The Church preached the principle of the indissolubility of marriage but did not universally practice it. After deep and lengthy heart-searchings, in the light of the scriptures, of various learned texts and of talks with Roman and Anglican priests, I was unable to feel that I should be doing wrong to marry again. In this I had the support of no less an authority than the Archbishop of Canterbury himself, who stated publicly: "I do not feel able to forbid good people who come to me for advice to embark on a second marriage."

I had never asked the archbishop's advice. Perhaps I should have done so. He was at this time being fiercely and, I think, unjustly criticized. His view was that the Church's duty was to bear witness to Christ's word, which was that marriage was meant to be lifelong. A divorced person whose former spouse was living must get married elsewhere than in church.

The Law and the Church were the bones and the sinew of the Establishment. Both had allies. *The Times* was one of the most powerful among them. On October 24, in a lengthy leading article, lucidly argued in splendid, sweeping phrases, *The Times* gave its views on Princess Margaret's intention to marry me. The heart of the matter, it said, did not lie in legal or theological argument. The real crux was that the Queen was a symbol for her subjects throughout the Commonwealth. These millions of people saw their better selves reflected in the Queen and, since part of their ideal was family life, the Queen's own family was involved. In this context, *The Times* argued, Princess Margaret's marriage with me could not be regarded as a marriage at all by vast numbers of her sister's people.

No one could possibly contest *The Times'* sentiments concerning the Queen and the Royal Family. But who were these vast numbers? Certainly, they were not as vast as those even vaster numbers of Christians whose elected representatives had legislated in parliament for divorce and the remarriage of divorced people. Nor was the Commonwealth composed entirely of Christians. They were, in fact, a vast minority, compared to the hundreds of millions of Buddhists, Moslems and Hindus, all of whom acknowledged the right of a divorced person to remarry.

The Times' arguments, so superbly couched, were specious and based on false premises. They did not, however, lessen its impact. The article has been taken as the turning-point in our story. That may well be so for the readers of *The Times*, but not for us. *The Times'* magisterial leader never swayed me. My mind was made up before I read it.

Where were we then, the Princess and I? The previous week had ended with our feeling hardly able to endure any longer the solemn pontifications, the debates which raged, at home and the world over, for and against our marriage.

On Saturday evening, October 22, the Princess and I had met at Clarence House. We were both exhausted, mentally, emotionally, physically. We felt mute and numbed at the center of this maelstrom. Later, the Princess had left London to spend the weekend with the Queen and the Duke of Edinburgh at Windsor Castle.

Next day, Sunday, we had spoken on the telephone. The Princess was in great distress. She did not say what had passed between herself and her sister and brother-in-law. But, doubtless, the stern truth was dawning on her. One is at a loss to comfort people over the telephone, and above all people one loves. I felt helpless, unable to reassure her, but when we spoke again later she seemed calmer; we promised to meet on the morrow.

That Sunday night I had hardly slept. My mind had turned incessantly on the sadness of the Princess. In just over a week the smile had vanished from her face, her happiness and confidence had evaporated. Events had put us to a rude test, and the clamor, louder than ever, still continued about us. It was time to put an end to an unendurable situation.

During the morning of Monday the 24th, the day *The Times* article appeared, I had sat mechanically dictating thanks to the scores of letters pouring into No. 19 Lowndes Square, where I was staying in London.

With rare exceptions, they were simple, touching expressions of sympathy.

I felt so played out that I tried to snatch a few winks before leaving to see the Princess at 4 P.M. But sleep evaded me. I was obsessed by the thought that the Princess must tell the world that there would be no marriage. Words, broken phrases turned in my head.

Of a sudden, I rolled off the bed, grabbed a piece of paper and a pencil. The words now came to me with clarity and fluency and I began to write: *I have decided not to marry Group Captain Townsend . . . It may have been possible to contract a civil marriage. But mindful of the Church's teaching . . . conscious of my duty to the Commonwealth . . .*

Less than an hour later I was with the Princess at Clarence House. She looked very tired, but was as composed and affectionate as ever. I told her quietly, "I have been thinking so much about us during the last two days, and I've written down my thoughts, for you to say if you wish to."

I gave her the rough piece of paper and she read. Then she looked at me and very quietly, too, said, "That's exactly how I feel." Our love story had started with those words. Now, with the same sweet phrase, we wrote *finis* to it.

For a few moments we looked at each other; there was a wonderful tenderness in her eyes which reflected, I suppose, the look in mine. We had reached the end of the road. Our feelings for one another were unchanged, but they had incurred for us a burden so great that we decided, together, to lay it down. As we did so, we both had a feeling of unimaginable relief. We were liberated at last from this monstrous problem.

The Princess was resolved to declare publicly what was on her mind and what she had decided. The message could have been put out within twenty-four hours and the wondering world would have been relieved of the suspense. But the royal advisers were against a statement, which meant that its publication was delayed for one more week, while speculation rose to a fiercer crescendo.

That Thursday afternoon Princess Margaret called at Lambeth Palace to tell the Archbishop of her decision. The drama was moving to its close, but still the *coup de théâtre* had to come.

The Princess and I spent the weekend with Rupert and Micky Nevill at Uckfield in Sussex. They, and John and Patricia Abergavenny, whose home, Eridge Castle, was nearby, were the staunchest and most hospitable of friends; without their help I could never have survived those days. It was a goodbye weekend for the Princess and me.

At last we could talk without that crushing weight of world opinion—the sympathy, the criticism, the pity and the anger—all the mass of emotion which had weighed so heavily on our minds. Uckfield House was a haven, though blockaded and besieged by the press and the public.

As at Allanbay Park, at the beginning of this tempestuous period, police and their dogs patrolled, reporters perched in trees or hid in ditches; the Princess and I could neither come nor go. We could only walk in the grounds, sniped at occasionally by long-range lenses.

On Monday, October 31, we returned separately to London. The Princess's statement was to be issued that evening at 7 P.M. About an hour earlier, I called to say a last farewell at Clarence House.

It was there, in the Princess's sitting room that we had met, so recently (but it seemed like an age) after our long, enforced separation. We had held out for more than two years to experience, not the unmitigated joys of a lovers' reunion, but a miserable trial by ordeal, held in public. The hard facts had prevailed and now that we were released, to be separated, sentimentally at least, forever, we felt as if we needed a stiff drink.

We did not feel unhappy. Without dishonor, we had played out our destiny. We were back where we started, that evening long ago at Windsor Castle. The story was ended, the book was closed. There remained only the glow, once shared, of tenderness, constancy and singleness of heart.

Then we, who had been so close, parted.

As I drove back, under a friendly moon, to Uckfield, the Princess's statement was broadcast to the world:

> I would like it to be known that I have decided not to marry Group Captain Townsend. I have been aware that, subject to my renouncing my rights of succession, it might have been possible for me to contract a civil marriage. But mindful of the Church's teaching that Christian marriage is indissoluble, and conscious of my duty to the Commonwealth, I have resolved to put these considerations before others. I have reached this decision entirely alone, and in doing so I have been strengthened by the unfailing support and devotion of Group Captain Townsend. I am deeply grateful for the concern of all those who have constantly prayed for my happiness.
>
> (Signed) Margaret.

Monday, October 31, 1955.